Strategic Organizational Communication

In a Global Economy

Sixth Edition

Charles Conrad
Texas A&M University

Marshall Scott Poole
Texas A&M University

THOMSON
WADSWORTH

Australia • Canada • Mexico • Singapore • Spain
United Kingdom • United States

THOMSON

WADSWORTH

Publisher: Holly J. Allen
Acquisitions Editor: Annie Mitchell
Assistant Editor: Aarti Jayaraman
Editorial Assistant: Trina Enriquez
Senior Technology Project Manager:
　Jeanette Wiseman
Senior Marketing Manager: Kimberly Russell
Marketing Assistant: Andrew Keay
Advertising Project Manager: Shemika Britt

Project Manager, Editorial Production:
　Jane Brundage
Print/Media Buyer: Doreen Suruki
Permissions Editor: Stephanie Lee
Production Service / Compositor:
　G & S Book Services
Cover Designer: Bill Stanton
Cover Image: Getty Images/PhotoDisc
Text Printer: Quebecor World/Kingsport
Cover Printer: Coral Graphic Services, Inc.

For more information about our products,
contact us at:
**Thomson Learning Academic
Resource Center
1-800-423-0563**

For permission to use material from this text
or product, submit a request online at
http://www.thomsonrights.com.
Any additional questions about permissions
can be submitted by email to
thomsonrights@thomson.com.

Library of Congress Control Number:
2004103543
ISBN: 0-534-63621-7

**Thomson Wadsworth
10 Davis Drive
Belmont, CA 94002-3098
USA**

Asia
Thomson Learning
5 Shenton Way #01-01
UIC Building
Singapore 068808

Australia/New Zealand
Thomson Learning
102 Dodds Street
Southbank, Victoria 3006
Australia

Canada
Nelson
1120 Birchmount Road
Toronto, Ontario M1K 5G4
Canada

Europe/Middle East/Africa
Thomson Learning
High Holborn House
50/51 Bedford Row
London WC1R 4LR
United Kingdom

Latin America
Thomson Learning
Seneca, 53
Colonia Polanco
11560 Mexico D.F.
Mexico

Spain/Portugal
Paraninfo
Calle Magallanes, 25
28015 Madrid, Spain

To:
Helen and Cecil,
who gave me a love of knowledge,
BJ,
who has given me knowledge of love,
and
Travis and Hannah,
our gifts of love.
Ed, Helen, and Kim,
who are the foundation,
Lisa,
who built the home,
and
Sam,
who keeps it warm
with all my love.

Contents

Preface

From its beginning almost twenty years ago, the goal of *Strategic Organizational Communication* has been to provide a unified description of the incredibly diverse array of ideas that make up our rapidly expanding field. Responses to the first five editions have been especially gratifying. Readers have been particularly complimentary about the level of sophistication of the book and its ability to integrate research from a number of academic disciplines. Those responding to the later editions also have praised our efforts to place organizations and organizational communication within a broader social, economic, and cultural context and have appreciated our relaxed, engaging writing style. Of course, we have retained or expanded each of these characteristics.

We also have tried to maintain and strengthen the theoretical framework that has been central to the book since its inception. Each edition has focused on the two-level concept of *strategic choice making*. We believe that people make choices about the overall strategies that they will use to operate the societies and organizations they will live within. Ironically, people tend to normalize and naturalize these choices, transforming them from a conscious selection among a number of available options into assumptions, taken-for-granted facts of life. These overall choices, in turn, create the specific situations that people encounter every day—the challenges they face, the resources they have available to manage those challenges, and the guidelines and constraints that limit the options that are available to them. People adapt strategically to the situations that they create, but in adapting, they tend to reproduce those situations; the result is a complicated cycle of acting, creating situations, and adapting to them.

Understanding this action-situation-adaptation cycle requires people to realize these things:

- *Organizations are embedded in societies and cannot be understood outside of a society's beliefs, values, structures, practices, tensions, and ways of managing those tensions.* For example, U.S. society is defined in part by a tension between **community** and **individuality**. This tension arises from many of the challenges faced by contemporary U.S. organizations—challenges as diverse as the attitudes of Generations X and Y (Chapter 1), the blending of traditional (Chapter 3) and cultural (Chapter 5) strategies of motivation and control, the implementation of feminist and other so-called alternative forms of organizing (Chapter 7), and the need to understand non-Western forms of leadership (considered throughout the book).

- *Each overall strategy of organizing includes a characteristic organizational design, a system of motivation and control, a particular form of leadership, and a particular relationship to communication technologies.* Each strategy of organizing is a choice, however; for example, bureaucracies are bureaucracies because people in them choose to act like bureaucrats. Each strategy also includes opportunities to resist the organization's strategy of organizing.
- *Members of organizations can manage organizational situations strategically.* They can exploit fissures and contradictions in social and organizational power relationships. Even in the turbulent world created by the new, global economy, members of organizations can manage organizational situations in ways that achieve their personal goals and the goals of other members of their organizations.

Responding to Reader Suggestions

Readers also have been very open about changes that they would like to see us make. As a result, each new edition really has been a *new* edition. This one is no exception.

The New and Improved

The most obvious change involves our efforts to locate organizational communication within the new, global economy. We focused on globalization in the fifth edition. In this one we have foregrounded the concept in Chapter 1 and incorporated it throughout the book. Similarly, in the fifth edition we treated communication technology in a separate chapter. In this edition we have discussed both concepts in each chapter, because it is increasingly clear that globalization and technology are woven into the fabric of contemporary organizations. In addition, we streamlined and combined the chapters on decision making and on communication and conflict. We have added a chapter on "Communication, Ethics, and Organizational Rhetoric" (Chapter 12). We both have long been interested in ethical issues facing contemporary organizations, as evidenced in Charley's *The Ethical Nexus* (1993) and a special issue of *Communication Research* on "Communication in the Era of the Disposable Worker," that we co-edited in 1997. However, the U.S. "corporate meltdown" that followed the bankruptcy of Enron in 2001, and that seems to be spreading throughout the developed economies, gave increased urgency to these concerns.

Other changes are more subtle, and each one reflects recent advances in organizational communication theory and research. Our treatment of feminist, postmodern, and cooperative forms of organizing continues to grow and deepen (see Chapter 7), as does our presentation of critical perspectives on organizing. The chapters in Unit I have been streamlined and reorganized to increase readability. Readers told us that the first chapter of the fifth edition covered too many complex concepts too quickly, so we have broken it into two chapters. The chapter on managing membership in organizations had become increasingly separated from the rest of the book. The first topic it covered—entering organizations—now is treated in Chapter 5, "Cultural Strategies of Organizing." The second topic—persuasive strategies available to members of organizations—has been incorporated into Chapter 8, "Communication, Power, and Politics in Organizations." Eleven of the twenty-six case studies in this edition are new, and three of the ones we retained from the fifth edition have been revised. Copies of the cases in the fifth edition that are absent from this one are available on the book's Web site (http://communication.wadsworth.com/conrad6), as are other teaching materials.

Oldies but Goodies

There are two aspects of *Strategic Organizational Communication* that we never want to change. One is the extensive research base for the book. The Bibliography for this edition is abbreviated in comparison to those in earlier editions, but like them it identifies readings that are especially appropriate for graduate students. In general, we have focused on works published after 1990, and have cited earlier sources only if they are classics in organizational communication research and theory. As a result, the endnotes for each chapter provide a number of additional readings on virtually every facet of contemporary organizational communication research and theory.

The second aspect that we hope always to retain is the conceptual coherence of the analysis. Two beliefs underlie all that we say in this book. The first is that organizations (and societies) are *sites* in which various tensions and contradictions are negotiated through communication (this idea is explained at length in Chapter 1). The second belief is that understanding organizations and organizational communication requires an analysis of *both* symbolic *and* structural processes. We realize that this both-and perspective is an anomalous position in a discipline that relishes either-or distinctions between functionalism and interpretivism, qualitative and quantitative research methods, and so on. We also realize that advocates of each of these polar terms often will feel that we are too sympathetic with the opposite pole and spend too little space examining their favored position. But we have consistently tried both to balance various perspectives and to indicate how each can be enriched by the key concepts of the others. Life is simply too complex for either-or thinking to capture its nuances; organizations are far too fluid and complicated for bimodal or trimodal paradigms to reveal much of importance.

Organization of the Book

Like the earliest editions, this book is divided into three units. Unit I introduces the theoretical framework that unifies the book, and it develops the concept of

strategies of organizing in detail. Unit II examines those strategies of organizing in more detail, discusses the communicative strategies that members of organizations might use to *strategically manage* the situations created by applications of those strategies of organizing, and offers a critical analysis of each.
Unit III examines key issues facing organizations during the early twenty-first
century—organizational power and politics, organizational decision making
and conflict, issues related to workforce diversity, globalization, and ethics and
organizational rhetoric.

Thanks

If they are to be effective, all communicative acts must be interactive. This dictum includes the writing of books. Consequently, our greatest vote of thanks
goes to the many readers of the earlier editions who made thoughtful and valuable suggestions for improvement.

Of the advice that we received on the different drafts of this edition, the
comments of many colleagues were exceptionally helpful: Stacey Connaughton,
Rutgers University; Stephen Cox, Murray State University; Chris J. Foreman, Eastern Michigan University; Annika Hylmö, Loyola Marymount University; and
Meina Liu, Purdue University. Linda Putnam is a constant source of support, providing insight, expertise, and resources that only she can provide, while Kathy
Miller's and Joel Iverson's superb teaching of our organizational communication
course constantly challenges us to be at our best. George Cheney, Ted Zorn,
Steve Corman, Bob McPhee, Gerry DeSanctis, Peter Monge, and Joe Folger
are constant sources of exciting new ideas. Our students are a constant source
of insightful questions and valuable suggestions. Holly Allen, Jane Brundage,
Trina Enriquez, Aarti Jayaraman, and Annie Mitchell have made working with
Wadsworth-Thomson a joy—we have never encountered more supportive and
capable people in any organization. Private encouragement was provided by
Betty Webber Conrad and Lisa O'Dell, and in even the most hectic of times,
Travis, Hannah, and Sam help us keep our priorities straight.

Charles Conrad
Marshall Scott Poole
College Station, Texas
February 2004

UNIT I

Underlying Concepts

Chapter 1

Strategic Organizational Communication

Don't ask me. I just work here.
—Anonymous

Central Themes

- Organizational communication is strategic in two senses. Organizations emerge from strategic choices about how they will be designed and operated. These choices create the situations that employees encounter at work. Employees must then make their own strategic choices about how to manage those situations.
- Societies and organizations face a fundamental dilemma. They must control and coordinate the activities of their members. But doing so frustrates their members' needs for autonomy, creativity, and sociability.
- As employees make their choices about how to communicate within the guidelines and constraints created by their organization's strategies of organizing, they reproduce those strategies, as well as the guidelines and constraints.

Key Terms

reification	chain of command
specialization	informal communication networks

At one time or another almost everyone has responded to the question "How did this (disaster) happen?" with a statement like "Don't ask me. I just work here." In some cases the excuse is legitimate. The person giving the answer is not allowed by his or her organization to make even simple decisions or take any initiative. "I just work here" means that the person knows the answer or is aware

2

of a solution to the problem but has too little power to make the necessary changes. In other cases, someone else failed to inform the person of the policy, problem, or procedure that is in question. "I just work here" means that the speaker simply does not have the information needed to answer the question. But sometimes the person acted in ways that caused the problem and the response is merely an excuse. Although viable excuses are often available in organizations, in the final analysis it is the employee's own choices that create the situations she or he faces.

This book is about the choices and choice-making behaviors of members of formal organizations. It concentrates on communication because it is through communication that employees obtain information, make sense of the situations they encounter, and decide how to act. And it is by communicating that employees translate their choices into action. Organizations must maintain at least an adequate level of communication effectiveness in order to survive and prosper. People who have developed an understanding about how communication functions in an organization, who have developed a wide repertoire of written and oral communication skills, and who have learned when and how to use those skills seem to have more successful careers and contribute more fully to their organizations than people who have not done so.

As a result, the number of college courses and professional training programs concerned with organizational communication has mushroomed. Of course, employees cannot function effectively unless they possess the technical skills that their positions require. But more and more it appears that being able to recognize, diagnose, and solve communication-related problems is vital to the success of people in even the most technical occupations. Accountants must be able to obtain complete, accurate, and sometimes sensitive information from their clients. Supervisors of production lines must be able to gather adequate and timely information on which to base their decisions. Managers of all divisions must be able to give their subordinates clear instructions, make sure those instructions are understood, create conditions in which their commands will be carried out, and get reliable feedback about the completion of the tasks that they have assigned.[1]

Understanding organizational communication has advantages above and beyond career advancement. At many times during their careers, people feel powerless because they simply do not understand the events taking place around them, or they understand but do not know how to deal with those events. In the worst cases they are victimized by such circumstances and do not understand how they became victims. As the title of a popular book says, bad things do happen to good people (and vice versa), both inside and outside of organizations. People need to be able to take a critical perspective on organizational events; that is, they need to examine the situations they find themselves in and understand the many pressures and constraints that make up those situations. People can learn from their experiences only if they understand the situations they face and the communication strategies that they might use to manage them effectively. In short, understanding organizational communicative processes is itself empowering—it allows people to determine which events are their responsibility and which ones are outside of their control and to discover new strategies for responding successfully.

The primary goal of the book is to give readers a sense of how organizational communication is used strategically, that is, how employees can analyze the organizational situations they face and choose appropriate communication strategies. It assumes that all employees are goal-oriented and that if they understand how communication functions in their organizations, they will be better able to achieve their own objectives and those of their organizations. It explains when it is appropriate to use a variety of communication strategies, including the denial of responsibility and the claim of ignorance ("Don't ask me. I just work here") and, just as important, when not to use them. In this chapter, we will introduce the core concept that underlies the rest of the book. We will observe that organizational communication is *strategic* and explain the two dimensions of that concept. This concept will become more and more clear as you progress through the book.

Organizational Communication as Strategic Discourse

One way to understand a complicated phenomenon is to begin with definitions of key terms. The simplest definition of organizational communication is that it is communication that occurs within organizations, but that definition is not very informative. Communication is generally defined as a process through which people, acting together, create, sustain, and manage meanings through the use of verbal and nonverbal signs and symbols within a particular context. Of course, the key terms in this definition are *people, acting together, meaning,* and *context.* In even a simple conversation, individuals bring a number of things with them. They each have histories of past conversations with one another or with people they perceive as similar to the other person. For example, conversations with one's boss are in some ways influenced by one's past conversations with bosses and other authority figures. They also bring expectations about future conversations with one another, goals for the conversation and for their relationship, assumptions about how people are supposed to communicate with one another, different kinds and levels of communicative skills, and so on. During every conversation people create and exchange a complex set of messages with one another and in doing so create meanings for each message and for the interaction. Some meanings that emerge are consistent with what the communicators intended; others are not. The systems of meanings that individuals create together influence their impressions of one another, their interpretations of their relationship, and the meanings that they attach to their communication. As their conversation continues, their goals may change as they discover that the other person is more (or less) sympathetic to their position than they expected. Similarly, people's assumptions about how civil they should be toward one another may change when they notice others are more civil than ever before, and so on.

For example, one of our graduate students studied a committee that was charged with designing guidelines for the sex education program of a city school district. To represent both sides of the issue, the committee was composed of some members who were liberal, in the sense that they supported a fairly extensive sex education program, and others who were conservative, that is, opposed to most types of current sex education programs. Both the liberal and the conservative subgroups came to the first meeting of the committee with little direct knowledge of each other. But each thought they knew what the other would be like based on their interpretations of the public debate in the United States over teenage sexuality and abortion. Conservatives feared that the liberals would want a program that encouraged sexual promiscuity among teenagers and would advocate abortion as a primary method of birth control; liberals were convinced that the conservatives would want a program that gave students little information and a great deal of fear and guilt.

During an early meeting the conservative group gave a number of long speeches arguing that the district's sex education program should persuade students to abstain from sexual activity. To the surprise of both groups, everyone in the room agreed. Although it took a while for the two groups to recover from the shock of finding that they agreed on something important, the rest of the committee's deliberations were different than they otherwise would have been. The liberals and the conservatives continued to be suspicious of one another throughout the next six months, but at least they listened to one another. In doing so, they discovered many other areas of disagreement and some additional areas of agreement. In the process of communicating with one another, members created, sustained, and modified a system of meaning that was uniquely their own. Their discussions were always influenced by the context in which they took place, both the local situation faced by the school board and the national debate over sexual issues. But the messages they exchanged and the meanings that they attributed to those messages could be understood only within the communicative process that they created.[2] In this committee, people with varying degrees of communicative skills acted together through the use of verbal and nonverbal cues to create, sustain, and modify systems of meaning. That is, they communicated.

Our definition of organizational communication differs from this definition of communication primarily in the complexity of the context and people dimensions. Organizational relationships are both like and unlike "normal" interpersonal relationships. We communicate with people at work because we like them or because our tasks require us to do so, or sometimes both. Thus, our relationships at work have both an interpersonal and an organizational dimension. As later chapters will explain, we constantly have to negotiate an appropriate mix of these two dimensions. We may have a strong personal relationship with our supervisor but have to maintain the kind of relational distance, detachment, and subservience that is appropriate to our organizational relationship. We may like one of our subordinates very much, but his or her inability to do the job well may create constant stresses in our interpersonal relationship. Work relationships are interpersonal relationships, but they also are different from relationships outside work.

CASE STUDY
How to Handle the Scarlet E-mail?

In some ways, the interpersonal relationships that we form at work are like the other interpersonal relationships that we form throughout our lives. But in other ways they are different.* Natural relationships seem to be voluntary—we encounter people, discover that we are attracted to one another, and begin to develop a relationship. We learn about them, develop expectations about how they will act, and begin to trust them when those expectations are fulfilled. If they violate our expectations, we interpret their behavior as a negative comment on them or as a negative comment on our relationship. If the relationship continues, we develop psychological contracts about how we will act toward and communicate with one another, and we make sure that those contracts are understood by both parties. The nature of our relationships is influenced by our relational histories and our anticipated future, and by our expectation that our relationships should be mutually fulfilling. We continue them because they fulfill what leadership expert Fredric Jablin has called "psychological-individual" functions.

Being members of the same organization complicates our relationships in many ways. Some organizational relationships are imposed on us, at least initially. We enter into them because they fulfill "formal organizational" functions. Some of those are with people we would have voluntarily formed relationships with; others are not.† The differences in power and status that accompany different organizational roles also complicate relationships—buying lunch for someone in the next cubicle does not mean the same thing as buying lunch for the vice president of sales. We communicate differently with people of different power or status, and we expect to be treated differently by them. Friends usually provide comfort and support to one another. But supervisors are required to evaluate their subordinates' work (and in some organizations, subordinates also evaluate their supervisors), and those evaluations may involve uncomfortable assessments of one another's competence, performance, and personality. Working relationships are also complicated by a "fishbowl" effect; they are public in a way that natural relationships are not.

The work situation also complicates normal aspects of relationships. All friends have to balance autonomy and connectedness. If friends work together, they may be forced to spend *too much* time together or to work *too closely*. Friends also tend to be more open and honest with one another because of their higher levels of trust. But organizational roles often require people to keep information secret, even from their closest friends. For a number of reasons, the "blended relationships" that people form at work simply are more complicated than natural relationships. As they develop, some become close friendships because the parties help one another solve work-related problems and find areas of similarity and attraction. Co-workers become trusted confidants and their communication becomes more personal and less cautious. Eventually some co-workers become important in one another's personal life.

The complications are easiest to see in romantic relationships at work. Although most experts on office etiquette flatly advise that if you care about your career, you should keep romance out of it, about 40 percent of workers admit to dating a colleague. With 50–60-hour workweeks, people simply do not have the time or opportunity to look elsewhere for romantic partners. Perhaps more importantly, people can gather accurate information about a potential mate by working with him or her—much more than they can learn at a singles' bar or from a classified ad. In recent years a few organizations (about 15 percent in 1999) have had written policies forbidding dating between supervisors and their subordinates, and more than 70 percent of employees say that people should never date their bosses or people who report to them. In spite of these policies and attitudes, most office romances involve supervisors and their subordinates (about 70 percent), often married, male supervisors and single, female subordinates. Most seem to be based on "true love" (about 80 percent) rather than on job- or advancement-related motives. In general, research indicates that romances do not harm organizational performance, unless they generate a high level of gossip that interferes with task performance. But obviously, perceptions of favoritism are more likely for employees involved in a romantic relationship with their supervisors. Gossip and discomfort among co-workers are extremely likely. If the relationship is terminated, it becomes difficult to see one's ex every day.[‡]

There are a number of commonsense steps that people can take to manage the complications created by office romances. First, all employees should learn their organization's view of workplace relationships. Seventy percent of organizations have no official policies, so it is sometimes difficult to obtain this information. But even in that case, once a relationship becomes serious, a frank conversation with your supervisors is warranted. Second, decide when and how to go public. Advisers differ on this issue. Some say that it's best to come clean about the relationship as soon as it gets serious. Others say that keeping it private is the best strategy. According to this perspective, your goal should be to minimize hearsay and innuendo, and especially to make sure your relationship doesn't interfere with your work. In some situations, those goals can best be achieved by keeping quiet; in others the open approach is less disruptive. Third, have an exit plan. Discuss what the two of you will do if the relationship ends. Then, if you break up, follow the plan. Finally, be discreet. Maintain a professional relationship at work. Richard Phillips, a career counselor in Palo Alto, California, reminds employees that "what you consider to be lovey-dovey between the two of you may make your co-workers retch. You're forcing them into a situation they don't want to be in."[§] Don't hold hands in the hallway, play footsie at meetings, or anything else that is perfectly appropriate in romantic relationships but completely inappropriate in professional relationships. And make sure your partner knows that your "aloof" behavior at work is not an indication that you're cold and uncaring toward him or her.[**]

Washington Post columnist Marc Fisher once wrote a column that vividly

(continued)

(Case Study, continued)

described how awkward office romances can be to co-workers. One of his co-workers accidentally sent him an e-mail that was meant for her romantic partner, probably by clicking the wrong line of her address directory. The message started out in a friendly tone, but very quickly became erotic. To make things worse, Marc knew the woman and her husband (who was not the recipient of the message); in fact, he had been invited to their home for dinner. What should he do? Respond in a businesslike tone ("Your message of 9:46 on Sunday morning was misdirected to me. Cheers.")? Notify the husband of what was going on? Keep quiet? Find some excuse for canceling the dinner date? He asked his friends for help. Most of the women told him to stay out of it; most of the men wanted him to find out all the sordid details and then let them in on it. He decided to do nothing.

Then another message arrived, one that was more intimate than the first. He went to dinner, sat between husband and wife, and felt very nervous throughout the evening. He squirmed during a private after-dinner conversation when the husband told him about his dreams for future years with his wife. He went home rattled and vowed to not have anything more to do with either of them. Then he went to a stationery store and bought note cards and envelopes—the appropriate medium for private messages.[††]

Applying What You've Learned

1. In what ways did the characters in Fisher's account violate the advice typically given to romantic partners in organizations? In what ways did they follow it?
2. Would a formal organizational policy about office romances have prevented this problem? What effects did the romance seem to have on the functioning of the organization?

Questions to Think About and Discuss

1. What would you have done had you been in Marc Fisher's place? What should you have done had you been in his place?
2. What does your answer to question 1 reveal about your personal values? About your view of the extent to which you have different values for working relationships than for nonwork relationships?

*See K. Bridge and L. A. Baxter, "Blended Relationships: Friends as Work Associates," *Western Journal of Communication* 56 (1992): 200–225; and B. A. Winstead, V. J. Derlega, M. J. Montgomery, and C. Pilkington, "The Quality of Friendships at Work and Job Satisfaction," *Journal of Social and Personal Relationships* 12 (1995): 199–215; Patricia Sias and Daniel Cahill, "From Coworkers to Friends," *Western Journal of Communication* 62 (1998): 273–299. Jablin makes the distinction between these two functions in "Organizational Entry, Assimilation, and Disengagement/Exit," in *The New Handbook of Organizational Communication,* Fredric Jablin and Linda Putnam, eds. (Thousand Oaks, CA: Sage, 2001).

[†]Jon Hess, "Maintaining Nonvoluntary Relationships with Disliked Partners," *Human Communication Research* 26 (2000): 458–488.

[‡]James Dillard and Katherine Miller, "Intimate Relationships in Task Environments," in *Handbook of Personal Relationships*, Steve Duck, ed. (Chichester, NY: Wiley, 1997), pp. 449–465; James Dillard, J. L. Hale, and Chris Segrin, "Close Relationships in Task Environments," *Management Communication Quarterly* 7 (1994): 227–255; Sue DeWine, Judy Pearson, and Carol Yost, "Intimate Office Relationships and Their Impact on Work Group Communication," in *Communication and Sex Role Socialization*, Cynthia Berryman-Fink, D. Ballard-Reisch, and L. H. Newman, eds. (New York: Garland, 1993), pp. 139–165; Dennis Powers, *The Office Romance* (New York: American Management Association, 1999).

[§]Sherri Eng, "Love in the Office Can Be Risky Affair," *Houston Chronicle*, March 14, 1999, C1.

[**]Bridge and Baxter, pp. 200–225; Winstead et al., pp. 199–215; Sias and Cahill, pp. 273–299; Jablin.

[††]Marc Fisher, "What's the Proper Etiquette for a Scarlet E-mail," *Houston Chronicle*, June 1, 1999, C1.

Just as we create relationships through conversation, we also create organizations through conversation. Thirty years ago, scholars thought of organizations as "things" or "containers" within which people sent chunks of information to one another through stable "channels" or "conduits" in order to meet shared goals. There is a grain of truth in this view. In fact, it is the view of communication that characterizes the traditional strategy of organizing that we will examine in Chapter 3. But it also depicts organizations as much more stable than they really are, and casts employees largely as inactive automatons who merely react to the messages they receive. By the late 1970s organizational theorists started to view organizations as dynamic, ever-changing groups of people who were actively trying to make sense out of the events that took place around them, while pursuing their own individual goals as well as goals they shared with their co-workers. At the same time, organizational communication theorists started viewing communication as more than the transfer of information; they saw it as a complex, multidimensional process through which organizing took place.[3]

By the late 1990s, an influential group of organizational communication scholars went even further, arguing that organizing and conversing are the same thing. Through communicating, we create shared views of organizational life. Until people start talking about the people around them as a work group, or their department as a department, or their organization as an organization, no work group, department, or organization really exists. Once everyone starts to view an organization as an organization, it takes on something of a life of its own. We talk about "what this organization does" or declare that the "auditing committee says" or "the legal department thinks" as if organizations can act, committees can speak, or departments can think, when it is the people who make up those groups who do all of those things. This process of treating something that we have created as if it was "real, live, and capable of acting" (which communication theorists call **reification**) is one of the most important dimensions of communication. For example, it is much more difficult to question the decisions of "the auditing committee" than it is to disagree with "John, Julie, Fred, and those folks from Arthur Andersen whom they hired to go over the books with them," and much more likely that an employee will be seen as credible when she or he speaks for "the organization" than when he or she speaks alone. In fact, the miracle of organizational communication processes is that they allow large numbers of people from very different backgrounds, ways of thinking, needs, and goals to coordinate their actions and create "organizations" that at least *seem* to be stable containers within which information flows from person to person.[4]

CASE STUDY
Can You Trust Anyone under Thirty? Part I

When managers, professors, and reporters think about workforce diversity, they usually think in terms of race, gender, ethnicity, or nationality. Each of these sources of difference is important, and we will examine them in detail in Unit III. But an often overlooked source of difference in today's organizations involves age and the experiences that accompany being part of a particular generation. The most common contrast is between the baby boomers, who were born between 1946 and 1964, and Generation X, born between 1969 and 1979. Boomers were raised in the post–World War II era of social stability and relative prosperity. Divorce was relatively rare; schools were safe, and jobs secure. Single-earner households with a clear division of labor between men and women were normal, for perhaps the only time in U.S. history. Boomers' parents or role models were the "organization men" described in William Whyte's 1956 book by the same name. They were loyal and committed to their organizations, learned to pay their dues patiently and wait for the opportunity for advancement, and largely defined themselves and their success in terms of their organizational rank. It was an era when white-collar workers in U.S. organizations believed and acted as if they had an unspoken contract with their organizations. If they worked hard, were loyal and productive employees, and followed the rules of their organizations, they expected to stay with their organizations as long as they chose to do so, to be rewarded for their contributions, and eventually to be supported during their golden years by an adequate pension.*

In contrast, Xers, who now make up about one-third of the U.S. workforce, grew up in two-career families, where divorce rates were increasing rapidly. They are the products of daycare, technology, including television, and perhaps most important, downsizing. During the period 1985 to 1995, the Xers' formative years, two-thirds of white-collar employees experienced downsizing or major restructuring. The fastest growing sector of the labor market between 1990 and 1995 was the category of temp employment agencies. (The next fastest growing categories were restaurants and bars, local government, recreation, and hospitals.) Richard Florida, a Carnegie Mellon University professor who studies employee retention, observes that "my students expect corporate disloyalty. A 24- or 25-year old says 'I am responsible for my own life. No one's going to take care of me, because they threw my dad out of work.'"† Adding to the fear and insecurities that Xers' parents felt was a growing resentment that stems from the disparity between skyrocketing firm profits and upper-management incomes on the one hand and the experiences of both white-collar and blue-collar workers on the other. Average worker pay rose 28 percent between 1990 and 1998, only 5.5 percent faster than the inflation rate. But average compensation of the top two managers in large companies rose 481 percent over the same time period. Consequently, the ratio of the base salaries of CEOs of U.S. firms to their average employee's salary in 1992 was 140:1, compared to 15:1 in Germany, 13:1 in Japan, and 40:1 in the United States twenty years earlier. In 1995 the ratio in the United States rose to 187:1 overall and 212:1 at the thirty largest U.S. companies; in 1999 the ratio was approximately 350:1; in 2002 it was around 530:1, even though there is very little evidence that CEO salaries are related to organizational performance.‡

As a result, Xers are advised everywhere to "consider themselves to be free agents" and keep their résumés polished and their network connections alert to opportunities in other firms. They must plan their own careers and seek out opportunities to develop new, marketable skills and opportunities to grow. And they seem to be listening. Traditional values like long-term commitment and loyalty to the firm aren't very popular with them. They refuse to make the kinds of sacrifices that their parents made—being subservient to their bosses, accepting multiple cross-country moves, putting in long hours, or accepting overnight travel. They are fiercely independent, aggressive, hard-working entrepreneurs, even if they are working in corporate structures. They concentrate on developing computer, leadership, and communication skills, in part to make them valuable to their current firms but also as a means of going out on their own as soon as possible. They move on quickly, changing jobs nine times by the time they're in their thirties. They are willing to take the risks of self-employment or job changes to get the greater rewards and freedom that accompanies being their own bosses. But they also tend to form relatively superficial and inauthentic relationships in the workplace. Knowing that they may not be around very long, they make little investment in getting to know their supervisors and co-workers as people, and their supervisors and co-workers spend little energy getting to know them. This makes it easier to exit the organization—they can do so without leaving close friends or commitments behind—and makes it more likely that they will do so. Ironically, they need to be given clear road maps about organizational life and want lots of performance feedback.

Some supervisors call them slackers—one J.C. Penney manager complained that "when I started out, I worked long hours. I did whatever they wanted me to do. They come in at 8 and leave at 5." The Xers are unrealistic about how long it will take them to be promoted—"if they don't get what they want, they'll leave—they're just not loyal." They question their supervisors' decisions and authority. They ask questions that are unheard of to the boomers, such as *If I don't like what my boss says, can I go to the next level?* and even do so during job interviews. Xers often view their boomer bosses as burned-out relics of a bygone era. They want rewards to be based on performance, not seniority. They want to know what

(continued)

those rewards will be, and know them in advance of taking on a task. They communicate in ways that boomers find excessively blunt—a direct, bold, cut-to-the-chase style. Boomers like to think that the Xers are just in a passing phase, that in time they'll settle down into a traditional mold. But Xers plan to retire long before they settle down. Some organizations are already encountering serious conflicts between the two groups. A U.S. Army report, released in early 2001, predicted that turnover among Generation Xers would make it difficult for the service to fill leadership positions within a few years. In 1989, 6.7 percent of the army's captains left the service voluntarily. The figure rose to 10.6 percent in 1999, and it reached 13 percent in 2000. Why the increase? Tensions between baby boomer senior officers and Gen X junior officers. Leonard Wong, a retired lieutenant colonel who authored the report, said, "Today's senior officers do not understand today's junior officers or their perspectives."[§]

As if dealing with the boomers isn't challenging enough, the Xers also will have to deal with a younger generation that has different experiences, expectations, and demands. Tentatively labeled the Y Generation, Next Generation, or Millennials, they were born between 1982 and 2002. There are more of them (81 million) than any other generation in U.S. history save the boomers (87 million), and they have had more disposable income and are more technologically sophisticated than any other group of teenagers in U.S. history. As a result they are highly optimistic and see a world of opportunities in front of them. They are already trying to distance themselves from the Xers—softer music, different clothing. Like the boomers, they are maturing in a time of sustained economic growth, have become accustomed to material possessions—cars, stereos, phones, computers, the right clothes—and believe in working hard in the short term for the promise of a big payoff in the long term. They are team-oriented and obsessed with planning—many of them knew what they wanted to do with their lives when they were in middle school. They are like the depression/World War II generation in their willingness to conform to social norms, like the boomers in their core values—in one poll 94 percent said they shared their parents' values—and like Gen Xers in being highly individualistic. Some observers say they are cynical and disconnected from their communities and the political process. Others say that they do not trust institutions and really are socially active—more than any other generation since the 1960s—and will bring their activist values to the workplace. Xers often view them as demanding, self-absorbed, and presumptuous.[**] They do not trust existing political institutions.

Bosses complain about their short attention spans and habits like talking to friends via cell phone or instant messaging or downloading music while at work. They seem to think they are entitled to special projects rather than being willing to "pay their dues" doing mundane tasks. And they think everything is negotiable:

Mr. Lankford, a health care recruiter, said that young workers often challenged company policies on matters like tuition reimbursement. "Their attitude is, 'Why won't you pay for this?' he said. 'Instead of accepting that these are our policies, they'll say: 'Let's talk about making an exception.' Or, 'Let's change the policies.'"

Education and training are other areas of negotiation because they know that they have to keep their skills current if they are to remain competitive. Many experts think that this model of constant negotiation cannot be sustained over the long run because it focuses attention on individual gain and away from the organization's needs. But bosses also admire their willingness to "take on tasks they know nothing about . . . and fearlessly march ahead."[††]

But their world also is changing. They are the safest generation in U.S. history—their parents were obsessive about car safety seats, bicycle helmets, and so on. The events of September 11, 2001, may have undermined their sense of invulnerability, though. The recession of the early 2000s has put their optimism to the test, especially because unemployment and underemployment among younger workers is even higher than it is in the general population. The series of corporate scandals that has characterized the new century may have increased their cynicism about established institutions. And there are those baby boomers and Gen Xers who still seem to be hanging around.

Applying What You've Learned

1. What expectations does each of these generational groups have about life and about organizations?
2. What messages and experiences have contributed to those expectations?
3. Over what issues are the three groups likely to have conflicts? Why?

Questions to Think About and Discuss

1. To which, if any, of the three generational groups do you belong? (Remember, it's the experiences you've had more than your age that influences generational membership.) How do your expectations and experiences correspond to theirs? Over what issues are you likely to have conflicts with members of the three groups? Why?
2. Are the strategies chosen by Generation Xers appropriate to the situations they face? Generation Yers?
3. What effects are their strategies likely to have on their relationships with their supervisors in traditional firms? with their co-workers? with their subordinates? Why?

---

[*]Chip Walker and Elissa Moses, "The Age of Self-Navigation," *American Demographics* 18 (September 1996): 36–42.; Shelly Donald Coolidge, "Boomers, Gen-Xers Clash," ABC News, September 1, 1999, http://www.abcnews.go.com/sections/business; Maggie Jackson, "Business Bends to Include Generation X Workforce," *Bryan/College Station (TX)*

(continued)

(Case Study, continued)

Eagle, January 31, 1999, E1. For analyses of these trends, see Patrice Buzzanell, "The Promise and Practice of the New Career and Social Contract," in *Rethinking Organizational and Managerial Communication from Feminist Perspectives,* P. Buzzanell, ed. (Thousand Oaks, CA: Sage, 2000); David Neumark, ed., *On the Job: Is Long-Term Employment a Thing of the Past?* (New York: Russell Sage Foundation, 2000).

†Stephanie Franken, "Corporations' Quest to Create a Happy Workplace," *Houston Chronicle,* October 15, 2000, D3.

‡"Executive Pay Remains Tops," ABC News, August 30, 1999, http://www.abcnews.go.com/sections/business; Joel Blau, *Illusions of Prosperity* (New York: Oxford University Press, 1999). These trends are analyzed in more detail in Chapter 12.

§"Top, Junior Officers Vie, Study Says," *Houston Chronicle,* November 19, 2000, A11.

**Don O'Briant, "Move Over, Gen-Xers," *Houston Chronicle,* August 13, 2003, D1; Neil Howe and William Strauss, *Millennials Go to College* (Washington, DC: American Association of Collegiate Registrars and Admissions Officers, 2003); and *Millennials Rising* (New York: Vintage, 2000); Peter Cappelli, *The New Deal at Work: Managing the Market-Driven Workforce* (Boston: Harvard Business School Press, 1999).

††Julie Connelly, "Youthful Attitudes, Sobering Realities," *New York Times on the Web,* October 28, 2003, p. 3, http://www.nytimes.com/.

The Fundamental Paradox

The concept of strategy enters into our perspective on organizational communication at two levels. One level is that of the organization. Most people have learned to think of organizations as places where a large number of members efficiently cooperate with one another to achieve some shared objectives. According to this view, disagreements, conflicts, inefficiencies, and communication breakdowns are aberrations—failures that could have been avoided if the organization and its members had only worked as they are supposed to work. When errors are made, they only need to be analyzed and corrective actions taken. In this book we take a different perspective. We will suggest that the notion that organizations normally run like "well-oiled machines" is not only unrealistic, but it can be damaging to organizations and to their members. It is more realistic and in the long run more productive to view organizations as sites where multiple tensions exist—tensions that must be managed successfully if the organization is to succeed in meeting its members' goals. Some tensions are specific to individual organizations; others are characteristic of the relationship between organizations and the surrounding society. But all organizations face at least one fundamental tension: a tension between individual members' needs and the needs of their organizations. People have needs for autonomy (the feeling that they are in control of their actions and destinies), creativity (the feeling of pride that comes from making something that did not previously exist or in doing something better or in a different way than anyone else), and sociability (the feeling that they have meaningful interpersonal relationships with other people). They also need an adequate degree of structure, stability, and predictability in their lives. They need to know who they are, where they fit in their organizations and society, and how they and their peers are likely to act in different circumstances.

Organizations also have needs. The most important of these are control and coordination. Organizations exist because the tasks that people must perform are sufficiently complex that members must cooperate with one another to achieve their goals. In essence, organizations require us to sacrifice some of our independence—our ability to be self-sufficient—and replace it with interdependence. In modern societies, few persons have the skills, experience, or opportunities to do everything personally that is necessary to live a productive life. Most modern people actually can do very little. We are constantly at the mercy of electricians, plumbers, appliance-repair technicians, auto mechanics, and organizations in which we work. What we can do, we do very well. Modern human beings have traded independence for **specialization** and have become far more efficient as a result. But our efficiency depends almost wholly on coordinating our activities with the activities of others.

Different cultures vary in the degree of interdependence that exists within them, as do different organizations and the various departments within them. Research-and-development divisions usually have low interdependence, relying only on computer operators, purchasing and receiving departments (which order and deliver raw materials), and the physical plant operators (who keep equipment secure and functioning). For them, coordination within the division is crucial; coordinating their activities with outsiders is less important. For other divisions, coordination is a more complex and critical problem. But to some degree, all organizations need to coordinate their members' activities.

Organizations also need to control their members' interpersonal relationships, both who they form relationships with and how they communicate within their work relationships. Some version of the military command that officers must not fraternize with enlisted personnel exists within almost all organizations. For example, Intel Corporation forbids dating between supervisors and their subordinates and enforces the rule by transferring offenders to different departments, but does not restrict relationships among peers. Often the command is never spoken because it need not be. Associates (recent graduates) in law firms learn by observation that they should not initiate conversations with senior partners, but should respond immediately when partners initiate communication with them. Assembly workers at Dana Corporation learn that they are expected to have lunch with upper management, and individuals in upper management learn that they are expected to have friendly but relatively superficial interpersonal relationships with rank-and-file workers. In both cases, the organization subtly controls the kind of interpersonal relationships that employees form and maintain. Organizations vary in how tightly they control their members' actions and relationships, but all organizations must exercise at least a minimal level of control if they are to survive.

However, these two sets of needs—those of a society or organization and those of their individual members—create a fundamental dilemma. If a society or organization successfully controls its members, the individual needs for autonomy, creativity, and sociability are frustrated. But if the society or organization fails to control its members, it loses the ability to coordinate its members' activities, and fails to achieve its central objectives. So societies/organizations must find ways to meet their members' individual needs while persuading them to act in ways that meet the society/organization's needs. They do so through adopting various *strategies of organizing.* Conversely, if members of organizations are to meet their own needs, they must find ways to *communicate strategically* within the situations they face in their organizations. This book is about this fundamental paradox and the role that communication plays in managing it.

Strategies of Organizing

In Unit II we will discuss at length the major organizational strategies that are employed in modern organizations. Each strategy has a different design and structure, a different system of employee motivation and control, different communication systems, and different ways of using communication technology. Of course, no organization corresponds perfectly to any of the strategies of organizing that we will discuss. All organizations have a mixture of strategies in place. Similarly, no strategy works exactly as it is supposed to work. But thinking about real organizations in terms of the available strategies of organizing can help members make sense out of their particular organizations.

The first and most important step in understanding strategies of organizing is to realize that they are strategies—choices made by powerful members of an organization about how it will be designed and how it will operate. It is easy to forget that organizations are constructed through strategic choices, for two reasons. First, the organizations of a particular society, and of a particular sector of an economy, are very much alike. In the United States, organizations tend to be large, privately owned, and only loosely regulated by government. This was not always so. Two hundred years ago there were very few large organizations; in the 1890s there were only a few, and they operated railroads or manufactured textiles or steel. Suddenly, things changed—within five years the 200 biggest corporations of the time were formed, and many of them still exist.

There are a number of reasons for this change—the United States was rich in natural resources and had a seemingly inexhaustible supply of inexpensive labor from Europe, a culture that celebrated individual achievement and entrepreneurship, and mass markets that were accessible because of improving transportation and communication technologies. The rapid economic growth following the Civil War concentrated wealth in the hands of a much smaller number of people than ever before in U.S. history. The economic power of these "robber barons" quickly exceeded that of other institutions. The United States was settled by immigrants, who brought with them a deep distrust of the dominant institutions of Europe and Asia—the official church and government. Initially, laws required corporations to be operated in the interests of the public as a whole and to have public representatives on their boards of directors.

In 1819, however, a group of New England businessmen, represented by Daniel Webster, persuaded the U.S. Supreme Court to rule that those requirements were unconstitutional. In the same year, owners persuaded courts and legislatures to create "limit liability," which says that if a company goes bankrupt and cannot pay its creditors or workers, the individuals managing the company do not have to pay its debts out of their own pockets, regardless of how wealthy they might be. The Supreme Court also declared that only the federal government had the power to regulate interstate commerce, which was important because at that time the federal government was much less powerful than the governments of the largest states. Finally, owners obtained the legal right to sell stock in their companies, and to do so in a way that limited individual stockholders' influence over their decisions or operations. This legal change gave them almost unlimited access to the funds they needed to enlarge their organizations. Taken together, these actions gave the executives of U.S. firms a unique ability to increase the size and independence of their organizations. Of course, to do so the owner-managers had to persuade policymakers that the changes they preferred were more efficient, better at generating jobs, more capable of meeting the overall society's needs, and so on. The fact that their firms often were *not* any more efficient, productive, or socially responsible than the governmental systems or alternative forms of organizing that they replaced is testimony to the success of their persuasive appeals. The result was a unique "American system," which was not duplicated anywhere until the expansion of U.S. economic and political power after World War II took it to much of the rest of the world.[5]

Organizations in the same sectors of an economy also tend to look very much alike. This is partly because their managers tend to be educated in the same way, which leads them to have similar views of what organizations are supposed to "look like" and how they are supposed to operate. But another reason is that organizations seem to be credible to various stakeholders only if they seem to be "normal." Prospective employees do not want to work for organizations that are too different from the norms in their "organizational fields." Bankers and stockholders do not want to invest in firms that do not have the up-to-date systems and practices that their competitors have. So, in order to legitimate themselves and their organizations, managers tend to mimic what other organizations do. Chapter 12 will explain the link between organizational communication and perceptions of credibility in more detail; at this point it is sufficient to realize that legitimacy is not automatic. It is earned by adopting familiar strategies of organizing and by strategically communicating that the organization is "normal."[6]

Eventually a single strategy of organizing comes to dominate each sector of an economy, and often of the entire society. Because it is the dominant strategy, it *seems* to be the best strategy, to be natural and normal. Because it is normal and natural, it need not be justified. In fact, there is no need to justify the choice; furthermore, it no longer *seems* to be a choice. Only those organizations whose leaders want to adopt a different strategy have to justify their choice, to legitimate their decisions to act in ways that are "abnormal" and "unnatural" (see Chapter 7). When people encounter organizations from other societies where the "normal" strategy of organizing is different—as often happens in a global economy—they may realize that their ways of doing things are indeed the result of choices that have been made in the past and that they repeat every day. But the rest of the time they take for granted the strategy of organizing that is normal to them.

Strategic Communication and Life in Organizations

The second sense in which organizational communication is strategic involves the actions of individual employees. For more than two thousand years, communication scholars have believed that people communicate most effectively if they adapt their communication strategies to the situations they face.[7] To communicate effectively, employees must be able to analyze the situations they encounter in their organizations, determine which communication strategies are available to them in those situations, select the best of those strategies, and enact them effectively. However, selecting appropriate communicative strategies is a complex process. All organizational situations contain *guidelines* that tell employees how they are supposed to act and communicate and *constraints* that tell them how they are not to act and communicate. Fortunately, organizational situations also provide *resources* for acting—potential lines of argument, acceptable forms of persuasive appeal, and so on—that allow employees to pursue their goals strategically. Strategies of organizing create particular kinds of organizational situations. As a result, the relative importance of guidelines/constraints and resources differs in different situations. In most organizational situations, employees have the resources available that they will need to meet at least some of their goals and at least some of their organization's objectives simultaneously. In these cases, choosing productive communication strategies is not particularly difficult.

For example, one of the most important guidelines/constraints in bureaucratic organizations is that communication should follow the **chain of command.** That is, subordinates send messages to their immediate supervisors, who relay the information to their immediate supervisors if they deem it appropriate to do so, and so on. No one goes over her or his supervisor's head. However, communicating via the chain of command is slow, cumbersome, and vulnerable to many different kinds of communication breakdowns (see Chapter 3 for more details). As a result, employees who follow this guideline/constraint are likely to feel that they do not know what is going on in their organization, and may even lack the basic information that they need in order to do their jobs. So they learn to compensate for weaknesses in formal, chain-of-command communication by forming **informal communication networks**—links to other employees that allow them to obtain and send information without following the chain of command. By using this strategy, they are able to find out what is going on in the organization, meet their needs for autonomy, and, ironically, make their organization work better than it otherwise would. And, in organizations in which the chain-of-command rule is taken *very* seriously, they learn to hide or disguise their informal networks.

In other situations, however, choosing the appropriate communication strategy is more difficult, perhaps impossible. Organizational situations sometimes paralyze employees, at least momentarily. One kind of paralysis occurs when the guidelines and constraints in a situation are clear, but the resources available to meet them are unclear, unknown, or insufficient. For example, an organizational situation may include the command for psychotherapists to "do good work," hospital administrators to "cut costs," or elementary schoolteachers to "stimulate all the students' interests." These guidelines may tell employees what they are supposed to do, but they tell them little about how they are supposed to accomplish the tasks. As a result, employees may become paralyzed while trying to make sense out of their situations and discover the resources that are available to them. A newly graduated student who had become a stockbroker once called and asked, "What do I do next?" after being given a desk and a "training session" that included only the comment "I hope you'll like it here. Just don't screw up like George (your predecessor) did." This kind of paralyzing situation seems to be common for new employees and has been shown to be a major source of organizational stress.

A more extreme form of paralysis occurs when action is called for, but constraints leave the employee with no available resources. Presumably, Linus's purpose (in Figure 1-1) is to gain the childlike fun that comes from a friendly snow-

FIGURE 1–1

PEANUTS reprinted by permission of United Feature Syndicate, Inc.

ball fight. But Lucy's comments leave him with both a command to act (dropping the snowball is an act) and no productive way to achieve his purpose. Throwing the snowball will fail; so will not throwing it. Lucy has taken the fun out of the snowball fight and has robbed Linus of any opportunity for meaningful choice.

Organizational situations sometimes parallel the Peanuts situation. Supervisors may find that they have only one position to allocate and two departments that desperately need help, have equally strong claims on the position, and will be justifiably angry if they do not receive it. Subordinates may be told to do one thing by one superior and the opposite by another. They may know that one supervisor has a higher rank than the other and that in their organization they are always expected to follow the orders given by the higher-ranking person. But they may also know that the lower-ranking supervisor might retaliate against them in ways that will never be detected by anyone else if they violate his or her order. Here the subordinate has no realistic options because no adequate resources are available. Between the two extremes of simple situations and paralyzing ones are those that employees normally face at work: situations that provide a range of options that can serve both the employees' purposes and those of their organizations, situations in which employees can act and communicate strategically.

Finally, employees' strategic choices create, reproduce, and in some cases change their guidelines/constraints and resources. For example, bureaucratic strategies of organizing continue to exist only because employees act like bureaucrats. The organizational strategy of making decisions by applying established, written policies and regulations (a key element of the bureaucratic strategy) exists only because members of some organizations actually make decisions based on established policies and regulations and have come to believe that decisions should be made in this way. In doing so, they choose to follow a rule that limits their actions to those prescribed by the organizational situation. And in doing so, they use that rule as a resource for managing demanding people. But in the process, they reproduce and legitimate the guidelines and constraints that they face.[8]

Conclusion: The Complexities of Organizational Communication

All societies, and all organizations, must find ways to successfully deal with a fundamental paradox: If they are to survive, they must control and coordinate the actions of their members. But control and coordination frustrate individuals' needs for autonomy, creativity, and sociability. A number of strategies of organizing have been developed that strive to achieve the organization's goals while managing this fundamental paradox. Each of these strategies relies on communication, because it is through communication that organizations emerge, are maintained, and change. Chapter 2 focuses on the process of making sense out of organizational situations. The chapters that make up Unit II examine the dominant forms of organizing used in contemporary organizations. Chapter 3 discusses what we call the *traditional* strategy of organizing. Chapters 4–7 cover *relational, cultural, network,* and *alternative* strategies of organizing. Although we strive to present each strategy as clearly as possible, we also continually caution readers not to lose sight of the complexity of organizational life. No strategy of organizing appears in a pure form in any modern organization. This is partly because every organization has its own unique history, membership, and mode of operating. As a result, every organization is a distinctive mixture of traditional, relational, cultural, and network strategies. Complexity also results from the strategies themselves. Each strategy focuses on one dimension of organizational communication while de-emphasizing the others. But the de-emphasized dimensions cannot be ignored completely. They are integral parts of organizational communication and have an important impact even if they are not central to the dominant strategy that is used in the organization. As a result, organizational life is much messier than any overall strategy envisions. That messiness makes organizational life interesting. It also makes strategic communication especially challenging.

In addition, members of organizations in the early twenty-first century face an increasingly complex array of challenges. The chapters in Unit III examine what we believe are the most important of them—dealing with organizational power and politics (Chapter 8), making effective decisions and managing conflicts surrounding them (Chapter 9), dealing with the challenges and opportunities created by the increasing diversity of organizations' members (Chapter 10) and the increasing globalization of their operations (Chapter 11), and managing ethical challenges (Chapter 12). At this point, all of these ideas may seem a little overwhelming. At least, we hope that most readers feel a little overwhelmed at this stage. Communication is an exceptionally complex process; organizational communication is an especially complex type of communication. There are a depressingly large number of books, training programs, and consultants' gimmicks that depict effective organizational communication as the simple application of "five foolproof techniques" or some equivalent. Unfortunately, these depictions are as misleading as they are glib. A number of principles are available for employees to learn and use in most organizational situations. But they are neither simple, foolproof, nor applicable in every case. Our goal in this book is to explain those principles and indicate how people can analyze the complexities they face at work and choose appropriate strategic responses, recognizing all the while that it was their choices and the choices made by other members of their organizations that created and reproduce the situations they face.

Notes

[1] See, for example, Patricia Hayes Andrews and Richard T. Herschel, *Organizational Communication* (Geneva, IL: Houghton Mifflin, 1996), pp. 16–18. For similar results in studies of Australian organizations, see Henry Irwin, *Communicating with Asia* (Sydney, Australia: University of New South Wales Press, 1997).

[2] See Nina Anderson Legg, "Other People's Kids: Decision-Making about Sexual Education" (master's thesis, Texas A&M University, 1992).

[3] Linda Putnam, Nelson Phillips, and Pamela Chapman, "Metaphors of Communication and Organization," in *Handbook of Organization Studies,* Stewart Clegg, Cynthia Hardy, and Walter Nord, eds. (London: Sage, 1996); Karl Weick, *The Social Psychology of Organizing*, 2nd ed. (Reading, MA: Addison-Wesley, 1979); Bonnie Johnson, *Communication: The Process of Organizing* (Boston: Allyn and Bacon, 1977).

[4] François Cooren and James Taylor, "Organization as an Effect of Mediation: Redefining the Link between Organization and Communication," *Communication Theory* 7 (1997): 219–260; James Taylor and Elizabeth van Every, *The Emergent Organization: Communication as Its Site and Surface* (Mahwah, NJ: Lawrence Erlbaum, 2000).

[5] Charles Perrow, *Organizing America* (Princeton, NJ: Princeton University Press, 2002).

[6] Neil Fligstein, *The Transformation of Corporate Control* (Cambridge, MA: Harvard University Press, 1990); and *The Architecture of Markets* (Princeton, NJ: Princeton University Press, 2001); William Powell and Paul DiMaggio, eds., *The New Institutionalism in Organizational Theory* (Chicago: University of Chicago Press, 1990).

[7] See George Kennedy, *Classical Rhetoric in Its Christian and Secular Traditions from Ancient to Modern Times* (Chapel Hill: University of North Carolina Press, 1980). A similar concept has been developed by rhetorical theorist Lloyd Bitzer in "The Rhetorical Situation," *Philosophy and Rhetoric* 1 (1968): 1–14; and "Functional Communication," in *Rhetoric in Transition,* Eugene White, ed. (University Park: Pennsylvania State University Press, 1980), especially pp. 27, 36–37.

[8] For a case study of how face-to-face communication reproduces strategies of organizing, see Teresa Harrison, "Communication and Interdependence in Democratic Organizations," in *Communication Yearbook 17,* Stanley Deetz, ed. (Newbury Park, CA: Sage, 1995), pp. 247–274.

Chapter 2

Keys to Strategic Organizational Communication

Don't look back . . . something might be gaining on you.
—Satchel Paige, Baseball Hall of Famer

Central Themes

- Systems models can be used to describe organizations and to explain their processes.
- Principles of systems thinking include the complexity of causation, the importance of indirect effects, the need to look carefully for the levers that can change systems, the fact that the whole is greater than the sum of its parts, the need to understand the system by analyzing its subsystems and suprasystem, and the importance of organizational learning and renewal.
- Critical analysis is designed to discover and escape from the limitations of assumptions that are embedded in organizations.
- Diversity presents a challenge because organizations tend to value homogeneity, but it is important to take advantage of the resources that diversity provides for the organization.
- Globalization may lead in any of three directions—homogenization, polarization, or hybridization of cultures.
- Over the past fifty years, there has been a transition from a production economy based on physical production of goods in factories to a knowledge society, in which most value is added through information and knowledge-related activities.
- Impacts of information and communication technologies (ICTs) on organizations and their members are neither simple nor deterministic but are shaped by social processes in the organizations and by the strategy of organizing they utilize.

- A number of ethical and policy problems arise from organizational use of ICTs, including privacy issues and the degree of surveillance that organizations should be allowed to undertake.

Key Terms

organizational system	information work
process system	convergence
principles of systems thinking	Internetworking
wholeness	intranet
levers	extranet
suprasystem	firewall
subsystem	portal
hegemony	bandwidth
laissez-faire capitalism	wireless
futility thesis	ubiquitous computing
perversity thesis	electronic data interchange
jeopardy thesis	CAD/CAM
heterogeneous	office workflow system
cultural homogenization	enterprise resource planning system
polarization	knowledge management
hybridization	telework
knowledge work	outsourcing

Effective strategies respond to the demands of the situation. In general, the situation facing today's communicators is more complex, more dynamic, and more uncertain than ever. With each new edition of this book, we have had to include more material on dealing with change and responding to complex challenges. This chapter presents five keys to effective organizational communication in a complex and changing world. These are not "tips" for how to communicate better, but ways to think about organizations that will foster more intelligent and discriminating responses to the challenges we face day to day. Following these will help you understand the forces shaping today's organizations and respond to them in a creative and positive way. Basically, we believe that effective organizational communication rests on cultivating the ability to

Discover connections among seemingly unconnected phenomena

Identify and critically assess the assumptions, often unknown to you, that shape your behavior

Take advantage of the new ideas and different skills that diversity brings to organizations

Understand how globalization is changing organizations and society

Understand the critical role information and communication technology has played in transforming modern organizations and how it can be used to make organizations more effective and enrich organizational life

This chapter introduces these keys, which are developed throughout the book.

Seeing Connections: The Importance of Systems Thinking

People Express Airlines was an amazing success story that turned into a spectacular failure.[1] It provided low-cost, high-quality air service on the East Coast throughout the early 1980s and grew to be the nation's fifth largest air carrier. It had a reputation as a corporate pioneer, based in part on its emphasis on its people. The airline had a number of innovative human resource policies, such as job rotation, team management, employee stock ownership, and a flat hierarchy, that have since been widely adopted. These innovations kept its employees happy and committed to the organization and enabled the airline to offer excellent low-cost service. The airline grew rapidly and took over Frontier Airlines to help provide the capacity it needed to continue growing.

Despite its enviable position, People Express ran into trouble. Demand for the airline's flights far outstripped the available seats, and the overload resulted in delays and passenger complaints. Service on the flights deteriorated, and its customers left in droves. By 1986 the airline had lost over $130 million and was "rescued" (read absorbed) in a buyout by Texas Air Corporation.

At the time, many theories were advanced to explain People Express's collapse. Some commentators traced the problems to a human resource policy that was "too lenient" and did not control employee costs enough. Others argued that the takeover of Frontier had been poorly planned and left the company strapped for cash, so that when its debtors called in loans, it was unable to pay them.

However, these accounts do not give much insight into how the troubles at People Express developed. It is always easy to identify "causes" of an organization's problems from the outside, but to really understand the situation, it is important to consider the processes that created and worsened the problems.

People Express "crashed and burned" because of a complex system of factors. The first of the "low fare" airlines, People Express introduced an innovative concept—low prices, no frills, and high-quality air service. It gained a reputation that led to an increasing number of new customers. In its early days, People Express's innovative human resource practices and employee stock ownership kept morale high and motivated its employees to work hard to maintain excellent service levels. However, as the number of customers rose, there were not enough staff to handle them, and current employees were overworked. Bringing more employees into the firm was slowed by its progressive human resource practices, which required lengthy training and development of new employees.

At the same time, demand for bookings continued to increase, because reports in the media and by word of mouth continued to tout the airline as a great bargain. This drove the price of People Express's stock higher, to more than twenty dollars a share. As a result, many of People Express's employees were wealthy. Though they were fatigued, they were happy and positively motivated.

Nevertheless, the crush of new passengers led to increasing customer complaints about service problems, ticketing delays, overbooked flights, and overloaded employees. The overworked staff had few resources with which to address these problems. For many, the passenger complaints soured the one thing they had to hold onto, their love of working with people. As problems persisted, customers began turning to other airlines. The resulting decreased revenues led to a fall in the stock price. Once employees realized that their hard work was not going to be rewarded by stock appreciation, their motivation began to shrink. There was a further decline in service quality, and still more customers gave their business to other airlines, which further worsened the bottom line. Paradoxically, the very human resource plans that had originally made People Express distinctive eventually brought about lower motivation and declining service.

Increasing the size of its fleet by acquiring Frontier Airlines promised to help address the airline's capacity problems and offered an opportunity to improve service. But implementing the progressive human relations policy in Frontier meant a delay in utilizing this new capacity, because Frontier's employees needed to be trained. Service quality continued to erode, and the new capacity really just added to the problem because employees were overworked and saw little reward from working still harder. The end result of this complex set of processes was a worsening spiral that led to the ultimate demise of the airline. These processes are shown in Figure 2-1.

People Express did not necessarily have to fail. Studies of People Express and similar airlines showed that it could have turned these negative processes around by either raising ticket prices by 25 percent (not an excessive increase in view of the economical prices it offered) or maintaining its high level of service, if it had acted soon enough. However, by the time the downward spiral developed momentum, raising ticket prices would have driven the airline's most loyal customers away, and maintaining high levels of service is difficult with a demoralized and overworked staff. These measures should have been enacted well before the spiral worsened.

People Express failed because of a lack of systems thinking.[2] Its managers should have realized that if rising stock prices made workers happy and motivated, falling stock prices might do the opposite. They should have recognized that growing as fast as the company did would stress service quality. Managers should have known that in the face of demand a slight increase in ticket prices would not have been a problem and might even have reduced customer overload somewhat, giving a window of time in which to renew service quality. Employees should have recognized that they were the key to turning the airline around and causing stock prices to rise. Unfortunately, neither the employees nor the managers were able to see these things. Instead, they stayed focused on

FIGURE 2-1
The System of Factors Influencing the Effectiveness of People Express

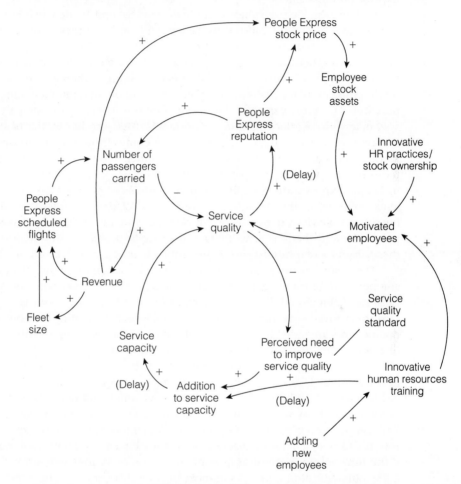

A plus sign by an arrow means "The greater the X, the greater the Y." For example, the greater the fleet size, the more flights People Express can schedule. A minus sign by an arrow means "The greater the X, the lower the Y." For example, the more passengers carried, the lower the quality of service (more passengers put more stress on flight attendants; they are rushed and their quality of service declines). Any cycle with all positive signs (for example, Service quality —+→ Perceived need to improve service quality —+→ Addition to service quality —+→ Service capacity —+→ Service quality) is a reinforcing cycle. These cycles result in ever-increasing values, a "runaway" system. Any cycle with an odd number of negative signs (for example, Service quality —+→ People Express reputation —+→ Number of passengers carried —→ Service quality) is a dampening cycle. The negative links counteract the influence of the positive ones, creating a "balanced" cycle. These can sometimes counteract runaway cycles (but there were not enough of them in the People Express case).

their immediate jobs, assuming that what worked in the past would work in the future. They were not able to recognize the forces that ended up driving People Express out of business.

Systems thinking does not come naturally. Several tendencies prevent us from seeing the system. Most of us have been taught to break things into manageable parts, to focus on a single problem and look for its cause. This is useful in some cases, because it enables us to act relatively quickly and in a straightforward manner. However in the case of People Express, there was not a simple single problem, but a chain of interconnected factors that interacted in a complex way. This is the way it is in most organizations. Focusing on one part of the system leads to overlooking other important factors. Another barrier to systems thinking is the narrowing of perspective that comes from working in a particular position in an organization. Over time members tend to see things mostly in terms of their position or department and reduce problems to their perspective. In People Express, for example, the human resource people viewed the problems confronting the organization as human relations problems, while the finance people viewed them as cash-flow issues and the operations management people viewed them as scheduling and capacity problems. Although each of these diagnoses captured a part of the problem, none grasped the whole system.

The basic constituents of a system are its components and the relationships among them. In thinking about organizations, two important types of systems must be distinguished. First, the *organization itself* can be viewed as a system. **Organizational systems** can exist at several levels, depending on whether the components are individual members of the organization, departments or units, or even entire organizations. The types of relationships that hold the system together may vary depending on the nature of the components. If the components are individuals, then the relationships among them include authority (who reports to whom), communication (who talks to whom about what), work roles (who works with whom and what do they do), and interpersonal relationships (who is friends with whom). A common way to map such systems is in the form of a network diagram, which is called a communication network if the relationship in question is communication of various types. We will discuss communication networks in more detail in Chapter 4. If the components are units or departments, relationships include authority (which departments have authority over which others), communication (which departments communicate with one another), and work (where departments fit into the workflow of the organization; which departments work with which). The same types of relationships hold when the components of the system are organizations. We will discuss systems of organizations in more depth in Chapter 6, which introduces the networked organization. Figure 2-2 depicts several different organizational systems.

Second, the *processes* that affect the organization and its members can be modeled as a system of interacting factors, as we did in the People Express example. In this case the components of the system are variables that play a part in its operation. The relationships among the variables include causation and influence in this type of system. Figure 2-1 presented an example of a **process**

FIGURE 2-2
Examples of Organizational Systems

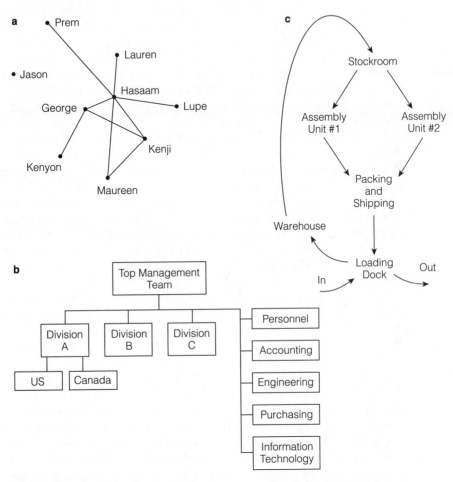

(a) A communication network, (b) a multidivisional organization, and (c) a workflow system in a small assembly plant. The two units build products, which are shipped from the loading dock.

system. Whereas the organizational system gives a description of the organization, the process system gives us an understanding of the processes that influence the organization. Most of the theories presented in this book are process systems theories. Several **principles of systems thinking** help in understanding organizations and developing strategies for organizational communication.

1.   *The whole is more than the sum of its parts.* Systems are more than just the parts that make them up. A cake is created from separate ingredients, but the cake is totally different from the assembled raw ingredients. In much the same way, an organizational system is more than the sum of its individual mem-

bers and units or their particular relationships to one another. For example, most charitable fund-raising agencies are composed of office staff, telephone and personal fund-raisers, advertising and promotion staff, accountants and bookkeepers, managers, and a board of directors. Each individual member has particular skills, values, strengths, and weaknesses. Joined into units, such as the accounting department, individuals' skills and strengths can compensate for others' weaknesses, and together they can achieve things they could not do separately. The units become wholes in their own right; they evolve their own goals and operating procedures, and they develop a set of values and a culture of their own. Joined into an organization, the units, too, can achieve different outcomes and have different values than they could on their own. Accounting units keep the fund-raisers honest. Advertising and promotion keeps the whole charity visible in the community, increasing revenues. But advertising and promotion would have no budget for their operations without the fund-raisers (nor would the accountants be paid without those they monitor). In a very real sense, the charity functions as it does only because of its entire configuration of people and units. But the people and units would not be what they are without the whole. It is through their place in the charity that they realize their potential. This process, through which a dynamic interdependence of parts and whole creates a unique overall system, has been called *emergence* by systems researchers.

Wholeness also applies to process systems. The variables can be defined independently, but their influence is due to how they interact with each other in the system. The set of relationships in Figure 2-1 forms a whole system of influences that drove People Express. The variables act as a set, and if the organization is altered to introduce another variable, the entire system changes its character.

2. *Cause-effect relationships in systems are complex.* Because all of the parts of a system are interconnected, it is not possible to find a single, simple cause for events or problems in the system. In the People Express process system, service quality affects the reputation of the airline. However, is it the ultimate cause of reputation? Quality is influenced by the number of passengers carried and by service capacity, which are themselves influenced by the flight schedule and additions to service capacity. But because the system runs in loops, these variables are influenced by service quality. Where is the cause for the system's behavior? The answer is: In the entire system. Because all variables are linked together, it is impossible to find a single ultimate cause for a problem or, for that matter, for success. Systems thinking warns us against trying to find a single variable or process to blame for a problem or to attribute success to. Although individual variables or processes certainly play an important role in the organization, problems or success stems from the system as a whole.

In the same vein, trying to find a person or a unit in an organizational system that is responsible for a problem or for success is fruitless. Organizations often place blame on a person or a unit or reward someone or some unit for successes, but because all the people and units are interconnected, they all play a role in problems or successes. This is why a commonplace of quality improvement programs is "Don't assign blame, change the system."

Many important effects in organizational systems are indirect. In Figure 2-1 additions to service capacity have an effect on reputation, but the effect is indirect. In Figure 2-2 George may well influence Maureen, but this effect will come indirectly through George's effect on Hasaam and Kenji. It is easy to overlook such indirect effects, but they are often quite important. This is particularly likely if the effect is delayed, because the further apart things are in time, the easier it is to miss the connections between them.

3. *It takes time to find the right levers.* Because indirect effects are hard to uncover and often overlooked, we often fail to find the really important variables, people, or units in the system. Although systems are wholes and their parts are interdependent, some variables, people, and units are particularly important. These parts stand at central points in the system where they are in a position to influence a number of other variables, people, or units or where they can filter or moderate the effects of other variables. In Figure 2-1 service quality is a centrally located and hence important variable. In Figure 2-2 Hasaam is particularly important because he ties together a number of other members. These critically important parts of the system represent **levers** that can be used to change and control the system. Finding a way to maintain service quality or adding other variables into the system that can increase quality would have given People Express a better chance of survival. Of course, key parts of a system are not always easy to change or control, compared to other parts. If we cannot change or control some element of a system, it cannot serve as a good lever.

4. *To understand a system, don't just focus on the system itself.* Every system is embedded in a group of larger systems (**suprasystems**), and every system is made up of a number of smaller, interdependent **subsystems.** For example, the loading crew of a freight company is a system made up of a number of subsystems (workers, their interpersonal relationships, and so on), which are made up of smaller subsystems (each worker's perceptual processes; tasks; information-processing activities; memories; expectations; family, church, and social ties; and so on). But the loading crew is only one part of the production suprasystem of the organization, which is only one part of the freight company (supra-suprasystem), which is part of the even larger trucking industry, and so on. At any given time, the actions of any of the many employees or subsystems of employees in the organization (the loading crew, for example) may be influenced by the actions of any of the other interrelated subsystems or suprasystems of people. Information is input into a system through one or more of its subsystems. As information moves through the system, it is interpreted, acted upon, and communicated to other members of the system. In systems-theory language, it becomes output that is interpreted, acted upon, and communicated to other systems and subsystems.

5. *Systems must adapt or they perish.* To thrive, and sometimes to survive, organizations must adapt to their environments. If an organization's environment changes, or if it moves into a new environment, the organization must

change as well. During the early 1990s, fast food chains adapted to the healthy-lifestyles movement by adding salad bars and vegetarian burgers and by moving into high schools and colleges, where their customers were less concerned with health issues and regularly went through french-fry withdrawal. Some chains shut down their outlets in health-conscious areas and reopened new ones where health was not such a hot issue. Now that the healthy-lifestyles movement has faded, many of the salad bars and almost all of the veggie burgers have disappeared (except in a number of different varieties in India).

In adapting to environmental pressures, an organization must balance the need for change with the stability provided by the older systems. Because organizational systems are made up of people and not parts, they cannot always change on a dime. People who have worked in the organization may resist some types of changes, and they may be slow in adopting even those they accept. The organization's culture may preclude some types of change, or at least make them difficult to implement. Organizations that successfully adapt are able to acknowledge that stability as well as change is needed.

6. *History is important in organizational systems.* It is important to remember that organizational subsystems, systems, and suprasystems are made of people, not things. Each organizational member brings a complex set of beliefs, values, history, and expectations into the system. These beliefs, values, histories, and expectations have an important effect on how members interpret, respond to, and communicate the information they obtain. For example, if employees believe that dishonesty is the normal way of conducting interpersonal relationships in their organization, inevitable communication breakdowns (like those discussed in Chapter 3) are likely to be interpreted as dishonest manipulation. It matters little that the breakdowns may actually be the result of harmless organizational processes. Within the interpretive frameworks of employees of this organization, they will be interpreted as intentional manipulation. Conversely, in an organization whose employees value openness and honesty, the same breakdowns might be interpreted quite differently; employees will act differently on that information, and they will communicate it to others in very different ways.

Consequently, employees define the situation(s) they face at work in their own ways. Those definitions change as the employees perform new and different tasks, participate in interpersonal relationships that develop and grow, receive and interpret new information, and confirm or disconfirm interpretations. Their strategic choices are influenced by the entire matrix of pressures, goals, and concerns that they experience, all of which also are emerging and changing. As a result, individual employees may make decisions that are difficult for other employees to understand. From the position they occupy in their organizational system, their choices probably make perfect sense to them, but they may not make sense to someone in a different position.

7. *Systems must constantly learn and renew themselves.* A vigorous, adaptive organizational system remains so because of the processes of learning and self-renewal. Organizations, made up as they are of people and machines, need to replace these parts when the parts grow old, unable to perform, or un-

willing to adapt. One way organizations renew themselves is by bringing in fresh, new people and technology. The danger here is that the new people and machines will too radically challenge a structure and culture that has worked well. In many cases, self-renewal is most effective if it replenishes and refreshes rather than making wholesale changes in the organization. How new members can be integrated into organizational relationships and how cultures can be produced and sustained are important topics discussed in later chapters.

However, an organization must learn too, and this is also an important part of self-renewal. It is important not only to maintain, but to expand perspectives, to try out new things, to experiment. For years 3M Corporation has had a reputation as one of the most innovative firms in the United States. A standard policy at 3M is to let its employees "steal" time for work on new ideas and to reward people even for failures, as long as they keep trying to generate new ideas and products. Another form of learning is to take advantage of unexpected opportunities and events. Open systems expose themselves to their environments and thus are open to many unanticipated happenings. They can use these surprises to make themselves stronger and more adaptive. Sometimes these unexpected opportunities come through apparent failure. The story is told that one of 3M's biggest successes, the ubiquitous Post-It Note, came about because of an accident that produced an adhesive that held only temporarily; papers that it was used on could be easily peeled apart. Rather than throwing out this batch of adhesive, creative 3M staff members tried to figure out what it could be used for. The result has replaced many a thumbtack, paper clip, or piece of tape. Opening up organizational systems to learning is critical to their growth and survival. Remaining open to new ideas and opportunities to learn is not always easy or even pleasant. But the organizations that are able to do so reap great benefits.

CASE STUDY
There Go the Lights, Here Come the Babies

In 1984 Yale University organizational sociologist Charles Perrow published a very influential book entitled *Normal Accidents*. Perrow's interest in accidents started in 1979 when he testified before a presidential commission established to examine an accident at the Three Mile Island nuclear power plant near Harrisburg, Pennsylvania. The committee concluded, as most of these investigations do, that the accident had resulted from operator error.* Perrow disagreed with the findings of the committee because the available evidence indicated that the power plant operators acted in completely sensible ways given their training and the (ambiguous, incomplete, and incorrect) information that was available to them. Blaming *individuals* for organizational failures and crediting *individuals* for organizational successes is completely consistent with the *individualistic* assumptions of U.S. society. Sometimes it *is* both fair and accurate—people do make mistakes that they

(continued)

(Case Study, continued)

should have avoided. But the assignment of blame to individuals often is misleading and counterproductive.

Accidents in complex organizations occur, Perrow argued, as a result of unique combinations of events, pressures, and incentives. The more complex a system is, the larger the number of possible unique, accident-producing combinations. In retrospect it is easy to see how all of the elements came together to create a particular situation, and to determine what the operators *should* have done. But it is virtually impossible to anticipate all of these unique combinations ahead of time, or even to recognize that they are taking place when one is in the middle of a crisis. When the systems also are tightly coupled (which means that when something goes wrong in one part of the system, other parts are affected almost instantly), operators have no chance to obtain the information they need to correctly diagnose the problem, much less to intervene and stop the process.

In some cases, systems actually encourage the "errors" that lead to accidents. For example, in the maritime industry, getting a ship to its destination on time or (better yet) early can mean thousands of dollars to the company. Most shipping companies share this windfall with the captains of the ships that arrive on time. As a result, on the one hand, shipping companies and ships' captains have significant financial incentives to take risks. On the other, they have few disincentives to do so. Unlike automobile insurance rates, which go up significantly if a driver has an accident, shipping insurance rates are not based on accident records. Although some countries use safety records in decisions about licensing of ships or companies, other countries do not. So shipping companies can simply obtain licenses in the least demanding countries (traditionally, these have been Panama and Liberia). In addition, the costs of accidents usually are shared with many people outside of the company, and companies can limit their liability through a variety of legal tactics. Consequently, the occurrence of accidents like the 1989 wreck of the *Exxon Valdez* in Prince William Sound, Alaska (and the more than fifty even larger maritime oil spills that have occurred worldwide since 1989), is virtually guaranteed. Preventing them would require a complete redesign of the "accident-inducing system," to use Perrow's phrase, something that in many situations simply is not possible.

The 2003 electricity blackout in the northeastern United States and southern Canada is an example of a systems error. It was not the first such blackout—similar events took place in 1965 and 1977—and a systems-level analysis suggests that it almost certainly will not be the last. And the initial investigation, like that for the Three Mile Island accident, concluded that no one could have anticipated a massive power outage on a calm, warm day—an event that could only happen if multiple safeguards broke down simultaneously. Secretary of Energy Spencer Abraham commented:

> When the procedures are followed and equipment works properly, the grid's delicate balance is maintained—even when things go wrong. But, when something does go wrong—and very important procedures aren't followed and critical trans-

mission monitoring and control equipment fails—the likelihood of major problems intensifies.[†]

The primary cause, concluded the committee, was "operator error."

At 3:06 p.m. on August 14, 2003, a power line owned by FirstEnergy of Ohio came into contact with untrimmed trees and shorted out. Power was automatically redirected to another line, which could not handle the load, overheated, and failed. Power was again redirected, and that line also failed at an energy breaker that connected FirstEnergy to the larger power grid. Had the operators known, they could have intervened, but the alarm system in their control room was not working, and they did not know that it wasn't working. Nevertheless, the committee concluded, if they had been adequately trained, they would have notified the other utilities in the grid that they were experiencing failures and would have conducted "contingency analyses" to detect those unknown failures so that appropriate action could be taken. By cutting 1,500–2,500 megawatts of power to the Cleveland and Akron area, they could have contained the outage. But they had not been trained to assume that their systems were malfunctioning even when no alarm had sounded, or to assume that automatic safety systems can cause problems rather than prevent them. By 3:46 p.m., forty minutes after the first power-line failure, it was too late to stop the blackout from cascading throughout the web (similarly at Three Mile Island the bulk of the damage was done in the first eight minutes).

Two minutes later, power surged wildly throughout the grid. The power system in upstate New York automatically acted to shut itself off from the surge by disconnecting itself from the Canadian grid. This prevented New York power plants from sending power outside of the state, which caused power plants in neighboring states to overload (including two nuclear plants), and they shut down. At 4:10 p.m., the blackout spread to Michigan, where a coal-fired power plant shut down and two transmission lines failed. A minute later, a power plant and several more lines failed in Ohio. Toronto and New York City went black; one-fifth of the U.S. power grid shut down, closing twelve airports, darkening more than 100 power plants, leaving 50 million people in the dark, and causing over $6 billion in economic losses.

If anyone had been able "to see the whole picture and put the pieces of the puzzle together" to connect the dots, using the phrase that became popular after September 11, 2001, all of this could have been avoided.[‡] But no one did. To understand why, we need to examine the suprasystem of the power industry. From 1900 until 1975 "electric companies dwelt in a stable and predictable realm where steadily declining costs of production and steadily increasing consumption were natural complements."[§] Although the electrical power market was tightly regulated, private companies were able to enter the market and succeed. In fact, the protections provided by regulation actually encouraged them to innovate and take risks, because they knew that they would be able to recoup the costs of doing so in the long run.

(continued)

(Case Study, continued)

The federal regulatory system was created during the 1930s in response to widespread abuses in the industry during previous decade. Power companies had grown so large that they crossed state boundaries and thereby avoided state-level regulation. Rate increases during the 1920s led to multiple government hearings that uncovered prevalent fraud and monopoly abuse in the industry. The federal regulation that was instituted in response allowed companies to retain the efficiencies of monopolies while protecting customers and suppliers. However, after the energy crises of the 1970s and in a political atmosphere that encouraged deregulation (the Carter administration deregulated the airline industry in 1978, and other industries quickly followed), controls were weakened, both in the United States and in the United Kingdom. Because of the nature of the industry, it is virtually impossible to create a completely free market in electricity—it makes little sense to have separate power lines from competing utility companies go to the same house, for example. So the level of deregulation is different for the three activities involved: producing power, distributing it over long distances, and marketing it to individual consumers. This mixed system is an open invitation for fraud and abuse, as California residents learned in the summers of 2001 and 2002. It also creates a maze of interconnected but independent firms, each trying to maximize its profits, with no overall control. For example, in the U.S. Midwest there are twenty-three different companies that share responsibility for maintaining the grid. Unfortunately, maintenance is an expensive proposition. Mark Mills, a partner in Digital Power Capital, a venture capital group that invests in utilities, noted that the problems leading to the 2003 blackout are easy to cure, but, he continued, "in this environment we've created in the last decade, utilities don't invest in expensive things."** It simply may make more financial sense for a company to set up systems to protect itself from other companies than to spend money on maintaining its part of the grid. Similarly, each company could share information about strengths and weaknesses in its part of the grid with other companies, but in a competitive market divulging that information could be used by competitors to the company's disadvantage.

The Midwest Independent System Operator watches over the grid, but membership in it is voluntary, as is obeying its recommendations. The Federal Energy Regulatory Commission (FERC) has been trying for years to force utilities to join regional grid organizations and follow their recommendations, but the effort has generated strong opposition among utility companies. In fact, the utilities persuaded their congressional representatives to insert a provision in the 2003 energy bill that would delay implementation of FERC's plans until after 2007. Although the bill did not pass during the 2003 session, its history suggests that the electrical power industry will continue to be fragmented and only loosely regulated.

Six months after the Ohio accident, no changes had been made to the system. No federal agency can compel the companies that were involved to take corrective action, or even to reveal what they have (or have not) done to prevent future blackouts. In October 2003 the North American Electric Reliability Council, a voluntary agency founded after the 1965 blackout to "prevent recurrences and fend off government regulation," asked each of its 167 member companies to describe how they manage swings in power, communicate with other companies, train their employees, and keep trees trimmed.[††] By mid-December only 55—less than one-third—had responded. Most consumer advocacy groups, as well as state (and provincial) public utility commissions, would like to see stronger regulations, but that would require federal legislation, which the industry is likely to oppose quite strongly. In January 2004 FERC chairman Pat Wood announced that his agency would act to force the utility companies to comply with standards that currently are voluntary. As predicted, industry spokespersons opposed the plan.[‡‡]

Applying What You've Learned

1. Using the terms described in this section, assume that FirstEnergy of Ohio is the system that you are examining. If that is so, what is the suprasystem? What are the important subsystems? How are they interrelated?
2. What pressures and incentives does FirstEnergy have to focus on prevention of future breakdowns? What pressures and incentives does it have not to do so?

Questions to Think About and Discuss

1. Whose "fault" was the 2003 blackout? If one takes a systems perspective, does this question make sense?
2. On April 5, 2004, the panel investigating the blackout issued its final report. It listed forty-six recommendations for changes designed to prevent another blackout. The first was that the voluntary rules that had been in place for years, but strongly opposed (and largely ignored) by the industry, be written into federal law and linked to significant penalties if they are violated.[§§] Given what you know about the blackout, how likely do you think it is that this recommendation will be implemented? Why? (After you read Chapter 8, on organizational power and politics, and Chapter 12, on organizational ethics, return to your answer to this question and evaluate it given the new information provided in those chapters.)
3. Oh, about the babies. About nine months after the 1965 and 1977 blackouts, the maternity rooms of hospitals in the affected areas experienced overload crises—women literally having babies in waiting rooms hurriedly converted into delivery rooms, on gurneys in hallways, and almost everywhere else. Evidently, when the power goes out and the televisions go off, people find other ways to entertain themselves, and local pregnancy rates skyrocket. Did the same thing happen in May 2004? If so, was the baby-

(continued)

(Case Study, continued)

delivery system prepared? Should it have been? Why or why not? (We wrote this case in January 2004, so we really don't know the answer to these questions).

---

*A case study of the TMI accident based on Perrow's book is available on our Web site at http://communication.wadsworth.com/conrad6.

†"U.S.-Canada Power System Outage Task Force, Washington, D.C.," November 19, 2003. Online at http://www.energy.gov.

‡P. Behr, "Blackout Report Cites Ohio Utilities: Michigan Panel Points to Failure to Isolate System," *Washington Post*, November 6, 2003, E5.

§Robert Kuttner, *Everything for Sale* (Chicago: University of Chicago Press, 1999), p. 270.

**Quoted in Matthew Wald, "Few Indications That Efforts to Cut Blackout Risks Are under Way," *New York Times on the Web*, December 13, 2002, p. 2, http://www.nytimes.com/.

††Wald, p. 1.

‡‡"FERC Says Grid Fix Can't Wait for New [Energy] Bill," *Houston Chronicle*, January 8, 2004, B2.

§§R. Perez-Pena, "Utility Could Have Halted '03 Blackout, Panel Says," *New York Times on the Web*, April 6, 2004, http://www.nytimes.com/. Behr, E5.Kuttner. Charles Perrow, *Normal Accidents* (New York: Basic Books, 1984).

Uncovering Assumptions: The Importance of Critical Thinking

The society from which an organization draws its members provides a context—a complex web of taken-for-granted meanings, expectations, and interpretive processes—through which people make sense out of their experiences at work. This context guides and constrains their actions at work and in turn guides and constrains the kinds of organizational strategies they will enact. These assumptions tend to be accepted uncritically; in fact, that is the primary source of their power. But understanding the organizations that exist within a society and understanding how communication functions in them involves assessing them critically, that is, *not* taking them for granted.

Societal Values and Social Myths

The dominant values of a society are articulated in social myths. These myths may or may not be true in an empirical sense, but they are believed to be true by members of a society. They are important because they tell citizens what their values are, how they should think, and how they should act. They also are important because they function as a powerful form of control, one that social theorists have labeled **hegemony.** Of course, no set of assumptions is accepted by all of a society's members all the time. Some people will constantly question some of the assumptions, and during times of social change, large numbers of people may question many of the taken-for-granted assumptions of a society. But assumptions are amazingly stable, because members of a society are constantly exposed to messages that support them, learn to interpret ambiguous information so that it confirms them, and tend to ignore or rationalize information that disconfirms them. By learning and accepting the assumptions of a society, its members become qualified to participate in that society. By learning how people are supposed to think and act, members of a society also accept limitations on how they think and act.[3]

Because organizations exist within particular societal contexts, the communication strategies that their members choose are strongly related to the assumptions of the societies from which they come. Those strategic choices in turn lead people to act in ways that make their assumptions seem normal and natural, accurate, and legitimate. Societal myths provide people with stable and predictable lives, both inside and outside of their organizations. This concept often is difficult to understand because doing so forces us to quit taking for granted the assumptions of our society. It asks us to treat our most basic beliefs about what is natural and normal as societal choices, not as absolute truths. Normally we do not think about such things, and as a result, the assumptions provide powerful guidelines and constraints on our actions and the actions of our organizations.

Two examples from Anglo-U.S. society will help to clarify these ideas. The first assumption involves the "proper" nature of an economic system. Historically, and increasingly since 1980, U.S. citizens have been taught that the optimal economic system is **laissez-faire capitalism.** This theory is based on the assumption that a free-market economic system has sufficient checks and balances in place to ensure that the legitimate interests of all members of a society will be met. As individuals compete with other individuals, and organizations compete with other organizations, in pursuit of their own self-interests, an invisible hand ensures that over the long term, good individuals and organizations will triumph and bad ones will disappear. If left alone, markets will move toward an equilibrium, and an equilibrium is the most efficient way for a society to allocate its resources. The competitive dynamics of a free marketplace ensure that no individuals or organizations can unfairly impose their own wills on others. According to this theory, government should have only a limited role in the economy. It may sometimes need to ensure that economic markets remain competitive (through antimonoply laws, for example) or that property rights are protected. But with these few exceptions, an economic system is best when government does the least.

This view of government's role in the economy is grounded in three assumptions. The **futility thesis** states that governments simply cannot effectively direct a society or an economy. The presumed "miracle" of the free market is that its processes work "invisibly" and thus do not have to be understood or managed. The presumed lesson of the demise of the Soviet Union is that centralized economic planning by a government is doomed to fail. When governments act, they do so on the basis of an incomplete understanding of social and economic processes and often base their decisions on considerations other than market values (that is, what one person is willing to pay another in a free economic exchange). In very rare instances, governments may actually do what the market needs to have done at a particular moment, but these instances are purely accidental. It is much more likely that government "intervention" will worsen the condition that the action is designed to solve (this is the **perversity thesis**). Even more important, government activities inevitably produce serious, perverse, unintended, and unanticipated consequences. As a result, whenever government acts, it is likely to jeopardize the virtues of a society or the economic gains that have been achieved through the free market (this is the **jeopardy thesis**).[4]

For individual citizens, free-market assumptions foster a focus on individualism that is articulated in a "Horatio Alger" myth, named after the writer of a series of short books published during the late nineteenth century. In Alger's books, the key character, always someone from a highly disadvantaged background, faces a series of challenges. But thanks to personal grit, talent, and determination, plus the unbounded opportunity provided by the U.S. free-market economy, he (all of the Horatio Alger heroes were male) eventually overcomes these challenges to become an economic and social success. Unlike Europe, the stories say, the United States is a classless society in which the only limits to success are individual competence and effort. Recent individuals who could have been Alger characters, with a high-tech twist, are Apple Computer's Steve Jobs, Microsoft CEO Bill Gates, and Dell Computer's Michael Dell. A fictional example is the character played by Jennifer Lopez in *Maid in Manhattan.*

However, like all social myths, Alger's assertions should not be taken literally. Very few sectors of the U.S. economy fit a strict definition of laissez-faire capitalism. Although the model works well in some sectors, in other sectors a mixture of government regulation and free-market principles is more effective and efficient than a pure free market, and in still others government is more efficient than the private sector. In addition, the claims about the success of laissez-faire systems depend on making a number of unrealistic assumptions (see Chapters 11 and 12).[5] There are a wide variety of capitalist economies in the world, each with a distinctive mixture of governmental and private-sector operations, and all of them fulfill the very different goals of their citizenry quite well.

At an individual level, the viability of the Horatio Alger myth has generally been exaggerated (in part because the United States has fewer overt symbols of class differences than other societies), and its accuracy has varied significantly over time. During the thirty years after World War II it reached its peak—among men whose fathers were in the bottom 25 percent of the country's social and economic status, 23 percent made it into the top 25 percent. But since 1973 income and wealth distribution in the United States has become more and more unequal (especially if inflation and total tax burden is taken into account): the average real income of the lowest 90 percent has fallen by 7 percent while the income of the top 1 percent has risen 148 percent, the income of the top 0.1 percent has risen 343 percent, and the income of the top 0.01 percent has risen 599 percent. As a result, the upwardly mobile percentage of the male population has fallen to 10 percent, roughly the same level as during the 1890s when Horatio Alger's books were written.[6] However, the empirical "truth" of the laissez-faire and Horatio Alger myths is much less important than their persuasive power. As long as the societal myths are believed, they guide and constrain public policies, organizational strategies, and individual actions.

Communication and Societal/Organizational Tensions

Core beliefs and values make up only one dimension of the context surrounding organizations. Just as societies shape dominant values and beliefs, they also are composed of tensions and contradictions within and among those beliefs. For example, although Anglo-U.S. society is highly individualistic, a number of social scientists have long observed that even there, a fundamental tension exists between individuality and community. Alexis de Tocqueville toured the United States soon after it became a nation. He observed that its people were so individualistic that they found it difficult to recognize their common needs and interests and to develop a sense of community. Almost two hundred years later, sociologist Robert Bellah and his associates interviewed hundreds of people from all walks of life. They found that European-Americans' obsession with individualism and their isolation from one another had expanded and deepened since the end of World War II.[7]

Of course, tensions between and within a society's core values can be managed, sometimes through organizations and sometimes through communication. For example, de Tocqueville concluded that the United States remained cohesive because so many people were involved in informal nonwork organizations that provided a sense of community—churches, lodges, and so on—which compensated for the extreme individuality that European-Americans faced in their work organizations. Sociologists like Robert Putnam recently have noted that declining participation in these informal organizations has further isolated U.S. residents from one another.[8] This decline in involvement in nonwork organizations has made communication an even more important means of managing societal/organizational tensions. It is not accidental that Horatio Alger–type stories are most prevalent in the mass media during eras of limited upward mobility. In sum, all societies have characteristic myths, expressions of core beliefs and values that are rarely even questioned, much less examined carefully and critically. Myths may or may not be true in an empirical sense, but they are treated as if they are true by members of a society. Articulated in stories and rituals, societal myths both express the core values and beliefs of a society and manage its core tensions (see Chapter 5).

Valuing Differences: The Advantages of Diversity

At least since the Industrial Revolution, organizations have been viewed as "containers," separated from their environments and from other organizations.[9] Of course, all the members of an organization recognize that other people are out there, supplying their organization with raw materials, purchasing the organization's products or services, regulating its activities, competing with it in the market, and welcoming its members home at the end of the day. But each organization is separated from the others in its environment, and each group of employees is separated from the other groups by space and time. Within each organization managers control workers in an effort to maximize performance through rational decision making and the efficient use of resources. Thinking is separated from doing, and the people responsible for one activity are assumed to be very different from the people charged with the other. Each group is relatively homogeneous in gender, education, class, and race. This homogeneity enhances communication within each group and makes it unlikely that a member of one group will ever occupy a position within the other.

In the United States, the positive value of homogeneity has been supported by an additional societal myth, the melting pot. This myth suggests that all people—regardless of their race, gender, ethnicity, or country of origin—can become Horatio Alger figures if they only embrace the distinctively European-American values of hard work, determination, and loyalty. Any hierarchies and inequities that exist in the society are attributed to individual differences in merit, not to different opportunities based on race, ethnicity, gender, or class. As we learn our society's assumptions, we come to accept its hierarchical relationships as *natural* (that is, inevitable) and *normal* (that is, expected and morally correct). As people *internalize* the values and assumptions of their society, they also internalize its hierarchies based on class, race, gender, and ethnicity. Educated middle- and upper-class men of the dominant race and ethnic backgrounds have been (and often still are) assumed to be superior to everyone else, at least in the skills and attributes needed in organizations. However, during the past decade, this dominant perspective has been challenged by two processes—diversification and globalization. Unfortunately, increased proximity does not automatically produce increased understanding or increased cooperation. It does mean that the dominant perspective is under increasing pressure. Modes of operating, social and organizational power relationships, and systems of control and resistance all are being changed.

In many ways the dominant view is based on notions of *distance* and *separation.* Managers are physically, sociologically, and psychologically separated from workers. Each group tends to view the other as fundamentally different people with different tasks, interests, personalities, and motivations. This way of viewing organizational reality simplifies and stabilizes everyone's organizational world and provides a degree of comfort and predictability. But today's organizations are becoming increasingly **heterogeneous,** especially in the industrialized world. The *proximity* between these groups of "others" has increased significantly, creating new challenges, new opportunities, and new demands on communicative processes. White, male, middle-to-upper-class managers are no longer separated from nonwhite people or from women. These "others" comprise an increasing percentage of their employees and sit with them in executive dining rooms. Moreover, the internal separation between workers and managers—who in the United States traditionally have been white, educated, middle-to-upper-class, heterosexual males—has started to dissolve as women and nonwhite employees have moved into professional and managerial positions. Simultaneously, many employees have rejected the arbitrary elevation of work over home that characterizes the dominant view. For many people, relationships and family take precedence over work and career, and balancing the two has become a significant challenge. No longer are employees willing to treat home and work as "containers" that are separate and independent of each other.

Unfortunately, organizational policies and practices have often been slow to adapt to these new realities (see Chapter 10 for a detailed analysis). For example, in the United States, women long have been and still are paid substantially less than men for the same or comparable work. There are a number of reasons for this difference, although one of the most important is that women tend to be concentrated in sectors of the economy that have relatively low salary rates (for example, teaching or nursing). As the proportion of women in these occupations increased, the level of prestige afforded the occupations, and the wage rates paid to the people in them, fell steadily until the occupations were approximately 50 percent women. When the proportion exceeds 50 percent, wages plummet. There are two possible explanations for this phenomenon: First is an explanation based on societal myths, in this case the myth that women's work is worth less than men's work. The second is an economic explanation that says that when the number of applicants for a particular type of job increases, the heightened competition forces wages down. The societal explanation has been shown to be more valid. Women are paid less than men in comparable jobs because their work is perceived to be less valuable, and our society has taught us that women's work is less valuable because they are paid less. The assumptions of our society/organizations lead us to believe that hierarchical relationships are normal and natural. In turn, we act and think in ways that support those assumptions.[10]

Similarly, supervisors tend not to offer married women managers promotions that require relocation, because they *assume* that wives will not ask their husbands and families to endure the stresses of moving, even when accepting transfers is necessary for promotion. Eventually these supervisors, their supervisors, and their employees notice that women managers do not move very often and in turn assume that this is because women managers value their families more than their careers (though the tendency is more closely related to the lower number of offers they receive). There is little objective evidence to support any of these assumptions. Today women managers do not turn down promotions that involve relocating any more often than men do.[11] But as long as managers *assume* that their beliefs are accurate, they will act on those assumptions.

In other cases, it is a combination of societal myths that is important. For example, the dominant ideology among European-American people is still that white men are more rational than women (and that women, African Americans, and Latinos[12] are more emotional than Anglo men). These assumptions alone have little relevance to organizations. But a second societal myth is that organizations are (and should be) rational enterprises, especially at managerial levels (in spite of substantial evidence to the contrary, as summarized in Chapter 9). This assumption, in itself, has little relevance for a diverse workforce. But when the two assumptions are combined, they generate a further assumption that Anglo men are inherently better managers than white women, African Americans, or Latinos. Whether they are direct or indirect, the dominant assumptions of a culture establish hierarchical relationships, and as long as the members of a culture believe that the hierarchies are normal and natural, they tend to act in ways that perpetuate those hierarchies. When a workforce is homogeneous, these different inequities can be glossed over; when it is diverse, they create challenges that must be managed through communication.

We often tend to view diversity in terms of the challenges it poses, and this blinds us to the potential advantages of diversity. As we will see in Chapter 10, diversity brings the potential for new ideas and different views of the situation, different ways of interacting, and different orientations to taking action. Diversity, in short, is an opportunity if properly handled. Getting past the myths that keep people from appreciating the contributions of those who are different from them is one key to strategic organizational communication.

Thinking Globally: The Challenges of Globalization

More and more, new technologies and the elimination of cold war barriers to economic activity mean that organizations also are becoming *globalized.* Increasing levels of education in the non-Western world, especially among women, have combined with the creation of a truly global flow of capital and trade to create a new environment for organizations the world over.[13] The increasing diversity of the employees of contemporary organizations challenges traditional modes of operating from the inside. The globalization of major organizations is challenging them from the outside. Workers, and organizations, compete directly with people half a world away as well as with people down the street. The insulation, comfort, and predictability provided by traditional barriers is rapidly disappearing and the "others" who once were so far away are now right next door. When multinational organizations based in Western societies enter a new geographic area, they bring with them a distinctively Western set of values—individualism, commercialism, separation of church and state, liberty, and laissez-faire economics—that are alien to Islamic, Confucian, Daoist, Hindu, Buddhist, or Orthodox Christian cultures. Many of their products, from rock music to fast food to cosmetics, are also distinctively Western.

Some observers argue that these trends will lead to **cultural homogenization,** a bland world in which the rich cultural diversity that currently exists will be squeezed into a single, standardized, Western or U.S. pattern. Different writers have created their own clichés for these trends—McWorld, Coca-Colonization, McDonaldization, or McDisneyization—but they all refer to the same processes. Other observers offer a **polarization** thesis, warning that people in non-Western societies will be progressively more alienated and angered by this cultural invasion, resulting in an increasingly hostile world. A third group argues that culture is far more resilient and flexible than either of the extreme positions suggests. Historically peoples throughout the world have accepted some characteristics of "invading" cultures, modified others to fit their core values, and maintained their distinctive character. This **hybridization** thesis suggests that the challenge imposed by globalization is for countries and individuals to find a healthy balance between preserving a sense of identity, home, and community while living and acting within a global economic system.[14] Each prediction suggests different challenges for multinational organizations.

There is a great deal of anecdotal evidence to support the homogenization thesis—McDonalds, Wal-Marts, Coca-Cola, and so on now exist in every conceivable corner of the world. Western consumerism is distinctively oriented toward consistency and name-brand identification. Everyone who discusses globalization has his or her own story. Sociologist Peter Berger talks about a visit to Hong Kong. He went into a Buddhist temple and found a middle-aged man in a business suit and stocking feet, standing in front of an altar, facing a large statue of Buddha, burning incense and talking on a cell phone. Cultural homogenization is fueled by mass advertising and the status that accompanies Western (or U.S.) products in much of the world. In fact, the phenomenon seems to be closely linked to the emergence of a global economic elite, people who have become wealthy as a result of the global economy and who are increasingly tied to one another and increasingly isolated from non-elite people in their own societies. In the long run, homogenization will minimize the challenges faced by global organizations—once the process is complete, differences will be minimized. The challenge has to do with the short term.

A second group of observers see much more negative forces at work. When the world becomes a smaller place, cultural differences become *more visible* and *potentially more alienating.* Cultural conflicts are much more difficult to resolve than economic or political ones—compromise on the terms of a trade contract is a fundamentally different thing from compromise on moral or religious truths.[15] When globalization creates or exacerbates disparities of wealth and income, as it has done in much of the developing world, these cultural differences may lead to an increasing polarization both within societies and between them. The current backlash against globalization is most intense in societies suffering both economic and cultural dislocation, and it tends to be focused on the United States and U.S.-based organizations. The targets of the September 11, 2001, attacks were not chosen at random—they were the headquarters of the U.S. military and U.S. global organizations. Whether or not it is accurate or fair to single out the United States and U.S. organizations, it is quite clear that polarization is significant and, in some areas, growing. Ironically, the same forces that created globalization can be used to resist it. Protests held outside meetings of the World Trade Organization and international trade and finance organizations were organized via the Internet, and the size and scope of those demonstrations was transmitted instantaneously throughout the world by CNN and Al Jazeera.

A final group of observers argue that the most likely outcome of globalization will be the development of a number of hybrid societies that combine local and Western cultural characteristics. This, they argue, has been the primary lesson of history—from Hellenization to Christianization, local societies have found ways to accept some aspects of outside cultures while retaining the core of their culture. Throughout his work, Thomas Friedman calls this process "glocalizing," a term that originally was developed in Japan as a label for marketing products to fit local tastes. John Tomlinson explains:

> Culture simply does not transfer in this [simple linear] way. Movement between cultural/geographical areas always involves interpretation, translation, mutation, adaptation . . . as the receiving culture brings its own cultural resources to bear . . . upon cultural imports.[16]

The use of English as the global language of commerce provides an excellent example. On the one hand, it is obvious that English dominates the global economy. There is no inherent reason for English to dominate—it is not easier to learn, more precise, more flexible, or more capable of expressing emotions. One-third of the world's population (1.6 billion people) use English in some form today. Eighty percent of the content posted on the Internet is in English (although that percentage is declining), even though one-half of Internet users speak a different language at home. Corporations in English-speaking countries account for 40 percent of the world's economic activity. English dominance reflects the political, economic, and military power of English-speaking countries. In many ways, it has created a new system of global haves and have-nots. Being able to speak and read English opens up opportunities for knowledge and career advancement that are not available to people who do not speak the language. Career ads in French newspapers published in Belgium are in English, because multi-national corporations (MNCs) increasingly require English-language skills of their professional employees.

But regional languages have not disappeared. In fact, differences among dialects of non-English languages are becoming more pronounced, and regional languages are increasingly popular ways of bridging linguistic differences. Mulitlingualism is becoming the worldwide norm, everywhere except in the United States. The language that a person uses with family and friends may be different from the one used with co-workers, which may be different from the one used with bosses or government. Many countries have reacted to the growing use of English by forbidding its use in settings where it is not required. As a result, local language use is becoming hybridized, just as local cultures are becoming "glocalized." Instead of becoming impoverished, as the homogenization thesis suggests, world cultures are being enriched by processes of hybridization. Instead of creating an increased potential for hostility, globalization has provided more opportunity for connection. However, glocalization may present the greatest challenge for multinational organizations. Cultural hybridization is a slow, highly selective, and context-dependent process.[17] It maximizes proximity and difference, while creating an infinite number of issues that must be negotiated successfully for the organization to thrive.

Understanding the impacts of globalization on organizations and society is a key to strategic organizational communication. The effects of globalization are felt not only around the world, but in the United States as well. Manufacturing job losses in recent years are one effect of the global economy. But globalization has also opened up markets to U.S. firms, so that U.S. computer sellers such as Dell are prospering in Europe and India. Effective organizational communication and organizational effectiveness depend on taking globalization into account, however difficult it might be to project its influence.

Understanding Technology: A Radical Force for Change

Peter Drucker, an astute observer of society and of organizations, wrote in 1994:

> No century in recorded history has experienced so many social transformations and such radical ones as the twentieth century. . . . In the developed free-market countries—which contain less than a fifth of the earth's population but are the model for the rest—work and work force, society and polity, are all, in the last decade of this century qualitatively and quantitatively different not only from what they were in the first years of this century, but also from what has existed at any other time in history: in their configurations, in their processes, in their problems, and in their structures.[18]

Perhaps the most far-reaching change has been the transformation of the United States and most of the developed world into a knowledge society. For most of this century and the previous one, the economy focused largely on production, on the laborious work in farm and factory that resulted in tangible products. Before World War I, farmers were the largest single group of workers in most countries. From 1920 to 1950, the farm population declined, although the production of food increased. In the 1950s, blue-collar workers accounted for 40 percent of the American workforce, representing the emphasis of that period on factory production through manual labor. However by 1990, blue-collar workers accounted for less than 20 percent of American workers and farmers for less than 5 percent. The largest classes of workers in 1990 were those employed in what Drucker terms "knowledge work" and what has also been called "information work."

Knowledge work involves creating and applying knowledge. Examples range from the work done by research scientists, engineers, attorneys, and financial analysts on the high end of the scale to that of teachers and X-ray technicians on the low end. Several things differentiate knowledge work from production work. People who do knowledge work perform abstract operations, and the product—knowledge—is intangible. Indeed, the only tangible outcome of much knowledge work is a document. However, despite its intangible nature, knowledge is the critical factor in the development of new products and the delivery of services such as legal and financial advice. Knowledge work organizes other forms of work, including production work. Knowledge work adds value to materials and to information, making them more useful or desirable or effective. An engineer's designs turn sand, copper, and aluminum into computer chips; an attorney's interpretive and negotiation skills create business partnerships from indecipherable (to any ordinary person) legal tomes and discussions among the parties involved. Knowledge-based work requires formal education (as opposed to apprenticeships or trade school) and an ability to acquire and apply abstract theoretical and analytical knowledge. It also requires a commitment to continuous learning; the knowledge worker's best and only asset is her or his expertise, which must be developed constantly through experience and further schooling.

Information work supports knowledge work. It involves gathering, entering, formatting, and processing information. Examples of information workers include those doing clerical jobs, data entry, and telemarketing. These jobs are generally lower paying than the lowest rungs of knowledge work. They have been called "pink-collar" work, because they are often office positions staffed largely by women.

Together, knowledge and information workers comprise about 40 percent of the workers in manufacturing firms and up to 80 percent in service organizations. They have become the largest class of workers in our society. This does not mean that production work is no longer important. It is, after all, what actually creates the products that knowledge workers design and that information workers catalog and sell. However, production work has become subsidiary to knowledge work in the new social arrangements. Advances depend far more on increases in knowledge than on production per se.

The increasing importance of knowledge and information work has put a premium on information and communication technologies. The last twenty years of the twentieth century and the first years of this century will surely be remembered as the time when information and communication technology exploded. The most obvious indication of this is the phenomenal and continuing growth of the Internet. This is only the tip of an iceberg of changes that include the spread of business integration systems, the takeoff of wireless telecommunications, extraordinary advances in communication technologies such as interpersonal messaging and videoconferencing, the advent of virtual organizations, and the reengineering of countless private, public, and nonprofit organizations to incorporate information technology.

Some scholars argue that information and communication technology (ICT) does not really change organizations.[19] They regard it as simply another variable that influences organizational communication by increasing the speed, accuracy, and efficiency of information exchange. However, the experience of the past five years indicates that this position vastly underestimates the potential of ICT to transform organizations and communication. A great many organizations could not operate effectively without ICT. Wal-Mart, for example, could not deliver such low costs without its computerized supply chain management systems. And many organizations could not even exist without ICT. Amazon.com and eBay are examples of organizations that exist only on the Internet. Take away ICT and these organizations would disappear. In most large businesses and a growing portion of small ones, ICT has become so much a part of everyday operations that it is difficult to imagine how the work would get done without it. The countless examples include farmers who rely on ICT to sell their crops, law firms that do their research through online services, and local government agencies that collect bills and taxes through online payments. ICT plays just as important a role in today's organizational communication as a face-to-face conversation or a telephone call.

We use the abbreviated term *ICT* to refer to computerized systems and advanced telecommunication systems. Relevant computerized systems include those used to manage databases containing budget, order, or inventory information; to provide communication through electronic mail and conferencing; and to coordinate work processes. Advanced telecommunication systems include voice mail systems, fax technology, proprietary telephone systems (for example, PBX systems), teleconferencing, videoconferencing, and wireless communications. All these systems enable organizations to operate much more rapidly and (sometimes) to adapt more quickly than they could if human communicators and traditional modes of communication (memos, letters, phone calls) made up the entire communication system. ICT gathers and transmits information so quickly, thoroughly, and reliably that it enables human links in the communication system to focus more on quality thinking, reasoning, and service, the tasks for which they are best suited.

Trends in the Development of Information and Communication Technologies

Everyone is aware of how rapidly ICT is changing. As consumers we are amazed at the variety and increasingly sophisticated functionality of devices like camcorders, televisions, and personal computers. The diffusion of ICT into organizations has been equally rapid, though sometimes we are not as directly aware of it. Although the process began rather slowly in the 1970s and 1980s, it has consistently picked up speed through the 1990s and early 2000s and shows no sign of slowing. The increasing rate of ICT implementation and its growing impact on organizations and society can be traced to several developments.[20]

The **convergence** of formerly separate technologies, such as computers and telephones, has been hastened by the development of digital technology. Once information like text, audio, and pictures has been converted into digital form—as it is, for instance, when we type into our computers or take a picture with a digital camera or camcorder—it can be easily moved from one kind of ICT to another. For instance, a digital picture can be sent along with an e-mail message or to a printer to make a paper copy. Convergence makes it possible to link together and sometimes even merge separate applications, which makes integration of information in organizations much easier. For example, electronic medical records can combine textual notes made by physicians with digitized radiological pictures and other types of documents in a single database. Another example is the cell phone that has a personal digital assistant (a small computer for personal use) built in. Still another is the growing number of organizations that are moving their telephone systems to the Internet rather than relying on the phone companies' dedicated lines.

Internetworking, the use of the Internet to deliver and access ICT applications, has grown beyond anyone's expectations during the past ten years. Technologies discussed in the previous edition of this text—office automation, electronic data interchange (EDI), groupware, videoconferencing, workflow management—previously were implemented in stand-alone proprietary systems that were difficult to connect to each other. Since the last edition, however, these applications and many others have moved to the Internet. Organizations have implemented **intranets,** internal, private internets that operate essentially in the same way that the public Internet operates. For example, an organization might install an intranet to handle its electronic mail, allow employees to move documents around the organization rather than passing paper copies, and retrieve needed information from the company database. **Extranets** are private internets that allow authorized people outside the organization to use them. Examples of extranets are business-to-business commerce sites that allow selected suppliers to offer products to an organization via the Internet. American Hospital Supply, for example, offers its products to hospitals via an extranet: authorized hospitals can place orders on the site, and there is even an automated system that monitors the level of supplies a hospital has and places a reorder automatically when they fall below a certain level. Both intranets and extranets are typically protected by **firewalls,** hardware and software systems that allow only authorized users to access them and prevent unauthorized use.

Intranets, extranets, and sites on the public Internet are usually accessed through **portals,** gateways to the Web site, that have an index of what is available through the site and other features. When you browse the Web, the first page you find for a site is its portal. The human resource portal on the Texas A&M University intranet, for instance, contains information about insurance and other benefit plans, forms that can be downloaded or filled out online to enroll or change coverage, announcements about workshops, contact addresses for counselors and other human resource personnel, and links to other Web sites at the university that are related to human resource concerns. In order to access this portal, it is necessary to enter a university-approved account name and password. It is designed to provide useful services and information but to protect the security and privacy of university employees.

Organizations have been embracing Internetworking. Building applications on the Internet makes it much easier for people to access them and enables organizations to reach customers or clients from a distance. For example, an increasing number of banks are offering online banking to any of their customers who have a standard Web browser, enhancing service and convenience. The Internal Revenue Service offers tax return forms and tax filing online, which greatly reduces paperwork and enables the IRS to provide refunds much more quickly than in the past (to the delight of many taxpayers). Organizations are also able to give their employees access to needed information and applications more easily via the Internet. For instance, online forms enable employees to enter information in standard formats that goes directly into the organizational database. This is valuable for employees working on site in the organization, but even more valuable for those working off site, such as telecommuters who work at home or salespeople who work in the field. They need only connect via their Web browsers, a cheap, easily available technology.

The growth of the Internet has also been driven by the increasing **bandwidth** it offers. Connections between ICTs, whether a telephone wire or a fiberoptic cable, can be likened to pipes through which digital signals "flow." The diameter of the pipe determines how much water can flow through it: more water can flow more quickly through a nine-inch pipe than through a two-inch one. Bandwidth is analogous to the diameter of "pipe" (the connection) between ICTs. The greater the bandwidth, the more information can flow and the more quickly it can move. When the Internet was first developed, it could only support transmission of small amounts of information, such as that included in text messages. Transmissions that included greater amounts of information, such as an audio recording or a video picture, moved so slowly that they were not satisfactory. Each new generation of the Internet increased bandwidth and was capable of more satisfactory transmission of richer information. Today streaming video on the Internet sometimes yields pictures similar to the video signals received by television sets. In the next few years there will be yet another upgrade of the Internet that should provide adequate bandwidth for almost any type of communication or data that can be envisioned. This will fuel still further growth.

Another major development has been the emergence of **wireless** technologies that allow ICTs to connect without cables or wires. The rapid spread of cell phones and other handhelds is the most obvious indicator of the speed with which wireless ICT is diffusing throughout society. Unlike most ICTs, which typically are implemented first in the most advanced countries—the United States, Japan, Europe—and then come much later to less developed areas, cell phones and other wireless communication devices are being implemented rapidly all over the world, in Africa and the Middle East nearly as much as in the United States. This is because there is no need to build up the costly infrastructure of transmission lines and switching boxes that traditional wired telephone systems require. Instead, cell phones can be supported by transmission towers, which can be built relatively quickly and do not take up as much real estate, and satellites, which are costly, but once in operation are easily and constantly available. This infrastructure is much easier to build and maintain in less developed areas than wired phone systems. Cell phones also operate on batteries and are less likely to be rendered inoperable by power outages. Thus, the unreliable electric utilities common in less developed countries are not as much of a problem as they would be for a physically wired telephone system, which must have continuous power to operate. Wireless communication truly is integrating the world.

Wireless phones are only a small part of the wireless revolution. Wireless devices are becoming more and more common in organizations. Wireless markers attached to pallets and even individual products help organizations keep track of inventory. The clips attached to clothes that set off alarms when the clerks forget to remove them are "dumb" examples of these devices. Handheld computing devices, such as personal digital assistants and palm computers connected into wireless networks, make computer networks much more flexible and adaptable. For example, garment maker VF Corporation is using wireless devices to tie its entire production and distribution system together.[21] Wireless networks are used to track sales rates of various garments, so that materials can be reordered and additional garments produced as needed. Wireless networks and factory input devices can ensure perfect color matching of the various pieces of fabric that go into garments, reducing quality problems. Wireless devices to be integrated into this system include mobile computers, wearable computers, bar-code scanners, and vehicle-mounted computers. This array of devices will greatly increase VF's ability to innovate and respond to market changes. In another example of wireless applications, utility companies supply employees with wireless computers that tell them what their next repair job is, give them directions to the location, and provide maps and diagrams of the installed utilities to guide their work and make sure they don't accidentally cut through the wrong wires or pipes. Wireless locators connected to global positioning systems enable organizations to know exactly where their workers are at a given moment. There is almost no limit to the range of uses to which wireless ICT can be put.

The advent of wireless ICTs, combined with their ever-increasing miniaturization, is likely to fuel the spread of **ubiquitous computing,** in which computers are embedded in almost everything. Computers are being developed that can be sewn into clothing, incorporated into sheets of paper, and painted onto almost any surface. Envisioned applications of these devices range from the mundane (keeping track of inventory and preventing theft, monitoring a diabetic's blood sugar level continuously) to the exotic (triggering changes in room temperature and lighting as a person walks from room to room). Although most applications of ubiquitous computing are only ideas at this point, it seems safe to assume that ubiquitous computing will have major impacts on the way we live and on organizations over the next decade or two.

CASE STUDY
Working in the Virtual Future: An Optimistic View

As her train picked up speed on its trip from Philadelphia to Boston, Tara Rodgers linked her personal digital assistant to the onboard computer via the connection in the armrest of her seat. Tara was on her way to Boston to facilitate a meeting for a scientific team that Worldwide Consulting Group was organizing for InuitAid International. InuitAid International (IAI) was a network organization of social service and health agencies that was being developed to address a health crisis among the Inuit peoples of Northern Canada. For the past three years, starting in 2008, Inuit children and elders had been contracting respiratory infections at three times the rate of 2007. Deaths in both groups had increased sharply, and a number of Native American tribes and organizations had urged the governments of Canada and the United States and the United Nations for help with this crisis.

Tara had a degree in communication, with a specialization in intercultural and group communication, and seven years experience working with international scientific teams. She had started with a major accounting firm but soon left to set up her own private agency with two of her colleagues. They had begun working with medical research teams in Boston and later expanded to include the entire East Coast. They developed expertise in helping teams whose members worked in several locations develop virtual organizations. Tara specialized in teamwork and facilitation, and her partners were experts in contract law and information technology, respectively. The partners learned from each other and each pitched in to help with all sides of the business, but having these three deep specialties enabled the partners to cover most of the important aspects of scientific collaboration. Tara's firm affiliated with Worldwide's group of consulting agencies three years ago and had worked on several contracts for Worldwide. Tara and her colleagues liked having their own independent firm, because it gave them flexibility to work on projects they believed in, like this one. Being one of Worldwide's affiliated partners had brought their firm a good deal of business, plus some wonderful opportunities like this one.

Tara's immediate job was to facilitate the organizing meetings of the diagnostic group of the IAI. She envisioned that the first set of meetings for this group would take about two months. Following this, Tara (and her associates if they were needed) would continue to work with the IAI to facilitate meetings, assist with problems and help manage conflicts, and help to keep project teams on schedule for the remainder of the project.

The IAI had been quickly assembled by Posi Sistrunk, the broker from the UN Agency for International Relief. She succeeded in getting commitments from the Centers for Disease Control, the UN Health Service, the Canadian Health System, and the Novosibirsk Hospital in Russia. The Centers for Disease Control brought expertise in tracking down the causes of outbreaks of disease or mortality; the UN Health Service had years of experience in delivering care in rugged terrain; and the Canadian Health System had first documented the problem and would be in the front line of care provision. The Novosibirsk Hospital had dealt with a similar incident among native peoples in Siberia four years before. In that case the cause had been found to be heavy metals from industrial sites in southern Siberia. Two major drug companies had agreed to provide medicines for the network, if any were needed. As with all network organizations, it was important that all partners commit themselves fully and develop good working relationships and clear ground rules from the beginning.

Using the onboard computer, which had a brighter and larger display screen than her personal digital assistant, Tara downloaded her e-mail and found she had received biographies of the seventeen people who would attend the workshop.

(continued)

(Case Study, continued)

This was a diverse group, and Tara knew that their different nationalities and scientific backgrounds would make coordinating the group a challenge. From hard-won experience, Tara knew that it was particularly important that everyone agree on definitions of key concepts, such as quality control. Scientists from different disciplines often assumed that others assigned the same meanings that they did to terms. As a result, needless disputes could arise; one scientist might disagree with another's quality assessment, for example, because the two had different definitions of the type of data needed to measure quality. Tara knew that it was important to spend several meetings establishing agreement on definitions and standards, even though the scientists might grumble that all they were doing was talking about words.

Tara knew three of the scientists well, and had heard of several others. She patched through a video call to Stanley Marsh, an epidemiologist with another firm in Worldwide's network who knew most of the scientists. After inquiring about each other's families, Tara and Stanley discussed the members of the group. Tara realized that Stanley was getting more and more interested in the project, so she asked him if he'd like to come on board as cofacilitator. His scientific expertise and evident trust in Tara would give extra weight to Tara's attempts to guide this group. Tara then put in a video call to Scientific Associates International, a nonprofit group dedicated to promoting scientific cooperation among nations, and downloaded case studies of effective scientific health teams and statistics on how long start-up periods for multidisciplinary scientific groups typically were. These would help her make her case for a slow but thorough start-up period for IAI.

In Boston Tara walked from the train station to Worldwide's telecommunications station. Participants would be linked into a virtual meeting tomorrow, and Tara wanted to familiarize herself with the meeting room. On one side of the room was a video screen that could hold full pictures of up to eighteen separate meeting sites; the three-dimensional holographic technology made them seem as though they were just different parts of the same room. She knew that not all sites had this technology; the Russians, in particular, had only two-dimensional videoconferencing walls with a capacity for four meeting sites. She knew she would have to make sure to indicate carefully who wanted to be recognized to speak in the meeting so that the Russians could switch to that site if it was not up on their screen already. Tara also spent some time setting up the conferencing software that would link the group's work over the next year. It allowed textual and data transfer, online data analysis, and video links for impromptu meetings of a few of the scientists in the network. This conference environment would be the team's virtual home for the next year. Finally, Tara arranged for a direct video interview of several Inuit leaders. She planned to lead off the meeting this way to highlight the plight of the Inuit, thus providing a common ground for fast, cooperative action in IAI.

Tara walked out of Worldwide a happy woman, looking forward to the meeting tomorrow. Sure, there would be some problems and unpleasant arguments, but she was eager to tackle them. Making IAI work was a challenge, but it would help so many people.

Applying What You've Learned

1. What advantages of information and communication technologies for working in the global world does this case illustrate?
2. IAI will bring together people from very different organizations, each of which will have a different organizational culture. What might Tara do to help these cultures work together?

Questions to Think About and Discuss

1. Will these technological advances help us to address the challenges posed by diversity?
2. What might be the downside of working in this organization for Tara? Can you identify any problems she might face or stresses she might experience?

Functions of Information and Communication Technology in Organizations

ICTs play a number of important roles in today's organizations. Most obvious is their capacity to *facilitate communication* within and between organizations. ICTs that support communication include e-mail, computer conferencing, audio and video conferencing, instant messaging, weblogs, and group support systems (see Chapter 9). These technologies vary considerably in the richness of information they can transmit and the immediacy with which responses come (see Chapter 6), and they can facilitate communication in several respects. They can speed up communication by making it more efficient to contact others (as e-mail and instant messaging do) and to convene meetings of people in different locations (as conferencing and group support systems do). E-mail, computer conferences, and weblogs facilitate communication between people who are on different schedules, because messages and entries can be read and answered whenever convenient for the receiver. Several of these ICTs also allow the sending of broadcast messages—requests or memos sent to a large group of recipients, even to the whole organization. This capability enables people who do not know whom to ask to gather information and form relationships.

A second use of ICTs is in *coordination and integration* of work processes. The improvements in quality and efficiency of work provided by ICTs are well known. Even greater benefits can be realized when ICTs are used to integrate organizational work processes. VF Corporation, discussed in the previous section, is one example of work integration via ICT. **Electronic data interchange**

(EDI) systems enable the management of data exchange between units, divisions, and companies that have to coordinate their work. Organizations use EDIs to set up automated exchanges of information needed to coordinate key tasks. For example, Chrysler Corporation uses an EDI linking its suppliers and plants for supply chain management.[22] This EDI keeps track of inventory and is used for parts requests by managers; as parts are needed, suppliers are informed, and orders arrive at the factory just in time to be installed. This just-in-time parts system eliminates the cost of keeping large inventories and helps avoid purchase of unneeded parts; as a direct link between suppliers and Chrysler, the EDI also helps the suppliers avoid manufacturing parts that go unsold and increases production quality through immediate feedback. Customers may also be included in EDI systems. American Hospital Supply (AHS) was a leader in utilizing information technology for customer orders. It placed terminals into health care organizations to enable them to order supplies directly from AHS, resulting in huge sales growth. Another type of workflow integration, **computer aided design/computer aided manufacturing (CAD/CAM)** systems, integrates the design of parts and products with their manufacturing. In an integrated system, design and manufacturing are done in a seamless process mediated by the information technology. This enables much easier redesign and correction of problems than do traditional methods. **Office workflow systems** help organizations manage the flow of information when their work involves information processing. For example, an oil exploration company in Houston uses imaging to store diagrams of geological formations, move these images into a videoconference with a client half the world away in Nigeria, process a contract negotiated in the videoconference and attach the geological images, send it via e-mail or fax to the client, get the signed and authenticated contract back via e-mail, and finally store it in the contract database, which has special links to various work notification messages sent via e-mail that inform exploration employees of the new job, who then e-mail back to verify assignments, call up the images to help them plan drilling, and so on. The ideal office automation system would link all the information processing and "paperwork" of the firm into a seamless whole. EDI, CAD/CAM, office workflow, and other applications such as inventory and supply chain management systems are currently being integrated into even larger systems called **enterprise resource planning (ERP) systems.** ERP systems are multipurpose integration tools and have been quite popular with large organizations during the past five years.

The monetary cost of electronic workflow integration is substantial, because it typically involves design of complex hardware configurations and integrating software across many applications. Even with substantial investment, problem-free integration of the various parts of a system is difficult. Many office automation projects remain unfinished, for example, because incompatible software and hardware make it impossible to link the various subsystems together. There may also be human resistance to workflow integration. Automation may eliminate jobs. It also tightens up surveillance, which may cause resentment, even as it increases quality and control. However, the gains from electronic workflow integration can be substantial, in terms of effectiveness and efficiency. As long as the process being integrated constitutes a substantial part of the organization's critical work and the implementation of the integration is competent, the gains outweigh the costs.

A third application of ICT is to help organizations *manage knowledge* that has been developed and accumulated over the years.[23] As we note in Chapter 5, over the past fifty years work with information and specialized knowledge has grown more and more important. One of an organization's greatest assets is the knowledge that its employees develop. Two kinds of knowledge can be distinguished. One important type of knowledge, *organizational knowledge,* consists of accumulated experience in an area, such as an extensive database of customers or experience with developing and operating a specialized product, for example computer-assisted inventory systems. A second type of knowledge is the *expertise* of employees. Although this knowledge may seem to be solely the property of the employee, the organization has a stake in it as well, because the organization often pays for employee education and training and gives the employee a context in which to develop this knowledge. For example, an employee who develops expertise in Web site design has done this using his or her talents and initiative; but the organization has supplied the computers and software and time for programming that enabled the employee to become an expert. Both organizational and employee-based knowledge have come to be regarded as assets that organizations can use to add value to their products and services, and organizations have attempted to develop knowledge-management processes to capitalize on these assets.

Knowledge management refers to the practices and procedures that organizations use to identify, catalog, harness, and utilize valuable knowledge. ICT plays an important part in knowledge management, because once an organization identifies key knowledge, it wishes to preserve it in a form that makes it easily available and manipulable. Knowledge-management systems can take a number of different forms. In some cases, organizations compile databases listing customers, problems that have occurred with products, and other organizational knowledge. Linking these together provides an elementary knowledge-management system. Other organizations actively solicit information and knowledge from employees, who enter it into a shared system such as Lotus Notes. This, however, is quite time-consuming for employees, and they are not always willing to comply fully with such requests. (Some are probably afraid that if they put everything they know into the system, they themselves would not be needed and would be fired!) Noshir Contractor developed a system to identify knowledge networks that did not rely on cataloging knowledge but rather discovered expertise among the members of an organization. He used a two-part mapping strategy: the first part involves identifying networks of who-knows-what knowledge that is relevant to a project; the second is to identify people "who know who knows what," that is, individuals who are particularly knowledgeable about where expertise lies in the organization. If you could not locate a needed expert from the first map, you could go to the second map to find a person likely to know someone else who had the knowledge you needed.

Knowledge management is still relatively new, and several problems must be solved before it can reach its full potential. As we have already mentioned, knowledge management requires cooperation of organizational members. In this time of overworked, overstretched workers, it may be difficult to obtain the needed inputs. Second, knowledge itself is often difficult to identify. Much knowledge exists in a form that can be expressed verbally and written down or stored in databases; just as much or more knowledge is tacit knowledge, know-how that cannot be put into words but instead rests in the hands of the experienced worker or the judgment of the manager or expert. Most organizational knowledge-management systems cannot capture this type of knowledge. It is possible that Contractor's approach is the best that can be done for tacit knowledge. Finally, some have doubted that effective knowledge management is even possible, given the fact that knowledge is a community property and changes constantly.

Finally, ICT can be used *strategically* by organizations. In the late twentieth and early twenty-first centuries, ICT have enabled organizations to offer new services and to expand into new markets or service areas.[24] Because of its potential to give private organizations an advantage over their competitors and to enable public and nonprofit organizations to deliver higher-quality services more effectively, ICT has increasingly played a major role in organizational strategy.

One of the earliest and most famous examples of strategic use of ICT is the American Hospital Supply (AHS) extranet mentioned in the previous section. This system, originally developed by a regional sales manager, enabled hospital clerks to order supplies over telephone lines using punch cards and primitive computers. It was extremely successful and increased sales markedly. When the executives of AHS realized that the system gave them a direct connection to their customers that competitors did not have, they developed the organization's strategy with this system in mind, reorganizing their sales force and inventory around the computerized purchasing system. They refined and improved the system until it became so simple and reliable that customers "self-served" themselves, relying on the sales force less than they had in the past. This strategy enabled AHS to reduce costs and increase market share and made it the leader in its industry. It also transformed the organization. Sales representatives no longer devoted most of their time to selling supplies, but instead sold the purchasing system. The sales function became much less important in the company, while the information systems function became much more important. Facilities and personnel were organized around supporting the purchasing system, which required redefinition of jobs and changes in work processes. AHS also used the information flowing from the automated sales transactions to help it predict demand from its customers; it was then able to adjust inventory levels to keep up with demand and reduce wastage. AHS customers, too, were changed by the system; AHS helped them redesign their purchasing and supplies systems to fit the new online process.

Of course, no strategy is effective forever. Eventually AHS's competitors offered their own purchasing systems and AHS lost its competitive edge. Today online supply systems are standard in the hospital supply industry (and many others), and they no longer offer the strategic advantage of the original AHS system. The next major strategic advance went well beyond AHS's proprietary system. In March 2000, five major health care suppliers—Abbott, Baxter, GE Medical, Johnson & Johnson, and Medtronic—started the Global Healthcare Exchange (GHX).[25] GHX was designed as an electronic marketplace for the purchase of health care supplies, but it also offered much more. It promised to enable hospitals to increase the efficiency of their entire health care supply chain, from placing orders to receiving delivery. The five founding partners handled more than 70 percent of the supply business at the time of GHX's founding, and they were joined by seventy additional firms in the next few years. This "one-stop shopping" approach was attractive to hospitals, but it was also beneficial to suppliers, who no longer had to compete in an open market. They could set prices higher than they might have been in open competition, and they could also count on having "captive" customers, once hospitals redesigned their purchasing procedures around the GHX system.

These two examples illustrate how strategic use of ICT transforms organizations and gives rise to whole new types of organizations, such as GHX. These organizations are literally designed or redesigned around ICTs. Rather than being just a tool for organizations to use, ICT is *the* major component of the organization. Other examples of strategic uses of ICT abound, including online reservation and travel services such as American Express Interactive, Taco Bell's use of ICTs to streamline work and make its franchises more efficient, and Dell Computer. These are all major corporations, but smaller organizations can also make strategic use of ICT. The College Station Independent School District in College Station, Texas, involves parents in their children's education by posting homework assignments on school Web sites and using e-mail to facilitate teacher-parent contact. Increasing involvement of parents in education has been shown to lead to improved student outcomes and thus helps the school district fulfill its mission of effectively educating its students.

Impacts of Information and Communication Technologies

The widespread use of ICT in modern organizations has several important effects. First, use of ICT tends to *open up communication and increase accessibility* of people in organizations. Studies show that e-mail, for example, tends to increase lateral communication (contacts across organizational levels) and the flow of ideas compared to more traditional communication media.[26] Sara Kiesler reports a case in which a broadcast request for ideas in a large organization elicited more than one hundred replies in two days, and several of the replies solved or significantly improved the problem.[27] Moreover, rather than just substituting for traditional channels such as face-to-face communication, e-mail usually adds to the total communication flow in organizations. As we will see in

Chapters 4 and 6, the more open the communication system, the more adaptable and responsive the organization is likely to be.

Second, ICT promotes the *spatial dispersion of organizations.* Organizations whose members are highly independent yet spread around different locations can use ICT to coordinate their work. Before the advent of ICT, organizations either had to situate employees working on highly independent tasks in the same place or allow for delays because of the time required to manage interdependence via letter, memo, or phone. However, electronic linkages are so fast and reliable and provide such rich interaction that organizations can now plan to have work dispersed to the locations where it can be done most effectively and integrate via electronic communication. For example, the sales team of a firm purchasing industrial equipment can work directly with engineers back at the home office to determine if alterations desired by customers are feasible and to price the changes. Whereas this may have taken a week or more in the "old days," electronic linkages make it fast and relatively easy. **Telework,** a work arrangement in which employees spend at least part of their time working at home or off site, is a growing trend supported by new ICTs. The capability of ICT to facilitate coordination and support work is also one major reason for the globalization of organizations.

A third impact of ICTs has been to foster *interorganizational linkages.* Organizations have always entered into joint ventures, alliances, and other types of collaborative agreements with other organizations. However, ICT has made it much easier for them to develop integrated activities, particularly since the spread of Internetworking. Ventures such as GHX, described in the previous section, would be much more difficult to manage without the Internet, which enables the companies to easily combine their product listings, make them available to customers, take and route orders, and share the accounts for the venture with each partner. Network and virtual organizations, discussed in Chapter 6, are often comprised of allied organizations linked together through the Internet. Another type of interorganizational linkage that is increasingly common is **outsourcing,** in which one organization contracts with another to perform certain functions. For example, it is becoming common for organizations to hire contractors to set up and maintain help desks. In many cases calls or e-mails are routed to help desk contractors located in other countries. Until recently Dell Computer had its help desks run by a subcontractor in India.

Recent developments in ICT have raised issues related to *privacy.* ICT enables organizations to monitor their employees relatively unobtrusively. Employees working on networked computers may have their keystrokes counted, e-mails perused, and the Web sites they visit recorded. Managers often justify these measures on the grounds that they have a right to make sure their subordinates are actually working. However, employees may feel violated in that what were previously private activities are laid open to scrutiny. We will explore issues related to privacy and surveillance in organizations in Chapter 3. ICT also enables organizations to collect and integrate personal information in unprecedented ways. Records can be made of the Web sites a person visits and the resulting Internet purchases. ICTs can also compile databases of information on individuals, such as major purchases, credit ratings, and travel. In the United States, this information is not the property of the individual, but of the organization compiling it. The recent dispute over plans by the Department of Homeland Security to employ Carnivore, a powerful search engine, to scan e-mail and other Internet communications for suspicious activity is one example of how an organization may compromise private information and intrude on citizens' privacy.

The spread of Internetworking also raises the issue of *security*.[28] The many computer viruses and other types of attacks that have plagued the Internet over the past several years underscore this issue. The interconnections enabled by the Internet also expose organizations and computer users to attacks from viruses and from hackers who "hijack" their computers for their own purposes. Previously secure databases with sensitive private information have become accessible to attackers who can penetrate extranets or intranets. As a result, identity theft and related intrusions have become growing problems.

In concluding this brief discussion of the impacts of ICT, we want to register an important qualification. If one thing is certain from the research, it is that effects are strongly dependent on the context in which the ICT is implemented — which include the organizational culture, the goals of the different parties involved in its implementation, the specific problems or opportunities the ICT is brought in to address, and social-influence processes at work-group and individual levels. To be sure, ICT has certain potentials or tendencies, but managers and planners need to be aware that technology is not a silver bullet. Managers who assume this will find that the bullet often hits different targets from those at which they aim.

Closing Note

ICT has opened up a whole range of possibilities for organizations in the twenty-first century. The steady development of ICT from stodgy mainframe computers of the 1960s to the dynamic, flexible network and wireless technologies of the 2000s has greatly enhanced organizations' ability to innovate and change. At this point it seems apparent that technology will continue to advance at a dizzying pace into the foreseeable future, so we should be ready for even more changes in work and organizations.

ICT has promoted the emergence of new strategies for organizing, including the network form discussed in Chapter 6 and the virtual organization. These new forms are communication intensive and provide some features of control that the traditional strategy offered but have the flexibility, adaptability, and empowerment offered by the relational strategy. What is less clear is whether these forms can evolve coherent organizational cultures.

These technologies have also changed the way work is done. Telework, either on the road or from home, gives both organizations and employees more options. In addition, organizations are increasingly trying to harness their employees' knowledge. However, there are potential problems with both of these developments. Telework threatens to erode workers' private time even further. Knowledge management asks employees for something they have never had to provide before, their special knowledge and insights accumulated over the years. This represents a new extension of the organizational domain over the individual. Other contentious issues pertain to possible infringements on privacy and confidential information.

The impacts of implications of ICT are not determined by the technology. They are worked out in human use of the technology, and in the balance of organizational and individual forces that put the technology into action.

Conclusion

The term *strategy* derives from the ancient Greek for "artifice" or "trick," and its early use referred to surprising the enemy in battle.[29] The person who conceived the strategy, the *strategos,* was a general. The roots of the word imply that the strategist is a person with sufficient insight to devise a trick and enough control to carry it out. But the ancient Greeks were subtle. They knew that situations often changed and that the *strategos* had to adapt. In our day too, strategy has an element of improvisation and cannot follow a rigid plan.

The five keys to strategic organizational communication suggested at the beginning of this chapter do not offer a simple formula. In our rapidly changing world, formulas are unlikely to work. Rather, the keys are what rhetoricians call commonplaces or topoi, issues to start from and ways of thinking that will help to generate insights into the challenges facing today's organizations. In complex and dynamic situations, it is important not to freeze one's thinking by trying to adhere to a few simple rules. Maintaining an open mind and responsiveness to the cues in the immediate situation is the key to intelligent and flexible response.

Although they deal with different aspects of organizations, the five keys are interrelated. Systems thinking works in synergy with critical thinking to help people become aware of unacknowledged structures that influence organizations. Both of these help us to understand globalization, diversity, and ICT, which are often driven by subtle forces that are difficult to fathom. ICT is an enabler of globalization, and globalization feeds into the development of ICT. In turn, globalization is one of the trends that confronts us with the challenges and opportunities of diversity.

As you read on and think about the organizations in your life, we hope you will come to understand these connections and uncover insights of your own.

Notes

[1] This example draws on the account by Peter Senge in his excellent book *The Fifth Discipline: The Art and Practice of the Learning Organization* (New York: Doubleday, 1990), chapter 8.

[2] The principles of systems thinking are discussed in much greater depth in Senge, *The Fifth Discipline.*

[3] Goran Therborn, *The Ideology of Power and the Power of Ideology* (London: Verso, 1980); and Dennis Mumby, *Communication and Power in Organizations* (Norwood, NJ: Ablex, 1988), especially chapter 4.

[4] Albert Hirschman, *The Rhetoric of Reaction* (Cambridge, MA: Belknap Press, 1991). For an extended summary of this argument and an excellent application of it to the recurring debate in the United States about increasing the minimum wage, see James Aune, *Selling the Free Market* (New York: Guilford Press, 2001), especially chapter 1.

[5] Robert Kuttner, *Everything for Sale* (Chicago: University of Chicago Press, 1999).

[6] For a brief summary of these data, see Paul Krugman, "The Death of Horatio Alger," *Nation,* December 20, 2003, http://www.thenation.com/. More extensive analyses have been published by authors across the political spectrum. At one pole is conservative economist and lifelong Republican Kevin Phillips (see his books *The Politics of Rich and Poor* [New York: Broadway Books, 1990] and *Wealth and Democracy* [New York: Broadway Books, 2002]); at the other pole is a series of reports issued by the liberal Economic Policy Institute: Lawrence Mishel, Jared Bernstein, and Heather Bousley, *The State of Working America, 2002/2003* (Ithaca, NY: Cornell University Press, 2003).

[7] See Robert Bellah, R. Madsen, W. Sullivan, and S. Tipton., *Habits of the Heart,* 2nd ed. (Berkeley: University of California Press, 1995); C. W. Reynolds and R. V. Norman, eds., *Community in America: The Challenge of Habits of the Heart* (Berkeley: University of California Press, 1988); and Warren Bennis, Jagdish Parikh, and Ronnie Lessem, *Beyond Leadership: Balancing Economics, Ethics, and Ecology* (Cambridge, MA: Basil Blackwell, 1994), especially chapter 10. For a summary of de Tocqueville's observations and their applicability today, see John Cawelti, *Apostles of the Self-Made Man* (Cambridge, MA: Harvard University Press, 1974); and Stanley Deetz, *Democracy in the Age of Corporate Colonization* (Albany, NY: State University of New York Press, 1992).

[8] Robert Putnam, *Bowling Alone* (New York: Simon and Schuster, 2000).

[9] Steve Axley, "Managerial and Organizational Communication in Terms of the Conduit Metaphor," *Academy of Management Review* 9 (1984): 428–437.

[10] Jeffrey Pfeffer and Alison Davis-Blake, "The Effect of the Proportion of Women on Salaries," *Administrative Science Quarterly* 32 (1987): 1–24; Robin Clair and Kelly Thompson, "Pay Discrimination as a Discursive and Material Practice," *Journal of Applied Communication Research* 24 (1996): 1–20.

[11] Lynn Martin, *Pipelines of Progress* (Washington, DC: U.S. Department of Labor, August 1992), p. 12; see also "Corporate Women," *Business Week,* June 8, 1992; and Korn/Ferry International, "The Decade of the Executive Woman," *Houston Chronicle,* February 19, 1996, B1.

[12] In general, we have chosen to use the terms that we do to refer to different groups of nonwhite employees because they seem to be preferred by members of each group. The reasons for our choice of terminology for persons of Spanish descent is a bit more complex. We use the terms *Latino* and *Latina* as *generic* terms to refer to men and women of Spanish descent, respectively. We use the term *Mexican American* to refer to residents of the United States who were born in Mexico or whose families immigrated from Mexico. We do not use the term *Hispanic* at all, because it is used in so many different ways, even in the scholarly literature, that it is inevitably confusing. These terminological distinctions are important because the experiences of Latino persons in American organizations are very different depending on their heritage. In particular, people who immigrated from or whose families immigrated from Central and South America or the Caribbean face different attitudes and have had different experiences than those with roots in Mexico.

[13] See Anthony Giddens, *The Consequences of Modernity* (Cambridge, UK: Polity Press, 1990); *Modernity and Self-Identity* (Cambridge, UK: Polity Press, 1991); and *Beyond Left and Right* (Cambridge, UK: Polity Press, 1994); John Tomlinson, *Globalization and Culture* (Chicago: University of Chicago Press, 1999). An excellent introduction to the related issues is provided by a special issue on globalization, edited by Louis Ferleger and Jay Mandle, *Annals of the American Academy of Political and Social Science* 557 (July 2000).

[14] Key advocates of the homogenization thesis are D. Howes, ed., *Cross-Cultural Consumption* (London: Routledge, 1996); George Ritzer, *The McDonaldization of Society* (Newbury Park, CA: Pine Forge Press, 1993); George Ritzer and A. Liska, "McDisneyization and Post-Tourism," in *Touring Cultures,* C. Rojek and J. Urry, eds. (London: Routledge, 1997). Advocates of the polarization thesis include B. R. Barber, *Jihad vs. McWorld* (New York: Random House, 1995); Edward Said, *Orientalism* (New York: Penguin, 1978); and Samuel Huntington, *The Clash of Civilizations and the Remaking of World Order* (New York: Simon and Schuster, 1996). Advocates of the hybridization thesis include Thomas Friedman, *The Lexus and the Olive Tree* (New York: Farrar, Straus and Giroux, 1999); and Ulf Hannerz, *Cultural Complexity* (New York: Columbia University Press, 1992).

[15] Samuel Huntington, "The Clash of Civilizations?" *Annals of the American Academy of Political and Social Science* 570 (2000): 3–22; Benjamin Barber, "Jihad vs. McWorld," *Annals of the American Academy of Political and Social Science* 570 (2000): 23–33; Robert D. Kaplan, "The Coming Anarchy," *Annals of the American Academy of Political and Social Science* 570 (2000): 34–60.

[16] Tomlinson, p. 84.

[17] Madeline Drohan and Alan Freeman, "English Rules," *Annals of the American Academy of Political and Social Science* 570 (2000): 428–434; Joshua Fishman, "The New Linguistic Order," *Foreign Policy* 113 (Winter 1998–1999).

[18] Peter Drucker, "The Age of Transformation," *Atlantic Monthly,* September, 1994, p. 53.

[19] This opinion is expressed by Susan J. Winter and S. Lynne Taylor, who argue that new IT-supported organizational forms resemble those found in the preindustrial era. See their article in *Information Systems Research* 7 (1996): 5–21.

[20] Linda M. Applegate, Robert D. Austin, and F. Warren McFarlan, *Corporate Information Strategy and Management,* 6th ed. (Boston: McGraw-Hill, 2003).

[21] Bob Brewin, "Garment Maker Donning Wireless," *Computerworld,* September 11, 2000.

[22] Henry C. Lucas, *The T-Form Organization: Using Technology to Design Organizations for the 21st Century* (San Francisco: Jossey-Bass, 1996), pp. 144–146.

[23] Knowledge management is one of the most rapidly growing areas of interest in information systems and management. The discussion in this section is based upon several sources, including Peter Monge and Noshir Contractor, *Theories of Communication Networks* (New York: Oxford, 2003); Bruce Kogut, W. Shan, and Gordon Walker, "Knowledge in the Network and the Network as Knowledge: Structuring of New Industries," in *The Embedded Firm: On the Socioeconomics of Industrial Networks,* G. Grabher, ed. (New York: Rutledge, 1993); Clyde Holsapple and K. D. Joshi, "In Search of Descriptive Framework for Knowledge Management: Preliminary Delphi Results," in *Kentucky Initiative for Knowledge Management, Research Paper No. 118* (Lexington: University of Kentucky, 1999).

[24] Applegate, Austin, and McFarlan, chapters 1–3.

[25] Applegate, Austin, and McFarlan, pp. 35–38. For more information about Global Healthcare Exchange, go to http://www.ghx.com.

[26] R. Johansen, *Teleconferencing and Beyond* (New York: McGraw-Hill, 1984).

[27] Lee Sproull and Sara Kiesler, *Connections: New Ways of Working in the Networked World* (Cambridge, MA: MIT Press, 1992); Sara Kiesler, Jane Siegel, and Timothy W. McGuire, "Social Psychological Aspects of Computer-Mediated Communication," *American Psychologist* 39 (1984): 1123–1134.

[28] "Knowledge Center: Security," *Computerworld,* July 14, 2003, pp. 30–40.

[29] C. T. Onions, ed., *The Oxford Dictionary of English Etymology* (Oxford, UK: Oxford University Press, 1966).

UNIT II

Strategies of Organizing

Chapter 3

Traditional Strategies of Organizing

The foreman should never be authorized to enforce his discipline with the whips
if he can accomplish it with words.
—VARRO OF ROME, C. 100

If the words of command are not clear and distinct, if orders are not
thoroughly understood, the general is to blame.
—SUN TZU OF CHINA, 500 BC

Central Themes

- Traditional strategies of organizing attempt to control employees through rules, norms, and systems of rewards and punishments, all of which rely heavily on communication. But all control systems lead to resistance.
- If information is filtered as it passes through the formal chain of command, decision makers may have too little relevant information to make good decisions; if it is not filtered, they may be too overloaded with information to make good decisions.
- Both structural and personal/interpersonal factors lead to omission and distortion of information as it passes through formal channels.
- When the environment surrounding an organization is stable or not competitive, traditional strategies of organizing may function well; when the environment is turbulent or competitive, weaknesses in formal communication systems make it difficult for traditional strategies to succeed.
- In traditional strategies of organizing, leadership primarily involves managing, that is, designing and implementing formal systems of communication, motivation, and control.
- Information and communication technologies (ICTs) offer ways for traditional organizations to avoid some of the problems that the strategy creates.

Key Terms

specialization	trained incapacity
hierarchization	counterbiasing
centralization	face management
bureaucracy	distributive justice
legal authority	procedural justice
time-motion study	surveillance
information overload	regression
decentralization	working to rule

As the ancient comments at the beginning of this chapter suggest, neither the study of organizations nor concern with communication in organizations is terribly new. Whenever people have depended on one another to complete tasks or meet their needs, they have formed organizations. By the time human beings joined together into families and clans, they had become involved in the economic activities of hunting and gathering. They had started to organize, which required them to communicate with other workers. After humans became farmers, they developed more complex organizations with more complicated communication needs. With farming came villages and the need to govern large groups of people; with villages came the concepts of citizenship and community welfare, which created the dual needs of defense and the management of the village's economy.

As villages turned into city-states, it became necessary for their managers to plan the operation of the society and to keep permanent records of the rules and procedures that they developed. The oldest written documents in existence deal with religion, management, and government, a combination that makes great sense when one realizes that the earliest managers also were governors and priests. As ancient religious and political civilizations expanded, their needs for effective economic organizations and effective organizational communication multiplied. As early as 2000 BC, leaders recognized the importance of communication. Pharaoh Ptah-hotep instructed his sons and managers in the importance of listening skills, the need to seek advice and information from their subordinates, the importance of staying informed about what was taking place around them, and the necessity of clearly explaining each worker's tasks and documenting these instructions in writing. The Chinese emperors Yao and Shun (c. 2300 BC) also searched for ways of opening communication channels between themselves and the peasants. They also encouraged managers to actively consult with their subordinates about the problems faced by the government. By the time of Christ, Greek and Roman scholars had suggested many of the key concepts of modern organizational communication theory. But it was the growth of the nation-state and the mercantile system that created separate roles for governors, managers, and priests. Within the large and complex firms of the Industrial Revolution, it became very clear that control and coordination could be achieved only through effective communication.

Unfortunately, the people who operated these organizations had few reliable guidelines. They had some experience in business and thus could rely on hunch and intuition. But people's memories often blank out or redefine their failures and overemphasize successes, so experience is an unreliable guide. Managers also could try to apply the principles used to run military organizations, which were the major large, complex organizations that existed before the Industrial Revolution. But overall, owners' decision making suffered from a lack of concern for efficiency and a virtual absence of reliable information.

In addition, owner-managers often treated their employees in arbitrary, capricious, and even inhumane ways. In the United States, proslavery politicians of the 1800s defended slavery by arguing that the lives of slaves were better than the lives of workers in Northern textile mills. There was enough of a parallel to make the argument credible. As a result, workers began to organize politically and form unions. Labor-management relations became increasingly hostile, and confrontations between labor and management were often violent. The broad, rapid economic growth of the 1800s came to a screeching halt in a series of economic depressions during the 1890s. By the early 1900s, both managers and scholars recognized that Western organizations faced serious problems in design and operation. In response to these observations, a group of organizational theorists proposed an alternate strategy of organizing, one that sought to manage the paradox between organizational and individual needs by enhancing efficiency, creating stable and predictable organizational situations, eliminating arbitrary supervisory behavior, and motivating workers through economic rewards and a sense of personal achievement.

Traditional Strategies of Organizational Design

A large number of people were involved in the development of the traditional strategy of organizing. One group, the *bureaucratic theorists,* attempted to improve organizations from the top down, by enhancing the effectiveness of administrative employees. These theorists are associated with sociologist Max Weber. A second group developed *scientific management,* an approach that tried to improve organizations from the bottom up, by reforming workers' tasks, efficiency, and rewards. They were inspired by an engineer, Frederick Taylor. Both groups had the same primary concern—replacing the arbitrary, capricious, and inefficient practices of contemporary organizations with systematically designed, objective, and fair systems of management and supervision.

Traditional Structure and Communication

All organizations are structured. It is structure that distinguishes organized enterprises from disorganized ones. Structure is important to members of organizations because it clarifies each member's areas of responsibility, it makes formal authority relationships clear to everyone involved in the organization, and it lets everyone know where different kinds of organizational knowledge are located. It makes life predictable, and with predictability come feelings of stability and trust.[1] But the specific structure that emerges in an organization depends on a series of choices that employees make.

Bureaucracy and Structure   Both the scientific managers and the bureaucratic theorists believed that organizations should be segmented into a matrix of formal positions defined by the specific tasks for which their occupants are responsible. The labor that must be performed in the organization is *divided* among various groups of employees who have the **specialized** skills necessary to complete their assigned tasks efficiently and effectively. The organizational chart also shows how the various positions are arranged, so that lines of authority are clear to all. Usually this arrangement is **hierarchical;** supervisors are directly responsible to their own immediate supervisors for their own actions and for those of their immediate subordinates. It also implies that decision making and control are **centralized.** This means that all the major decisions facing the organization are made by the people who occupy the positions at the top of the organizational hierarchy. Of course, all members of the organization are responsible for making *routine* decisions in their areas of responsibility. But they must base their decisions on *policies* and *procedures* that are established at the top. When communication does take place outside of the immediate work group, it is formal, both in tone and in the way in which it is communicated. Because this organizational structure is so widespread, it is easy to forget a number of basic facts about it. The most important fact is that structure is a choice. There are a large number, perhaps an infinite number, of ways in which an organization can be structured.

The kind of structure that we have just described is called a **bureaucracy.** As sociologist Max Weber noted a century ago, it is especially appropriate to Protestant, capitalistic, democratic societies. To people raised in those societies, bureaucratic structures *seem* to be *natural* and *normal* (recall Chapter 2). As members of these societies mature, they learn that formal rules are necessary for the efficient operation of societies and organizations because they protect people from arbitrary or harmful treatment by more powerful people. They are taught that societies "of law" are better than societies of people and personal connections. They come to value individuality, to believe that individuals have rights, and to feel that individuals are responsible for their actions. They learn to accept what Weber called **legal authority,** the notion that societies and organizations should be organized around a formal, objective (and thus impersonal), written set of rules, policies, and procedures. They come to value themselves in terms of the formal roles that they play in their societies and organizations and to accept the notion that with different roles come different rights and obligations. But these assumptions mask the fact that the bureaucratic structure is only one of a large number of available strategies of organizing. They also tend to obscure the fact that traditional strategies of organizational design have distinctive strengths and particular weaknesses.

In an organization that is structured bureaucratically, the positions are arranged in a hierarchy. Applicants are hired for a position solely because they demonstrate the special expertise needed to perform their required tasks. Employees base their decisions solely on the written policies, procedures, and rules of the organization, and all their actions are to be documented in writing. Employees are empowered to make decisions in their areas of expertise, as long as they follow established policies and procedures. Only those employees at the top of the organization may actually establish policies and procedures or make major decisions. To prevent favoritism, all employees must maintain detached, impersonal relationships with clients and co-workers and keep emotional considerations from influencing their decisions and actions. Communication is to be formal and restricted to the chain of command, because only then can responsibility for communication breakdowns be assessed and remedies taken.

The bureaucratic theorists valued this kind of structure primarily because they thought it would bring fairness and accountability to organizations, although they also believed that it would increase organizational efficiency. People would be hired based on their abilities, not their political or personal connections. Everyone involved in the organization would know who was responsible for each task that needed to be performed. If those tasks were performed well, the correct people would be rewarded; if not, the responsible people would be punished. Every employee would also be held responsible for communicating relevant information up and down the chain of command. After they successfully completed a probationary period, employees would be guaranteed a job for life (assuming their performance continued to be adequate) and an adequate pension. As a result, they could not be pressured to show favoritism to powerful clients or supervisors. Organizations, and all their members, would be accountable for their actions, and the organization would be efficient.

Scientific Management   The second group of people who helped develop the traditional strategy of organizing focused on *scientific* management. Like the bureaucratic theorists, they were concerned with accountability. In fact, Frederick Taylor, the father of scientific management, was very disturbed by a common managerial practice of blaming and punishing workers for management's bad decisions. That practice reduced organizational efficiency because managers who are not held accountable for *their own* errors have no incentive to improve. It also inevitably drove a wedge between labor and management, and management's primary goal should be to foster cooperative relationships with workers. For Taylor, accountability bred efficiency.[2]

Although these attitudes may not seem to be all that radical today, they were startling to Taylor's contemporaries. They were palatable only because Taylor coupled them with a set of efficiency-enhancing techniques that had significant short-term economic benefits. Taylor believed that by using these techniques, firms would be able to increase their profits and the incomes of all their employees, including managers. Over time they would be able to reduce their prices, and the entire society would benefit. The best known of these techniques was the **time-motion study,** in which a supervisor or a consultant observes workers completing a task, breaks the process down into its elements or motions, and then redesigns it to minimize the number of movements necessary to complete it. By using the improved techniques, workers could increase their productivity and income, and thereby increase the organization's profits. Today a number of consulting firms, armed with sophisticated video technology, still conduct time-motion studies and make recommendations that improve efficiency and reduce worker strain and fatigue. For example, Charley Conrad helped fund his college education by working summers and vacations in a metal-processing foundry. Initially he operated a drill press. But when the company conducted a time-motion study, it found that workers taller than six feet could not efficiently operate the equipment. They had to bend over to reach some of the levers and as a result got tired sooner than the shorter workers did. Like every other operator who was taller than six feet, Conrad was transferred to a section that had tasks that could be efficiently performed by people of his height. Taylor stressed that time-motion studies, and all of the other techniques he developed, should be used in close consultation with workers and in an atmosphere of cooperation and mutual gain. If they are used without first consulting workers, as they often are, they generate strong resistance, especially if there is a low level of trust between labor and management.

Today firms such as the ones Taylor envisioned are often viewed as sweatshops where workers are treated like parts of a giant industrial machine. In addition, the term *bureaucracy* carries negative images: inefficient bureaucrats producing little except exhaustive expense accounts; customers and employees alike being buried in red tape and treated without dignity in a vast administrative morass; and stubbornness when action is required, blind obsession with unchangeable policies when flexibility is necessary, and interminable delays when speed is crucial. These pictures of the traditional strategy of organizing are really quite ironic, because the original purpose of this strategy was to create efficient and productive organizations in which people were treated fairly and equitably. The arbitrariness and capriciousness that Taylor and Weber observed in the organizations of their time were to be replaced by policies and procedures that treated everyone—workers, customers, and clients—in the same way. The inefficient decision making of early firms was to be replaced by objective, data-based considerations. Although the strategy focused on meeting the organizations' needs for coordination and control, it also was intended to meet individual employees' needs for stability and autonomy. Bureaucratic structure is clear, stable, and predictable. But the traditional strategy is also problematic in two ways. Perhaps most important, its key elements—specialization, hierarchization, and centralization—place a great deal of pressure on an organization's formal communication system. Consequently, communication breakdowns are highly likely. Second, the strategy sacrifices flexibility and responsiveness for consistency and predictability. Although this is an appropriate trade-off for some organizations, it creates serious problems for others.

Communication Breakdowns in Formal Communication Systems

For the traditional strategy of organizing to succeed, information must flow freely through the chain of command. The decision makers at the top of the organization must receive accurate, complete, concise, and timely information about the extent to which orders have been carried out and tasks have been completed. They must also be informed about problems that have developed or are likely to develop in the future. In addition, decision makers must benefit from the specialized expertise of each employee along the chain of command. If that expertise is not available to individuals in upper management, their decision making will suffer. Similarly, information must flow from supervisors to subordinates, including information about policies, procedures, reward/rule systems, and the optimal means of performing assigned tasks. If any of these communication processes break down, the organization will function at less-than-optimal efficiency. If the margin of error within the organization is small, these communication breakdowns may threaten its survival.[3]

The Filtering Paradox   Unfortunately, processes of information exchange create a fundamental paradox. On the one hand, upper-level decision makers depend on receiving accurate, timely information from employees lower in the hierarchy. However, if information were to flow freely through the chain of command, the upper-level managers would soon be overloaded and overwhelmed by the amount of information they receive. For example, envision a moderate-sized hierarchical organization (one in which each supervisor has only four subordinates and the organization chart has seven levels). Each employee sends only one message a day up the chain of command. If no messages are filtered out, 4,096 messages would reach upper management each day, creating serious problems of **information overload**.[4] But if every employee screens out only half of the information received, 98.4 percent of the information generated in the organization never reaches its decision makers. Consequently, the traditional strategy of organizing requires employees to rely on formal channels for the information they need while simultaneously restricting the flow of information through these channels.

Structural Barriers to Information Flow   A number of factors complicate the filtering paradox. Some of these barriers to information flow involve the people who make up the organization—their background and training, personal characteristics, and interpersonal relationships. But others involve the formal structure of the organization and the nature of human communication. The structural barriers would exist regardless of who worked in the organization.

When one person communicates a message to another, each of them interprets it. The words that make up the message are meaningless until some human being makes sense out of them.[5] When people communicate, they exchange their *interpretations* of information, not information in a "pure" form. When they interpret messages, they alter the messages' meaning. People *condense* messages, making them shorter and simpler; people *simplify* messages into good or bad, all or none, or other extreme terms; they *assimilate* new messages so that their meaning is consistent with information received in the past; they *whitewash* messages, so that they will not upset the people to whom they are sent; and they *reductively code* messages by combining them with other information to form a sensible overall picture. In the process of interpreting a message, people simplify and clarify it. They absorb some of the uncertainty and ambiguity in the message. But in the process they also change it. Interpreting information is inevitable because all messages carry some degree of ambiguity and some degree of uncertainty about how they should be interpreted. When messages are interpreted, they are changed.

Interpersonal Barriers to Information Flow   Personal and interpersonal factors also complicate information flow (see Table 3-1). The amount of communication flowing through the chain of command is reduced by power and status differences among members of an organization. Messages are communicated in writing instead of face-to-face, and they focus on tasks, with little informal or social content. Written messages are more ambiguous than exchanges in open, face-to-face encounters, making differences in interpretation more likely.[6] Differences in interpretations tend to reduce trust, leading employees to rely even more heavily on written communication to protect themselves, and so on in a downward spiral. Supervisors can offset these effects by de-emphasizing status

TABLE 3-1
Factors That Distort Vertical Communication

Structural	Personal and Relational
1. Processes of interpreting messages 　　Condensation 　　Accenting 　　Assimilation to past 　　Assimilation to future 　　Assimilation to attitudes and values 　　Reduction 2. Number of links in communication chain 3. Trained communication 　　Incapacity 　　Perceptual sets 　　Language barriers 4. Large size of the organization 5. Problems in timing of messages 6. Problems inherent in written communication	1. Power, status differences between parties 2. Mistrust between parties 3. Subordinates' mobility aspirations 4. Inaccurate perceptions of information needs of others 5. Norms or actions that discourage requests for clarification 6. Sensitivity of topics

differences, training their subordinates in communication skills, rewarding their subordinates for keeping them informed, and encouraging them to seek clarification of ambiguous messages. However, they often do the opposite by verbally or nonverbally communicating *"I don't want to hear about it now."* They may talk only while on the run, use an annoyed tone of voice, physically move away from the subordinate, and allow other people to interrupt the conversation. Or they may simply fail to acknowledge or act on the information their subordinates provide.[7] If subordinates do not trust their supervisors, other factors come into play. Subordinates who wish to be promoted or recognized for past achievements and believe that the supervisor will have an influential voice on promotions are especially likely to withhold negative information from supervisors they do not trust. Those effects are increased when subordinates believe that their supervisors do not pass negative information on to them. They are especially unlikely to communicate negative information or information that deals with controversial or sensitive issues—precisely the kind of information that supervisors most need to have. In highly political organizations, withholding information is even more likely, especially when it is negative. As Chapter 8 explains, information is a potent source of power, but only if it is not widely available. Political battles—among individual employees and among units of the organization—often are information battles, and the side that has obtained and exploited secret information wins.[8]

This section has focused on barriers to the upward flow of information through the chain of command, but downward communication is limited by the same factors and processes. One of the most consistent findings in research on organizations is that subordinates want their supervisors to keep them informed and feel that they receive too little relevant and useful information from their supervisors, especially about events, policies, and changes directly involving them or their jobs. Many supervisors simply do not provide their subordinates with sufficient job-related information, especially feedback about the subordinates' performance. Downward communication is selected, filtered, and interpreted in much the same way as upward communication. In addition, when supervisors believe that they should give their subordinates only the absolute minimum necessary amount of information, they filter an even higher proportion of downward communication, frequently withholding even crucial information. Destructive, or productive, cycles are formed and perpetuated. Supervisors whose communication is considerate, frequent, and reliable tend to have subordinates whose communication is similar. Because they better understand their supervisors' information needs, they can better summarize the information they receive without leaving out important details. These subordinates keep their supervisors informed, which makes them seem trustworthy, and perceptions of trustworthiness reduce the distorting effects of status differences. Conversely, supervisors who withhold information from their subordinates have subordinates who withhold information from them. The subordinates may interpret their own actions as an appropriate way to defend themselves against an untrustworthy supervisor; the supervisor may see the subordinates' actions as compelling evidence that they are hostile or unmotivated, which justifies the supervisor's withholding information, and so on. No individual is to blame (or should receive credit) for these patterns of action, although supervisors' higher formal power means that they have a greater effect on the direction the cycle will take. These patterns result from complex, interacting systems of meaning-creation and should be understood as complex systems of communication.

How Traditional Strategies Complicate Information Flow   Each of the sources of communication breakdown described in this section are present in all organizations. But they are more of a problem in organizations that employ traditional strategies of organizing than in organizations that rely on other strategies. One of the key characteristics of traditional strategies is centralization of power and decision making. If an organization is highly centralized (that is, if its organizational chart is "tall"), messages will be exchanged, interpreted, and altered many times before they reach the decision makers at the top of the organization. The decisions that are made—the policies and procedures that are created—will be exchanged, interpreted, and altered many times before they reach the people at the bottom of the organization who will implement them. If decision making is distributed throughout the organization (that is, if it is **decentralized**), messages will be exchanged fewer times before action is taken on the information they contain. Fewer exchanges mean less interpretation and less alteration. In addition, communicating through the chain of command is very time-consuming, as any student who has needed to change a registration for a course or searched for a "lost" student aid check is painfully aware. In highly centralized organizations, information may reach decision makers (or implementers) too late for it to be useful.

A second element of the traditional strategy of organizing is specialization. It increases organizational efficiency by making sure that tasks are performed by people with the relevant expertise. But specialization also complicates information flow. As people are trained in an increasingly specialized set of skills, they become less and less capable of performing other tasks. They develop a kind of **trained incapacity.** The most obvious incapacity involves differences between upper management and lower-level workers. Managers often become incapable of understanding the processes through which their workers perform their tasks and are rarely able to actually do those jobs themselves. Conversely, lower-level workers become less able to understand complex, abstract thought. However, trained incapacity permeates the entire organization. Employees who play specialized roles interpret the messages they receive in a manner appropriate to those roles. Personnel officers interpret messages in terms of what they imply about future needs for hiring, firing, or training employees; and financial officers attribute meaning to messages based on the economic impact that they imply. As their training and experience progress, employees become less capable of taking the perspectives of other members of the organization when interpreting or sending messages. Sometimes they may even create their own languages. As employees become literate in the artificial language of their position or unit, they become less capable of translating their ideas into a language that other people can understand.[9] As a result, misunderstanding between specialties is quite common. The size of an organization in itself does not seem to increase problems of trained incapacity, but when an organization is highly specialized, trained incapacity can create severe problems.

Finally, traditional strategies of organizing attempt to formalize communication, which highlights power and status differences and stipulates that relationships between supervisors and subordinates should be impersonal and governed by established policies and procedures. As a result, trust and shared interpretations of information are reduced and written communication dominates. It is precisely in this kind of situation that the personal and interpersonal sources of distortion are most potent. In short, traditional strategies rely heavily on formal, chain-of-command communication and paradoxically create barriers to successful information flow. If organizational communication really did function as it is supposed to in the traditional strategy, most people would not know what was going on most of the time.

CASE STUDY
Feel Safer Now?

Within days of September 11, 2001, pundits and politicians alike were trying to explain the intelligence breakdowns that allowed twenty or more terrorists to carry out attacks on the World Trade Center and the Pentagon. As in the case of accidents (recall the blackout case in Chapter 2), the dominant impulse was to blame "operator error":

> there were people at the borders who let these people in even though they didn't
> have proper papers. . . . There were F.B.I. people who, when they got reports from
> Phoenix and Minnesota and elsewhere, didn't think they were important enough
> to buck up to the higher-ups. There were security officers at the airports who let
> these people onto airplanes even though they were carrying materials that weren't
> allowed on airplanes.*

However, there also was a second tendency: almost as soon as the investigations began, informed (and uninformed) experts started attributing those breakdowns to "communication problems." Although the bulk of the information about the hijacking and hijackers still is not available to the public—and is not likely to be available for many, many years—some items have been made public. The story begins at the end of World War II, not in 2001.

Myriad federal agencies are in some way involved in national safety, from the Department of Agriculture to the Immigration and Naturalization Service. The most visible, and most important, are the Federal Bureau of Investigation (FBI), the Central Intelligence Agency (CIA), and the National Security Agency (NSA). When World War II ended, a proposal was made to continue the wartime Office of Secret

Service as the CIA. The head of the FBI, J. Edgar Hoover, fought the creation of the CIA, primarily on the grounds that the two bureaucracies were unnecessarily duplicative.[†] Hoover lost the battle, but he was able to ensure that the two agencies would have separate intelligence functions: one for targets outside of the United States and one for internal targets. Even at the time, critics questioned this division of labor, because spies and saboteurs regularly cross national borders, but it did make sense politically. Over time the two bureaucracies developed different ways of doing business and different rules for operating and making decisions, and they even attracted different kinds of employees. During the same era the operations of the CIA became progressively more secretive, even after the creation of the even-more-secret NSA. And all of the relevant agencies developed norms of sharing information with one another only on a "need to know" basis. Throughout the intervening decades their operations often were criticized. Much of the criticism focused on the FBI, which, under Hoover, had engaged in spying and various "dirty tricks" against antiwar groups and the leaders of the Civil Rights movement, but it included the CIA. Occasionally Congress would act to restrict their powers, as when it forbade the CIA to attempt to assassinate the leaders of foreign governments or acted to reduce racial bias in the FBI's decisions about whom to target for its investigations. In the process, the FBI's mandate was clarified—it was to investigate crimes that had already been committed, not try to prevent crimes from occurring.

Sometimes leaders of one or more of the agencies would complain that current counter-terrorism intelligence gathering was inadequate; a 1998 report has often been cited. But there is little question that, when taken together, the $30-billion-per-year (because the budgets of the NSA and the CIA are secret, this figure is only an estimate) U.S. intelligence agencies do an excellent job of generating information. Indeed, former FBI director Louis Freeh concluded that there is so much information available that "analyzing intelligence information can be like trying to take a sip of water coming out of a fire hydrant."[‡]

The "communication breakdown" explanation for the U.S. intelligence community's "failures" before 9-11 is the observation that various government agencies possessed items of information on the attackers that (1) were obvious clues regarding their plans and (2) were not shared with other agencies. These conclusions are based on three items of information.[§] Evidently, no government agency had any relevant information on sixteen of the nineteen hijackers prior to September 11. However, some information was available on the remaining three—Khalid al-Midhar, Nawaf al-Hazmi, and his brother Salim al-Hazmi (all three were aboard the plane that crashed into the Pentagon). The intelligence community began a worldwide effort to monitor people connected with al-Qaida and Osama bin Laden during 1999. The community closely monitored a meeting in Malaysia, from which the CIA discovered new information about al-Midhar (his full name, passport number, and so forth) and learned that he was leaving Malaysia on a plane with Nawaf al-Hazmi. Eventually they decided that none of this information was important

(continued)

(Case Study, continued)

enough to pass on to the other agencies. The NSA's (secret) database also included the name Nawaf al-Hazmi, along with information indicating that he was linked to al-Qaida. A lower-level employee, whose job it was to improve communication between the CIA and the FBI, did brief the latter agency and summarized the briefing for other CIA agents. Later, an overseas CIA agent notified his headquarters that al-Hazmi had entered the United States, but the information was not communicated to the FBI because he had done nothing illegal or threatening (in fact, this report evidently was not read by many people within the CIA).

While investigating the attack on the USS *Cole,* the CIA uncovered additional links to al-Qaida, and in at least one case passed the information on to the FBI. When the FBI agent asked why the CIA was following al-Midhar, he was told that the information could be given only with permission from the CIA agent's supervisor, which permission never was formally requested. The CIA had so many resources tied up investigating the attack on the USS *Cole* that it could not follow up on these leads, and the FBI could not do so because no crime had been committed and because if it investigated a group of Middle Eastern men, it risked litigation or at least criticism for racial profiling.

The most egregious example of "not connecting the dots," at least according to the U.S. press, involved a presumed almost-hijacker, Zacharias Moussaoui. He had been in the United States for some time attending various pilot schools. When he made it clear to a trainer in Egan, Minnesota, that he did not want to learn how to take off or land, the instructor became suspicious and called the local FBI office. When Moussaoui refused to allow agents to search his laptop computer, he was arrested on a charge of visa violations, constructed by the FBI in order to hold him while conducting an investigation. They learned from French intelligence officials that he had connections to al-Qaida. Local agents asked the Washington office to obtain a search warrant for Moussaoui's computer. The Washington office made the request to the special U.S. national security court but did not include the French reports in the request. The request was denied, leading to a heated, and now famous, memo from Minneapolis Special Agent Coleen Rowley to the Washington office. Other agencies experienced similar errors—the NSA intercepted a message, believed to be a recorded telephone conversation, that referred to a "big event" planned for September 11, but it was in Arabic and was not translated until after the attacks.

By June 2002, President Bush reported that "the CIA and the FBI are now in close communications, there's better sharing of intelligence." The next day White House spokesman Ari Fleischer amended the president's comments to contend that the needed changes were gradually being implemented.** Eighteen months later the independent Markle Task Force on National Security in the Information Age was less optimistic, concluding that information sharing "remains haphazard and still overly dependent on . . . personal relations among known colleagues." In addition, there seems to be some confusion about the roles of two agencies created since September 11, the Terrorist Threat Integration Center, created to coordinate information gathered by the CIA, FBI, and other agencies, and the Department of Homeland Security.[††]

Using What You Have Learned

1. Which of the sources of breakdowns in information flow described in this chapter seem to have been present prior to September 11? To what extent were the identified problems a function of insufficient amounts of information, inadequate flow of information, or errors in interpreting the information that was available?
2. As we indicated in Chapter 2, one of the difficulties in assessing the causes of accidents arises in separating actual system problems from what only seem to be problems because of the advantages gained by hindsight. For example, airport screeners were trained to search for bombs and the materials that could be used to build bombs, not to think of an airplane filled with fuel *as* a bomb. Of the "errors" made before September 11, which ones were errors, and which ones merely seem to be errors in hindsight?

Figure 3.1 shows the organizational chart of the Department of Homeland Security (which does not include the FBI, CIA, or NSA).

Questions to Think About and Discuss

1. Using what you know about the sources of communication breakdowns in bureaucratic organizations, assess the likelihood of communication breakdowns in the new department and among the new department and the FBI, CIA, NSA, and Terrorist Threat Integration Center.
2. What strategies would you recommend in an effort to compensate for any potential sources of communication breakdowns? Why would they work?

---

[*]Thomas Kean, chairman of the September 11 investigating panel, in Philip Shenon, "Chief of Sept. 11 Panel Assesses Blame but Holds Off on Higher-Ups," *New York Times on the Web*, December 19, 2003, p. 1, http://www.nytimes.com/. The best single source for the events leading up to 9/11 is the transcript of this commission's hearings and its final report, which is scheduled to be released during the summer of 2004. Both are available on the Web site of any major U.S. newspaper.

[†]See Mark Riebling, *Wedge: The Secret War between the F.B.I. and C.I.A.* New York: Knopf, 1994.

[‡]Cited in Mark Helm, "Former Director Defends FBI," *Houston Chronicle*, October 9, 2002, 7A.

[§]This summary is drawn from Eleanor Hill, *The Intelligence Community's Knowledge of the September 11 Hijackers Prior to September 11, 2001* (Washington: Government Printing Office, September 2002); and the U.S. Senate Select Committee on Intelligence and U.S. House Select Committee on Intelligence, *Joint Inquiry into Intelligence Community Activities before and after the Terrorist Attacks on September 11, 2001* (S. Rpt. 107-351, JH. Rpt. 107-792), 107th Cong., 2nd sess. The full report is available at www.gpoaccess.gov.

[**]Bennet Roth, "Information Gap between FBI, CIA Closed, Bush Says," *Houston Chronicle*, June 5, 2002.

[††]Laurence Arnold, "Sharing of Terror Intelligence Still 'Haphazard,' Study Finds," *Houston Chronicle*, December 3, 2003, A8.

FIGURE 3–1

ORGANIZATION CHART: OFFICE OF HOMELAND SECURITY
Agencies it must coordinate

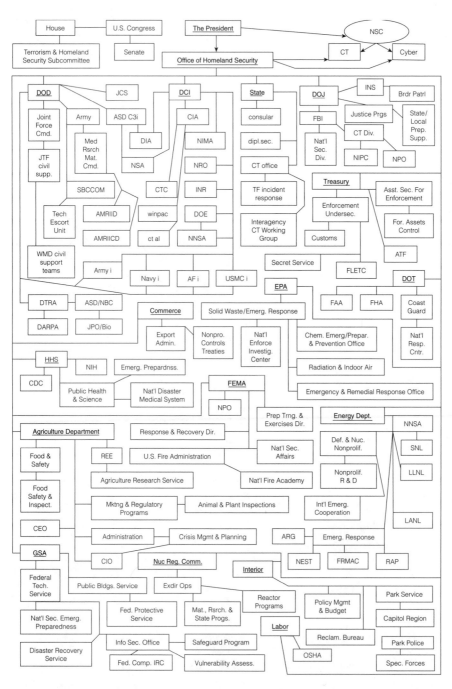

Copyright Dr. Jay Jakub and the Monterey Institute of International Studies 2001. Reprinted with permission from Dr. Jay Jakub, professional staff member of the House Permanent Select Committee on Intelligence.

Compensating for Communication Problems of Traditional Strategies of Organizing

So far in this chapter, we have argued that traditional strategies of organizing rely heavily on formal systems of communication and that it is normal for these systems to break down. That analysis may lead readers to wonder just how these organizations manage to survive. The answer is that many organizations have minimal needs for rapid and accurate task-related communication. Some organizations exist in extremely stable environments that place limited demands on communication. Problems can be anticipated and situations can be understood rather easily because they almost always are like those faced in the past, and tried-and-true solutions are generally available. Expertise, decision making, and authority can be centralized, communication can be restricted to the chain of command, and so on. Information can usually be obtained through formal channels, and the kinds of communication breakdowns that are discussed in this chapter can be anticipated and offset. In stable environments, traditional strategies of organizing cope quite well with the limited amount of uncertainty that they face. In contrast, organizations in highly competitive, rapidly changing, turbulent environments are effective when their work and communication structures allow a free, open, and rapid flow of information, not the restricted, formal, and slow chain of command. Organizations in turbulent environments often face complicated problems unlike any they have faced in the past. Lynda St. Clair, Robert Quinn, and Regina O'Neill state the case simply: "Both practitioners and theorists agree that organizations today face enormous competitive pressures and must be highly responsive to rapid changes in the external environment if they are to survive."[10] Open communication structures (such as those of the relational, cultural, and network strategies described in Chapters 4, 5, and 6) allow information about sudden environmental changes to be diffused more rapidly throughout the organization.

Fortunately, there are steps that members of organizations can take to compensate for the communication problems inherent in the traditional strategy of organizing. Because competition and turbulent environments magnify these communication problems, managers can find ways to reduce those pressures. Large firms can pay other organizations not to produce competing products. They can purchase, and then dissolve, competitors, or they can become even larger. Monopolies and oligopolies are able to influence (perhaps even control) the prices and availability of inputs and sales in ways that reduce the environmental turbulence they face. Pharmaceutical firms have used all these strategies to prevent the development or production of low-cost generic drugs.[11] Managers also can often persuade government to insulate them against environmental pressures by placing patent or copyright restrictions on their competitors or by using tariffs or other restrictions to make foreign competitors' products excessively expensive. Or they can focus some of the organization's activities on sectors of the economy that have relatively stable environments. For example, the largest U.S. tobacco firms diversified their activities during the 1980s, often linking with stable industries such as food production. Not only does diversification reduce the impact of a volatile environment; it allows firms to apply political and financial pressure on potentially problematic elements of their environment. For example, television news organizations might be tempted to air highly popular exposés of the tobacco industry if not for the massive advertising revenues that they receive from the tobacco companies' food subsidiaries. Of course, in a society that presumably values "free and open competition," many of these activities raise important ethical and legal questions (see Chapter 12). But they reduce the environmental pressures that organizations face. Finally, organizations can rely on information and communication technologies to help them get around some of the liabilities of the traditional mode of organizing.

Managers can also relax organizational rules about following the chain of command during crises or when rapid flows of information are important. Subordinates can compensate for problems of the traditional strategy. Once they isolate recurring patterns of communication breakdowns, they can offset problems of filtering and structural distortion by building *redundancy* into their own communication networks. They break down personal and interpersonal barriers through **counterbiasing,** in which they determine the probable biases of each person who communicates with them, adjust their interpretation of the message to compensate for this bias, and then talk about the topic with people who have different biases. Fortunately, these compensating networks seem to emerge quite naturally unless managers actively suppress them.[12] By acting strategically in their own interests, employees compensate for the weaknesses of traditional strategies of organizing.

Traditional Strategies of Motivation, Control, and Surveillance

One of the goals of the traditional strategy of organizing was to replace the arbitrary and capricious treatment of workers that often took place in organizations of the late 1800s and early 1900s with a scientifically designed and rationally implemented system of incentives and disincentives. All employees work to achieve goals, primarily economic ones, and a system that rewards them for following established rules and procedures and maximizing their individual performance would seem to be in everyone's self-interest. If appropriate rule-and-reward systems could be created, workers would choose to act in ways that met their needs and the needs of their organizations. Labor-management hostility would be replaced with cooperative, mutually rewarding relationships. But rule-and-reward systems succeed only if they are supported by effective communication.

Traditional strategies of organizing are defined in part by a particular organizational design and in part by a distinctive system of employee motivation and control—systems of rules and rewards. Rule systems make our worlds stable, predictable, and in some ways simpler. Organizational theorist Karl Weick has noted that rules place parameters around our interactions with other people. Without those rules, we would constantly have to negotiate and renegotiate how we act toward one another, leaving little time and energy for accomplishing tasks or pursuing other goals. For example, when hospitals provide parents of pediatric patients with a written list of rules about who (parents or nurses) will be responsible for different aspects of their child's care, both the parents and the nurses are more satisfied. The rules make an ambiguous and stressful situation less difficult and allow the parties to spend their time and energy making detailed decisions about the child's special needs.[13] But even with these advantages, it is still difficult to implement rule-and-reward systems successfully. Doing so depends on communication and on being able to persuade members of an organization that the rules and rewards in the system are *legitimate* and *fairly administered.* Success also depends on the systems themselves, and how they deal with *unintended consequences.*

Rules, Rewards, and Persuasive Communication

To work, rules must be clear enough to be easily understood, specific enough to give employees precise guidelines for acting, and general enough so as not to seem trivial and persnickety. Rules will be seen as legitimate only if members believe that they are applied fairly equally to everyone in the organization and are produced by the organization, rather than by an individual supervisor acting on his or her own whim. Rules will be perceived as illegitimate if they are applied outside an accepted range of activities. For example, rules about employees' private lives will not be accepted if employees perceive that their employer does not have a legitimate right to enforce them. At one time employees, especially managerial and supervisory personnel, gave their organizations the right to control much of their private lives. Today employees often refuse to accept company rules about where they should live, how they should spend their income, or what they should do with their leisure time. For example, the management of Dell Computer Company recently created an uproar when it distributed a memo informing employees that their "Code of Conduct" for behavior at work also applied to the games of the local AA baseball team, the Round Rock Express (which plays its home games at the Dell Diamond). Heckling visiting players or booing members of the home team were forbidden because they were "disruptive, unprofessional, offensive, or potentially slanderous"; acting "responsibly with respect to consumption of alcohol" was required. Dell employees are accustomed to rules that impinge on their private lives—sixty-hour work weeks for its sales staff or mandatory overtime for tech support people—and generally view those intrusions as legitimate business requirements. But many of them believe that this application of the code of conduct goes too far.

Rules systems succeed only if they are supplemented by a credible reward system. Employees must perceive that the rewards they receive are both substantial and important. Pay seems to have these characteristics, especially for employees whose incomes are low, whose tenure in the organization has been brief, whose commitment to the firm is low, and who feel that their pay is inappropriate when compared to the pay of other workers. The promotions and status that usually accompany pay increases also seem to be important to most people, especially those with a high need for achievement. Praise also is valued by most people and is positively related to both improved performance and job satisfaction.

Employees must be persuaded that the reward system is fair. They must believe that rewards are based on performance, rather than on friendships or biases, and that individual employees are primarily responsible for their level of performance and the rewards they receive. This is a difficult undertaking because people tend to attribute their successes to themselves or to factors within their control and their failures to others or to factors they cannot control.[14] These problems are reduced when objective, quantifiable measures of an employee's performance are available. In the end, however, the key is a supervisor's ability to provide persuasive performance feedback.[15] Feedback should both clearly confront a problem (or clearly encourage continuation of excellent performance) and allow all parties to save face. **Face management** is complicated by an employee's status, race, gender, and ethnicity. Face-saving is especially important to people who have communitarian orientations—women and people from Latin, Asian, and Middle Eastern backgrounds.[16]

At least for people from Western societies, a reward system is seen as fair only if it also seems *equitable.* Employees do not evaluate the rewards (or punishments) they receive in a vacuum; they compare them to what others receive and what they believe others *should* have received. If they see **distributive justice,** that the rewards allocated by the organization are just, their job satisfaction is higher than if they believe the distribution of rewards is unjust. If they perceive that the *process* through which the rewards are allocated is fair (**procedural justice**), their trust in and evaluation of their supervisors, as well as their commitment to the organization, will be higher.[17] If they think the reward system is not just, they will be frustrated and may respond by reducing their effort, negotiating for increased rewards, leaving the organization, or rationalizing the inequity.

Supervisors have several persuasive strategies available to convince their subordinates that the reward system is just. Some strategies are overt, such as giving workers information that proves that they are being treated equitably; others are covert, such as withholding information about the other employees' rewards. It is difficult to employ the first strategy successfully, as professors remember each time they try to respond to a student's complaint that "I worked much harder than so-and-so and received a lower exam grade." It is equally difficult to implement the second strategy, although organizations often try to do so through rules that forbid employees to discuss their raises (or salaries) with others. The primary effect of these rules seems to be to encourage employees to obtain the forbidden information, as the very existence of the rules creates the impression that the reward system is inequitable. Thus the confidentiality rules give employees incentive to share salary information covertly. The fact that such rules often fail may be the best evidence in support of the equity theory's assumption that people are very much concerned with the equity of reward systems.[18]

Evidently, supervisors recognize the importance of issues about equity when they make decisions about rewards. When they believe they have reliable performance information on their employees and they can realistically determine which employee was responsible for which outcomes (positive and negative), they do try to allocate rewards based on performance, although they realize that doing so can create competition and hostility within a work group. Equity considerations are especially important in large departments where people work alone and do not have close personal ties with one another. But when the situation is less clear-cut, or when the supervisors are concerned about "team building," they tend to give approximately equal rewards to each of their subordinates. As a result, in departments where people work closely together and have similar backgrounds, experience, and interests, rewards are more alike and there is less difference among the salaries of the various employees.[19]

To complicate matters even further, employees' responses to issues of equity seem to be culture-specific. In a study of employees in two individualistic and masculine cultures (the United States and Japan) and a culture that is less individualistic and less masculine (South Korea), Kim and his associates found that all three groups of employees preferred equity-based reward systems over across-the-board systems, although the preference was stronger with the U.S. and Japanese employees. Weber noticed that in traditional Catholic, European peasant communities, raising the sum that workers received for each item they produced often actually *reduced* their output. Workers found that with the increased pay rates, they could maintain the same income with less effort. Because leisure time was more important to them than increased income, increasing their pay had a paradoxical effect. With the coming of Protestantism, and its emphasis on wealth and consumption as evidence of moral goodness, increases in pay have a more predictable effect on performance.[20] In sum, there is no doubt that organizational control systems influence employees' actions and attitudes. However, there also is a great deal of evidence that control systems may have many unanticipated consequences. Implementing control systems requires that a number of requirements—communicative and otherwise—be met, and even if these requirements are met, employees will still make their own decisions about how to interpret and respond to them.

CASE STUDY
The Power of Rewards at Industry International

Industry International is a manufacturing firm with about twenty-five hundred employees in a number of plants. It is often touted as a monument to the power of financial reward systems. In an industry that has been battered by foreign competition for three decades, it has remained highly profitable, in large part because its workers are 2½ to 3 times as productive as those of its competitors. Their com-

(continued)

(Case Study, continued)

pensation is also three times the average salary for U.S. manufacturing employees. They are not unionized, have no paid vacations, and work 45–50 hours per week. Much of their income comes from a year-end cash bonus. Each year, after company taxes and dividends have been paid, the board of directors determines the size of the bonus pool, which is divided among the employees based on their base salary and individual merit ratings. From 1943 to 1994 the bonus percentage ranged from 55 percent to 104 percent; in 1994 it was 61 percent, meaning that an employee earning a $30,000 base salary and receiving a 100 percent merit rating would receive a bonus of $18,300.* The bonus is kept secret from October until a meeting/celebration in December. When the meeting ends, the employees rush to their cars, bonus checks in hand, and tie up traffic for hours going to their favorite places of celebration.

Most employees use the money to pay accumulated bills; in fact, many spend far in excess of their base salaries and then put off paying bills and loans until the bonus checks come in. Other employees use the money for less mundane activities. One got his bonus in $100 bills, spread them on the living room floor and, along with his wife, rolled around on them (among other activities) in celebration. Some made major purchases like houses, cars, and luxury items in cash. A few (mostly younger employees) used the money to gamble, hire prostitutes, or buy illegal drugs. When asked why they spend the money as they do, three answers were commonly given: to live the good life so valued in the United States, to assert their autonomy (one said "spending bonus money is the one thing they [management] ain't telling me what and how to do"), and for the social status that money provides. Other employees commented, "As soon as they [friends and neighbors] find out you work there, they think you have money coming out of your ears," and "They think I'm the richest s . . . o . . . b [ellipses added] in the world." A worker recalled, "Years ago we made more money than professional football players."

What they don't tell their envious neighbors is what they go through to get the bonus. Merit points are based on output, quality, dependability, and personal characteristics. The first two can be quantified, leading employees to "work like dogs" until they are dangerously exhausted by long hours and difficult working conditions; the latter two cannot, creating a highly political atmosphere in the plant. Most echoed one worker's conclusion that "if you don't go along with the system [managers], you could be the hardest worker in the world . . . and you would still be way short because you have not gone with the flow and you would be blackballed, and they give you what they want to give you."

But things have changed for Industry International. The recession of the mid-1980s led to low bonuses (55 percent). Many workers lost their homes and cars because they were relying on large bonuses to pay mortgages and loans. Workers attributed the decline to many things, but primarily to management greed and incompetence—a "fat managerial level and more men at the top," embezzlement, and mismanagement of overseas accounts. Whatever the reason, the recession made it clear to workers just how dependent they were on Industry International and how much things had changed: "The whole philosophy [established by the founder and maintained until 1983] was that you worked hard and got compensated for it. You busted your ass, but you got compensated. Now you bust your ass and you don't get compensated for it." The employees have very few options, however. Most are too old to start over somewhere else and are limited by their education and training to manufacturing jobs. Furthermore, high-paying manufacturing jobs are becoming very rare in the United States (see Chapters 1 and 11).

So workers talk about resisting management. They fear that management will eliminate the bonus system, replacing it with a form of profit-sharing that is not as lucrative for the workers. Many predict a massive walkout or work stoppage if that happens. Others consider unionizing the firm. Management has persuaded them that the bonus system relies on a nonunion shop, but if the bonus system is eliminated, they have no reason not to unionize. Others predict that without the bonuses, employees would quit the company; still others predict plummeting productivity and quality; others threaten physical violence against management and sabotage of the plant. "If they got rid of bonus, they wouldn't have the control over anyone. Bonus is what they have to keep the hold on you."

Applying What You've Learned

1. A number of factors need to be present for rule-reward systems to succeed. Which of those factors were present at Industry International? Which, if any, were absent?

2. What resistance strategies are available to these employees? What could they do to keep from being so dependent on the system? What effects would those actions have on the system? Why?

Questions to Think About and Discuss

1. There is a substantial amount of research evidence indicating that pay is the most powerful motivator for U.S. workers, more so than for workers in some other countries.[†] Why?

2. Would this kind of motivation/control system work differently in different societal contexts, for example, in a society that was not as consumption-oriented as the United States or in a country with extensive social support systems for unemployed workers and their families?[‡]

3. If you were the CEO of Industry International, what kinds of public economic policies would you want the government to follow? (Would you want the Federal Reserve Board to focus on keeping inflation low or keeping unemployment low? Would you want corporate income taxes to be a primary source of government funding, or personal income taxes?) Why?

(continued)

(Case Study, continued)

This case is based on Melissa Hancock and Michael Papa, "Employee Struggles with Autonomy and Dependence: Examining the Dialectic of Control through a Structurational Account of Power," Paper presented at the International Communication Association Convention, Chicago, 1996.

*Because Hancock and Papa have never identified the real company that they called Industry International, it is impossible to update these figures. However, the Lincoln Electric Company, which operates very much like Industry International, and which had comparable bonuses during the years covered in this case, gave out average bonuses of $11,800 in 2002 and $10,800 in 2003. The reduced size resulted from the recent recession.

†See John Campbell and Robert Pritchard, "Motivation Theory," in *Handbook of Industrial and Organizational Psychology*, Marvin Dunnette, ed. (Chicago: Rand-McNally, 1976); and Charles Greene and Philip Podsakoff, "Effects of Withdrawal of a Performance-Contingent Reward on Supervisory Influence and Power," *Academy of Management Journal* 24 (1981): 527–542.

‡This question is examined in Richard B. Freeman, ed., *Working under Different Rules* (Washington, DC: Russell Sage Foundation, 1994).

Avoiding Unintended Consequences of Rule-Reward Systems

Unfortunately, rule-reward systems may inadvertently encourage behaviors other than those that were intended. In what has become a classic essay on reward systems, Steven Kerr provided examples of "the folly of rewarding A while hoping for B." For example, in politics, U.S. citizens presumably want candidates for office to make their goals, proposals, and funding systems perfectly clear so that they can make informed choices. But repeatedly, voters reject candidates who do so and reward those who deal with images and personalities rather than issues and solutions. Citizens want state adoption agencies to place children in good homes, but they enact regulations that base their administrators' budgets, prestige, and staff size on the number of children enrolled (that is, the number *not* placed). Consequently, administrators are encouraged to make it difficult to adopt children—requiring that prospective parents not smoke, be of the same religion, have never been divorced, have a separate bedroom for the child, and so on. Universities are supposed to teach students, but they reward research activities that have only an indirect positive effect on teaching quality. Students are supposed to go to college to learn something but are rewarded by employers and graduate schools largely for the grades they receive, regardless of what they have learned; so students are encouraged to take easy classes (reducing their opportunities to learn), adopt a goal of passing a course instead of working for mastery of the material, and so on. Lower-level employees in a manufacturing firm perceive that they are rewarded for "apple-polishing" and "not making waves" when upper management sincerely believes that it is encouraging all employees to be creative and innovative.[21]

Reward systems may also ignore the intangible rewards that employees receive from their jobs. Some professors in research universities actually do spend time and effort on undergraduate teaching, in spite of the organization's formal reward system, because they receive intangible rewards from their interactions with their students. Kerr studied a medical insurance company that rewarded claims adjusters for quickly and accurately paying good claims and rejecting bad ones. But the size of the reward was too small to offset the hassles they received from turning down a claim. So newcomers quickly learned the tactic "when in doubt, pay it out!"

Finally, some tasks are complicated in ways that make it virtually impossible to design an effective reward system. For example, William Ouchi examined the reward systems in a number of retail stores.[22] He found that the salespersons who were paid on a commission basis sold a lot of merchandise but did no other necessary tasks—ordering and arranging inventory or training new salespeople. In contrast, people paid an hourly wage completed all the necessary tasks but didn't sell much merchandise. People paid on commission also had strong incentives to engage in unethical behavior. Presumably, management can discourage unethical activities and encourage employees to complete support tasks. But if salespersons receive no rewards for maintaining high ethical standards or completing support activities, especially in the short term, they will do what they *are* rewarded for doing.[23] In sum, rule-reward systems are complicated because human beings are complicated. People actively perceive, interpret, and strategically respond to the guidelines and constraints that they face. The people who design the systems clearly do not *intend* the systems to have negative effects; indeed they cannot even *predict* that they will have them. Reward systems are powerful motivating agents, but their impact is determined more by the employees who interpret them than by the systems themselves.

Surveillance and Rule-Reward Systems

All organizational control systems require some form of **surveillance,** some process through which supervisors can determine the extent to which employees conform to policies, procedures, rules, and motivational systems. This is particularly true of traditional strategies of organizing because the primary function of supervision is worker control and because they exercise control over everything from major policies and procedures to microscopic elements of task design and completion. The simplest form of control has supervisors constantly looking over the shoulders of their subordinates. This kind of surveillance is still common in newly industrialized economies. In a Malaysia-based microchip plant, male supervisors constantly pressured female workers to increase their productivity; even trips to the locker-room were penalized. Workers complained about being constantly spied upon and felt that they had no place to hide. The company set up an in-house "union" to serve as an additional watchdog.[24] Simple surveillance systems have two important disadvantages. First, they are highly inefficient, requiring organizations to hire and pay large numbers of supervisors to watch over their employees. This managerial overhead is especially large in U.S. firms (almost three times as large as in Japanese organizations and almost four times as large as in European firms), and it has steadily increased since the end of World War II. Second, these supervisors are very *obtrusive* (visible and "in your face"), which generates a great deal of antagonism between supervisors and subordinates.[25]

Today supervisory surveillance is made much easier by the advent of sophisticated computer technologies. A 2000 study by the American Management Association found that almost 80 percent of U.S. firms used some form of electronic surveillance during the previous year, a number that had increased by an astonishing 67 percent over the previous year. The most common activities were monitoring Internet use, listening in on or recording telephone conversations, storing and reviewing computer files, and recording computer use (number of keystrokes per minute, time taken between entries, and so on). Indeed, computer monitoring is more common in the workplace than in any other sector of society, in part because modern organizations are technology intensive, making it easy to monitor employees, and partly because of widespread acceptance of the doctrine of "employment at will," which means that employers have the right to set almost any condition of employment and to fire workers for almost any reason. Women are more likely to be monitored than men, and minority women are the most heavily monitored group. This is because it is easiest to monitor people whose jobs can be quantitatively measured—clerical work, data entry, or routine computer programming—and those tasks are largely performed by minority women. Some computer monitoring is widely accepted (for example, videotaping for security purposes), some is widely condemned (monitoring and posting the number of bathroom breaks employees take and the amount of time they spend in the bathroom), some involves normal managerial activities (keeping track of inventory), but most involves employee control.

Assessing the effects of computer surveillance systems is difficult. They have often been linked to negative outcomes—lower job satisfaction, higher absenteeism and turnover, adverse health effects (including increased stress and anxiety), feelings of lost privacy, lower commitment to the organization, and high levels of resentment about being monitored. Heavily monitored employees often feel that management does not trust them and treats them like children and fear that they are being set up for punishment or dismissal. Some systems are interactive and flash messages like "work harder" or "concentrate" on the workers' computer screens when they slow down. All the negative feelings and attitudes are increased when these systems are used. Surveillance systems can also harm performance, especially for employees who perform complex tasks. Employees begin to believe that management is concerned with quantity of output *but not quality,* and they respond accordingly. They provide lower-quality service to customers and find ways to bypass complicated or otherwise time-consuming clients or activities.

However, properly designed and implemented electronic surveillance may have net positive effects. Monitoring is perceived favorably if it is restricted to legitimate, performance-related activities, if it increases the fairness of the organization's rule-reward system, and if it is linked to effective performance feedback. In these senses, employee responses to computer monitoring are very much like employee responses to rule-reward systems in general.[26]

Resistance to Rule-Reward Systems

Resistance is an inevitable aspect of social or organizational control, because control systems inevitably reduce members' autonomy and creativity (recall the dilemma discussed in Chapter 1).[27] The simplest forms of resistance are withdrawal and open rebellion. The former leads people to be progressively less involved in and committed to their jobs; the latter can culminate in sabotage. The disastrous chemical leak at Bhopal, India, in 1985 resulted in part from an employee's rebellion against being punished (fired) for breaking what he perceived as illegitimate rules. A cleaning woman once admitted that she retaliated against an especially controlling employer by using her employer's toothbrush to clean her commodes—for years. Employees also may resist rules through **regression,** that is, by reducing their performance to the minimum acceptable standard that the rule-reward system allows. Employees resist electronic surveillance systems by finding ways to fool the computers, sabotaging the systems, or filing lawsuits.

Other forms of resistance are more complex. Employees sometimes rebel against their organizations by following rules exactly, robbing their organizations of the common sense and flexibility to make rule systems work. In Mexican maquiladoras, workers covertly resist pressures to speed up production by engaging in *tortuosidad,* literally "working at a turtle's pace." Because their supervisors (U.S. and Mexican) view the workers as lazy, they often fail to recognize that the slowdowns are strategic.[28] During 1991 a small number of American Airlines pilots resisted management by following FAA regulations to the letter—filing very complete flight plans, requesting detailed weather reports, and engaging in other activities that are completely legal but rarely absolutely necessary for flight safety. The number of flight delays and cancellations skyrocketed. Management retaliated by giving the pilots assignments that reduced their income (while denying in public that they were doing so). Pilots countered by following the rules even more exactly, eventually paralyzing the airline through their strategy of malicious obedience. Similar actions in 1997 and 2000 cost Americans $70 million and $225 million, respectively. In 1997 United Airlines pilots virtually shut that airline down by obeying rules regarding overtime exactly; in 2000 the same strategy cost the airline $225 million. Even flight attendants, who have substantially less bargaining power, were able to force concessions from U.S. Airways in 2000 after costing the company $40 million by **working to rule.**[29]

Whether the consequences are massive or minor, all forms of resistance serve the same purpose: they allow employees to rebel against rule-reward systems. Unfortunately for organizations, supervisors often respond to resistance by tightening the rule-reward system, which increases the probability of further resistance. The organization then finds itself immersed in destructive cycles of disobedience and dictatorial management. Unfortunately for employees, resistance rarely leads to major changes in organizations or organizational rule-reward systems. The nature of the traditional strategy makes it difficult to locate and resist real sources of organizational control. When resistance actually does threaten to force changes on an organization, high-powered members are usually able to change the rules or rewards. For example, strikes have long been a potent way for unionized workers to resist management. But, first in the 1981 air traffic controllers' strike and increasingly since then, management has been able to hire (or threaten to hire) permanent replacements for striking workers, thus virtually eliminating strikes as a viable means of resisting management. In addition, resistance is exhausting, much more so than enforcing rule-reward systems. Eventually workers lose the strength necessary for further resistance. Finally, resisting rule-reward systems focuses attention on them and can in effect legitimate them. Resistance usually raises questions about the legitimacy of a particular rule-reward system or the way in which it is being implemented. But it also accepts the legitimacy of having *some* system of organizational control. Thus the relationship between control and resistance is paradoxical: control inevitably creates resistance, which often ends up supporting systems of control.[30]

Traditional Strategies of Leadership

Most contemporary organizational theorists view leadership as a process of developing a vision that challenges an organization to excellence and change, a concept that contradicts the traditional strategy of organizing (see Chapters 4 and 5 for more detail on contemporary views of leadership). The traditional strategy dictates that supervisors will be *managers,* people who implement an existing set of plans, or *administrators,* people who develop routine techniques for accomplishing particular tasks. However, it de-emphasizes *leadership,* at least in the modern sense of that term.[31] In fact, the politics of traditional organizations may produce the opposite kind of behaviors. Traditional strategies of organizing create a kind of class or caste system that fosters clear distinctions among a managerial power elite, a "new working class" composed of lower-level managers and people with technical skills, and lower-level workers. To advance through the organizational hierarchy, employees must concentrate on conforming to the demands of upper management. Most of those demands involve creating and maintaining a certain kind of image. To move up the hierarchy, workers must appear to be "like" upper management, both in overall attitudes and behaviors and in the images they project. They must learn to please their superiors by accommodating their every whim and meeting their every need. Subordinates are expected to anticipate superiors' demands, prevent or solve the problems they encounter, and "help a superior perform well and look good," even if doing so involves taking blame for the superior's errors and giving her or him credit for the subordinate's successes.[32] They must demonstrate loyalty, both to the organization and to their sponsors in the power elite. They must keep their distance from people below them in the hierarchy. They tend to develop a near obsession with following rules, because rules are their only source of protection. People who advance through traditional hierarchies tend to come from the same schools, wear the same clothes, and develop the same communication styles and mannerisms of their higher-ups. Above all, they do not make waves; creative approaches and new ideas threaten the stability and predictability that are hallmarks of the traditional strategy of organizing. As a result, the people who are hired for upwardly oriented jobs tend to already have the appropriate credentials and behavioral styles. And "fitting in" gets progressively more important as one moves up the organizational hierarchy.

Omar Aktouf has provided an excellent example of these processes in a study of two breweries, one in Montreal and one in Algiers. Although there were some differences in the two settings, there were striking similarities in how one became promotable in these two very traditional organizations. From the day they arrived in the organization, employees who eventually became worthy of promotion engaged in a particular pattern of behavior. They were obsessed with doing more—a machinist who used his breaks to clean his machine or a quality-control officer who repeatedly phoned the plant on his days off to make sure things were going well. They showed a strong capacity to keep lower-level workers in line and demonstrated unconditional obedience and submission to their superiors. They kept their distance from the regular workers and took care to master the language of the elite—managerial jargon, including the most recent managerial fads, and upper-class accents. They zealously enforced rules and quotas, boycotted all unionizing activities (or informed on pro-union workers), appeared to suffer from their workload and worries, and constantly stayed on their bosses' coattails. In both plants the formal job descriptions of managers and the official reward/evaluation system focused on objective performance criteria such as production per machine or number of equipment breakdowns. But upper management described a "good" (promotable) subordinate in terms that had little to do with technical expertise or objective performance. To them, good subordinates were submissive, punctual, serious (absorbed in their tasks), malleable, and ambitious. As a result it is not surprising that the workers in these plants complained about the technical incompetence of their supervisors as well as about their untrustworthiness and political game-playing.[33]

Consequently, by the time people are promoted to managerial positions in traditional organizations, they have developed ways of thinking and acting that preclude their being leaders in the contemporary definition of the term. The only legitimate vision is that of maintaining the existing systems and structures; the only possible challenge is to do what the organization has always done, more rapidly and efficiently. Such people are likely to be excellent managers and administrators, but not leaders.

Information and Communication Technology in Traditional Strategies of Organizing

As the discussion in this chapter emphasizes, the principles of the traditional strategy of organizing often create problems in their own right. To reap the efficiencies of bureaucracy, organizations must manage employees through hierarchical arrangements that can lead to resentment and resistance on the part of workers. The friction generated by intrusive managers reduces efficiency and saps employee energy. In order to avoid constant oversight by managers, the traditional strategy relies on rule-governed coordination of work, often supported by technologies such as assembly lines. However, the rules must be kept relatively simple, or employees will lose track of them, and simple rules promote a degree of inflexibility. When organizations try to build flexibility into rules by making them more complex, the rule books become dense and time-consuming to consult. Almost any college catalog is a good example of this; aside from the standard curriculum, the rules are somewhat different for each major and degree, and the result is a tome that must be carefully consulted when contemplating graduation or changing majors. And finally, applying complex rules often requires access to information that frontline employees do not have access to. When the authors bought their first houses more than twenty years ago, they filled out applications that listed assets and debts and documented credit worthiness, but the bank employee who took the application had no idea whether this information was correct or not. It took several days, sometimes as much as a couple of weeks of telephone calls and formal requests for information, to verify that the authors were not deadbeats out to cheat the bank or ne'er-do-wells who would default on their loans.

These problems have in the past imposed limits on organizations employing the traditional strategy. However, in the past twenty years, the new developments in information and communication technology (ICT) have enabled organizations to minimize the effects of these problems. ICTs make it much easier to monitor employees in an unobtrusive manner, to support consistent use of complex rule systems, and to provide needed information to frontline employees than has previously been the case.

Overcoming the Limitations of the Traditional Organizational Strategy

As we noted in Chapter 2, ICTs offer an unprecedented opportunity for organizations to monitor their employees, in order to facilitate the type of coordination and control the traditional strategy is designed for without incurring the problems they have traditionally faced.[34] For instance, it is possible for a secretarial supervisor to monitor statistics on every keystroke that employees take to make sure they are working up to standards. As noted in a previous section, if monitoring systems are applied fairly and with some tact, employees for the most part do not find them objectionable. Indeed, some organizations use statistics on errors to give their employees feedback on needed training, developing better workers in the spirit of Taylor's original philosophy.

Workflow systems can route documents through channels just as efficiently as the assembly line routes physical objects. In some insurance companies, for instance, a claim application submitted by a field adjuster at her portable PC is automatically evaluated by a machine-based expert system to determine whether it needs further scrutiny by higher-level employees. If it does not, the claim is routed through the system for direct payment; if it requires another look, it is routed to a manager, who evaluates it and may communicate via e-mail with the adjuster regarding any questions, finally sending it on for payment or further scrutiny. The documents and related messages are all handled by the workflow system and the routing is almost instantaneous. The system uses a complex set of rules more rapidly and consistently than any person with a manual could.

ICTs can be used to provide frontline employees with information that enables them to do their jobs better and more flexibly. For example, in today's loan process, the information that the authors provide is entered into a workflow system that enables the loan officer to verify information and check credit status much more rapidly than in the past. Often a same-day response is possible for even complicated loan applications. In a different field, sales of large computers, servers, and networks are facilitated by systems that the frontline sales associate can use to customize complex systems and networks via his or her laptop. These systems enable sales associates to give quotes for complex networks of computers and memory devices in real time, greatly enhancing the sales process. Many of the most compelling examples of how ICT revolutionizes traditional organizations are in the sales sector, but they abound in manufacturing as well. In the 1950s and 1960s, machine tools were limited in the number of parts they could manufacture. It often took hours to "retool" a machine so that it could make a different part, and this often had to be done with the assistance of a foreperson or engineer. Modern computer-controlled machine tools can make literally hundreds of different parts. "Retooling" is done by programming and the operator is generally trained to do this. Computerized machine tools enable the frontline worker to control the process, increasing responsiveness and efficiency, yet still delivering adequate control over the work.

Aviall Inc., an aviation parts distributor headquartered in Dallas, implemented an integrated IT inventory management system to give the company more control over its work processes. In 1999 the company lost 20 percent of its accounts and $70 million in business, in part because of a botched effort to implement an enterprise resource plan. The company conducted a major overhaul of its systems in 2000, installing an extranet for customers to use in purchasing parts. This system allowed the company to offer 380,000 parts to its 17,000 customers, using 20,000 different pricing schemes. Web sales rose 60 percent and cost per order declined from seven dollars by phone to thirty-nine cents via the Web. Aviall also upgraded its inventory control and warehouse system, enabling managers to track products in inventory and move them around more effectively. Sales managers knew what was in stock and could initiate sales incentives on overstocked products. The system also supplied information about what sorts of parts customers ordered, allowing salespeople to target their sales pitches. Customers were able to cut expenses in the order process and track shipments using the system. They were even able to download invoices before receiving their order. This system enabled Aviall to greatly enhance its ability to control and monitor inventory and deliver service more efficiently, while allowing its employees to operate more autonomously.[35]

In short, ICTs enable traditional organizations to "have their cake and eat it too." Organizations can exert control over work processes in a very efficient, complete, and relatively unobtrusive manner. They can implement systems of rules to regulate work that are complex enough to be flexible. They can give frontline employees detailed information and support so that the employees can operate independently using the rules.

Enforcing Company Policies

ICTs can also be used to detect and prevent behavior counter to company policies. It is becoming increasingly common for organizations to employ systems that sweep through e-mail files to find evidence of employees sharing proprietary information with outsiders or private use of e-mail. E-mail systems often keep copies of erased messages, so there is no way for members to hide their activities, as Oliver North, President Reagan's aide who planned secret arms sales to the Iranians via e-mail, discovered to his chagrin. Network software can keep records of all activity on the Internet from each computer station, enabling employers to discover when employees are surfing the net on company time, visiting pornographic sites, or even applying for jobs online. We discussed some of the negative effects of hidden surveillance on employees and the organizations previously in this chapter.

These surveillance capabilities raise important ethical and policy questions. How far should organizations be able to go in monitoring employees? Some argue that if an organization provides the ICTs to employees, it should be able to monitor and control everything that goes on in the system. The organization is not paying for personal facilities for its employees; they should use the system for work and nothing else. Furthermore, if an employee engages in illegal or questionable behavior—sexual harassment of a co-worker, fraudulent use of the Internet, lobbying a politician—the organization will be held liable, because it provided the means to the perpetrator. The other side of the argument holds that even in the workplace employees have some expectation of privacy. Although it is true that the organization provides the ICT, personal use within reasonable bounds should be allowed, particularly because the company often expects employees to check their e-mail or voice mail from home on their personal time and may request that employees work extra hours. Being able to take a few minutes to order Christmas gifts from the office is reasonable compensation for the organization's infringement on personal time and private life. The vast majority of employees do not engage in questionable activities using ICT, and they should not be penalized for the misdeeds of a few. Moreover, employees will always make some personal use of organizational resources; they make phone calls related to private matters and use the photocopier for their tax returns. Is there really any difference between this and some private use of the Internet? There is no clear resolution to this issue at present.

A recent study showed that an overwhelming proportion of employees report using the Internet for personal reasons.[36] This study indicated that costs to the organization of this behavior can be substantial. A company with 1,000 Internet users who do personal Web surfing for one hour per day can lose more than $35 million in productivity each year. However, the study also indicated that the great majority of firms were not concerned about this type of cost, because they believed that increased morale among employees more than compensated for it. Most organizations in the survey indicated that they tolerated private use of the Internet as a perk for their employees. More than 80 percent of the firms surveyed indicated that they have a written Internet use policy to guide employees.

A second privacy-related problem concerns organizations' use of private information about customers and employees. The increasing integration of computer networks enables information from different databases to be linked and shared within and across organizations. Information about employees' health histories, for example, might be compiled and shared among companies. Because employees' health problems often result in higher insurance costs and time missed from work, some organizations might use this information in their hiring decisions. There has long been a debate about the appropriateness and legality of compiling and using this type of information, and laws and standards have been proposed. This issue is clearly on the public's mind. Fear of having health problems included in a company database and ultimately disclosed has led some people to avoid seeking treatment for serious maladies or to seek private treatment that they pay for themselves. Although Congress and state legislatures recently have passed laws protecting patient privacy, gaps in those laws and ambiguities regarding employer access to records ensure that the issue will continue to be important and controversial.

Information about consumer preferences can also be captured by ICT. A group of seventy electronic commerce companies, including IBM and First Union Corporation, have been developing a data-sharing specification called Customer Profile Exchange,[37] which promises to enable companies to compile massive databases on customers and to comb through them to discover purchasing patterns, lifestyle information, and other information about customers. This possibility has raised concerns that the companies are overstepping the bounds of their customers' privacy. The chairman of the Senate Select Committee on Intelligence, Richard Shelby, has written to the Federal Trade Commission (FTC) regarding concerns for lack of privacy protection. It is unclear whether the FTC has legal authority to develop regulations for such efforts, and the debate continues. One part of the solution to this problem came late in 2001, when Internet browsers incorporated the Platform for Privacy Protection, a program allowing consumers to set privacy preferences in their Internet browsers. However, legal and policy issues still remain to be determined.

CASE STUDY
Scenes from the Electronic Sweatshop

Barbara Garson, playwright and investigative journalist, investigated how computers were transforming office work. Her book *The Electronic Sweatshop* documented some negative consequences that occurred when ICTs were used to coordinate and control work in traditional organizations. Here are two vignettes based on her book that illustrate the dark side of ICTs.

The Automated Airline Reservation Agent

Until the late 1970s, airline reservation agents were valued, long-term employees of the major airline companies. They had to learn and remember the companies' fares, routes, and policies and apply this knowledge to solve problems for customers on an individualized basis. This made them highly skilled employees who were difficult to replace. Some made as much as fifteen dollars per hour in the early 1980s, good money at that time.

However, once computerized reservation systems were developed, companies attempted to redefine the work of the reservation agent. Much of the problem solving was built into the system: the agent simply had to type in the place of departure and the destination, and the computer listed the available times and seats. There was, however, still need for a human in the loop, because each customer's circumstances were so different that adjustments had to be made.

Although the airlines still had to have people online, they wanted to regulate their behavior as much as possible to maintain strict cost and quality control. Based on studies of the work processes involved in making a booking, conversations between agent and customer were broken into typical segments, with recommended scripts and prompts assigned to each. For example, if a customer called up knowing what he or she wanted, agents were instructed in ways to get the reservation down as quickly as possible, so they could go on to the next customer. In cases in which customers were fare-shopping, agents were taught ways to probe for a sale. One strategy was to tell the customer that there were limited seats at the low fare and that a seat could be held for twenty-four hours at no cost, thus ensuring that many customers would call back and offer another opportunity to close the deal. Agents were also told never to ask yes-or-no questions such as "Would you like to book?"; instead they were to ask "Would you like the 10 a.m. or the 2 p.m.?" All transactions between agents and customers were tightly scripted. Supervisors listened in without the agents' knowledge and graded them on how well they kept to the script and efficiently booked passengers. Too much small talk or empathy could get the agent a lower grade. The companies also set performance targets: in the company Garson studied, agents were supposed to make a sale during 26 percent of their calls.

Time online and offline was carefully monitored by the computer system as well: AHU ("after hang-up") time, the time between calls, was supposed to be fourteen seconds on average, if the agent wanted a raise. To keep her or his job and get raises, the agent had to be available, plugged in for bookings, 98 percent of the time.

For this, new agents were paid $5.77 an hour.

The Automated Social Worker

When New York state installed a computer system to keep track of its welfare system, it took a job that one would think is impossible to automate and turned it into a series of steps. Most social workers adopt the profession because they want to help people. They are taught in school that every person is an individual and that it is important to take each individual's needs into account to help him or her. People attracted to this field typically enjoy working with others and hope to make a difference in people's lives. However, the computerization of work in New York did not take this approach.

Job analysis divided the social worker's tasks into units and assigned a time value to each. For example, making a food stamp change counted .5, authorizing funeral and burial expenses counted .7, and replacing a lost or stolen welfare check counted .4, where the numbers stood for tenths of an hour. As a worker does each of these tasks, they are toted up to give a figure for hours of work done. Once a worker reaches her or his allotted 160 hours (actually the target is about 120 hours per month, because 40 hours are required for staff meetings, maintaining work records, and other activities), he or she is done for the month. An experienced worker can do most of these tasks in much less time than the official time figure, so it is possible to get credit for 160 hours with much less work.

So do the workers stop working when their credits reach their limit? Although we have not provided a full list of tasks here, suffice it to say that activities such as making exceptions for clients, trying to help them with their special problems when the help goes outside procedures, and providing sympathy are not on the officially sanctioned list of tasks. The task list includes only bureaucratic operations involved in registering parties for welfare and delivering their services, not the human side of welfare. Garson found that the social workers spent the time they had left after satisfying their hourly credits on these other activities—coaching clients in how to get the best benefits, giving them sympathy and support, working around the system—and also in helping and counseling each other. The social workers made the system human by "gaming" the system.

Sadly, social workers who really try to help clients within the system often receive poor performance evaluations. If they diligently carry out their work, it takes more time than is allotted in the work analysis. One social worker commented,

> Now if you is a person with a problem, you don't want to just tell it to everyone. You want to feel it out first. "This [social] worker, does she have some sensitivity to my problem? Can she hear me?" But I can't hear her. I can't listen to her. I'm just trying to get my points. The whole system is survival. And she goes away feeling

(continued)

(Case Study, continued)

as bad or worse than when she came down here. . . . [S]ome people come here, they are at the end of their rope. They think, "You is a social worker. That's something. Maybe you can help me." And they start telling me about a child that is getting out of hand, starting to drink, not coming home . . .

This woman was a dedicated social service employee, who wanted to do the best she could for her clients. But engaging a client in this way was not efficient and did not earn her the points she needed to make her hours. She had been "written up for Corrective Action" three times in the previous four months. Garson concluded, "The fact is that Jo Martin is not an efficient [social worker]. But a human service department that's organized so it can't use her true skills is profoundly inefficient."

The system used to organize social workers was very similar to the scientific management systems set up to control work under the traditional strategy of organizing. However, unlike the studies of physical labor conducted by management scientists, New York's studies made a profound error. Sympathy for the client and advocacy for her or his needs are important parts of the social worker's job that were simply omitted from the analysis; the system captured all the physical motions of being a social worker but ignored the spirit of the profession. This may have been inevitable in a system that was intended to enable computerization of social work. Behaviors that could be counted were emphasized because number-crunching is what the computers at that time did best.

A good deal of the social worker's time was spent filling out papers that documented all the papers they filled out for clients, so that their work records could be entered into the computerized system. The next step was to set up the system so social workers could enter their activity records into networked computers themselves. As the system developed further, the workers would enter data about their clients directly, and the system would guide the social worker through the steps of authorizing burial expenses and other activities. In theory this might eliminate the labor of filling in forms, freeing the social workers to engage their clients. However, judging by how the system had been developed at the time of Garson's interview, it is doubtful that this was the direction it took. Instead, the social workers would simply have their case loads increased.

Ironically, the dedication of the workers to their clients kept this system going. Garson had the following conversation with one of the supervisors:

G: What do you think of the time standards and point system?
S: I blame the union for the way it's operating.
G: You mean because they're sabotaging it?
S: No, because they're *not* sabotaging it.
G: What do you mean?
S: If they followed the rules the department issued them, this system would have collapsed in three months. . . . If I were a worker and a union activist, the first time I did 100 percent in the first three weeks of the month I'd stop work. And if they tried to make me do anything over 100 percent, I'd fill out an over-

time form. The problem is that all the workers have developed systems of their own to get the points they need and still deliver timely service. That's what keeps this place going.

Applying What You've Learned

1. Are the airlines and the social work agency automating or informating their work? (Answer this question again after you read the section "Postscript: Automating versus Informating" that appears later in this chapter.)
2. How do these organizations apply the principles of the traditional bureaucracy in their systems? What are likely reactions of employees to the system controls?

Questions to Think About and Discuss

1. What are some of the benefits of the computerization of work discussed in these cases for the employees involved? For customers or clients? For the organizations?
2. Would you like to work in these jobs (assuming that the pay was up to your standards)? Why or why not?
3. Do you agree with the supervisor's suggestion concerning how the social workers could shut down the system? What might management do if the social workers tightly conformed to the rules?

This case is based on Barbara Garson, *The Electronic Sweatshop: How Computers Are Transforming the Office of the Future into the Factory of the Past* (New York: Penguin, 1989).

Telework

Telework refers to a wide range of working arrangements in which employees work outside the traditional office, conducting a large portion of their work via computer or telecommunications linkages. Although not all telework is performed in traditional organizations, a good deal is, and this raises some issues that are worth considering at this point. The nature of telework varies widely. Some teleworkers conduct all their business from home; the telephone salespersons for some catalog companies mentioned in a previous section are one example; but many other professional employees work out of their homes as well. Some employees telecommute only part time, working at home a few days a week or month, and going into a regular office the rest of the time.[38] The advent of reliable ICTs, as we have seen, makes it possible to coordinate complex work, such as sales of high-ticket items, with complex specifications at distant locations or in the field. The number of teleworkers was estimated at 19.8 million in 2002, and it has been projected to be as many as 60 million by 2010. In 2002 one survey found that 37 percent of employees worked remotely at least part of the time.[39]

Many insurance firms have done away with central offices, assigning agents and underwriters to the field, where they work out of cars and hotel rooms via telecommunications and e-mail. At AT&T, about 5 percent of the company's 373,000 employees do their work from cars or hotels. These "road warriors" save their companies millions in overhead each year. But they also complain of the lack of a feeling of belonging to their organizations and of the stress of living on the road many weeks a year.

Telework is feasible for any job that centers around paperwork and information processing. There are a number of incentives for telework. For organizations, the attraction stems from lower overhead because they don't have to maintain office buildings and, for the many teleworkers who work on a part-time basis, don't have to pay benefits. For the worker, advantages include closer contact with home and family (except for the road warrior), a more relaxed lifestyle away from the formality of the office, avoidance of office politics, and fewer long commutes. There are also advantages for the public: less commuting means less expense for highways and other infrastructure and less automobile pollution. Evaluations of telework support its advantages. The majority of studies suggest that teleworkers are more productive and less costly than workers based in the office.

There are several prerequisites for teleworking arrangements to succeed. First and foremost, the technological infrastructure must be developed. Often this means that high-speed transmission lines must be installed by the phone companies or other communication carriers. The organization must also purchase the proper technology (computers and high-speed modems) for processing and moving the information. Second, all individuals involved must have developed "communication discipline," that is, they must be in the habit of using their e-mail, workflow, and other ICTs to stay in contact and coordinate their work. These new media require users to develop new patterns of behavior based on communication modes (usually written) different from the verbal channels with which most people are accustomed. Managers must be able to trust that commands issued via communication technology will be followed; employees must learn to understand what managers mean in media such as e-mail that do not offer the direct personal contact that often provides extra information and detail. A final prerequisite for effective telecommuting is that home workers must create a work environment in their homes. Provisions must be made so that family matters do not constantly intervene in work. Some employees take on considerable expenses in setting up and equipping home offices. Because some office equipment is too expensive to be installed in the homes of all workers, many companies have established satellite offices where employees can work when they need office facilities. Satellite offices are also places where employees can work with information too sensitive to transmit over public media.

A major barrier to effective telework arrangements is the discomfort of managers who can no longer see what their employees are doing. Before they become accustomed to electronic media, many middle and upper managers are wary of supervising employees they cannot see. "Management by walking around" is premised on visual contact and face-to-face communication. Managers do not know what they will find, but they walk around to see what is happening; in the process they see things that work and should be done more and problems that have to be addressed. Management is very different with teleworkers. The information technology provides ways to monitor work, but understanding and working with the information requires managers to learn new procedures and skills. Managers who do not have these, or who are uncomfortable with new technologies in general, are likely to perceive a loss of control because of telework. A manager at a major truck manufacturing company learned that sending blunt e-mails similar to the orders he gave in person could cause problems. "People would say, 'Why did you ask me that? Are you angry at me?'" said the manager. "If you see them every day, they figure 'That's just Dave—he has to get stuff done.' But if you're not seeing them on a frequent basis, you have to explain yourself." Managers in new telecommuting programs are often counseled to take communication courses to avoid this type of problem.[40]

Telework may also present some problems for the employee. The line between work and private or family time often blurs for teleworkers. Telework may be convenient in the sense that it gives the employee a more informal and flexible work environment; but it also makes it more convenient for other members of the organization to reach the employee. Television commercials showing an employee on vacation, relaxing on the beach or around a pool, only to be interrupted by a cell-phone call, are designed to show how convenient new technologies are for employers. But they also show that the technologies also may mean that workers never really are able to leave work—they always are in a position where their supervisors can reach out and touch them. As a result, most teleworkers—and almost all road warriors—report that they work more hours than non-teleworkers. When work intrudes into the family space, there is nowhere for employees to escape work-related stress and get a break from the pressure. Teleworkers must exert considerable effort to keep their nonwork lives intact.

Despite these disadvantages, telework is here to stay. It is simply too attractive to both organizations and employees. Some futurists predict that telework will reverse the growth of cities and suburbs. If a travel agent can work as effectively from a farm 100 miles away from Minneapolis as in the city, there is nothing to keep her or him in the city. A corporation that can locate satellite offices around the country in cheaper rural locales could be sorely tempted to vacate its high-priced suburban campus. It is possible that telework will encourage dispersion of the population and a general move away from the cities. The result may be further deterioration of cities and, eventually, suburbs, as those holding the highest paying jobs disperse more evenly around the country.

Postscript: Automating versus Informating

The impact of ICTs on organizations and their employees depends in part on how they are used. Once applications are available in the office or on the work floor, employees can begin to master computers themselves. They can use the computers to analyze their work and improve it. Shoshanna Zuboff argued that the preferred strategy for organizations is not simply to use computers to *automate* work and replace employees with machines.[41] Instead she advocated using information technology to *informate* work, to enable workers to learn which processes are effective and which are not. Informating is possible because computers—properly programmed and utilized—can generate information on how the work is done and the output associated with different configurations of steps or methods. This makes workers smarter about their work and also better able to suggest and make improvements. As the case on the electronic sweatshop illustrates, computers are sometimes used in a very different way, to de-skill employees and turn them into servants of the machine.

For informating to succeed, those at the top of the organization must be willing to share power with those lower down. Those at lower levels must feel some control over their work and some power to make changes before they are willing to take the initiative to change how they work based on the new information. Whereas management often initiates the empowerment of workers, distributed technologies themselves may also shift the balance of power downward. Enhanced communication via e-mail and other telecommunications facilities make it possible for lower-level employees to form coalitions and share information that increases their power in the organization.

Conclusion: Communication and Traditional Strategies of Organizing

We have spent a substantial amount of space discussing traditional strategies of organizing because they are so relevant to modern employees. The traditional strategy, with its tight hierarchy, focus on the structural dimension of communication, and written policies and procedures, is still the dominant strategy used in the United States for governmental agencies, educational institutions, and many private firms. Bureaucratic modes of management are the norm rather than the exception throughout the world. Although very few organizations conform completely to the strategy, many employees entering organizations today find themselves in situations much like the traditional bureaucracy. Procedures and policies are documented in writing; job-related communication flows through the chain of command; positions require specialized skills and are filled at least in part because applicants fulfill established, written criteria; and decision making is centralized near the top of the organization. The development of ICT promises to enhance the effectiveness of the traditional strategy and has in a real sense revitalized it.

Of course, real organizations—even those in which the traditional strategy is in evidence—deviate in important but predictable ways from what the traditional theorists envisioned. But understanding the traditional strategy is important because many people will spend most of their lives working in organizations that are traditional in many ways.

Notes

[1] D. A. Morand, "The Role of Behavioral Formality and Informality in the Enactment of Bureaucratic versus Organic Organizations," *Academy of Management Review* 20 (1995): 831–872; C. Handy, "Trust in Virtual Organizations," *Harvard Business Review* 73 (1995): 40–48. This section is based on two sources: Robert McPhee, "Vertical Communication Chains: Toward an Integrated View," *Management Communication Quarterly* 1 (1988): 455–493; and Robert McPhee and M. Scott Poole, "Organizational Structure, Configurations, and Communication," in *The New Handbook of Organizational Communication,* F. Jablin and L. Putnam, eds. (Thousand Oaks, CA: Sage, 2000).

[2] For excellent summaries of Taylor's ideas, see Frederick Taylor, "The Principles of Scientific Management," in *Classics of Organizational Theory,* Jay Shafritz and Philip Whitbeck, eds. (Oak Park, IL: Moore, 1978); and Edwin Locke, "The Ideas of Frederick Taylor," *Academy of Management Review* 7 (1982) 14–24.

[3] Robert Snyder and James Morris, "Organizational Communication and Performance," *Journal of Applied Psychology* 69 (1984): 461–465.

[4] This is why computerized management information systems, recently installed in virtually every major organization, have had perplexing effects. Computer information systems do not filter information. In theory, they allow every employee, no matter where in the organization, to instantly access any part of its information base. However, no one can process all the information. Unfiltered formal communication will literally bury upper-level managers in information, at least until they learn to use the equipment to screen out messages. High-speed computer systems may only allow them to be buried more quickly. The "solution" to the problem of communication overload is for upper management not to use the systems, which defeats the purpose of installing them in the first place. See Ron Rice and Urs Gattiker, "Communication Technologies and Structures," in *The New Handbook of Organizational Communication,* F. Jablin and L. Putnam, eds. (Thousand Oaks, CA: Sage, 2000). Also see Fredric Jablin, "Formal Organizational Structure," in *Handbook of Organizational Communication,* Fredric Jablin, L. Putnam, K. Roberts, and L. Porter, eds. (Newbury Park, CA: Sage, 1987).

[5] Eric Eisenberg, "Ambiguity as Strategy in Organizational Communication," *Communication Monographs* 51 (1984): 227–242.

[6] Terrance Albrecht and Betsy Bach, *Organizational Communication* (Ft. Worth, TX: Harcourt, 1996).

[7] Cal Downs and Charles Conrad, "A Critical Incident Study of Effective Subordinancy," *Journal of Business Communication* 19 (1982): 27–38; Gail Fairhurst, "Dialectical Tensions in Leadership Research," in *The New Handbook of Organizational Communication,* F. Jablin and L. Putnam, eds. (Thousand Oaks, CA: Sage, 2000). For an extended analysis of how one's nonverbal cues influence interpersonal communication, including communication by the other members of the relationship, see Judee Burgoon, David Buller, and W. Gill Woodall, *Nonverbal Communication: The Unspoken Dialogue* (New York: Harper and Row, 1995); and Valerie Manusov and Julie M. Billingsley, "Nonverbal Communication in Organizations," in *Organizational Communication: Theory and Behavior,* Peggy Yuhas Byers, ed. (Boston: Allyn and Bacon, 1997).

[8] Janet Fulk and Sirish Mani, "Distortion of Communication in Hierarchical Relationships," in *Communication Yearbook 9,* Margaret McLaughlin, ed. (Newbury Park, CA: Sage, 1986).

[9] Larry Spence, *The Politics of Social Knowledge* (University Park: Pennsylvania State University Press, 1978); Fredric Jablin, "Communication Competence and Effectiveness," in *The New Handbook of Organizational Communication,* Fredric Jablin and L. Putnam, eds. (Thousand Oaks, CA: Sage, 2000).

[10] Lynda St. Clair, Robert Quinn, and Regina O'Neill, "The Perils of Responsiveness in Modern Organizations," in *Pressing Problems in Modern Organizations (That Keep Us Up at Night),* Robert Quinn, R. O'Neill, and Lynda St. Clair, eds. (New York: American Management Association, 2000), p. 244. An excellent summary of the underlying research for this section is available in Kathy Sutcliffe, "Information Processing and Organizational Environments," in *The New Handbook of Organizational Communication,* F. Jablin and L. Putnam, eds. (Thousand Oaks, CA: Sage, 2000).

[11] Sheryl G. Stolberg and Jeff Gerth, "Drug Makers Fight Generic Rivals and Raise Questions of Monopoly," *Houston Chronicle,* July 23, 2000, A4.

[12] See Peter Monge and Noshir Contractor, "Emergent Communication Networks," in *The New Handbook of Organizational Communication,* F. Jablin and L. Putnam, eds. (Thousand Oaks, CA: Sage, 2000).

[13] Karl Weick, *The Social Psychology of Organizing,* 2nd ed. (Reading, MA: Addison-Wesley, 1979); Rebecca Adams and Roxanne Parrot, "Pediatric Nurses' Communication of Role Expectations of Parents to Hospitalized Children," *Journal of Applied Communication Research* 22 (1994): 36-47.

[14] Explanations of these processes are part of "attribution theory," a model summarized effectively and applied to organizational reward systems in J. Bettman and B. Weitz, "Attributions in the Board Room," *Administrative Science Quarterly* 28 (1983): 165-183; and B. Staw, P. McKechnie, and S. Puffer, "The Justification of Organizational Performance," *Administrative Science Quarterly* 28 (1983): 582-600.

[15] Karen Tracy and Eric Eisenberg, "Giving Criticism," *Research on Language and Social Interaction* 24 (1990-1991): 37-70.

[16] Barry Nathan, Allan Mohrman, and John Milliman, "Interpersonal Relations as a Context of the Effects of Appraisal Interviews," *Academy of Management Journal* 34 (1991): 352-369.

[17] Dean McFarlin and Paul Sweeney, "Distributive and Procedural Justice as Predictors of Satisfaction with Personal and Organizational Outcomes," *Academy of Management Journal* 35 (1992): 626-637.

[18] An excellent summary of the importance of equity in Western societies is available in Edward E. Sampson, "Justice, Ideology, and Social Legitimation," in *Justice in Social Relations,* H. W. Bierhoff, R. L. Cohen, and J. Greenberg, eds. (New York: Plenum, 1986); a fine cross-cultural comparison may be found in Ken Kim, Hun-Joon Park, and Nori Suzuki, "Reward Allocations in the United States, Japan, and Korea," *Academy of Management Journal* 33 (1990): 188-198. Summaries of the effects of perceived distributive and procedural justice are available in J. Brockner, T. R. Tyler, and R. Cooper-Schneider, "The Influence of Prior Commitment to an Institution of Reactions to Perceived Unfairness," *Administrative Science Quarterly* 37 (1992): 254-271; and McFarlin and Sweeney, pp. 626-637.

[19] James Meindl, "Managing to Be Fair," *Administrative Science Quarterly* 34 (1989): 252-276; Jeffrey Pfeffer and Nancy Langton, "Wage Inequality and the Organization of Work," *Administrative Science Quarterly* 33 (1988): 588-606.

[20] Cited in Francis Fukuyama, "The End of History?" *National Interest* 481 (1989): 117-142.

[21] Steve Kerr, "On the Folly of Rewarding A While Hoping for B," *Academy of Management Journal* 19 (1975): 769-783.

[22] William Ouchi, "The Relationship between Organizational Structure and Control," *Administrative Science Quarterly* 22 (1977): 95-113. This concept is developed in greater detail in the final sections of Chapter 9.

[23] Jeffrey Kerr and John Slocum, "Managing Corporate Culture through Reward Systems," *Academy of Management Executive* 1 (1987): 99-108.

[24] Aihwa Ong, "The Gender and Labor Politics of Postmodernity," *Annual Review of Anthropology* 20 (1991): 196-214.

[25] The best source for data on managerial overhead is David Gordon, *Fat and Mean* (Ithaca, NY: Cornell University Press, 1996). Superb summaries of these ideas are available in Stanley Aronowitz, *False Promises* (New York: McGraw-Hill, 1973); Harry Braverman, *Labor and Monopoly Capital* (New York: Monthly Review Press, 1974); Michael Burawoy, *Manufacturing Consent* (Chicago: University of Chicago Press, 1979); and Richard Edwards, *Contested Terrain* (New York: Basic Books, 1978).

[26] G. Stoney Adler and Phil Tompkins, "Electronic Performance Monitoring," *Management Communication Quarterly* 10 (1997): 259-288; J. R. Aiello, "Computer-Based Work Monitoring," *Journal of Applied Social Psychology* 23 (1993): 499-507; J. R. Aiello and C. M. Svec, "Computer Monitoring of Work Performance," *Journal of Applied Psychology* 23 (1993): 537-548; J. J. Balitis Jr., "Care Needed with Electronic Monitoring," *Business Journal (Phoenix)* 18 (21) (1998): 71; Carl Botan, "Communication, Work, and Electronic Surveillance," *Communication Monographs* 63 (1996): 294-313; Carl Botan, "Examining Electronic Surveillance in the Workplace," paper presented at the International Communication Convention, Acapulco, Mexico, May 2000; R. E. Kidwell Jr. and N. Bennett, "Employee Reactions to Electronic Control Systems," *Group and Organization Management* 19 (1994), 203-219.

[27] Hannah Arendt provides an explanation of the inevitability of resistance in *The Human Condition* (Chicago: University of Chicago Press, 1958). Michel Foucault, a theorist whose work we cite frequently in this book, draws similar conclusions in *Discipline and Punish: The Birth of the Prison,* A. Sheridan, trans. (1977; New York: Vintage, 1990); *Power/Knowledge,* C. Gordon, trans. (New York: Pantheon, 1980); and *The Practice of Everyday Life* (Berkeley: University of California Press, 1984). Foucault's work is difficult to understand. An excellent summary is available in James Barker and George Cheney, "The Concept and Practices of Discipline in Contemporary Organizational Life," *Communication Monographs* 61 (1994): 20-43.

[28] D. Pena, "Tortuosidad," and G. Young, "Gender Identification and Working-Class Solidarity among *Maquila* Workers in Ciudad Juarez," both in *Women on the U.S.-Mexico Border,* V. L. Ruiz and S. Tiano, eds. (Boston: Allen and Unwin, 1987).

[29] Laura Goldberg, "Slowdowns Hit Airlines," *Houston Chronicle,* December 6, 2000, C1.

[30] Charles Conrad summarizes the research underlying these conclusions in "Was Pogo Right? Communication, Power, and Resistance," in *Communication Research in the 21st Century,* Julia Wood and Richard Gregg, eds. (Cresskill, NJ: Hampton Press, 1995). The most important sources are Michel de Certeau, *The Practice of Everyday Life* (Berkeley: University of California Press, 1984); Burawoy; Stewart Clegg, "Power, Theorizing, and Nihilism," *Theory and Society* 3 (1976): 65–87; and Kathy Ferguson, *The Feminist Case against Bureaucracy* (Philadelphia: Temple University Press, 1984).

[31] Marlene Fine and Patrice Buzzanell, "Walking the High Wire," in *Rethinking Organizational and Managerial Communication from Feminist Perspectives,* P. Buzzanell, ed. (Thousand Oaks, CA: Sage, 2000).

[32] Roy Smith, "How to Be a Good Subordinate," *New York Times,* November 25, 1970, F16. The primary source for this section is Ferguson.

[33] Omar Aktouf, "Defamiliarizing Management Practice," in *Understanding Management,* Stephen Linstead, Robert Grafton Small, and Paul Jeffcutt, eds. (London: Sage, 1996).

[34] For more detail on the arguments in this section, see McPhee and Poole.

[35] Kathleen Melymuka, "Going for Broke," *Computerworld,* March 26, 2003.

[36] Dan Verton, "Employers OK with E-Surfing," *Computerworld,* December 18, 2000.

[37] Dan Verton, "Senator Attacks Data Sharing," *Computerworld,* December 11, 2000.

[38] Kirk Johnson, "Many Companies Turn Workers into High-Tech Nomads," *Minneapolis Star-Tribune,* April 3, 1994, J1.

[39] Mary Brandel, "Distant Messages," *Computerworld,* December 9, 2002.

[40] Brandel, p. 50.

[41] Shoshanna Zuboff, *In the Age of the Smart Machine* (New York: Free Press, 1988).

Chapter 4

Relational Strategies
of Organizing

If thou art one to whom petition is made, be calm as thou listeneth. . . . Do not rebuff him before he has . . . said that for which he came. . . . It is not [necessary] that everything about which he has petitioned should come to pass, [but] a good hearing is soothing to the heart.
—Pharaoh Ptah-hotep to his managers, c. 2700 BC

If a leader maintains close relationship with his soldiers, they will "be more eager to be seen performing some honorable action, and more anxious to abstain from doing anything that was disgraceful."
—A lesson learned by Alexander the Great from the Persian King Cyrus, c. 325 BC

Central Themes

- Relational strategies of organizing substitute decentralization and participatory decision making for the centralized, hierarchical, specialized organizational design of the traditional strategy. Employees sometimes resist these strategies, and the effects of the strategies depend on a number of factors.
- Informal communication networks are an inevitable aspect of organizations, and they can benefit organizations and their members in many ways.
- Teams are a basic building block of the relational strategy. Teams enable relational organizations to respond flexibly to their challenges, but they may also function to control their members rather than empowering them.
- Relational strategies rely on creating open and supportive supervisor-subordinate relationships, achieved through "transactional" leadership tactics.
- ICTs that support groups and relationships include e-mail, instant messaging, and group support systems.
- Critical theories of organizational communication argue that relational strategies obscure differences among the interests of owner, managers, and workers.

Key Terms

work group	gossip
project team	weak ties
quality-improvement team	boundary-spanning activities
integrating team	routinized
uniplex relationship	de-skilling
multiplex relationship	ratebusters
clique	team
closeness	self-managing team
centrality	concertive control
prestige	transactional leadership
liaison	unified messaging
bridge	groupware
isolate	systematically
density	distorted communication

In the modern world, people can accomplish relatively little acting alone. In fact, the reason formal organizations developed after the agricultural revolution was that the everyday tasks societies needed to perform could not be accomplished efficiently by individuals or family groups acting on their own. Organizations are made up of people involved in complex webs of relationships with one another. Relational strategies of organizing focus on interpersonal relationships as the key to managing the "fundamental paradox" described in Chapter 1.

Like Chapter 3, this chapter discusses organizational design; motivation, control, and surveillance; leadership; and technology. However, the amount of space that we devote to each of these topics is quite different. Traditional strategies of organizing focus on organizational design and motivation, control, and surveillance at length, and de-emphasize leadership. *Communication* is defined very narrowly, as the movement of information from one point in the organization to another. Relational strategies of organizing reverse that priority, largely taking organizational design for granted and focusing on motivation, control, and surveillance along with interpersonal relationships among workers, including leadership. *Communication* is defined more broadly, to encompass both information exchange and the development and maintenance of interpersonal relationships.

Relational Strategies of Organizational Design

There is one important design-related difference between relational and traditional strategies—decentralization. In traditional strategies of organizing, centralization and hierarchization—the notions that organizations should be shaped like a multilevel triangle and decision making should be located at the top of the triangle—are central concepts. Lower-level employees are allowed to make decisions, but only about implementing the rules, policies, and procedures that are established on high. The relational strategy relaxes both assumptions, asserting instead that organizational hierarchies should be "flattened" and decision making should be decentralized. There are far fewer exchanges of messages between the sources of information and the people who use that information. This means that lower-level employees are empowered to make decisions about a wide range of issues that directly affect them and their jobs, and that there are far fewer links in the formal chain of command.

Decentralization and Participation

Decentralization and participatory decision making (PDM) are two sides of the same coin. If an organization adopts a decentralized organizational structure, the number of managers drops significantly, as does the number of levels of management. As a result, lower-level employees must be allowed to make everyday decisions because there is no one else available to do so. In addition, the managers that are left in the organization are required to supervise much more "loosely" than are managers in the traditional strategy. "Tight" supervision is alienating and increases the likelihood that workers will resist management. Loose supervision involves granting workers more autonomy, allowing them to determine how to accomplish their assigned tasks, and expecting them to make the decisions that influence them most. Supervising loosely allows each supervisor to manage a much larger number of employees. Furthermore, decisions are made by the employees who are most directly concerned with them and most expert in the day-to-day activities of the organization. Formal communication crosses fewer levels, thus reducing the potential for structural breakdowns (recall Chapter 3).

Necessary Features for Successful PDM   Participatory decision making is time-consuming and costly for organizations, but these costs are often more than offset by the heightened morale, improved decision quality, and enhanced information flow that results. PDM comes in a variety of different forms with different labels. Regardless of the particular form, PDM will increase organizational performance only if certain requirements are met:

1. Subordinates must want to be involved in decision making, must be involved in complex tasks, and must be given substantial control over how they complete their tasks.
2. Supervisors must be willing to allow their subordinates to participate legitimately and must listen and respond to their ideas and encourage them to contribute.
3. The issues being discussed must be important to the participants. Workers usually believe that any decisions that directly affect them or their jobs are important and that decisions about more general company poli-

cies are less important. They especially would like to have influence over decisions about how to do their own work, scheduling of work, awarding raises and promotions, and hiring and firing of co-workers.

4. All the participants must have expertise and information relevant to the problems being discussed.

5. Managers must foster and support the beliefs, values, and attitudes necessary to legitimate participatory systems. Publicly recognizing employees' contributions and creating positive feelings of success give employees a feeling of empowerment: they believe that they really do have the authority to act on their own.[1]

Resistance to PDM   Sometimes resistance to PDM is grounded in the societal context surrounding an organization. It seems logical to expect PDM systems to be more successful in societies that have a strong democratic tradition, like the United States. However, U.S. society has long separated the political and business realms—political rights that are taken for granted (freedom of speech and dissent, majority rule, due process, and so on) have never been required in private-sector organizations.[2] Because the United States also has had adversarial relationships between workers and management, it is difficult to achieve the level of trust and cooperation necessary to make PDM systems work well. In some societies, people learn that supervisors should make and enforce decisions simply because they are supervisors (a concept that Max Weber labeled traditional authority).[3] For example, Asian workers often find it difficult to challenge higher-status members of their organizations. For them, PDM can be alien and frustrating. Sometimes resistance is based on a lack of trust or skill. Many workers, especially blue-collar workers, do not wish to participate in decision making because they would rather not share the responsibilities that accompany the systems. This is especially true early on, before workers are persuaded that management will not use the systems to penalize them when they make inevitable mistakes. It also is true later on, when people with high levels of expertise but weak communication skills are often frustrated by PDM. They expect to have a great deal of impact on decisions because of their expertise. But their limited communication skills reduce their impact and they become frustrated. People with high levels of communication anxiety may also find participation threatening and may respond by withdrawing. The organization loses the expertise of such employees, and their satisfaction with their jobs drops. In less participatory arrangements, these people would have opportunities to communicate privately with a single supervisor. Because privacy provides a backstage area where they can plan and rehearse their messages for this single, known listener, their anxiety may be reduced. For them, nonparticipatory decision making may be more satisfying and may allow the organization to benefit more from their expertise.

Participation may also increase employee stress by creating communication overload. When participatory strategies are used, everyone involved is required to increase his or her communication. Some PDM systems ask employees to meet after work or on weekends. Especially when their jobs place extreme demands on them, they may not be able to handle the increased communication and the time it takes away from other activities. The problem is even greater when employees, for whatever reasons, wish to participate less than they are asked to do. When the amount of participation is either more or less than employees desire, they show higher stress, lower job satisfaction, and poorer performance than when participation matches their preferences.[4]

Supervisors also resist PDM. People become supervisors, at least in part, because they have a desire for power and an ability to obtain and use it to their advantage. They gain substantial rewards from their superior positions—salary, status, and most important, the legitimate right to exercise authority over others. PDM works best, both in terms of enhancing productivity and in terms of increasing job satisfaction, if supervisors reduce the power "gap" between themselves and their subordinates. If the strategies succeed in equalizing power, they threaten the superiority, and thus the self-esteem and self-images, of precisely those people who hold power most dear and who have the greatest personal and practical reasons to want to hold on to the power they have gained over the years.

Power holders may overtly resist sharing their power by refusing to use participatory strategies, using them only for trivial issues, acting in ways that split the group or otherwise impede its ability to make effective decisions, refusing to carry out the group's decisions, or sabotaging a decision when it is implemented. Other methods of resistance are more subtle, for example, withholding valuable information from subordinates and thereby leading the subordinates to make bad decisions. Based on the withheld information, supervisors can (accurately) predict that their subordinates' decisions will fail. When their predictions turn out to be accurate, their subordinates perceive that the supervisors are exceptionally expert and competent. Thus their ability to control the group's decisions in the future is increased. In this way, power holders may actually be able to use participation to increase their influence and enlarge the power gap between them and their subordinates. In a series of studies of power-sharing strategies in European firms, Mauk Mulder found that in addition to having greater access to information, supervisors typically also have greater communication skills than their subordinates. They are more persuasive, argue positions more effectively, and are more adept at interpreting other employees' communication and responding appropriately. In participatory systems, these advantages allow them to influence the views of other employees. In time a "power elite" develops, whose membership seems to be determined by the members' greater communication skills, but it also is related to their formal positions. Eventually less powerful members communicate less and less and more powerful members begin to dominate the decision-making process. Thus, the opportunity for more open communication, which is the strength of participation, may lead to increased power gaps rather than to power sharing.[5]

CASE STUDY
Going South

USA Home Products (a pseudonym, like all the other company names in this case study) is a U.S. multinational company that has been operating in Mexico for more than forty years. It has more than one hundred thousand employees in eighty countries and markets more than two hundred brands to nearly 5 billion consumers worldwide. Unlike many U.S. firms, which move to Mexico solely to reduce labor costs, USAHP did so because it long ago saw Latin America as an important market for its products. In order to expand its operations in Mexico, the company purchased a state-of-the-art plant in Lourdes state (also a pseudonym) from a Mexican corporation, MEXCO.

The two companies had very different ways of doing business. MEXCO valued having a local workforce, so it hired largely through family connections (like Industry International, one of the case studies in Chapter 3). Lourdes state is a unique place. Its largely native population is very proud of the fact that Lourdes was never conquered by the Aztecs. It allied itself with the conquistadores and gained special treatment by the Spanish. As a result, it is culturally and economically very different from neighboring states, especially Azteca state (another pseudonym), which surrounds Lourdes on three sides. Azteca is much more sophisticated (the home of a number of universities), much more accepting of foreigners, and wealthier than its smaller neighbor. The two peoples eat different foods, have different forms of entertainment—the Aztecans' most important sport is soccer, which is not that important in Lourdes. Citizens of Azteca are "foreign," almost as foreign as Anglos from the United States.

MEXCO's management believed that employees could learn by trial and error and did not need more than an elementary school education. Salaries, especially of managers, were based more on interpersonal relationships with the owner and the board of directors than on performance. Both practices are completely consistent with the Latin concept of *familia*—strong values attached to family and community, as well as a commitment to hard work, achievement, and aiding people who are in need as ways of honoring one's family. These practices had a major effect on the plant's reward system. The favored managers had salaries much higher than employees of USAHP who held a similar rank in the company, whereas the salaries of lower-level employees (especially the technicians who operated the high-tech machinery) were much lower than USAHP standards. Mexico is a high power-distance culture, which means that its people learn to accept very hierarchical power relationships. For the technicians this meant they accepted that management would make decisions and they themselves would follow orders, and they gained a sense of pride from their technical skills, especially in comparison to workers who cleaned the plant and its equipment and staff personnel who worked in the

(continued)

(Case Study, continued)

company's offices. They also gained a degree of pride from their ability to "make do," an attitude that is quite common in societies that experience scarcity. The plant never had allocated much money for maintenance and repair of equipment. When things broke down, the technicians found ways to get them running again. Most of the solutions they discovered were nonstandard—"spit and bailing wire"—but they worked. In effect their motto became "if it ain't broke don't fix it," and when it did, the "fix" was almost never anything that would be included in an operations manual or a university course.

When USAHP took over the plant, it immediately moved to change the plant's operations to accord with those in its other plants, both in the United States and in Latin America. Part of the change was a complete revision of the selection and reward system. USAHP wanted its machine operators to have technical training, preferably a degree from a respected university, and fluency in both written and spoken English. Very few people with this level of education lived in Lourdes, which has one of the weakest educational systems in Mexico. Instead of helping improve Lourdes's educational system, something that local leaders expected, US-AHP decided to hire new employees from the universities in Azteca. To make matters worse, the expatriates (U.S. employees that USAHP transferred to the new plant) decided to live in Azteca, where the schools are better, the climate cooler, and the lifestyle more sophisticated. Suddenly, the plant was being run by people who were doubly foreign—Anglos allied with Aztecans. In addition, many of the overpaid managers were fired, and the ones who had the technical skills USAHP desired had their salaries frozen until the rest of the employees caught up to US-AHP's salary scale. USAHP's headquarters saw these changes as making the plant's salary structure more fair; many of MEXCO's workers had a very different definition of "fairness," one based on tenure and loyalty, not technical qualifications. The supervisors who stayed were unhappy, but glad they still had jobs; the workers who remained were afraid because the interpersonal connections that had given them a sense of security suddenly were irrelevant.

However, the biggest change involved USAHP's "Active Management" system. It was based on two principles borrowed from Japanese managerial practices (practices drawn from the work of American J. Edwards Deming), "continuous improvement" and constant monitoring of performance using advanced statistical techniques. For the technicians this meant that they would now be responsible for cleaning and maintaining their own machines. They could no longer blame equipment breakdowns on the maintenance department, and they suddenly were responsible for performing tasks that were "beneath them." They were evaluated in part on a very ambiguous criterion of "support for the AM" system, even though Mexican culture is known for its low tolerance of ambiguity. (Interestingly, the company's efforts to shift to AM in its U.S. plants during the 1990s had failed because it violated U.S. workers' "if it ain't broke" attitudes and because it was a Japanese system. The company had greater success in Latin America, because, they believe, the culture is more supportive of following orders sent from "the top down.") Upper management realized that they had to persuade local management to support AM or they would not be able to overcome resistance by the workers. The parent company transferred managers from other Latin American plants that had successfully shifted to the AM system, and paired them with local plant managers.

Unfortunately, they failed to persuade Mr. Suarez, a supervisor from Lourdes state who had worked in the plant for decades. Management also failed to explain the changes and the reasons for them to the workers, evidently assuming that in a "top-down" culture, they would quickly accept changes that were mandated by their supervisors. The technicians resisted the changes in every way they could. After 2½ years, only one of forty teams had successfully completed the first phase of the program.

It is somewhat surprising that USAHP's upper management realized that the new system was failing—U.S. managers have long been known for a tendency to persist in failing courses of action long after failure is abundantly clear.* But USAHP learned from its mistakes and started implementing Active Management/Preventive Maintenance in a way that was appropriate to Mexican and Lourdian culture: they completely revamped the reward system so that it could encourage acceptance of the change, broke down the solidarity around the previous opposing leader, and improved the skill level of the workforce.

In order to recover from the initial failure, USAHP replaced the ambiguous practice of rewarding people for showing their commitment to the new system with rewards based on achieving a set of clearly stated objectives. New procedures and metrics to evaluate the involvement of the personnel in AM were implemented, such as attendance at AM-related meetings and activities. All AM teams meet each week to share their results and assign each member specific responsibilities, ensuring that all of the employees were actively involved in the implementation process. The operators still have a lot of pressure to produce, but now they have preestablished hours to receive training in AM. Teams were given small rewards for achieving the set goals, and recognition will be given to those completing important milestones in the AM process. The team decides when it will be audited to see if it is ready to move on to the later phases of implementation, and teams are told ahead of time precisely what criteria will be used in the evaluation.

Mr. Suarez was relocated outside of the production division, where he could be consulted for technical advice but no longer supervised the technicians. He was replaced by two production managers who are familiar with and committed to the new system. Three technicians with long histories in the plant were selected to receive initial training and then to train the other technicians in the division. In order to break the tight solidarity among the workers from the previous company, a new leadership team was formed, which included members from all of the production areas. New subcommittees were created in each area, composed of a functional leader (a worker with AM experience), the leader of the area, and a PM planner.

(continued)

(Case Study, continued)

Applying What You Have Learned

1. In general, why do people resist participatory programs? Which of those sources of resistance were evident in this case?
2. What aspects of Mexican/Lourdes culture made the shift to a more participatory system more complicated? What aspects made it (or should have made it) easier?

Questions to Think About and Discuss

1. Is this case study primarily about cross-cultural differences, or about resistance to change, or about attitudes toward participation? How are these factors interrelated?
2. If you were to develop a manual on cross-cultural communication based on this case, what would it say? Why?

The research on which this case is based was partially funded by both the Consejo Nacional de Ciencia y Tecnología (CONACYT—Mexico), contract no. 35981-U, and the National Science Foundation (NSF—USA), contract no. DMI-0116635.

*For example, see Alan Tegar, *Too Much Invested to Quit* (New York: Pergamon, 1980).

The Organization as a Tier of Groups

The group is the basic unit of the relational strategy of organization. The relational strategy does not do away with managerial structure altogether. There are still top managers and some middle managers, as well as line-level work groups. However, the concept of the hierarchy so critical to the traditional strategy is replaced by the concept of the organization as a tier of groups. One of the primary advocates of the relational strategy, Rensis Likert, developed a model of relational organizational design that may help clarify these concepts. He proposed that organizations should be structured around overlapping groups of employees instead of with the independent divisions of the bureaucratic model. Each group would make any decisions that affected it or its members. Each group would be linked to every other group with which it was interdependent by a "linking pin," an employee who was a member of both groups (see Figure 4-1). In this structure, each group could better understand the needs and problems of the other groups. The problems of trained communication incapacity and specialized languages (discussed in Chapter 3) would be minimized because the groups would always have a translator available. Intergroup conflict could be reduced because communication breakdowns between groups would be less frequent. Group decision making would be enhanced because each linking pin would have access to different kinds of information as a result of her or his contact with other groups. In effect, this system (which Likert called System Four)

FIGURE 4–1
Likert's Multiple Overlapping Groups

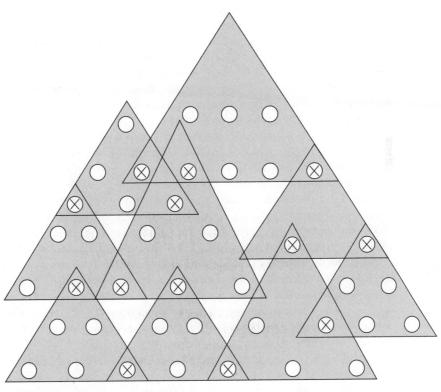

⊗ Linking pins

created an organizational structure designed around the concept of PDM. Unfortunately, linking pins are placed in difficult and stressful positions. When things go wrong, they are handy scapegoats, and they are often not rewarded for their efforts.[6]

Several different kinds of groups can be distinguished in the linking pin model of organization. The most common form of group in organizations is the **work group,** such as a hospital emergency room unit or a sales team. Work groups are formal units that range in size from three to more than fifty members. Work groups have definite goals and tasks, and their relationships with other work groups and the larger organization are often specified in formal terms. For instance, in an office-equipment business studied by Scott Poole, production was organized around six-to-eight-member teams that crafted pieces of office furniture. Each team developed its own methods of working together to assemble the furniture (that is, the teams were self-organizing) and to coordinate two teams in the shipping department that packed and shipped the orders.

These lower-level teams were coordinated by a management team. Under the relational strategy this coordination is carried out through direct communication between the groups, sometimes through linking pins and sometimes via informal representatives. The informal communication system, discussed in the next section, may also play a role in coordinating work groups.

Note that some work groups are composed of frontline workers who are carrying out production or service tasks, whereas others are management groups that coordinate the work of lower-level groups. There may be several tiers of these groups in a typical organization that follows the relational strategy. **Project teams** are formed on a temporary basis to carry out specific tasks within specified time frames, which may vary from a few months to several years. Members are typically assigned to project teams on a limited basis and are often on loan from their home department or group. Organizations often create project teams to develop new products and activities or to solve persistent problems, as when McDonald's Corporation formed the Chicken McNugget team to bring this interesting fast food to market.[7] The Chicken McNugget team had members from the product development and marketing departments, which made it a cross-functional project team. Cross-functional teams are constituted to ensure that the perspectives of different departments or functions are brought to a project and that all aspects of the organization that must participate in the project are involved. Other examples of project teams include **quality-improvement teams** (sometimes called quality circles), which are charged with studying and solving problems in some organizational process, and task forces, which focus on important, high-profile problems or issues and are composed of high-status members who bring credibility to the group.

In addition to work groups and project teams, there is one other important type of group in most organizations, the **integrating team.** Integrating teams, which are discussed in more detail in Chapter 6, are set up specifically to coordinate activities of different groups or departments in an organization. Examples of integrating teams include the executive committee of a college within a university, made up of department heads who discuss issues that affect more than one department or the college as a whole, and a merger team, composed of members from two organizations that are set to merge, which attempts to coordinate the combination of the organizations and address problems as they develop.

Informal Communication Networks

Communication networks are an important part of all organizational systems, as we noted in Chapter 2.[8] The formal structure of the organization constitutes part of the organizational network. The hierarchy specifies who should talk to whom in the chain of command. Information flowing up and down the hierarchy helps to coordinate and control work. Traditional organizations try to limit the flow of communication in the organization to formal channels, on the assumption that other types of communication detract from job performance and are therefore not desirable.

However, informal communication networks emerge in every organization. They formed even in the prisons and concentration camps of World War II. Because communication through informal ties is outside of management's control, supervisors in traditional organizations often try to suppress the development of informal ties. Relational strategies suggest that informal communication networks are an important part of the organization's structure. Through informal networks employees form meaningful interpersonal relationships, gain a sense of self-respect, meet their sociability needs, and exercise some degree of control over their working lives. People who are actively involved in informal networks have higher morale, job satisfaction, and commitment to their organizations; know more about how their organizations operate; and are better able to meet others' communication needs than employees who are not so involved.[9]

At this point we will introduce some basic communication network terminology that we use in the remainder of this book. There are two types of ties in organizational communication networks. Some relationships are **uniplex,** which means that the parties always talk about the same topic (for example, work or sports). Others are **multiplex** relationships, in which the parties communicate about a wide variety of topics and play a number of different roles with one another (for example, boss, collaborator on a key project, tennis partner, and so on). Multiplex relationships tend to be long-term, emotionally intense, influential, trusting, and more predictable than uniplex relationships. Communication tends to be deep, involving a good deal of self-disclosure, and rich, providing much emotional and cognitive detail. Multiplex relationships offer social support and opportunities to vent frustrations, thus helping manage stress and make positive changes. They also may increase stress, however, because it takes time and emotional energy to maintain intense relationships. Informal communication networks tend to have more multiplex ties than formal communication networks do.

Sets of people who are tightly interconnected are called **cliques.** Cliques can arise from formal work groups or units whose members interact a lot, but they may also result from informal interactions. Figure 4-2 shows a communication network in which there are three interconnected cliques. There are also other important properties related to the position that an individual has in a communication network. **Closeness** refers to the ease with which a person can reach others in the communication network. The more people one can reach without having to go through others, and the fewer others one has to go through, the higher one's closeness. An example of a person high in closeness is the administrative assistant of a unit; typically that person has close contacts with all others in the unit and can contact them immediately to route a phone call or request. **Centrality** is the degree to which an actor is central to a network. The more one can "control" the flow of information in a network, the more central one is. The administrative assistant in a department is typically highly central. Centrality and closeness are often correlated in organizations. **Prestige** is the degree to which a person is contacted by others as opposed to having to contact them. Studies have shown that people with high status and power are sought

FIGURE 4-2
A Communication Network

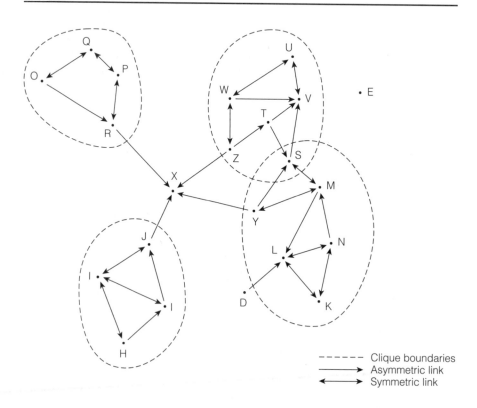

out by lower-ranking, less powerful people and therefore typically receive more contacts and communications than they must send. It is interesting to note that prestige is not necessarily correlated with closeness or centrality. Some prestigious people are high in centrality and closeness, but others are not.

Several key roles in communication networks have been identified by previous research. A **liaison** links cliques that would not otherwise be linked but is not a member of either clique. Person X in Figure 4-2 is a liaison. Liaisons have important roles in networks because they provide linkages between groups that would not otherwise be linked. Liaisons are often managers or highly respected people, and they tend to score high in prestige (they are contacted a lot, but they may not directly reciprocate those contacts). They may also be members who perform a specialized role, such as one of the linking roles described in Chapter 6. A **bridge** also links two cliques but is a member of both of them. An **isolate** is someone who has few or no links to others in the network. It is tempting to think of isolates as people who are not valuable to the organization, but some are isolated because they are so committed to their work that they do not communicate with many others. Other people are isolates because of their work schedules. The janitor who cleans after hours may be an isolate, but he or she performs an important duty.

One important characteristic of communication networks as a whole is their centralization, the degree to which one or two members can control most of the flow in the network. Networks with a few members very high in centrality, where most others have relatively low centrality, tend to be centralized. The organizational hierarchy characteristic of traditional organizations is centralized, whereas participatory networks characteristic of the relational strategy are lower in centralization. **Density** refers to how dense the communication network is and is measured by the ratio of how many links are actually in the network and how many links there could potentially be between members. The organizational hierarchy of the traditional organization is low in density on purpose, because the traditional organization wants to restrict information flow to a relatively few formal channels. It regards additional links beyond what is required to maintain the hierarchy as wasteful. In contrast, the relational strategy seeks to create denser networks. Table 4-1 summarizes key terms used to characterize communication networks.

TABLE 4-1
Properties of Communication Networks

Measure	Definition	Example in Figure 4-2
Measures of Network Ties		
Frequency	How many times or how often the link occurs.	X talks to Y 5 times per week.
Multiplexity	Extent to which two members are linked together by more than one relationship.	X and Y work together, belong to the same club, and share gossip.
Strength	Amount of time, emotional intensity, intimacy, or reciprocation.	X and Y interact a lot and spend a lot of time together.
Direction	Who initiates the link.	In an asymmetric link, Y asks X for advice, but X does not ask Y for advice. In a symmetric link, M and Y both ask each other for advice.
Measures Related to Individuals in the Network		
Centrality	Extent to which member is centrally located in a network (there are lots of ways to measure this).	X is central.
In-degree	Number of directional links coming to a member from other members.	X has 4 in-degrees.
Out-degree	Number of directional links going from the member to other members.	Y has 3 out-degrees.
Closeness	Extent to which member is close to or can easily reach all the other actors in a network.	X has high closeness. K has low closeness.

(continued)

TABLE 4-1
Continued

Measure	Definition	Example in Figure 4-2
Measures Related to Individuals in the Network		
Prestige	How many asymmetric links an actor has in which he or she does not initiate contact measured by in-degree).	X is high in prestige.
Network Roles		
Star	An actor highly central to a network.	X is a star.
Liaison	An actor who has links to two or more cliques that would otherwise not be linked, but is not a member of either clique.	X is a liaison.
Bridge	An actor who belongs to two or more cliques.	S is a bridge.
Isolate	A person who has no links or relatively few links to others.	D and E are isolates.
Gatekeeper	A member who mediates or controls the flow between one part of the network and another.	X, Y, and Z could be gatekeepers.
Measures of Entire Network Properties		
Density	Number of links in the network compared to the number that could potentially form. Dense networks have lots of links.	The network is moderately dense.
Centralization	Degree to which a few members could control most links in the network.	The network is highly centralized.
Connectivity (also called Reachability)	Extent to which actors in the network are linked to one another by direct or indirect paths.	The network is moderately high in connectivity.

It takes effort to develop and sustain dense, connected informal networks. It takes time for people to find one another, and much successful communication must occur before they come to understand and trust one another. Sometimes they must learn to compensate for the problems of trained incapacity that were discussed in Chapter 3. Informal networks must regularly be used or they tend to atrophy. Unless two people communicate on a fairly regular basis, they will forget each other's language and frame of reference. Just as competence in a foreign language wears off with disuse, knowledge of the frame of reference of other employees also wears off. Then, when a crisis occurs in which employees need to communicate, they find it difficult to do so. Typically, informal networks are maintained through **gossip,** the sharing of personal information that is irrelevant to specific tasks or organizational decisions. But without gossip, informal networks dissolve.[10]

Generally speaking, informal networks help organizations in three ways: by compensating for the weaknesses in formal communication, by improving organizational decision making, and by fostering innovation. Formal communication networks allow people to handle predictable, routine situations, but they are inefficient means of meeting unanticipated communication needs, for managing crises, for dealing with complex or detailed problems, for sharing personal information, or for exchanging information rapidly. In a now classic study, Keith Davis found that during a quality-control crisis in a large firm, the information that was needed to solve the problem was rapidly disseminated using informal networks, not formal channels. Informal communication may also be more reliable than formal communication. Because informal communication is less restricted by differences in power and status, it is richer in content than formal communication. Mutual give and take is less inhibited in informal communication, so communicators provide more detail in their messages and are more willing to give and receive feedback. Even gossip and rumors—messages whose accuracy cannot immediately be determined by management—usually provide accurate information. Job-related rumors originate because employees are not adequately informed through formal channels. Although some gossip and rumors may be false, when compared to formal communication, with its inherent problems of withholding and distortion (recall Chapter 3), informal communication may often be more accurate. Informal networks also tend to be self-correcting. Once an employee is caught spreading false rumors, his or her credibility is reduced. Formal communication networks are not based on interpersonal relationships, so they tend not to self-correct.[11]

Informal networks can also foster innovation. Sometimes people have access to a wealth of valuable information that they are not "officially" supposed to possess. Informal relationships with those people provide an invaluable source of information, especially information that is not supposed to be public knowledge. Employees can release a "trial balloon" and monitor other employees' reactions without ever having to admit officially that the proposal was even being considered. Being able to talk off the record seems to improve organizational decision making, especially when organizations are in the early stages of defining problems and searching for solutions. Through his twenty-year study of bureaucratic organizations, Peter Blau found that informal communication allowed employees to obtain advice and assistance without "really" admitting that they needed it, and that informal communication provided them with politically safe opportunities to think out loud about new ideas or experiences. In general, the more dense and less centralized an organization's communication system is, the more innovative its employees will be. Through informal networks, people share innovative ideas, obtain feedback that allows them to improve those ideas, and eventually obtain support for innovations. Informal networks allow people to come to a shared understanding of new ideas and their importance to the organization and thus stimulate them to take collective innovative action. But there is no guarantee that these benefits will result from an informal network.[12]

Whereas dense, connected communication networks enable organizations to implement new ideas more effectively, the *source* of new ideas is more often the **weak ties.** Weak ties are connections to others with whom one has only occasional contact. Because they represent ties that are seldom used, weak ties typically do not show up in network diagrams like the one in Figure 4-2. However, they are critical for moving new information into existing networks. People tend to talk about the same types of things and have much in common with those to whom they are strongly tied. Continuous communication in formal and informal networks tends to homogenize thinking. New ideas more often come from the outside, from someone we meet on an airplane, or at a conference or a party, someone who has a different perspective and different ideas and knowledge. Sociologist Mark Granovetter conducted one of the first studies of weak ties and found that, contrary to common expectations, most people found a new job not through contacts they regularly communicated with, but through weak ties.[13]

Boundary Spanning: A Key Component of Group Effectiveness in Organizations

Deborah Ancona and David Caldwell have conducted important research on factors that make groups effective in organizations.[14] Their research establishes the importance of external, **boundary-spanning activities** in communication networks. Groups must interact with individuals and groups in the organization who are important to the group's effectiveness, such as superiors who must evaluate the group, resource providers, customers and clients, and parties affected for good or ill by group activities. Four types of external activities that span the group's boundary with the organization are particularly important:

> *Scouting or scanning activities* through which group members gather intelligence and information that can help them make better decisions.
>
> *Liaison activities* with those who evaluate and consume the group's work or products to ensure that requirements are understood and needs met.
>
> *Campaigns* to form good impressions of the group, its activities, and its products in the organization and the external community.
>
> *Buffering* activities that protect the group from external threats and events that might prevent it from attaining its goals. This includes a wide range of protective behavior, for example, keeping group activities secret until the group is ready to go or defending the group from negative comments made by a supervisor in another unit.

Depending on the group's context, some of these four types of activities may be more important than others.

Relational Strategies of Motivation, Control, and Surveillance

Traditional strategies of motivation and control are based on the assumptions that workers find work to be alienating and must be tightly controlled and motivated by the promise of economic gain (the view that James McGregor once labeled "Theory X"). Relational strategies are based on what McGregor called a

TABLE 4–2
McGregor's Theory X and Theory Y

Theory X

1. Workers must be supervised as closely as possible, either through direct oversight or by tight reward and/or punishment systems.

2. Work is objectionable to most unless it is made offensive by the actions of organizations.

3. Most people have little initiative, have little capacity for being creative or solving organizational problems, do not want to have responsibilities, and prefer being directed by someone else.

4. People are motivated by economic factors and a need for security.

Theory Y

1. People usually do not require close supervision and will, if given a chance to control their own activities, be productive, satisfied, and fulfilled.

2. Work is natural and enjoyable to people.

3. People are ambitious, desire autonomy and self-control, and can use their abilities to solve problems and help their organizations meet their goals. Creativity is distributed "normally" across the population, just as is any other characteristic.

4. People are motivated by a variety of needs only some of which involve economics or security.

"Theory Y" (see Table 4-2) view of human beings and work—people have important needs for autonomy, creativity, and sociability, needs that are frustrated by organizations' (and societies') needs for control and coordination. Supervisors can align those individual needs with the needs of their organizations by making work meaningful and fostering positive supervisor-subordinate relationships. They can do this by enlarging and enriching jobs, and by adopting transactional leadership strategies.[15]

Job Enrichment and Enlargement

Three of the most influential advocates of this approach to motivation and control were Abraham Maslow, Frederick Herzberg, and Chris Argyris. Maslow's model of human motivation is widely known: people have five kinds of needs that are arranged in a hierarchy: physiological (expressed in feelings of thirst, lust, and so on), safety (feeling free from danger, harm, and the fear that physiological needs will not be met), belongingness (a desire for meaningful relationships with other people), esteem or ego (feelings of accomplishment and recognition), and self-actualization (a concept that Maslow never explained clearly but that seems to be related to the feeling that one has done or is doing what one is meant to do). Once lower-level needs are fulfilled, upper-level needs become salient. Herzberg refined Maslow's model by differentiating lower-level needs (which he called hygiene factors) and higher-level needs (which he called motivators). Hygiene factors motivate people by allowing them to avoid pain. When these needs are not met, people feel discomfort; when they are met, the discomfort is reduced, but once an adequate level of fulfillment is reached, no additional pleasure is felt. Motivators create pleasure when they are provided, but their absence does not cause frustration or pain. Although neither Maslow's nor Herzberg's conclusions have been supported consistently by subsequent research, their perspective became the basis of a number of strategies for increasing workers' job satisfaction by enlarging and enriching their jobs.[16]

One of the earliest and most influential advocates of job enrichment/enlargement was Chris Argyris. He argued that many of the key characteristics of traditional models of organizing frustrated the needs of normal, psychologically healthy people. Jobs that are specialized or **routinized** (performed in the same way day after day), supervisors who control their employees "tightly," and highly competitive, individualistic atmospheres are especially frustrating. People respond to these situations by acting in ways that are counterproductive for their organizations—becoming defensive (attacking or withdrawing from co-workers) or apathetic (for example, daydreaming), socializing with other frustrated workers instead of focusing attention on their work, leaving the organization, or attempting to advance to positions that are less frustrating. The traditional strategy focuses on creating precisely these kinds of situations. Managers are charged with **de-skilling** jobs—segmenting, simplifying, and routinizing them—making them as "impoverished" and "small" as possible.

Presumably, this de-skilling of jobs is designed to increase organizational efficiency. But it is so alienating for employees that it often leads to a net loss in individual and organizational productivity. In fact, the real reason for de-skilling often is to enhance supervisory control rather than to improve efficiency. Direct surveillance is easiest when jobs are de-skilled. In addition, organizations with many de-skilled jobs can hire employees who have few alternatives and thus cannot resist management regardless of how alienated they are—high school students, disabled people, or, most recently, residents of Third World countries (including children). De-skilled tasks can easily be outsourced (contracted to outside organizations who use their own workers to do the job, often at much lower rates of pay) or assigned to part-time or other "contingent" workers (people who are hired for a specific project only). And because workers perform tasks requiring few skills, they are easy to replace when they are fired. Arraying de-skilled tasks along an assembly line provides workers with little or no opportunity to communicate with one another and forces them to adjust the pace of their activities to the pace of the machines. This keeps them from sharing grievances, comparing the way management treats them, or making plans for collective action. New technologies can be developed solely for the purpose of simplifying and routinizing jobs even further. For example, at one time the service jobs of grocery-store checker and fast-food sales clerk required at least minimal arithmetical, keyboarding, and memory skills. Today computerized cash registers—which, like all other de-skilling technologies, can increase output per person hour—make it possible to hire people without these skills. The next time you visit your local McDonald's, look closely at the keyboard on the cash registers and ask yourself what skills are necessary to operate it. To see just how de-skilled these jobs are, order something that is not represented by a button on the keyboard and see what happens. By the mid-1960s most production workers in the United States were involved in this kind of routine, repetitive, de-skilled activity, which failed to fulfill individual needs for creativity, autonomy, or sociability. By the mid-1980s many white-collar workers were involved in similar jobs.[17]

Although de-skilling does increase productivity for a time, it also decreases job satisfaction and encourages resistance. Sometimes resistance is informal. For example, salesclerks have long resisted de-skilling by creating and using their own informal relational strategies. They are friendly and supportive of one another, huddle together on the floor to foster in-group communication, ignore management's efforts to make them compete against one another, share duties that management assigns to individuals, and meet together outside of work to engage in "rituals of women's culture," such as wedding and baby showers.[18] Other forms of resistance involve more overt hostility between labor and management.

An alternative to de-skilling is for management to do just the opposite—to "enlarge" or "enrich" jobs. Doing so increases efficiency because it allows organizations to decentralize. It also increases profitability by substituting the upper-level rewards of enhanced creativity and autonomy for expensive lower-level rewards, such as salaries and wages. But successful enlargement/enrichment relies heavily on relational communication. If a job is too complex, it is frustrating and unsatisfying. If it is too simple, it is boring. Successfully matching workers and jobs, as Fredrick Taylor realized a century ago, requires a high level of open communication and feedback between supervisors and their subordinates. In addition, workers seem to figure out how rich their jobs are both by monitoring what they do and by talking with other workers. Unless people believe that their tasks are stimulating, they will not be stimulated. Workers develop these beliefs when other workers tell them that they envy their jobs. In fact, job satisfaction in general is influenced both by the objective features of employees' jobs and by what their co-workers say about their jobs. Thus, successful job enlargement/enrichment requires both careful job design and active and supportive relational communication.[19]

Group Influence, Teams, and Team-based Surveillance

The groups an employee belongs to have an important influence on her or his attitudes and actions. Attention to group influences on motivation goes back at least as far as the Hawthorne studies of the 1930s. Groups influence employees in several ways. First, work groups play an important role in socializing members to the organization. Organizations often spend considerable time on formal orientation and training for new members in attempts to socialize them. However, once orientation and training are over, employees spend most of their time in their work groups, which also teach them a great deal about the organization. In work groups employees informally learn things like shortcuts and special techniques for getting their work done properly, which rules the organization will enforce and which are simply window dressing, which supervisors are fair and which are unreasonable. In some cases this learning actually counteracts the formal orientation and training sessions. Employees also join other groups in the organization, such as the company baseball team, the Windows user's group, and informal groups (cliques) such as the group of other employees they typically have lunch with. These groups shape the way in which the employee makes sense out of work experiences. For example, if a company institutes a quality-improvement program and an important group interprets these attempts to motivate employees as exploitative, its members are likely to resist the program, no matter how attractive it may seem to those who devised it. If groups buy into job enrichment or other programs, however, their attitude may significantly increase the motivational impact of the programs.

Work groups also influence their members' productivity. In some cases, these pressures lead individual members to be less productive. **Ratebusters,** people who produce too much or who go along with management too readily, may be punished by co-workers. Sanctions can range from "tutoring," to warnings, to the "silent treatment," and even to physical violence. In other cases the pressures may increase production. Leonard Sayles notes, "We have other instances on record where the group has sanctioned increasingly high productivity, rejected fellow workers who could not maintain high output, and resisted threats to existing high quality standards." This line of thought is behind recent advocacy of team-based organizations. In theory, properly composed and motivated teams may create a more effective organization than more traditional forms of organizing.[20]

A **team** is a formally established group that has a clear focus and an effectiveness-driven structure in which members are aware of their own and others' roles and are motivated to work together to help the team succeed. As this definition implies, not all groups are teams, and becoming a team is something of an accomplishment.[21] Although many organizations may use the label *team* to refer to any formal group, merely applying the label does not mean that the group functions as a team.

Carl E. Larson and Frank M. J. LaFasto conducted an in-depth study of fifty effective teams, ranging from a field team from the Centers for Disease Control to the 1988 Notre Dame football team. They found that effective teams have eight common characteristics:

1. A clear, elevating goal that is meaningful and significant to members, clearly stated in familiar terms, measurable, and challenging. Larson and LaFasto concluded that the main reason for failure in the fifty teams they studied was that personal goals superceded group goals.
2. A results-driven structure with clear role definitions, accountability, methods for monitoring performance, and an effective communication system that fosters fast and complete information exchange and documentation of issues and decisions.
3. Competent team members who have technical knowledge and skills necessary for the team's work. Members must also have social compe-

tencies. They must be able to work with others, desire to contribute to the group, and appreciate others' differences and contributions.

4. Unified commitment to the team and its success. This is fostered, first, by promoting participation of all members in making important and day-to-day decisions. Second, members must develop "high expectations for each other, expect that everyone else on the team will contribute to the extent that each is capable, and . . . become disturbed if a member pursues individual objectives at the expense of the team goal." [22]

5. A collaborative climate, characterized by open communication operating on the following principles: honesty (bringing all issues before the group and not hiding problems or exaggerating what one has done); willingness to share and receptivity to ideas, opinions, and positions; consistency in behavior; and respectful and dignified treatment of all people.

6. Standards of excellence that create pressure to perform at very high levels. Pressure to perform stems from having members who have a high motivation to excel, encouragement by other members to perform, a clear sense of the positive consequences of success and the negative consequences of failure, and external pressure from the organization. High standards are encouraged by models of excellence, especially other high-performing teams. Effective teams also continuously upgrade their standards as they meet or exceed them.

7. External support and recognition from the larger organization. The team must be given the resources and authority to succeed, and the organization must recognize and reward high performance.

8. Principled leadership that establishes a vision for the team and empowers members. The leader must also create change by realizing the need for change, reminding members that change is normal, and helping members through the change process. The goal of the effective team leader is to unify the team and enable members to "unleash their talent" in the team's work.

A group that organizes itself around these principles is designed to motivate its members to contribute to the organization and also to improve their knowledge and skills so they can contribute even more. Teams like this do not just spring into being with little or no work, but instead are cultivated over a period of time.

In line with the emphasis on participative decision making in the relational strategy, many organizations, including corporations such as Xerox and Proctor and Gamble, are attempting to promote the development of teams by setting them up so that they are "self-managing." **Self-managing teams** are intended to empower team members by enabling them to organize and govern themselves as they see best. In many cases, the team is also allowed to set its own goals. In a real sense, the team members serve as their own managers and leaders. The philosophy behind self-managing teams takes a page from the principles of empowerment discussed previously: If members are told what to do and kept in dependent positions, they are unlikely to develop the skills and motivation needed to create an effective team. But if members are given power and responsibility, they will see them as a privilege and rise to the occasion, learning the skills and attitudes of leaders by making their own mistakes and correcting their course. The self-managing team is currently the pinnacle of the relational strategy of organizing.

CASE STUDY
Empowerment or Iron Cage?

Xel Communications, a telecommunications manufacturing company located in the Denver suburbs, changed its manufacturing plant from a traditional hierarchy to a flattened design that depended on self-managed teams.* Xel made this change because Vice President Joe Painter became convinced that the company could survive in the highly competitive telecommunications market only if it was adaptive and innovative. He concluded that self-managed teams that harnessed all employees' energy and creativity were the most effective way to increase Xel's flexibility.

Self-managed teams are peer groups of ten to fifteen people totally responsible for the manufacture of major components. Members of the team make all the decisions and undertake all the work involved in manufacturing the components; they are also responsible for hiring and firing, obtaining materials, and general management of the team. If a self-managed team has a problem coordinating with another team, members of the two teams meet to come to a workable decision. J. R. Barker, C. W. Melville, and M. E. Pacanowsky observe, "These teams fit best in organizations characterized by interdependent tasks, complex processes, time sensitivity, and the need for rapid change and adaptation."

Xel implemented the new program gradually, starting with a trial team that performed well beyond anyone's expectations. Within eight months the plant had been reconfigured to accommodate three self-managing teams, labeled the red, the white, and the blue teams. Painter's role became that of a "coach," a consultant the teams could call on for advice and problem-solving suggestions. Otherwise the teams called their own shots, and were proud of their independence. In fact, at one point the white team encountered a crisis and sent their coordinator to ask Joe for advice. When she returned with an "order" from Joe about how to handle the situation, the team rebelled—they were angry and resentful that Joe would "order" a self-managing team to do anything. They confronted Joe and aired their grievance, at which time Joe told the white team that they were absolutely correct that they should make their own decisions and that Alma had misinterpreted his suggestion as an order. The members of the white team were pleased when their independence was confirmed. They felt they had learned to stand on their own two feet and take responsibility. They also had started to feel that the fate of the company rested in their hands. They were responsible for decisions that could make or break Xel.

Over time the team's empowerment confronted it with a thorny issue: what was it to do with members who had their own ideas about work and did not go along with the group's sense of what should be done? No longer were there supervisors around to write up employees who did not act as the team wanted them to. One particular problem was employees who arrived late and left work early. In theory members could set their own hours now that the team managed itself, and a degree of flexibility was seen as desirable by some members. However, when these members worked fewer hours than other members but received the same pay, it impaired the white team's ability to deliver orders in a timely fashion. At one of the team's daily 7:00 a.m. meetings, when the day's activities were planned and other decisions made, the members decided that everyone should arrive before the 7:00 a.m. meeting and work until 5:00 p.m. to meet the backlog of orders. A worker who arrived five or more minutes late would be docked a day's pay. When one late-arriving member protested the penalty, team members scolded her and refused to relax their rules. This and similar incidents had an interesting effect on the members of white team. They noted their fellow members' strictness and became afraid of it themselves. Moreover, having seen the team be hard on its own members, they were also not inclined to let other members "get by" by relaxing the norms. Over time, some members began to resent the rigidity of the white team, but it steadily increased its focus on the control system. Eventually the team wrote more and more rules, which were more and more concrete and restrictive. They began to talk more about following their very bureaucratic rules than about teamwork and commitment to Xel.

Stitchco,[†] a textile plant in the United Kingdom, underwent a similar change. Prior to the institution of a team system, all decisions were made by managers, and employees were rewarded individually based on their output. Workers who produced more than the "standard minute," determined through the "time-motion" studies described in Chapter 3, were rewarded; workers who did not were sanctioned. In the early 1990s the British textile industry was hit hard by foreign competition. Stitchco responded by closing half of its plants, without warning to the employees or the community, and converting the other half to a teamwork system. Management's goal was to increase flexibility and speed of manufacturing. One division was told that it would constantly be in competition with external suppliers, with a clear threat that manufacturing would be completely shifted outside the firm if the division failed to compete successfully. It was clear that an influential contingent of the company's top managers wanted to close manufacturing altogether, and that the division had been excluded from the decisions to close some operations and restructure the others. A complex accounting system was implemented to monitor the performance of the division in comparison to external producers.

Teams were made up of members who were classified as high, medium, and low performers based on their previous records. Workers were paid a flat rate, and bonuses were based on the performance of their teams as a whole. Initially the high performers resisted the change because they feared that their incomes would decline, but once the system was in operation, those fears dissipated. Team

(continued)

(Case Study, continued)

performance was monitored twice a day, and the results were posted where everyone in the plant could see them. Management hoped that the combination of team-based rewards and public displays would motivate the strongest performers in each team to teach and motivate the weaker performers to improve. Unfortunately, the strategy failed: "team members were not necessarily committed to improving or maximizing their collective output, especially if it meant compensating for . . . other team members [or resolving] conflicts over the allocation of work within the teams."[‡] In short, the self-managing teams refused to self-manage.

The failure stemmed from a number of factors. Perhaps most important, the workers understood the system too well: one machinist explained, "I prefer line work and piecework. . . . [Under teamwork] you've got to be the supervisor as well as the machinist. When you're working in a line you earn the money that you get. If you're having a bad day . . . the other girls don't suffer." The machinists received no training in supervisory skills and no separate rewards for playing that role. Others simply were not interested in the bonus system—they knew that they would get the "flat rate" if the group performed at 80 percent of the expected rate, and because they didn't have families to support, that was fine with them. Interpersonal problems also were quite frequent. Management placed workers on teams based solely on their past performance, which meant that some teams had members who had long-standing grievances with one another over issues like boyfriends. As a result, plant managers spent much of their time sorting out disagreements over issues that had nothing to do with the tasks being performed. In something of a paradox, the groups never coalesced into "teams" because they felt too connected to one another to "order one another around," but not connected enough to feel responsible for their peers' incomes.

Applying What You've Learned

1. What forms of control are characteristic of relational strategies of organizing?
2. How do those forms of control differ from control in traditional strategies?
3. A basic assumption of the now-extensive literature advocating the use of team systems is that teamwork provides a better quality of work life for employees, while improving organizational efficiency. Was this assumption true of these two companies? Why or why not?
4. What personal and interpersonal factors are involved in the success (or failure) of "relational" strategies like teamwork?

Questions to Think About and Discuss

1. Were the members of white team empowered, or trapped in a control system of their own creation?

2. Barker, Melville, and Pacanowsky conclude that employees who strongly identify with a firm are generally tougher managers for each other than hierarchical supervisors are. Do you agree or disagree with this?

3. Why might employees entrusted with managing their own team develop the strong surveillance and control system over other members that they did at Xel? Why might they refuse to do so, as they did at Stitchco?

4. Barker, Melville, and Pacanowsky argue that excessive (and even exploitative) control of self-managing teams over their members is harder to recognize and resist than the same type of control by managers. This is because members believe that the rules they are enforcing are legitimately made by a democratic process. As a result, they see the rules as more objective and legitimate than they might if a manager imposed them from outside. This seemed to be true of the white team at Xel but not the machinists at Stitchco. Why were the machinists able to avoid the cycle that appeared at Xel? Is it possible for the white team to break out of the spiral of control it has fallen into? What recommendations do you have for how it could do this?

*The first part of this case is based on J. R. Barker, "Tightening the Iron Cage: Concertive Control in Self-Managing Teams," *Administrative Science Quarterly* 38 (1993): 408–437; and J. R. Barker, C. W. Melville, and M. E. Pacanowsky, "Self-Directed Teams at Xel: Changes in Communication Practices during a Program of Cultural Transformation," *Journal of Applied Communication Research* 21 (1993): 297–313. Similar findings, in an overseas operation of a Japanese-owned electronics manufacturing plant, are available in Graham Sewell, "The Discipline of Teams: The Control of Team-Based Industrial Work through Electronic and Peer Surveillance," *Administrative Science Quarterly* 43 (1998): 397–428.

†The second part of the case is based on Mahmoud Ezzamel and Hugh Willmott, "Accounting for Teamwork: A Critical Study of Group-Based Systems of Organizational Control," *Administrative Science Quarterly* 43 (1998): 358–396. For a similar study of an organization in which team-based control was rather ineffective, see Alan McKinlay and Phil Taylor, "Power, Surveillance, and Resistance: Inside the Factory of the Future," in *The New Workplace and Trade Unionism,* Peter Ackers, Chris Smith, and Paul Smith, eds. (London: Routledge, 1996).

‡Ezzamel and Willmott, p. 379.

Although teams can be quite rewarding to participants and for the organization as a whole, as the Xel case study shows, they may also exert their own form of control over their members, control that may cause stress and even lead members to act against their best interests. Several characteristics of teams—the emphasis on unity and commitment and on high levels of performance, their ever-increasing standards, and the high levels of mutual responsibility among members—can set the stage for the development of extreme pressure to conform on members who are out of line with the group. When groups strongly identify with the organization, as at Xel, this pressure can serve as a stronger controlling force than a traditional hierarchical manager exerts. Philip K. Tompkins and George Cheney call this **concertive control** because, although it has many of the same results as control by top managers, it arises from the concerted action of peers.[23] In such cases, the team becomes just another body that represents managerial interests at the expense of worker development, empowerment, and other desirable results of the relational strategy. Members of controlling teams tend to fall back into a cycle of doing things the organization wants them to do, powerlessness, and in some cases the same type of resistance to the team that is common in hierarchical structures. However, concertive control is particularly effective because it is often much harder to recognize than control by managers or top-down rules. This is because members of the team have inadvertently developed the control system themselves, and they see it as a normal outgrowth of their work and tend not to recognize how it undermines participation. Concertive control is a special case of unobtrusive control, a strategy of control that figures importantly in the cultural strategies of organizing (the topic of Chapter 5).

Other kinds of teams, such as quality-improvement teams, have been criticized for similar reasons. Cynthia Stohl argues that though quality circles are often intended to enable employees to improve their work through participation, they frequently become tools of managerial control.[24] Only those suggestions that management is comfortable with are implemented, which in effect takes participation out of employee hands and turns quality-improvement efforts into instruments of organizational control. This is why former members of quality circles are among the least satisfied employees.[25] Scott Poole found examples of this in a large medical organization; several members of quality-improvement teams commented that had they known their efforts would be used to promote the agendas of management, they would not have participated in the first place. However, this reaction was not uniform: other members found the quality teams a great source of satisfaction and felt that their voices had been heard; some also believed participation had helped them develop their leadership skills and would help their careers. As with all systems of surveillance and control that develop in participative programs, control is less than perfect, resistance is possible, and some participation is real and meaningful.

Relational Strategies of Leadership

Although there are many different relational strategies of leadership, they all focus on improving supervisor-subordinate relationships through making them more trusting and more predictable. These goals are achieved by fostering open and supportive communication and by engaging in **transactional leadership.**

Fostering Open and Supportive Supervisor-Subordinate Communication

Early research on relational strategies of leadership found that high-producing organizations had supervisors who were highly competent in the technical aspects of their jobs and were also employee-centered and considerate. Effective supervisors express respect for, trust in, and a genuine concern about their subordinates. They set high but achievable performance goals for their units and communicate a kind of contagious enthusiasm about achieving them. They supervise loosely and actively encourage their subordinates to participate in decision making. They do not engage in superficial "pat-on-the-back" or "first-name" gimmicks, but emphasize a deeper concern for the group members' needs. They also do not make their subordinates feel uncomfortable or defensive.

When people feel that they are being judged (even praise creates discomfort if it is excessively strong or too public), manipulated (tricked into believing that they have an important role in the organization when they do not), controlled, "preached at," or otherwise treated as an inferior, they become defensive and withdraw from the relationship. Supervisors can create supportive, nondefensive climates by communicating in ways that are descriptive and objective rather than evaluative; that focus on working together to solve important problems; that are spontaneous, open, and honest; that affirm the subordinates' competence; and that encourage subordinates to initiate communication, even if doing so involves negative topics or information. Even orders can be given in a supportive way. The orders themselves need to be clear and specific, be perceived as logical and appropriate, and be legitimate in the sense that Weber used that term (that is, accepted as normal and proper by workers). Orders also need to be communicated in a way that allows subordinates to retain a sense of personal pride, self-respect, and autonomy—to feel that they are making a free and open choice to obey the order.[26]

Supportive communication also depends on the supervisor's listening skills and his or her ability to avoid disconfirming communication. Messages carry meaning at both content and relational levels—they provide information and they make a statement about the interpersonal relationship that exists between the communicators (see Chapter 7 for a more detailed discussion). Disconfirming communication occurs when a supervisor communicates in a way that does not acknowledge a subordinate's worth. For example, a young accountant waited two weeks to see her supervisor. After having meetings canceled, rescheduled, and canceled again; telephone calls cut off; and chance meetings in the hallway in which the supervisor did not even stop walking to say hello, the accountant finally got into a meeting. She explained that she did not understand the new tax laws on capital gains rates, and her supervisor responded, "This isn't my problem. Talk to the training department." Her long-awaited meeting lasted three minutes. Clearly, she concluded, her supervisor did not recognize that she existed, much less that she was an important part of the team. This does not mean that supervisors cannot disagree with their subordinates, because one can reject or question the content of persons' communications without rejecting their identities.[27] Open and supportive communication enhances trust, reduces withholding and distortion of information, and serves as a basis for transactional leadership.

Transactional Leadership

Supervisor-subordinate communication is a two-way, interactive process. Although supervisors tend to have a greater impact on communicative relationships than their subordinates because of their formal authority, interpersonal relationships develop because of the mutual exchanges that take place between the parties. This is the primary assumption underlying transactional views of leadership. Leaders, according to this model, must legitimate their position—formal rank alone does not make one a leader—but legitimation is a two-way street. Leaders and each of their followers negotiate working relationships. Both parties align themselves with each other; they converge toward the same set of values, are able to solve complex and unprecedented problems together, and have a relaxed, mutually supportive relationship. Eventually, they become co-oriented—they reach agreement on the rules that guide their relationship (for example, what topics they will discuss and what topics they will avoid, whether they must schedule meetings or can just pop into each other's office, whether to use first names or titles, whether they interrupt each other or quietly wait until the other is finished talking to respond). They negotiate a trusting relationship, one in which their motives, intentions, openness, and integrity are consistent, in which they are dependably competent, willing, and able to help each other with job-related problems, and in which they consider each other's judgment reliable.

Even supportive communication is mutual and transactional. Trust, respect, and task factors, such as risk-taking and innovation, have all been shown to be greatest when supervisors are supportive of their own supervisors and their subordinates perceive that they receive high levels of support. In other words, both the level of support and the level of agreement about the level of support are important factors. Supervisors and subordinates support one another by talking about how organizations work (for example, discussing potential career moves and their likely effects); by helping develop new skills or giving one another tangible assistance when it is needed (for example, a director of programming jumping in to help solve a knotty language problem and doing so cheerfully without a this-will-cost-you-later attitude); by providing an outlet for venting anger or frustration (serving as a sounding board); or by offering praise, acceptance, or reassurance. Regardless of the specific technique that is used, it is the mutual support that supervisors and subordinates give one another that is important.[28]

In sum, transactional views of leadership focus on the development of particular kinds of supervisor-subordinate relationships. They recognize that neither person is wholly in charge of the process and that supervisors will often have different kinds of relationships with different subordinates.

Leadership and Group Decision Making

In Western societies people are taught to assume that groups must have a designated leader or leaders. In most organizations, the leader is identified before the group begins its work, either explicitly when person X is ordained as chairperson, or implicitly when members realize that person X is the group member who has the highest status in the organization. If no leader is appointed or selected for the group, the group has three options: designate one person as leader from the outset, take a chance that a leader will emerge, or hope that the different members of the group can share leadership tasks efficiently and smoothly. The second and third options have their advantages, but they are also risky. When the group allows a leader to emerge naturally, the person best suited to the task and the group often rises to the occasion. Emergent leaders are generally more effective than leaders appointed by management. However, the danger in the emergence option is that no leader will emerge or that competing candidates will split the group. Sharing among all members develops every member's skills and commitment to the group; but members must be very conscientious, or important issues may slip through the cracks.

Groups with clearly identified leaders are often more efficient, have fewer interpersonal problems, and produce better decisions, provided the leader is competent and can effectively organize the group. This does not mean that leaderless groups are doomed to failure. It just means that they will have problems unless members have the right mix of leadership skills and exercise them effectively. Another strategy for a leaderless group or self-managed team is to rotate leadership; this builds all members' skills and also gives the team one clear point of responsibility without assigning power to one person on a permanent basis.[29]

What role should a leader play in group decision making? Leaders have three options: they can make the decision themselves, they can consult with the group and then make the decision themselves, or they can have the group make the decision. An important model developed by Victor Vroom and Peter Yetton advanced some rules to help leaders decide which method to use. According to their model, either consultation or group decision making should be used when the quality of the decision is critical and when the leader does not have sufficient information to make the decision herself or himself. The group model should be used when members' acceptance of the decision is important. But the leader should make the decision singly or after consulting the members if the members do not share the organization's goals. If quality is not important, any of the methods can be used, depending on what seems best for the group at the time.[30] Two additional factors that must be considered are the amount of time the group has to make a decision and the cost of convening the group. If time is short and cost high, the recommendation is to have the leader make the decision or consult in an efficient manner.

When the group is making the decision, the leader's role should fulfill three functions. Leadership means influencing members' *perceptions of themselves* — motivating them to contribute to the group and to feel committed to it and its task. Leadership also involves influencing members' *perceptions of the group*. It means focusing the group's attention on the group's goals and the role that each step has in the group's meeting those goals. The leader needs to make members feel that the group is an autonomous entity by minimizing references to outside pressures, involving members in decisions about tasks and procedures, taking each member's comments seriously, and building the group's confidence that it can make a good decision.

Finally, leadership means influencing the *pace* and *direction* of the discussion and the *decisions* made by the group. In general, leaders should avoid acting like advocates, especially early in the group's history; they should adopt a participative style that invites members' contributions and follows their ideas.[31] If the leader jumps in too early or too forcefully, members are discouraged from sharing their ideas and expertise, reducing the advantages of group decision making. However, leaders are generally selected because of their perspective or expertise, and there are times when the group needs to have the benefit of the leader's resources.

Members who are not identified as leaders also play important roles. Group tasks are too large or complex to be performed by individuals. Consequently, the group needs the expertise and efforts of all members. But commitment is rarely high in all members or equal among all of them. One problem in groups, especially those larger than six or seven members, is the "free-rider" problem, wherein several members do not contribute their effort fairly and take advantage of other members' work.[32] You may have experienced this yourself with classroom group projects. The opposite extreme, when members are excessively committed to the group, is equally damaging. Groups benefit from disagreement, from constructive conflict. When members agree for the sake of agreeing, the group does not benefit from their expertise or from the careful testing of ideas and evidence that comes from positive confrontation. The primary obligation of group members is to act as valuable members of a cooperative activity and to undertake communication functions, such as summarizing, contributing ideas, encouraging other members, and energizing the group.

Information and Communication Technology and Relational Strategies of Organizing

Several information and communication technologies (ICTs) support participation, groups, and informal networks, the keystones of the relational strategies. The most familiar is e-mail. E-mail is a fast and effective linking mechanism, for several reasons. It enables communication between people who are on different schedules, because it can be read and answered whenever convenient for the receiver. It is also less intrusive than a phone call or face-to-face contact; the recipient can reply on his or her own schedule. Hence, e-mail encourages communication between people who do not know each other well, who differ in status, or who are in different units that do not have formal relationships. E-mail also allows the sending of broadcast messages—requests or memos sent to a large group of recipients, even to the whole organization. This capability enables people who do not know whom to ask to gather information and create links. The end result is that e-mail tends to increase lateral communication between people at the same level of the organization and contacts across organizational levels, enhancing relational linkage in organizations.[33]

When e-mail systems are implemented, the total amount of communication within an organization or work group increases and the use of the telephone and written memos decreases somewhat, although face-to-face communication increases. Thus the electronic media seem to supplement, rather than replace, traditional media.[34] The information exchanged via electronic media does not seem to be any more or less accurate than information exchanged through other media, although people tend to be less confident of its accuracy. In face-to-face communication, we rely on vocal cues (pitch, rate of speech, loudness) and nonverbal cues to confirm our interpretations of the meanings of the words that people use. Because these cues are less readily available or are absent in mediated communication, we feel less secure in our interpretations.

Use of e-mail seems also to be affected by the user's relationships. Studies have shown that the adoption and degree of use of e-mail are significantly influenced by the user's closest co-workers and others in the same communication network. These effects are even stronger in cohesive groups.[35] Once formed, groups joined by e-mail seem to reinforce members' continued use.

There are also costs to e-mail, notably message overload. In e-mail-intensive organizations, it is not unusual to receive more than fifty messages a day. (One manager in an information technology firm came back from a two-week vacation to find more than a thousand messages waiting!) Sorting through this to separate the junk mail from the important messages can take much time and energy. Some have worried about the impersonal nature of computer-mediated communication. However, studies have generally shown that this medium can be as personal as any other, once users master it.[36] The style of electronic messages often is less formal than that of written messages, and people seem to think less about social norms and hierarchical relationships when constructing electronic messages than when constructing messages for other media. Their communication may be less inhibited—they may express extreme emotions overtly (a process called *flaming*) and swear more often. Of course, groups of people develop and enforce cultural expectations that require users to refrain from flaming or to engage in other patterns of communicating, such as reading and responding to e-mail messages within a specified period of time.[37]

The availability of electronic message networks also allows people to address messages by topic rather than by the name of the recipient. Employees who are unhappy about a recent management decision can instantaneously locate other people who also are unhappy, share their gripes, circulate résumés, and help one another look for new jobs, as R. Emmett observed in a large computer organization.[38] Of course, this highly efficient means of letting angry employees know that other people share their sentiments was probably not what upper management had in mind when it purchased the systems.

Other ICTs that enable messaging, including instant messaging, short messenger services, wireless mobile devices, paging, and voice mail, have a similar effect to that of e-mail. All enlarge the social networks of users and hence enable relational connections to be made more easily.[39] One exciting advance that is just beginning to diffuse through U.S. organizations is **unified messaging,** systems that integrate e-mail, voice mail, and faxes in a single message system. This technology has the potential to reduce the complexity of current communication systems, which often require multiple systems.[40]

There are also ICTs that support participation and decision making in groups. **Groupware** refers to various technologies that support the work of groups or teams. Groupware is typically used for two purposes: to help groups generate ideas and make decisions and to help teams coordinate projects.

To help groups make better decisions, some groupware incorporates formal decision tools, such as idea generation (brainstorming), problem-solving sequences, analysis methods, and evaluation tools (such as voting and rating). These systems, called Group Support Systems (GSSs), have enjoyed increasing use over the past ten years. GSSs are often used to help groups that meet face-to-face make important decisions or resolve conflicts; but they can also be used to help coordinate dispersed groups. Figure 4-3 shows a typical GSS for rela-

FIGURE 4–3
Small Decision Room with Group Decision Support system

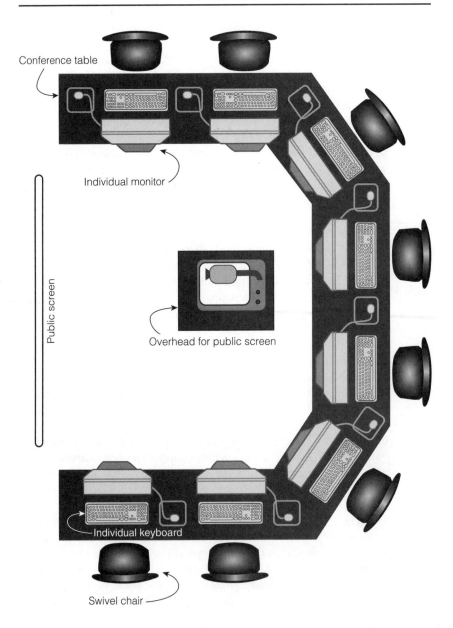

Conference table

Individual monitor

Public screen

Overhead for public screen

Individual keyboard

Swivel chair

tively small face-to-face groups. In recent years Internet-enabled GSSs for distributed or virtual groups have been developed as well.

Each member has her or his own computer, and the group can view on a public screen the results of activities such as brainstorming or a vote. The menu for this GSS gives the group a number of decision procedures to work with, including idea generation, idea evaluation, and decision procedures, such as multi-attribute decision analysis (which enables groups to evaluate options on many criteria), stakeholder analysis (which enables groups to conduct analysis of the political climate surrounding a decision), and problem formulation. GSSs have been shown to increase the number and quality of ideas considered by groups, to enable more effective conflict management, and in some cases to promote more effective decision making.[41] However, this depends on whether the group uses the GSS to promote member input and participation. In groups that do not use the GSS in this way, the benefits are not as likely to materialize.

A second, more common, use of groupware is to support work groups in carrying out both short- and long-term projects. Lotus Notes and Microsoft Exchange are two of the systems that have been developed for this purpose. These systems combine features from office automation, electronic workflow linkage, and computer conferencing systems into a bundle of tools for a group; these tools can be used by groups working in the same office or building or by geographically dispersed groups. A typical work-group support system, such as Lotus Notes, includes document management, scheduling features, e-mail notification, and computer discussion groups. The discussion groups are similar to computer conferences in that they contain discussion threads, which are lines of discussion on a single topic arranged in statement-response format. Figure 4-4 contains an example of threaded discussions organized by topic. Under each topic a response to a statement is indented to indicate what it is addressed to. Discussion topics can vary widely, from a general discussion of policies to specific updates on a particular task. Other features that may be incorporated into a work-group support system include audio- or videoconferencing over the Internet, project-management tools that keep a diagram of the project and monitor progress, and libraries to store commonly used documents. In addition, organizations may program their own specific applications into the system; an accounting firm, for example, may want to have its software connect with the work-group system. At present, the most widely used work-group softwares are Lotus Notes and Microsoft Exchange, which require organizations to buy and support specialized software. However, during 2003 and 2004 , several work-group systems that can be used through Internet browsers were developed and implemented.

Teams that use work-group support systems typically have to change their mode of operation, because the systems require members to diligently check in and enter their own work and documents. These systems generally encourage groups to be more structured in how they work and make decisions, because the group has to "think out loud" about how it is going to proceed as it decides how to break up its work into tasks and decides on discussion topics. Although

FIGURE 4-4
An Example of a Threaded Discussion from a Workgroup Support System

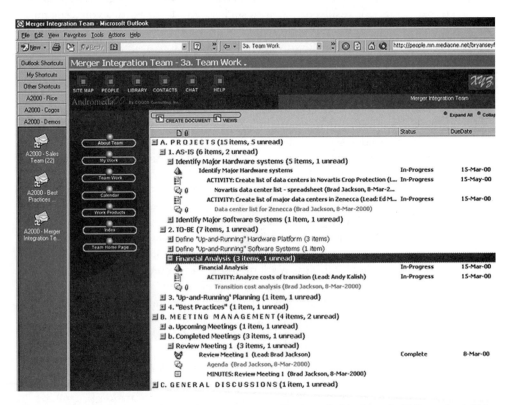

This is an example of a team work space in a groupware application called Andromeda (© Cogos, Inc.). This is a team at Cogos, Inc., whose members are in four different places, Boston, MA, Houston, TX, rural Pennsylvania, and Minneapolis, MN. There are two major topics in this space, Projects and Meeting Management. The entries under "Projects" refer to various companies that this team is working with. The entries under "Meeting Management" refer to virtual meetings the team will conduct online.

The Projects are divided into two types, "As-Is" and "To-Be," which reflect special meanings for this team's members. Under "As-Is" there are two major topics of discussion, which refer to actions the team is taking. "Identify Major Hardware Systems" has under it five comments. A comment is indented if it is a response to a previous comment. So "Activity: Create a list of data centres in Novartis Crop Protection . . ." is a response to the topic "Identify Major Hardware Systems." Items are labeled according to whether they are simply comments (which have no prefix) or refer to activities (which have the "Activity" prefix to the comment). To read a comment a team member would simply click on the heading and it would come up in his or her screen with options to reply, vote, etc.

This type of software also enables members to remind each other when an activity is due, update each other as to whether it has been done, enter items in a library, monitor other teams' work, and many other activities.

groups initially try to use their own typical procedures in the system, over time, their style of working adapts to the system itself. For example, a team that typically did not get feedback from all members on an idea would be likely to develop a norm favoring more input and feedback if it faithfully used the discussion features of a work-group system.

The most direct application of work-group support systems is for the groups themselves, but the systems can also be used to link teams and people across entire organizations. Teams can be given access to each other's discussions and time lines, and discussion groups that anyone who is interested may join can also be set up. For example, a major oil company used Lotus Notes to set up project support for more than thirty teams and gave members of other teams limited access to most of these "team spaces." This enabled members of related teams to find out what other teams were doing, helped coordinate work between teams, and allowed teams to learn from each other. In addition, general discussion groups were initiated on various topics, including general-interest topics such as movies and the company's charitable projects, and specific topics such as Microsoft Office and techniques for three-dimensional analysis of oil deposits. These general discussion groups enabled people from all over the organization to get to know one another and share ideas; they also built organizational cohesiveness. A few executives complained that the general discussion groups wasted company time, because they were not related to specific project support. However, the chief information officer argued for and succeeded in preserving the discussion groups on the grounds that they encouraged employees who otherwise might be unwilling to learn the new technology to try it out and that they generally led to a more connected organization.

Work-group support systems are used by more than 10 million people, according to the combined estimates of sales by Lotus and Microsoft. The number is larger than this if we include the increasing number of groups that are using groupware provided by online companies such as Yahoo. However, despite the impressive figures in terms of sales and signups for online companies, the actual number of users is probably a good deal smaller, because in most cases some team members either do not learn the software (which is difficult and confusing at first) or are low-level participants. Such members are more common in teams located in a single facility than in teams dispersed over several different locations, because the co-located teams also have the option of meeting face to face. The browser-based systems, which are expected to be the future of groupware, are more likely to have larger proportions of members actually using them, because they are more familiar to people already using the Internet.

Assessing Relational Strategies

There are many criteria that might be used to evaluate a strategy of organizing and its associated motivation and control strategy and approach to leadership. Two commonly used criteria are employees' job satisfaction and organizational performance and profitability.

Relational Strategies and Employee Job Satisfaction

Relational strategies, both PDM and transactional leadership, do lead to increased job satisfaction. This impact has been shown to be rather small from a practical standpoint, but it does seem to occur consistently, regardless of the kind of organization being studied or the specific research method employed. The effect is strongest for employees near the bottom of the organizational hierarchy and for people who need large amounts of information to do their jobs well. But whatever the specifics of a work situation, employees in open, supportive communication climates are satisfied employees.[42]

Creating and maintaining high levels of job satisfaction is important for many reasons. Perhaps most important, work groups composed of satisfied people simply are more pleasant to work in. Because most people spend much of their lives at work, this may be sufficient justification for the use of relational strategies. There also are some more tangible benefits. Job dissatisfaction has consistently been linked to high levels of absenteeism and voluntary turnover. When employees who perform important tasks are missing, other employees feel increased stress, and organizational performance declines. When the costs of searching for and training replacement personnel are high, voluntary turnover is costly. When the economy is strong, as it was in the United States during the 1990s, voluntary turnover can be extremely expensive. For example, in 1999 Ford Motor Company agreed to establish thirty round-the-clock "Family Service and Learning Centers" at their largest locations. These centers provide child and elder care, formal and informal education programs, health screenings, and limited health care. They are primarily designed to address the lack of affordable child care for working parents, especially for those who work the night shift. Former Ford president Jacques Nasser said, "It's not low cost, but we're not wasting a cent. This is an effort to attract and retain talent because turnover costs money."[43] Of course, other factors also influence turnover. Relationships with co-workers are important, especially to lower-level employees. So are factors such as the legacy of downsizing and the end of loyalty described in Chapter 1. But the primary factor seems to be satisfaction with supervision. In a 1999 survey by Lou Harris associates, employees who were dissatisfied with their supervisor-subordinate relationship were four times as likely to be looking for other jobs than were satisfied employees. A 1999 Gallup poll found that a caring boss is a more important determinant of job satisfaction than either money or fringe benefits. The researcher in charge of the study concluded that "people join companies, but they leave managers."

PDM and Individual/Organizational Performance

Participatory systems have a number of positive effects. In U.S. firms, formal, company-wide programs of participation still are rare, although their popularity has increased during the last few years (see Chapter 3). Informal programs of participation, in which supervisors ask their most productive employees for advice or information, are more widespread. Subordinates respond with useful advice, which increases their supervisors' trust in their judgment and encourages them to seek further advice, and their job satisfaction increases, which reduces absenteeism and voluntary turnover. Somewhat surprisingly, these positive effects do not result from subordinates feeling that participation gives them greater power, primarily because PDM in U.S. firms is structured and operated in ways that largely maintain gaps in power. Instead, positive effects arise from subordinates' sense of being better informed about what is going on in the organization. During participatory interactions, supervisors provide information and a more open and satisfying communicative relationship is created.

Systems of participation have more limited effects on performance and productivity. In general, the quality of decisions made by participatory groups is better than that of decisions made by the "average" member of the group but is worse than the decision that would be made by the group's most expert individual. This does not suggest that better decisions would be made by a supervisor acting alone, for the simple reason that the supervisor may or may not be the most expert member of a work group. It just suggests that the positive effects of PDM depend on various factors, including the distribution of expertise in the group. Research on the effects of participation on productivity is less favorable. Some studies have found that participation does motivate workers to perform more effectively and more efficiently. In other cases, participation gives supervisors an opportunity to persuade their subordinates to accept high performance goals. But overall, research on participation indicates that participation does not automatically increase organizational productivity.[44]

Cynthia Stohl and George Cheney have explained these results by focusing on the paradoxical nature of participatory systems. One group of paradoxes involves the design and operation of PDM systems (what they call "paradoxes of structure"). Typically, PDM systems are imposed by management, so that the overall message given to employees is "be spontaneous, creative, vocal, and assertive *in the way that we have planned!*" (emphasis added). A secondary message usually is "be democratic, but don't take much time doing it." Over time, the process becomes so tightly constrained, and so routine, that its advantages disappear. "Paradoxes of agency" are similar and occur because employees are told to "do things in your own way, but make sure that's it's our way." Individuals often wind up handing the limited power that is made available to them over to the group. "Paradoxes of identity" hark back to the "fundamental paradox" that we described in Chapter 1, because the message sent is "Be *self*-managing, but do so in order to meet the goals of the organization." "Paradoxes of control" occur when participatory groups are more controlling than traditional strategies, a process that we will examine in the following section. We would add a final paradox, that managers tend to adopt PDM systems because they are a popular fad and thus help legitimate managers as "up-to-date" experts in their fields (see Chapter 12), or as a last resort when their firms are failing. Although properly designed and implemented PDM systems can enhance organizational performance and profitability, they rarely are able to offset the economic strains or unwise managerial strategies that pushed a firm to the edge of bankruptcy. Ironically, some very successful PDM systems were created after firms closed. For example, when Argentina's economy collapsed in early 2002, many managers simply shut the doors of their factories and walked away, often owing their employees months of back pay. Instead of giving up, many workers, backed by neighborhood associations, persuaded the bankruptcy courts to let them reopen the plants. After eighteen months, at least 150 factories employing more than ten thousand people were being run as cooperatives. They are run by plant councils, which, like plant managers, are elected by the workers. By equalizing wages— everyone from the plant manager to custodians gets the same salary—they have been able to double the average wages paid to the workers. They are willing to make sacrifices for the organization because of "the commitment we feel to something that is our own." Of course, the cooperatives face challenges (we will discuss the difficulties facing alternative forms of organizing in Chapter 7). Their ability to expand is limited because the banks are unwilling to make loans to them, but they have managed to find other sources of funding. Now that the economy has improved, many of the former owners have gone to court in an effort to regain control of the properties. But at this point, the Argentinean cooperatives provide testimony to the effectiveness of truly participatory systems.[45]

Transactional Leadership and Individual/Organizational Performance

Transactional leadership is based on the assumption that improving communication will increase morale and motivation, which in turn will increase individual and organizational performance. Ironically, at least in production-oriented firms, relational strategies do have positive effects on performance—but not for the reasons described in the strategy. First of all, the primary assumption of the relational strategy does not seem to be accurate: high levels of job satisfaction do not inevitably lead to high levels of individual or organizational performance. Of course, it does makes sense intuitively that satisfied workers will work harder and perform better than dissatisfied workers; if people are happy at work, they should be more committed to their organization and thus should want to work harder to make sure their organizations succeed. However, fifty years of research on the relationship between job satisfaction and performance has not found strong relationships between the two. The average correlation is 0.14, which means that about 2 percent of differences in employees' performance can be attributed to differences in their job satisfaction. Instead, this research indicates either that high performance leads to high job satisfaction (because workers feel pride in a job well done) or that other factors simultaneously increase both satisfaction and performance. For instance, if workers value hard work and high levels of performance for their own sake, or if they believe they will receive tangible rewards from high performance, they tend to be both satisfied and productive. If they do not hold these beliefs, they tend to be both dissatisfied and relatively unproductive regardless of the strategy of organizing used in their organizations. People who are trapped in an autocratic, alienating organization because they have few employment opportunities; because of their race, gender, ethnic background, lack of education, or disabilities; or because of the general economic situation are often dissatisfied but highly productive because they are afraid of losing their jobs. Conversely, people whose nonwork lives are fulfilling may expend only the minimum amount of effort necessary to keep their jobs regardless of how satisfied they are at work. In short, the work world seems to be relatively full of people who smile a lot and do very little and people who smile not at all and do a lot.[46]

So relational strategies do not necessarily improve productivity by increasing morale. But they do seem to pay off for other reasons. Open and supportive supervisory communication helps compensate for the problems in formal communication that are described in Chapter 3. Openness creates trust, and trust reduces the withholding or distorting of information. Open and supportive communication is especially valuable for subordinates who have complex and ambiguous jobs. They need a great deal of task-related information and advice that only their supervisors can provide. It is difficult to ask for help from a closed and unsupportive supervisor. If they do not ask for information or help, it is more difficult for them to master their complex tasks, which makes it more likely that they will make errors. Subordinates who make frequent mistakes lose their supervisors' trust, which perpetuates the negative cycle.[47] As Chapter 6 will explain in more detail, these advantages are especially important to organizations in highly competitive, turbulent environments. Relational leadership (as well as decentralized structures and PDM) creates open, relatively free-flowing communication systems. Boundary-spanners can obtain information from the environment and rapidly disseminate that information to other employees who will be able to draw on multiple kinds of expertise to solve complicated, unprecedented problems. For example, Taiwan and Hong Kong, and more recently mainland China, have built their economic success around family businesses. These organizations have thrived in highly competitive, global environments because they are more flexible, less bureaucratic, and have greater employee commitment than large private or state-owned companies. They also innovate more rapidly and are quicker to adopt new product lines.[48]

Relational strategies also seem to have a positive influence on the performance of service-related organizations, which now constitute more than half of U.S. firms. When employees communicate with clients or customers, they tend to mirror their communication relationship with their supervisors. If their supervisors are not warm, supportive, and open with them, they will not be so with their clients and customers. Alienated subordinates create alienated customers, who may take their business elsewhere. For example, the late 1990s were a disastrous time for Northwest Airlines, the fourth largest carrier in the United States. Beginning with serious labor problems in 1995, the public's opinion of the airline plummeted, culminating in a 1999 snowstorm in Detroit when angry passengers were left sitting in planes for eight hours. Faced with economic disaster, members of Northwest's management asked some of its best customers (then a small and rapidly declining number of people) to tell them what they could do to turn the airline around. The customers blamed the airline's image problem on poor supervisor-subordinate relationships. One told them that "your employees do care and a lot of them are frustrated by lack of response from Northwest's management"; another advised them to "focus on respect for your employees and they will undoubtedly deliver." Management responded by trying to improve supervisor-subordinate communication. Within a year, Northwest's regular customers saw a difference. Tom Bagget, a customer from Memphis, Tennessee, noted, "Northwest is going from an almost adversarial relationship with employees to cooperation." Northwest's experience, and the experiences of similar firms like Southwest Airlines and Kaiser Permanente of Oakland, California, makes it clear that improving superior-subordinate communication pays immediate dividends in improving employee-customer relationships. For service organizations, high customer satisfaction yields bottom-line benefits: it increases profit margins, reduces marketing costs while increasing them for the competition, enhances the organization's reputation, and lowers many of the costs of doing business.[49]

Thinking Critically about Relational Strategies of Organizing

Throughout this chapter we have examined relational strategies largely in terms of their effect on organizational performance and effectiveness. The dominant assumption among managers and management theorists is that there should be positive effects. However, an important part of understanding organizations and organizational communication is being able to think critically about taken-for-granted views. On the surface, relational strategies do seem to create better work situations than traditional strategies, but that impression masks some important realities about all strategies of organizing. Two key concepts are especially important for understanding critical theories of organizing—interests and legitimate participation.[50]

Thinking Critically about Interests

At one level, owners, managers, and workers all seem to have many interests in common, including the long-term survival of their organization. On a closer look, it becomes clear that all three groups have some self-interests that are different from, and contradictory to, the interests of the other groups. For example, workers almost always have a strong vested interest in the continued operation of their firms in a particular locale and with stable or increasing real (adjusted for inflation) wages. When plants are closed or relocated, workers usually lose their jobs and have difficulty finding comparable employment elsewhere. Even if they are offered employment in other plants, relocating is psychologically and financially costly, especially for workers who have not previously moved. Similarly, reductions in wages or benefits can be devastating for workers, and programs to increase organizational productivity through technological innovations often lead to layoffs or a lowered standard of living.

Managers usually benefit little from maintaining the long-term viability of their organizations or increasing their workers' job security. This is because managers rarely are owners, especially in large firms. They are not entrepreneurs whose vision, ideas, and hard work built an organization to which they are psychologically and financially committed. Indeed, their careers usually involve moving rather often from one organization to another. Their rewards are based on the short-term profitability of the firm, especially now that a large proportion of managers' total income is based on year-end performance bonuses. Consequently, they may have little self-interest involved in the firm's long-term success and a great deal of interest in downsizing, reducing workers' wages and benefits, and replacing workers with new technologies. Because each of these steps is likely to increase the firm's short-term profitability, they will increase the managers' economic gains. They also may increase managers' salaries, bonuses, and job security because they also serve the financial interests of investors. For example, Alan Downs found that in U.S. firms during the 1990s, the number of jobs that a CEO eliminated was a better predictor of his or her compensation than the overall performance of her or his firm.[51] Similarly, successful strategies of motivation and control tend to serve management's interests much more than workers' interests. Even if they do lead to increased organizational effectiveness and profitability, most of the resulting rewards will go to management and investors, not to workers.

Two highly publicized cases illustrate this point. During the 1980s, Frank Lorenzo was the CEO of Texas Air, the parent company of Continental Airlines and Eastern Airlines. Although Continental and Eastern regularly lost $200 million or more each year and entered bankruptcy proceedings three times, Lorenzo regularly received annual performance bonuses of more than $1 million. When Eastern finally went out of business, its owners (creditors) received approximately three cents for each dollar they had invested in the airline. Similarly, during the late 1980s and early 1990s, Lee Iacocca decided to move much of Chrysler's production operation overseas (primarily to Mexico and the Far East). These steps cost thousands of autoworkers their jobs, but they also increased Chrysler's profits (or, initially, reduced its losses) and the value of its stock. Iacocca was rewarded with multimillion-dollar annual performance bonuses and one of the largest retirement bonuses in American history. Iacocca could have taken a different approach to revitalizing Chrysler—reducing stock dividends and reinvesting the funds in improved production technologies, as many German automakers did, or reducing the massive gap between worker income and managerial salaries, as Japanese automakers did, or reducing overhead by restraining managerial salaries. There is little evidence that Chrysler's management (or the management of virtually any large U.S. organization) ever seriously considered these approaches. In sum, actions that may be in management's self-interest may violate the short- and long-term interests of workers and owners and vice versa. Most of the corporate scandals that rocked the United States during 2001–2003 (see Chapter 12 for a more detailed analysis) involved egregious behaviors that enriched upper management at the expense of all other stakeholders.

However, the conflicting nature of these interests is often disguised by the discourse of modern organizations, a process that Jürgen Habermas has labeled **systematically distorted communication.**[52] One way of disguising the contradictions is to treat one set of interests (for example, management's) as everyone's interests. Installing a computerized system for monitoring employees'

work is usually justified in terms of its increased efficiency and the firm's enhanced ability to compete (recall Chapter 2). Efficiency and increased competitiveness are presented as being in everyone's interests. In the long run, they may
or may not be, depending on a large number of considerations. But in the short
term, the new system increases management's control and workers' stress and
has no guaranteed effects on either workers' or stockholders' incomes, because
management may not choose to pass the savings on to either group. Another
way of disguising the contradictions is to simply deny that they exist.[53] Simple
forms of denial include refusing to discuss a topic or denying that one's actions
meant what they seemed to mean. ("Of course I wasn't trying to get rid of you.
I just wanted you to have the excitement of working in Kandahar.") A more
complicated mode of denial is pacification, a process through which legitimate
conflicts are treated as unimportant, or mere communication breakdowns, as
when managerial discourse suppresses grievances through defining the organization as a team or family in which all the members are in it together. Another way
of disguising contradictory interests is disqualifying some interest groups, as in
"This is a managerial problem, and you just don't have the information necessary to understand it fully." If events are also defined as inevitable or unavoidable
(layoffs during recessions, for example) or value-neutral ("We have to base our
personnel decisions on the data, not on how we feel"), they cannot be discussed,
much less challenged. (Recall the discussion of hegemony in Chapter 2.)[54]
Whatever the specific technique, the effect of organizational discourse often is
to disguise or redefine the conflicting interests of workers, managers, and owners. Relational strategies often disguise this conflict.

Thinking Critically about Empowerment

Legitimate programs of participation and transactional leadership empower
workers throughout the organization. To be legitimate, relational strategies must
be valued for their own sake, as a means of ensuring that the legitimate interests
of all organizational groups are represented in decisions. This means that the
strategies cannot be justified solely because they increase organizational efficiency, unless they involve guarantees that increased efficiency will fulfill the interests of all organizational stakeholders. Legitimate participation entails equal
opportunities to communicate. This sounds simple, as when women's con-
sciousness-raising groups use "talking sticks" (a system adopted from Native
Americans in which someone must be holding a particular object in order to be
allowed to speak) to ensure that all members get an equal number of speaking
turns. Contrast this system with Michael Huspek's study of communication in a
lumberyard. Although the company presumably had an "open door" policy for
workers to express their grievances, managers demanded that those discussions
take place in the technical, legalistic language of management. Because the workers literally did not know how to speak that language, they were often literally
unable to say a word during grievance sessions. As important, their inability to
express themselves led them to believe that they did not know enough to have
the right to challenge their supervisors.[55] The research on supervisory resistance

to PDM that was summarized earlier in this chapter provides additional examples of relational strategies that de-power instead of empowering.

Legitimate empowerment programs also ensure equal opportunities to influence a work group's decisions. Doing so involves giving all employees all of the information that is relevant to the decisions being made and valuing all of the conceptions of truth expressed by members of the group. For example, single parents' reports of their own frustrating experiences in seeking adequate child care must be respected as much as the results of management's surveys on child-care issues. Empowerment also means that conflicts within the group will not be resolved through appeals to some external higher authority (as in "It's a great idea, but the CEO will never buy it"). The relational strategies that are used in contemporary organizations often include only an illusion of empowerment. As long as participatory systems are used without making major changes in organizational power relationships, managerial interests will be privileged. The existence of the hierarchy and the right of management to make final decisions—including how, when, where, over what issues, and with what outcomes participation will occur—will continue to be treated as natural and normal. When workers are trained to participate in decision making (or quality-control programs, or quality-of-working life groups), they are taught to make decisions on criteria (such as efficiency) and through processes that favor the interests of management.[56] But the discourse surrounding relational strategies of organizing often presents them as systems for fulfilling the interests of all stakeholders.

Notes

[1] Angela Michelle Chiles and Theodore Zorn, "Empowerment in Organizations: Employees' Perceptions of the Influences on Empowerment," *Journal of Applied Communication Research* 23 (1995): 1-25. The concept of empowerment is popular in contemporary organizational theory and will appear repeatedly throughout this book. One of the most important lines of research underlying the relational strategy was conducted by Arnold Tannenbaum and his associates. They found that in many kinds of organizations in both capitalist and socialist countries, employees believe that they exercise far less influence over decisions that affect them directly than does upper management. Tannenbaum found, however, that the most productive organizations and departments were ones in which all employees, even those at the bottom of the organizational hierarchy, perceived that they had substantial influence over decisions (see Arnold Tannenbaum, "Control in Organizations," *Administrative Science Quarterly* 7 [1962]: 17-42).

[2] See George Cheney, Lars Christensen, Theodore Zorn Jr., and Shiv Ganesh, *Organizational Communication in an Age of Globalization* (Prospect Heights, IL: Waveland Press, 2004); Cynthia Stohl and George Cheney, "Participatory Processes/Paradoxical Practices," *Management Communication Quarterly* 14 (2001): 349-407.

[3] See Cheney et al.; Cynthia Stohl, "European Managers' Interpretations of Participation," *Human Communication Research* 20 (1993): 108-131.

[4] David Jamieson and Julie O'Mara, *Managing Workforce 2000* (San Francisco: Jossey-Bass, 1991). Also see David Seibold and Christine Shea, "Participation and Decision-Making," in *The New Handbook of Organizational Communication,* Fredric Jablin and Linda Putnam, eds. (Thousand Oaks, CA: Sage, 2000); Virginia P. Richmond and K. David Roach, "Willingness to Communicate and Employee Success in U.S. Organizations," *Journal of Applied Communication Research* 20 (1992): 95-115; and Chris Foreman, "The Reality of Workplace Democracy: A Case Study of One Company's Employee Involvement Process," paper presented at the International Communication Association Convention, Chicago, May 1996.

[5] See Bernard Bass, *Bass and Stogdill's Handbook of Leadership,* 3rd ed. (New York: Free Press, 1990); Mauk Mulder, "Power Equalization through Participation?" *Academy of Management Journal* 16 (1971): 31-38; and Mauk Mulder and H. Wilke, "Participation and Power Equalization," *Organizational Behavior and Human Performance* 5 (1970): 430-448.

[6]Dennis Organ, "Linking Pins between Organizations and Environments," *Business Horizons* 14 (1971): 73-80. For an extended critique of Likert's model, see Alfred Marrow, David Bowers, and Stanley Seashore, *Management by Participation* (New York: Harper and Row, 1967).

[7]Carl E. Larson and Frank M. J. LaFasto, *TeamWork: What Must Go Right/What Can Go Wrong* (Newbury Park, CA: Sage, 1989).

[8]This section draws heavily on Peter R. Monge and Noshir S. Contractor's excellent book *Theories of Communication Networks* (New York: Oxford, 2003). They provide a definitive discussion of this topic.

[9]Terrance Albrecht, "An Overtime Analysis of Communication Patterns and Work Perceptions," in *Communication Yearbook 8,* Robert Bostrom, ed. (Beverly Hills, CA: Sage, 1984); Fredric Jablin, "Task/Work Relationships," in *Handbook of Interpersonal Communication,* Mark Knapp and Gerald Miller, eds. (Beverly Hills, CA: Sage, 1985); and Eric Eisenberg, Peter Monge, and Kathleen Miller, "Involvement in Communication Networks as a Predictor of Organizational Commitment," *Human Communication Research* 10 (1983): 179-201.

[10]James March and Guje Sevon, "Gossip, Information, and Decision Making," in *Advances in Information Processing in Organizations,* Lee Sproull and Patrick Larkey, eds., vol. 1 (Greenwich, CT: JAI Press, 1982).

[11]See Sally Planalp, Susan Hafen, and A. Dawn Adkins, "Messages of Shame and Guilt," in *Communication Yearbook 23,* Michael Roloff, ed. (Thousand Oaks, CA: Sage, 1999). Davis's study is "Management Communication and the Grapevine," *Harvard Business Review* 31 (September–October, 1953): 43-49.

[12]See Terrance Albrecht and Bradford Hall, "Facilitating Talk about New Ideas," *Communication Monographs* 58 (1991): 273-288; Terrance Albrecht and Bradford Hall, "Relational and Content Differences between Elites and Outsiders in Innovation Networks," *Human Communication Research* 17 (1991): 535-561; Betsy Bach, "The Effect of Multiplex Relationships upon Innovation Adoption," *Communication Monographs* 56 (1991): 133-148; David Bastien, "Change in Organizational Culture," *Management Communication Quarterly* 5 (1992): 403-442; Beth Ellis, "The Effects of Uncertainty and Source Credibility on Attitude about Organizational Change," *Management Communication Quarterly* 6 (1992): 34-57; Ronald Rice and Carolyn Aydin, "Attitudes toward New Organizational Technology," *Administrative Science Quarterly* 36 (1991): 219-244.

[13]Mark Granovetter, "The Strength of Weak Ties," *American Journal of Sociology* 81 (1973): 1287-1303. See also Monge and Contractor, pp. 147-148.

[14]Deborah G. Ancona and David F. Caldwell, "Beyond Task and Maintenance: Defining External Functions in Groups," *Group and Organization Studies* 13 (1988): 468-494; Deborah G. Ancona and David F. Caldwell, "Demography and Design: Predictors of New Product Team Performance," *Organizational Science* 3 (1992): 321-341.

[15]McGregor found that supervisors really do tend to communicate to their subordinates in ways that are consistent with one of these two sets of assumptions. Also see John Courtright, Gail Fairhurst, and L. Edna Rogers, "Interaction Patterns in Organic and Mechanistic Systems," *Academy of Management Journal* 32 (1989): 773-802.

[16]Edwin Locke, "The Nature and Causes of Job Satisfaction," in *Handbook of Industrial and Organizational Psychology,* Marvin Dunnette, ed. (Chicago: Rand-McNally, 1976).

[17]See Richard Edwards, *Contested Terrain* (New York: Basic Books, 1978); and Christopher Dandeker, *Surveillance, Power, and Modernity* (New York: St. Martin's Press, 1984). An excellent example of the alienating effects of de-skilling is provided in "The Lordstown Auto Workers," in *Life in Organizations,* Rosabeth Moss Kanter and Barry Stein, eds. (New York: Basic Books, 1979).

[18]S. Benson, "The Clerking Sisterhood," in *Gendering Organizational Analysis,* A. J. Mills and P. Tancred, eds. (Newbury Park, CA: Sage, 1992).

[19]Timothy Pollock, Robert Whitbred, and Noshir Contractor, "Social Information Processing and Job Characteristics," *Human Communication Research* 26 (2000): 292-330.

[20]Elton Mayo, *Social Problems of an Industrial Civilization* (Boston: Graduate School of Business Administration, Harvard University, 1945). In *The Human Group* (New York: Harcourt Brace, 1950), George Homans gives a readable account of the information provided by the Hawthorne Studies on work-group influences on members. For examples of the processes described in this paragraph, see Jane Freeman, "The Tyranny of Structurelessness," in *Women in Politics,* Jane S. Jaquette, ed. (New York: Wiley, 1974); Leonard Sayles, "Work Group Behavior and the Larger Organization," in *Research in Industrial Human Relations,* W. F. Whyte, ed. (New York: Harper, 1957); and Susan A. Mohrman, Susan G. Cohen, and Allan M. Mohrman, *Designing Team-Based Organizations: New Forms for Knowledge Work* (San Francisco: Jossey-Bass, 1995).

[21]Starting in the late 1980s, there has been an upsurge in the research and popular literature on teams. See Larson and LaFasto; Jon R. Katzenbach and Douglas K. Smith, *The Wisdom of Teams* (New York: HarperCollins, 1993); J. Richard Hackman, *Groups That Work (And Those That Don't)* (San Francisco: Jossey-Bass, 1990).

[22]Larson and LaFasto, pp. 82-83.

[23] Philip K. Tompkins and George Cheney, "Communication and Unobtrusive Control in Organizations," in *Organizational Communication: Traditional Themes and New Directions,* Robert D. McPhee and Philip Tompkins, eds. (Beverly Hills, CA: Sage, 1985).

[24] Cynthia Stohl, "Bridging the Parallel Organization: A Study of Quality Circle Effectiveness," in *Communication Yearbook 10,* Judee Burgoon, ed. (Beverly Hills, CA: Sage, 1985).

[25] Cynthia Stohl, *Organizational Communication: Connectedness in Action* (Thousand Oaks, CA: Sage, 1995).

[26] Much of this foundational research is summarized in Rensis Likert, *New Patterns of Management* (New York: McGraw-Hill, 1961); and in the first and second editions of *Studies in Personnel and Industrial Psychology,* Edwin Fleishman and Associates, eds. (Homewood, IL: Dorsey, 1961 and 1967). An excellent summary of research on leadership communication is provided by Gail Fairhurst in "Dialectical Tensions in Leadership Research," in *The New Handbook of Organizational Communication,* F. Jablin and L. Putnam, eds. (Thousand Oaks, CA: Sage, 2000).

[27] Virginia P. Richmond and James C. McCroskey, "The Impact of Supervisor and Subordinate Immediacy on Relational and Organizational Outcomes," *Communication Monographs* 67 (2000): 85–95; Martin Remland, "Leadership Impressions and Nonverbal Communication," *Communication Quarterly* 19 (1987): 108–128; Fredric Jablin, "Superior-Subordinate Communication," in *Communication Yearbook 2,* Brent Ruben, ed. (New Brunswick, NJ: Transaction Books, 1979); and "Communication Competence and Effectiveness," in *The New Handbook of Organizational Communication,* Fredric Jablin and Linda Putnam, eds. (Thousand Oaks, CA: Sage, 2000).

[28] Terrance Albrecht and J. Halsey, "Mutual Support in Mixed Status Relationships," *Journal of Social and Personal Relationships* 9 (1992): 237–252; Terrance Albrecht and Mara Adelman, *Communicating Social Support* (Newbury Park, CA: Sage, 1988).

[29] Ernest Bormann discusses the dynamics of leadership emergence insightfully in *Small Group Communication: Theory and Practice,* 3rd ed. (New York: HarperCollins, 1990). Also see Bass, *Handbook.*

[30] The classic source on this model, which is simplified in this discussion, is Victor H. Vroom and Peter W. Yetton, *Leadership and Decision Making* (Pittsburgh: University of Pittsburgh Press, 1973).

[31] Bass, *Handbook,* pp. 452–455.

[32] John M. Levine and Richard L. Moreland, "Small Groups," in *Handbook of Social Psychology,* 4th ed., Daniel Gilbert, Susan Fiske, and Gardner Lindzey, eds. (New York: Oxford University Press, 1998).

[33] Ron Rice and Urs E. Gattiker, "New Media and Organizational Structuring," in *The New Handbook of Organizational Communication,* Frederic M. Jablin and Linda L. Putnam, eds. (Thousand Oaks, CA: Sage, 2000).

[34] Ron Rice, *The New Media* (Beverly Hills, CA: Sage, 1984).

[35] Janet Fulk, "Social Construction of Communication Technology," *Academy of Management Journal* 36 (1993): 921–950. Rice and Aydin.

[36] Lee Sproull and Sara Kiesler "Reducing Social Context Cues," *Management Science* 32 (1986): 1492–1512; Tom Finholt and Lee Sproull, "Electronic Groups at Work," *Organization Science* 1 (1990): 41–64; Ron Rice and G. Love, "Electronic Emotion," *Communication Research* 14 (1987): 85–108; Joe B. Walther, "Interpersonal Effects in Computer-Mediated Interaction," *Communication Research* 19 (1992): 52–90.

[37] Joanne Yates and Wanda J. Orlikowski, "Genres of Organizational Communication," *Academy of Management Review* 17 (1992): 299–326. Also see Lee Sproull and Sara Kiesler, "Reducing Social Context Cues"; and Charles Steinfeld, "Computer-Mediated Communication in the Organization," in *Cases in Organizational Communication,* Beverly Sypher, ed. (New York: Guilford, 1991).

[38] R. Emmett, "Vnet or Gripenet," *Datamation* 27 (1981): 48–58. This capacity sometimes can cause problems for new users of the systems. When Charley Conrad was first learning to use e-mail, he sent a relatively personal note to Ted Zorn (whose work is often cited in this book) congratulating him on his promotion to associate professor. He accidentally told his computer to send the message to everyone on the organizational communication network, which, of course, includes Charley. Conrad knows this because some kind people recognized what he had done and sent him instructions about how to keep from doing it again. He has never admitted his error to Ted, who may never know unless he reads this note.

[39] Monge and Contractor, "Emergent Communication Networks," pp. 229–231.

[40] Drew Robb, "Unified Messaging Boosts Productivity," *Computerworld,* November 4, 2002, pp. 32–33.

[41] Gerry DeSanctis and Brent Gallupe, "A Foundation for the Study of Group Decision Support Systems," *Management Science* 33 (1987): 589–609; Brent Gallupe, Laura Bastianutti, and W. H. Cooper, "Unblocking Brainstorms," *Journal of Applied Psychology* 76 (1991): 137–142; Jay F. Nunamaker, Alan R. Dennis, Joey George, Joe Valacich, and Doug Vogel, "Electronic Meeting Systems to Support Group Work," *Communications of the ACM* 34 (1991): 40–61; V. Sambamurthy and Marshall Scott Poole, "The Effects of Variations in Capabilities of GDSS Designs on Management of Cognitive Conflict in Groups," *Information Systems Research* 3 (1993): 224–251; Janet Fulk and Lori Collins-Jarvis, "Wired Meetings: Technological Mediation of Organizational Gatherings," in *The New Handbook of Organizational Communication,* Fredric Jablin and Linda Putnam, eds. (Thousand Oaks, CA: Sage,

2000); Craig R. Scott, "Communication Technology and Group Communication" in *Handbook of Group Communication Theory and Research,* L. Frey, D. Gouran, and M. S. Poole, eds. (Newbury Park, CA: Sage, 1999).

[42] Ruth Guzley, "Organizational Climate and Communication Climate," *Management Communication Quarterly* 5 (1992): 379–402; Dominic Infante and William Gordon, "How Employees See the Boss," *Western Journal of Speech Communication* 55 (1991): 294–304.

[43] "Ford, Union to Open 30 Child-Care and Family-Service Centers for Workers," *Houston Chronicle,* November 22, 2000, C1; Amy Zipkin, "Bosses Become Nice to Try to Keep Employees from Leaving," *Houston Chronicle,* June 4, 2000, D5. Denise Segura argues that what satisfies workers varies with their level in the organization, but not with their gender or ethnicity ("Chicanas in White-Collar Jobs," in *Situated Lives,* Louise Lamphere, Helena Razoné, and Patricia Zavella, eds. [New York: Routledge, 1997]). Craig R. Scott and his associates ("The Impacts of Communication and Multiple Identifications on Intent to Leave," *Management Communication Quarterly* 12 [1999]: 400–435); and Mike Allen ("The Relationship between Communication, Affect, Job Alternatives, and Voluntary Turnover Intentions," *Southern Communication Journal* 61 [1996]: 198–209) both found that there also is a direct relationship between communication and turnover—communication in itself influences turnover intentions and also influences satisfaction, which has an additional effect on turnover.

[44] Bass, *Handbook;* Teresa Harrison, "Communication and Participative Decision-Making," *Personnel Psychology* 38 (1985): 93–116.

[45] Larry Rohter, "Workers in Argentina Take Charge of Abandoned Factories," *New York Times on the Web,* July 6, 2003, http://www.nytimes.com/.

[46] Cynthia Fisher, "On the Dubious Wisdom of Expecting Job Satisfaction to Correlate with Performance," *Academy of Management Review* 5 (1980). Also see Bass, *Handbook.* For summaries of the relationship between organizational communication and voluntary turnover, see M. W. Allen, pp. 198–209.

[47] Dennis Gioia and Henry Sims, "Cognition-Behavior Connections: Attribution and Verbal Behavior in Leader-Subordinate Interactions," *Organizational Behavior and Human Performance* 37 (1986): 197–229. Also see Fairhurst.

[48] L. P. Dana, "Small Business as a Supplement in the People's Republic of China (PRC)," *Journal of Small Business Management* 37 (1999): 76–81.

[49] Karen Mills, "Northwest on a Flier-Satisfaction Mission," *Houston Chronicle,* May 14, 2000, D6; Kim Cameron and Michael Thompson, "The Problems and Promises of Total Quality Management," in *Pressing Problems in Modern Organizations (That Keep Us Up at Night),* R. Quinn, R. O'Neill, and L. St. Clair, eds. (New York: American Management Association, 2000); Thom Weidlich, "Who Says Unions Must Dislike the Chief?" *New York Times on the Web,* December 15, 2002, http://www.nytimes.com/.

[50] The best analysis of the development of critical theory and its many versions is David Held, *Introduction to Critical Theory* (London: Hutchinson, 1980). An excellent application to organizational theory is Mats Alvesson and Hugh Wilmott, eds. *Critical Management Studies* (Newbury Park, CA: Sage, 1992); and an application to organizational communication is Stan Deetz, "Critical Theories of Organizational Communication," in *The New Handbook of Organizational Communication,* Fredric Jablin and Linda Putnam, eds. (Thousand Oaks, CA: Sage, 2000); and *Transforming Communication, Transforming Business* (Cresskill, NJ: Hampton Press, 1995).

[51] Alan Downs, *Corporate Executions* (New York: AMACOM, 1995); also see Stanley Deetz, *Democracy in the Age of Corporate Colonization* (Albany: State University of New York Press, 1992), especially chapter 9.

[52] See Jürgen Habermas, *Knowledge and Human Interests* (London: Heinemann Educational Books, 1972); and *Communication and the Evolution of Society* (London: Heinemann Educational Books, 1979).

[53] See John Forester, *Planning in the Face of Power* (Berkeley: University of California Press, 1989). This section is based in part on Goran Therborn, *The Ideology of Power and the Power of Ideology* (London: Verso, 1980). A fine summary of the issues regarding the concept of ideology is available in Astrid Kersten, "Culture, Control, and the Labor Process," in *Communication Yearbook 16,* Stanley Deetz, ed. (Newbury Park, CA: Sage, 1993).

[54] Richard Jehensen, "Effectiveness, Expertise, and Excellence as Ideological Fictions," *Human Studies* 7 (1984): 3–21. For analyses of how seemingly objective organizational "data" are manipulated symbolically to privilege management's interests, see S. Ansari and K. Euske, "Rational, Rationalizing, and Reifying Uses of Accounting Data in Organizations," *Accounting, Organizations, and Society* 12 (1987): 549–570; and David Sless, "Forms of Control," *Australian Journal of Communication* 14 (1988): 57–69.

[55] Michael Huspek, "The Language of Powerlessness" (Ph.D. diss., University of Washington, 1987).

[56] See, for example, Mats Alvesson, "Organizations, Culture and Ideology," *International Studies of Management and Organization* 17 (1987): 4–18; and *Organization Theory and Technocratic Consciousness* (New York: Walter de Gruyter, 1987). Classic studies of nonlegitimate participatory systems are available in B. Abrahamsson, *Bureaucracy or Participation* (Beverly Hills, CA: Sage, 1977); Charles Perrow, *Complex Organizations,* 3rd ed. (New York: Random House, 1986); and Stewart Clegg, *Power, Rule, and Domination* (London: Routledge and Kegan Paul, 1975).

Chapter 5

Cultural Strategies
of Organizing

The reality of the [social] world hangs on the thin thread of conversation.
—PETER BERGER AND THOMAS LUCKMANN

Central Themes

- Cultural strategies of organizing assume that managers can influence employees' beliefs, values, and perceptions of reality and that employees actively create their own beliefs, values, and perceptions.
- Organizational cultures are communicative creations, embedded in a history and a set of expectations about the future. They are usually heterogeneous, composed of multiple subcultures.
- Cultural strategies of motivation and control rely on self-surveillance, which is accomplished through systems of unobtrusive control, emotional regulation, and discursive practices.
- Cultural strategies of leadership focus on "transformational" processes through which leaders communicate a vision of the organization and help employees "frame" everyday events.
- Organizational symbolism—metaphors, stories, myths, and rituals—facilitates unobtrusive control.
- Communication technologies have cultural assumptions embedded in them, and the way in which they are used in a given organization is influenced as much by the organizational culture as by the characteristics of the technologies themselves.

Key Terms

subcultures	storytelling
externalization	rituals
objectification	ceremonies
internalization	display rules
identities	surface acting
reality shock	deep acting
anticipatory socialization	obtrusive control
identify	unobtrusive control
stories	self-surveillance
myths	charisma
mythologies	leadership moments

In Chapter 1 we suggested that in all societies there is a central tension between *individuality* and *community*. The traditional strategy of organizing focuses on the individual pole of this tension and relies on the structural dimension of communication to manage it. The traditional strategy assumes that rewarding employees for their *individual* competence and performance will motivate them to act in ways that meet their organizations' needs for control and coordination. Feelings of connection to one's co-workers are either ignored or treated as a potential threat to organizational control. Although some versions of the traditional strategy have noted that people do feel pride from successfully performing their tasks, traditional strategies view human beings as predominantly rational, not emotional, beings. In contrast, relational strategies retain the rational, individualistic focus of traditional strategies but also recognize that human beings are emotional, community-oriented creatures. For this reason they offer a more complete view of human experience. Their recognition of the power of work groups and teams admits that sociability and interpersonal relationships are important aspects of working life. But even these changes offer an impoverished view of the rich texture of feelings and personal connections that characterize life in modern organizations.[1]

The cultural strategy suggests that humans are emotional beings and that feelings of connectedness and community are important aspects of all social structures, including organizations. Emotional ties, both to one's organization and to one's co-workers, are powerful influences on how people choose to act and communicate at work. Cultural strategies do not ignore individuality or rationality. Indeed, they suggest that employees make reasoned, strategic choices based on their individual beliefs, values, and sense-making processes. Motivating and controlling employees' behavior depends on persuading them to accept the organization's core beliefs, values, and frames of reference as their own. Creating a sense of community within work groups is depicted as a primary means of managing the tension between individual and organizational needs. Like the other strategies of organizing, cultural approaches also incorporate a distinctive form of leadership and posit unique relationships with communication technologies.

Cultural Strategies of Organizational Design

Although most advocates of cultural strategies of organizing were comfortable with relational conceptions of organizational design[2]—decentralization, participation, and so on—issues of organizational design were relatively unimportant to them.[3] The values, beliefs, language, symbols, and meaning systems that hold the organization together are much more significant. Initially they argued that organizational cultures could be managed strategically, and rather easily. Upper management merely had to communicate persuasively the core values of the organization to all employees and provide tangible and intangible rewards to employees who acted in accordance with those values. Eventually, a homogeneous and harmonious "strong" culture would emerge, one in which employees throughout the organization—regardless of their rank, tasks, networks of interpersonal relationships, or formal roles—would share the same goals, have the same kinds of feelings about the organization, and interpret the culture in the same way. This strong culture would be the key to managerial control, worker commitment, and organizational effectiveness.[4]

However, studies of organizational cultures soon discovered that the reality was much more complicated than the culture-management theories suggested. This research reminded us that organizations are composed of active, thinking human beings. Employees sometimes interpret management's attempts to mold beliefs, instill values, and manipulate perceptions and emotions as offensive and manipulative (regardless of how management interprets them). Even if they are not offended, they may interpret and respond to management's messages in completely unanticipated ways. In other cases, they may resist even positive changes in their organization's culture, and generally make culture management or planned cultural change exceptionally difficult. Even if a strong culture exists, not all employees will participate in it equally or in the same ways. Employees tend to form communicative ties with people who share their view of their organization. Different **subcultures** emerge—groups of people whose shared interpretation of their organization helps bind them together and separate them from other groups of employees. Consequently, it is more likely that an organization will be composed of many distinct and different subcultures rather than a homogeneous culture consciously defined and guided by upper management.[5]

For example, Charley Conrad once visited the technical writing division of a major computer firm as part of a consulting project. He entered through the front door and was examined by the security team at the front desk. Then he was led down corridor after corridor past each of the major divisions of the firm into a separate building that housed the writing staff. One of the first things he noticed was the staff's coffee room. On the wall was a poster of the firm's newest product, an exceptionally powerful portable computer that was not yet on the market. But unlike the hardware division, which had an entire wall covered with the posters, or the software group, which had arranged to have one of the posters professionally framed and displayed in the center of its workroom, the technical writing group had only one poster and displayed it in a dark corner. In front of the poster was a Norfolk pine that all but obscured it from view.[6]

Prominently displayed in the center of the room was a poster of a penguin jumping off an ice cliff into the ocean with a long row of penguins following it. Someone had written the division head's name next to the lead penguin and the other writers' names next to the others. Significant symbols reveal a great deal about the culture (or subculture) of an organization. These poster symbols suggested that Technical Writing was a subculture—a strong and stable one—that was separate from the other units of the organization. Members of the division perceived themselves as writers, not as employees of Computer Firm X. They proudly told Conrad that they were in their isolated building because they had asked to be there. Sometimes the different subcultures in an organization coexist peacefully; in other cases their values, patterns of acting, sense-making processes, and so on are conflicting and irreconcilable. Subcultures, like the communication networks that underlie them, are fluid and changing. The existence of multiple, ever-changing organizational subcultures does not mean that implementing cultural strategies of organizing is impossible. In some cases, the organization's core beliefs and values are so powerful and are communicated so persuasively that individual interpretations and subcultural differences are overwhelmed. Cultures are communicative creations. They emerge and are sustained by the communicative acts of all employees, not just the conscious persuasive strategies of upper management.[7]

Cultural Strategies of Motivation, Control, and Surveillance

Cultural strategies of control rely on three communicative processes—socializing newcomers into the assumptions of the organization; reinforcing those assumptions through organizational symbolism, and regulating emotions. The goal of all three processes is to encourage employees to monitor and control their own behavior in ways that meet the organization's needs.

Socializing Newcomers

Sociologist Peter Berger has described the process through which people learn and accept the core values and beliefs of their society. In the first phase, **externalization,** people notice the ways in which others interpret and respond to their surroundings. To fit in, they begin to act as the "locals" do. Eventually, they may enter the second phase, **objectification.** They begin to believe that the way the people act in their society/organization is the only correct (that is, normal and natural) way of acting. As they "objectify" the thought processes and action patterns of their society/organization, they are not consciously aware of how those societal/organizational assumptions influence their everyday lives. Eventually they forget that the people in their societies *choose* to act as they do and that they could have chosen any number of different courses of action. The concept of objectification implies that societies (and organizations) are maintained nonconsciously, as much through habit as through conscious deliberation. Routine decisions can be made automatically and with little expenditure of time or energy. In the final, **internalization** phase, people begin to evaluate themselves and their actions in terms of the society/organization's assumptions. They begin to see themselves as good, productive, or righteous only if they think and act in accordance with the core beliefs and values of their society. Their self-concept begins to depend on continually thinking and acting in ways that are normal in their organizations. Their self-esteem depends on doing what is valued by their society/organization. If they ever do act in ways that violate those core beliefs and values, they will view themselves negatively and be motivated to change their behavior. As we explain later in this chapter, their sense of who they are as people—their **identities**—are tied to their society and its accepted assumptions.

When people enter a new organization or a new division of their existing organization, they go through a similar process. They bring with them a lengthy and complex history.[8] They have learned to perceive their organizational world in their own ways and have developed patterns of acting and communicating that have succeeded in the past. But every organization is unique in some ways. Consequently, all newcomers experience some degree of **reality shock**—the sudden realization that what they took for granted in their previous organization is not what people take for granted in their new one. So the first challenge that newcomers face is *making sense out of* their new organization, coping with the surprises that their new experiences bring. When situations do not make sense, people seek out information and perspectives from other people. Through *interacting* with others, newcomers begin to manage the ambiguities and uncertainties that they feel. Eventually, the new situation makes enough sense that individuals can begin to seek out additional information about how the organization works.[9] Of course, some newcomers are better able to cope with new situations than others. Newcomers who have had many and varied work experiences deal with the reality shock of the entry experience more successfully than people with few work experiences. They also are better equipped to see the culture of their new organization as a chosen strategy. Among employees with limited experience, certain personality characteristics may also influence their ability to cope. For example, people who are inner-directed, that is, who rely on their own beliefs, values, and analytical skills, cope more easily than people who are outer-directed, who usually rely on the opinions and interpretations of others.[10] Consequently, outer-directed people are more likely to be influenced by cultural strategies of control than inner-directed people are. However, the need to make sense out of a new situation makes all newcomers susceptible to persuasion from their new organizations.

Anticipatory Socialization   As we suggest throughout this book, expectations are influenced by the accepted assumptions of a person's society, as well as by a person's individual needs and experiences. Some societal assumptions involve work and organizational life (recall the "Under Thirty" case study in Chapter 1). In Chapter 3 we introduced Industry International, an organization with an especially powerful system of financial rewards. But Industry International also relies on organizational socialization as a mechanism of control. Industry's employees learn to accept its core beliefs and values long before they ever enter its doors. The organization hires its workers, who are frequently relatives of its current employees, from the local blue-collar communities. From childhood, they learn that Industry is a stable and highly successful organization. By the time they are adolescents, they have learned a strong work ethic—to be dependable, conscientious, and concerned about the quality of their work, and to work very, very hard. They learn that real men put food on their family's table, and that only "real men can make it at Industry International."[11] In fact, being able to withstand the body-punishing rigors of blue-collar life and being willing to celebrate the strength, stamina, and manual dexterity required by Industry work is the source of the worker's identity and self-esteem. For Industry's employees, these attributes make them superior to people who make a living by shuffling papers. Industry's employees internalize the organization's values at their dinner tables and look forward to someday becoming one of "the mud, the blood, and the beer guys."

By the time people apply to work at Industry, they know what will be expected of them, what it means to be part of a cohesive work group, and what kinds of financial rewards they can obtain. This preemployment indoctrination makes it easy to adopt the core beliefs of the organization. As Roy, a seventeen-year-old employee notes:

> You walk in there and you know you're not going to get days off. You know you're not going to get sick days. You know that you don't just say "I'm not feeling well and I'm going home." If the person after you doesn't show up [for the next shift], you know that you're not leaving. Your group depends on you to keep the line going.

Employees also know that if they ever slack off, they will be reminded by the men with whom they are working. Deon (an old-timer at twenty-five) explains, "When I see these kids in here who do not know how to work, I kinda' take them under my wing. I show them how to work hard." Jim personalizes the issue: "If my kid or relative went there and wasn't working hard, I'd go down and kick his ass. No way he's shamin' me by not working as hard as I said he could." Some of the most powerful identification messages come from employees' supervisors and co-workers.[12] But if workers really have identified with their organization, few messages are necessary. They act as the organization wants them to because they believe that it is natural and normal to do so.

Our system of higher education seems to provide the same kind of **anticipatory socialization** for potential white-collar employees that messages from family members and neighbors play for workers at Industry International. Students in U.S. universities are taught to expect that they will someday get a "real job," one that pays well (the realest ones have six-figure salaries), is full-time, involves managerial tasks and perks (independence and a large private office), includes the possibility of advancement, and is with a reputable company.[13] In real jobs, supervisors are competent and do not mistreat their subordinates. These expectations are elitist, and they are stereotypically masculine because the "realness" of a job depends on traditionally male considerations, such as financial gain and upward mobility. Stereotypically feminine values like improving society or nurturing and caring for others are characteristic of jobs that are not quite "real" jobs. Students' perceptions of real jobs include a particular kind of organizational life and a specific set of criteria for evaluating organizations, jobs, and the people who fill them. But some of the first jobs that new college graduates obtain—as many discovered during the recession at the beginning of the twenty-first century—are not "real" jobs, and their expectations will not be fulfilled.

Other expectations are more specific. As soon as a person has accepted a new position, she or he begins to anticipate what the new job will be like. For some people these expectations will be relatively accurate; for others they will not be. Sometimes selection processes and negotiations over terms of employment create inaccurate expectations. During these processes, the firm and the applicant engage in communication that is similar to romantic courtship, where each party strives to present the best possible image. But as in many marriages, the reality may be quite different from the expectations.[14] Sometimes unfulfilled expectations involve organizational tasks and perks. Just as often they involve the employee's personal life or family—his or her subdivision was not as welcoming, or her or his children's' schools were not as good, or the weather was not as balmy, or the local theater not as good, as he or she had anticipated. Organizations do a great deal to help newcomers prepare for their jobs, but they often fail to realize that people also have identities and lives that go beyond the workplace. Failing to adequately prepare newcomers for their nonwork lives is just as alienating as failing to prepare them for their tasks—perhaps more so. The most memorable experiences that people have in their organizations involve their first few weeks. Unfortunately, if these memories involve unmet expectations, the disappointment and hurt feelings may never disappear.[15] When expectations are violated, people feel betrayed, and their trust in the other parties is reduced. As Chapter 3 explained, low levels of trust reduce the amount of and accuracy of communication. As the quality of communication between newcomers and old-timers is reduced, it becomes progressively more difficult for either side to understand the other. New expectations are formed, based on patterns of withholding or distorting information. Because these expectations are unrealistic, they are easily violated. As employees become less predictable to one another, they tend to withdraw, making it even more difficult for them to communicate effectively. Their expectations become less realistic, their orientations toward one another less trusting, open, or cooperative. In contrast, if the original expectations are fulfilled, the newcomers are likely to feel psychologically connected to their organization and begin to identify with it.

Identification and Organizational Socialization   Organizations encourage employees to **identify**—to begin to see their membership in the organization as part of who they are as people—through a number of communicative strategies. Identification is a significant dimension of much formal organizational discourse—newsletters, annual reports, and so on. Sometimes these documents laud a *team atmosphere* between workers and the organization. Other identification strategies involve *expressing concern for individual employees* and *recognizing contributions* made by individual employees or work groups to the organization or to the larger society. Other messages *invite* employees to become involved (or remain involved) in some worthwhile organizational activity, or *brag* about the dedication shown by an individual or work group successfully completing a task. The Bank of America newsletter includes a regular feature in which employees talk about their contributions to the company. Sometimes an organization's messages encourage employees to identify with the organization by identifying a common enemy. When Steve Jobs served his first term as head of Apple Computer, he expressed respect for IBM as a "national treasure" but galvanized Apple's employees by telling them that he was concerned that Apple was the only thing that kept IBM from "total industry domination." Each of these communicative strategies creates a corporate "we" between workers and the organization—a feeling that "we" are inextricably tied together, teammates in the struggle against common enemies. Through overt persuasive efforts, organizations attempt to move employees toward identifying with them.[16]

However, employees may respond to these efforts in different ways. Many do identify with their organizations. They feel close ties to the employees who are mentioned in the messages and feel connected to the organization through their positive feelings about those people. They may feel as though they really are part of the organization or feel pride in being involved in an organization that cares for its members. Or they may feel a strong connection to their peers or to their organizational community. Other employees may interpret the messages as mere sources of information or entertainment and even complain that they don't achieve either of those goals very well. Others actually may "disidentify" with the organization because of the messages. They may feel that their own experience contradicts the messages, may see the messages as a waste of organizational resources, or may feel that their work group or its members are not given enough recognition.

In many cases identification strategies fail because people have complex and multifaceted identities. For example, both authors of this book simultaneously are husbands, fathers, researchers, teachers, organizational communication scholars, members of a communication department, part of a College of Liberal Arts and a university with a distinctive culture and tradition, and have a number of other roles. Scott Poole also is a faculty member in the College of Business, and Charley Conrad works with colleagues in the College of Engineering. Our selves are constantly being created and recreated as we receive and interpret messages from people who see only one or two of our many identities. The boundaries between those selves are blurry and constantly changing.[17] As a result, it is unlikely that we will ever identify completely with any of the organizations or groups of which we are members. We tend to identify most closely with the people who are most central in our communication networks—

our immediate families and our immediate work groups (our department). And we identify most closely with organizations and relationships that we have been involved with for a long time, because we have developed closer communicative relationships within them. We interpret each identification message we receive through lenses that are made of complex webs of attachment and identification.

Finally, the extent to which people identify with their organizations depends on tangible considerations. If they become dissatisfied with their pay, their working conditions, or the degree of autonomy they have at work, they are less likely to identify with their organization and more likely to interpret identification messages as manipulation.[18] Some people identify with their organizations completely and constantly. Others identify only in part, for example when their own beliefs, values, and interests happen to coincide with those of the organization. They understand where they fit in the organization, take pride in their contributions to its success, and feel commitment to its continuation. They may accept some of the assumptions of the organization; but they do so because they actually believe in those values, not because the organization tells them they should. They may believe and proudly say "I am an IBMer" in a way that suggests that they have identified completely with the organization and at the same time realize that their commitment is primarily based on coinciding goals and functional ties. Even true-blue IBMers call their generous retirement programs and benefits packages "golden handcuffs" (because they would lose so much money by moving to another firm that they are effectively tied to IBM). They learn the assumptions of the organization but do not accept them uncritically. An employee's level of identification also varies across time and with different organizational experiences. A handsome reward or especially moving integration ceremony may lead an employee to temporarily identify more strongly with the organization; a negative performance evaluation or conflict with a co-worker may reduce such identification. But even during those times, identification is a powerful mode of organizational control.

Organizational Symbolism and Cultural Strategies of Motivation and Control

Organizational symbolism—metaphors, stories, myths, rituals, and ceremonies—have a dual relationship to cultural strategies; they express the assumptions of the culture and, when articulated, reproduce those assumptions. Some advocates of the cultural strategy of organizing assume that upper management can motivate and control employees by strategically managing organizational symbols. Unfortunately, this view seriously oversimplifies the nature of symbolism and organizational cultures. Employees are human beings, and humans actively perceive, process, and choose to respond to messages in their own often idiosyncratic ways. They interpret stories and other symbolic forms precisely as they interpret identification messages, in terms of their own needs, experiences, and frames of reference. Different employees or different subcultures of employees may interpret the same symbolic act in different ways. They also may tell different stories, create their own independent rituals, or describe their organization or unit through the use of different metaphors. Upper management may tell a different story to explain an organizational disaster (or success) than production employees do; employees in a subculture dominated by marketing employees may tell a story that blames the research and development division for a failed product line; research and development employees may tell the same story in a way that satirizes members of the marketing division. In these cases, organizational symbolism may actually reduce managerial control and motivate employees to act in ways that are not preferred by management.

Metaphors   These are symbols in which one image is used to describe another one. They are often used to describe an entire organization. Frequent organizational metaphors are military machines (working here is like being in the army), families (these people are my closest friends, my family, or this desk is my home away from home), and games (to survive here you have to play the game, pretend to be what the big shots want you to be). For fifty years, a large West Coast toy manufacturer has been described by its employees as an "army under siege." Although the enemy has changed many times, from profit-hungry East Coast companies, during the 1950s; to wily foreign importers who keep their workers in poverty, during the 1960s and 1970s; to computer firms that care about wires and chips, not children, in the 1980s, the guiding metaphor has remained the same. Employees talk about "fighting the battle," which means constantly working hard to maintain efficiency; "taking no casualties," which means that everyone constantly monitors quality (including a company program in which samples are donated to employees if they will take them home and see how long it takes their children to destroy them); "everyone being a spy," which leads most employees to regularly take their children to toy shops just to see which of their competitors' products are popular and ought to be duplicated; and "foot soldiers in the battle," which both involves every employee in the mission of the organization and justifies a hierarchical, rule-governed style of management. But the most powerful expressions of the metaphor are borrowed from the larger culture: "be all that you can be" is used to justify voluntary overtime, and "lean, mean fighting machine" is used to explain reductions in the number of middle managers. Almost every normal work experience is explained in language reflecting the army-under-siege metaphor; almost every behavior desired of workers can be justified by referring to the metaphor. In cases like this one, management and employees share the same metaphorical description of their organization and define that metaphor in the same way. Motivation and control are enhanced.

However, metaphors are highly ambiguous—they can be interpreted in different ways.[19] If employees think their organizational family is like the Taylors (*Home Improvement*) or the Camdens (*7th Heaven*) they are likely to respond very differently to the metaphor than they would if their image of "family" is the Hills (*King of the Hill*), the Cartmans (*South Park*), or the Simpsons, or any other mythical family whose attributes are like those of the employee's organization. If they believe their organization is a family, they will perceive employees who behave in unfamily-like ways as being bad family members. Only in rare cases do these events lead employees to question the accuracy of the metaphor itself. The meanings attributed to metaphors also change over time and with events. Metaphors are important, because they guide and constrain peoples' interpretations of everyday events. They also provide stability, because people tend to perceive reality in ways that confirm their metaphors. When metaphors are interpreted in different ways, or when management relies on an outdated metaphor to motivate and control its employees, the power of metaphor may lead to very different outcomes.

Stories and Storytelling   Human beings are *storytelling* animals. From childhood fairy tales to the tales told during executives' weekend retreats, stories provide concrete, vivid images of what life is or will be like and what behaviors our culture values or prohibits.[20] **Stories** present events in sequence rather than in a list or chart, which makes some events seem to be the causes or effects of other events. At least in Western cultures, stories are based on a dramatic conflict between a protagonist and an antagonist. Stories are relevant to the needs and experiences of members of the organization. Stories are told most often and are most powerful, when people are confused and concerned about what is going on in their organizations (for instance, when a person is entering a new organization or when the organization is undergoing major changes). They provide explanations of events, policies, procedures, and so on that are beyond doubt or argument. They function as social **myths,** not in the sense that they are untrue (although they may be), but in the sense that their "truths" are taken for granted by the people who tell and listen to them. The power of myths, like that of stories, stems from their coherent, vivid details, their ability to help people make sense of their surroundings, and their consistency with other organizational stories and myths.[21]

Stories and myths usually coalesce to form **mythologies,** groups of interconnected symbols that support one another. In short, stories and myths tell people how things are to be done in a particular group and provide a social map that points out potentially dangerous topics, events, or persons present in at least one of an organization's subcultures. To be credible, stories must express a value, purpose, or philosophy that is consistent with the assumptions of the culture or subculture and must provide employees with guidelines for acting. They often tell employees what management wants them to believe is valued and rewarded in the organization; they sometimes tell employees what management really rewards and who really has power. And sometimes they may do both. Stories and myths also gain power from the processes through which they are told. **Storytelling** (and mythmaking) is an interactive process in which the teller presents his or her version of a story, usually leaving out many details, while others jump in and challenge, reinterpret, and revise the storyteller's version. The process allows each of the storytellers to link her or his own experiences to the experiences and interpretations of other storytellers. Through this process of mutual interpretation and reinterpretation, the accepted assumptions of the group are shared and reproduced. During the storytelling process, differences and tensions among interpretations may be expressed and managed. Thus, through a complicated process, the values and assumptions of the group are produced, reproduced, and revised.[22]

Of course, the observation that organizational symbolism can be powerful does not imply that its effects are always positive. Tom Hollihan and Patricia Riley's study of a "Toughlove" group provides an excellent example. Toughlove is a self-help voluntary organization composed of parents who have troubled teenagers. Toughlove meetings are like "testimonial services" in Protestant churches. Members come to tell stories about their experiences and their successes in overcoming their problems. Their individual stories combine to form a complicated mythology that unifies the members through their common experiences. The core experience is suffering brought on by the actions of their delinquent children; the common salvation is recognizing that adolescent children choose to behave as they do, realizing that parents have rights to peaceful homes and productive lives, and taking action to regain control of their lives instead of remaining victims of the tyranny of their children. Their stories are filled with villains and nostalgic images of a peaceful past. The villains are child-service professionals—teachers, social workers, therapists, and counselors—who are too quick to blame the parents for their children's delinquency and who are responsible for the modern "permissive" view of child-raising that the parents believe has created the problem of delinquent children. The nostalgia is of their childhoods when visits to the woodshed led them to both fear and respect their parents and learn to behave in socially acceptable ways.[23] By listening to stories, members of organizations learn the values that bind the culture together and discover what they must say and do if they are to become accepted members of the culture.

Rituals and Ceremonies   A final form of organizational symbolism involves rituals and ceremonies. Like storytelling, these gain their power from the act of participating in them, as well as from the meaning that people extract from them. Because the meaning of rituals and ceremonies is located in the doing, they can be especially powerful symbolic acts. **Rituals** are informal celebrations that may or may not be officially sanctioned by the organization, and **ceremonies** are planned, formal, and ordained by management. When a work crew gets together at a local bar on Friday evenings, it is a ritual—an informal gathering. When all the employees of a department store are asked to appear at a media event designed to kick off a new line of clothes, it is a ceremony. Participating in rituals and ceremonies helps individual employees understand the political and interpersonal nuances of their organization. If they perceive that the ritual or ceremony is meaningful, participating may increase their commitment to the organization because it makes them feel that they are a part of the organizational community.

Harrison Trice and Janice Beyer have observed that there are five primary types of organizational ceremonies. *Ceremonies of passage* tell everyone that a person has changed organizational roles and now has a new set of responsibilities, behavioral guidelines and constraints, and interpersonal relationships. *Degradation ceremonies* assign responsibility for errors or problems, refocus attention on the kinds of performance that are expected by management, and remove the guilty party from the power structure of the organization (usually through demotion, reassignment, or resignation). *Enhancement ceremonies* (for example, Mary Kay Cosmetic seminars) reemphasize the goals of the organization and create instant heroes who symbolize those goals. Regular awards ceremonies for the top salespersons can serve this function. *Renewal ceremonies* (such as annual executive retreats, complete with motivational speakers) create an image of action and deflect attention from underlying organizational problems. *Integration ceremonies* (for example, giving every employee an identical Thanksgiving ham) redefine the organization as a community and tell each employee that he or she is a part of it.[24]

Of course, the power of ceremonies to motivate and control employees depends on the meaning that employees extract from them and the extent to which they are meaningful. Like all symbolic forms, ceremonies can be interpreted in many different ways. The foundry that Charley Conrad worked in during his undergraduate years (recall the time-motion study described in Chapter 3) had a Christmas ceremony during which hams were distributed by the owner to each worker from the back of a truck—every worker except him. After his first Christmas ceremony, the owner quietly took him aside and explained that he was excluded because he was a part-time employee (summers and holidays). The owner feared that giving Conrad a ham would make the ceremony less meaningful (or might even cause resentment) for the full-time workers. Ironically, a group of workers later took him aside and told him that they felt bad that he had been left out. They explained that they thought the oversight was because he was not the head of a family as they were and thus didn't need the gift. And they presented him with a ham that they had purchased during lunch with a pool of money they had collected among themselves after the ceremony. Although the two meanings were very different, they both recognized that the ceremony was meaningful to the owner and workers alike.

CASE STUDY
It's My Party and I'll Do What I Want To

Subtle and covert political games often take place in settings that on the surface do not seem to be political settings at all. Chapter 4 explained that organizational ceremonies function to maintain the assumptions of an organization. Because those assumptions underlie the view of "reality" that its members take for granted, and because power relationships are grounded in employees' views of reality, maintaining an organization necessarily involves maintaining its power relationships. In

(continued)

a study of annual ceremonies at a Philadelphia-area advertising agency—a Christmas party and an annual breakfast—Michael Rosen has shown the subtle and powerful ways in which ceremonial events serve as covert power games.

Organizational ceremonies are part party (a celebration of a sense of community that binds people together) and part work (a reminder of the status and power hierarchy that separates people from one another). The Shoenman and Associates annual Christmas party had characteristics of both. Although it was held after hours on the Friday before Christmas, attendance was required. No spouses or family members were allowed to attend (except the boss's family), and a formal program—a four-page list of the evening's activities printed on heavy yellow paper—was provided. But the event also was a party. It was held at a rustic bar away from work, where people seemed to eat, drink, and "make merry" with one another as equals regardless of their formal rank, and where the boss acted more like a host than like a supervisor—wearing casual clothes and circulating from table to table making small talk at each stop. But the tension between the two identities is also quite clear. As one married member put it, the structure of the event tells employees that "your work is your life, and these are your friends. It's so f—— weird. There's dancing later. I don't want to dance with people that I work with." The party *did* require employees to be away from their families for an extended period during the most family-oriented time of the year. Nevertheless, perhaps because of the timing—the holiday season—or the location, most of the employees seemed to think of the event as more party than work.

After dinner was over, the program began—a series of jokes and skits that were carefully prepared and professionally executed. All of them were funny; all were ambiguous; most made fun of the higher-ups in the firm. Together they created a joking relationship that seemed to help bridge or flatten the hierarchy of the firm. They celebrated the bosses' problems. All three top managers were going through divorces. The employees joked about the divorces and presented a skit entitled "The Mating Game" (a take-off of the TV series *The Dating Game*) that included a voluptuous blonde asking pointed questions about the sexual appetites and exploits of the three divorcing upper managers. Other jokes and skits made fun of the managers' status symbols and of one manager's inability to keep secretaries because he was so obnoxious. The humor also commented on the crazed pace and work hours of the agency—one skit raffled off a coupon for electroshock psychotherapy treatments, and many of the jokes were about the craziness of the work environment. They also made fun of other workers. One skit spoofed the large number of female employees who dyed their hair blond; another made fun of the different attire of the business side of the operation (dark blue suits and ties) and the creative side (almost anything else).

At one level, the humor made it seem that the organization's hierarchy had disappeared and it was a community of equals. After the program ended, the participants adjourned to the bar and dance floor. During this very informal part of the ceremony, bosses and subordinates buddied around the bar, arms on shoulders, joking and laughing. Workers commented on how the humor had skewered the bosses. Some were even honest with management. The obnoxious manager asked the office manager what people thought of him. Thinking "what the h—," she told him that he was considered to be a bastard and was the most disliked person in the agency, something she admitted that she never would have said at work. She could get by with saying it because they were at a party. In Western societies eating signals community, and drinking alcohol symbolizes freedom, especially from the drudgery of work. Parties are times of unusual license, and frictions encountered in the presence of alcohol tend to be forgiven. It *seemed* that the rules of the game were very different at the party than they were at work.

But behind the scenes things were different. Hierarchy and formal power/authority relationships were subtle, but still in place. People seemed to dance with one another as equals; but even during the most informal part of the party, the women (most of whom are secretaries) danced with males who were their own age or older and who occupied higher positions in the organization. The skits that skewered upper management were written by a skits committee only after a lengthy negotiation process, and they were revised many times before being approved by the committee chair. As one member put it, "We really had to watch our asses, but we had a f—— ball putting this thing together." A skit at the previous year's party had superimposed a picture of the boss over a picture of a farmer in overalls, boots, and pitchfork, with the title "Big Wally (boss) Sells B—s— (advertising) Cheaper." Walter had made it very clear that the picture was out of bounds, primarily because it was a permanent record that could leave the party, not a joke or skit that could be remembered but not reproduced. Through censorship, the rules of the work game invaded the party game, and actions that were permitted under the party rules were not allowed to be carried back to the work game. In addition, much of the party celebrated and legitimated the rules of the work game. One of the most important work rules was that work comes before anything else—that all employees were expected to sacrifice their personal and family lives to meet deadlines and satisfy clients' every whim. Much of the humor at the party focused on the frenetic pace of the organization—even divorces could be celebrated, because everyone knew that they resulted, at least in part, from the demands of the workplace. Even the party itself required employees to sacrifice time that could be spent with outside relationships.

Interactional rules were constantly being negotiated, but negotiated in a way that maintained the underlying power relationships. Subordinates *could* make fun of their supervisors, but only in approved ways. Supervisors *could* fraternize with their subordinates, but only in ways that maintained the hierarchy of the firm. Supervisors *could* ask for frank reports on how they were perceived by others; but they alone could decide what to do with that information. Subordinates *could* give frank responses, but only in private and only when asked. Some kinds of commu-

(continued)

(Case Study, continued)

nication were out of bounds and other kinds were permitted. Although the bounds were different at the party than at work, boundaries did exist, and in negotiating them everyone was reminded that underneath it all was a power relationship that could not be challenged.

Whereas the Christmas ceremony was a party that retained vestiges of the power and authority relationships at work, the breakfast ceremony was work with some of the trappings of a party. It was held at one of Philadelphia's most posh hotels, and everyone was dressed in formal attire—even the servers. In one way everyone was alike—even the lowliest employees could experience opulence at least once a year just by being part of the team. For a moment, they were being served instead of serving. But in other ways the opulence focused attention on hierarchy—most of the employees could never have afforded this place on their salaries, and for a short time everyone was looking and consuming *as if they were managers,* not as if they were regular employees. It also obscured differences between the business and artistic sides of the organization.

After breakfast, the speeches started. The boss (Walter) was in control of the entertainment part of this ritual. Walter congratulated everyone for the firm's success and noted that it occurred in spite of the recession, in spite of "problems" in the public relations division, and because of their hard work and sacrifice (late hours and frenetic work pace). Walter gave gifts to retirees and recognized their loyalty to the firm. Walter talked about the "things the agency does for *us,*" like funding the pension program (not mentioning that the "agency" [that is, Walter] has a legal obligation to do so, that "it" did so instead of giving year-end bonuses that were customary in other advertising agencies and had been customary in their firm, or that it could do so because of the work and skills of the workers). After a slide show that made fun of the creative side of the firm, Walter announced that the money that would have gone to bonuses reluctantly had to be retained "for the good of the firm." Although managers would benefit from the decision, because it would increase the value of their stock in the firm, it meant that the workers' incomes actually fell because of the effects of inflation. Raises and bonuses would be given only when management decided that they should be given, and no one knew when that might be. One accountant referred to this tendency to leave potentially troubling details out of his announcements about the munificence of management as a "Walterism."

Finally, the vice president of public relations spoke. He talked about how important the division was, admitted that it had problems and failures, and confessed that all of those problems were his fault. After the confessional, Walter returned to the podium and led the celebrants in a pep rally, focusing on telling versus listening ("If everyone in this agency told and listened, we'd have fifteen percent more revenue"); me versus we ("If we can get all of the ambitions of the Me under the We, Shoenman and Associates could add another 15 to 20 percent to our revenues"); and drive/win ("Laid-back people have no place in this agency . . . drive is what it takes to win . . . let's get back to work").

Although still subtle, the discourse at breakfast enacted the organization's power relationships in a much more overt form than the Christmas party did. *Walter* decided who would be rewarded, who would be chastised, and who would be allowed to talk. *Walter* defined and celebrated the values of the organization and legitimated them in terms of increased revenues. And *Walter* decided how those revenues would be distributed. Although at least some of the employees understood all of these things, they said nothing, for saying nothing is how *they* played the Walter game.

Applying What You've Learned

1. What were the assumptions about supervisor-subordinate relationships at Shoenman's?
2. How did the behaviors at the parties enact those rules? How did they undermine them?

Questions to Think About and Discuss

1. Rosen argues that these political rituals are important because they obscure the organizational power relationships while enforcing them. How would the employees' interpretations and responses have been different if Walter had been overt and direct about his expectations about employee performance and his evaluations of their work? Why?
2. What would have happened if an employee who understood what was going on had spoken up? How would the other employees have responded? Why?

This case is based on Michael Rosen, "You Asked for It: Christmas at the Bosses' Expense," *Journal of Management Studies* 25 (1988): 463–480; and "Breakfast at Spiro's," in *Reframing Organizational Culture*, Peter Frost, L. Moore, M. R. Louis, C. Lundberg, and J. Martin, eds. (Newbury Park, CA: Sage, 1991), pp. 77–89.

Emotion Regulation and Unobtrusive Control

So far we have discussed cultural control in terms of employees' thoughts—the ways in which they come to identify with the dominant beliefs and values of their organizations. But human beings are not only thinking creatures; they also are emotional beings. Emotions are relevant to cultural forms of motivation and control in three ways. At the simplest level, organizations can overtly manipulate employees' emotional responses. The emotions may be positive, as in ceremonies of enhancement. Often employees receive recognition based as much on complying with the organization's demands as on making tangible contributions. In any case, public recognition of subordinates serves to solidify the supervisor's power position, because she or he makes the decision about whom to recognize and how to do so. Negative emotions serve similar control functions. For example, many observers of the downsizing and outsourcing of tasks that dominated U.S. firms during the 1990s believe that both practices are designed more to control workers through fear and anxiety than to enhance organizational efficiency.[25] Manipulating negative emotions reduces employees' self-esteem and makes them more compliant; they follow orders more readily and are less likely to see emotional manipulation as a control strategy. For example, Pan American airline flight attendants who had been made to feel shame about their age, weight, or sexual orientation were more likely to refuse to go along with a union slowdown and vote against their co-workers than those who had not experienced degradation. Supervisors who are made to feel embarrassed for mixing with their subordinates tend to withdraw from them and become more autocratic.[26]

Control also is exercised when employees learn to interpret emotions in ways that are preferred by the organization. Emotional responses are highly ambiguous. Fear and excitement *feel* very much the same, so they must be interpreted. The core beliefs and values of an organization often tell employees how to interpret their emotional responses. They may learn to feel pride only when the organization's goals are met, not when their own objectives are fulfilled. For example, flight attendants may be successfully taught to interpret their anger at obnoxious passengers as care and concern for their helpless and dependent charges.

Finally, employees may learn to actually feel the emotions that are desired by their organizations. The process begins when employees are taught to obey particular **display rules** as part of their jobs. For example, people who work in the leisure/tourism industry are required to constantly display positive emotions and to elicit them in their clients or customers. Flight attendants and cruise ship employees are expected to be happy, perky, and concerned about meeting their customers' needs and to make the customers feel the same positive emotions. In contrast, bill collectors are expected to display negative emotions, such as disgust, in order to elicit other negative emotions (guilt) from the people they contact. Other employees must display neutral (or no) emotions, even in crisis situations, to calm the people around them. No matter how trivial a call to 911 might seem to be (the Chicago-area 911 gets many calls regarding parking just before Bears' home games), or how much of a crisis is involved (for example, a burglar is actually in someone's home), operators are expected to remain calm, collected, and emotionally distant. Employees can manage these demands in three different ways. They may pretend that they feel the emotions that they display, a process that usually is labeled "**surface acting.**" This kind of acting is exhausting. In many ways, it is easier to manage the dissonance and discomfort created by surface acting by learning to actually feel the desired emotions, to engage in a kind of **deep acting.**

For example, Arlie Hochschild's study of flight attendants found that emotions often are not just responses to work, but that emotion control *is* the work. Flight attendants learn to experience only the feelings that are required by their organizational roles and to suppress other feelings. They create a package of emotions and emotional displays in which genuinely felt emotions are transformed into organizationally acceptable emotions. In a way, this is the easiest response to organizational demands for emotion regulation. Acting, in either its surface or deep forms, creates dissonance. It is uncomfortable to feel one thing (for instance, disgust at a client's lifestyle) and display another (warmth and concern). And it is exhausting to continually do so—acting takes a great deal of effort. This dissonance is lowest, and the amount of effort is reduced, when one actually feels the emotions that he or she is supposed to feel and express. Emotion management can lead to burnout, reduced self-esteem, depression, and cynicism. But if employees learn to deal with it, emotion management can increase job satisfaction and enhance feelings of connectedness and community at work, as well as causing workers to believe that they are performing their tasks well and having a major impact at work. This is why employees who have been in careers that require emotion management for a long time experience less dissonance and less effort than newcomers to such a profession.[27]

CASE STUDY
The Hidden Emotions of Tourism

As we indicate throughout this book, resistance is an inevitable aspect of systems of motivation and control. This is true even of cultural forms of control, although if unobtrusive control is working, it is largely invisible. Consequently, resistance is less likely than in other forms, but it still is possible. Some modes of resistance may be overt and public. For example, some of the stewardesses in Hochschild's study admitted "accidentally" spilling hot coffee in the laps of especially obnoxious travelers. But it is more likely that resistance to unobtrusive control will occur in private places and times. This case is about emotional control and resistance in three tourism-related organizations, an airline (FWA), a cruise ship (the *Radiant Spirit*), and *Pairs,* an upscale, all-inclusive Caribbean resort. The names have been changed to protect the innocent—and the guilty. *Pairs* and *Radiant* cater to people from all over the world but primarily from Europe and North America. FWA has a less exclusive clientele but also operates largely in North America. Their marketing rhetoric, from brochures to television ads, depict all three businesses as catering to tourists in every way. At *Pairs* frontline employees, all of whom are black, are taught that they are to display the "happy-go-lucky" attitude that tourists expect of Caribbean people. Employees on the *Radiant,* all of whom are white, learn to mimic the behaviors of the crew of the television series *The Love Boat,* which above everything else means to constantly be smiling and "perky." In all three, employees learn that the customer is always right and that employees will always be smiling, happy servants. They also learn that these duties have no limits. One *Pairs* staff member said, "A guest coming here could be a thief or a murderer, but we have to be nice to them no matter what." Cassie, a *Radiant* employee, told about a man at the ship disco who

> asked me to dance. He was grabbing and holding me close . . . and saying these
> weird things . . . [like] "have you ever thought of coming over to the dark side?" I

(continued)

(Case Study, continued)

just played dumb. . . . In this type of situation you don't want to piss someone off. . . . I didn't know what I could get away with and what I could not. I was so frustrated that I had no control.*

When Cassie reported the incident to her supervisor, she was told to walk away when things like that happen. But after a training program that included the motto "We never say no," she really didn't know what to do, and she blamed herself for not knowing.

All three organizations use a variety of mechanisms to enforce their behavioral rules. At *Pairs* each guest is given an evaluation sheet that includes a section where she or he is asked to comment on the performance of the staff by name. Twice a month the public relations office posts the comments for all employees to see. Cash rewards are given to employees who receive many positive comments, and punishments are given those with negative comments. The *Radiant* uses a similar system, and it works so well that employees believe that the passengers are their "second bosses," who control the employees' actions and emotions. But their cash awards seem to focus on control as well as service—one employee won an award by suggesting that mirrors be installed throughout the ship so that employees could constantly monitor their appearance. FWA uses "ghost riders," supervisors who fly disguised as customers.

The employees themselves help discipline one another. *Pairs* posts summaries of customer comments. When the sheets are posted, all the desk staff excitedly huddle together behind the reception desk to read the results. Workers read positive comments aloud for all to hear; workers with the highest points received congratulations from their peers; workers with negative comments and low points are talked about behind their backs for the rest of the week. When Ken, a bellman, walked by the desk, Simone teased him by saying "I don't see your name here." He immediately turned the pages of the report until he found a remark that included his name: "It only takes one," he said. If any of the *Radiant*'s workers complain, their co-workers will tell them, "It's a tough job. If you can't handle it, go home."

The control system does *seem* to work. Most of the workers are like Trendy, about whom a *Pairs* worker commented, "I have never seen Trendy get mad. I'm not telling a lie. In all the years I've been here I've just seen her smile [when guests or supervisors are present]." A *Radiant* employee said, "Our job is to be happy, and there will be times when you don't feel that way. You have to put it aside and look as though you're enjoying your job."† The employees' performances are so fluid and so convincing that they seem to be scripted. One script welcomes new guests: "Hi, I'm Laura, your concierge [big smile]. I am here to help. If you have any questions don't hesitate to call. If any situations arise (I won't say problems because we don't have problems at *Pairs*), please call. We are out of the office a lot, but we have a radio, so just call the operator and he will get in touch with us." Even the actor's voice is scripted. When the staff members talk to one another or to guests from the Caribbean they use the local patois, with its rhythmic tone and colorful metaphors. But with most guests only standard English is used.

Perhaps most important, most of the workers see their act as just that, a strategic way of behaving that fulfills management's commands while making their lives easier. *Radiant* employees complained bitterly that management shoved the customer service program down their throats. And behind the scenes—in the galleys of airliners, the back rooms of resorts, and the tiny employee staterooms on cruise ships—"servanthood" is a different thing entirely. When safely out of the hearing of guests or management, *Pairs* staffers talk about anything and everything, and they often complain about the customers, making it clear that it simply isn't true that the customer is always right. A *Radiant* employee told all his peers about a customer who asked if the ship generates its own electricity; the employee wondered "what if I would have told him, 'No, we run an extra long electric cord back to port.'" Simone was working at the *Pairs* registration desk with Sandy one day, and a U.S. tourist interrupted and asked Sandy if he could mail his postcards with U.S. stamps. Sandy, in his best British English, explained that he would have to use local stamps, "because each country uses its own stamps and postal system." As the guest departed, Sandy immediately shifted into his local dialect, and the employees talked at length about how little U.S. residents, including Sandy's friends at school, knew about Caribbean or West Indian culture. In fact, one of the dominant topics of conversation involved the various failings of the guests—their stupid questions ("Why is it raining?" or "What language are the staff members speaking?" [the answer is English]), their arrogance (for example, one U.S. resident repeatedly demanded that the desk clerk check his bill for unauthorized long-distance calls after seeing his maid using his phone, even after being told that the maids *always* use the room phones to notify the desk when they have finished cleaning a room), their paranoia (a German couple would not leave their luggage for a moment lest a staff member steal a tacky palm-leaf hat, and another couple demanded to know the location of the American embassy in case of civil unrest, something that had not happened on this island in almost a century), and their racism (all staff members are black; almost all guests are white). Telling these stories to one another seemed to have three purposes—they place the worker in a superior role vis-à-vis the guest, thus reversing the complete subservience demanded by their organization; they help cushion the worker from negative comments by the guests, making it less likely that they will blame themselves when they encounter rude behavior; and, paradoxically, they allow the worker to continue to play his or her assigned role while simultaneously rejecting it.

Employees also share with one another strategies for resisting the control system. FWA old-timers tell new employees how to detect ghost riders and how to use privacy laws to short-circuit managerial strategies, such as making random checks of the flight attendants' bags. They teach one another to follow the most alienating rules only when management is around. Terry was told to never again wear her

(continued)

(Case Study, continued)

Santa earrings on flights during the holidays. To get around the policy, she took them off when management was around and put them on when she stepped on a plane. They fulfill the requirement to wear makeup only during their annual performance reviews and wear the required high-heeled shoes only when flying through a hub city where managers are likely to be hanging around. They teach one another to use humor to keep overbearing pilots in their places and to combat the sexism that often accompanies their jobs: they bring beverages to the pilots before takeoff as ordered, but poke fun at the rule by asking them if they need to be "hydrated." Or they devise systems that allow them to escape the housemothers who are assigned to women's dormitories during training—for example, signing one another in and out in order to resist curfews that the airlines impose on adults—and satirically label the experience "Barbie Bootcamp."

The goal of this case study has been to contrast employees' public performances—those that take place in the view of people who have the organizational right to control them, supervisors and customers—and their private or "hidden" performances. The greater the power gap between controllers and controlled, the more different these two types of performances will be. If one looks at public performances alone, it seems that unobtrusive control is total—employees' beliefs, values, and feelings correspond with the desires of their organizations. But if one also examines their hidden messages, a much more complex picture emerges. Workers in all three organizations do seem to have internalized the core beliefs and values of their organizations and do seem to be willing to enforce behavioral constraints on themselves and their peers. This is especially true in public but also seems to be true to some degree in private. However, they also engage in complex processes of resisting, sometimes in public and often in private. Organizational life seems to involve a "dance of resistance and domination."[‡]

Applying What You've Learned

1. What evidence is there that the employees of these tourist organizations have identified with their organizations and roles in them? What evidence is there that they have not done so?
2. How does surveillance work in these organizations? Who does it? How do they do it, and with what effects?

Questions to Think About and Discuss

1. How do the various forms of control used at *Pairs, Radiant,* and FWA support one another? How would the points/bonus system work differently if there was no system of managers watching the employees? No system of guests being encouraged to watch and report on the employees? No training program or messages that support the organizations' core beliefs and values?

2. What functions does resistance play for the workers? What effects does it have on the functioning of the organization? On the organizational control system? Why?

3. Some theorists argue that unobtrusive control soon will go the way of the dinosaurs. Recent trends toward short-term employment (recall Chapter 1) mean that employees will not be in a company long enough to even learn its core beliefs and values, much less identify with it. Others argue that people are getting more and more isolated from one another, so that their workplace is the only source of community that is available to them. As a result, unobtrusive control will be even more powerful. What do you think? Why?

This case is based on Simone Carnegie, "The Hidden Emotions of Tourism: Communication and Power in the Caribbean" (master's thesis, Texas A&M University, 1996); Alexandra Murphy, "Hidden Transcripts of Flight Attendant Resistance," *Management Communication Quarterly* 11 (1998): 499–535; and Sarah J. Tracy, "Becoming a Character for Commerce," *Management Communication Quarterly* 14 (2000): 90–128. The key source for all three studies is James Scott, *Domination and the Arts of Resistance* (New Haven, CT: Yale University Press, 1990). For an analysis of resistance in a very different kind of organization, see D. Collinson, *Managing the Shop Floor* (New York: DeGruyter, 1992).

*Carnegie, p. 110.

†Carnegie, p. 106.

‡Tracy, p. 99.

Summary: Unobtrusive Control and Self-Surveillance

Both the traditional and the relational strategies of organizing rely on systems of motivation and control that are **obtrusive,** that is, known by and visible to workers. Indeed, if employees are not aware of and do not understand systems of reward and punishment, or policies and procedures, those systems will not succeed.[28] Similarly, concertive control—when peers monitor and control one another in some kind of team arrangement—relies on workers' awareness of the rules and regulations, although workers may perceive that they had a voice in creating those rules. Obtrusive control systems are difficult to administer because employees may interpret them in unanticipated ways, and because they often have unintended consequences. In addition, the more obtrusive a control system is, the more it robs employees of a sense of autonomy and the opportunity to be creative. As a result, they often choose to resist obtrusive motivation/control/surveillance systems. In contrast, cultural strategies of organizing focus on **unobtrusive** forms of control—in which employees choose to act in ways desired by the organization while perceiving that they are freely choosing to do so. In effect, organizational surveillance becomes **self-surveillance,** a process in which employees act in ways that are desired by the organization because they have internalized its core beliefs and values, identify with it, and feel positive emotions when they comply with its commands. Unobtrusive control is simultaneously the most potent and most fragile form of control. Persuading people to change deeply held values, beliefs, and identities is an exceptionally difficult process. Core beliefs and values will not be seen as legitimate if they contradict the experiences workers have had and messages they have received outside of the work setting. If unobtrusive control is perceived as manipulation, it is likely to fail, and to alienate. In addition, negative events at work can lead people to critically analyze the organization's core beliefs. Overt resistance by a handful of employees can have the same effect. In extreme cases, employees may "dis-identify" with their organizations. Consequently, organizations tend to rely on a mixture of obtrusive and unobtrusive control systems, but that practice may also lead employees to view unobtrusive strategies as manipulation.

Cultural Strategies of Leadership

We noted earlier in this chapter that there is a key tension within cultural strategies of organizing. On the one hand they assume that organizational cultures can be managed strategically. But on the other hand they assert that employees actively perceive, interpret, and strategically respond to their organizational situations. Thus, employees may come to believe, feel, and act in different ways than management assumed they would. Cultural strategies of leadership recognize that this tension exists and strive to deal with it through what have been labeled "transformational" processes. The most important of these processes are called *visioning* and *framing*.

Visioning and Transformational Leadership

Both transformational and transactional leaders are characterized by their consideration for employees and their needs, by their willingness to actively involve their subordinates in decision making (even encouraging them to question the basic assumptions of the organization or unit), and by their willingness to supervise loosely. Both forms of leadership involve similar communicative strategies: leaders clarify the challenges that the organization or unit faces while encouraging, supporting, and inspiring their subordinates to use their own abilities to meet those challenges. Transformational and transactional leaders both maintain close communicative ties with their subordinates.

But transformational leaders also differ from transactional leaders. Their authority is based on what Max Weber called **charisma,** the image that they possess some divine, supernatural, or otherwise special talents or attributes. At the heart of charismatic leadership is the ability to create a vision of where the organization or unit is going and how it is to achieve those goals and persuade others to accept that vision.[29] Visionary leadership involves communicating a mission for the organization or unit that is noble or otherwise meaningful for employees. The vision encompasses each employee's hopes, desires, and so on (even if it requires the leader to sacrifice some of her or his own gains). Visionary leadership involves a great deal of impression management—displays of personal integrity and a willingness to take reasonable risks and give of oneself for the good of the organization and demonstrations of personal warmth and charm, including showing concern for employees and their nonwork lives.[30] Transformational leaders are able to transform their subordinates' creative ideas and actions so that they further the mission of the organization or unit and do so without embarrassing them or claiming ownership of their ideas.

Of course, not just any vision will do. A transformative vision is realistic and credible. It is consistent with the history of the organization or unit and fits the realities of the current situation, and it is attractive. It provides targets that beckon. The genius of transformational leadership is the ability to "assemble— out of all the variety of images, signals, forecasts, and alternatives—a clearly articulated vision of the future that is at once simple, easily understood, clearly desirable, and energizing."[31] Visions provide a picture of the future, an explanation and sense of purpose, and guidelines for acting on an everyday basis. They allow each employee to find his or her own role in the organization, his or her own way to contribute to the mission, and in doing so, they release new energies and enthusiasm. Visions emerge over time, with experience, and through mutual consultation with subordinates. They are flexible and adaptive. They include long-term goals that help define a series of short-term goals, which in turn both guide and are influenced by goals that emerge out of everyday experience. For example, when Dr. Barbara Barlow was appointed chief of pediatric surgery at Harlem Hospital Center, her goals focused on successful treatment of patients. But she and her staff noted that many patients were hospitalized because of injuries suffered from falling out of buildings, playing on unsafe playground equipment, and improperly operating their bicycles. So her goals changed to focus on preventive care as well as acute care—increasing the number of window gates in apartment buildings, teaching children safety rules and street smarts, and so on. Her unit now pursues long-term, short-term, and emergent goals simultaneously, and each kind of goal influences the pursuit of the others.[32]

Finally, visions are *appropriately* ambiguous. It is somewhat ironic that transformation leadership *relies* on ambiguity, because ambiguity complicates cultural strategies of motivation and control. When situations and symbolic acts are ambiguous, employees have much more freedom to reinterpret them and act in ways that differ from what the leader intended. But ambiguity may be intentional and strategic. This may seem to be a somewhat strange concept for members of Western societies, because they have been taught to value clear communication. In many non-Western societies, ambiguity is treated as something that should be managed strategically. Some situations call for a high level of clarity and specificity—communicating technical standards for precision equipment or delivering negative performance feedback, for example. In other cases, ambiguity can actually be helpful. It allows different people to interpret the same message in different ways, helping to maintain a diversity of viewpoints within the same organization. When the organization faces problems that are new or particularly difficult, or when it goes through major organizational changes, this diversity can lead to innovative solutions. Ambiguity may also allow parties involved in conflicts to avoid having to blame anyone for an impasse or escalation, thus saving face. *Teamwork,* an important dimension of both transactional and transformational leadership, is an ambiguous but appealing concept in many societies. In Japan it is associated with loyalty to one's company; in Sweden it refers to one's membership in a work group; in Anglo societies it evokes images of team sports—rugby, cricket, soccer, baseball, or basketball. Good visions are both sufficiently focused to energize employees and give them a sense of direction and ambiguous enough to allow flexibility. According to cultural/transformational strategies of leadership, this dilemma is managed through processes of framing.

Framing and Transformational Leadership

In addition to persuading employees to accept a particular set of beliefs and values, transformational leadership involves persuading them to see their organizational world in a particular way. It may be as simple as getting them to view a new situation as a challenge rather than a problem. The ambiguities of organizational life create spaces within which transformational leaders can act. Framing begins when a leader develops her or his own view of reality and makes sense of the organization's past, present, and future in terms of that view. It continues when she or he communicates that view to subordinates. In this sense, the key to framing lies in employees' memories. If a leader's interpretation makes sense and seems to be spontaneous, honest, and motivated by a legitimate concern for the organization and employees, it may be credible. However, if it is perceived as being manipulative, controlling, or uncaring, it will not be.[33] If the supervisor has conveyed a credible interpretation, then when employees later encounter a new situation, they will automatically approach it through the supervisor's frame of reference. Eventually the entire work group or organization will begin to share the same way of making sense out of the world.

In some cases, members of the organization may develop a language that is consistent with their frame of reference. They will think in terms of a particular set of metaphors and categories, interpret events in accord with stories and myths that they share, and infuse their new language with beliefs and values that are especially meaningful. Thus, the key to persuading subordinates to accept a transformational leader's frame of reference is not overt persuasion. Instead, persuasion occurs when a leader uses a particular frame of reference in his or her everyday activities to make sense out of events. By paying attention to some things and ignoring others, expressing honest emotions of anger in response to some things and joy in response to others, and reacting to critical incidents and crises in particular ways, we let other people know how we make sense out of life, and in the process we let them know what we really value. The supervisor-subordinate relationships that emerge can be empowering for workers, because they capitalize on enthusiasm and create feelings of significance, competence, and connectedness to others who share a common purpose.[34]

For example, a new resort was about to open. The employees were anxious because they knew about a neighboring resort that had recently experienced a disastrous opening day; everything that could have gone wrong did. Recognizing how nervous everyone was, the CEO convened a meeting of all employees and said:

> We have all noticed the bad press about [the other resort's] opening day. You can't help but feel the pressure. Despite our confidence and all that we've done to get ready for tomorrow, you can be sure that something will go wrong. But that's not what makes a bad opening day. It's how you deal with what goes wrong that makes the difference. Tomorrow, you will see people walking around looking lost. You'll be lost too. Instead of sitting there feeling insecure, walk up to our guests and introduce yourself. Say, "I'm new here too, but I'm going to do my best to try to help you."

He went on to tell other stories about people bringing order out of chaos and thereby replaced the failure scenario that the employees had been circulating with a more positive one. The exchange helped put people at ease and contributed to a successful opening day.[35]

Of course, leaders do communicate their frames of reference in more formal ways. During planning sessions, a leader sets an agenda for a group by guiding the discussion toward a certain set of priorities or suggesting that the group view a particular event or problem in a certain way. Leaders also send powerful messages about what they actually value when they appraise employees' performance and distribute rewards. But the most powerful way to communicate a frame is by everyday behavior, by seizing what Gail Fairhurst and Robert Sarr call **"leadership moments,"** opportunities to suggest a particular way to view events, messages, and communication.

Technology Information and Communication in Cultural Strategies of Organizing

It is common to think of information and communication technologies (ICTs) as neutral products of science and engineering. Certainly science, engineering, and design are important factors in the production of technologies. However, ICTs also embody cultural assumptions and political influences.[36] Take the personal computer, for example. Until very recently the PC was designed for people with good vision; a person with a visual impairment was unable to use most of the features on a PC. Voice activated computers were an accommodation that developed in response to problems that people with visual impairments had with PCs, which are still largely visual in orientation. PCs are also difficult to use for people who have trouble understanding or processing visual information of the type that appears on the computer screen. While most people younger than fifty find PCs fairly natural, to the authors' parents and to many of your grandparents the PC seems unnatural and alien. Some of them have never managed to grasp what an icon is or how word processors work. PCs also are heavily oriented to those with good typing skills. Despite the graphical interfaces of most PCs today, the most efficient mode of inputting large amounts of information is still via keyboard. People who favor handwriting and have never learned to type and those who prefer or are forced to speak their input have been, until recently, out of luck. Further, PCs are organized around an office metaphor. Microsoft explicitly uses the desktop metaphor in its software, and other operating systems implicitly model the computer screen as a table. For those who do not work in offices, this is an unnatural metaphor, and it takes such users considerable time to master the desktop idea. Systems designed for use in warehouses and other active workplaces typically have a different type of interface, often organized around buttons, that seems more natural to these users.

It was not inevitable that PC designs favor vision over other senses or the office or table over other work areas. Their makers were not forced to adopt these designs. The designers' thinking was channeled by choices that seemed natural and obvious to them but also reflected certain values. The dominance of visual thinking in Western scientific inquiry tended to favor visual over other approaches to PC design. The IBM PC, which set the standard for design, was designed for office workers because this was the biggest market for PCs at the time; a desktop metaphor seemed natural. However, as we have observed throughout this chapter, what seems natural to one person or culture may seem strange and artificial to another.

ICTs, like all cultural artifacts and symbols, play an important role in creating and sustaining organizational culture. They embody assumptions of the broader culture, as the PC illustrates, but they also are tailored to embody the organizational culture. In an organization that seeks to create a highly work-focused professional culture, PCs are likely to have standard logos and applications. The software on them and the use of the software are likely to be tightly controlled by the information systems department. An organization with a looser culture that looks to its employees for creativity may allow users to put whatever graphic they want—however strange or irreverent—on their PC screen and may allow employees to play computer games and surf the Internet while they incubate ideas.

Organizations also use ICTs to symbolize and shape their cultures. Over the past five years customer relationship management (CRM) systems, a type of work-integration ICT that enables companies to keep track of and provide enhanced customer service, have been growing in popularity. Implementing a CRM requires the organization to redesign how its employees work with customers, and this often requires redesigning the entire work process. For example, a CRM enables companies to identify their most loyal customers and calls up a special script for dealing with them, which may contain special offers or extra services. Installing a CRM is a strong signal that the organization has a customer-service orientation and is cultivating a customer-centered culture. Some organizations use this to reinforce already existing aspects of their cultures, whereas others may implement a CRM in an effort to change their culture. The CRM not only changes member behavior; it is an expensive and potent symbol of the value of customer service.

Culture also has a reciprocal effect on ICTs. ICTs not in line with organizational culture will often meet with resistance. For example, a university system

whose culture stressed the autonomy of local campuses attempted to implement a financial management system that was uniform across all units in the system. The new system met considerable resistance from the campuses, especially
those that were large and brought in large amounts of research funding. The end
result was that three of the twenty units in the system did not use the system
and some of the other units used it, but kept their own unique accounting systems that ran in parallel with the financial management system.[37]

ICTs are also used differently in different organizational cultures. An interesting study of a computerized calendar system found that use varied according
to organizational culture. An organization with a very work-oriented, rigid culture used the calendar system as a control device. They set it so that everyone
could see everyone else's calendars. In this culture a blank spot on an employee's calendar was interpreted to indicate that the employee was free for a
meeting or (worse) that she or he was not working hard enough. And heaven
help the employee who typed "gone golfing" into a time period when others
were working. In a different organization, whose culture emphasized autonomy
and flexibility, calendars were used quite differently. Large blank spaces were interpreted to mean the employee was taking some time to think through a new
idea or design a new product. Managers did not check calendars to make sure
they were filled and the employee was working hard. Instead the calendar was
mainly used as a coordination device for the many meetings required in this participatory culture.

Thinking Critically about Cultural Strategies

In chapters 3 through 5 we have examined three common strategies of organizing in isolation of one another. We did so because each strategy is so complicated
that it is impossible to treat them together. But doing so may be a bit misleading,
because it makes these strategies seem to be mutually exclusive. There are few,
if any, real organizations that use only one strategy of organizing. Organizations
emerge and develop in their own, distinctive ways as their members collaborate
and compete while dealing with the situations they face. In Chapter 6 we present a fourth strategy of organizing, one that often generates organizations that
do not really seem to be organizations. And, as Chapter 6 explains at length, processes of organizing often lead to the creation of organizations that are filled with
tensions and contradictions that must be managed through communication.
Sometimes, those tensions are managed by creating relatively independent subcultures, as this chapter explained. In other cases, the tensions become the primary principle that energizes members and links them together.

We also recognize that we have presented a somewhat paradoxical view of
motivation, control, and leadership in organizations. In some ways, traditional
strategies may seem to be the most "ethical" form of organizing because they are
"honest" and open. Control and reward structures are clear to everyone—indeed, they fail if they are not visible and clearly understood. But they also are

based on inequality and domination. Conversely, relational and cultural strategies are more satisfying and seem to be more empowering than traditional strategies, but their success depends on their not being viewed as systems of control. In extreme cases, they may be implemented in exceptionally manipulative ways. In short, while some system of motivation and control must exist for a society or organization to function (recall the "fundamental paradox" described in Chapter 1), assessing their ethicality is a very difficult proposition. All strategies of organizing are value-laden, and how they are evaluated depends not only on the values that are applied, but also on the relative importance that is afforded to different values.

Notes

[1] Stephen Fineman, "Emotion and Organizing," in *Handbook of Organization Studies,* Stewart Clegg, Cynthia Hardy, and Walter Nord, eds. (Thousand Oaks, CA: Sage, 1999).

[2] Joanne Martin, *Cultures in Organizations: Three Perspectives* (New York: Oxford University Press, 1992).

[3] Karl Weick has argued that decentralization and participation are necessary for cultural strategies to succeed ("Organizational Culture and High Reliability," *California Management Review* 29 [1987]: 112–127). Also see Weick's *Making Sense of the Organization* (London: Blackwell, 2000).

[4] For an extended analysis of the development of the cultural strategy, see Eric Eisenberg and Patricia Riley, "Organizational Culture," in *The New Handbook of Organizational Communication,* F. Jablin and L. Putnam, eds. (Thousand Oaks, CA: Sage, 2000). The primary proponents of this view were Tom Peters and Robert Waterman, *In Search of Excellence* (New York: Harper and Row, 1982); Terrance Deal and Alan Kennedy, *Corporate Cultures* (Reading, MA: Addison-Wesley, 1982); and William Ouchi and A. Jaeger (see their "Type Z Organization," *Academy of Management Review* 3 [1978]: 305–314; and William Ouchi, *Theory Z* [Reading, MA: Addison-Wesley, 1981]). The two foundational works in the area were Deal and Kennedy; and Peters and Waterman. *In Search of Excellence* still is the most popular book on organizations ever published (selling more than 5 million copies in its first three years). It generated a series of follow-up books, videotapes, and consulting programs, and by 1987, three years after its publication, Peters's consulting firm was grossing about $3.5 million. In 2003 Peters admitted that the authors had made up the "data" that supported the claims made in the book, which did not surprise its critics. The popularity of the perspective is explained in Charles Conrad, "Review of *A Passion for Excellence,*" *Administrative Science Quarterly* 30 (1985): 426–429). The dominance of the perspective is examined by Stephen Barley, G. W. Meyer, and Debra Gash, "Cultures of Culture," *Administrative Science Quarterly* 33 (1988): 24–60.

[5] William Ouchi and Alan Wilkins, "Efficient Cultures," *Administrative Science Quarterly* 28 (1983): 468–481; Kathleen Gregory, "Native-View Paradigms," *Administrative Science Quarterly* 28 (1983): 360–372; Mary Jo Hatch, *Organization Theory* (Oxford: Oxford University Press, 1997); and Shirley Willinghanz, Joy L. Hart, and Greg Leichty, "Telling the Story of Organizational Change," in *Responding to Crisis,* Dan Millar and Robert Heath, eds. (Mahwah, NJ: Lawrence Erlbaum, 2003).

[6] For examples of subcultural differences, see Michael Rosen, "Breakfast at Spiro's," *Journal of Management* 11 (1985): 31–48; Ed Young, "On the Naming of the Rose," *Organization Studies* 10 (1989): 187–206; and Leslie Baxter, " 'Talking Things Through' and 'Putting It in Writing,' " *Journal of Applied Communication Research* 21 (1994): 313–328.

[7] Alan Wilkins, *Managing Corporate Character* (San Francisco: Jossey-Bass, 1989).

[8] The entry experience usually is thought of as occurring in stages, but that view can easily be misleading. The entry experience is made up of the processes that occur throughout a person's experience in an organization—they are continuous, overlapping, and do not occur in a fixed sequence. There do seem to be key "turning points" that, in retrospect, signaled the declining importance of some thoughts, emotions, and communication processes and the increased importance of others (J. Kevin Barge and G. W. Musambria, "Turning Points in Chair-Faculty Relationships," *Journal of Applied Communication Research* 20 [1992]: 54–77; Connie Bullis and Betsy Wackernagel Bach, "Socialization Turning Points," *Western Journal of Speech Communication,* 53 [1989]: 273–293). Excellent summaries of research on the entry experience include Vernon Miller and Fredric Jablin, "Information Seeking during Organizational Entry," *Academy of Management Review* 16 (1991): 92–120; and Fredric Jablin, "Organizational Entry, Assimilation, and Exit," in *The New Handbook of Organizational Communication,* Fredric Jablin and Linda Putnam, eds. (Newbury Park, CA: Sage, 2000). Two classic articles are Meryl Reis Louis,

"Surprise and Sense-Making in Organizations," *Administrative Science Quarterly* 25 (1980): 226–251; and John van Maanen and Edgar Schein, "Toward a Theory of Socialization," in *Research in Organizational Behavior,* Barry Staw, ed., vol. 1 (Greenwich, CT: JAI Press, 1979).

[9] For fine summaries of newcomers' information-seeking tactics, see Miller and Jablin; Debra Comer, "Organizational Newcomers' Acquisition of Information from Peers," *Management Communication Quarterly* 5 (1991): 64–89; and Michael Kramer, R. R. Callister, and D. B. Turban, "Information-Receiving and Information-Giving during Job Transitions," *Western Journal of Communication* 39 (1995): 151–170.

[10] A summary of these personality variables is available in Terrance Albrecht and Betsy Bach, *Organizational Communication: A Relational Perspective* (Fort Worth, TX: Harcourt Brace, 1996), especially chapter 7; also see Renee Edwards, "Sensitivity to Feedback and the Development of Self," *Communication Quarterly* 38 (1990): 101–111; and Meryl Reis Louis, "Acculturation in the Workplace," in *Organizational Climate and Culture,* B. Schneider, ed. (San Francisco: Jossey-Bass, 1990). Personality variables seem to not be important for people involved in job transfers (see Fredric Jablin and Michael Kramer, "Communication-Related Sense-Making and Adjustment during Job Transfers," *Management Communication Quarterly* 12 [1998]: 155–182).

[11] Cited in Melissa Gibson and Michael Papa, "The Mud, the Blood, and the Beer Guys," *Journal of Applied Communication Research* 28 (2000): 78. The classic study of anticipatory socialization of blue-collar workers is Richard Sennett and James Cobb, *The Hidden Injuries of Class* (New York: Vintage Books, 1972). For a similar case study in organizational control at the U.S. Forest Service, see Connie Bullis and Phil Tompkins, "The Forest Ranger Revisited," *Communication Monographs* 56 (1989): 287–306. For analyses of the processes through which identification occurs, see Michael Pratt, "The Good, the Bad, and the Ambivalent," *Administrative Science Quarterly* 45 (2000): 456–493.

[12] Michael Kramer and Vernon Miller, "A Response to Criticisms of Organizational Socialization Research," *Communication Monographs* 66 (1999): 362–368.

[13] Robin Patric Clair, "The Political Nature of the Colloquialism, 'A Real Job,'" *Communication Monographs* 63 (1996): 249–267.

[14] Steven Ralston and William Kirkwood, "Overcoming Managerial Bias in Employment Interviewing," *Journal of Applied Communication Research* 23 (1995): 75–92. It also is disorienting when the organization changes around its employees, as in mergers (see David Schweiger and Angelo Denisi, "Communication with Employees Following a Merger," *Academy of Management Journal* 34 [1991]: 110–135).

[15] Connie Bullis and K. Rohrbauck Stout, "Organizational Socialization: A Feminist Standpoint Approach," in *Rethinking Organizational and Managerial Communication from Feminist Perspectives,* P. Buzzanell, ed. (Thousand Oaks, CA: Sage, 2000); Cynthia Stohl, "The Role of Memorable Messages in the Process of Organization Socialization," *Communication Quarterly* 34 (1983): 231–249; Jablin and Kramer.

[16] Louis Pondy, "The Role of Metaphors and Myths in the Organization and the Facilitation of Change," and Joanne Martin and Melanie Powers, "Truth or Corporate Propaganda: The Value of a Good War Story," both in *Organizational Symbolism,* L. Pondy, P. Frost, G. Morgan, and T. D. Dandridge, eds. (Greenwich, CT: JAI Press, 1993); Kenwyn Smith and Valerie Simmons, "The Rumpelstiltskin Organization," *Administrative Science Quarterly* 28 (1983): 377–392.

[17] See J. R. Di Sanza and Connie Bullis, "Everybody Identifies with Smokey the Bear: Employee Responses to Newsletter Identification Inducements at the U.S. Forest Service," *Management Communication Quarterly* 12 (1999): 347–399; Robin Patric Clair, "Ways of Seeing," *Communication Monographs* 66 (1999): 374–381. Also see George Cheney, *Rhetoric in an Organizational Society: Managing Multiple Identities* (Columbia: University of South Carolina Press, 1991); Craig Scott, Steven Corman, and George Cheney, "Development of a Structurational Model of Identification in the Organization," *Communication Theory* 8 (1998): 298–336; Linda Larkey and Calvin Morrill, "Organizational Commitment as Symbolic Process," *Western Journal of Communication* 59 (1995): 193–213; Craig Scott, "Identification with Multiple Targets in a Geographically Dispersed Organization," *Management Communication Quarterly* 10 (1997): 491–522.

[18] Traci Callaway Russo, "Organizational and Professional Identification," *Management Communication Quarterly* 12 (1998): 72–111.

[19] Pondy, "Role of Metaphors"; Martin and Melanie Powers; Smith and Simmons.

[20] A number of sources have investigated the relationship between stories and cultures, organizational and otherwise. An extended treatment of the relationship between stories and societal control is available in Dennis Mumby, ed., *Narrative and Social Control: Critical Perspectives* (Newbury Park, CA: Sage, 1993). For extended analyses of organizational stories, see Harrison Trice and Janice Beyer, *The Cultures of Work Organizations* (Englewood Cliffs, NJ: Prentice Hall, 1993). For an extended distinction between lists and stories, see Larry Browning, "Lists and Stories in Organizational Communication," *Communication Theory* 2 (1992): 281–302; and Karl Weick and Larry Browning, "Argument and Narration in Organizational Communication," *Journal of Management* 12 (1986): 243–259.

[21] Walter Fisher, "Narration as a Human Communication Paradigm," *Communication Monographs* 51 (1984): 1-22.

[22] The distinction between stories and storytelling is developed at length in Michael Pacanowsky and Nick O'Donnell-Trujillo, "Performance," and in Michael Pacanowsky, "Creating and Narrating Organizational Realities," in *Rethinking Communication,* vol. 2, Brenda Dervin, Lawrence Grossberg, Barbara O'Keefe, and Ellen Wertella, eds. (Beverly Hills, CA: Sage, 1989). Also see Joachim Knuf, "'Ritual' in Organizational Culture Theory," in *Communication Yearbook 16,* Stanley Deetz, ed. (Newbury Park, CA: Sage, 1993); and David Boje, "The Storytelling Organization," *Administrative Science Quarterly* 36 (1991): 106-126.

[23] Thomas Hollihan and Patricia Riley, "The Rhetorical Power of a Compelling Story," *Communication Quarterly* 35 (1987): 11-20.

[24] See Harrison Trice and Janice Beyer, *Cultures;* and "Studying Organizational Cultures through Rites and Ceremonials," *Academy of Management Review 9 (*1984): 653-669. For an excellent analysis of the ritualized nature of the concept of communicating via the chain of command, see David Golding, "Management Rituals," in *Understanding Management,* Stephen Linstead, R. G. Small, and P. Jeffcutt, eds. (London: Sage, 1996).

[25] Dennis Tourish, N. Paulsen, and P. Bordia, "The Downsides of Downsizing," *Management Communication Quarterly* 17 (2004): 485-516; M. Casey, Vernon Miller, and J. Johnson, "Survivors' Information-Seeking Following a Reduction in Force," *Communication Research* 24 (1997): 755-781; Manfred Kets deVries and K. Balazs, "The Downside of Downsizing," *Human Relations* 50 (1997): 11-50; Richard Burke and Cary Cooper, eds., *The Organization in Crisis: Downsizing, Restructuring, and Privatization* (Oxford: Blackwell, 2000).

[26] H. Flam, "Fear, Loyalty, and Greedy Organizations," in *Emotion in Organizations,* Stephen Fineman, ed. (London: Sage, 1993). For the examples presented in this section, and others, see Sally Planalp, Susan Hafen, and A. Dawn Adkins, "Messages of Shame and Guilt," in *Communication Yearbook 23,* Michael Roloff, ed. (Thousand Oaks, CA: Sage, 2000).

[27] Emotion management is a relatively new topic for organizational communication scholars. The classic study is sociologist Arlie Hochschild's study of stewardesses in *The Managed Heart* (Berkeley: University of California Press, 1983). Alexandra Murphy revisited flight attendants in "Hidden Transcripts of Flight Attendant Resistance," *Management Communication Quarterly* 11 (1998): 499-535. And Sarah Tracy and Karen Tracy examined 911 operators in "Emotion Labor at 911," *Journal of Applied Communication Research* 26 (1998): 390-411. A recent special issue of *Management Communication Quarterly* summarizes recent trends. See Susan Kruml and Deanna Geddes, "Exploring the Dimensions of Emotional Labor," 14 (2000): 8-49; Sherianne Shuler and Beverly Davenport Sypher, "Seeking Emotional Labor," 14 (2000): 50-89; and Sarah J. Tracy, "Becoming a Character for Commerce," 14 (2000): 90-128. Excellent additional case studies are available in Kruml and Geddes; Shuler and Sypher; B. E. Ashford and R. H. Humphrey, "Emotional Labor in Service Roles," *Academy of Management Review* 18 (1993): 88-115; and Gideon Kunda, *Engineering Culture* (Philadelphia, PA: Temple University Press, 1992).

[28] The ideas that we present in this section are similar to those of Mats Alvesson, "Cultural-Ideological Modes of Management Control: A Theory and a Case Study of a Professional Service Company," in *Communication Yearbook 16,* Stanley Deetz, ed. (Newbury Park, CA: Sage, 1993), pp. 3-42.

[29] See J. Kevin Barge, *Leadership* (New York: St. Martin's, 1994); Bernard Bass, *Leadership and Performance beyond Expectations* (New York: Free Press, 1985); M. Z. Hackman and C. E. Johnson, *Leadership: A Communication Perspective* (Prospect Heights, IL: Waveland Press, 1991); and C. Pavitt, G. G. Whitchurch, H. McGlurg, and N. Peterson, "Melding the Objective and Subjective Sides of Leadership: Communication and Social Judgments in Decision-Making Groups," *Communication Monographs* 62 (1995): 243-264; and Warren Bennis, Jagdish Parikh, and Ronnie Lessem, *Beyond Leadership: Balancing Economics, Ethics, and Ecology* (Cambridge, MA: Basil Blackwell, 1994).

[30] William Gardner and Dean Cleavenger, "The Impression Management Strategies Associated with Transformational Leadership at the World-Class Level," *Management Communication Quarterly* 12 (1998): 3-41.

[31] Bennis, Parikh, and Lessem, p. 58; Peter Senge, *The Fifth Discipline* (New York: Doubleday, 1990).

[32] The example and the analysis of different kinds of goals is from Gail Fairhurst and Robert Sarr, *The Art of Framing: Managing the Language of Leadership* (San Francisco: Jossey-Bass, 1996), who based their analysis on Steve Wilson and Linda Putnam, "Interaction Goals in Negotiation," in *Communication Yearbook 13,* James Anderson, ed. (Newbury Park, CA: Sage, 1990); and Pamela Hellman, "Her Push for Prevention Keeps Kids Out of ER," *Parade,* April 19, 1995, pp. 8-10. An excellent discussion of the need for visions/goals to be adaptive and flexible is available in Michael Hitt, B. W. Keats, H. F. Harback, and R. D. Nixon, "Rightsizing: Building and Maintaining Strategic Leadership and Long-Term Competitiveness," *Organizational Dynamics* 23 (1994): 18-32.

[33] Joseph Sgro, Philip Worchel, Earl Pence, and Joseph Orban, "Perceived Leader Behavior as a Function of Trust," *Academy of Management Journal* 23 (1980): 161-165.

[34] Marlene Fine and Patrice M. Buzzanell, "Walking the High Wire," in *Rethinking Organizational and Managerial Communication from Feminist Perspectives,* Patrice Buzzanell, ed. (Thousand Oaks, CA: Sage, 2000).

[35] Ellen O'Conner, "Discourse at our Disposal," *Management Communication Quarterly* 10 (1997): 395–432.

[36] Stanley Deetz, "Representation of Interests and the New Communication Technologies: Issues in Democracy and Policy," in *Communication and the Culture of Technology,* Martin Medhurst, Alberto Gonzales, and Tarla Rai Peterson, eds. (Pullman, WA: Washington State University Press, 1990). James W. Chesboro, "Communication Technologies as Cognitive Systems," in *Toward the 21st Century: The Future of Speech Communication,* Julia Wood and Richard B. Gregg, eds. (Cresskill, NJ: Hampton, 2000).

[37] Bongsug Chae and Marshall Scott Poole, "A Tale of Two Systems: Technology Acceptance of Mandated Technologies," Department of Management, Kansas State University, 2003, unpublished manuscript.

Chapter 6

Network Strategies of Organizing

*The connective mechanism that enables parts of the [network] organization
to coordinate with one another and with other organizations is communication.*
—Janet Fulk and Gerardine Desanctis

Central Themes

- Over the past fifty years, there has been a transition from a production economy based on physical production of goods in factories to a knowledge society, in which most value is added through information and knowledge-related activities.
- The knowledge society gives rise to different types of organizations than the production economy did and to two new types of workers, knowledge workers and information workers.
- Along with the knowledge society came an increased rate of change in the growth of knowledge and in markets, products, and competition, much of it spurred by the globalization of the economy.
- The increased complexity and required speed of response have led organizations to emphasize flatter structures with more lateral links; different types of integrating mechanisms have been developed to coordinate these organizations.
- The network organizing strategy has evolved to handle very high levels of uncertainty caused by complexity and rapid change in the environment.
- The network organization has four characteristics: flexible modular structures, team-based units, flat organizational design, and use of information technology to integrate the organization.
- Motivation and control in network organizations is handled through developing trust, through making sure that tasks are engaging and significant, and through formal control systems.

- Network strategies of organization rely on leaders to be symphony conductors rather than top-down managers. The manager must be coach, negotiator, problem solver, and improviser, rather than simply a director.
- Several problems confront network organizations, including their complexity, a tendency for power to "recentralize" despite efforts at empowerment, and the disadvantages of permanent "temporariness."

Key Terms

network organization
technology
knowledge work
knowledge society
liaison roles
task forces
integrating teams
managerial linking roles
matrix organization

dual-authority systems
contracts
interdependence
trust
full-disclosure information systems
broker
centralization
information work

One of the striking developments of the past twenty years has been the increased instability, complexity, and turbulence of organizational environments. We discussed the roots of these changes in Chapter 2, but it is useful to review them in a more focused manner in order to lay the groundwork for understanding the emergence of an increasingly common organizational form, the **network organization.**

One driver of the increased pace of change has been the continuing and accelerating growth of knowledge about the physical and biological environment. Products now change much more quickly than they once did. Product life cycles—the time from introduction to the point at which the product is outmoded or dated—have grown shorter and shorter. The life cycle of a computer chip has decreased from five years to one. Even refrigerators have product life cycles of only three years now, as opposed to ten or more, years ago. Services are also changing rapidly. The number of options for telephone or banking service today compared with what was available ten years ago is striking.

The pace of change in products and services is partly a response to the rapidly increasing rate of technological change. The stunning advances in medical **technology** in the past three years—the sequencing of the gene; new understandings of the roots of diseases such as arthritis, Alzheimer's disease, and addiction; and new therapies such as noninvasive surgery—clearly show the ever-accelerating growth of knowledge, know-how, and innovation. To keep up with their competition, organizations have to improve their operations and innovate continuously. Rapid technological change makes the continuous learning characteristic of **knowledge work** particularly important.

Along with increased instability has come increased complexity of organizational environments. Globalization of the economy has introduced many new competitors into the United States and, in turn, has made opportunities available in many more places than U.S. organizations envisioned previously. The rapid change and growth in knowledge and technology have increased competition as well, as companies strive for advantage. The public, too, has become more aware of the impacts of organizations on the quality of life in general. As a result, organizations have to deal with increasing regulation, lawsuits from disgruntled parties, and consumer protests. As time goes by, the environment of many organizations becomes more crowded with stakeholders who are more tightly interconnected.

Although organizations in the private sector, such as manufacturers, food companies, and retailers, have been most immediately affected by these changes, they are reverberating through the government and nonprofit sectors as well. Vice President Gore implemented the "Reinventing Government" initiative that promoted innovation and work redesign in more than half the U.S. federal government agencies. Governments at all levels are using information technologies and going online. In the United States and most developed countries, government agencies are also having to compete with private organizations bidding to provide the same services. This tendency also affects nonprofit hospitals, charitable organizations, consumer advocacy groups, and many other organizations in the nonprofit realm. Indeed, the first decade of the twenty-first century seems likely to bring about changes in public and nonprofit sectors comparable to those in the private economic sector in the 1990s.

The upshot of these cumulating and accelerating changes is that many organizations must deal with extremely uncertain conditions. They employ changing technologies and face environments that are unstable and highly complex. None of the strategies for organizing that we have introduced thus far are well suited for this situation. The most flexible of the three strategies, the relational strategy, is appropriate for organizations facing moderately high rates of change, but not the rates of flux that confront a significant number of today's organizations.

In the "good old days" organizations would have had to throw up their hands and cope as best they could. However, now there is a wild card—information and communication technologies (ICTs). As we have seen, ICTs open many options to organizations that were previously simply too time-consuming or costly. The advent of information technology is also one of the enabling forces behind the emergence of the **knowledge society.** It facilitates both the management of existing knowledge and the growth of knowledge. Information technology has also facilitated the emergence of the network strategy of organizing as a major trend in the twenty-first century.

Network Strategies of Organizational Design

Network strategies of organizing are premised on the need to balance integration and change. As previous chapters have observed, a major purpose of organizations is to integrate the activities of many people and units to achieve goals too ambitious for smaller, informal groups or individuals. Organizations achieve this coordination by integrating members and their work through structures, relationships, and cultures, using the strategies discussed in Chapters 3, 4, and 5. But as the world changes around them, organizations must change how they operate if they are to achieve their goals, and this often means that they must change their structures, relationships, and cultures.

A major problem faced by organizations is balancing the flexibility needed for change with the structure needed for integration. An organization faced with a low to moderate amount of change in its environment can often effectively change by simply tinkering with structures, relationships, and cultures as described in the earlier chapters of this unit. A bureaucratic organization can amend its procedures and rules to take new circumstances into account. An organization using a relational strategy can involve its employees in a change program whereby they diagnose needed alterations and implement them. Organizations also undertake steps—sometimes more and sometime less successfully—to alter their cultures. However, tinkering has its limits, and when the need to change passes a certain point, it becomes difficult to use the three strategies to integrate organizations.

There have been other times when organizations faced the need to integrate in the face of great change and uncertainty. The Manhattan Project, which created the atomic bomb in World War II, and NASA's project to put a human on the moon in the 1960s both confronted these conditions and had to develop new strategies and tactics for integration. These have continued to develop, culminating in the growth of the network strategy from a specialized approach to a common form of organizing in the 1980s and 1990s. To understand the network strategy, it will be useful first to make a short detour to consider ways of integrating organizations.

Methods for Integrating Organizations

More than thirty years ago Jay Galbraith identified a number of methods organizations use to cope with uncertainty through integration, and based on recent developments in information technology, we can add several others.[1] Galbraith was concerned with how the organization can reduce to manageable levels its uncertainty about how to respond to changing environments while minimizing money and time spent communicating. Of particular interest to us are methods for creating lateral relationships, relationships that facilitate communication and coordination across different units or organizations. One limitation of Galbraith's analysis is that it focused primarily on linkages within organizations. However, today linkages between different organizations are just as important, so we have expanded his discussion to include interorganizational linkages as well as intraorganizational ones.

Structural Integration Mechanisms   These mechanisms of linking organizations rely on organizational structure and people to do most of the work of integrating the units or organizations. Structural mechanisms differ in the costs—

money, time, effort—involved in implementing them; we have arranged them in order of increasing cost.

Liaison roles. Personnel are assigned specifically to link two units or organizations. This may be a part-time or a full-time assignment. For example, the assistant to the director of a local social service agency was asked to be liaison to the County Health Department. This assignment took one day a week and involved keeping in contact with the Health Department to ensure that the social service agency's soup kitchen and homeless shelter complied with codes and to represent the agency to the Health Department. "Yep, it'd be a real PR problem to have the local soup kitchen shut down for rat droppings." By having a "person on the spot," the social service agency ensured that it had some input in the writing and enforcement of regulations. Filling the liaison role usually has beneficial career development consequences, because it broadens the liaison's outlook and sharpens his or her communication skills. The major disadvantage is that the liaison may come to identify more with the unit she or he visits than with the home unit or organization. This is a formal version of the informal liaison role described in Chapter 4.

Task forces. As mentioned in Chapter 4, these are short-term teams set up to deal with a specific problem or project. Members are drawn from several different units based on special knowledge about the issue and the interests their units have in it. Task forces typically dissolve after a set time or when the project is finished. A key challenge for the team is to overcome communication barriers resulting from the fact that its members come from different units (and sometimes different organizations) and differ in experiences, terminology, and interests. If this problem can be surmounted, task forces often outperform other teams. When Texaco faced charges that it systematically discriminated against black managers (see Chapter 12), it formed a blue-ribbon task force to find the roots of this problem and work out a solution. The task force went to work, quickly made some recommendations, and was dissolved. Interorganizational task forces are also common. For example, standards for new technologies such as DVD recorders are typically worked out by task forces representing the manufacturers, government regulators, and professional information technology standards bodies, such as the International Standards Organization.

Integrating teams. Sometimes a problem or project continues indefinitely or recurs regularly. In this case, a dedicated team is formed on a permanent basis. Assignments to this team become a permanent part of the members' jobs. Many universities have ongoing committees dedicated to increasing the number of women and minorities they hire. These integrating teams have representatives from all parts of the university. In the technology standards area, some task forces have been in existence such a long time, because of the complexity of the technologies, that they have evolved into integrating teams.

Managerial linking roles. Often the integrating team has a special in-between status. Everyone agrees it is dealing with an important problem, and upper management agrees to back up its recommendations and actions; but the team itself is still not regarded as a legitimate unit on a par with long-established departments or units. To give the integrating team more legitimacy and power, a formal manager may be added. This managerial integrator is directly connected into the hierarchy of authority and has a budget. He or she represents the team to the organization and serves as a symbol. Having an integrating manager gives the team more legitimacy and resources to work on its own.

One company that designed integrated computer hardware and software systems had several teams working on different parts of its new System Alpha. To deliver System Alpha on time and in shape, it was vital that each team's work be compatible with that of the others. The company created an Alpha Management Team, whose assignment was to coordinate the work of the System Alpha teams. An engineer who had informally worked on coordinating the teams involved in System Alpha was appointed manager of the Management Team. She was given a budget for personnel to test the compatibility of products that the different teams were creating and to provide extra help for teams having problems. This extra heft that the manager had enabled her to stimulate the teams to action, and System Alpha was delivered on schedule.

Joint ventures between organizations are often managed by integrating teams with special managers. For example, NASA and the 3M Company negotiated a joint venture to conduct materials engineering experiments in the vacuum of outer space. It was handled by a team of people drawn from both organizations and headed by a 3M manager.

Matrix organizations. Sometimes organizations face tasks of high complexity that require them to constantly adjust and coordinate the activities of a great many specialties and departments. In these cases it is useful to shift to a **dual-authority system** in which members of specialized departments are assigned to one or more projects and report to both the integrating manager of their project team and their department manager. The most common type of dual-authority structure is called the matrix.[2] As Figure 6-1 illustrates, the matrix is literally a matrix structure in which members of project teams report to two managers: the project manager and their department manager.

To accomplish the incredibly complex and daring feat of landing a person on the moon, NASA developed one of the first matrix organizational forms. Members of various departments were assigned to one or more special projects. For example, a materials engineer specializing in forming parts from metal alloys might be assigned to the Nosecone Team for 50 percent of her or his time, to the Booster Team for 30 percent, and spend the remaining 20 percent back in the Materials Engineering Laboratory. On both teams, the engineer would lend his or her special expertise in materials to creating the best possible nosecone or booster, working closely with other engineers and scientists with different specialties. Back at the home lab, the engineer could consult with other materials engineers about problems that needed solving on the two teams and catch up on the latest knowledge in materials engineering.

The advantage of dual structures, such as the matrix, is that teams keep the

FIGURE 6–1
Diagram of a Dual-Authority Matrix Structure

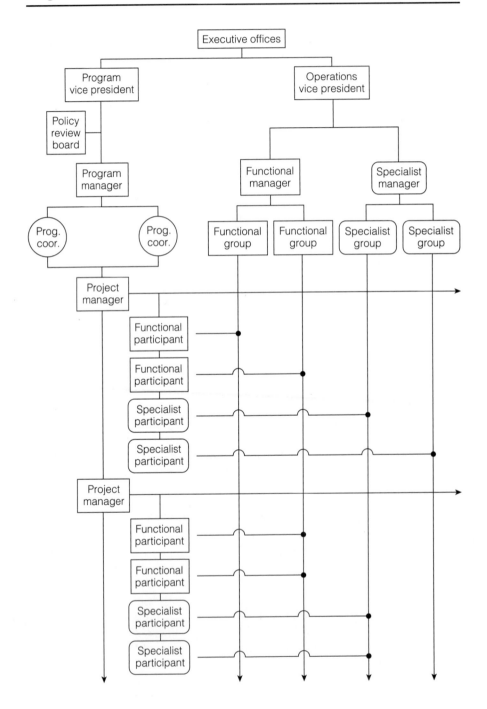

work focused on tangible products and outcomes (nosecones and boosters). Reporting back to their home department helps members keep their skills sharp and stay up to date on the latest developments in their fields. So our engineer is kept focused on nosecones by the project emphasis of the Nosecone Team. Other members of this team keep the engineer from applying only a materials perspective to the problem, and she or he will keep other team members "honest" by making sure that materials issues are considered each time the team makes a decision. Upon return to the materials department, the engineer is able to consult with other materials engineers about the materials-related problems that the team has encountered. This sharpens the engineer's own expertise and makes him or her more valuable to the project team.

The matrix structure as a whole also helps ensure that the various project teams and departments are coordinated. The project managers meet as a team and with their integrating managers to ensure that the various projects come together into an effective whole. Using a structure such as this, NASA succeeded in putting a man on the moon by 1969, after starting almost from scratch in 1961. No one, not even NASA managers, thought it could be done. But the matrix organization was up to the task. Giant corporations, such as Dow Corning, have put permanent matrix structures into operation to integrate their international operations.

The matrix structure attempts to ensure effective performance on complex tasks by dividing them among highly focused project teams. However, to ensure that the personnel on these teams are highly qualified and current in their fields, they are drawn from specialized departments with which they keep in touch.[3] The overall structure of the matrix coordinates the work of the various project teams. The glue that holds the matrix together is intensive communication. Through many team meetings, liaisons between teams, integrating teams across projects, and communication with functional departments, members of the matrix create a deep and complicated flow of information and ideas throughout the organization. For the matrix to work, communication within project teams and in specialized departments must create team and organizational cultures that promote open communication, innovation, constructive criticism, and high standards of excellence.

This communication-intensive organization has costs as well. Serving more than one supervisor can create ambiguities in the chain of command and tensions for workers who are torn between the mandates of two or more bosses. The requirement of continuous open communication can cause overloads and stress in its own right. Meetings, meetings, meetings can drive workers to distraction. And the solution to these problems is often even more communication. The matrix keeps all workers on their toes but can be exhausting as well. In addition, this form works only if the integrating managers can coordinate the various projects, bringing them to completion on schedule so that one project does not hold up other interdependent ones.

Matrix structures proliferated during the 1970s and are still common today in large complex organizations, where they are not as open as the NASA matrix just described. These corporate matrix structures have formal reporting mechanisms and use the matrix to organize the divisions of the organization. For example, in the 1980s Dow Corning set up a matrix in which the organization was divided into groups representing different regions of the world (Africa, East Asia, North America, and so on) and divisions representing the different product types the company offered (industrial chemicals, agricultural chemicals, glass, and so on). The units within Dow Corning reported to both group and division managers. For example, the manager of Dow's pesticide plant in India was responsible both to the division management for agricultural chemicals and to group management for South Asia. The rationale was similar to that for the NASA matrix: local plants need to be both excellent in their function (for example, manufacturing pesticides) and responsive to their region (for example, South Asia). However, at the plant or facility level within the matrix, each plant or facility was organized along either structural or relational lines, depending on what it did. For instance, the pesticide plant used continuous production processes similar to those in an oil refinery and was staffed mostly by professional engineers and mechanics and so used a relational strategy for organizing. Continuous adaptation, quality control, and problem solving were best served by the flatter, team-oriented relational strategy. A pesticide warehouse would more likely be organized in a traditional fashion, with managers exerting hierarchical control over lower-level employees.

The corporate matrix is thus a hybrid with a matrix for higher-level management and other strategies for particular plants or facilities. Although it uses matrix principles to some extent, it has lost the flexible, open-communication orientation of the original matrix structure. These days organizations needing flexible, adaptive structures are more likely to adopt the network strategy, which is described below.

ICT Integration Mechanisms   As we discussed in previous chapters, ICTs offer a wide variety of ways to integrate organizational units and organizations. Here we will mention some again and distinguish three different ways to integrate organizations—through communication links, through work process integration, and through developing a shared knowledge base.

Communication technologies. As discussed in Chapters 2 and 4, technologies such as e-mail, computer conferencing, audio-conferencing, videoconferencing, blogging, and instant messaging can be used to knit disparate parts of the organization together. These technologies typically increase linkages both within and across units and organizations at all levels. They are advantageous for the formation of informal relationships and networks. But they are perhaps more valuable as linking mechanisms when combined with one of the structural mechanisms, as when a liaison uses e-mail or a computer conference to maintain contacts with the units or organizations she or he is responsible for.

Today many integrating teams are "virtual teams" that maintain contact and meet mostly via e-mail or conferencing because their members are spread over geographically dispersed units or belong to different organizations.

Work integration. We have discussed many examples of ICTs used to integrate organizational work processes. Each of these, of course, is an integrating mechanism. So enterprise resource planning (ERP) systems, electronic data interchange (EDI) systems, and office automation systems can be used to integrate organizational units and organizations.

For example, CNA Insurance Corporation uses a virtual office to integrate employees in its many units and divisions.[4] Any employee can access an intranet portal, which runs a steady feed of insurance industry news and company announcements, as well as links to a corporate knowledge base and an e-learning area that offers training modules in different aspects of the virtual office. On the left of the portal are buttons that employees can use to go to the virtual teams they are members of or to go into the virtual office that has their applications, such as tools for calculating rates, a word processor, and forms that can be entered into the office document workflow system. The virtual office also gives workers access to a general discussion space, project management and budgeting tools, and status reports on how the company and various projects are progressing. The CNA information systems department is constantly working to improve and further integrate this office portal.

Work integration can also link together different organizations. Jones and Stokes, an environmental consulting firm, uses an extranet to link staff, clients, and subcontractors from the Western United States to prepare Environmental Impact Reports to submit to the Environmental Protection Agency for major construction and reclamation projects.[5] The virtual office application used by Jones and Stokes has a library with thousands of references and manuals useful in preparing environmental reports. Once a document is authored, the virtual office application automatically notifies the next person in the workflow that it's ready to be reviewed and edited.

An exchange like GHX, the medical supply purchasing exchange, is another type of work integration technology that provides linkages among firms. As we noted in Chapter 2, this exchange brings together more than seventy-five suppliers and many health care organizations that want to purchase their products. Interestingly, once an exchange or other ICT that links two or more organizations is in place, it is common for the services it offers to be expanded in response to supplier and customer needs. For instance, an order tracking system might be added so that customers can monitor their delivery schedules themselves.

Another form of work integration system is the interorganizational accounting systems that are discussed in this chapter. This kind of system is used to monitor and enforce contracts in networks of different organizations.

Knowledge management systems. Another way to integrate organizations through technology is to develop a knowledge management system. Whereas work integration systems link people and units through the common work they perform, and communication systems integrate people by enabling contact and communication, knowledge management systems link people by building a common knowledge base that they can draw on in their work.

Intec, an engineering and project management firm that serves the petroleum industry, provides one example of how integration through knowledge management can be done.[6] In 2002 the company found that it was becoming more and more difficult to keep track of and access information and knowledge that had been accumulated over years and in the course of many projects. The company formed a Learning Team to put together a knowledge management system that would compile useful knowledge and make it available so that Intec engineers could learn from one another's experiences and weren't always reinventing the wheel when they undertook a new project. The Learning Team put together a database system that integrated existing knowledge resources such as manuals and previous bids, automatically located experts on various topics, facilitated the identification of best practices, and captured information from engineers' work automatically, all with an easy-to-use interface. Although this sentence makes it sound easy, it took the Learning Team more than a year to do this, and they had the assistance of an excellent knowledge-management vendor. The resulting system enabled engineers to capitalize on the firm's knowledge and saved the company more than two hundred thousand dollars, not to mention improving the quality of its work.

A knowledge management system integrates an organization not by directly linking work processes or people, but by providing a shared resource that employees come to. When they draw on the system in their work, employees are bringing a common stock of knowledge and experience to bear and adding to it as well. The system is a growing shared resource for the organization, a contact point to draw its members together.

Legal Integration Mechanisms   **Contracts** are the third class of integrating mechanisms. Legal agreements are, of course, a common means of specifying how two different organizations will work together. For example a building contractor might contract with a food service company to feed its employees on site. Traditionally, contracts have been thought of as means of keeping organizations independent of one another: the contract specifies each organization's rights, responsibilities, and rewards, and each treats the other as a separate entity. However, this is an idealized view of contracts; there is an increasing emphasis on the contract as a basis for a relationship. Contracts have often been viewed as mechanisms for integrating organizations, as when one organization contracts with another for some service. However, many large organizations are moving to models that treat each unit as its own organization with internal and external customers. The information systems department of an organization, for example, might have to bid competitively against outside companies for a job to develop a database for another unit in the organization. If the department wins the bid, it will sign a contract with the unit, just as an outside organization would.

Contracts vary in how specific they are. Some are basically just "handshakes" that are rather general and rely on the goodwill of one or both parties. Others are much more detailed, specifying not only what products or services are to be delivered but also levels of quality and service. For example, when an organization contracts with a company to maintain its computer network, it is common to put in the contract the bandwidth of the network, what percentage of downtime will be accepted, and what penalties the provider will incur if these requirements are not met. The rule of thumb is, the more detailed the better, when it comes to contracts. However, it is impossible to be completely specific; interpretation and negotiation are always involved when people or organizations work under contract.

Which Integration Mechanism to Use?   Organizations often combine more than one integrating mechanism. For example, an organization might employ an integrating team and communication technology to link personnel involved in a particularly important project. Two organizations entering a joint venture might use work integration technology for routing key documents, a managerial linking role to manage the project, and liaisons between units of the organizations that need to coordinate.

How does one choose among and combine these integration mechanisms? One thing to consider is the cost of the method compared to the benefits it offers. Benefits of the structural mechanisms depend on each method's effectiveness in handling the level of uncertainty the organization experiences. Liaisons and task forces are effective for moderate to moderately high levels of uncertainty. Organizations facing high levels of uncertainty may need to utilize approaches further up the list, including integrating teams, managerial linking roles, and matrix designs. Costs due to these mechanisms include personnel expenses, the time spent learning to use the method and getting it to work smoothly, the information load imposed by the method, and the amount of stress that members experience.

Some benefits and costs of ICTs vary depending on the situation. Workflow integration will work better under conditions of moderate uncertainty, though it can be useful when uncertainty is high. Both communication and knowledge management ICTs work fine with higher levels of uncertainty. In terms of costs, integrating technologies that are already installed, such as electronic mail or Internet applications that are standard, such as Internet messaging, are more economical than purchasing a special system, like the knowledge management system used by Intec. Maintaining security for ICTs to avoid attacks or intrusions also adds to their cost, as does training users, providing support, and maintaining the systems. Contracts, too, have costs in addition to the benefits they offer in terms of uncertainty reduction. Monitoring whether the other party is living up to its side of a contract is one cost, and another is enforcing the contract in the courts, if it comes to that.

From the cost-benefit standpoint, an organization should select the least costly mechanism that meets its needs. For example, an organization in a very complex, unstable environment with an extremely difficult task may have to choose a highly flexible, yet costly system, such as the matrix. An organization in a more stable situation that has one difficult problem may be able to handle things with a task force.

A second variable to consider in choosing integration mechanisms is the degree of geographical dispersion of the organization, that is, how many different locations the employees and units that need to be linked are spread across. Organizations that are widely dispersed must often choose an ICT-based linkage system.

Another variable to consider in choosing a linking mechanism is the culture of the organization. The values, traditions, and history of an organization may predispose it to be more comfortable with some integration methods than others. Selecting a method the organization is not accustomed to requires a period of learning and change. For example, implementing a task force is not simply a matter of assigning people. More important is getting people from different departments that have very different views on an issue to work together. In an organization that emphasizes teamwork and inclusion, this will be easier than in one built around competition and individualism.

No single integration method will work under all circumstances or for all organizations. The balance among cost-benefit considerations, geographical dispersion, and culture depends on which is more important to the organization or the task at hand. In many cases, organizations settle on integration modes after a period of experimentation in which different methods are tried and rejected.

Limitations of the Integrating Mechanisms   The integrating mechanisms have proved extremely useful. However, they do not offer a complete solution to problems of uncertainty. Many of these mechanisms are suitable for addressing limited individual problems but not capable of integrating an organization as a whole by themselves. The matrix and the ICTs offer solutions for the whole organization, but they tend to work best for moderately high uncertainty and not for extremely uncertain conditions that require flexibility. The matrix tends to become inflexible after it is used for some time. Members learn to think of it as a framework much like the bureaucracy. The matrix is flexible as long as managers keep it so, but once they start to think of it as a standard operating procedure, it can become as much of a cage as a bureaucracy. ICTs offer some degree of help in dealing with high levels of uncertainty, but they must be supplemented by structural measures and contracts as well.

The Network Organization

Network organizations are aggregates of organizations whose component units are assembled to meet a particular set of demands. They are referred to by a number of names including *dynamic networks, federated organizations, "cloverleaf" forms, virtual organizations,* and *post-bureaucracies.* Network organizations take a wide variety of forms: in some cases the units are from the same organization, whereas in others, different organizations make up the network; some network organizations are assembled on a long-term basis, and others are set up for temporary projects. The Japanese *keiretsu,* a dense network of interrelated organizations that develops lasting and stable business relationships, is a good example of a long-term networked organization. In the Japanese automobile industry, firms such as Nissan and Toyota develop networks of suppliers,

FIGURE 6-2
A Network Organization: Textbook Publishing

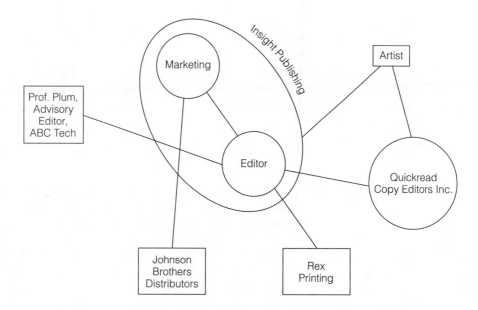

shippers, and financial institutions that depend on the central firm's business for their livelihood and in turn give the central firm exceptional quality, effort, and dependable support.

Some textbook publishers offer examples of temporary, project-centered networks, illustrated in Figure 6-2. Older publishing companies have traditionally consolidated the acquisition of new books, their design and layout, printing, and sales in a single organization. More recently publishers have been farming out some, or even all, of these functions. The publisher may acquire the book and then hire a graphics firm to handle layout, an independent printer to produce the books, and several firms, including the publisher's own staff, to market the book. Special types of books are produced for the publisher by smaller independent firms, themselves dynamic networks, often founded by former employees of the publisher who have gone out on their own. Publishing is a very different game today than it was thirty years ago.

Whereas the example of textbook publishers shows how a number of different organizations can be combined into a network, large firms often create networks within themselves for special projects. In one common case, a firm assembles a temporary dynamic network to develop a new product and bring it to market. The network might be put together by an integrating project manager who assembles units for the project: design might be carried out by a team assigned from engineering, and production by a particular plant with excess capacity; inventory might be handled by suppliers on a just-in-time basis; marketing might be the responsibility of a sales team reassigned from a downsizing division; and the accounting department would handle bookkeeping. The project manager would start with no organization and through negotiation and competitive bidding get units together to bring the product out. After the product was out and sales had begun, it might be transferred to an existing functional unit of the organization and the dynamic network might be disbanded.

Characteristics of Network Designs   The network is not a new organizational design.[7] Building contractors have long employed this structure. They assemble reliable subcontractors into a temporary structure that they coordinate according to the needs of each unique project. Before the 1980s, network structures were utilized mostly by specialized industries such as construction; but in more recent years, they have become ubiquitous. The modern network organization generally has four characteristics:[8]

1. Flexible, modular organizational structures that can be readily reconfigured as new projects, demands, or problems arise. As noted previously, these structures may be composed of units of a single larger organization, or they may be different organizations joined through various types of interorganizational alliances. A flexible arrangement of organizational units is important to the ability of networked organizations to adapt. For example, a network of community mental health agencies might find that its clients need help with job placements. It could then approach a job-training and placement agency and arrange for it to join the network.

2. Team-based work organization that emphasizes autonomy, self-management, and initiative. This is generally combined with emphasis on quality and continuous improvement. To be effective, network organizations must be designed so that they promote effective teamwork, as discussed in Chapter 3. They must work to define clear goals that specify the overall mission of the organization and the contribution of each unit, so that units can manage their own processes to contribute to the overall mission. Team-based work organization also involves empowerment of employees, just as in the relational strategy, because only if they have the necessary resources and authority, can teams adapt to the needs of the situation. Cross-functional teams that bring together people from different units and organizations are particularly important in network organizations. There is also an expectation that members of network organizations will be proactive and work hard to deliver quality and excellence to the product or service being delivered.

3. Flat organizational structures that rely on coordination and negotiation rather than hierarchy to manage relationships among teams and units. As organizations move to network structures, they lose layers of middle managers and generally have fewer employees than traditional organizations.

4. Use of information technology to integrate across organizational functions and geographically dispersed units to reengineer production and

service processes and to create tighter **interdependence** among activities. Technologies such as e-mail and telecommunications, discussed in Chapter 2, can be used to ensure that people from different units coordinate their activities. These units may be different departments in a single location, units spread across a wide distance, or a combination.

One pharmaceutical company that Scott Poole worked with used a computer conferencing system and teleconferences to develop a team of eleven salespeople, each stationed in a different Asian or African country. The team members met face-to-face a few times a year but conducted all other business through the Internet and teleconferences. Members of the team not only had to manage their own sales strategy; they also had to coordinate with other sales teams that had responsibility for other geographical areas and with production units in Europe and the United States on a frequent basis. Without ICTs, this team could not possibly have managed its work.

ICTs also enable organizations to redesign and rethink how they do their work. As networked organizations rely more and more on ICTs, their work is changed. For example, an organization may decide to use an automated inventory-control system that relies on input of stock levels through hand-held computers. It also is likely to find that it does not have to keep as many parts on hand, because the computer system enables it to keep track of them easily and automatically reorders them through the Internet. As a result, it might enlarge the jobs of stockroom clerks so that they are also responsible for reordering needed parts; this action would eliminate some jobs in the procurement department but greatly reduce the costs incurred in storing parts.

Finally, ICTs can also enable units to automate their coordination. For example, a group of companies planning a complex offshore oil project can automatically share design updates through computer networks. When a unit in charge of designing the pipes that bring the oil from the seafloor to the platform changes the pipes' design and specifications, the plans of all other units would be automatically altered to reflect this change. Unit members could then determine whether the alterations would cause any problems or require any action on their part. In all three functions, information technology speeds up production and response time and enables the organization to adapt to customer needs and environmental demands in highly specific ways.

CASE STUDY
Al-Qaida: A Network Organization?

It is well known that many underground movements set themselves up as networks. News reports in the wake of the September 11, 2001, attacks have repeatedly described al-Qaida and related Islamic terrorist groups as networks. But what is it about the network strategy that makes it so useful for underground groups?

(continued)

(Case Study, continued)

The members of al-Qaida are organized into small cells, groups of five to twenty members, who communicate only with each other and often do not know the members of any other cell. Cells are linked through their connections to a few prominent members. The resulting network has densely connected groups that are linked to other groups only through their contacts, who do not move information between cells unless absolutely necessary. The result is a network of moderate density in which groups are relatively close to other groups in the network but do not directly relate to them.

For example, the cell in Madrid, Spain, that trained a number of the September 11 hijackers was led by a used-car salesman, Imad Yarkas, who had a Spanish wife and five children. Muhammed Zouaydi, the cell's financier, ran construction and real estate companies that funneled money from Islamic supporters to the cell. Other members of the cell had normal businesses such as carpentry shops and a ceramics factory. Members were recruited by Yarkas, and Yarkas and Zouaydi were the primary contacts to the larger al-Qaida organization. Occasionally higher-level cell members would meet with members of other cells to plan large-scale operations, like the September 11 attacks. However, for the most part the cell kept to itself. The members of the cell have cultivated very strong ties to one another—many had met one another years before in school or on the job—and interact with others outside the cell only on a more superficial level unconnected with the cell's mission, selling them cars, for example.

Networks made up of cells like the one in Madrid are very efficient communication mechanisms. The cells are linked by a number of central liaisons, and the number of links between any two cells is very small. So information about operations, attempts to capture the members of the network, and related issues moves very quickly from cell to cell.

Such a network is a remarkably resilient organization. If the members of one cell are captured or destroyed, the other cells can go on basically undisturbed. They are insulated because the members of other cells do not know them or what they are doing well enough to supply useful information. So, although the Madrid cell is now broken up, it is likely that there are other cells unknown to us going about their business.

The most logical approach to breaking up a terrorist network would seem to be to capture or kill the most prominent members, on the assumption that if the leaders are taken out of action, the group will founder. Paradoxically, taking out the leaders of a terrorist network will not necessarily disable it. The leaders are important links, but the cells can survive without them because they are so strong by themselves. Studies of networks similar to al-Qaida suggest that eliminating the central leader would not disable the network, because there are multiple connections between cells. In time one or more of the liaisons would emerge as a new leader. Capturing the person who is the most central link in this type of network may even strengthen the power of individual cells for a while. They may take more initiative than they might have when linked to a leader from whom they felt a need to seek permission. Hence, rather than disabling the terrorist network, capturing the central leader may stimulate more attacks. These attacks might be interpreted by leaders of the opposing forces and the media as "revenge attacks," when in fact they are simply a product of the cells' feeling more potent and in control of their own affairs. Network research suggests that the capture or killing of Osama bin-Laden, however satisfying to the West, will hardly end al-Qaida's activity. Arquilla, Ronfeldt, and Zanini issue this caution:

> It is important to avoid equating the bin Laden network solely with bin Laden. He represents a key node in the Arab Afghan terror network, but there should be no illusion about the likely effect on the network of actions taken to neutralize him. The network conducts many operations without his involvement, leadership, or financing—and will continue to be able to do so should he be killed or captured.*

Indeed, there is reason to believe that terrorist organizations form a "network of networks." Al-Qaida is linked to other terrorist organizations in the Philippines, Kurdistan, and Morocco that have their own bases and causes to fight for. The organizations exchange information and sometimes resources. In the late 1970s there was a formal agreement among the Palestine Liberation Organization, the Red Brigades in Italy, the Irish Republican Army, and other terrorist groups to assist one another with training, procuring arms, and planning attacks. There is less evidence that this holds true today, but there are ties among the various terrorist networks.

Information and communication technologies are very important to the maintenance of terrorist networks. E-mail and telephones are important tools for maintaining a far-flung network. ICTs also offer a way to locate members of terrorist networks and trace their activities, but the terrorists have become very good at using pseudonyms and other means of disguising their accounts and use of these technologies. ICTs enable networks to operate over vast distances, whereas without the technology members would need to be located close together. This makes terrorist networks even more difficult to disrupt. Some authorities have argued, for example, that the invasion of Afghanistan has made terrorism even harder to deal with, because it dispersed the terrorist groups that were moving to Afghanistan all around the world, as they fled to escape UN forces.

Applying What You've Learned

1. In what way is al-Qaida like the network organizations described in this chapter? How does it differ?
2. What are some of the weaknesses of an organization like al-Qaida? Is it subject to any of the problems that network organizations face, as discussed at the end of this chapter?

(continued)

(Case Study, continued)

Questions to Think About and Discuss

1. Drawing on the principles and practices of a network organization, what suggestions would you have for stopping al-Qaida and disrupting its network?
2. Networks are complex systems. Which of the principles of systems thinking discussed in Chapter 2 might give us insights into al-Qaida and how it might be stopped?

This case draws on a number of sources, including Cynthia Stohl and Michael Stohl, "Networks, Terrorism, and Terrorist Networks," paper presented at the National Communication Association Organizational Communication Pre-conference, Denver, CO, November 20, 2002; Daniel Woolls, "Al-Quaida Suspects Had Normal Lives," *Houston Chronicle,* January 20, 2004, A9; Peter Bergen, "Defining Al-Qaida: Is It a Group? Is It a Movement?" *Houston Chronicle*, January 4, 2004; Peter Bergen, "Al Qaeda's New Tactics," *New York Times*, November 15, 2002; and J. Arquilla, D. Ronfeldt, and M. Zanini, "Networks, Netwar, and Information Age Terrorism," in *Countering the New Terrorism*, A. Lesser, B. Hoffman, J. Arquilla, D. Ronfeldt, and M. Zanini, eds. (Santa Monica, CA: Rand, 1999).

*Arquilla, Ronfeldt, and Zanini, p. 63.

Network Organizations and Boundaries   Peter Monge and Noshir Contractor have commented that "network organizations create what have come to be called 'boundaryless' organizations."[9] In network structures, it is not always clear where one organization leaves off and another begins. Organizations and units in networks share practices, knowledge, and often members. No longer is it necessary to think of organizations as self-contained entities with definitive structures. Instead they can be composed, rearranged, and stuck together by various integrating mechanisms, as the occasion demands. Organizations become "mix-and-match" systems. The network offers a good description of the various joint ventures, cross-firm alliances, and consortia that are becoming increasingly prevalent today.

An example of this type of venture network is SEMATECH, the Austin, Texas–based research-and-development consortium developed by more than ten leading information technology companies.[10] Typically firms assign researchers to SEMATECH, where they work with employees of other companies to develop cutting-edge products and share insights into solving production problems. The rationale behind such a consortium is that the United States needs a prosperous, technically advanced group of information technology companies if it is to remain among the world leaders in this area. Such firms are usually seen as temporary ventures; but some are so successful that they exist for a long time. SEMATECH now is more than ten years old.

Virtual Organizations   A virtual organization is one that has no physical location.[11] It has no building, no campus, no office. Instead it exists across a computer network. Many catalog companies' sales divisions are virtual organizations, with independent individual sales agents operating out of their homes.

The catalog companies link them via high-speed computer lines to a central database that handles order delivery and other functions. Compaq Computer Corporation moved its sales force into home offices and reported a 50 percent reduction in sales expenses as a result.

The California flower company Calyx & Corolla is a good example of a virtual organization.[12] The organization is really a virtual network composed of a negotiated agreement between three organizations. Calyx & Corolla mails catalogs showing flower arrangements to potential customers and takes orders using an 800 number and an order center located in a suburb of San Francisco. The orders are then forwarded via computer network or fax to flower growers who have agreed to package the flowers in arrangements. Calyx & Corolla has negotiated an agreement with Federal Express to pick up the arrangements and deliver them the next morning to any place in the continental United States. Orders are tracked and monitored via a computer system that also handles accounting and distribution of payments to the various components of the organization. Calyx & Corolla itself is relatively small, but the virtual organization it has put together is much larger and includes the growers and Federal Express. Consumers cannot differentiate the different organizations that make up Calyx & Corolla; from the point of view of the customer, Calyx & Corolla looks like a traditional florist that delivers.

One characteristic of virtual organizations is that to outsiders they appear to be like older self-contained organizations. They deliver the same or better product or service with the same or better efficiency. Information technology and telecommunications enable these dispersed organizations to coordinate their activities and maintain coherent work processes. Each part of the virtual organization is able to focus on its particular function, resulting in competent and even excellent performance. By staying small, the component organizations keep their costs for management and overhead down, enhancing efficiency. Smallness also makes communication easier within the components, opening them up for fast development and testing of new ideas.

Like other network organizations, the virtual organization requires the development of **trust** among members, often by cultivating long-term relationships among component organizations. Kingston Technology, one of the most successful firms in Silicon Valley, has only 220 employees, with the rest of the organization spread out over a network of subcontractors.[13] However, rather than hiring subcontractors on a temporary basis, Kingston maintains long-term, solid ties with its partner companies. Kingston designs systems that speed up PCs and data transfer. These are assembled by Express Manufacturing, which works closely with Kingston, and then they are shipped by Federal Express. When Kingston needed more manufacturing capacity, Express Manufacturing built more because it knew it could depend on the business from Kingston. Although Express has other customers, Kingston always comes first. When Kingston needed more advertising material shipped, it worked with its printer to expand that business, again guaranteeing work. As the companies work together and develop stronger and stronger communication ties, trust grows.

Kingston often does business without contracts and pays ahead of time on its orders so that its small affiliates will have the money to do their work. It also maintains open books, so that all its employees maintain trust in management. Kingston has created a virtual organization by building a family of firms and a family of its own employees. It has developed an enduring culture that spans a number of companies.

CASE STUDY
Evolving into a Network Organization

Industrial controls maker ICG has long been in the forefront of its industry. It was among the first firms of its kind to implement a computer-aided design and manufacturing (CAD/CAM) system. The CAD/CAM system enabled engineering and manufacturing units to work on a common set of plans stored in a database; as units made alterations and adjustments in either design or manufacturing, the changes were automatically entered into the plans. This system met some resistance from engineers who were used to paper drawings, but the engineers' enhanced ability to consult with manufacturing noticeably improved the quality and time-to-market for the various product lines offered by ICG. These teams worked in a paperless environment with the CAD/CAM system as the linking pin for their efforts.

As ICG worked with the CAD/CAM system, top managers realized that the company was not capitalizing on its potential. To take advantage of the system, they felt, it would be necessary to develop cross-functional teams that would own product development from womb to tomb, so to speak. ICG constituted product teams with representatives from marketing, engineering, manufacturing, scheduling, and quality assurance that would be responsible for product performance in terms of quality, cost, time-to-market, and profit. These product teams were formed by top management and charged with managing a set of products and allocating resources among them. Although many ICG employees were skeptical about the new teams because they had been ordered by top management, they were eventually won over as it became clear that management was going to give the teams full control over their own decisions. Working on product teams enabled employees to develop their skills in management, teamwork, communication, and leadership; it also increased their commitment to ICG.

Its experience as a leader in CAD/CAM led to ICG's next advance. It worked with a major computer maker to create the Pyramid Integrator, a computer system that incorporated CAD/CAM and had the ability to integrate all of a company's design and manufacturing across multiple products. The Pyramid Integrator facilitated standardization of designs across products, reducing costs and enabling companies to build on previous designs as they created new products in a rapid and flexible process. It also made it much easier to tailor products to customer needs, because customers could work with ICG personnel, in effect designing their own systems. The first product lines ICG designed with the Pyramid Integrator were a great success and won the company national recognition and an award from a manufacturing publication. The Pyramid Integrator also became a profitable product for ICG.

ICG had moved to a team-intensive organization, but it was still hierarchically organized around divisions that corresponded to product lines. The excessive amount of work entailed by the various teams and the fine-tailoring of products for customers put pressure on the product-oriented divisions, which were better suited for relatively large production runs of similar products. Moreover, the divisions tended to be concerned mainly with their own success and did not think in terms of the success of the entire enterprise of ICG. Each division focused on its narrow line of products, which utilized a certain technology, and sought to be a world leader in its own products. This narrow focus sometimes put divisions at odds with each other, as they introduced products that conflicted or went in very different directions. It also confused the sales force and ran the risk of overstretching resources across too many product lines.

The executive vice president decided that ICG needed to reorganize. He argued that success no longer depended on technologies or new products, because technology was beginning to diffuse rapidly through the industry; rather, success would depend on how well the company could respond to the particular needs of its customers. Therefore, ICG should be organized around its customers and projects for them, not around product-focused divisions. After considerable analysis of customer needs, the management group determined that the core business for ICG lay in two product lines and that everything else the company did basically added value to these lines.

ICG was reorganized as a concentric organization with the two core control businesses at the center. A second ring, Communication and Information Systems, would focus on tying these core technologies together using information systems. The third and outer ring, Application Services, would package integrated control systems according to customer needs. General service functions, such as human resources, marketing, planning, and operations, were consolidated from the old divisions into single units in orbit around these three rings to provide support for them as needed.

As the company reorganized, it reduced its number of projects to about one-third of those in the old divisionalized structure. Self-managed teams handled various projects and customer groups. Teams sometimes operated at only one layer of the concentric circles; for example, a team might specialize in controls for canning companies and work with teams in the control and communication and information systems layers to tailor these. Some teams bridged layers; for example, a team attempting to develop new control devices to combine with other company products in an integrated system might be composed of personnel drawn from the core and second layers of ICG. Teams could be formed only with the approval of an upper-level management team, which was called the executive sponsor team. The executive sponsor team scanned for business opportunities and identified person-

(continued)

(Case Study, continued)

nel and resources for the teams that undertook them. Once formed, the teams were largely self-managing. Supervisory business teams were formed to coordinate sets of related teams and to argue for and make decisions about resources and other organizational-level issues for their teams. The result was a network of teams and a shallow three-level hierarchy with little direct authoritarian control over the bottom-level teams. Just as teams were created at need, they were phased out when their projects had run their course, and the personnel were reassigned to other teams.

ICG also included personnel from its suppliers on some teams, creating networks with suppliers. As it developed deeper relationships with some particularly effective suppliers, ICG reduced the total number of suppliers it dealt with by about 50 percent. Interorganizational teams of ICG and supplier personnel worked on quality improvement projects to make sure that parts and materials met the highest quality specifications; they also embarked on some joint ventures in which both the supplier and ICG developed parts of a new product. ICG reached out to competing firms as well, to engage them in developing standards and sometimes in joint ventures.

Over a fifteen-year period, ICG moved from a traditional divisionalized form to a networked organization best characterized as a team of teams.

Applying What You've Learned

1. What characteristics of a network organization does ICG exhibit? Which ones are missing, if any? Is ICG a "poster child" for network organizations?
2. Why did ICG evolve from a divisionalized form to a networked organization? Were any of the forces discussed at the beginning of this chapter in operation?

Questions to Think About and Discuss

1. Based on the discussion in Chapter 4, we would expect that working on ICG teams is not always completely satisfactory for their members. What are some of the problems that might arise in ICG's teams? How might these problems carry over into networks of teams?
2. The change at ICG was instituted on the initiative of top management. What measures did management take to ensure that employees accepted and cooperated with these changes? What might management have done to increase the probability that employees would go along with the changes at ICG? What would have happened to ICG if it had not changed? Would it have been as successful? Why or why not?

This case is based on Nitin Nohria and James D. Berkley, "Allen-Bradley's ICCG Case Study," in *The Post-Bureaucratic Organization: New Perspectives on Organizational Change*, Charles Heckscher and Anne Donnellon, eds. (Newbury Park, CA: Sage, 1994).

Informal Network Organizations   Just as there are informal networks between people in organizations, there are also informal networks of organizations. In some cases, these form around a particular purpose, and interaction is regular enough that though they are not held together by formal contracts or structures, these networks can be called network organizations. In industries where technology is rapidly changing, knowledge is complex, and expertise is distributed among a number of organizations, knowledge networks often form whereby organizations can uncover new knowledge and insights. The biotechnology industry—to which we owe the new advances in DNA analysis and development of new bioengineered therapeutic drugs—is an example of this type of field. Studies of small biotech firms have documented that they develop densely connected networks for the exchange of new knowledge, information about competitors, and new directions in the biotechnology industry.[14]

No doubt, some of these informal connections eventually evolve into more formal connections. However, the absence of formal contracts or connections among these organizations increases their flexibility to seek new connections and also decreases the potential problems associated with sharing information that might be proprietary if developed in a formal network organization.

Other areas around which informal network organizations might develop include organizations that are heavily dependent on certain ICTs, such as the GHX medical supply exchange discussed in Chapter 2 (in response to the power that this exchange gives the suppliers, several informal buyer groups have formed, and they are beginning to develop more formal ties); organizations developing standards for new technologies, products, or services; and school districts attempting to deal with the unusually demanding budget and legislative restrictions of the past few years (for example, as a result of the "No Child Left Behind" Act).

Network Strategies of Motivation, Control, and Surveillance

The lack of hierarchy and the empowerment of members in network organizations poses new challenges for coordination and control. Although members of the units that make up the network are likely to feel loyal to their units, there is no intrinsic reason for them to feel the same loyalty toward the network. Consider the case of a computer programmer whose software firm contracts to develop a new inventory system for a major company. This software firm is part of a temporary network formed to bring a major new product to market. The programmer's future is with the software firm, not the major company; any raises come from the firm, and personal ties exist with co-workers in the firm, not with "those other guys" in the big company. The software firm and the project itself form the programmer's frame of reference when planning work. The programmer uses the standards of her firm and profession when planning and evaluating work. The big company's standards are relevant only if her managers emphasize them. The programmer is influenced by the software firm's culture, and much less by the culture of the distant company. To the extent that she orients to the big company at all, her main concern is to ensure that the software firm delivers on its contract and is judged favorably by the larger company.

Motivation in Network Organizations

How do network organizations motivate the members of individual units to collaborate and be innovative? This problem cannot be solved by a leader's dictates, because the relatively flat network organization does not have hierarchical authority over its constituent units or their members. Indeed, hierarchical authority would undermine the flexibility and adaptability that are the greatest advantages of the network form. Another challenge arises from the fact that the network gives units a degree of freedom in how they organize their work and the effort they put into the larger enterprise. This situation makes it possible for some units to take advantage of the others by "free riding" and taking shortcuts—putting in the bare minimum that others will accept, in order to maximize their profit.

Network organizations motivate and control their units and their units' members through three complementary routes. First, they attempt to cultivate trust in the network. Trust is the ideal cement for the network organizations. They have little or no hierarchy, so hierarchy cannot be the source of authority to coordinate and control. Moreover networks are often composed of numerous different organizations, each with its own culture, so culture cannot be the basis for control. Trust is a special property of the relationships among members of the network that enables them to act on the assumption that others will fulfill their own responsibilities in good faith. It is achieved through engaging in cooperative action with others and through observing their competence and their willingness to live up to their commitments. To cultivate trust, the managers of the new-product network might ask the programmer to work in the field for a couple of weeks with programmers from other components of the network. If their work goes well, programmers from the various firms come to trust each other and carry back good reports to the rest of the network. Trust will also be built in this network as various units carry out their responsibilities on time and effectively.[15]

Trust can also be based on reputation; we tend to trust people who are recommended by those we trust or who have a reputation for integrity. If the programmers report back to their managers that other firms' programmers are competent and good to work with, this in turn enhances the managers' trust in the network. Generally trust is assessed informally through direct experience of others. Hence organizations are most likely to enter into networks with those they already know and respect. Research shows, for example, that managers and decision makers tend to turn first to well-established networks of associates and advisers, rather than broadly searching for "strangers" who might be competent.[16] However, there are also formal indicators of trustworthiness. Professional credentials and certifications, such as those a computer programmer is likely to have, can also form the basis for trust. Some have envisioned that in the future companies and professional associations will develop reputational rating systems that record the projects that individuals and firms participate in and the reactions of their managers and peers in the network to their work. Those interested in building network organizations could then consult the ratings for advice as to which individuals and companies might be suitable for a project.[17]

A second source of motivation in network organizations is an inspiring, meaningful task. Network organizations typically focus on a task or a product, and this gives all members a common frame of reference. A meaningful task or goal can inspire the units and individuals in the network to work hard and ensure that they coordinate with other units. For example, the goal of the networked floral company Calyx & Corolla is to deliver the best possible flower arrangements faster than any other company and at a good price. This goal unifies the efforts of each part of the network: the flower growers try to deliver high-quality flowers; the arrangers work out innovative designs; the express delivery companies configure their operations to make sure the flowers arrive fresh; and the coordinating unit, Calyx & Corolla itself, works hard to make sure that the parts of the network connect smoothly with each other as the process moves from flowers in the field to flowers on the table.

One important thing to bear in mind, however, is that an inspiring task can hold a network together only for so long; in the longer term, members must also develop trust in each other. If some part of the network does not deliver—for example, if a grower contributes poor-quality flowers—the best efforts of the other units will not make the project succeed. In this case, the network either begins to malfunction and fall apart or finds another, better grower.

A third source of motivation and control in network organizations is network-based formal systems for monitoring and control of members and their activities. Networked organizations may attempt to develop structures to formally coordinate unit activities. These systems are based on contracts among the units in the network that provide a formal, written understanding concerning the units' responsibilities and compensation. Because contracts are legal documents, any unit that does not fulfill its contract can, of course, be sued. However, legal actions often take years to complete, so they are not effective in coordinating ongoing activities. A more effective means of coordination is to first develop a project or workflow plan that specifies what should be done and in what sequence; second, provide methods to enable units to monitor each other's activities; and finally, utilize a **full-disclosure** accounting information system such as those discussed previously that enables units to know what other units are contributing to the network and what earnings they are getting from it.

The accounting information system is simply a set of databases accessible to all participating units that shows them whether other units are meeting their responsibilities and indicates the level of return obtained by the organization as a whole and by each unit. For example, units in the new-product venture could determine from this data whether suppliers are on time with their deliveries, whether other units are putting in a fair effort (based on their expenditures and the payments they have received), and where they stand vis-à-vis other units in the network in terms of expenses and profits. This accounting information system reassures units that others are holding up their end of the bargain and puts pressure on them to hold up their own end. As units see that others are faithfully fulfilling their obligations, they come to trust them, and trust builds over time. Also important in this trust-building process is timely and effective use of electronic communication systems such as e-mail, teleconferencing, and groupware, discussed in Chapter 2. Direct, rapid communication and response help the network coordinate work and iron out problems. Both the accounting and the communication systems help to build trust, and trust is a self-reinforcing cycle: open communication enhances trust, which leads to more open communication and to more trust, in an ever-increasing spiral.[18]

Problems with Control Systems in Network Organizations

Systems for motivation and control in network organizations are an amalgam of methods used in the relational strategy (trust and an involving task) and the traditional strategy (formal control systems). The network strategy, however, extends relationships over a much greater distance than does the relational strategy, and it calls for more flexibility in the control system than is typical in the traditional strategy.

Just as team control sometimes becomes overwhelming in the relational strategy, control can be excessive and uncomfortable in the network. The project management system and full-disclosure information systems give information to all parties. This information can be used to make judgments about the effort of any given unit and bring pressure on that unit to get into line. The fact that these systems and their plans were approved by all units and are open to everyone gives negative information an objective force that can be used to embarrass and harass individuals or units. The resulting control structure can be just as oppressive as the team-based systems discussed in Chapter 4, creating defensiveness that makes the network less flexible than it could be if each unit were not holding all the others to strict standards of accountability.

There is also a mismatch between the types of rewards and incentives acceptable in U.S. culture and those needed to make a network organization function properly. Team-based organizations should give rewards to teams rather than basing salaries and promotions on individual performance. But most people are accustomed to expect rewards on an individual basis, as specified in the traditional strategy and passed on to the relational strategy. Anne Donnellon and Maureen Scully argue that organizations like the network form must move beyond traditional assessment and reward practices in which the manager assesses the employee, who receives an individual reward based on the assessment.[19] They argue for assessment by fellow team members and team-based rewards supplemented by individual rewards. In addition, they assert that organizations ought to avoid using terms like *merit,* a symbol that implies that individual characteristics are responsible for good performance. Such a term is misleading in network organizations, where good performance is dependent on collaboration and teamwork among individuals and units. In such systems, performance cannot be traced to individuals, and it is a mistake to continue to use the language of merit, which implies that it can.

Network Strategies of Leadership

Leadership in network organizations is not as clear-cut as it is in the traditional, relational, or cultural strategies, simply because networks are, by definition, somewhat diffuse. It is useful to distinguish top leadership, within which there is a central figure who provides leadership for the network, and leadership at the unit and interunit levels.

In most networks there is a salient person or persons who can emerge as leaders. Many network structures are assembled by **brokers,** a manager or firm that identifies appropriate units and builds them into a network. The broker may be an integrating project manager, as in the new-product development example introduced earlier in this chapter. Alternatively, the broker may be an independent agent or organization. Building contractors, who coordinate the work of carpenters, plumbers, electricians, and others, are brokers. Or leaders may emerge as symbols or spokespeople for the central organization in a network. The president of SONY, for example, could serve a leadership role for the keiretsu that developed in association with SONY.

These top leaders may take either transformational or transactional roles in the networked organization. A founder or renewer of the network may play the role of a transformational leader, described in Chapter 5. The founder/renewer sets the values and basic directions for the network, and its members look to him or her as an inspirational model. A broker or manager of a network will take a transactional approach, as detailed in Chapter 4. The role of transactional manager in newer designs, such as the networked organization, has been described as more like that of a symphony conductor than anything else. The individual units and their members have high levels of specialized knowledge and skill, and, like individual musicians, they know best how to perform their part in the organization. A good leader sets up conditions that enable units and members to perform up to their capabilities—rather than telling them what to do (micromanaging)—and helps them to coordinate their work with other units.

With respect to leadership within units, the network form poses several challenges for managers.[20] The team-based structure of network organizations implies that leaders must be able to promote teamwork, as described in Chapter 4. Because teams are self-managing, leaders should take on the role of coach rather than directive leader, advising the team and helping it to solve problems. The flatness of networked organizations necessitates a negotiator role for the manager as well. The negotiator must be able to represent the unit and its interests in negotiations over schedules, division of labor, and problems between units. The flexibility of network organizations means that managers must be able to deal with workforce management in a responsive, creative manner. For example, if serving a client means that someone has to travel to a distant plant and fix something, who in the unit is to do it? How does that person get compensated for her or his time within a fixed budget without causing perceptions of unfairness on the part of other employees? These and other sorts of issues arise during the process of constant adjustment necessary for flexible response. So the manager in the networked organization must be coach, negotiator, problem solver, and improviser, rather than simply a director.

Managers and members of units in networked organizations must also manage relationships with other units and organizations, because integrating functions are so important. Some of the communication functions involved in spanning the boundaries between units were discussed in Chapter 4. In addition, units in network organizations face a new problem. Whereas previously the problem was how to relate to another set of units that one is more or less stuck with, in the network it becomes how to maintain credibility in a network of units when some of them may be potential competitors seeking to replace your unit. The challenge in this case is how to project an image of competence, efficiency, and quality. In a real sense each unit—even within intact organizations—becomes an independent small business vying with many potential competitors. This situation requires a very different strategy for communicating with other units than do the three strategies discussed in Chapters 3, 4, and 5.

Challenges and Problems for Network Organizations

Organizations employing network strategies face a number of problems. For one thing, network organizations—with their flexible structures and complicated relationships among units—are extremely complex. This complexity introduces problems. It is often not easy to determine who is responsible for what in network organizations. Unless units specifically work out how they will coordinate activities and constantly communicate with each other, important things can fall in the cracks.

In complex systems, as we noted in Chapter 2, it is often impossible to determine the cause of problems. Consider a relatively simple organization composed of three units: one that designs widgets, a second that produces them, and a third that markets and distributes them. The marketing unit may find that there is not enough of product X to meet the demands of an important customer. Its initial tendency is to blame production, which has immediate responsibility for making the Xs. But production may be having trouble resulting from a design problem that causes a part of the product to break when it is removed from the stamping presses. The blame then seems to shift to design. However, the design unit used the flawed plan for product X because it had not received any feedback from production on the problem. Moreover, design understood from marketing that customers really appreciated the part of X that tended to break off in production's machines, so they wanted to keep it. Does the problem then trace back to production's lack of feedback or to marketing's insistence that the part of the design that caused problems be retained? The answer is that none of these can be said to be the sole cause of the problem. Causality in networks is ambiguous. The problems persist because of the organizational system as a whole, a system in which design does not communicate with the other units, in which production is not particularly proactive about problems it encounters, and in which marketing is out there selling stuff without considering whether other departments can meet the delivery schedules it sets. When it is difficult to determine the causes of problems, it is also difficult to solve them. When eliminating the source of a problem means changing the entire system, the problem may recur, because systems change slowly at best.

Network organizations also have a tendency to become more limited, rigid, and inflexible over time. One reason for this is that "once organizations have chosen partners, they tend to spend less time seeking other partners." [21] A lot of effort is typically put into finding suitable network partners, ascertaining whether they can be trusted, and negotiating working relationships with them. Once organizations find suitable partners, they are not as likely to put new effort into finding additional ones. As a result, networks tend to contain the "same old" organizations, which are not likely to bring new ideas or new skills to the table. Another reason networks tend to become rigid is that the units highest in prestige, centrality, and closeness tend to grow more powerful over time. They have information that other units do not have; they enjoy status due to their centrality; and they can control the flow of information. The extent of their power is in direct proportion to how much they control the key communication paths in the network. This slight (and sometimes not-so-slight) advantage can set up a self-reinforcing cycle whereby the more **centralized** units use their power to exert some control over the network, thereby increasing their reputation and power still more, and so on. However, centralized control over the network weakens the ability of units to adapt flexibly to the demands of the situation, defeating the purpose of using a network system. Centralization also takes power away from some units, sapping the initiative that self-management gives them. The heterarchy, described in the next chapter, is an adaptation of the network form that promises to be more flexible and responsive.

Another problem with network organizations is that, although they may enable their members to develop their own professionalism and careers, they do so at the expense of making "temporariness" permanent. No longer can employees assume they'll be working for the same company for thirty or forty years. By their very nature, network organizations force their employees to think of a future in which they'll have to find new contacts and new positions in a new organization. This can undermine loyalty to the organization, making it hard to develop and sustain an organizational culture. It is also an uncomfortable situation for individuals who desire stability in their lives. Although it may seem something of a paradox, stability in employees is critical for maintaining the flexibility and adaptability that the network emphasizes. When employees know the organization and their jobs well, they are generally better able to see what needs changing and how to change it.

Conclusion

Network organizations have become more prominent in the past twenty years, but they have always been with us. As we noted, building contractors typically operate network organizations. Acting as brokers, they contract with carpenters, plumbing companies, electrical contractors, and others to perform the work necessary to build a house or store.

There have also been times in the past when network organizations were just as common as they are becoming today.[22] The textile industry was the first major industry to emerge in the United States. During the period of 1820–1880 there was much uncertainty and change in this industry. Technology was changing fast; concentrated work in factories was a novelty, because most people were used to working on farms, in small workshops, and at home; and new entrepreneurs were uncertain about where to get capital to start new ventures. As a result several different types of industry organization emerged. In Massachusetts, the heavily capitalized, large corporations we are familiar with today were beginning to develop. They favored large plants that concentrated workers. But around Philadelphia a network of textile companies developed. They were smaller and required less capital, and they formed and went out of business relatively rapidly. They regularly worked together for periods of time without merging or consolidating. For example, if one weaver won a larger order than he could deliver, he would often have several other weaving companies help to fulfill the order. Companies specialized in certain aspects of textile preparation and cooperated with others who fulfilled other functions to produce the finished product. One company might dye and make the yarn, another weave it into cloth, and a third finish the cloth and sell it to local stores.

The large factories of Massachusetts were fairly inflexible because they had to invest a great deal of money and time in machinery suitable for a single type of textile. During the Civil War, when the supply of cotton from the South dried up, the factories in Massachusetts had to shut down, because they were only set up to handle cotton. The textile firms around Philadelphia were more flexible and could adapt better to the current demand for cloth. If wool was in oversupply, they could shift to cotton or linen fairly easily. They were not as dependent on inflexible technologies and could adjust their looms accordingly. And some companies would simply go out of business when demand changed; their owners or employees would either start up new companies suited to current demand or find jobs with other firms in the network.

The network of textile firms around Philadelphia in the mid-1800s was much like the network organizations we see today. So in a real sense, today's firms are "reinventing the wheel."

Charles Perrow argues that the Philadelphia network model might have become the pattern for our economy if the large, heavily capitalized firms like those in Massachusetts had not influenced legislation and the structure of the economy and if our federal government had not been so weak.[23] As a result of these factors, we developed an economy that favored the types of firms that are described in the chapter on traditional organizations. Many argue that today our economy is undergoing a fundamental change that will increasingly favor network organizations.

The gradual evolution of the knowledge society in the last half of the twentieth century set the stage for the explosive rate at which the emphasis on knowledge and **information work** has developed over the past twenty years. Along with this came the globalization of the economy, rapid growth in knowledge and technology, and increased environmental turbulence. The rapid development of ICTs has facilitated and fed on these changes. Computer and telecommunications technologies have permeated organizations and made many types of structures and communication systems possible that were only visions before 1980.

To deal with the increased pace of change and adapt to turbulent environments, organizations must incorporate integrating communication mechanisms for coordination. We discussed a number of different methods for integrating organizations and suggested that they be evaluated on the basis of benefits and costs to the organization, the degree of geographical dispersion of the organization, and the organization's culture. Ideally, the least costly method that can adequately meet the organization's needs should be chosen. In practice this is not always possible because of limitations in member knowledge and willingness to use a given method and because of lack of fit with the organization's culture. These coordination methods will help organizations employing the traditional, relational, and cultural strategies to deal with changing technologies and environments; but they can only go so far. When uncertainty is high, as a result of environmental change, internal complexity, or other factors, a different strategy of organizing is needed.

The network strategy of organizing is appropriate for organizations that must cope with high levels of uncertainty. It is a highly relational strategy that designs the organization with a flexible, modular structure that links units in a network, a relatively flat hierarchy, an emphasis on teams and self-management, and the use of information technology to coordinate units. Networks can be changed relatively easily to incorporate new units; they can rearrange themselves to respond to new demands from their work or environment. The network organization relies on employees to be independent, knowledgeable, and team-oriented. Rather than rigid structures, the network uses mutual trust among members, members' commitment to their work, contracts, and open communication systems to hold the network together. Units in the network coordinate through communication and negotiation rather than through authority.

Notes

[1] Jay Galbraith, "Organizational Design," in *Handbook of Organizational Behavior,* J. Lorsch, ed. (Englewood Cliffs: Prentice Hall, 1987).

[2] A readable account of the matrix organization can be found in Robert Youker, "Organization Alternatives for Project Managers," *Project Management Journal* 8 (March 1977): 18–24. Also see Galbraith.

[3] Richard Daft, *Organization Theory and Design,* 3rd ed. (St. Paul, MN: West, 1989).

[4] Drew Robb, "Collaboration Gets It Together," *Computerworld*, December 9, 2002, p. 30.

[5] Robb, p. 30.

[6] Kathleen Melymuka, "Smarter by the Hour," *Computerworld,* June 23, 2003, pp. 43–44.

[7] Susan J. Winter and S. Lynne Taylor, "The Role of Information Technology in the Transformation of Work: A Comparison of Post-Industrial, Industrial, and Proto-Industrial Organizations," in *Shaping Organization Form: Communication, Connection, and Community,* Gerardine DeSanctis and Janet Fulk, eds. (Newbury Park, CA: Sage, 1999).

[8] Marshall Scott Poole, "Organizational Challenges for the New Forms," in *Shaping Organization Form: Communication, Connection, and Community,* Gerardine DeSanctis and Janet Fulk, eds. (Newbury Park, CA: Sage, 1999). Deborah Ancona, Thomas Kochan, Maureen Scully, John Van Maanen, and D. Eleanor Westney, "The New Organization: Taking Action in an Era of Organizational Transformation," in *Managing for the Future: Organizational Behavior and Processes* (Cincinnati: South-Western College Publishing, 1999).

[9] Peter Monge and Noshir Contractor, *Theories of Communication Networks* (New York: Oxford University Press, 2003).

[10] Larry Browning, Janice Beyer, and Judy Shetler, "Building Cooperation in a Competitive Industry: SEMATECH and the Semiconductor Industry," *Academy of Management Journal* 38 (1995): 113–151.

[11] Henry C. Lucas, *The T-Form Organization: Using Technology to Design Organizations for the 21st Century* (San Francisco: Jossey-Bass, 1996).

[12] Lucas.

[13] Michael Meyer, "Here's a 'Virtual' Model for America's Industrial Giants," *Newsweek,* August 13, 1993, p. 40.

[14] Woody W. Powell, Ken Koput, and L. Smith-Doerr, "Interorganizational Collaboration and the Locus of Innovation: Networks of Learning in Biotechnology," *Administrative Science Quarterly* 41 (1996): 116–145. Julia P. Liebeskind, A. L. Oliver, Lynne Zucker, and M. Brewer, "Social Networks, Learning, and Flexibility: Sourcing Scientific Knowledge in New Biotechnology Firms," *Organization Science* 7 (1996): 428–443.

[15] Dale E. Zand, "Trust and Managerial Problem-Solving," *Administrative Science Quarterly* 17 (1972): 229–239.

[16] Monge and Contractor, *Theories of Communication Networks*.

[17] Poole, "Organizational Challenges."

[18] Zand.

[19] Anne Donnellon and Maureen Scully, "Teams, Performance, and Rewards: Will the Post-Bureaucratic Organization Be a Post-Meritocratic Organization?" in *The Post-Bureaucratic Organization: New Perspectives on Organizational Change*, Charles Heckscher and Anne Donnellon, eds. (Thousand Oaks, CA: Sage, 1994).

[20] Ancona et al., chapter 1.

[21] Monge and Contractor, *Theories of Communication Networks*, p. 192.

[22] Charles Perrow, *Organizing America* (Princeton, NJ: Princeton University Press, 2002), chapter 4.

[23] Perrow, *Organizing America.*

Chapter 7

Alternative Strategies of Organizing

New organizational forms arise to cope with new environmental conditions.
—RAYMOND E. MILES AND CHARLES C. SNOW

Central Themes

- The effectiveness of an organization's structure and communication system depends on the nature of the organization's work, its interdependencies with other organizations, and its environment.
- Contingency design theory attempts to explain which structures are most effective under various conditions and gives advice on how to design an effective organizational communication system.
- The design of organizations and their communication systems is also influenced by social institutions.
- In choosing which communication medium to use, one should consider information richness, fit with the organization's culture, and the symbolic value of the medium.
- Postmodern, cooperative, feminist, and heterarchical organizations are emerging strategies of organizing that offer alternatives to the four strategies discussed in Chapters 3–6 of this book.

Key Terms

contingency design theory	routine technology
formalization	nonroutine technology
centralization	interdependence
span of control	pooled interdependence
technology	sequential interdependence

reciprocal interdependence
environmental complexity
institutional theory
social institution
coercive influence
normative influence
mimetic influence
media richness

symbol-carrying capacity of a medium
simulacra
deconstruction
postmodern organization
cooperatives
feminist organizations
heterarchy

Now that we have defined four strategies for organizing, several questions arise: Are some strategies better than others? How do we select a strategy? If strategies can be combined, as noted in previous chapters, how do we pick which ones to combine? Are these all the possible strategies? This chapter addresses these questions. It also recognizes that there may be many reasons for choosing a particular strategy of organizing. Of course, at least in for-profit organizations in capitalist economies, the most frequent basis for choosing a strategy is organizational effectiveness. Consequently, we begin this chapter by presenting the most important effectiveness-based model of strategic choice, **contingency design theory.** It offers advice concerning when to choose different strategies, when one strategy is likely to be more effective than others, and when strategies might be combined. We conclude this section with a discussion of forms of organizing different from those traditionally studied under contingency theory.

However, many alternative forms of organizing are based on ideologies that reject the notion that "effectiveness" or "efficient seeking of profits" is the only, or even the most justifiable, basis for operating organizations. Some of these focus on creating societies based on cooperative action; others are based on feminist theory. All three forms challenge the assumptions underlying the vast majority of contemporary organizations. These thought-provoking alternative strategies of organizing may well become more common in the future.

Contingency Design Theory

This theory is concerned with the question, What conditions determine which strategy of organization will be most effective? Advocates of traditional and relational strategies thought they had found the one best way to organize. So did the early proponents of cultural strategies, who viewed building strong cultures as a universally applicable strategy. However, much research and practical experience has shown that they were mistaken. Under some conditions, the bureaucratic strategy works best, whereas under other conditions, the relational, cultural, or networking strategies are superior. This was first noted in the late 1950s by two English sociologists, Tom Burns and G. M. Stalker.[1] They found that when conditions are stable, a well-planned, efficient organization, which is epitomized by the bureaucracy, outperforms all other types because it is the most efficient organization. Other types of organizations may do well for a while, but ultimately the bureaucracy outraces them because it produces the best results with the least input. It will have superior profitability and efficiency and more funds to reinvest in improving its product or service.

However, Burns and Stalker found that when the environment is unstable and turbulent, the bureaucracy is too slow to adapt. Its formal structures, standard operating procedures, and centralized decision making limit its members' ability to recognize the need for change and make it inflexible when change is necessary. The relational strategy, which features decentralized decision making and informal structures, and cultural strategies that focus on change are much better at adapting. Of course, if employees become too committed to one another (as sometimes happens with relational strategies) or identify too completely with the organization's core beliefs and values (as in some strong culture organizations), they have trouble changing. Under conditions of high instability and turbulence, when adaptation is at a premium, the network strategy is more effective than the relational or cultural strategies. Contingency design theory helps to explain why some organizational systems are more effective than others. It also gives useful advice about the design of organizational structures and communication systems.

Design Features That Can Be Managed Strategically

Viewing organizations as systems suggests that they must adapt if they are to survive. The following are some of the features of organizational structures and processes that can be altered in an effort to adapt to situational pressures.

- **Formalization,** as defined in Chapter 3, is the degree to which the organization has well-defined roles, strict division of labor into relatively small tasks, and rules and procedures that apply to most activities. Bureaucratic structures are high in formalization. An organization lower in formalization would have more flexible role definitions, more flexible adjustment and redefinition of tasks, and few codified rules and procedures. The structures associated with the relational strategy are typically low in formalization. Network structures are intermediate in their degree of formalization because they often have formal control systems but also need to have flexible response and therefore as few rigid rules as possible.
- **Centralization** refers to the degree to which control is centralized in top management. As Chapter 3 notes, bureaucratic structures tend to be highly centralized. Power is more widely distributed in relational and network strategies, and they are therefore less centralized.
- **Specialization** is defined as the degree to which workers and staff have to obtain specialized training or degrees to carry out their work effectively. For example, engineering firms need a highly trained staff with a great deal of experience to function. Fast food restaurants and department stores do not. Most employees are hired with minimal screening, because the organization believes it can easily train them to do an adequate job.
- **Span of control** is the number of employees who report to a single manager or supervisor. Managers with wide spans of control supervise many

employees; those with narrower spans supervise fewer. Narrow spans of control are important when managers must check for details, special problems, or errors. Wider spans of control are workable when there are not many exceptions and the work is pretty much the same all the time.

- Communication and coordination, that is, the frequency, formality, and medium of communication among members, may be adjusted by an organization. If members frequently experience coordination problems, communication must be more frequent, less formal, and more immediate. A preset chain of command may be sufficient for routine communication, but more direct and unregulated interaction is required to solve problems and deal with exceptional circumstances. Although routine communication can be handled through written media (memos, e-mail), communication about problems, exceptional circumstances, and nonroutine matters is more effectively dealt with through face-to-face discussion, telephone calls, and meetings.
- Interorganizational relationships have to do with the degree to which an organization forms and maintains stable relationships with other groups or organizations. Some organizations have well-defined boundaries and remain self-contained, whereas others form contracts, joint ventures, or partnerships with other organizations.
- ICT intensiveness is the degree to which organizations choose to rely on ICTs to support their work. Some organizations may purposely remain "low-tech," choosing to use ICTs minimally. Others may choose to utilize them more extensively, as an increasing number of organizations have been doing in recent years. Of course, what constitutes high technology differs as time passes. Twenty years ago a telecommunications system with features such as voice mail and multiple lines was regarded as fairly high-tech. Fifteen years ago, e-mail was high-tech, but today it is considered a necessity.

These features do not vary independently of one another; they tend to come in "packages" that are consistent with the different strategies of organization. For instance, in the traditional strategy an organization typically has high formalization, high centralization, low to moderate spans of control, formal communication, few and well-defined interorganizational relationships, and moderate ICT intensiveness, where the ICT is used for control and coordination of work. Does this particular package of features represent the traditional strategy as you understand it? Try working out the packages of features for the other three strategies (answers are in note 2).[2]

Variables That Should Be Considered When Choosing Organizational Design Strategies: Contingencies

Contingency design theory builds on the observations outlined in Chapters 3–6 about the organization-environment relationship. Research has identified three characteristics that are particularly important in determining organizational design: technology, interdependence between units, and the organizational environment.

Technology   In contingency design theory, **technology** is broadly construed as the tools, techniques, and actions used to transform organizational inputs into outputs.[3] This definition means that technology includes more than just machinery, computers, or chemicals; *technology* refers to the means by which the work of the organization is done. According to this way of thinking, a social service agency has a technology just as much as an automobile plant does. The social service agency's technology comprises the procedures followed for patient intake and record-keeping, the service procedures (for example, such things as client counseling or therapeutic methods), and procedures for discharge and billing. This technology enables the social service agency to serve its clients, which in turn ensures a flow of funds to the agency.

In general terms, technology varies along a continuum from routine to nonroutine.[4] In a **routine technology,** the process by which the work must be done is well understood, and there are few unexpected problems or exceptions. Routine tasks can be broken down into steps and programmed. In many cases, routine tasks can be automated, reducing the organization's reliance on human labor. For example, fast food restaurants offer limited menus, so the procedures for preparing the food are highly standardized. This is true even in those that claim to let you "have it your way." Machines often do the cooking, and workers follow tightly regimented recipes and portion-control formulas. Routinization ensures a consistent product and good returns for the franchise. In fact, the primary appeal of McDonald's is that Big Macs taste the same almost everywhere in the world (except India). Even exceptions can be easily planned for. "Having it your way" involves a relatively limited set of ingredient variations and preparation steps, each of which is planned well in advance. Workers have little or no discretion or control over the work. Engineers, operations management specialists, and other experts analyze the work and determine how it should be done.

At the other end of the scale are **nonroutine** tasks. Because there are many exceptional cases, and because the procedures for doing nonroutine tasks are not well understood, human judgment and discretion must be applied to each case. As the old phrase goes, the work is more an art than a science. Skilled workers are needed to exercise finely trained judgments in solving problems and doing the work. Strategic planning requires extensive know-how and background. However, planners do not always understand exactly what is the right way to respond to the situation they face. Nor do they know what the situation will be like in the future. Hence they must improvise and project based on their own knowledge and experience.

Generally speaking, uncertainty increases as we move from routine to nonroutine technologies. As a result, traditional strategies of organizing are most effective for routine technologies; relational strategies are most effective for nonroutine technologies. Cultural strategies that emphasize continuity and stability are more effective for routine technologies; but those that emphasize change and innovation are more effective with nonroutine technologies. Intermediate cases are more difficult. In such cases, there is less-than-perfect knowledge of how to do the work and more than a few exceptions occur; however, these intermediate cases do not have the extremely high degrees of uncertainty that nonroutine technologies are designed for. Examples of intermediate cases are clothing design and pattern making, specialty steel manufacturing, legal work, and the performing arts. A typical intermediate strategy is to develop a repertoire of methods or techniques that can be mastered and applied to different cases. The challenge is selecting and combining the right routines to get the job done properly. So the surgical team knows many different procedures (anesthesia, opening the patient, tying off blood vessels) and combines different sets of them in different ways, depending on the type of operation being done and the particular characteristics of the patient.

Organizational communication is quite different in organizations that have routine technologies from that in organizations that have nonroutine technologies. The greater the uncertainty, the greater the need for direct, intensive communication and many adjustments. Although most people prefer face-to-face communication, such direct and intense communication is costly. It takes a great deal of time to communicate and come to an understanding, to adjust work and plans, and to manage the conflicts that may arise along the way. For best results, a balance must be struck between communication needs and cost: the organization should enact the least costly communication system that can adequately meet its needs for communication and coordination. If people need to exchange only standard information, such as an order for a meal, placing the order through an impersonal medium, such as a checklist or a computer system, is adequate because it conveys the information with little communication cost. (Of course, the computer system is costly in its own right, but for high volumes of communication the cost per message comes out to be quite low.) For routine technologies, vertical, formal, written communication is most adequate. Because these tasks are predictable and repeatable, there is usually a wealth of documented information and analysis concerning how best to do the work and handle problems. This can be expressed in formal manuals or work procedures that substitute for direct communication between workers or between workers and managers. For routine tasks, most communication follows the chain of command as managers give orders to and solve problems for subordinates. Low levels of task variety suggest that exceptions requiring extended discussion will be rare and that instructions for handling those that do can be built into procedural manuals.

For nonroutine technologies, uncertainty reaches very high levels. There is high variety and low analyzability, so each task must be approached with a great deal of direct, often unscheduled communication. Face-to-face consultations and long, intense meetings are often the only adequate form of communication to meet the needs of nonroutine work.

For intermediate cases, there is a need for higher levels of communication than routine organization allows for but less than the nonroutine case. The lowest-cost method for increasing communication beyond formal channels in such cases is the scheduled meeting, because this can be planned into the work. Some of the simpler methods for lateral coordination discussed in Chapter 6 are appropriate for intermediate cases.

To sum up, depending on the nature of the technology employed in a unit, the unit will have different levels of uncertainty and different communication needs. To remain effective and viable, the organization must develop a communication system that is adequate for the demands placed on it. Assessing a unit's technology can help a person understand why its communication is effective or not and what needs to be done to improve communication.

Interdependence   Technology influences the communication systems of intact units. However, units do not always work in isolation; they are **interdependent** with other units. Three different types of interdependence can be distinguished:[5] pooled, sequential, and reciprocal. Each imposes different communication requirements on the organization. In the case of **pooled interdependence,** work does not flow between units. Instead, the units each work on their own product or services and the total output of the organization is the pooled work of the individual units. Franchise restaurants, such as Denny's or McDonald's, are good examples of pooled interdependence. Franchises in different locations do not need to coordinate with each other; each does its own work and contributes independently (more or less) to the return of the whole chain. Other organizations with pooled interdependence include personal tax preparation services and independent long-haul trucking firms.

Because the degree of interdependence is low, communication among units or people linked in pooled interdependence can be handled through standardization, the creation of rules, and formal written plans to ensure that each of the parallel units is adequately supplied and turns out work of adequate quality. These plans and rules serve as substitutes for communication and reduce the need for other forms of communication. Managers above the pooled units provide sufficient coordination to keep them operating smoothly, and vertical communication between managers and units is the final ingredient in an effective coordination system. Units with pooled interdependence do not require strong communication links with each other; hence they do not have to be located near each other or linked by telecommunications.

Sequential interdependence exists when units are arrayed in a series and the output of one department is the input for another. In this case, how well each successive unit can perform depends on how well the previous units have done their work. Sequential interdependence increases coordination needs and requires higher levels of communication than pooled interdependence (see Figure 7-1). Because there is a one-way flow of materials, people, or information, extensive planning and scheduling is required, and feedback concerning problems is needed to ensure that earlier steps have been performed properly. The classic example of sequential interdependence is the assembly line. Other examples include college admissions offices, financial institutions, and unemployment offices.

Sequential interdependence is best coordinated by active planning among participants, guided by management. Managers use vertical communication channels to do a great deal of the coordination work for sequential units. Under

FIGURE 7–1
Three Types of Interdependence among Organizations or Units

Type of interdependence	Communication requirements
POOLED Work in 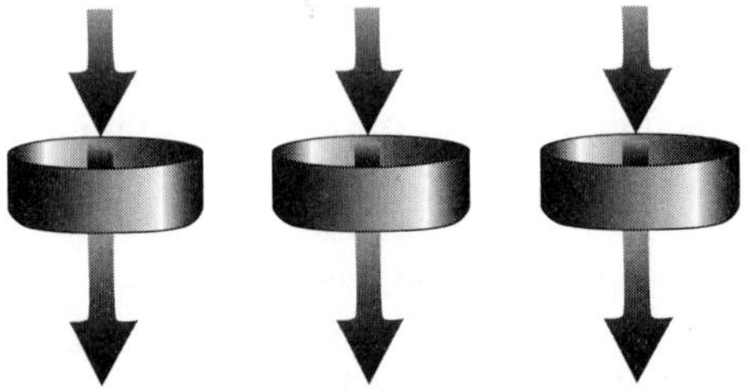 Work out	Low
SEQUENTIAL Work in 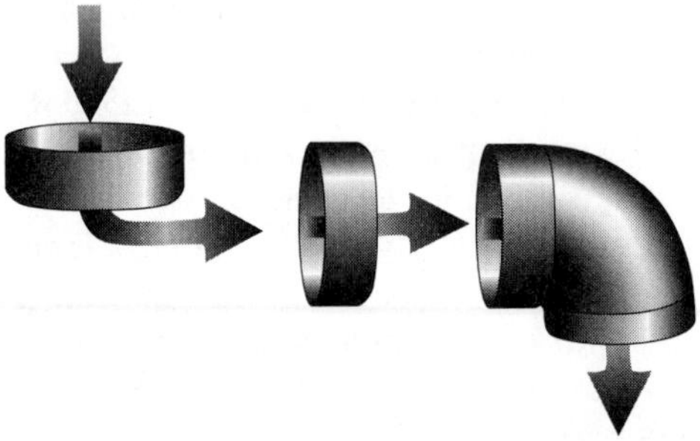 Work out	Moderate
RECIPROCAL Work in 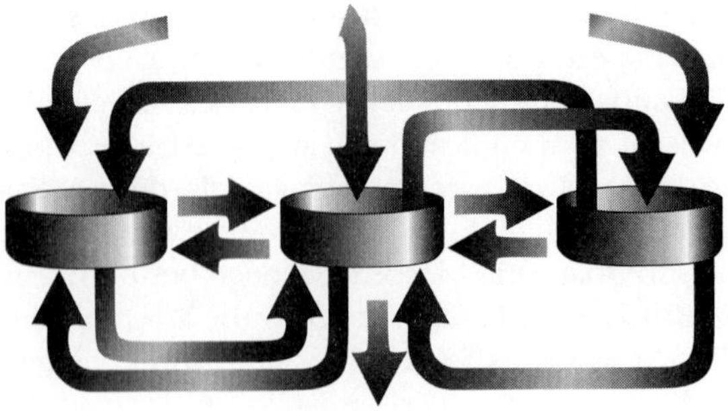 Work out	High

the auspices of management, representatives of these units also come together in scheduled meetings to form plans that ensure smooth operation and minimize problems. Problems that arise are dealt with either by management or through horizontal communication among units.

The highest level of interdependence is **reciprocal interdependence.** In this case, all units are involved together in the work; the outputs of each unit become the inputs of the others, and vice versa. Units work together intensively when there is reciprocal interdependence, so they require a great deal of communication and coordination. It is not always possible to predict the types of operations or problems that will occur under reciprocal interdependence, so it falls to the units to manage coordination through direct interaction as the need arises. The extensive coordination that reciprocal interdependence requires is best handled through mutual adjustment of the units, though the modes of coordination employed for pooled and sequential cases (standardization and planning) can help as well. Coordination needs for reciprocal interdependence tend to arise on the fly and must be met by horizontal communication via unscheduled meetings, face-to-face communication, and electronic channels. Managers can help resolve coordination problems for reciprocally linked units, but the units themselves are in the best position to actually suggest and try out solutions.

To sum up, at low levels of interdependence, substitutes for communication are sufficient; as interdependence increases, plans, scheduled communication, and vertical communication are needed; and at high levels of interdependence, horizontal, unscheduled, and continuous communication is required. Organizations that want to coordinate their units adequately (sufficient communication with minimum cost) would do well to follow these guidelines.

Environment   The third variable affecting organizational design and communication structures is the organization's environment. The notion of organizational environment has been introduced in earlier chapters. In this section, we define environment more systematically and relate it to the design of organizations and their communication systems.

Literally, environment refers to everything outside the organization's boundaries. However, for purposes of analysis, environment can be defined as those institutions, organizations, groups, and people outside the organization that affect it. Environments are made up of many elements, including domestic and foreign competitors, customers and clients, government agencies and regulators, general economic conditions, technological developments relevant to the organization, financial resources, the labor market, raw materials suppliers, and the general culture surrounding the organization. Not all of these elements are similar or equally important for every organization; depending on its purpose and location, each organization has a particular mix of these elements as its environment.

Organizational environments can be described in terms of two basic dimensions, complexity and stability.[6] The **complexity** of an organization's environment refers to the number of elements in the environment with which the organization has to deal. An organization with a simple environment may have only a few elements to deal with, whereas one in a complex environment may deal with dozens or hundreds of elements. For example, a university library has a relatively simple environment; it has to deal with the university's administration, the library's student and faculty clientele, publishers and other publication sources, and other libraries. Many of the library's dealings with other agencies, such as the Occupational Safety and Health Administration and the Social Security Administration, are handled for it by the university administration, greatly reducing the environmental complexity. A publishing house has to deal with a much more complex environment—stockholders or owners (who may change frequently as a result of mergers), competing publishers, authors (who often miss deadlines), customers, an assortment of government agencies, the financial institutions that provide its capital and operating moneys, labor unions, and new technologies that compete with published books, magazines, and journals. Clearly, university libraries and publishing houses experience different environmental demands.

The other dimension of organizational environment, *stability*, can be defined as the rate of change in the elements of the environment and their relationships, a concept mentioned in several previous chapters. Some environments are stable or, if not, they change in a predictable fashion. Before deregulation, the telephone company AT&T had a stable environment. Suppliers and customers were predictable; the company's monopoly status gave it a guaranteed market, and its relations with the regulators ensured that it would make a reasonable profit. Change came mainly in the form of new technologies and services that the phone company itself developed. On the other end of the continuum are organizations whose environments are changing rapidly and continuously. These organizations must adapt constantly, and unpredictability is expected and factored into their operation. To deal with instability, such organizations develop special positions and units to monitor and plan reactions to the environment. Firms in the information technology field offer a good example of life in an unstable environment. Driven by the fast pace of technological change and cutthroat international competition, they often change their products, their markets, and their own structures in order to survive and remain competitive.

Together environmental complexity and stability define four basic situations that can be arranged in order of increasing uncertainty. Simple, stable environments create relatively low levels of uncertainty. Organizations in these environments can focus on setting up the most effective and efficient organizational design. Examples of organizations in this cell include soft drink distribution companies and law offices. Complex, stable environments offer medium levels of uncertainty. As a result, the organization must evolve special units or procedures for dealing with uncertainty and must anticipate a certain amount of change. Examples of organizations with complex, stable environments include universities and chemical companies. Moderate to high uncertainty is experienced by organizations in simple, unstable environments. Whereas these environments are relatively simple, they undergo continuous change, and organizations must change to survive in them. Examples of organizations with unstable, simple environments include firms in the clothing industry and manufacturers of personal computers that supply the big retail outlets. Unstable, complex environments create the highest level of uncertainty. In these environments, the organization must constantly plan for change and react to circumstances beyond its control. To do this, special positions and units are created to monitor and guide reactions to environmental change, and a flexible organizational structure is needed to promote adaptation. Examples of organizations in this quadrant are software, telecommunications, and airline firms.

To be effective, organizations in stable environments should adopt the traditional strategy; those in moderate to highly unstable environments should adopt the relational strategy, and those in environments with very high instability should adopt the network strategy.[7] Cultural strategies that value stability are more effective in stable environments; those that emphasize innovation and change are more effective in unstable environments. Because of the traditional form's advantage in efficiency, it is the most effective choice when the organization can plan its structure and procedures carefully. However, when the environment is changing, the flatter, more interconnected relational form is preferred because of its adaptability.

As environmental complexity increases, the number of departments in the organization generally increases. Organizations typically have units to deal with critical aspects of their environments, and the more of these there are, the greater must be the number of units. The only bank in a small rural town has a relatively simple internal structure: officers to deal with regulators and make major decisions, accountants and auditors to keep track of the money, tellers to deal with customers, and janitors to keep the place clean. However, if another bank moves into town, the first one may add a marketing unit to compete for customers; if a large plant relocates to the town, the bank may add a commercial lending unit. As the environmental elements increase in number and interrelationships, the structure of the organization becomes more complex. In the same vein, organizations facing complex environments may add boundary-spanning personnel who directly relate to various organizations or groups in the environment. The small-town bank, for example, may add a special position dedicated to contacting and serving the relocated plant.

As instability and complexity increase, the need for communication and integrating roles in the organization increases. Integrating roles are those that help different units coordinate their efforts and resolve actual and potential conflicts. Organizations with high levels of instability and complexity in particular have many integrating roles.

Interrelationships among the Variables

Each of the three variables affects somewhat different features of organizations and their communication systems. Technology influences the communication system within units; interdependence influences the communication between units within the organization; and the environment influences the communication system that crosses the boundaries of the organization. If we can assess the values of these variables for a given organization, we can know what an effective communication system should be like. Contingency theory can also help pinpoint possible problems in an organization's communication system and suggest ways in which it can be made more effective.

CASE STUDY
Steeling Away into a Different Structure

From the days of Andrew Carnegie and the other steel barons up to the late 1960s, the steel industry was dominated by large, vertically integrated companies. The industry existed in a stable environment and the rate of technological advance was steady and gradual. If steel manufacturers could produce steel of good quality at a reasonable price, it could be sold.

Excelsior Steel is 125 years old, employs 2,200, and makes 250,000 tons of steel a year. Located in northern Indiana, it is housed in a huge plant where all operations are consolidated under one roof. Excelsior had a centralized, hierarchical structure. From its offices in downtown Gary, top management, with the aid of engineering, made decisions regarding the products Excelsior would manufacture and the level produced. Separate departments handled manufacturing, marketing, metallurgy, field sales, and support for these units. Over the years, top managers forged close contacts with unions, and the unions often worked with Excelsior to determine work rates and how the work should be done.

But all that changed starting in the late 1970s. The inflation of that period, coupled with the recession that followed it and fierce competition from Germany, Japan, and Brazil, brought Excelsior to the edge of bankruptcy. It was in danger of following many of the other steel giants that lined the southern edge of Lake Michigan out of the steel business. But Excelsior did not become another of those huge abandoned buildings north of Hammond, Indiana. Instead it took aggressive steps to solve problems.

After extensive diagnosis, Excelsior's managers found that their products were no longer keeping pace with the market, 60 percent of the firm's orders ran behind schedule, and profits were eaten up by materials, energy, and labor costs. In this more turbulent environment, the stable, hierarchical structure was not nimble enough. Moreover, technological advances had rendered much of Excelsior's plant outdated. Smaller furnaces equipped with the latest computer-assisted manufacturing devices could turn out many of Excelsior's products at a much lower cost.

In conjunction with outside experts and the union, management at Excelsior concocted a strategy to save the plant. The strategy hinged on shifting production to high-value products tailored for separate markets, while upgrading technology and research.

To get started, Excelsior set up three product task forces: sheet metal, special alloys, and open-die forgings. These task forces had representatives from all departments involved in the products, and their charge was to determine how each product could be produced in an independent product group. The task forces formed the basis for permanently integrating teams headed by product managers; each team was responsible for all aspects of one of the three product areas, including sales. Each product area was also responsible for introducing new products and trimming products that were not successful.

Over time, there were so many orders for different types of specialty steel that the special-alloys group subdivided into multiple project teams, instituting a mini-matrix structure within the group. Because it was important to keep the personnel in the special-alloys groups trained in the latest technology and metallurgical research, the functional departments assumed increased importance. Functional managers, such as the manger of metallurgy, were responsible for keeping abreast of the latest technical developments and for keeping personnel trained. These personnel were then assigned to one or more projects, under the supervision of the project manager. This structure greatly enhanced communication both within and between specialties.

Excelsior installed electronic mail and voice mail when it implemented an order and inventory tracking system. These greatly increased the ability of Excelsior's employees to keep in touch with each other and increased the flow of ideas. Along with this, Excelsior created a program to cultivate new ideas: employees who had brainstorms could set up project teams to develop them, provided they could make a good case with the management team. From this program came several new product lines.

Implementation of this new structure was not painless. The company had to lay off workers, because the three product lines did not require as many employees as Excelsior had in its heyday. By the end of the reorganization, Excelsior had only 1,300 employees; however, as production increased, it hired back about 300 more. Many of the laid-off employees were replaced by technology. The union still hung on, but union and management were much less adversarial than in the past. Union and management worked together to reorganize the plant. Middle managers and foremen were especially confused by the transition to product units and the matrix-based structure. Not accustomed to dealing with ambiguity, they initially resisted the increased number of meetings and negotiation required. Over time the most disgruntled managers and foremen retired, and the new structure, which emphasized horizontal and integrative links as well as vertical communication, took over. Many of the managers who initially resisted this shift have found it to be a growth experience; they try to involve younger employees in new product development and problem-solving to develop them for the future.

Excelsior Steel is now back on track. Deliveries are on time better than 95 per-

(continued)

(Case Study, continued)

cent of the time. An average of twenty new products are introduced each year, and profits are up. Market share has recovered as well. Excelsior employees gladly embrace their new motto, "Change or Die."

Applying What You've Learned

1. How did Excelsior respond to changes in its environment and technology? Which of the integrating methods did Excelsior use?

Questions to Think About and Discuss

1. It is not clear that a company in Excelsior's position can ever stop changing. What are some of the disadvantages of continuous change? How could Excelsior minimize them?
2. What communication problems would you expect to have occurred as Excelsior moved from its old structure and culture to the new one?

This case is a composite of several cases describing companies both inside and outside the steel industry. It was inspired by Richard Daft, *Organization Theory and Design,* 3rd ed. (St. Paul, MN: West, 1989), pp. 244–245.

This discussion of contingency variables also suggests a problem: what if the variables are inconsistent with each other? An organization might, for example, have a nonroutine technology but confront a simple, stable environment. The technology suggests that the relational strategy should be used; but the environment suggests the traditional strategy. Two possible outcomes have been suggested for organizations in this situation. Some scholars say that the organization should adopt the most complex organization indicated by the three variables. At the cost of some inefficiency, the organization would be able to deal with its toughest challenge. Other scholars believe that when the variables are inconsistent, the organization must "suboptimize" or underperform, because it is faced with contradictions. The heterarchy, one of the emerging organizational forms, has been advanced as a response to just this sort of case, in which the situation confronting the organization is both contradictory and highly changeable. (See "Heterarchies," a subsequent section of this chapter.)

An Alternative Influence on Strategy Selection: Institutional Pressures

Contingency design theory implies that a rational process guides the adoption of organizing strategies. The theory explains how strategy and structure can be selected so that the organization is best suited to respond to demands of technology, interdependence, and environment. However, in practice, nonrational processes also influence decisions about organizational structures and practices. Fashion has been shown to be one important ingredient in the choice of organizational strategies and structures. Organizations often latch onto ideas discussed in the leading business publications, such as *Harvard Business Review*, *Fortune*, and the *Wall Street Journal,* and on television and radio to help them respond to problems or become more effective. In many organizations the thinking behind adoption of innovations such as quality management, the matrix form, and videoconferencing was based more on the fact that organizations they admired had adopted these innovations than on a rational search for evidence that the features actually improved organizational effectiveness.

Institutional theory offers an explanation for organizational decisions about strategy and structure that takes fashion and other nonrational processes into account. This theory is premised on the fact that organizations respond to social institutions when they make decisions about adopting structures and practices. A **social institution** is a major organizational force in society. Some social institutions are actual organizations, such as the Federal Communications Commission, which has legal power to regulate organizations in the communications industry; the Congress; and the courts. Other institutions are ideals, values or norms that represent accepted practices in society. For example, the elementary school is influenced by one set of such ideals. There is a general expectation that elementary schools should have teachers who work closely with the children to build their basic skills in reading and writing and in physical activities involved in games and the like. An ideal elementary school would teach our children a love of learning and respect for our government and for others. There is also an expectation in the United States that elementary schools should treat each child as an individual with individual strengths and needs. To carry out these duties, elementary schools have certain basic structures in common. They have teachers who work with relatively small numbers of students, five to thirty depending on age. They have principals who make sure the teachers are following a sound curriculum, handle problems, and otherwise manage the school. Classrooms vary a great deal, but they are expected to have educational materials to interest the students, books, blackboards, materials for projects, the teacher's desk at the front, and so on. This description does not exhaust the ideals, values, and norms associated with the elementary school. It would be difficult to do so in less than a chapter. However, it illustrates the common expectations we have about organizations. Common expectations cover a wide variety of organizations ranging from elementary schools to the military. It is worth noting that actual organizations often deviate from these ideals. However, if they do so, it is at the risk of being judged inadequate because they do not live up to the ideals, values, and norms associated with them.

Institutional theory argues that organizations adopt structures and practices in response to institutional influences rather than solely to improve their performance. Three types of institutional influences have been identified. **Coercive** influence occurs when organizations are forced by institutions to adopt certain structures or practices. Federal and state legal codes forbid organizations to discriminate against women or minorities. Wal-Mart is currently forcing all its suppliers to use wireless digital identification devices on all goods shipped to the merchandiser. Although this is quite expensive for the suppliers, they really have no choice in the matter, because losing Wal-Mart's business would be a major blow. In Texas, local schools must have special education teachers on staff or lose state funding. These examples illustrate the role of institutional coercion in organizations' adoption of practices and structures. To be sure, doing these things may also make the organizations in question more effective. However, they are not acting for reasons of effectiveness, but because of coercion from larger institutions.

A second source of institutional pressure is **normative influence**. Organizations are sometimes moved to adopt a structure or a practice by normative pressure from organizations like themselves. This pressure comes through associations among similar types of organizations and through other channels that indicate what organizations should do to live up to the value systems they subscribe to. To continue our school example, there are numerous organizations that seek to promote effective education; school district administrators, principals, teachers, school counselors, school nurses, and other staff belong to them, attend their meetings, and read their publications. These organizations have codes of values regarding how to be effective educators, administrators, counselors, nurses, and so on. In accordance with these codes, they advocate adoption of various types of innovations and practices, and there is pressure for people who value and want to live up to the norms of these associations to follow their recommendations. In addition, most school personnel go through special educational programs to learn how to be a good teacher, principal, and so on, and one of the goals of these programs is to instill a sense of professionalism. Values and expectations are an important part of learning to be a professional. When professionals go to work for an organization, they bring these values with them and influence the organization to adapt in ways consistent with professional norms.

Mimetic influence is the third type of institutional effect on organizations. Organizations often seek to imitate exemplary organizations of the same type. In the early 1990s Eastman Kodak, a high-tech company with a very good reputation for its ICTs, decided to outsource its information systems to a major contractor, which took over management of Kodak's ICTs. This unusual move, to turn over management of a very important function to another company, was widely reported in the press and grabbed the attention of other large corporations. In the next three years a number of other firms imitated Kodak and outsourced their information systems functions. This sudden move toward outsourcing was dubbed "the Kodak effect," because rather than being driven by independent rational thinking, it was traced to imitation of Kodak. Mimetic influence is strongest in situations with high uncertainty, when organizations may not be able to determine the likely consequences of their actions well enough to make a rational decision. When it is difficult to make sense of a situation, organizations often turn to models for guidance. At the time of Kodak's decision, outsourcing of information systems was not well understood by most organizations, and so they turned to exemplary cases such as Kodak for advice. Because it seemed to work out well for Kodak, other companies began to outsource their information systems functions.

Why do organizations respond to institutional influence? In some cases they respond because they will be penalized if they do not. When institutions require certain structures or practices, not adopting them can lead to legal action or fines. Organizations have to attend to worker safety, regardless of whether this reduces efficiency, because the federal Occupational Safety and Health Administration will penalize them if they do not. Organizations also respond to institutional pressures because they want to excel: they want to be like companies they admire because they assume this is the key to success. Finally, organizations respond to institutional influence because their resources depend on it. As our example of the elementary school illustrates, there are institutional patterns that represent ideals, values, and practices typical of a legitimate organization. In order to continue to receive funding from the school system, a school must conform to the pattern. If it does not conform, for example if it does away with grades and hires uncertified teachers, the school is likely to have its funding cut or its principal fired by the school system. A school system that allowed many of its schools to depart from the pattern would be unlikely to win tax increases from voters. By conforming to the pattern, the school shows that it is a legitimate school, deserving of public confidence and support. In a real sense, the school system is being rhetorical: it is symbolically indicating that it is a good, legitimate school system by setting its schools up to conform to the ideal pattern for schools.

Institutional theory argues that the choice of organizational structures and practices is often not based on rational judgments of what will improve efficiency or effectiveness, but on what institutions require of the organization. This is not to say that following institutional influences will not result in benefits for the organization. In some cases, accommodating institutional influences will enable the organization to obtain funding or other resources that it needs, or avoid legal sanctions attached to deviating from typical forms. However, the ultimate decisions are not rational, but instead based on what institutions demand or imply.

Reflection: Things Will Not Always Be Clear

It is important to acknowledge that many organizations are a pastiche of more than one strategy. Many large transnational companies, for example, combine a (shorter) hierarchy built on the traditional strategy with a network strategy.[8] Organizations making a transition between strategies also usually exhibit characteristics of two (or more) strategies. As the case of ICG discussed in Chapter 6 illustrates, organizations commonly maintain aspects of their previous strategy of organizing as they search for a new strategy that works for them. In the course of evolving toward a network form, ICG kept aspects of the traditional hierarchy in place and gradually shed some of the traditional structures as it networked. It is important to bear in mind that the four strategies are ideal types, and that the "real world" is a blurry, confusing place. Many organizations that we encounter will not display the strategies in the pure, clear way we have discussed them.

Media Choice: An Individual-Level Contingency Theory

Contingency design theory is a theory about organizations. However, there are also contingency theories to guide individual behavior. A particularly useful contingency theory that has developed in recent years is media choice theory, which is intended to guide us in our choice of which medium to use in communicating.

People now have many more options for communicating with one another than they previously did.[9] These options include face-to-face conversation, a face-to-face meeting, a speech to a large assembly, memos (handwritten and typed), formal reports and documents (similar to essays in form), telephone, fax, e-mail, audio-conference, videoconference, and computer conference. How should we decide which mode to employ?

Linda Trevino, Ralph Lengel, and Richard Daft developed a framework for media choice based on the relative richness of the media.[10] **Media richness** depends on the number of cues the medium can carry, the timeliness of feedback via the medium, the variety of languages that can be used in the medium, and the degree to which the medium allows the message to be personalized. A very rich medium would carry many cues and allow immediate feedback, a wide variety of language forms, and a high degree of personalization of messages. Less rich media are deficient in one or more of these respects. Based on this definition, media can be ranked according to richness. The richest medium is face-to-face conversation, because it allows people to exchange a wide range of vocal, nonverbal, and verbal cues. Telephones screen out nonverbal cues and thus are less rich than face-to-face conversation. E-mail also screens out vocal cues. Personal written messages are also less rich than phone calls, and identical written messages sent to a number of people are the leanest medium of all.

Simple, routine messages such as requests for information (lunch at Fred's at 1:15?) can be communicated in either rich or lean media; complex messages or sensitive processes, such as negotiating or managing disagreements and conflicts, need to be handled face-to-face.[11] To communicate with parties who are unfamiliar with electronic media, people should use richer media than they would with those who are experienced and comfortable with the new technology. Of course, this assumes that the communicator wants to be understood as fully as possible. Employees who wish to be ambiguous may want to choose leaner media.[12] But *in general,* when communicators want immediate feedback, need to monitor emotional responses or determine how a message influences their interpersonal relationship with the other person, or are communicating equivocal or ambiguous information, they should rely on rich media.[13]

However, media richness theory fails to take into account the ways in which organizational situations guide and constrain choices of communicative media. Like everything else, perceptions of what are appropriate media for different kinds of messages and different communication processes are socially constructed. Employees learn the accepted assumptions of their cultures or subcultures about media use the same way that they learn other assumptions— indirectly, by observing what other people do, and directly, through conversations with others, particularly those in their immediate work groups.[14] After an advertising account representative lost an important account because the representative was offended by the brevity and impersonality of an e-mail message, all the executives started using the telephone or face-to-face meetings with their clients. An engineer asked his associates how to deliver bad news to the manager of another division of the organization. One colleague advised using lean media for this message, another recommended a written memo sent through the normal chain of command to signal respect for the other division, and still another told a story about what happened the last time an engineer communicated with the other division via a memo. Together, the engineers established a set of their own "rules" for choosing appropriate media. Although considerations such as the inherent richness of a medium are important, those considerations must be interpreted within the cultural context of the organization.

A final consideration is raised by Sim Sitkin, Kathleen Sutcliffe, and J. R. Barrios-Choplin: one should also consider the symbolic impact of media choice.[15] They note that immediate goals and norms are not the only influences on communicators' media choices. Instead, communicators also consider the **symbol-carrying capacity** of the medium. Symbol-carrying capacity manifests itself in at least two ways. First, media vary in their ability to transmit the core values of the organization. For example, an organization that values efficiency will find e-mail, which can deliver a message almost instantaneously, a better device for signaling this value than snail mail, regular postal delivery that could take several days for the same message. Symbol-carrying capacity is also evident in the symbolic value that the medium itself comes to hold. During World War II, parents of a soldier serving at the front shuddered when they saw the Western Union delivery person, because the news of deaths was sent via telegrams; telegrams came to symbolize death and mourning. For many of today's communicators, e-mail symbolizes being technologically savvy and innovative, whereas sending the same message in a handwritten note indicates backwardness. Because the form of a message is often as important as its content, symbol-carrying capacity is an important criterion to consider in choosing a medium. Of course, organizational cultures and co-worker attitudes also shape what a medium symbolizes. Symbol-carrying capacity may vary a great deal from organization to organization.

Together, richness, cultural norms, and symbol-carrying capacity provide a useful set of criteria to guide media choice. As with the contingency design variables, described at the beginning of this chapter, the only problem arises when recommendations based on different criteria conflict with one another. Probably the most basic criterion is the organization's culture. There are indications that it shapes perceptions both of richness and of symbol-carrying capacity.

Postmodern Forms of Organizing

One of the most influential and most controversial views of society and organizations that has developed during the past thirty years is postmodernism. Although it is impossible to describe this perspective at length in this chapter, it is based on the assumption that sometime during the twentieth century human society underwent a fundamental change. For millennia human beings had looked for a source of stability, an explanation of natural and human events that made sense in all situations and could thus be used to predict future events and prepare for them. In some societies that explanation was primarily religious; in others it was primarily philosophical; in the West it was primarily scientific, at least after the Enlightenment. Of course, in all societies the three forms of explanation mixed together in complex and often contradictory ways, but there was a common assumption that *some* stable explanation was possible—that a "grand narrative" could be constructed that made sense out of human experience. Eventually, this changed. People realized that the world had become fragmented and more interconnected and was rapidly changing. The narratives that we now construct are unstable, so much so that they are illusions (postmodernist theorist Jean Baudrillard calls them **simulacra** because they are mere simulations of a "reality" that does not really exist). They also are highly political, in that they legitimate some form of domination of one group of people by other groups. Authority should not only be examined critically, as the student movements of the 1960s through 1990s claimed; it should be resisted. In fact, there is no such thing as "fact"—all "truth" is constructed through communication, and its claims should be taken apart (through techniques usually labeled **deconstruction**) and examined.[16]

How, one might ask, could an organization be **postmodern,** considering that the whole idea of postmodernism is a rejection of the concept of organizing? First, in postmodern forms of organizing, image is central—in fact, it may be all there is. Postmodern organizational theorists Eric Eisenberg and H. Lloyd Goodall point to a BMW plant in South Carolina as a stereotypical example of postmodern forms of organizing. BMW makes automobiles, but doing so is only a sidelight, or a mechanism, for selling a corporate image. Its logo means wealthy, sophisticated, European, and technological (even though its actual operations are much less technologically sophisticated than those of its competitors). BMW is so completely focused on adapting its products to different global markets that it can be "different things for different people." An automobile is an automobile, but that is a decidedly modern (as opposed to postmodern) way of thinking—BMW is not an automobile; it is an image.

Of course, if everything is image, then communication is crucial. It also is unlimited. BMW rejects the notion of boundaries. It is actively involved in every community it touches. It uses communication technology to keep each of its employees directly connected with its customers and suppliers. It emphasizes shared accountability among all employees. Everyone, regardless of rank in the organization, wears the same uniform and is accessible to everyone else. The company celebrates ambiguity and difference—cultural, linguistic, racial, ethnic—and emphasizes that what might be viewed as communication breakdowns (recall Chapter 3) are opportunities for dialogue and discussion.[17] In short, postmodern strategies of organizing take all of the trends that we discuss in this book—from globalization to technological change to organizational image—and extend them as far as possible.

Alternative Strategies of Organizing

The network and other new organizational forms continue to evolve. However, as we have noted, they did not spring up new and fully formed in the 1990s. Versions of the network organization have been around for decades if not centuries. Several alternative strategies of organizing should also be recognized. They are not as common as the four discussed in the previous chapters, but one or more of them may emerge as major types of organizing strategy in the future.

Cooperatives

Organizations have been designed and operated in accordance with distinctive philosophical beliefs for millennia. Historically in the United States alone, Christian monasteries long have produced wine; the Shaker communities once produced household products, including furniture, that continue to be valued—almost revered; and the Amana Colonies long produced appliances. In each of these cases, the operant organizational strategy was based on a particular set of beliefs, usually beliefs that in some way separated the believers from the surrounding society.

Throughout U.S. history, groups have formed **cooperatives** around specific economic philosophies. Many of them, especially in agriculture, were designed to empower small producers in the struggle against monopolies, primarily banks and railroads. The *tanda* (which means "to take turns") and the *cundina* ("to increase in volume" or "go a long way") in Mexico allow people to avoid the fees and interest charged by banks for personal loans. In these cooperatives, friends, relatives, or co-workers deposit a set amount of money per week into a communal pot. The participants determine when they will pay money out to members and what the money can be used for. Sometimes loans are used to start businesses. More often they are used for more personal projects—home remodeling, automobiles, and so on. These systems work because the members have trusting relationships with one another. Although banks have tried to compete by creating their own *tanda* systems, they have had limited success for the simple reason that the people trust one another more than they trust the banks.

The best-known alternative organizations among organizational communication scholars are on opposite sides of the world—Spain and Bangladesh. The first is the Mondragón Cooperative Corporation in the Basque region of northern Spain. For almost a decade George Cheney studied the Mondragón Cooperative Corporation, making extended visits in 1992, 1994, and 1997. Founded in 1956 by a priest and five young engineers, the cooperative is based on a radical strategy of organizing—democracy. Organizational decisions, including the selection of managers, are made on a one-person, one-vote system. Each of the 170 co-ops, which range in size from 8 to 9,000 employees, is worker-owned. A system is in place that is designed to ensure that employee welfare and relationships with the surrounding community are as important as productivity and profit in organizational decision making. Originally, only participants in the collectives could own stock in them. In Bangladesh, one of the poorest countries in the world, the Grameen Bank was created in order to help women gain a measure of economic independence. Bangladeshi women typically are confined to their homes, either by cultural limits or by the demands of child care. So the Grameen Bank established a system of giving them small loans in order to help them set up home businesses, usually producing textiles.[18]

These organizations face unique challenges because they are alternative organizations. Sometimes the challenges are internal. The educational programs at Grameen Bank were designed to challenge male domination over women, but they were presented in a paternalistic manner by dominant males—the women were given information to be used as a guide for better lives but were not empowered to use that information in their own ways. Although the bank's loans helped the women escape from the oppression of traditional moneylenders, they did not overcome cultural and economic barriers to selling their goods. As a result the impact on the women's incomes was limited. People who worked for the bank were so committed to its social-change-oriented values that they often made excessive sacrifices of their own needs. Other challenges came from the outside. After Spain entered the European Union in 1992, the Mondragón cooperatives suddenly had to compete with German, Swedish, Japanese, and U.S. firms. Pressures for greater productivity and faster responses to customers led to a more centralized, bureaucratic, strategy of organizing. Differences in wages grew, leading one group of co-ops to leave the association. Originally, "participation" (recall Chapter 4) meant the right or power to influence organizational decisions and policies. Today it has become more centered on daily tasks and on managing competition. Like many of the PDM programs described in Chapter 4, it has become participation without democracy.

Feminist Strategies of Organizing

Although there are a number of versions of feminism, both in the United States and in the rest of the world, feminists agree that masculine conceptions of reality, modes of organizing, and ways of communicating dominate the public realm in

Western societies. Masculine organizations are based on metaphors suggesting hierarchy, rely on "power over" views of interpersonal influence, define effectiveness as achieving goals in spite of resistance by others, and privilege centralized expertise and decision making. In contrast, feminine (as well as feminist) organizations are defined by metaphors that describe webs of interconnected interpersonal relationships, define effectiveness in terms of achieving consensus among organizational members, and focus on systems of shared leadership and diffuse expertise. The distinction between feminine and **feminist organizations** is important because many alternative organizations, though composed primarily or exclusively of women, are not based on feminist goals regarding social change, and their members may not espouse feminist values at all.

For example, Nancy Wyatt described a weaver's guild, a women's organization made up primarily of middle-class, conservative women unified by their common interest in sewing and weaving, who had never expressed an interest in feminist politics.[19] But they created and sustained an organization that was fundamentally different from any of the strategies of organizing discussed in this book. The women provided one another with mutual support and opportunities to learn new skills from one another; they considered failure and success as equally important parts of learning; they were avidly noncompetitive and maintained diffuse and nonhierarchical power relationships and modes of decision making. Leadership was shared by eight members of the weavers' guild, some of whom were leaders because they were uniquely able to articulate a shared vision for the organization; others were leaders because of their ability to organize the group's activities. But all eight were very much concerned that they not dominate the others—they provided advice and direction only when asked, for example. This was in part because of the history of the group. At one time it had a strong, centralized leader, and when that woman left the guild, it almost fell apart. But it also was because of their focus on maintaining a supportive community within the group. Formal roles rotated among the group's members so that a variety of talents and interests were represented in decision making, and the guild's activities were orchestrated so that each member's goals were met. There were tensions within the group, usually over the organization's unique form of organizing. One member once had been a weaver by profession and tended to withhold her expertise from the other members, because doing so had been a successful political strategy in her previous organizations. Members who wished to use the guild as a stepping-stone for a future career in "typical" weaving organizations were frustrated by the shared responsibility and shared credit characteristic of the guild. In spite of these tensions, the weavers' guild was able to create and sustain a fundamentally different kind of organization— one that was able to simultaneously be a community and address the needs and desires of its individual members.

Other feminist organizations have found it more difficult to maintain that kind of balance. Frequently, they begin with an emphasis on consensus, equality, collectivity, and legitimate participatory decision making; but more traditional, hierarchical strategies of organizing emerge, in which representative democracy replaces participation. This shift seems to stem from environmental pressures on the organization. Feminist organizations face an important dilemma: how can an alternative organization maintain a collective, nonhierarchical, participatory, egalitarian strategy of organizing while simultaneously pursuing other goals such as profitability? Some external pressures are overt and direct. In Western societies, organizations need funds to survive and especially to grow. A major donation or a grassroots political campaign may provide sufficient funding for an organization to be created and even to succeed at a relatively small size. But if it is to grow, other sources of funds become necessary, and significant funds are usually available only from traditional, bureaucratic organizations—government agencies, banks, and the financial markets. Decision-makers in traditional bureaucracies are comfortable with organizations that operate on the basis of similar strategies of organizing. So they pressure alternative organizations to be less alternative or at least to appear to be. Alternative strategies of organizing become less alternative, and if the organization is involved in social-change efforts, those efforts are moderated or made less visible.

For example, *Ms.* magazine faced a central tension from the day it was created: it drew its content from feminist publications but designed its format and marketing to be like mainline women's magazines. Its funding came from readers who were attracted to the magazine because of its feminist ideology and from advertisers who saw it as an opportunity to reach women readers. Advertisers pressured the editorship to focus content on career feminists, who had the disposable income that they coveted. But career feminists were only part of the *Ms.* readership, and many of them were attracted to its feminist ideology. As competition and costs increased during the 1980s, advertising revenues became more necessary, and the advertisers' influence over content increased. Readers found many of the ads offensive and resisted the shift. The opposition crystallized around a 1987 issue on women and addiction, which included none of the tobacco and alcohol company ads that had become common. Readers were irate about what they saw as blatant hypocrisy, and the editors' argument that the *Ms.* policies had led to improvements in advertising directed toward women fell on deaf ears. Although the magazine's content had become progressively less political as the advertisers exerted increased control, advertisers abandoned the magazine during the highly conservative political climate of the late 1980s. In 1989 the magazine folded, only to be reborn the following year with no advertising.[20]

People, regardless of their gender and regardless of the strategy of organizing that is in place, bring the dominant assumptions of their societies with them into their organizations. Thus, people in Western societies tend to value efficiency, expertise, and experience. Consensus decision making and participation consume a great deal of time and energy (recall Chapter 4) and thus seem to be inefficient, especially in the short term; differences in expertise and experience seem to warrant hierarchical power relationships. Members of alternative organizations are pressured by the many different traditional organizations in which they also are involved—churches, schools, clubs, and so on. These competing organizations work on a schedule and through a process that contradicts the flexibility and adaptability of the alternative organization. Consequently, it is difficult for members to continue to support forms of organizing that seem to be so non-normal, so unnatural. Several factors do help offset these pressures— small organizational size, common goals, relatively equal knowledge and experience, and a benign environment. As a result, there are a number of flourishing cooperatives and collectives that operate on the basis of alternative strategies; but sustaining them involves a constant process of managing tensions.[21]

Feminist organizational strategies face a second dilemma: can these strategies expand to successfully include people from diverse racial, ethnic, class, and gender groups? Alternative organizations tend to begin with local, grassroots organizing. These groups tend to have common interests and homogeneous backgrounds and experiences. For example, in the United States, feminist groups have primarily involved educated middle- and upper-middle-class Anglo women. Unless they actively reach out to men and to people of other classes, races, and ethnic origins, they tend to remain homogeneous. Because an alternative form of organizing does not in itself bridge racial, class, or ethnic differences, and because the concerns that bring middle-class Anglo women together in alternative organizations may not be salient to anyone else (and vice versa), diversifying alternative organizations is quite difficult. Doing so is more likely to succeed when the organization emerges from a multiclass, multiethnic community; but even then it takes a great deal of time and energy to sustain a truly diverse organization. Consequently, pressures for efficiency may be especially acute for these organizations, making factors like small size and common goals even more important.[22]

CASE STUDY
Trying to Stay Balanced

All organizations must deal with tensions and inconsistencies. In alternative organizations those tensions often are more visible because they are not obscured by underlying assumptions. In these two cases, separated by more than twenty years, feminist organizations confront and manage the tensions that they face.

Redwood Records began as a "mom and pop" (literally) operation designed to produce and market records by Holly Near. Although she had a sizable and stable following, major record companies refused to contract with Near because her anti–Vietnam war message was controversial and because her music was not as "submissive" as women's music was "supposed" to be. By the mid-1970s Near's parents tired of running the company, creating a need for a new organization. Near restructured Redwood Records into a feminist alternative organization: an all-woman, worker-run, nonhierarchical, social-change-oriented organization. All employees performed all of the necessary tasks—from licking stamps to making strategic decisions. Their ideology was explicitly antiprofit, and their goals focused on helping create a women's music industry designed to foster social change. Communication among members was excellent, information flow was good, and power

(continued)

(Case Study, continued)

really was shared among members, creating high levels of morale, effort, and commitment. But, like many alternative feminist organizations founded during the 1970s, Redwood's combination of participatory, consensual decision making and lack of formal structure created problems: service was inconsistent, salaries and job security were low, burnout and turnover among staff members were high, and financial problems were almost constant.* In short, Redwood Records was a social movement that happened to be a business.

After 1980 Redwood evolved to become a business that had an alternative strategy of organizing and a vision of social change. It signed a number of other women artists, and as Near's role in the organization declined, it began to rely more and more on profits to sustain itself. Redwood maintained an atmosphere of informality and support as well as its commitment to consensual decision making and open confrontation as a primary mode of conflict management. But it began to focus more on efficiency in order to keep up with growing demand for its products. Eventually a management team was formed, and day-to-day communication became more formal and bureaucratic—meetings involved the minimum number of people necessary rather than all employees, and meeting times were set in advance instead of being spontaneous, for example. After 1985 Redwood decided to quit limiting its selections to music designed for an audience of women, but it continued to have an all-woman staff.

Throughout its existence, Redwood has had to manage a tension between economic demands and its social-change ideology and commitment to an alternative strategy of organizing. It maintains a balance by being very strategic about the projects it takes on. Money and profits were redefined to be means to a social-change end. Profits gained from some products allow Redwood to support social-change activities that do not in themselves make money. Some members focus more on profits than politics; others more on politics than profits; and most are in the middle, trying to simultaneously maintain both. The company's continued openness and commitment to policymaking by consensus allows it to manage this central tension successfully. It has found a middle ground between bureaucratic structures and modes of operating on the one hand and a fluid and structureless mode of operating on the other.

Haven is a feminist organization that provides emergency help to survivors of domestic violence and tries to prevent future cases through education and counseling.† It has 25 paid staff members and 125 volunteers; some of them answer the organization's crisis hotline, others work with children staying at the shelter, and others serve as victims' advocates who respond to police calls and counsel victims at the scene. The paid staff emphatically say that what makes Haven different than other domestic violence organizations is its commitment to *ethical communication*. The key to ethical communication is empowerment that transcends the formal hierarchy of the organization. In training sessions, meetings, and everyday interactions among staff members, members learn to express emotions, deal openly with conflicts, and promote equality. However, there are important differences in how the two groups—staff members and volunteers—interpret and enact ethical communication.

Volunteers think of Haven as something unique, different from both home and "work" (where they obtain their livelihood). In a sense, it is a place where they can escape the responsibilities and decision-making challenges that they experience in the other parts of their lives. It is a place where the volunteers do make decisions, where they do feel autonomous and strong as persons, and where they can feel good about their contributions to others. But they also felt that their connections to Haven were temporary and that their tasks were unique—ambiguous, fluctuating, supportive, relationally oriented, part-time, and unpaid. For them, "empowerment" meant (1) being able to choose the level of involvement and responsibility that they want, (2) having access to the information and skills they need to do their jobs, (3) having an opportunity for personal and professional growth and a sense that they are making a contribution to others, and (4) the freedom that comes from someone else being ultimately responsible for things. They were not offended by the level of hierarchy that exists at Haven; in fact they found it to be comforting, especially because it seemed to be based on the degree of involvement and responsibility that different people had. They realized that the staff members were ideologically opposed to hierarchy—they talked about it almost every day—and some volunteers were a little disillusioned about the inconsistency between the staff's expressions of their ideology and the fact that there really was a hierarchy in place. But the volunteers were much more concerned about not receiving the kind of emotional support that they needed, and about their feelings that the support they did receive sometimes seemed forced and inauthentic. They also were frustrated that they rarely were told what happened to their clients once they left the shelter. They provided support to one another, but all in all they still felt isolated, and they felt guilty that they did not work as many hours as others did. For them, doing their jobs and feeling good about what they were doing were more important than enacting an ideology.

The staff members interpreted ethical communication and empowerment very differently. They talked about being antihierarchy and encouraged the volunteers to undercut hierarchy by taking care of themselves, challenging supervisory authority, and even poking fun at the supervisors. Ironically, one of the reasons they were so committed to fighting hierarchy was their belief that it could not be eliminated—the battle would never actually be won. A second irony was that they were committed to persuading the staff to practice empowerment and ethical communication, almost "whether they wanted to or not." Volunteers wished that staff members would spend more time and energy preparing them to perform their tasks, supervising them and providing feedback on their work, and giving them more guidance when they asked questions—in short, they wanted the supervisors to act more like supervisors and less like equally empowered peers.

(continued)

(Case Study, continued)

Applying What You Have Learned

1. What tensions existed at Redwood Records and at Haven? What were the source(s) of those tensions? How were they managed?

Questions to Think About and Discuss

1. Some critics of feminist organizations complain that they eventually "sell out" their political commitments in order to be economically successful. Evaluate this criticism, and explain how members of an alternative organization can "know" when they have tipped the balance too far toward ideology or too far toward success.
2. Other critics argue that feminist forms of organizations inevitably will fail if they maintain their alternative mode of operating. Others note that alternative forms of organizing are becoming so common that there is no longer any marketing advantage in being "different." Evaluate these criticisms.

This case is based on Cynthia Lott, "Redwood Records: Principles and Profit in Women's Music," in *Women Communicating,* Barbara Bate and Anita Taylor, eds. (Norwood, NJ: Ablex, 1988).

*See Jo Freeman, "The Tyranny of Structurelessness," *Ms.,* July 1976.

†This case is based on Karen Lee Ashcraft and April Kedrowicz, "Self-Direction or Social Support?" *Communication Monographs* 69 (2002): 88–110. For similar, also excellent case studies of the management of tensions within feminist organizations, see Paige Edley, "Discursive Essentializing in a Woman-Owned Business," *Management Communication Quarterly* 14 (2000): 271–306; J. Martin, K. Knopoff, and C. Beckman, "An Alternative to Bureaucratic Impersonality and Emotional Labor: Bounded Emotionality at the Body Shop," *Administrative Science Quarterly* 43 (1998): 429–469; Karen L. Ashcraft, "Organized Dissonance: Feminist Bureaucracy as Hybrid Form," *Academy of Management Journal* 44 (2001): 1301–1322.

Heterarchies

Heterarchies are organizations (or networks of organizations) in which different units (organizations) are allowed to choose and develop their own particular organizational strategy and practices. These practices may vary, and no uniformity is imposed on the units (organizations) that make up the heterarchy. Like feminist organizations, different voices and approaches to organizing are valued in heterarchies. However, there is a consistency in feminist organizations that is not present in heterarchies. In heterarchies, different units may adopt different ways of doing the same work, different ways of relating to other units, different methods of decision making, and so on. Units will have different value systems as well. Some units may emphasize efficiency and low cost, others quality despite cost, and still others development of their members' skills. The organization accepts and tacitly encourages these different approaches. However, it does not require them or try to organize them. Each unit is allowed to develop as it sees fit.[23]

One example of a heterarchical organization is a new media advertising firm that serves its clients through multiple media, including traditional channels, such as television and print media, and new channels, such as the Internet and blogs. In this organization, each department—the creative department, the designers, the marketers, the technologists, and top management—must organize itself as it sees fit to deal with the particular demands of its own task, which are continuously in flux. The ways in which departments organize themselves also may vary when they specialize on different media or sectors of media, because each medium has its own demands. The departments must still coordinate their activities with each other for the firm to be effective, and each will be held accountable by the value sets of all the departments it coordinates with, because there is no chain of command in a heterarchy. For example, the marketing department must initiate and sell ads in a way that enables the creative department to produce good, effective art and the technologists to deliver a reliable product via state-of-the-art technologies. It must meet two different sets of criteria and adjust its activity to satisfy them. In turn, the creative department and the technology unit must satisfy the marketing department and adjust their activities so that they smoothly fit. The various parts of the advertising firm are very much like the different animals in an ecological system; they go their own way, but they must also fit themselves into the system to continue to survive in it.

The rationale for a heterarchy is that it offers the best way to enable the organization to cope with extreme levels of uncertainty. In some cases, not only is the environment of organizations changing, but also the nature of the environment is changing. For example, the advance and spread of new ICTs are changing the work of the advertising firm so rapidly that practices that used to work no longer are guaranteed to work with new media such as wireless communications. These media are developing so fast that there is literally no standard practice as there once was for print ads, and they change so quickly that by the time a "standard" is recognized, it may be outmoded. At the same time as the technology is changing, new trends in public taste are developing, spurred and magnified by increasing concentration in media ownership that enables media firms to shape tastes much more strongly than previously. This type of radical change makes it difficult for organizations to understand their environments well enough to plan coherently. So numerous variations by different units offer the best way to hit on new ideas or practices. Each individual unit knows its own particular problems and its own situation best and therefore is able to adapt more effectively than if directed by a superior unit, common culture, or coordination mechanisms in a network. Heterarchies are truly self-organizing systems.

As our example of the advertising agency illustrates, though units may adapt independently, there are still interdependencies among units that must be carefully managed for the organization to be effective. Interdependencies tend to be managed by improvisation at first; as units come to understand each other better, they fall into more regular patterns. For instance, in the ad agency, the creative unit may want to try a new wireless campaign. In order to do so, it would need to coordinate with the technology department to make sure the ads were designed for the narrower bandwidth of cell phones. Members of the creative unit would need to work with the "wireless guys" in the technology department, which would involve working out ways to collaborate effectively; once all this was done, future contacts on wireless projects would be much easier. If this collaboration proved to be unusually fruitful, it might later be imitated by other units of the agency.

What is life like in a heterarchy? On the one hand, it is interesting and can be exhilarating because it involves continuously confronting situations and working out answers. There is no "rulebook" for a heterarchy. Members are free to organize in ways comfortable for them and to put their stamp on the organization. On the other hand, it is likely to be exhausting as well from time to time because of the need to satisfy many different units. Recall the ancient Chinese curse "May you live in interesting times." People with low tolerance for ambiguity will likely not be happy in a heterarchy. Those who like rules and clear structure will not function well either.

Do heterarchies eventually evolve into one of the other organizational forms? For example, if the rapid advance in the ICT industries slowed, the advertising firm might well eventually stabilize as the particular practices that were effective were preserved and others died out. In this case it might shift toward a relational or network strategy, which are the ones that best fit the type of work advertising firms do. However, if the environment continued to be uncertain and rapidly changing, the heterarchy would continue to renew itself. Heterarchies may also be preserved if the organization and its members value them. Some critics of the control organizations exercise over their members argue that heterarchies are an organizational form that preserves members' freedom and allows them voice.

Heterarchies must address several types of challenges to continue to be effective. For one thing, they require members and units to invest a lot of energy. If the matrix structure and network strategy are communication intensive, then the heterarchy is *really* communication intensive for its members. Problems of overload and burnout are likely to be common. Second, the heterarchy works only if its constituent units or organizations remain fairly equal in terms of power or influence over the system. Once one or a few units or organizations gain control, they may begin to favor some ways of organizing over others and impede the random variation of approaches taken by different units that is at the heart of the heterarchy's effectiveness. Third, coordination of units or organizations in a heterarchy is by no means a trivial matter. Because coordination depends on relationships among units, it will sometimes break down. Breakdowns can be the source of new ideas and practices that further enrich the heterarchy, but they may also lead to problems or even failure for the organization.

Conclusion

Organizations have always had a wide range of options for organizing themselves, and new technologies have broadened this range still further. Contingency design theory, which attempts to explain what makes different organizational structures effective, gives us some guidelines to use in determining which of the four strategies of organizing (or which mix) to use. It gives advice on how an effective organization and its communication system can be designed based on three variables: the organization's technology, its interdependence with other organizations or units, and its environment.

It is important to realize that contingency design theory assumes that organizations respond to their environments based on rational decisions about what will make the organization most effective. This may not always be the case. Institutional influences of various types may also shape the strategy of organizing that is adopted. There are also alternative organizational forms that are advocated for ideological and not for instrumental reasons. Cooperative, feminist, and heterarchical organizations offer alternative forms that address different issues from those raised in contingency design theory, issues related to the values that the organizational forms should embody or what happens when the contingency model breaks down.

Notes

[1] Tom Burns and G. M. Stalker, *The Management of Innovation* (London: Tavistock, 1961).

[2] The relational strategy typically has moderate to high formalization, low centralization, moderate to high spans of control, informal communication, and moderate ICT intensiveness. Interorganizational linkages vary for the relational strategy. The cultural strategy varies on all dimensions, depending on the particular nature of the culture, except that it has high levels of both formal and informal communication. The network strategy has moderate to high formalization, low centralization, moderate to high spans of control, both formal and informal communication, and high ICT intensiveness.

[3] Charles Perrow, "A Framework for the Comparative Analysis of Organizations," *American Sociological Review* 32 (1967): 194–208.

[4] Perrow divides technology into two dimensions: analyzability and variety. Analyzability refers to the degree to which the process the technology is designed to carry out is known and understood. The second dimension of technology is its variety, which refers to the number of exceptions encountered in the course of doing the work. In some work, exceptional cases are very rare; there are only small differences from case to case and the "inputs" to the organizational systems are relatively uniform. This defines four types of technology. Two are covered in detail in the main text: low analyzability coupled with high variety (nonroutine technologies apply) and high analyzability coupled with low variety (routine technologies apply). The other two cases are engineering and craft technologies. Engineering technologies, with high analyzability but also high variety, are complicated, because many exceptions are encountered. However, because cause-effect relationships are well understood for these tasks, it is possible to develop a set of formulas that can then be applied to the different cases. For engineering technologies, uncertainty is somewhat higher than that for routine technologies, but lower than that for nonroutine technologies. Manuals and standard procedures describe the various programs the unit can carry out, but members of the unit may need to consult each other regarding the specific programs that will be used, how they will be coordinated with each other, and what to do if problems arise. Hence, engineering technologies are most adequately served by a combination of written, standardized communication and verbal communication directed to coordinating work and problem resolution.

Craft technologies, with low analyzability and low variety, have a stable set of activities, but the transformation process is not well understood. Extensive training and experience is required to master work techniques and develop the judgment necessary for applying them. For example, in a group of performing artists putting on a play, the members know the script, but turning that script into a performance requires them to draw on years of slowly accumulated know-how that they cannot put into words. For craft technologies, uncertainty is still higher than for engineering technologies. Because these technologies deal with work of low analyzability, the use of manuals and standard procedures is less feasible. The most adequate way of coordinating craft work is through horizontal verbal communication among those who have to work together. This can often be scheduled. For example, a specialty steel-fabricating plant might have a scheduled weekly meeting to discuss formulations for new orders.

[5] This important distinction was developed by James Thompson, *Organizations in Action* (New York: McGraw-Hill, 1967).

[6] Robert B. Duncan, "Characteristics of Perceived Environments and Perceived Environmental Uncertainty," *Administrative Science Quarterly* 17 (1972): 313–327.

[7] R. Daft, *Organization Theory and Design*, 3rd ed. (St. Paul, MN: West, 1989), especially chapter 2; Howard E. Aldrich, *Organizations and Environments* (Englewood Cliffs, NJ: Prentice-Hall, 1979).

[8] Janet Fulk and Gerardine DeSanctis, "Articulation of Communication Technology and Organizational Form," in *Shaping Organization Form: Communication, Connection, and Community*, G. DeSanctis and J. Fulk, eds. (Newbury Park, CA: Sage, 1999).

[9] Excellent discussions of research on communication media choice can be found in Ron Rice and Urs Gattiker, "Communication Technologies and Structures," in *The New Handbook of Organizational Communication*, F. Jablin and L. Putnam eds. (Thousand Oaks, CA: Sage, 2000); and J. Fulk and L. Collins-Jarvis, "Wired Meetings: Technological Mediation of Organizational Gatherings," in *The New Handbook of Organizational Communication*, F. Jablin and L. Putnam, eds. (Thousand Oaks, CA: Sage, 2000).

[10] Linda Trevinio, Ralph Lengel, and Richard Daft, "Media Symbolism, Media Richness, and Media Choices in Organizations," *Communication Research* 14 (1987): 553–574.

[11] When messages are not complex, personal preferences seem to determine which media people use. Trevino, Lengel, and Daft. For example, people with high levels of oral-communication anxiety seem to avoid face-to-face media unless the complexity of the message absolutely requires them to use it. Elmore Alexander, Larry Penley, and I. Edward Hernigan, "The Effect of Individual Differences on Managerial Media Choice," *Management Communication Quarterly* 5 (1991): 155–173.

[12] Noshir Contractor and Eric Eisenberg, "Communication Networks and New Media in Organizations," in *Organizations and Communication Technology*, Janet Fulk and Charles Steinfield, eds. (Thousand Oaks, CA: Sage, 1990). There also is evidence that people quickly learn to manipulate the richness of a medium. C. Olgren and L. Parker, *Teleconferencing Technology and Applications* (Dedham, MA: Artech House, 1983), found that employees who regularly use videoconferencing learn to control vocal and nonverbal cues, so that they put on a performance rather than communicate the substance of their ideas.

[13] Ron Rice, "Evaluating New Media Systems," in *Evaluating the New Information Technologies*, J. Johnstone, ed. (San Francisco: Jossey-Bass, 1984); Richard Daft and R. H. Lengel, "Information Richness," in *Research in Organizational Behavior*, Larry Cummings and Barry Staw, eds., vol. 6 (Greenwich, CT: JAI Press, 1984).

[14] Janet Fulk, Charles W. Steinfield, Joseph Schmitz, and J. G. Power, "A Social Information Processing Model of Media Use in Organizations," *Communication Research* 14 (1987): 529–552.

[15] Sim B. Sitkin, Kathleen M. Sutcliffe, and J. R. Barrios-Choplin, "A Dual-Capacity Model of Communication Medium Choice in Organizations," *Human Communication Research* 18 (1992): 563–598.

[16] Jacques Derrida, *Speech and Phenomenon* (Evanston, IL: Northwestern University Press, 1976).

[17] Eric Eisenberg and H. L. Goodall Jr., *Organizational Communication: Balancing Creativity and Constraint* (Boston: Bedford/St. Martin's Press, 2001).

[18] Jenalia Moreno, "Old-Fashioned Savings, Loans," *Houston Chronicle*, September 17, 2002, B1; George Cheney, *Values at Work* (Ithaca, NY: Cornell University Press, 1999); Michael Papa, Mohammed Auwal, and Arvind Singhai, "Dialectic of Control and Emancipation in Organizing for Social Change," *Communication Theory* 5 (1995): 189–223.

[19] Nancy Wyatt, "Shared Leadership in a Weavers' Guild," in *Women Communicating*, B. Bate and Anita Taylor, eds. (Norwood, NJ: Ablex, 1988). An excellent, in-depth treatment of feminist organizations is Myra Marx Ferree and Patricia Yancey Martin, *Feminist Organizations* (Philadelphia: Temple University Press, 1995).

[20] Amy Farrell, "Like a Tarantula on a Banana Boat," in Ferree and Martin.

[21] See Joan Acker, "The Gender Regime in Swedish Banks," *Scandinavian Journal of Management* 10 (1994): 116–142; and "Feminist Goals and Organizing Processes," in Ferree and Martin; Joyce Rothschild-Whitt and J. A. Whitt, *The Cooperative Workplace* (Cambridge, UK: Cambridge University Press, 1986); George Cheney, "Democracy in the Workplace," *Journal of Applied Communication Research* 23 (1995): 167–200.

[22] Acker, "Feminist Goals"; Mary Pardo, "Doing It for the Kids," in Ferree and Martin.

[23] David Stark, "Ambiguous Assets for Uncertain Environments: Heterarchy in Post Socialist Firms," in *The Twenty-First Century Firm: Changing Economic Organization in International Perspective*, P. Dimaggio, ed. (Princeton, NJ: Princeton University Press, 2001); David Stark, "Heterarchy: Distributing Authority and Organizing Diversity," in *The Biology of Business: Decoding the Natural Laws of Enterprise*, J. H. Clippinger III, ed. (San Francisco: Jossey-Bass, 1999).

UNIT III

Challenges in the Twenty-First Century

Chapter 8

Communication, Power, and Politics in Organizations

Whatever else organizations may be . . . they are political structures. This means that organizations operate by distributing authority and setting a stage for the exercise of power.
—Abraham Zaleznik

Insofar as knowledge is power, communication systems are power systems.
—David Barber

Central Themes

- Power usually is thought of as the "ability to dominate" other people. Not only does this perspective ignore the "accomplishment" aspect of power, but it also seriously oversimplifies its multifaceted nature.
- Power has two components: a "surface structure," which consists of overt displays of power and conscious but unspoken decisions about who, when, and how to challenge power relationships; and a "deep structure," which consists of unconscious elements of power relationships.
- Power is in the eye of the beholder. Whenever people are able to control resources that others perceive they need, they have a potential base of power.
- Employees can develop power through developing personal characteristics (expertise, interpersonal skills, and access to symbols of power) and through controlling key resources (information, rewards and punishments, roles in coalitions).
- Power is obtained and exercised through a predictable group of communication strategies.
- One of the effects of social and organizational power relationships is to silence the voices of dissenting individuals. These processes help explain unethical and illegal organizational behavior.
- Power also serves to silence the voices of "different" employees. One of the most important sources of resistance to power relationships is raising those voices.

Key Terms

sovereign power	manipulation
disciplinary power	justifications
surface structure of power	rationalizations
open face of power	strategic ambiguity
hidden face of power	indirect questions
deep structure of power	self-disclosure
power	politics
public self	nullification
private self	whistle-blowers
open persuasion	practical questions
manipulative persuasion	technical questions

The words *power* and *politics* are used every day by almost everyone to explain much of what happens in life and at work. Consumers decry their powerlessness in the face of big business. Students complain that they are victimized by arbitrary professors and administrators and can do nothing in response. Subordinates vow to change their organizations for the better as soon as they advance to positions of authority (but they rarely keep such promises). Power influences employees' choices about which audiences to address (and which to avoid) and how to communicate with them. Political considerations tell people what actions must be taken in particular situations and what actions and emotions should be suppressed.[1]

If subordinates see their supervisors as powerful members of their organizations, their job satisfaction may increase and their tendency to withhold or distort information may decrease. Similarly, if subordinates perceive that their supervisors are actively involved in organizational politics, they may trust them less and be more likely to withhold information.[2] Employees base their choices about how to communicate on their assessment of organizational power relationships and politics and on their choices about how to reproduce power relationships.

A Perspective on Organizational Power

Many discussions of organizational power and politics are based on a misconception of what power is and how it functions in organizations. They focus on what Michel Foucault calls **sovereign power,** the processes through which sovereigns (kings, dictators, prison wardens, or directors of mental institutions) dominate their subjects. Historically, this kind of power is connected to the phrase *abuse of power,* because having total power often leads to its misuse. However, there are a number of problems with this "power over" view. One is that it fails to recognize that power is dispersed throughout societies and organizations. It exists in every relationship and every interaction, not just those that cross levels of the organizational hierarchy. As Chapter 3 explains, organizational control sometimes does involve direct surveillance by supervisors and

systems of control through rules and rewards. It also may involve team surveillance and control (Chapter 4) and self-surveillance and self-control (Chapter 5),
processes that Foucault calls **disciplinary power.** In modern organizations,
disciplinary power is at least as important as sovereign power, so "power over"
models seriously oversimplify organizational power relationships.³

Second, traditional views of power forget that abuse stems from *imbalances* of power, not power itself. The accent in Lord Acton's famous dictum that
"absolute power corrupts absolutely" should be on absolutism, not on power.
When people have a great deal of power over others, they begin to believe that
low-power people are inferior and untrustworthy. Conversely, if people feel
powerless, they tend to become depressed and helpless, feel higher levels of
stress, develop physical symptoms such as headaches and hypertension, and impede valuable organizational change and innovation. Powerlessness creates feelings of vulnerability, and vulnerability leads to abuse. People need to feel that
they have influence over their lives. One way to offset these negative effects is
to help people understand the relationships between power and communication. All power relationships involve opportunities and strategies for resistance.
Although knowledge is often used to dominate people, it also can lead to *empowerment.* Increasing the degree of balance in organizational power relationships reduces the potential for abuse.

Third, an "ability to dominate" view of power makes people overlook the
positive role that power plays in mobilizing people and resources to get things
done. If members of an organization define power as "accomplishment" rather
than "domination," nonproductive and personally destructive power games are
less likely. But because the "domination" view of power is an underlying assumption in Western societies, it is difficult for people to change their frame of
reference. The shift can happen, but only through understanding how communication, power, and politics are interrelated.

The final problem with "sovereign" views is that they focus on only the
overt, conscious level of power. We will call this level the **surface structure** of
power.⁴ It has two dimensions. One involves an **open face** that is composed of
overt displays of power—threats, promises, negotiations, orders, coalitions, gag
rules, and so on. The second dimension of the *surface structure* of power is its
hidden face. This face works by regulating public and private issues. In organizational life, employees must often make difficult decisions about when and
how to challenge power holders. Newcomers soon learn that some issues are
not to be discussed in public; some potential solutions are not to be considered
openly; and some arguments are not to be made. Open discussions are limited
to safe topics (those that power holders are willing to have discussed in public),
acceptable alternatives, and unofficially sanctioned premises for making decisions. As a result of these regulatory processes, consensus in open discussions
is the rule, not the exception. When disagreements are voiced, they tend to be
over minor issues and serve the purpose of perpetuating the myth that open, rational, and objective decision making characterizes the organization. If individuals violate these constraints, they may be either ignored or attacked by the rest

of the group. If they persist, they will be "educated" by an unofficial tutor. If they cannot be educated, they may be removed.

But power also has a second level, a **deep structure** that operates below employees' conscious awareness. Throughout this book, we discuss the processes through which the assumptions of a society guide and constrain employees' actions. People act in ways that they have learned are *normal* and *natural* and usually do so without being aware of it. A society's underlying assumptions tell people who they are, what their role is in society, and where they fit in the formal and informal hierarchies that constitute their society. It is through these nonconscious parameters of action that power is normally exercised. Usually employees do not realize that these societal assumptions are part of organizational power relationships.

For example, in Western societies people take it for granted that experts on an issue should have the greatest influence over decisions about that issue. This assumption ensures that people who control access to information or who have had training in argumentation will have the greatest degree of power. This is true even if the issue being discussed is one for which information and argument are largely irrelevant, for example, a highly value-laden issue. Deciding when to terminate life support for a terminally ill patient is a matter of values and emotion much more than one of information and expertise. But societal assumptions—codified into law in most states—treat it as an information-based decision to be made by medical experts.[5] By deferring to expert opinions, people support the societal assumption that medical experts should dominate decision making. In doing so, they reproduce the deep structure of power.

The underlying assumptions of societies and their organizations dictate that some people will have power over others. But power is not hierarchical; it is diffuse and dispersed. Some source of power is available to every member of a society or organization. Our goal in this chapter is to examine potential *sources* of power and to describe the communicative strategies that can be used to manage organizational power relationships. In the process, we will discuss the ways in which power is exercised in organizations, a process that we label *organizational politics.*

Societal Assumptions and the Bases of Organizational Power

Power is in the eye of the beholder.[6] It is the belief by some members of a society or organization that they should obey the requests or commands and seek the favor and support of other members. Power is not possessed by a person. It is granted to that person by others. One person may order another to act in a certain way. But the person giving the command has no power over the other until she or he accepts the first person's right to dominate. In this sense, power is a feature of interactions and interpersonal relationships, not of individuals or organizational roles.

Creating perceptions of power is important to every employee. But creating perceptions of power is particularly important for people who depend on other people to help them do their jobs. Even employees located near the bottom of an organization can have power if other employees depend on them. If an employee is relatively autonomous and independent, creating and maintaining power is less important. But only completely self-sufficient workers need not be concerned with developing power.

Traditional strategies of organizing assume that power and power relationships can be built into the formal structures of organizations; relational strategies assume they can be embedded in particular forms of leadership and tasks; cultural strategies inculcate beliefs and values that create distinctive kinds of power relationships; and networking strategies conceptualize power as stemming from one's position in the network and alliances among parties. But there are fissures, gaps, and contradictions in all systems of power. Employees can maneuver within these gaps and manipulate these contradictions by acquiring power on their own, independent of their formal position in their organizations.[7] They can do so by demonstrating that they possess one or more valued *personal characteristics* or that they have the ability to control the distribution of resources valued by other people. But characteristics and resources cannot be transformed into power unless they are *scarce* (available in supplies that are smaller than the existing demand), *significant* (employees depend on them to do their jobs), and *irreplaceable* (depletable and not easily replaced).

Gaining Power through Personal Characteristics

In Western societies two kinds of personal characteristics are assumed to be a legitimate basis on which some people can obtain and exercise power—*expertise* and *interpersonal relationships.*

Expertise as a Source of Power   In Western societies expertise has at least two dimensions. The first is a person's organization-related *knowledge.*[8] However, knowledge provides power only if other people depend on it and it is scarce, significant, and irreplaceable. This explains why people sometimes do not want to hire the most competent applicant for a job. If the newcomer has the kind of expertise that an old-timer has used to gain power, the newcomer is threatening. When you are the only person who can operate the computer system, you have almost complete power. When you are one of two people who knows how to do so, you have little power unless you can form and sustain an alliance with the other expert. It also explains why employees sometimes develop equipment or procedures that only they understand. Secretaries have known for millennia that if they devise filing systems that only they understand, they may be irreplaceable. In a group of tobacco-processing factories, the mechanics who repaired machines realized that they had a great degree of power; without their cooperation the factories would come to a grinding halt. Over time they trained new mechanics orally, making sure that there were no written diagrams of equipment or repair instructions around. They modified the equipment in ways that would make it difficult, if not impossible, for outsiders to repair it. As a result, as long as they cooperated with one another, they could virtually force management to act as they wanted. Although their power was fragile, it could be maintained as long as management depended on them to keep the equipment running.[9] More recently, middle managers who fear that the installation of computerized management information systems would eliminate their jobs have used similar strategies to increase their organizationally relevant expertise. They may create files that only they can locate, design systems that only they can operate, or enter data in forms that only they can interpret.

Communication is necessary to transform expertise into perceived power. Sometimes other employees do not understand why a particular employee's expertise is important to them and to their organization. This is one of the reasons why it is more difficult for staff personnel, who do important work "behind the scenes," to obtain and maintain power than it is for line personnel, who directly create the products or provide the services sold by the company. The activities of line personnel are visible to everyone, so it is much easier for them to obtain power in their organizations. In addition, the people who occupy the top positions of organizational hierarchies determine what "counts" as expertise, how much value is attached to different kinds of knowledge, and how it is supposed to be used. The upper managers of chemical firms are usually chemists, not human resource specialists. Engineering firms are usually controlled by engineers, not former directors of personnel. They can understand the value of being able to develop new chemicals or design new equipment. They often find it more difficult to understand why the ability to design and administer a new appraisal system is significant.

Image-Management as a Source of Power   For millennia communication scholars have recognized the impact that a communicator's image has on his or her messages. As early as 330 BC, Aristotle observed that the images speakers create of themselves are their strongest persuasive tools. Images are created through communication and can be altered by subsequent communication. The content of organizational communicators' messages, the justifications they provide for their recommendations, and the beliefs and values they espouse, all influence their images. Conversely, the images they create influence the way other employees interpret, evaluate, and respond to their messages. Employees cannot choose between creating an image and not creating one. They *can* choose between creating an image by chance or doing so by design. They can manage the images they present without being dishonest. Every person has various traits, abilities, and personality characteristics. Impression management means accenting some of those characteristics and de-emphasizing others. It involves putting on one's "best face" but not necessarily putting on a false face.

Because impression management is so pervasive in organizations, one employee rarely can know the "real" person of another employee. Erving Goffman, a sociologist whose research provides the most thorough analysis of image management, has differentiated the **public self**—the image that other people have of a person—and the **private self**—the self-image that a person has. To feel comfortable in relationships with others, Goffman argues, people need to be able to keep some of their self private. In organizational relationships, the barriers to self-disclosure are even greater than in others. Consequently, an employee can know only the surface person of other employees, the public image that they have created.[10] Hiring decisions are based largely on selection agents' conclusions about the extent to which candidates match the agents' images of the kind of person needed for a particular job. Promotions are granted or withheld primarily on the basis of how well an employee's image conforms to decision-makers' preferred images. Employees live in fishbowls (or, given the size of most organizations, in aquariums) in which they are constantly observed and their actions analyzed and interpreted.

Once employees learn the attributes that are valued by members of their organizations, they can begin to create situationally appropriate images. If the gap between a person's public and private images is too great, that person has to engage in a great deal of exhausting pretending. Employees who find themselves in that situation might be wiser to either change their aspirations or move to an organization in which their private image would be valued. For example, professors who enjoy performing in the spotlight probably should gravitate toward institutions that value undergraduate teaching; those who are most comfortable working alone or with small groups may be more successful and more comfortable in major graduate research universities.

Once an image has been created, it must be maintained. Doing so is made difficult by the dynamics of nonverbal communication. Some nonverbal cues are easy to manage; others are not. Personal appearance can be consciously managed and has been related to career success, although the size of the effect is small. In general, people who fulfill cultural assumptions about what constitutes attractiveness may be preferred over people who do not. For example, in U.S. organizations men who are tall (over 6 feet) and trim have been shown to have higher salaries than men who are short (5 feet, 5 inches) and overweight. Having long hair or a beard is negatively related to getting an initial job offer, especially in organizations or careers in which people are strongly expected to have a particular kind of appearance (for example, accounting). For women, the dynamic is more complicated. Hair that is too short may seem to be unfeminine and violate traditional cultural assumptions about sex roles; but hair that is too long (or blond) may be interpreted as sexy and contribute to perceptions of incompetence or low intelligence.

Other nonverbal cues are more difficult to manage consciously. Maintaining direct eye contact, active gesturing, a relaxed and open body position, responsive nonverbal cues (for example, nodding in agreement), and leaning forward while talking are all perceived positively and can be consciously controlled. In job interviews, interviewers' perceptions of an applicant's social skills seem to be more positive if the applicant is animated (gestures actively for a period of time during the interview), responsive (provides extended and relevant responses to questions), and conforms to expectations regarding attire and appearance (is moderately formally dressed).

Fortunately, "presenting an appropriate self" (as Goffman labels the image-maintenance process) is made easier by two elements of interpersonal communication. First, people usually establish working agreements to support one another's public images. Participants who violate the implied agreement risk having others retaliate by undermining their images. Image maintenance is also aided by the availability of front and back stages in interactions. Even in organizational fishbowls, there are times and places in which people can rehearse and perfect the communication patterns they are trying to establish. The need for back stages is one of the reasons that employees have resisted open-office arrangements: Walls and doors create back stages. Removing these physical barriers to communication robs employees of the vital spaces where they can rehearse their images.

Persuasive Skill as a Source of Power   A third dimension of expertise is an employee's ability to persuasively *articulate* positions, to argue successfully in favor of preferred courses of action. Analyzing organizational situations provides guidelines about what communicative strategies to use and how to turn those strategies into messages. Of course, one aspect of the situations an employee faces is her or his image, because it influences the credibility of any message that she or he might construct, just as the credibility of the messages influences image.

Fortunately, employees have a wide variety of message strategies available to them; unfortunately, they do not seem to be very good at selecting persuasive strategies unless they are specifically trained to do so.[11] These strategies can be grouped into three categories, *open persuasion, manipulative persuasion,* and *manipulation.* **Open persuasion** occurs when employees make their goals and methods clear to their target(s). Some open persuasion strategies are *cooperative,* as when an influencer bases appeals on rational arguments grounded in the available information. Bargaining may also be an open, cooperative strategy if both parties are interested in achieving a mutually beneficial outcome.

Other open persuasion strategies are *competitive,* as when an influencer simply orders someone to do something or threatens or promises sanctions. Threats, promises, and self-centered bargaining are available to all employees; even workers at the bottom of the organization can threaten to quit working or promise to work harder. As one might expect, subordinates rarely use competitive strategies to influence their supervisors; rational strategies are used instead. However, when resources are tight and competition for them is intense, competitive strategies are more common.[12]

A second type of influence strategy involves **manipulative persuasion,** when influencers disguise their strategies but not their goals. *"Going over someone's head,"* seeking support from co-workers, and manipulating interpersonal relationships are competitive versions of this strategy. *"Wearing a target down"* with repetitive influence attempts is another. *Ingratiation,* making others feel important or humbling oneself, is a common cooperative form. Although ingratiation rarely influences decisions or outcomes, it does seem to make target individuals like influencers more, which may benefit them in the long run.

The final category involves **manipulation,** disguising one's goals and one's strategies. A complex version of manipulation is to overload a target person with information until the target is confused. The influencer then offers a solution that he or she prefers. There is a substantial amount of evidence that manipulation is the most common organizational influence strategy. The reason is simple: the potential costs of failing to influence are smallest when one's intention to influence is hidden. If the influencer fails, she or he can merely claim not to have been trying to influence. Retribution then will be seen by others as arbitrary and capricious behavior.

Concern for retribution also seems to influence organizational persuaders' choices of *targets* for their efforts. The optimal target is someone who is powerful enough to actually influence the outcome of an issue, but who is not powerful enough to retaliate against an employee who tries to influence him or her but fails. Trying to influence one's immediate supervisor carries risks, because the superior can retaliate if the attempt is offensive. It is safer to choose a target who can impose smaller costs—a peer, a group of peers, or an employee in another unit of the organization. Thus, two supply sergeants at different bases are more likely to bargain with one another for desired materials than to bargain with their base commandants. If the negotiations go awry, neither one can punish the other. The optimal target for influence attempts is the weakest person in the organization who can give the influencer what she or he wants. But regardless of the target choice, in general, the softer influence strategies (open persuasion or ingratiation) seem to be more effective in persuading other employees to change their beliefs or actions than the harder strategies.[13]

Other factors that influence employees' choices of strategies include their *cultural backgrounds* and *goals,* and the *point in the influence effort.* For example, European-American managers in U.S. firms seem to use different strategies depending on the issue. When a matter clearly is within the manager's formal authority (for example, a subordinate not coming to work on time), managers tend to use highly individualistic and dominating strategies—issuing ultimatums or threatening the subordinate with punishment. When the issue is less clearly within the manager's range of formal authority, managers tend to use softer individualistic strategies—requests ("I want you to feel free to ask me for help"), promises ("I reward people who have good ideas"), and ingratiation ("I really trust your judgment"). In contrast, Japanese managers seem to use community-related strategies regardless of the issue—altruism and appeals to duty ("For the good of the company, please do it") or counseling ("Can I help you get here on time?"). Of course, European-American managers also occasionally use community-related strategies, and Japanese managers also sometimes use individualistic strategies. In addition, there is no evidence that all Japanese (or all European-American) managers are alike in their selection of influence strategies. But the tendencies of the two groups seem to be quite clear regardless of the kind of organization they work in and clearly related to their cultures of origin.[14]

Communicators' goals also seem to influence strategy selection, at least among European-American employees. When the goal is to improve performance or meet organizational objectives, cooperative strategies are more common; when the objective is to get personal assistance or rewards, ingratiation is most common. When the target has high formal status, rational argument is most common; when the target is of low status, competitive and manipulative strategies seem to dominate. Supervisors' personal preferences seem to be a more important influence on their choices of influence strategies than strategic considerations: they use friendly and attractive compliance strategies with subordinates whose communication is friendly and attractive, and they use unattractive strategies with subordinates who communicate in unattractive ways.

Finally, communicators seem to use different influence strategies at different points in the influence effort. Organizational communicators are similar to modern politicians, who do not try to sway voters with a single brilliant speech or television ad but instead hope to influence them through a lengthy persuasive campaign. Organizational politicians usually begin influence efforts with open and cooperative strategies and shift to competitive or manipulative communication when they encounter resistance or discover that cooperative strategies have failed.[15]

Three conclusions can be drawn about research on choices of influence tactics. The first is that employees really do engage in preferential treatment—they communicate differently with people they like than with those they do not like—although these differences may not be based on careful, strategic considerations. The second is that, as in virtually everything else about organizational communication, the choice of influence strategies is reciprocal. Supervisors mirror the influence styles of their subordinates, who in turn mirror the supervisors' influence styles. Third, the influence strategies used in organizations reflect their masculine character. They are individualistic and emphasize competition and achieving goals, usually by gaining or asserting control over other people. They focus on protecting one's identity and feelings. Like any other organizational strategy, a preference for masculine influence styles is a choice, a choice that employees may not be aware they are making because it is based on an underlying assumption. Other influence systems are possible. For example, organizations could adopt feminine influence tactics, ones that value the ideas of all members of the organization, focus on equality and openness, and emphasize tentativeness and flexibility. However, these tactics are appropriate only in particular contexts—where an organization makes sense to all of its members, where people feel *safe* to take risks and self-disclose, and where organizational control systems are not excessively constraining. These conditions do seem to exist in some alternative forms of organizing (see Chapter 7); but even there they are difficult to sustain, because masculine strategies are viewed as normal and natural in organizations.[16]

Once employees choose appropriate persuasive strategies, they must translate them into messages. Anyone can find facts and arguments to support a position on complex issues. But influence depends on articulating organizationally appropriate reasons. Some explanations are **justifications** (reasons presented in public before an action is taken, a policy is implemented, or an issue is resolved);

others are **rationalizations** (reasons presented after a decision or action). Both forms of explanation are essentially the same—they are presented by an image to an audience through some medium of communication and consist of reasons arranged in some order. In the best of times, employees carefully choose the reasons, structure, medium, and image. In the worst of times they do not.

If employees notice that in their organization rationalizations are often based on statistical data of a certain type, they can conclude that this kind of data is a source for reasons justifying favored policies and actions. Conversely, if they find that statistical data are *never* offered successfully as reasons, they can eliminate this kind of information from their list of potential justifications. Of course, some of the items in the acceptable list are more powerful than others in particular organizational situations. For example, moral arguments like fairness, equity, and honesty may be used successfully in personnel decisions but not in budget decisions. In other situations, none of the usually acceptable reasons are viable, forcing the employee to employ a usually unacceptable reason and create some plausible explanation of why is it appropriate in this case and only in this case. Our point is that the actions of employees determine which reasons are acceptable; employees sometimes change their minds; and naive employees can get caught in the middle of the shift if they are not careful.

Once employees choose a set of situationally appropriate reasons to support their ideas, they still have to express those reasons in a message. In Western societies and organizations, messages are more influential if they are clear, organized, include extensive supportive evidence, and generally create an impression of rationality. Creating effective messages involves a great deal of editing. In general, messages that offer simple, straightforward *expressions* of one's feelings or thoughts are minimally effective. Most organizational situations are complex and multidimensional, requiring people to pursue multiple goals simultaneously. For example, subordinates almost always want to construct messages that *both* preserve or strengthen their relationships with their supervisors and achieve one or more tangible goals. Even when a supervisor-subordinate relationship is hostile or otherwise negative, subordinates want to maintain at least the minimum level of civility needed to perform their assigned tasks.[17] Expressive messages tend to be too simple and blunt to achieve multiple goals simultaneously. And they tend to lock relationships into us-against-them patterns, polarize positions on the issue(s) being discussed, and create ill feelings. If reciprocated, they tend to create rapidly escalating conflicts (see Chapter 9).

Messages that draw on the *conventions* of a society or organization tend to be more effective than expressive messages. But by using the rules and resources that exist in a particular situation of a group, conventional messages reproduce situational rules and tend to create rigid, emotionally distant, formal work relationships. *Rhetorical messages* allow employees to pursue multiple objectives simultaneously—express feelings, create harmony, foster relational development, demonstrate sensitivity to others, and generate productive outcomes. They recognize the unique circumstances faced by the target person or the unique complications that exist in a particular situation. And they also tend to be **strategically ambiguous.**[18]

Students and employees are often told that clarity is a virtue. But in organizational situations, ambiguity can be strategic. It allows someone to speak without being held accountable for what he or she says. Employees sometimes may want to say, "Making a good decision on this issue is more important to this organization than pretending that we all get along." But they realize that the message must be presented in a way that ensures that only insiders will know its real meaning. One of the marvelous features of communication is that people can exchange a great deal of information without ever saying anything explicit. Items that are omitted often say more than items that are included. Messages can *imply* many things without ever saying them.

Strategic ambiguity also allows people to violate expectations—to say things that are not supposed to be said—without overtly doing so. For example, in contemporary organizations, recommendation letters are often left ambiguous for two reasons. Legal factors may make it impossible to keep recommendation letters confidential. If recommenders prefer not to spend time in court, they have three options: refuse to write a recommendation (which also may be cause for legal action), write only factual information (telling when a person worked at the organization, what jobs he or she held, and so on), or write a highly ambiguous letter. The second reason involves the circumstances surrounding a worker's termination. It is often in the best interests of the organization to persuade an employee to resign rather than be fired (the organization may be able to avoid paying unemployment compensation or fulfilling contractual obligations regarding severance pay). Typically, part of the arrangement that is negotiated involves giving future employers positive, or at least neutral, recommendations. Ambiguous messages allow these negotiations to succeed. But this ambiguity works only when both sender and receiver understand its value and are willing to tolerate its use.

Ambiguity helps maintain a diversity of perspectives within an organization. When the organization faces new or particularly difficult problems, diversity of interpretations can lead to innovative solutions. Interpretations differing from what was intended often reveal problems in the organization and can eventually lead to organizational change. If goals and procedures set in the past are clear, they are also constraining. If they are ambiguous, they can be changed without anyone having to admit that she or he has abandoned the past.

Finally, ambiguity also may allow people to take actions that are necessary but forbidden by existing policies and procedures. A supervisor usually cannot openly tell his or her subordinates, "OK, do it that way, but if you get caught I'll never admit that we had this conversation." She or he can, however, leave instructions so ambiguous that a sensitive subordinate will get the message. Ambiguity provides flexibility, and in highly structured organizations flexibility may be more important than clarity. However, ambiguity can also be used to manipulate employees. People are led to believe that commitments have been made that later are not carried out. They take risks and exert time and effort for promised rewards that do not materialize. They become angry and defensive, resorting to the destructive bureaucratic behaviors that are described in Chapter 3. Cycles of distorting and withholding information are established, and people become more concerned with creating a protective paper trail documenting their activities than with maintaining effective work groups.

In addition, constructing rhetorically *appropriate* messages creates an image of expertise. Being able to present masterful, logical arguments in support of a proposal is a wonderful skill. But if the proposal is rejected, the advocate's credibility is reduced, regardless of how brilliant his or her arguments might have been. Good proposals often fail solely for political reasons. They may involve scuttling a powerful member's pet (but failing) project or shifting the staff and budget of a powerful department to a less powerful one. Especially good proposals may even provide evidence that a subordinate is more expert than a supervisor. In all of these cases, the proposal threatens power holders and is likely to be resisted and, ultimately, rejected. In what may seem to be a kind of perverse logic, expert people are those whose ideas are accepted, and people whose ideas are accepted are perceived as experts.

Interpersonal Relationships as a Source of Power   The final source of personal power is the management of *interpersonal relationships.* People have learned that it is natural and normal to comply with the wishes of those with whom they have good relationships. If we believe that refusing to comply with a friend's request may threaten the relationship, we are more likely to comply. Maintaining effective interpersonal relationships also increases a person's power in less direct ways. People view those with whom they have good relationships as being more expert, powerful, and trustworthy than others. They communicate more freely with friends and give them information they can use productively. An employee who has many friends in the organization eventually knows a lot about what is going on and can use that information to create an impression of expertise and power. Because people are attracted to expert, powerful people, they form friendships and share information with them. Sharing provides them with additional information and expertise. In a complex cycle, creating and sustaining interpersonal relationships also enhances an individual's access to other bases of power.

Interpersonal relationships with groups of people also can provide power.[19] Coalitions are particularly important for employees or departments that lack other bases of power. Having allies includes the additional benefits of increasing employees' self-confidence and reducing their stress. Alliances are based on common interests, which are ever-changing. When salient issues and interests change, every member has the option of defecting and joining a different alliance. Coalitions are also unstable because of the dynamics of size. They are based on the expectation that some form of spoils will be divided up if the coalition is victorious. Each member's reward will be increased and obligations to the other members decreased if the alliance is of the smallest winning size. But employees also must think about the future and the need to implement the decision once it is made. Implementation often requires the cooperation of a large number of people. Their support will be stronger if they are part of the alliance that got the policy enacted. To gain their support, coalition members must give up some of their potential rewards to these persons. Each member of the coalition thus may be ambivalent about the presence of each other member. Coalitions are unstable, although for many people they may be the only available base of power.

Gaining Power through the Control of Key Resources

People control resources when they are *key communicators* or *gatekeepers* in communication networks, occupy formal positions that allow them to distribute *legitimate rewards* and *punishments,* or can obtain access to the *symbols* of power.

Controlling Information   Especially in societies that value rational decision making, information is a potent source of power. In fact, people who appear to be experts often have no more knowledge than anyone else; they merely have superior access to information. Information allows people to anticipate organizational problems and either prevent them or be ready with solutions when they occur. It helps them locate and exploit weaknesses in potential adversaries and locate employees with whom they have common interests. But knowledge is usually acquired only from other employees, primarily through informal communication networks. Employees who occupy a central role in these networks (the key communicators described in Chapter 6) have access to more information than people who occupy peripheral roles.

Being a key communicator and possessing information reinforce each other. When people are confused, they seek out people who are reputed to be in the know. Key communicators can also control the flow of information through their organization. Information gives people power only if it is scarce. If it is disseminated selectively, it can enhance an individual's image as an expert. For example, in a classic study of how an organization chose between two computer systems, Andrew Pettigrew revealed the strategies a middle manager used to ensure that his preference was purchased. The manager gathered information about both systems from his subordinates, passed little information about the system he opposed on to his supervisors (unless that information was negative), and sent on favorable information about the system he favored. In effect, he created uncertainty about one system and then provided the information needed to resolve that uncertainty. Because he was in a central position in the formal communication network and was able to prevent his subordinates from "going over his head," he was able to control communication. This control gave him influence over both the computer decision and subsequent decisions. Of course, in an organization with an active informal communication network, controlling information flow is very difficult. But because key communicators in formal networks also tend to play central roles in informal networks, it may not be impossible.[20]

There are many potential sources of information available to every employee, and there are different strategies that can be used to obtain it. Asking overt questions is the most *efficient* way to obtain information; but it is awkward because doing so reveals one's ignorance. It is especially difficult for employees who have been transferred from other parts of the organization, because they are *supposed* to know what is going on. Consequently, overt questions tend to be used only between people who have high levels of mutual trust. In other relationships, employees tend to avoid overt strategies of obtaining information until they perceive that the risks, including the possibility of being embarrassed, are small (see Table 8-1). Instead, they may devour all the written information that is available to them. Or they may ask **indirect questions** about a harmless topic that is related to what they really want to know. They may hint or ask other employees about their histories with the firm as a way of finding out about how people advance through the organizational hierarchy. *Joking* about key characteristics of the new organization or **self-disclosing** (revealing a relatively private aspect of one's experiences or identity) may generate informative responses from other employees. For example, an employee might tell a supervisor that she or he prefers all-nighters to missing deadlines in the hope that the supervisor will respond by revealing his or her preferences about deadlines and work styles. Newcomers also may simply *observe* other employees completing specific tasks and mimic their actions. As Chapter 5 points out, employees can obtain a great deal of insight into the beliefs and values of the organization by closely monitoring key symbolic forms—stories, myths, metaphors, rites, and rituals. Of course, they must be careful to remember that the official meaning of a symbol may be very different from the real meaning that employees attribute to it. Asking third parties is risky, because it may produce incorrect or misleading information or may lead an employee to view the organization in ways that conflict with the supervisor's views. An even more risky strategy involves *testing limits,* when employees intentionally violate the informal rules of the organization and observe and interpret other employees' responses to their actions.

However, even when an employee is able to elicit information-sharing, she or he must be able to listen effectively to the message if it is to become a source of power. Listening is a complex and difficult process. Effective listening depends on understanding the nature of messages and developing a specific set of skills. Every message includes multiple levels of meaning. Messages "mean" on a *cognitive* level—they convey bits of information. They also "mean" at *emotional* and *relational* levels. It is possible to detect a speaker's emotional tone and intensity during face-to-face communication, even though communicators often attempt to hide their emotions, especially in organizations where rationality is valued and emotional displays are frowned on. It is more difficult to assess emotional tone when messages are communicated in modes that do not include nonverbal cues, for example, in e-mail messages. Finally, messages say something about the sender's interpersonal relationship with the receivers, with other members of the organization, and with the organization itself.[21]

Simultaneously listening for cognitive, emotional, and relational dimensions of meaning is important for two reasons. First, it gives employees more complete and accurate information about the purposes that underlie communication from others. For example, when an old-timer tells a newcomer, "That's a

TABLE 8-1
Types of Information-Seeking Behavior

	Overt Questions	Indirect Quesions [hinting]	Observing	Testing Limits	Observation
Employee comfort level	High	Low	Low	High	Low
Fear of being embarrassed	High	Low	High	Low	
Source availability/ competence	High	High	High	High	High
Risks	High	Medium	Moderate to High (depending on degree of culture shock)	High	Moderate (because relies on newcomers' perceptions)

pretty good idea, for a rookie," the comment may reflect a variety of purposes. It could be intended to focus attention on a good idea (primarily a content purpose), to express a mentor's pride in the accomplishments of a mentee (an emotional purpose), to remind the newcomer that he or she is a subordinate (rookie, a relational purpose), or any combination of the three. The rookie can accurately understand the comment and its purposes only by thinking about what it means at content, emotional, and relational levels.

Second, listening for multiple levels of meaning also gives employees a sense of what responses are appropriate to different messages. For example, the effects of the rookie's responding "Yep. . . . Gee, I'm smart, aren't I?" will depend on the old-timer's purpose(s). If it was content, the response will have little impact. If it was emotional, the response might deny the old-timer's right to feel pride in the mentee. If it was relational, it might challenge the hierarchical relationship that existed between them. In any case, the response will alienate the mentor.

However, listening for multiple levels of meaning is a skill that must often be learned. For example, in Western societies men often do not learn to listen at the emotional and relational levels. Listening for content alone can easily lead to misunderstandings, frustrations, and communication breakdowns. In contrast, Western women often learn to focus on the relational level of meaning and to respond by expressing understanding, sympathy, and emotional support. They learn to treat the content of the message as less important. But focusing solely on the relational level of meaning can also create misunderstanding and frustration.[22]

Just as employees must listen for multiple levels of meaning, they also must listen for the *organizational functions* and *personal implications* that messages contain. Some messages serve a decision-making function. They call for a rational analysis of problems and give permission for some level of disagreement. Other messages *seem* to serve a decision-making function but are really organizational ceremonies (recall Chapter 5). For example, when upper-level personnel resign or retire, messages like "What can we ever do to replace Andy?" abound. They may sound like a call for analysis; but responses like "I think Fred, Jennie, or Stanley could easily move up and do quite well" or "Ah, come on . . . anyone could handle Andy's job" would miss the point entirely.

Messages also include *personal implications.* Every message can influence employees' public images and their private conceptions of themselves. A challenge that all employees face is to understand that the organizational functions and personal implications of messages often do not coincide. It is difficult to construct messages that fulfill organizational *and* personal purposes simultaneously, as illustrated by research on organizational friendships. Work fosters the development of friendships, because it places people in sustained contact with one another; because it makes it easier to find common interests, backgrounds, and so on; and because it creates opportunities for people to demonstrate their loyalty to and concern for one another. Contact, similarity, and emotional commitment are the basis of strong interpersonal relationships, in part because they foster high levels of trust.

But work also creates tensions within friendships. One tension is between individuality and community. Friends enjoy contact and interaction; but too much contact can smother the relationships and create tension. Other tensions involve organizational roles. Friendships are most stable if both parties are open, honest, and nonjudgmental. But organizational roles often require people to evaluate one another's work, especially in supervisor-subordinate relationships and in work teams, and organizational situations usually limit the kinds of information that co-workers can share with one another.[23]

Formal Control of Resources   Some positions in formal hierarchies involve officially sanctioned control of scarce resources. Resource control gives people power by enabling them to reward or punish (promise gains or threaten losses to) other employees. As long as they threaten subtly or promise tactfully, they will be able to exercise power. Resource control also allows employees to persuade others to share some of the assets that they control. Most societies have deeply ingrained norms of reciprocity. When a person voluntarily gives something to someone else, the recipient feels pressure to reciprocate.

Although any scarce resource can be used as the basis for a threat or a promise, the most important is money. Employees and groups who control funds invariably are the most powerful parts of an organization. In all organizations a substantial proportion of the budget is fixed. The allocation of the remainder (usually less than 10 percent) is flexible and can be distributed at someone's discretion. Once it is distributed, recipients begin to depend on it. They start payments on new equipment, hire new staff, or expand sales territories. If the discretionary funds are suddenly withdrawn, the person or unit faces serious problems. Payments will not be met, new staff will have to be fired, and new clients will have to be abandoned. Controlling discretionary funds is a potent source of power, and it provides an exceptionally strong basis for making threats, promises, or bribes. It's a golden rule: "The one who has the discretionary gold makes the rules."[24]

Obtaining Access to the Symbols of Power   At first glance it may seem strange to think of symbols as a resource. But power depends on perceptions, and symbols are powerful influences on perceptions. In all societies tangible materials symbolize power: large offices, large desks, royal blue carpets, the key to the executive washroom, invitations to social events that include high-status people, and even office windows. Symbols create the impression that the person who possesses them should be honored and obeyed. They take on meaning disproportionate to their "real" value.

As a result, some of the most intense and humorous battles ever observed have involved an office with a large window or office space that neither combatant really needed. While Charley Conrad was an undergraduate working in the foundry described in Chapters 3 and 5, the key symbol of power was a hard hat—lower-level workers had none; foremen had blue ones; supervisors had white ones. One day Conrad and a friend started wearing yellow plastic, nonprotective hard hats that they had borrowed from a child of his neighbor. For two weeks the foremen and supervisors puzzled over what to do about the toy hats, although they agreed from the outset that *something* had to be done. There was no official rule about wearing toy hard hats, so Conrad and his friend were violating no policy, but they were upsetting the power relationship by making fun of its most important symbol. Finally, after a one-hour high-level meeting, a new policy was enacted that forbade the wearing of unapproved hats, "because they provided no added safety for workers." Possessing symbols of power creates the perception of power, but only if some people are denied access to them.

Summary   Power is in the eye of the beholder. We have discussed a number of potential sources of power as if they were independent of one another. In real organizations they are interrelated. For example, people who occupy central positions in communication networks also tend to be perceived as experts and generally are part of many interpersonal relationships. Individuals who are thought to have powerful allies are often seen as being more expert and having access to more information than other people. Perceptions of others are not separate and discrete. They merge together and overlap into complicated overall images. The communication strategies that employees can use to establish one base of power also influence other bases. Individuals or units of organizations are seen as being powerful or powerless depending on the *composite image* that their communicative acts establish in the minds of other members of their organization.

CASE STUDY
On Death and Dying

Martha McJimsey was pulling brains out of cow carcasses coming down the line at IBP in Amarillo [TX] when she split one of her fingers wide open. But, before a nurse would stop the bleeding and stitch her up, McJimsey had to sign a waiver not to sue the company, now called Tyson Fresh Meats. It didn't matter that her right hand—her writing hand—was dripping blood. A company representative simply put a pen in her left hand and told her to sign.*

Like many southern and western states, Texas law does not require organizations to carry workers' compensation insurance, which would pay medical bills and, in some instances, pay for income lost while an employee was off work. The 65 percent of organizations that do are protected from lawsuits, even if the injury resulted from the company's negligence. For a time, the 35 percent that choose not to participate in the program (thereby saving hundreds of thousands of dollars in insurance premiums) were able to obtain the same protections by requiring employees to sign a waiver as a condition of getting a job, or by negotiating a waiver clause in union contracts. In 1991 the state legislature made pre-injury waivers illegal, but postinjury waivers, like the one Martha McJimsey was required to sign, are perfectly legal. Many organizations delay the signing longer than Tyson does. For example, one of the largest health care firms in Houston, Memorial Hermann, waits until after the victim's second doctor's visit before presenting him or her with the waiver form. The delay is more humane, but some of Hermann's employees doubt that it gives them any more realistic options. X-ray technician Gabriel Beltran was injured when a 250-pound patient fell on him and herniated a disk in his back. Before he was able to see a neurosurgeon, he had to sign a waiver. His medical insurance would not pay the bill because it was an on-the-job injury. The hospital would not let him show the waiver to an attorney before he signed it: "I was kind of stuck. I wouldn't have a paycheck, and who would pay for my medical costs?" Beltran complained, but district judge Patrick Mizell ruled that the waiver was binding because Beltran did not sign it under duress. Hermann estimates that it saves about $8 million per year as a result of the waiver system.

Other firms require employees with injuries—or any other grievances—to sign preemployment agreements to use company-appointed arbitrators who typically conduct secret hearings—in many cases the employee is not invited to attend—and issue a ruling that is never published, instead of using the legal system. Some organizations have shifted to an arbitration system after losing a major court case. For example, in 1991 Joseph Oncale sued a subsidiary of Nabors Industries for same-sex harassment on one of its offshore oil rigs. Initially, the U.S. Fifth Circuit Court ruled that laws against sexual harassment applied only to heterosexual relationships and that Oncale had no grounds to sue. Oncale appealed his case to the U.S. Supreme Court, which ruled that same-sex harassment was unconstitutional and Oncale could continue his lawsuit. However, Nabors responded by announcing a mandatory arbitration system, as did Halliburton, Circuit City, Waffle House, and others after losing major discrimination cases.

Ironically, there is little reason for firms to fear the court system. Texas appellate judges, who are elected in increasingly expensive political campaigns, once were perceived as very sympathetic to plaintiffs. But during the past two decades, corporations have invested millions of dollars in the campaigns of more company-friendly judges, shifting the orientation of the courts. In fact, a criminal defendant—in a state that executes more inmates than all other states combined—is much more likely to win an appeal than an employee is.[†] In addition, recent sessions of the state legislature have passed "tort reform" legislation that makes it much more difficult to win lawsuits against corporations and caps damages at such a low level that filing a suit is unlikely to be worth the effort. The laws in Texas are quite similar to those in many other states, and they are slowly being incorporated into federal law.

However, federal laws do exist to help employees equalize the power relationship that exists between workers and their employers. The primary agency is the much-maligned Occupational Safety and Health Administration (OSHA). Between 1982 and 2002, OSHA investigated more than a thousand cases of workers losing their lives because of employers' "willful violation" of safety laws. Although the companies paid fines, in 93 percent of those cases, OSHA decided not to pros-

(continued)

(Case Study, continued)

ecute, even when the case involved repeat offenders. For the more than two thousand deaths uncovered in a *New York Times* computer search of OSHA records, fines totaled $106 million (in comparison, in 2003 WorldCom paid $750 million in fines for misleading investors) and jail time totaled 30 years (the Environmental Protection Agency obtained prison sentences totaling 256 years in 2001 alone); 20 of those years came from one case, a chicken-plant fire in North Carolina where twenty-five workers died because management had locked emergency exits.[‡] State OSHAs have had a comparable record, although California seems to be a major exception.[§] However, this may change because of recent legislation passed in California "reforming" the state's worker compensation laws.

Perhaps the most egregious example of a company disregarding worker safety laws is the story of McWane Inc., of Birmingham, Alabama. McWane is one of the world's largest manufacturers of cast iron water and sewer pipes. Between 1995 and 2002 it has recorded more than 4,600 on-the-job injuries and 400 safety violations—four times the total of all its major competitors combined. Nine employees have died, three because of deliberate safety violations. The punishments meted out by the federal government were so small that McWane treats them as a normal cost of doing business; in fact, McWane "views the burden of regulatory fines as far less onerous that the cost of fully complying with safety and environmental rules,"[**] calculating their costs down to the penny per ton of pipe produced. Although the company has paid a little less than $10 million in fines, the amount accounts for less than 1 percent of its annual revenue. No McWane executive has gone to jail. Even if one was convicted of causing the death of a worker by willfully violating safety rules, the maximum jail time is six months, one-half the penalty for harassing a burro on federal lands.

However, with the exception of the magnitude of its violations, and the attention paid to it by the press, McWane's is a very typical story. The company has stellar safety and environmental policies on the books; the problem is that supervisors are not required to enforce them; in fact, the pressure for increased profits virtually requires the policies to be ignored. The company has become very adept at fooling regulators—"fudging" the results of voluntary tests, stalling inspectors at the gates of its plants while equipment is modified or violations are hidden—and lobbyists were paid to pressure elected prosecutors to drop cases or modify charges. When actions were taken, it was because of a whistle-blower. After reviewing a number of cases at McWane plants in his state, Utah environmental regulator Robert Sirrine admitted that "if a company intentionally wants to falsify records . . . there is no way we can catch them unless an insider decides to report it."[††] State worker compensation laws preclude civil lawsuits, and the company operates in states with laws that minimize union influence. Turnover at McWane plants is very high, which makes safety an even bigger problem because an increasing proportion of the workforce is inexperienced with the equipment and its operation. It also means that the only people who work for McWane are those who have no other options. Increasingly this means legal and illegal immigrants and inmates at state prisons whose labor is contracted out. These workers have almost no legal protections.

Things do seem to be getting better since the company received so much negative publicity in early 2003. Safety policies actually are beginning to be implemented within the plants. Bad publicity also has encouraged government agencies to act—in December 2003 the federal government obtained criminal indictments of McWane managers. Indictments are a long way away from trials, and an even longer way from convictions and punishment. But they are a start.

Applying What You Have Learned

1. What sources of power are available to management in the cases described here? What sources are available to workers?

Questions to Think About and Discuss

1. Contemporary models of power suggest that resistance to power always is possible. Albert Hirschman notes that there are four possible responses to objectionable practices: exit (leaving the organization), voice (speaking out against organizational practices), loyalty (quietly accepting the practices while working to change them), and neglect (ignoring the objectionable practices).[‡‡] Which of these options are realistically available to employees in these cases? What responses is management likely to make to each of the options?
2. What does your answer to question 1 suggest about the theory that resistance always is possible? Why?

---

[*] L. M. Sixel, "Sign Here If You're Injured—Or You Won't Get Treatment," *Houston Chronicle*, November 2, 2003, C1.

[†] L. M. Sixel, "Forced Arbitration Closing Court Doors to Employees," *Houston Chronicle*, December 27, 2002; Jane Elliott, "High Court Rulings Favor Business, Group Says," *Houston Chronicle*, October 31, 2003, A30.

[‡] See the series of investigative articles on OSHA enforcement in the December 2003 *New York Times*, available on the newspaper's Web site, http://www.nytimes.com/.

[§] David Barstow, "California Leads in Making Employer Pay for Job Deaths," *New York Times on the Web*, December 23, 2003, http://www.nytimes.com/.

[**] David Barstow and Lowell Bergman, "Deaths on the Job; Slaps on the Wrist," *New York Times on the Web*, January 10, 2003, p. 2, http://www.nytimes.com/. Thanks to an investigative report by a team from the *New York Times*, the Canadian Broadcasting System, and the *Frontline* PBS series in January 2003, McWane's practices became public knowledge. Extensive background information is available on both the *New York Times* and the *Frontline* (http://www.pbs.org) Web sites.

[††] David Barstow and Lowell Bergman, "Criminal Inquiry under Way at Large Pipe Manufacturer," *New York Times on the Web*, May 15, 2003, p. 2, http://www.nytimes.com/.

[‡‡] Albert Hirschman, *Exit, Voice, and Loyalty* (Cambridge, MA: Harvard University Press, 1970).

Organizational Politics: Overt Power in Communicative Process

Politics is power in communicative action.[25] In its simplest form, organizational politics involves using the influence strategies described in this chapter to pursue one's interests. Open politicking is relatively rare in organizations. Employees must appear to be cooperative members of their organizations or units, lest they be perceived as untrustworthy. If they undermine their trustworthiness, they risk destroying their credibility and losing their ability to gain cooperation from others.

When open politicking does occur, it usually is in situations that are confusing or ambiguous. Uncertainty and ambiguity create power vacuums that invite political activity. This explains why organizations are most politically active when changes are taking place—reorganization, personnel assignment (hirings, firings, and promotions), and budget allocation. These issues are directly related to organizational power, partly because they are important and partly because they involve high levels of uncertainty. But open politicking creates uncertainty and ambiguity, which feeds political activity. Politics depends on power, but power often depends on not seeming to be political.

Managing Organizational Politics

Politics is a central element of virtually all organizational situations. The greatest complication in managing organizational politics is its game-like nature.[26] In some ways game is an unfortunate metaphor. When used in the popular press, it tends to trivialize political action. It also suggests that there are stable rules that govern organizational politics. Neither notion is accurate. Even what seem to be incredibly trivial political games—fights over corner offices, the largest cubicle, and so on—often are serious processes of negotiating organizational power relationships. Similarly, although organizational political games may *seem* to have rules, the rules are always negotiable and can change at any moment. The old adage "When English gentlemen can't win playing by the rules, they just change the rules" applies not only to people from the United Kingdom or to gentle*men*. In all organizations manipulating the rules is an important part of political action.

Some political games involve the surface structure of power. The strategies used may be relatively transparent, or they may be more covert. When employees interpret events or actions, they label them as either legitimate or illegitimate. People who act in ways that are perceived to be legitimate tend to garner support from others, and because they act "legitimately" they tend to maintain or increase their power. People who act in ways that are defined as not being legitimate generate opposition and reduce their power. As a result, much of organizational politics is covert and subtle.

The Biggest Game of All: Taking and Silencing Voices

During the 1990s organizational communication theorists started to focus on the concept of *voice,* recognizing that a crucial element of social and organizational power relationships is regulating who gets to speak (and who does not), what they may speak about, and how they must speak in order to be heard. The process of regulating voice occurs at an individual level when organizations suppress dissent, but it also occurs at a broader level. Organizational discourse tends to be discourse by and for a particular group of people—primarily educated white male managers—and tends to exclude the voices of other groups— women, nonmanagement workers, and members of racial and ethnic minority groups. Because these concepts are developed in more detail in Chapters 10 and 11, we introduce them only briefly in this chapter. But because processes of privileging some voices and muting others are essentially political processes, it is important to think about them in terms of organizational power relationships.

Muting Individuals' Voices   W. Charles Redding, generally viewed as the father of organizational communication, once summarized a speech given to his class by a high-ranking officer of a Fortune 500 firm:

> A single dominant theme emerged from the speaker's lecture. . . . Although the company needs people who, of course, are intelligent and competent, our overriding objective is to find people who will *fit in.* . . . "Will this applicant become a Company Man or a Company Woman?" [a "loyal" employee who internalizes corporate goals and values]. . . . To be sure we heard the conventional wisdom that the company needed college graduates with "ideas," with "creativity and imagination." However class questions elicited the caveat that generating innovative ideas did *not* extend to challenging "basic corporate policies" or "managerial prerogatives." I wrote down at one point the speaker's exact words, which he emphasized with appropriately vigorous gestures: *We don't particularly need boat-rockers.*[27]

Twenty years later, Redding's point still is appropriate—in most organizations dissent is forbidden, regardless of how principled or correct it might be. Employees are expected to speak in the organization's (that is, upper management's) voice, both inside and outside of the organization.

Of course, in most organizations, most of the time, dissent is not even an issue. Every strategy of organizing (recall Unit II) has its own system of controlling employees. Every system of control covers what employees do *and* what they say. But no control system is perfect; there is always some space for resistance, and dissent is a potent form of resistance. However, resistance leads to counterresistance. When resisting voices are raised, surface-level power strategies come into play. These overt strategies of suppressing dissent typically are implemented in graduated phases. Initially, organizational power holders attempt to persuade the dissenters that they are wrong or mistaken (a process sometimes called **nullification**). If that fails, the dissenters are isolated from co-workers—disconnecting telephones or revoking computer access codes, re-moving the dissenters' names from invitation lists for social events, or transfer-ring them to the corporate version of Stalin's Siberia. If isolation fails (and it rarely does, because most people decide that dissent is not worth the costs), di-rect sanctions are applied—defaming the dissenters or expelling them from the organization.

The processes through which organizations suppress dissent are illustrated clearly by research on "unethical actions" in organizations and by the experi-ences of **whistle-blowers,** people who report unethical or illegal activities within their organizations to the authorities or the press. Many studies find that managers believe their jobs require them to compromise their own values. In a typical study, B. Z. Posner and W. H. Schmidt found that 72 percent of employ-ees face pressure to engage in actions that they perceive to be unethical and that 41 percent admit that they have succumbed to those pressures. A 1995 study of thirty Harvard MBAs revealed that twenty-nine of them had been ordered to vi-olate their own personal ethical standards at least once during the previous five years. Because pressure to act in unethical or illegal ways is so common, exam-ples of whistle-blowers are easy to find—every major newspaper publishes at least one story every month—even though only about 10 percent of people who could blow the whistle actually do so.[28] Whistle-blowers' stories are amaz-ingly consistent with one another. An employee detects something going wrong in the organization. It often involves illegal activity (a recent study in the United States found that 51 percent of such stories involved criminal activity, 19 per-cent involved health and safety problems, and 12 percent involved discrimina-tion)[29] and always involves something that the potential whistle-blower fer-vently believes is unethical. He or she first uses the organization's internal processes in an attempt to get the practice changed. When internal appeals fail, the whistle-blower goes public.

After that, the organization's response is easy to predict. A typical case is John Kartak, who reported fraudulent activities in a Minneapolis army recruiting office. Soon after he filed his report, he was ordered to report to a Veterans Administra-tion hospital for psychological evaluation. After being declared fit for duty, he re-turned to his unit. He was constantly watched by his supervisors and ostracized, threatened, and intimidated by his co-workers (many of whom were later proved guilty of fraud). Then he was ordered back to a military hospital for another psy-chological evaluation, which also declared him fit for duty. Studies in the United States have found that 90 percent of whistle-blowers lost their jobs or were de-moted, 27 percent faced lawsuits, and 26 percent experienced psychiatric or med-ical referrals. Similar studies in Australia have shown the same results.[30]

Unfortunately, whistle-blowers often are punished more by their peers than by their supervisors. This seems to be especially true in organizations that rely on cultural strategies of organizing. Employees who identify closely with their organizations are prone to interpret threats to it as personal threats, and respond accordingly. For example, Dr. Troy Madsen was on hour 32 of a 34-hour shift at Johns Hopkins Hospital, the top-ranked hospital in the United States. As a result

FIGURE 8–1

NON-SEQUITUR reprinted by permission of Universal Press
Syndicate.

of exhaustion, he made a mistake that could have killed a patient. His shift was
violating rules established in 2003 that limited medical residents to 30-hour shifts
and no more than 80 hours of work in a single week. He reported his experience
to the authorities and was immediately ostracized. Madsen recalled, "People I
worked with, people I knew very well, would not look at me, would not talk to
me." Unlike most whistle-blowers, Madsen won his case and forced Johns Hopkins to abide by the new regulations.[31] But he moved to Ohio State, not because
he was fired but because of the way he was treated by his co-workers.

The decision to "go public" is a very difficult one. People in the United
States have ambivalent attitudes about whistle-blowers. At one level, we know
that because organizations are adept at covering up their illegal and unethical
activities, whistle-blowers are absolutely necessary for our justice system to
work. Virtually every successful action against corporate corruption and illegal-

ity—from Texaco executives' openly racist remarks to environmental violations to corruption in the mutual fund industry—could not have happened without whistle-blowers. *Time* magazine celebrated three dissenters as its "people of the year" for 2003 (though none of them fit the technical definition of a whistle-blower because they decided not to take their concerns outside of their organizations after their internal dissents failed). But elementary-school children learn to view children who report wrongdoing at least as negatively as the wrongdoers themselves, and studies of peer harassment of whistle-blowers show that these attitudes carry over to adulthood.

Research by Jeffrey Kassing and his associates has found a complicated relationship among the issue, the dissenter's standing in the organization, and the audience of the dissent. Employees who express dissent to their supervisors tend to be supervisors themselves, enjoy arguing, have high levels of job satisfaction and identification with their organizations and better interpersonal relationships with their supervisors, and believe that their organization values freedom of speech, compared to those who express their concerns to co-workers. Those who dissent only to their co-workers have the opposite characteristics. All employees are very much concerned with the effects that dissenting has on their image in the organization; they have to balance those concerns against the risks of retaliation and their individual ethical codes. They realize that the risks to a whistle-blower's personal life, advancement, relationships with co-workers, and personal safety often are quite large and the potential gains quite small.[32]

There is a patchwork of legal protections for whistle-blowers, but they vary across industries, states, and topics. For example, there are relatively strong protections for people who report racial or sexual discrimination to federal agencies or who report safety violations involving airlines or nuclear power plants. The protections are much weaker elsewhere. A whistle-blower protection provision for the new U.S. Department of Homeland Security was defeated after strong opposition from the Bush administration. As the following case study indicates, even in the industries with the strongest protections, there is little effective protection. One-quarter of whistle-blowers become alcoholics; 17 percent lose their homes; 15 percent subsequently are divorced; 10 percent attempt suicide; and 8 percent go bankrupt. But the personal costs of not doing so—reduced self-esteem, guilt, and fear that someone else will report the matter, leaving the employee in the role of an accomplice—may also be great. For potential whistle-blowers, merely deciding whether to communicate is in itself a complicated problem. Most people do not speak up even when doing so promises equivalent gains and risks; very few do so when speaking involves substantial risks with little opportunity for gain. For example, after reflecting on his experiences, Richard Lundwall, the manager who blew the whistle on Texaco's racist promotion policies (see Chapter 12), now says, "If there are other Richard Lundwalls out there who have information contrary to their employers' best interest, they would be rather foolish to put themselves at risk." As a result of the experiences of people like Lundwall, whistle-blowing is relatively rare, and whistle-blowers' complaints are often withdrawn before any corrective action is taken.[33]

CASE STUDY
Suppressing Dissent in the Nuclear Power Industry

Because of the obvious risks to public health and safety, the nuclear industry has one of the strongest whistle-blower protection systems in U.S. industry. Since 1974, if a nuclear organization is convicted of discriminating against an employee for raising safety concerns, the U.S. Department of Labor can order reinstatement, back pay, promotion, and other compensation, and the Nuclear Regulatory Commission (NRC) can fine the company and refer the matter to the Justice Department for criminal prosecution. But the power relationships between nuclear organizations and their employees mean that "the system is stacked against you. . . . if you've got the law and the facts and God on your side, you've got a 50 percent chance of winning," says Larry Simmons, a former contact welder who blew the whistle at Florida Power Company's Crystal River plant in 1988. The results of the many complaints filed against nuclear firms seem to support Simmons's conclusion. (In January 1993, 142 such cases were pending nationwide, a figure that almost certainly underestimates the number of violations, because most people do not blow the whistle on their employers.) It is nearly impossible to win a case against a multimillion-dollar firm with a battery of skilled attorneys who can drag a case out for years while the plaintiffs' savings and resolve are depleted and their careers destroyed. Even in the relatively rare cases when plaintiffs receive a settlement, the vast majority of the money goes to cover their legal expenses, and fines levied against the organizations are small relative to the firm's size. (Fines of $25,000 to $250,000 are common for violations at plants that generate $1 million a day in revenues.)

Three cases are illustrative of the experiences of nuclear industry whistle-blowers. In March 1989, Len Trimmer (who had worked for the University of California division at Los Alamos National Laboratory since 1962, receiving numerous promotions) was assigned to inspect drums of radioactive material to see that they met safety standards. He complained that his test equipment was malfunctioning and later discovered about twenty leaking drums. The drums tested with the flawed equipment were labeled "certifiable" and the leaking drums were left to leak. He complained to the NRC and subsequently experienced a number of events that he believed were in retaliation: One co-worker kicked a chair out from under him, and he was ordered to move heavy drums, aggravating an old back injury. While he was on disability leave, his desk and locker were broken into; and on the day that the local newspaper ran a story about him, a large rock bounced off his parked car. He was never called back to work.

Martin Marietta Energy Systems, the primary contractor at Oak Ridge National Laboratory, transferred Charles Varnadore to a high-radiation chemistry lab and assigned him the task of manipulating radioactive materials with mechanical arms, something he couldn't do well because he had been blind in one eye since birth and didn't have the depth perception necessary to operate the equipment properly. After he made a number of messes, he complained. From then on he was a

(continued)

(Case Study, continued)

persona non grata, being transferred so often that he earned the nickname "technician on roller skates." He returned to work in July 1989 after surgery for colon cancer to find that his job had been filled by a younger man and his new office was a room "with mercury all over it," where drums of radioactive waste were stored. In June 1993 Judge Theodor Von Brand ruled in Varnadore's favor and wrote a blistering criticism of Martin Marietta that concluded that "they intentionally put him under stress with full knowledge that he was a cancer patient . . . particularly vulnerable to the workplace stresses to which he was subjected." Since the court decision, Varnadore has filed additional complaints, one of which accuses a company labor relations officer of saying during a training session that "someone should get a gun and take him out and shoot him."

One of the longest and most complicated cases involves Vera English, whose eight-year battle against General Electric's nuclear fuel plant in Wilmington, North Carolina, has included favorable rulings by the U.S. Supreme Court, NRC, Department of Labor, and a number of other judges; $250,000 in lost wages and legal fees; no financial gain; and a $20,000 fine paid by GE. In March 1984, after two years of complaining to GE management about safety-related violations, English charged GE with violations of company policy regarding safety. In April, GE told her that she would lose her job unless she applied to be transferred to the non-nuclear section of the plant. In July she was fired; in August she filed a complaint with the Department of Labor, which found evidence of discrimination in October. GE appealed the verdict. A year later an administrative law judge ordered GE to reinstate English to her original position and pay her $73,007 in damages plus back pay. GE appealed. In January 1987, the Secretary of Labor reversed the decision on the grounds that English had not filed the complaint within thirty days of being warned of the layoff. She appealed, arguing that she did complain within thirty days of being fired. After a number of other rehearings and appeals within the Labor Department, the secretary again dismissed her complaint.

But English had also sued GE in federal court. In February 1988, a federal district judge found that she had a valid claim but dismissed it on a technicality. In June 1990, after two additional appeals, the U.S. Supreme Court ruled in her favor and returned the case to the lower court. In October her case was dismissed because she had not proved GE's actions to be "outrageous," a decision that was upheld on appeal. Amount of time spent fighting the case: 7½ years with the Department of Labor; 5½ years in court. Outcome: no damages recovered. A Tennessee Valley Authority whistle-blower concluded: "We all discovered that the process doesn't do anything but put a big bull's-eye on your back."

However, sometimes the outcome is different. David Lamb and James Dean, who raised safety concerns about a south Texas nuclear power plant run by Houston Lighting and Power (HLP), were fired in 1992. In late 1993 an administrative law judge in the Department of Labor ruled that they had been harassed and fired because of their whistle-blowing activities, but the company appealed the ruling to the Secretary of Labor. In November 1996, HLP paid a $160,000 fine to the NRC as a result of the allegations, and on November 19, 1996—the day before the Secretary of Labor was to announce his decision—the company reached an out-of-court settlement with the two for an undisclosed amount of money. Neither man has been able to find employment in the nuclear power industry, but Lamb concludes that "[the settlement takes] a big load off our backs. No amount of money will ever pay for what they did to us or what I believe they have done to other personnel. But it sure goes a long way."*

Applying What You've Learned

1. There is a good deal of evidence indicating that whistle-blowers' co-workers place intense pressure on them to withdraw their charges once they become public. What accepted assumptions in Western societies underlie this response?
2. What sources of power do whistle-blowers have available in their efforts to change organizational practices? How can those sources be used?

Questions to Think About and Discuss

1. Pretend that you are the manager of a nuclear plant and are not especially constrained by ethical considerations. Also pretend that an employee keeps making complaints about safety problems at the plant. Although the likelihood of these problems becoming public knowledge is quite slim, they could be very expensive and embarrassing if they ever did. But solving the problems would be very expensive, and your supervisors already are pressuring you to reduce costs. So the "rational" strategy seems to be to silence the dissenter. What strategies are available that would allow you to do so? What are the likely costs and effects of each of those strategies?
2. Now pretend that your efforts to suppress dissent failed, and the employee has reported the problems to the Nuclear Regulatory Commission. What strategies are now available to you to deal with the problem? What are the likely costs and effects of each of those strategies?

The primary source for this case study is a series of articles published by the *Houston Chronicle* during March and September 1993. For a broad analysis of issues regarding the release of low-level radioactivity, see Jay Gould, *Deadly Deceit: Low Level Radiation, High Level Coverup* (New York: Four Walls Eight Windows, 1990); and Jay Gould and Ernest Sternglass, *The Enemy Within: The High Cost of Living near Nuclear Power* (New York: Four Walls Eight Windows, 1996).

*Jim Morris, "Whistle-Blower Claims Settled," *Houston Chronicle,* November 20, 1996, A24-25.

Muting Groups' Voices   One of the recurring themes of this book is that power and control in organizations depends on processes of perceiving and attributing meaning. Sense-making is guided by social and organizational power relationships; power relationships are managed strategically by creating shared sense-making. In turn, sense-making and strategic communication create, reproduce, and sometimes transform power relationships. At first glance, the interrelationships among meaning-creation, communication strategies, and power relationships appear to be the same for all groups of people. But contemporary views of social and organizational power suggest that a closer look will reveal that there are important power inequalities embedded in meaning-creation and communication. In short, in most U.S. organizations, what an act means is determined by the beliefs, values, and frames of reference of educated white male upper-level managers. Although employees who are nonwhite, lower-level, less educated, or female may make sense of an event or action in very different ways, the discourse of organizations tends to privilege the sense-making processes of dominant groups. For example, the meaning that is typically attached to the job cuts that accompanied organizational downsizing during the 1990s is that they were unavoidable adaptations to the pressures of a global economy. They will increase efficiency and productivity, thus making U.S. firms more competitive in the long term and protecting Americans' jobs. Of course, many other interpretations are possible. For example, one could persuasively argue that downsizing primarily benefits upper management (recall Chapter 1), not workers, stockholders, or society as a whole; or that downsizing has had little positive effect on efficiency or productivity. Only 26 percent of downsized firms report efficiency increases; 19 percent report decreases, and 39 percent report no change. Eleven percent of downsized firms report increased absenteeism; 62 percent report lower morale, and 39 percent report increased voluntary turnover. So for workers and middle managers—more of whom tend to be female, nonwhite, less well educated, and less wealthy than upper management—downsizing means lost income, reduced self-esteem, and increased stress and insecurity, not increased profits or a rosy future. But the discourse about downsizing, both within organizations and in the popular media, focuses almost completely on the managerial interpretation and almost completely ignores or mutes other interpretations.[34]

Another alternative interpretation involves the criteria of efficiency and effectiveness themselves. Roger Jehensen has called these concepts ideological fictions that foster the interests of some groups over the interests of others. Efficiency is not itself a goal or outcome. It is a means of reaching some other goal or outcome. Driving fast, or driving in a fuel-efficient manner (two possible definitions of efficient travel), are meaningless unless doing so gets people somewhere, specifically, where they want to go. Presumably, organizational efficiency is important because it produces something else of value—profits or the continued existence of the organization, for example. If efficiency is defined in this way, as a *means* to an end, it immediately raises questions about the value of the ends themselves. People will ask what communication theorist Jürgen

Habermas has called **practical questions,** questions such as "What level of environmental damage are we willing to accept in order to increase profits?" or "What proportion of a firm's profits should be reinvested in the publicly funded infrastructure (roads, education systems, and so on) that the organization uses to produce its profits?" But when efficiency is defined as an *end* in itself, as it usually is, these value-laden questions are inappropriate. Instead, people only ask what Habermas calls **technical questions,** about how best to maximize efficiency. Defining efficiency as an end transforms value-laden questions about goals and social costs into seemingly value-neutral questions about technique. In the process, narrow, technical kinds of expertise—the expertise that managers are presumed to have—are elevated in importance. And the voices of people who ask *practical* questions that are based on nonmanagerial expertise, experiences, and values—workers and members of the communities in which our organizations exist—are silenced.[35]

Focusing on *technical* questions instead of *practical* ones privileges the interests of some groups over others. So do the definitions of the key terms that make up the questions themselves. For example, the usual "technical" definition of efficiency is output per person hour. But what if efficiency is defined in terms of output per dollar of supervisory overhead? Both definitions are justifiable on economic grounds; but the former definition focuses attention on workers, places the burden for organizational success on controlling and motivating *them,* and legitimates management's efforts to do so. It also suggests that the returns created through increased efficiency should be given largely to management because it was *their* skill at motivating and controlling workers that created the efficiency. Similarly, the dominant definition justifies blaming workers for negative outcomes because it could only have been *their* lack of effort, ability, and productivity (in spite of management's best efforts) that caused the losses. This sense-making system further legitimates management's efforts to motivate and control workers in the future. In contrast, the second definition of efficiency focuses attention on managerial overhead, places the burden for organizational success on management's shoulders, suggests that the number of managers and their compensation should be kept as small as possible, and assumes that nonmanagerial personnel do the *real* work of the organization. The former definition elevates the interests and "voice" of managers over workers; the latter elevates the interests and voice of workers.

Conclusion

Traditional models define organizational power in terms of domination and through overt displays such as orders, threats, promises, and political strategizing. But power has additional, equally important dimensions. The surface structure of power also has a hidden face, the conscious processes through which employees decide which battles to fight and how to fight them. And power has a deeper structure. Power is perception; it exists in the minds of social and organizational actors, not in a realm independent of people's activities. It is inextricably linked to the underlying assumptions of our culture, both in general and in particular organizational cultures. It is exerted through disciplinary processes that permeate every corner of the organization.

Each of these dimensions of power must be considered if any one dimension is to be understood. Overt displays are influenced by the hidden face of power and its deep structure, and both of these dimensions are influenced by overt displays. Similarly, the hidden face is influenced by employees' perceptions of what actions are *normal* and *natural* in their cultures. Their decisions about which battles to fight and how to fight them determine how and when power is displayed in their organizations. Finally, the assumptions of a society are created, reproduced, and transformed by its members' overt actions and hidden decisions about power relationships. One dimension of power simply cannot be understood without simultaneously considering the others.

Notes

[1] Abraham Zalzenik, "Power and Politics in Organizational Life," *Harvard Business Review* 48 (May-June 1970): 47–60; David Barber, *Power in Committees* (Chicago: Rand McNally, 1966). The literature on social and organizational power is almost overwhelmingly large, and as a result it would be impossible to list even a small proportion of the important works here. Particularly valuable items are Henry Mintzberg, *Power in and around Organizations* (Englewood Cliffs, NJ: Prentice Hall, 1983); Jeffrey Pfeffer, *Managing with Power* (Boston: Harvard Business School, 1992); and Dennis Mumby, "Power in Organizations," in *The New Handbook of Organizational Communication,* Fredric Jablin and Linda Putnam, eds. (Thousand Oaks, CA: Sage, 2000).

[2] Fredric Jablin, "An Exploratory Study of Subordinates' Perceptions of Supervisory Politics," *Communication Quarterly* 29 (1981): 269–275.

[3] See Angela Tretheway, "A Feminist Critique of Disciplined Bodies," in *Rethinking Organizational and Managerial Communication from Feminist Perspectives,* Patrice Buzzanell, ed. (Thousand Oaks, CA: Sage, 2000); and James Barker and George Cheney, "The Concept of Discipline in Contemporary Organizational Life," *Communication Monographs* 61 (1994): 19–43. These sources summarize Foucault's *Discipline and Punish: The Birth of the Prison,* A. Sheridan, trans. (1977; New York: Vintage, 1990); and *The History of Sexuality,* R. Hurley, trans., vol. 1 (1978; New York: Vintage, 1990).

[4] Multilevel models of power are developed in a large number of contemporary writings. They are summarized in Stewart Clegg, *Frameworks of Power* (Newbury Park, CA: Sage, 1989); and Charles Conrad, "Was Pogo Right? Communication, Power, and Resistance," in *Communication Research in the Twenty-First Century,* Julia Wood and Richard Gregg, eds. (Cresskill, NJ: Hampton Press, 1995). For applications of multilevel models to interpersonal relationships in organizations, see Calvin Morrill, "The Private Ordering of Professional Relationships," in *Hidden Conflict in Organizations,* Deborah Kolb and Jean Bartunek, eds. (Newbury Park, CA: Sage, 1992); Robyn Clair, "The Use of Framing Devices to Sequester Organizational Narratives," *Communication Monographs* 60 (1993): 113–136.

[5] David Smith, "Stories, Values, and Patient Care Decisions," in *The Ethical Nexus,* Charles Conrad, ed. (Norwood, NJ: Ablex, 1993); and Marsha Vanderford, David Smith, and Willard Harris, "Value Identification in Narrative Discourse," *Journal of Applied Communication Research* 20 (1992): 123–161.

[6] Charles Berger, "Power, Dominance, and Social Interaction," in *Handbook of Interpersonal Communication,* Mark Knapp and Gerald Miller, eds., 2nd ed. (Beverly Hills, CA: Sage, 1994). For a classic application of this concept to organizations, see Chester Barnard, *The Functions of the Executive,* 30th anniversary edition (Cambridge, MA: Harvard University Press, 1968).

[7] Michel de Certeau, *The Practices of Everyday Life* (Berkeley: University of California Press, 1984).

[8] Michel Foucault presents a somewhat different analysis of the relationship between power and knowledge in *Power/Knowledge,* C. Gordon et al., trans. (New York: Pantheon, 1980).

[9] M. Crozier, *The Bureaucratic Phenomenon* (Chicago: University of Chicago Press, 1964).

[10] Erving Goffman, *The Presentation of Self in Everyday Life* (New York: Doubleday, 1959); and Erving Goffman, "On Face Work," *Psychiatry* 18 (1955): 213–231. Also see Anthony Giddens, *Modernity and Self Identity* (Palo Alto, CA: Stanford University Press, 1991).

[11] See Steven R. Wilson, John O. Greene, and James P. Dillard, "Introduction to the Special Issue on Message Production," *Communication Theory* 10 (2000): 135–138.

[12] For a summary of subordinates' influence strategies, see Kevin Lamude, Tom Daniels, and Kim White, "Managing the Boss," *Management Communication Quarterly* 1 (1987): 232–259. Also see Nancy Roberts, "Organizational Power Styles," *Journal of Applied Behavioral Science* 22 (1986): 443–455.

[13] Cecilia Falbe and Gary Yukl, "Consequences of Managers' Using Single Influence Tactics and Combinations of Tactics," *Academy of Management Journal* 32 (1992): 638–652.

[14] Randy Hirokawa and A. Miyahara, "A Comparison of Influence Strategies Used by Managers in American and Japanese Organizations," *Communication Quarterly* 34 (1986): 250–265. Also see Young Yong Kim and Katherine Miller, "The Effects of Attributions and Feedback Goals on the Generation of Supervisor Feedback Message Strategies," *Management Communication Quarterly* 4 (1990): 6–29. For an analysis of relational effects on supervisor strategies, see Michael Garko, "Persuading Subordinates Who Communicate in Attractive and Unattractive Styles," *Management Communication Quarterly* 5 (1992): 289–315.

[15] G. H. Morris, S. C. Gaveras, W. L. Baker, and M. L. Coursey, "Aligning Actions at Work," *Management Communication Quarterly* 3 (1990): 303–333.

[16] See Julia Wood, *Gendered Lives* (Belmont, CA: Wadsworth, 1994); and Sonja Foss and Cindy Griffin, "Beyond Persuasion," *Quarterly Journal of Speech* 62 (1995): 2–18.

[17] See Vince Waldron and Kathy Krone, "The Experience and Expression of Emotion in the Workplace," *Management Communication Quarterly* 4 (1991): 287–309; and Vince Waldron, "Achieving Communication Goals in Supervisor-Subordinate Relationships," *Communication Monographs* 58 (1991): 289–306.

[18] Eric Eisenberg, "Ambiguity as Strategy in Organizational Communication," *Communication Monographs* 51 (1984): 227–242; and Eric Eisenberg and Steven Phillips, "Miscommunication in Organizations," in *"Miscommunication" and Problematic Talk,* N. Coupland, H. Giles, and J. Wieman, eds. (Newbury Park, CA: Sage, 1991).

[19] Linda Putnam, "Conflict in Group Decision Making," in *Communication and Group Decision Making,* Randy Hirokawa and M. Scott Poole, eds. (Newbury Park, CA: Sage, 1986).

[20] Classic studies of how interdependencies and power are interrelated include Andrew Pettigrew, "Information Control as a Power Resource," *Sociology* 6 (1972): 187–204; and Richard M. Emerson, "Power-Dependence Relations," *American Sociological Review* 27 (1962): 31–41.

[21] Paul Watzlawick, Janet Beavin, and Don Jackson, *Pragmatics of Human Communication* (New York: Norton, 1967). Perhaps the most important aspect of the "relational" level of meaning involves the relative power that exists among the people who are communicating. Steven Lukes, *Power: A Radical View* (London: Macmillan, 1974).

[22] See Dennis Mumby, "Organizing Men," *Communication Theory* 8 (1998): 164–183; Julia Wood, "Engendered Relationships," in *Processes in Close* Relationships, Steve Duck, ed., vol. 3 (Beverly Hills, CA: Sage, 1993); and Wood's *Gendered Lives.*

[23] This section is based largely on Karen Bridge and Leslie Baxter, "Blended Relationships: Friends as Work Associates," *Western Journal of Communication* 56 (1992): 200–225. Also see D. J. McAllister, "Affect- and Cognition-Based Trust as Foundations for Interpersonal Cooperation in Organizations," *Academy of Management Journal* 38 (1995): 24–59; Michael Kramer, "A Longitudinal Study of Superior-Subordinate Communication during Job Transfers," *Human Communication Research* 22 (1995): 39–64; Patricia Sias and Fredric Jablin, "Differential Superior-Subordinate Relations, Perceptions of Fairness, and Coworker Communication," *Human Communication Research* 22 (1995): 5–38; and Patricia Sias, "Constructing Perceptions of Differential Treatment," *Communication Monographs* 63 (1996): 171–187.

[24] Jeffrey Pfeffer, *Power in Organizations* (Marshfield, MA: Pitman, 1981); Pfeffer, *Managing with Power.*

[25] Dennis Mumby, "Power, Politics, and Organizational Communication," in *New Handbook of Organizational Communication*, F. Jablin and L. Putnam, eds. (Thousand Oaks, CA: Sage, 2000).

[26] Peter Frost, "Power, Politics, and Influence," in *Handbook of Organizational Communication,* F. Jablin, L. Putnam, K. Roberts, and L. Porter, eds. (Newbury Park, CA: Sage, 1987); Karl Weick, *Sense-Making in Organizations* (Thousand Oaks, CA: Sage, 1995).

[27] Charles Redding, "Rocking Boats, Blowing Whistles, and Teaching Speech Communication," *Communication Education* 34 (1985): 245–258. Also see Marcia Miceli and Janet Near, *Blowing the Whistle: The Organizational and Legal Implications for Companies and Employees* (New York: Lexington Books, 1992).

[28] B. Z. Posner and W. H. Schmidt, "Values and the American Manager," *California Management Review* 26 (1984): 202–216. Also see Robert Sims, "The Challenge of Ethical Behavior in Organizations," *Journal of Business*

Ethics 11 (1992): 501–513. The MBA study and the cost estimates are summarized in Jim Barlow, "Ethics Can Boost the Bottom Line," *Houston Chronicle,* October 31, 1996, C1.

[29] Sam Hananel, "Whistle-Blowers Lack Protection," *Houston Chronicle,* September 2, 2002, A19.

[30] U.S. and Australian data are available in John McMillan, "Legal Protection of Whistleblowers," in *Corruption and Reform*, S. Prosser, R. Wear, and J. Nethercote, eds. (St. Lucia, Queensland: University of Queensland Press, 1990); and Damien Grace and Stephen Cohen, *Business Ethics* (Melbourne, Australia: Oxford, 1995).

[31] Jason Straziuso, "New Doctors Find Hours Still Long, but Abuses Fewer," *Houston Chronicle,* January 13, 2004, B10; Diane Vaughn, *Controlling Unlawful Organizational Behavior* (Chicago: University of Chicago Press, 1992).

[32] Jeffrey W. Kassing, "From the Look of Things," *Management Communication Quarterly* 14 (2001): 442–470; Jeffrey Kassing and Todd Armstrong, "Someone's Going to Hear About This," *Management Communication Quarterly* 16 (2002): 39–65. Also see "Executive's Concern Led to Investigation of Funds," *Houston Chronicle,* December 10, 2003, B3.

[33] The Lundwall interview is available in "Texaco Whistle-Blower: Much Trouble, Little Reward," *USA Today,* December 20, 1999, A24.

[34] The data presented are based on a September 1996 survey of 5,000 companies by the Society for Human Resource Management. A summary was published in the *Houston Chronicle,* October 1, 1996, B1. Additional data are provided by Melissa Gibson and Nancy Schullery, "Shifting Meanings in a Blue-Collar Worker Philanthropy Program," *Management Communication Quarterly* 14 (2000): 189–236. For an analysis of the effects of downsizing on both employees who are dismissed and those who stay, see Dennis Tourish, Neil Paulsen, and Prashant Bordia, "The Downsides of Downsizing," *Management Communication Quarterly* 17 (2004): 485–516. An excellent summary of muted-group theory is provided by Mark Orbe, "An Outsider within Perspective to Organizational Communication," *Management Communication Quarterly* 2 (1998): 230–279.

[35] Roger Jehensen, "Effectiveness, Expertise, and Excellence as Ideological Fictions," *Human Studies* 7 (1984): 3–21; and Barker and Cheney. Habermas's work is treated at length in a number of sources. Two communication theorists have done an especially thorough job of developing these ideas: Dennis Mumby, *Communication and Power in Organizations* (Norwood, NJ: Ablex, 1988); and Stanley Deetz, *Democracy in the Age of Corporate Colonization* (Albany, NY: State University of New York Press, 1992). For an analysis of the ways in which technical reason strengthens management's power, see Dan Gowler and Karen Legge, "The Meaning of Management and the Management of Meaning," in *Understanding Management,* Stephen Linstead, R. G. Small, and P. Jeffcutt, eds. (London: Sage, 1996).

Chapter 9

Communication, Decision Making, and Conflict in Organizations

Plans are important in organizations, but not for the reasons people think.
—KARL WEICK

Central Themes

- Both Western culture and traditional models of organizing view individual employees and organizations as rational actors. In contrast, many contemporary perspectives suggest that these assumptions are cultural myths and that actual decision-making processes are often not rational.
- Because our rationality is "bounded" and our choices are "intransitive," we cannot be rational actors. Consequently, we use communication to make choices that are acceptable and not necessarily rational.
- Traditional views of group decision making are straightforward applications of the rational-actor model; contemporary models focus on the processes through which groups deviate from strict rationality.
- To make effective decisions, groups must exchange and analyze information in a critical fashion, maintain a balance between group cohesion and conflict, and counteract hidden agendas.
- A number of situational and interactional factors influence the extent to which a particular organizational decision can or should be made through strictly rational processes.
- Because rationality is a core value of Western cultures, people need to rationalize their nonrationality. However, doing so tends to privilege the interests of managers over those of workers.
- Conflicts are an inevitable part of relationships characterized by interdependence and interaction. People may perceive that a conflict exists when there is no realistic basis for one, and vice versa.

- The ways in which people "frame" conflicts and the choices they make during the early phases of conflicts create parameters that guide and constrain the communication during overt conflicts.
- Destructive escalation occurs when major power imbalances exist. They can be prevented or controlled if all parties understand the communication strategies available to them.
- In productive conflicts many kinds of communication strategies are used; in destructive ones fewer strategies tend to be employed.
- In dealing with conflicts employees can employ avoidant or confrontive strategies. Confrontive strategies generally lead to better results.
- Organizational dispute systems are of three types: interest based, rights based, and power based.
- An alternative view of conflict based on feminist principles views conflict and negotiation as an opportunity for communication and transformation rather than as issue-based problem solving.

Key Terms

availability bias	conflict
optimizing	latent conflict
bounded rationality	mixed-motive situations
satisficing	perceived conflict
retrospective sense-making	conflict frames
group cohesion	avoidant strategies
groupthink	confrontive strategies
egocentric influence	aftermath
intuition	dispute resolution system
enactment-selection-retention	feminist approach to conflict

Communication and Organizational Decision Making

Many people, especially in Western societies, view organizations as rational, cooperative enterprises. According to this perspective, organizations exist so that people can pursue their goals through the most efficient means, and organizations are efficient only if the people who comprise them are trained to make and rewarded for making rational decisions. Rational employees encounter problems or challenges; they systematically seek out the information and expertise needed to choose among courses of action and then make careful, objective decisions based on the available information. In this chapter we take a somewhat different position about individual, group, and organizational decision making. We first present the rational-actor model of decision making. Then we contrast that *theoretical* model with research on how individuals, groups, and organizations *actually do* make decisions. We conclude that, except in the simplest decision situations, people are not and cannot be strictly rational actors and may sacrifice a great deal by trying to be. Our goal is not to disparage the decision-makers. Instead we want to suggest that strictly rational theories of decision making simply do not reflect the complex maze of personal, interpersonal, political, and ethical considerations that employees incorporate into their choices. In short, it is the "rational-actor" model that is in error, not the "nonrational" employees.

The Rational Model of Individual Decision Making

According to rational-actor models of decision making, people choose among all the available courses of action in a particular situation by comparing the probable outcomes of each alternative on the same criteria and selecting the one that promises the greatest return. For example, if a person is trying to choose among three job offers, she will begin by selecting a set of evaluative criteria. (For the purposes of this example, we have chosen the flexibility in working conditions and three items included in offers given to recent college graduates in the early 2000s—stock options, signing bonuses, and initial salary). Next, our decision-maker assigns a weight to each criterion and determines how important it is to her. Finally, she estimates the likelihood that accepting each offer will produce the outcomes that are implicit in each evaluative criterion. She then multiplies each weight by its associated probability, adds the products, and voilà, has her choice (see Table 9-1).

In our example, a hiring bonus is highly salient to our decision-maker because she has large unpaid college loans and plans to change firms or start a business as soon as possible. So she gives it a weight of 11. Starting salary is almost as salient (a weight of 9) because she wants to invest the bulk of it to make enough money to start her own business quickly. Stock options are a bit less important (a weight of 7) because she anticipates that the firms' stocks will skyrocket in value in the short term, level off by the time she changes jobs, and plummet soon after (like dot.com companies did during the late 1990s and 2000). Flexibility of working conditions is relatively unimportant (a weight of 2) because she is single and plans to work incessantly before age thirty and then get a life.

She estimates that the probability of receiving handsome stock options from company X is quite high (and attaches a probability of 0.9); getting them from company Z is moderate (a probability of 0.4), and the probability of getting them from company Y is quite low (probability 0.1). Negotiating for a large sign-

TABLE 9–1
A Rational Model of Career Decision Making

	Stock Options		Flexibility		Salary		Bonus		Total
Company X	0.9(7)	+	0.8(2)	+	0.1(9)	+	0.2(11)	=	11.0
Company Y	0.1(7)	+	0.5(2)	+	0.1(9)	+	0.1(11)	=	3.7
Company Z	0.4(7)	+	0.1(2)	+	0.3(9)	+	0.9(11)	=	15.6

ing bonus is relatively easy with company Z, because a recent and successful initial public offering of stock has given it a lot of cash (probability of 0.9); but the likelihood is low for companies X and Y because they are cash-strapped at the moment. Company X has won a number of awards for its family-friendly policies and flexible scheduling (so it receives a likelihood score of 0.8 for flexibility). Company Y has just started its flextime and telework programs and still puts lots of limits on them (resulting in a score of 0.5), and company Z still is living in the 1950s on these issues (a score of 0.1). Starting salaries are comparable across the industry, but they are a little bit higher in company Z. So it receives a probability score of 0.3; the other two companies receive scores of 0.1. When our decision-maker performs all the necessary computations, company Z wins.

For this system to lead to the best decision, our decision-maker must have quite a bit of information, including (1) sufficient self-awareness to know the criteria that are important to her, (2) accurate information about the probability that the various jobs will fulfill the criteria, and (3) the relative importance of these criteria to her so that weights can be assigned to the criteria. In the simplest life (and organizational) decision situations, these requirements may be met. However, most of the situations people face are more complicated.

Problems with the Rational Model and Alternative Viewpoints

Studies of individuals' actions during decision-making situations indicate both that humans cannot act in accordance with this rational-actor model and that they do not do so. At most, people act in ways that *appear* to be consistent with the model.[1]

Why Humans Cannot Be Rational Actors   People cannot be rational actors because they have limited analytical skills and because their decision making is handicapped by a variety of situational factors. For one thing, people rarely have accurate and complete information to base their decisions on. Obtaining information is costly in terms of time, money, and other resources. With limited resources, decision-makers are forced to settle for the information that it is feasible to obtain. Even with the increased access to information provided by the Internet, research is still generally limited. Think of the last time you did research on some topic on the Internet. Did you spend several hours looking everywhere you could possibly find information and trying different search strategies? Or did you settle for the first couple of Web sites that provided you information that was "good enough"? If you are like most people, you took the second route. Only when a decision is exceptionally important and resources are plentiful do people conduct the comprehensive search for information about the problem, solution alternatives, and probability that different alternatives will satisfy criteria that is presumed by the rational model.

Second, several cognitive biases tend to hamper human information processing. There is a tendency to overestimate the likelihood of "good" outcomes and underestimate the probability of "bad" ones. For example, no matter how much information students are given about past patterns of grading in a course and about their own academic records, they invariably seem to overestimate their chances of receiving A's and B's and underestimate their chances of getting C's, D's, or F's. There is also a tendency to assume that the examples one can call immediately to mind are the most likely to occur (this is called the **availability bias**). For instance, a manager trying to decide whether employees will adopt an innovation may call to mind a recent event in which several administrative assistants sabotaged a new word processing program because they wanted to stick with their old word processing application. With this example in mind, the manager is likely to conclude that resistance is very likely. However, the manager's judgment is based on one example; it may well be the case that in making the judgment based on the one example, the manager has overlooked ten other cases in which employees embraced innovations.

Third, circumstances can sometimes limit rationality. If a decision must be made in a very short time frame, there is not time to gather or fully process the relevant information. In organizations with cultures that place a high value on quick and decisive action, taking a rational approach can make one look bad.

Because of limitations in information, the nature of human information processing, and the situations decision-makers are in, the requirements of the rational-actor model are not often met. Humans sometimes try to choose the best possible course of action (a process that is called **optimizing**). However, because human rationality is **bounded** by the processes and conditions just discussed, they more often use a more limited approach to decision making. The **satisficing** process is one in which people consider a limited number of options on a few criteria with limited information until they find an acceptable choice. They search through a haystack of complicated options looking for a needle that is sharp enough to sew with, not for the sharpest needle available.[2] Although the rationality of some people does seem to be more tightly bounded than others, and although some decision situations are more complex than others, people can rarely rely on strictly rational processes to make choices in real situations.

We may not be able to be rational, but we still have to make choices. To do so we must simplify the complicated situations that we face. We can do so largely because we are able to communicate. Once two of Charley Conrad's students (an engaged couple) sought advice about purchasing a new automobile. They said their goal was noble—to shift from their old gas guzzler to a fuel-efficient model to do their part to forestall a worldwide energy crisis. Conrad suggested that this goal would be best achieved if they kept their old car. The amount of fuel they would save during the lifetime of their new car would be far less than the amount of energy and nonrenewable minerals that would be used in the manufacture of their new car. Besides, there was no guarantee that the person who purchased their old car would use it to replace an even less fuel-efficient vehicle. Thus the net effect of their buying a new car, regardless of how fuel-efficient it might be, would be to increase the depletion of nonrenewable resources, bringing the world even closer to eco-catastrophe.

Now the rational-actor model does not predict that the students would discover that Conrad was correct. But it does suggest that they should respond to his argument by seeking out information about the resources used in fabricating new automobiles, means of controlling the energy use of potential purchasers of their old car, and the relative scarcity of petroleum compared to the scarcity of the other resources used in the fabrication of cars. The model predicts that they would use their communicative and intellectual skills to obtain the information needed to find out whether he was right. However, the model fails to recognize that some of the needed information may either not exist or be so difficult to locate that it would not be worth the effort, that the decision-makers could not care less about the effects that their actions might have on other people's actions, that their friends are committed to energy conservation, or that a host of other intangible factors may influence their decision making.

Eventually the students chose a course of action that did incorporate some of these considerations. They returned after a lengthy discussion and produced the following changes in their position: they were going to be concerned only about gasoline (because it is too much work to determine the net effect their purchase would have on other resources); they were going to ignore the effects that their decision would have on anyone else's energy use; and they were going to buy a new fuel-efficient car because doing so would symbolize their commitment to conservation whether it actually had that effect or not. In retrospect their interchange (and their private discussion) did not lead to a strictly rational decision, at least not as the rational-actor model defines that term. But their communication with each other did allow them to (1) simplify their decision situation and make it more manageable, (2) provide mutual validation of their new view of the situation, and (3) provide social and emotional support for each other's decision-making processes. They were, in the end, able to make a decision and to make it with conviction. Communicating usually helps people make decisions, but not to make strictly "rational" decisions.

Why Humans Are Not Rational Actors   The rational-actor model presumes that people determine decision criteria and seek out relevant information before they actually make a decision. Observations of human decision making, and especially of organizational decision making, suggest that they often reverse the sequence, first making choices and acting on them and then seeking out the information needed to *rationalize* their decisions. They make a decision that seems to be correct and then construct a picture of their decision-making process that makes them seem to be rational actors. This kind of backward thinking (the academic term is **retrospective sense-making**) seems to occur in almost all kinds of human decision making.[3]

Groups Also Limit Rationality   One way to overcome the liabilities of individual decision-makers is to have a group make the decision.[4] Groups have several potential advantages over individuals. Members of a group, taken together, generally have a broader knowledge base than any individual. They can check one another's ideas by exposing flaws in reasoning, mistaken assumptions, and misinformation. Properly composed groups also have a broader range of interests and perspectives, and therefore their decisions may be more politically acceptable to different interest groups in the organization. Finally, groups can sometimes achieve synergy, so that the performance of the group as a whole is greater than the performance of the members' individual efforts combined. In this case the group is more competent and creative than any individual could be.

Traditional models of group decision making are based on rational models of individual decision making. Early-twentieth-century philosopher John Dewey argued that people confront problems through a five-step process: (1) a problem or general feeling of uneasiness is recognized, (2) the problem is located and defined, (3) the person sets standards by which to test a solution, (4) several response options are identified and tested, and (5) a solution is selected and implemented. From this individual model a standard-agenda model of group decision making developed. To make an effective decision, it was reasoned, groups should follow steps similar to those followed in individual rational decision making:

1. Define the task facing the group, making sure each member understands why the task is important, what its final product will look like, and what that product will be used for.
2. Reach agreement on group and individual responsibilities (who is to do what about what).
3. Seek out all the information needed by the group, arrange it for easy access, and evaluate its accuracy.
4. Establish criteria for evaluating possible courses of action, including recognizing what options and outcomes are realistic.
5. Discover and evaluate options.
6. Prepare to present the group's choice persuasively and defend it to people who will be involved in implementing it.

Each phase has characteristic goals, tasks that must be performed, and obligations for members and leaders. It is also important to define and understand the problem and establish criteria *prior to* considering options or solutions. Premature consideration of options or solutions may lead decision-makers to attend to only those aspects of the situation or problem that pertain to the solution. This procedure is designed to promote open-minded and full exploration of the situation and creative generation of apt solutions.

Traditional models of group decision making are based on the assumption that groups should and do follow this agenda. This implies that the group's decision process should evolve in a simple, consistent, and straightforward manner. Contemporary research indicates that this assumption is only partly correct. Groups are constantly dealing with pressures from their subsystems and suprasystems. Some of these pressures are constant throughout the decision-making process. For instance, the group's assigned task is a continual pressure. Other pressures are intermittent. They occur only at certain points during the process and pressure the group to change its direction, at least temporarily. Some are external, as when members discover and introduce new information from outside of the group. In organizational groups, external pressures are often political, and they often slow, sidetrack, or reverse decision-making processes.[5] Other pressures are internal, developing out of the group discussion. Groups seem to participate in "reach testing," in which they propose, develop, modify, drop, and then restart testing of ideas.

As a result, the linear, step-by-step standard agenda rarely is implemented in the way that the traditional model envisioned. Instead, group processes are idiosyncratic and cyclical. Different phases overlap: members move from one phase to another and back again; and roles change with the flow of the conversation. The key to effective participation is not adapting to the "phase" of group development, but adapting to the specific situations that emerge as the process continues. Participation is *strategic,* in the sense that this book uses the term. Participation involves monitoring and interpreting the communication of the group, choosing productive ways of responding to the situation at hand, and communicating effective strategic responses, while recognizing that each member's actions transform the situation and the communication of the other members.

Each of the tasks envisioned in the traditional model—establishing criteria, evaluating alternatives, seeking and presenting information, and so on—must still be fulfilled properly in order to make an effective decision. However, groups may take a number of missteps as they attempt to make decisions. Five errors can contribute to poor group decisions:

1. The improper assessment of the situation
2. The establishment of inappropriate goals and objectives
3. The improper assessment of the strengths and weaknesses of various alternatives
4. The establishment of a flawed information base
5. Faulty reasoning based on the group's information base[6]

Improper uses of information sometimes results from errors in information gathering. In complicated and ambiguous situations—the kind in which groups often can be better decision-makers than individuals—members often do not know what kinds of information are useful or when they have sufficient information to make the choice. Thus, they often unknowingly collect too little information, the wrong information, or so much information that they cannot process it adequately. In other cases, they may not evaluate the information they obtain accurately. Organizational power relationships and political considerations may also lead members to withhold or distort the information they provide the group. Groups may have to make a decision quickly, without sufficient time to properly understand the problem or the situation. This was the case when President Gerald Ford needed to respond to the swine flu epidemic of the mid-1970s. Feeling intense pressure from what seemed to be an impending disaster, the Ford administration set up an inoculation program on an emergency basis. Not only did it turn out that the inoculation program was unnecessary, because the epidemic was overstated and did not materialize, but the vaccine led to illnesses in some of those who were inoculated.

In addition, the communication processes that occur within the group may create distortions. Groups collaborate in creating realities based on the information they have gathered (recall Chapter 1). Once these realities begin to be shared, they influence subsequent interpretations of information. Citing Irving Janis, Dennis Gouran and Randy Hirokawa noted that this kind of process seemed to influence U.S. policy during the Korean War:

> The Chinese were seen by President Truman and his advisors as weak puppets of the Soviet Union. . . . The puppet like image created in presidential discussions, coupled with the belief that the Soviets were reluctant to become involved in a ground war, laid the foundation for predicting success in the contemplated action (crossing the border into North Korea). In reality, the decision proved to be one of the president's most costly. Something of the same mentality has been attributed to those in the Johnson administration who recommended increased military involvement (in Vietnam).[7]

Emotional connections among group members both help and hurt group decision making. **Group cohesion** refers to the degree to which members are attracted and committed to the group. There are at least three sources of group cohesion: *task cohesion,* which is due to members' beliefs that the group's work is valuable and significant; *attraction-based cohesion,* which is due to liking for other members of the group; and *status cohesion,* which is due to the rewards members receive based on the reputation and status of the group. Research suggests that task cohesion is positively related to group effectiveness; the other two forms of cohesion are unrelated to group performance but are positively related to member satisfaction. Overall, the value of cohesion is curvilinear; that is, it is valuable up to a point, but beyond that point it begins to do harm. In an important way *cohesion* is similar to *identification* as that term is explained in Chapter 5. When people identify fully with their organizations, they make decisions through the processes and based on the accepted premises of their organizations. If those processes are inappropriate, or if the premises are incorrect or irrelevant in specific situations, people make choices that are inappropriate. When group members identify fully with one another, that is, when the group is highly cohesive, they may make the same kinds of errors.

In all groups, but especially in highly cohesive groups, pressures develop that may reduce the range and quality of information presented and thus eliminate the advantage of having decisions made by groups rather than by individuals. Often these pressures are not deliberate. Groups may develop *norms of concurrence,* which pressure members into agreeing with other members rather than seeking the best solutions. If an individual member dissents from the group's position or questions the assumptions the other members seem to share, others respond by arguing with, ignoring, or in extreme cases (or if the deviant persists) expelling the dissenter from the group. As the discussion continues, the group shifts to the position initially taken by the majority or by its most vocal members. These "choice shifts" depend not on the information available to the group, but on in-group communicative pressures. As a result groups may make "extreme" decisions—ones that unquestioningly continue precedents and existing policies or that are inordinately risky. Because cohesion generates high levels of commitment to decisions and the high levels of motivation necessary to implement them, excessive cohesion may also lead groups to do everything they can to implement a foolish decision and to ignore or distort feedback indicating that their decision was unwise. The communicative processes that *should* lead to the generation of creative ideas, sharing of accurate and relevant information, and the critical analysis of options begin to support what often may be unwarranted and unwise decisions.[8]

Irving Janis and his associates have argued that these processes often dominate political decision making. Classic examples of what Janis called **groupthink** include the 1941 decision to ignore warnings that Japan might attack Pearl Harbor, the 1961 decision to invade Cuba at the Bay of Pigs, and the Committee to Re-Elect the President's 1974 decision to break into the Democratic Party's headquarters in the Watergate Hotel. In each case, extensive group deliberations preceded the decision, and ample information was available that suggested that the outcome was unwise. But as Julia Wood, Gerald Phillips, and Douglas Peterson conclude: "The transcripts of these committees' discussion[s] clearly demonstrate that some members knuckled under to group opinion, others rationalized going along with the majority, and still others could not see beyond the 'party line.'"[9] The intelligence, extensive experience, and power of these groups did little to compensate for the communicative pressures that prevented constructive dissent.

Cohesive groups may also develop an illusion of invulnerability. Not only does this illusion hamper decision making, but in organizational settings it leads members to see themselves as separate from and better than other work groups. The competitive orientation that develops increases intergroup conflict. In time, the errors that highly cohesive groups make and the conflicts they have with other groups may create dissension. Members may respond by even more intensely suppressing disagreement, which increases cohesion and its disadvantages. In a continuing cycle, highly cohesive permanent groups may become less and less capable of making good choices.

To counteract the negative impacts of group cohesion, groups should seek diverse points of view and cultivate disagreements and conflict (provided it is managed properly). In fact, a group's search for a mutually acceptable decision requires conflict if it is to succeed. Comparing and evaluating ideas—classifying, narrowing, refocusing, selecting, eliminating, and synthesizing—depend on the expression of divergent points of view. Properly managed, *substantive* conflict focused on the issues aids group decision-making processes.[10]

Group decision making can also be distorted by a member's need to control or impose his or her agenda on the group. Gouran and Randy Hirokawa illustrate this **egocentric influence:**

> As more than one observer has noted, former President Richard Nixon was ultimately responsible for his own political undoing in the Watergate case be-

cause of his inability to permit normal investigative processes to move forward in regard to the break-in at Democratic National Headquarters. Instead his need for control dominated discussions among members of his inner circle and culminated in the fateful decision to engage in a cover-up.[11]

Signs of egocentric influences on group decision making include (1) one or more members adopting a win-lose orientation and appearing to be preoccupied with getting the group to adopt their particular solutions; (2) highly defensive members; and (3) statements such as "Please, don't question me, I know what I'm talking about," "I have been dealing with this kind of problem for over ten years," or "It's the principle of the thing."

To counteract egocentric influences, a group should adopt procedures that force it to approach the problem systematically and that do not give one member's viewpoint too much weight. It is also important that other members clearly indicate to the egocentric member that they are not going to knuckle under to him or her. Working out creative decisions that meet the member's needs but also guard against problems in the hidden agenda is another way of handling egocentric influences without creating serious fractures in the group.[12]

Limits to Limited Rationality   The observation that individuals and groups cannot be strictly rational does not necessarily mean they cannot make good, reasoned decisions. An individual who conducts a reasonable search for information, takes her or his biases into account, and tries to be as rational as possible can do quite well. For complex decisions or decisions that impact a wide range of people and units, groups can be effective if they are aware of the processes that can hinder decision making and find ways to counteract them and ensure that they cover all the bases in the problem-solving model that we have presented.

However, it is important to realize that the tidy rational model of individual and group decision making is only a standard—an ideal that can be approached but not attained—and only one standard at that. In addition to rationality, individual and group decisions also must take other factors into account: the impact on people inside and outside the organization, building a stronger organization that is better able to cope with the changing world, and ethical concerns. Each of these three additional standards may require the organization to forgo an economically rational decision. As we move into the organizational arena, decision making becomes more complex.

Organizational Decision Making and Rationality

When it is applied to organizations, the rational-actor model depicts decision making as a systematic process that includes the following steps:

1. An employee recognizes that a problem exists and that it is caused by some unexpected, or as yet untreated, change in the organization's environment or by the actions of some of its members.

2. Each member of the organization who, because of his or her formal position, expertise, or available information, has an interest in the problem is told about it and invited to help solve it.
3. Alternative courses of action are compared through open, problem-solving communication.
4. The optimal solution is chosen and implemented.
5. The impact of the solution is monitored, and information about its effects is gathered and stored for use in similar situations in the future.

Through this feedback process the rational decision process is able to correct itself.[13]

As in the case of individual and group decision making, in some cases employees can and do make decisions in this way—decisions that are simple and politically unimportant, for example. But in many other cases, organizational decision-makers deviate from the rational-actor model, by making decisions either through "intuition" or through other processes that are nonrational according to the rational-actor model.

Nonrational Organizational Decision Making

The rational-actor model assumes that making the best possible choice is always the best organizational strategy. In contrast, nonrationality models suggest that situations in which the best possible choice can be determined are quite rare in organizations. This perspective does not advocate *irrational* decision making—ignoring the realities of a situation—but neither does it exclude emotions. Instead, it proposes that organizational decision situations are complex and multidimensional and that decision-making processes should be adapted to the complexities of those situations.

Nonrational models are difficult to accept because they violate many of the basic assumptions of modern Western societies. Consequently, fully understanding nonrational organizational decision making goes hand in hand with analysis of some societal myths about decision making.

Making Decisions through Intuition   According to the traditional mythology of Western organizations, the model for good decision making is the rational process associated with adult males in the workplace. In fact, says that mythology, it is rational decision making that differentiates the worlds of work and home: at home decisions are made by women, who base their decisions on emotion and "intuition."[14] At work, decisions should be made not on the basis of sentiment, but on the basis of factually informed reasoning.

Notwithstanding this myth, there is a great deal of research indicating that managers, regardless of their gender, often make decisions by **intuition.** Managers are often required to act quickly, especially in today's highly competitive global environments. Seeking out adequate and accurate information and devising and considering alternatives simply cannot be done. Markus Vodosek and

Kathleen Sutcliffe succinctly summarize the dilemma that managers face: "Although in some cases extensive [rational] analyses may lead to better decision making . . . it consumes valuable time and resources, decreases the speed with which decisions can be made, and creates a false sense of security."[15]

Instead of trying to make rational choices when it is impossible to do so, managers often play hunches. They are usually quite confident in the quality of their hunches and often make intuitive decisions that are quite successful, because experience in any endeavor teaches people to recognize meaningful patterns. Without that experience, the events and conditions that make up a decision situation are just random bits of information. For example, present a chess champion and a chess novice a board with 25 pieces arranged at random. Let them study the board. Then remove the pieces and ask the players to replace them in their correct positions. Both players will be able to replace about 6 pieces accurately. Later on, play a game of chess until there are about 25 pieces left on the board. Repeat the experiment. The novice will still be able to replace about 6 pieces, but the champion will correctly reposition 23 or 24 pieces. The difference lies in the champion's experience and the way that experience enables the recognition of meaningful patterns. When the pieces are randomly arranged, there are no patterns and the champion's experience does not help. Playing a game creates familiar patterns, which the champion can recognize instantly and intuitively. Managers' experience has the same effect. When confronted with a problem, managers draw on experience, recognize the pattern, and recall solutions that worked before. Of course, intuition is not foolproof: many situations only appear to be like past situations, and rapid recognition can be wrong recognition.[16]

In many situations that confront organizations, it is more important to *act* than to take the *best* action; accurate perceptions and decisions are nice, but often they are simply unnecessary. Acting also generates new information and encourages employees to communicate with one another in ways that correct misconceptions. As a result, organizations that prefer acting over rational decision making tend to understand the environmental pressures they face better; they are able to update their information more rapidly and do a better job of adapting quickly to future changes. In some cases acting may be the only way to solve a problem. Karl Weick tells a story about a small Hungarian military unit that became lost during maneuvers in the Swiss Alps. After they had been snowbound for two days, one soldier finally found a map in his pocket, and using it they found their way back to camp. Eventually, they discovered to their astonishment that the map was of the Pyrenees mountains, not the Alps. Weick concludes:

> This incident raises the intriguing possibility that when you are lost, any old map will do. . . . [Maps and plans] animate and orient people. Once people begin to act (enactment), they generate tangible outcomes (cues) in some context (social), and this helps them discover (retrospect) what is occurring (ongoing), what needs to be explained (plausibility), and what should be done next (identity enhancement).[17]

In short, intuition or quick decisions often generate effective solutions and may be the only form of decision making that is possible under intense time pressure or when other limiting factors are present.

The Myth of Understanding   The rational-actor model depicts communication as a process through which people obtain information to reduce uncertainty and ambiguity. According to nonrational models of decision making, communication is a process through which people *manage* confusion and ambiguity. Employees encounter nonsensical situations and act in response to them. But in acting they change those situations.[18] These changes create confusion and ambiguity for other members of their organizations, and perhaps for the decision-making employees as well. Other employees act in response, which also changes the situation. In time, these cycles of acting and interacting transform the situation, creating new ambiguities and confusion, and so on, in a continuous cycle of acting, confusing, and coping (see Figure 9-1). The situation never really becomes clear; ambiguity is never eliminated and often is not even reduced. But ambiguity is managed; people are able to make choices and take actions that satisfy their needs and the needs of their organizations. Because the underlying causes of the problems are not eliminated, they crop up over and over again. But for people who are paid to make decisions, having a never-ending supply of problems to be solved may not be all that bad.

As well as gathering information in nonrational ways, employees often manage information nonrationally. After all, organizational decision-makers are people who are often acting in groups and thus are subject to all the pressures

FIGURE 9-1
Acting, Coping, and Managing Ambiguity

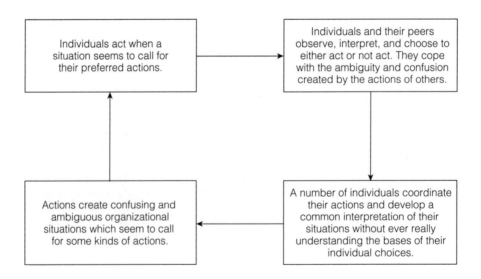

and nonrational processes described in the first parts of this chapter. They rationalize decisions already made, engage in groupthink, and persist in failing policies long after the available evidence makes it clear that the policies should be abandoned. Organizations are made up of people who have multiple goals that are constantly changing, frequently inconsistent, and often not clear to anyone. The "intelligence" of an organization is more a loose and transient collection of impressions than a systematic and logical group of tightly interlocked preferences and procedures. Each employee has a set of preferred "solutions" when looking for problems; each person is a decision-maker looking for work.[19] In normal organizational decision situations, employees make choices and then begin to construct, share, and publicize seemingly rational explanations and rationalizations of their choices. Like anyone else, managers often search more actively for relevant information after they make decisions than before. Research over a period of seventy-five years on the ways in which executives make decisions indicates that they, like anyone else, are as likely to use information to *rationalize* their decisions as they are to use information to make them. Even when their information searches precede decisions, they may use information as much because it is readily available as because it is accurate or relevant. Not only does it take time and effort to obtain information, but seeking information usually involves admitting one's ignorance. In organizations where appearing to be uninformed is punished, it may be wiser to rely on information that is easily accessible than to search for better information that cannot be obtained without publicly admitting one's ignorance.[20]

CASE STUDY
Managing the Ambiguity

A key assumption of nonrational models of organizational decision making is that ambiguities can rarely be eliminated, but they can be managed. One of the most ambiguous roles played in a hospital is that of the social worker. Usually hospital social workers work with terminally ill patients and their families. But what they do with their clients is multidimensional and ambiguous. Some social workers say they "get families to communicate better when someone is dying"; others "help people live better when they are under stress"; still others "prepare people to leave the hospital as quickly as possible." Although almost all say that their primary concern is with providing the best possible care for their patients, the meaning of quality care depends on a number of factors. Sometimes quality care means playing the role of a bureaucrat—getting people out of the hospital as quickly as possible (or at least before their insurance or HMO coverage ends) or dealing with the mountains of paperwork that are part of helping a family move their loved one to a nursing home. Sometimes quality care involves providing psychotherapy, either for the

(continued)

(Case Study, continued)

family members or for the dying patient. Sometimes it involves helping people work through religious issues regarding death and afterlife. But always, there is a great deal of ambiguity about what a hospital social worker does.

A social worker's role in the medical organization also creates ambiguity. Most hospitals operate on the basis of a medical model, the view that medicine is about curing people—fixing what's broken, treating a disease through objective, emotionally detached, scientific methods, sending the patient home when she or he is cured. In this view of medical care everyone with the same condition should receive the same treatment, and only outcomes—getting the patient well—matter. But social workers have often been trained to operate with a very different view of reality, a psychosocial model that calls for treating each individual patient as a whole person who has psychological, medical, social, and economic needs. This model values empowering the patient, giving him or her as much control over what happens as possible. It treats emotions and emotional responses as central to the healing process. It tells social workers to be empathic and focus on the treatment process as well as its outcomes. But because hospital social workers practice in organizations that are dominated by the medical model, they often are caught in the middle between two different views of patient care and must find ways to manage the ambiguities and tensions that result.

Finally, authority relationships create ambiguities. Social workers are taught to value egalitarian relationships, but hospital social workers work in bureaucratic, authoritarian organizations. An egalitarian supervisor might be more comfortable to work with but may not have sufficient credibility with the hospital administration to get the resources necessary for improving patient care. None of these ambiguities and tensions can be eliminated, because they are inherent in the nature of social work as a discipline and in hospitals as bureaucratic organizations. Managing them adds stress to an already stressful occupation, however. This does not mean that they cannot be managed. But the ways in which the tensions and ambiguities are managed have important implications, both for patients and for the social workers themselves.

One way of managing the ambiguity is through controlled chaos. In some social work units described by Debra Meyerson, people all talked at the same time, came and went as they pleased, communicated as if no one else was in the room, and held meetings that were unstructured free-for-alls. One social worker in a unit like this described life at work as "like you're trying to find a place to stand in the middle of a kaleidoscope"; others said that "life is gray, not black and white. If you want black and white go to Macy's, not to a social work unit." Not only did their confusing, chaotic madness allow them to manage incongruities; it even contributed to their satisfaction with work and with their careers.

Another way of coping was less chaotic but still not traditional. In these other units the social workers accepted the fact that they were part of a bureaucracy, but they felt that their role was to keep an elbow in the system's side, to constantly ad-

vocate for individual patients and their unique needs in a context that was designed
to treat everyone alike. They lacked the formal authority necessary to change the
hospital's rules, so they had to effect change by working within the rules. For them,
life involved constantly looking for opportunities to change the system from the inside, to rebel against the system while accepting their role in it. They coped with
this contradiction by developing a healthy cynicism, using humor to diffuse the
most frustrating situations, or expressing the group's shared emotions about un-
justifiable policies that they knew could never be changed. Neither chaos nor cynicism eliminated the ambiguities or resolved the contradictions that hospital social
workers faced, but these tactics did allow them to manage their situations.

Social workers also seem to adopt one of two approaches to making sense out
of their own experiences. Social work is a stressful occupation; stress that is sustained over long periods of time often leads to *burnout,* feelings of emotional exhaustion and psychological withdrawal from one's job. Stress and burnout also are
ambiguous experiences. They can be interpreted either as an individual employee's
problem or as a symptom of the organizational situation. In most hospitals, social
workers seem to use the medical model to make sense out of their own stress and
burnout—they are abnormal responses, caused by individuals' inability to manage
stress properly, that need to be treated and controlled. One social worker said, "I
think that they [people that burn out] will have the same problem wherever they
go. They probably had the problem before they came here. I see it as an internal
problem. I don't see it as job-situated at all." Another concluded, "Yeah that's my
professional job [to fight off burnout]. See, I would consider that if somebody said
to me, 'I'm burned out' then I would call them a very nonprofessional person. I
wouldn't deal with them anymore because they should quit." * Stress and burnout
are understandable during times of crisis or organizational change, or when someone is new to a job. But they can and should be cured. In the words of The Eagles,
"get over it." Viewing stress as an individual weakness has advantages for the organization: it means that the organization is not responsible for changing the conditions that create stress, and it gives supervisors permission to intervene in their
subordinates' lives to fix their stress.†

But stress and burnout can be interpreted through a socio-psychological model
that defines stress as a normal condition, a healthy response to stressful situations:
"There is no way not to have occasional bouts of burnout when you do this kind
of work. . . . Burnout is the need to detach and I think that there's something
healthy about needing to detach sometimes. . . . And just like stress, it's not a bad
thing when you start to feel the signs and symptoms of stress, it's a warning signal
to take care of yourself, and it can be a positive thing." It is an organizational and
situational problem, not an individual pathology. It should be addressed by the organization, by providing time off for people who are burned out, offering retreats
that provide training in stress management, and so on. One social worker noted, "I
read something somewhere that hospice has the lowest turnover rate in social

(continued)

(Case Study, continued)

work because it's a place that honors that [stress and burnout]. If you get really depressed you can honor that, take a few days off for mental health days. That saves you in the long run."[‡]

Although Meyerson does not indicate that any of the social workers in her study interpreted their experiences in this way, stress also can be viewed from a broad, social and political perspective.[§] Social work is a predominantly female profession. Like other helping professions, it has relatively low social status and correspondingly low rates of pay. Because many of hospital social workers' activities are not directly related to the profit streams of their organizations, social workers are relegated to marginal positions in the organizational hierarchy and their problems are not treated as legitimate organizational concerns. Their clients—elderly, poor, chronically ill, or addicted people—are similarly relegated to the fringes of society. Treating social-worker stress as an individual pathology tends to lump social workers and their clients together as sick people. Treating stress as evidence of how much they care about their careers and clients or as something that they should be allowed to get over quickly so that they can return to work defines them as means to organizational ends (profits). Both interpretations allow society and its organizations (hospitals) to keep social workers and their clients in marginalized positions. Their experiences can be treated as normal and natural elements of their career choices; their voices can easily be quieted or ignored.

Applying What You've Learned

1. In Chapter 1 we argued that organizations and organizational communication are contextualized within the broader society. What assumptions must be present in a society for the first interpretation of stress to make sense? The second interpretation? The final one?

2. Many scholars argue that organizational decision making can be better understood if it is treated as a ritual or a ceremony rather than as an effort to solve problems. What kind of ceremony is stress management in these hospitals (recall Chapter 5)? What functions does that ritual play?

Questions to Think About and Discuss

1. Try to recall the most ambiguous or confusing experience you have ever had in an organization. Briefly describe the actions taken by members of the organization that caused your confusion. How did you manage the frustrations that you experienced? How did the other members of the organization manage the confusion that you caused them?

2. Now try to recall the most confusing experience that you have had with an organization in which you were not a member. How did members of that organization deal with you (and thus with the confusion, ambiguity, and

frustration that you caused them)? Why might they have chosen those ways of dealing with you instead of other ways?

This case is based on Debra Meyerson, "'Normal' Ambiguity?" in *Reframing Organizational Culture,* Peter Frost, L. Moore, M. R. Louis, C. Lundberg, and J. Martin, eds. (Newbury Park, CA: Sage, 1991); and "Interpretations of Stress in Institutions," *Administrative Science Quarterly* 39 (1994): 628–653.

*Myerson, "Interpretations," p. 643.

†Stephen Barley and D. B. Knight, "Towards a Cultural Theory of Stress Complaints," *Research in Organizational Behavior* 14 (1992): 1–48; Stephen Fineman, "Emotion and Organizing," in *Handbook of Organization Studies,* Stewart Clegg, Cynthia Hardy, and W. Nord, eds. (Thousand Oaks, CA: Sage, 1999).

‡Myerson, "Interpretations," p. 648.

§Marifran Mattson, Robin Patric Clair, Pamela A. Chapman Sanger, and Adrianne Dennis Kunkel, "A Feminist Reframing of Stress," in *Rethinking Organizational and Managerial Communication from Feminist Perspectives,* Patrice Buzzanell, ed. (Thousand Oaks, CA: Sage, 2000).

The Myth of "Solving" Problems   The rational-actor model also presumes that the purpose of decision making is to solve problems. It may be more accurate to view problem solving and decision making as political rituals in which members of organizations demonstrate their competence, power, and commitment to the organization by participating. To an observer who believes that decision making should be rational, it will seem that nothing ever gets done in these decision-making events. If the observer is an anthropologist or sociologist, she or he soon will realize that what gets done is the doing, the act of participating. If the observer is a recently hired college graduate who has been trained in strategic decision making, it may take years to realize that what goes on in meetings is meeting. When former students return to their alma maters and complain to their mentors, "I'm always going to meetings where nothing ever gets decided" (as they often seem to do), they give testimony to the ritualized nature of organizational decision making.

Viewing decision-making events as rituals also helps explain the otherwise mystifying processes through which employees decide when and how to become involved in decision-making events. Employees have a variety of personal goals, favored actions, and pet plans. They move along during the day-to-day activities of their organizations until they discover a decision-making event relevant to one of their concerns. They then choose to participate in that event. Other members participate in the same event for different reasons. If they eventually do agree on a course of action, their consensus may be based on a long list of individual and often inconsistent goals. One supervisor may support a building plan because it gives his subordinates more overtime. A department head may support it because it gives her an opportunity to transfer two troublesome workers to another section. Other employees may like the plan because it diverts upper management's attention away from the large equipment purchases that they plan to make during the next week. They use the decision episode like a garbage can, dumping into the discussion a plethora of concerns, only some of which are logically related to the problem being discussed. Of course, it is not likely that the participants will admit their real motives in public. Instead, they search for a rationale for the building project that is acceptable to everyone and that can be stated in public. In this way, communication obscures the participants' real motivations rather than reveals them; but in the process, it also allows the participants to make what seems to be a rational decision. When an agreement is reached in organizations, it sometimes is an agreement over decisions and public justifications of them, not over the reasons or goals that lie behind the choice (see Figure 9-2).[21]

In fact, political considerations and power relationships may influence the decision-making process far more than the goal of making the best decision does

FIGURE 9-2
Coping with Multiple Aims and Multiple Decision Events

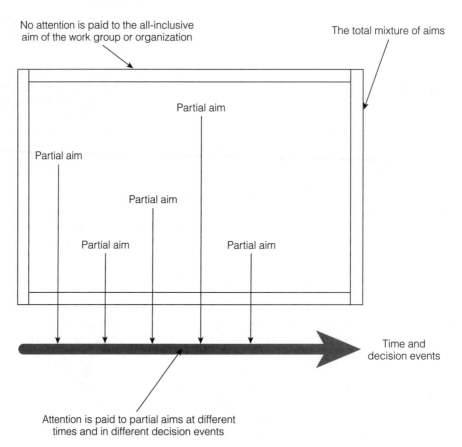

Source: Adapted from Gunnar Westerlund and Sven-Erik Sjostrand, *Organizational Myths* (Harper and Row, 1979).

(recall the hidden face of power discussed in Chapter 8). Powerful employees can push an issue through the process rapidly or can interrupt the process by pressuring for a longer information search, demanding that other interested parties be involved in the process, tabling the issue, or referring it to a subcommittee. For example, the president of a subsidiary of a large multinational corporation chairs an eleven-person committee that includes the vice presidents and department heads (remember, organizational groups tend to be larger than the optimal five to seven members because of political considerations). The group must decide between the terms of an existing contract and a new pricing system. After a half hour it becomes clear that the president and the executive vice president disagree on the proposal. One senior vice president adds information about international market conditions, but no other members speak up, because they realize that doing so may alienate one of the two top-ranking people in the organization. No action is taken, but another meeting is scheduled to discuss the issue further (and then another, and another . . .).[22] In many organizations, employees attend meeting after meeting, year after year, where the same issues are discussed and the same arguments and information are presented. This repetitiveness is irritating primarily to employees who believe our cultural myths that problem-solving rituals should solve problems once and for all. For employees who realize that the purpose of meeting is meeting, repetitive problem-solving is easy to understand.

The Myth of Plans as Solutions   Karl Weick has suggested that "plans are important in organizations, but not for the reasons people think."[23] Plans serve as *symbols,* signals to outsiders that the organization really does know what it is doing. They also are *advertisements,* tools with which to attract investors or mobilize workers. Plans also are *games,* means of determining how serious people are about their ideas. Planning takes time and energy. Unless a person or group is really committed to the idea, they will not expend the effort needed to plan. The 3M Company is famous for cutting off the funding for its new projects at least six times, to winnow the advocates of the projects so that only the real fanatics remain.[24] Finally, plans are often *excuses for further planning.* Because many decisions are too complex to be sorted out completely in a single decision-making episode, they must be managed incrementally. Decision-makers "muddle through" complex problems by making a series of small decisions. Eventually, the minor actions that they take provide new information and help them make sense out of complicated problems. In the process they act, and by doing so, they convince others that they really do understand those problems.[25]

Over the long term, the decision-makers do learn; but they do not learn through strictly rational processes. Karl Weick has described organizational learning as a process in which people first act (he calls this phase **enactment**); then they observe their actions and the effects of their actions (he calls this phase **selection**); and after that they construct explanations of their actions (a **retention** phase) (see Figure 9-3). Later, organizational decision-makers remember the solutions (actions) that succeeded in the past and a rough outline of the situations in which they seemed to work. This list gives them guidelines

FIGURE 9–3
Weick's Model of Organizational "Learning"

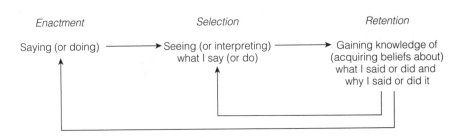

about when not to act and how and when to act. In fact, organizational learning and sense-making is largely a process of constructing a link between the present and the past, of making decisions by intuition.[26]

A Contingency Model of Organizational Rationality

The goal of the preceding pages has been to suggest that people often do not act in ways that conform to the rational-actor model, either in personal life or in their organizations. We do not intend to disparage employees. On the contrary, we want readers to understand that people violate societal myths of strict rationality for a number of good, understandable reasons. Some of these reasons involve the nature of the decision itself. We can array organizational decision situations along a continuum. At one end of the continuum are simple problems for which the effects of different courses of action can be quantified; where the information needed to make the decision is finite, well-defined, and readily available; where only a limited number of options are possible; and where the relevant communication networks are simple. At the other end are decision situations that are so ambiguous, problems so complex, and information so inaccessible that rational decision making is impossible (see Table 9-2). Using strictly rational decision-making processes is both possible and preferable at the simple extreme; it is either inappropriate or impossible at the other.

A second continuum reflects the need to implement organizational decisions once they are made. It *is* important for organizational decision-makers to make decisions of at least satisfactory quality. But it often is just as important to arrive at decisions that people will support actively. For example, in a six-year study of how hospitals make decisions about purchasing CT scanners and other equipment costing millions of dollars, Alan Meyer uncovered a recurring decision-making process that combined rational and ritual processes in a complicated maze.[27] In general, the decision-making episodes started with careful consideration of program needs, equipment costs, projected payoff periods, and other objective factors. Necessary information was gathered before the decisions were made, important people were involved in the process, and so on. In short,

TABLE 9-2

A Continuum of Forms of Decision Making

"Rational Decision Making"— Both Possible and Preferable	"Rational Decision Making"— Either Impossible or Inappropriate
Quantifiable outcomes	Ambiguous outcomes
Clear decision-effect links	Ambiguous decision-effect links
"Finite" communication	Unknown or ill-defined parameters
Redundant available sources	"Infinite" communication
Defined information needs	Unknown or indefinite information needs
Limited communication networks	Diverse or undefined communication networks

Minimal organizational and environmental
  change
	Constant organizational and/or environmental
	  change

Precedented and/or simple problems	Unprecedented and/or complex problems

the early phase of the decision-making process approximated the rational-actor model.

But eventually, in most of the episodes, the process deviated from the rational model. Communication among participants became more vague and started to focus on abstract topics like the parties' shared beliefs, values, goals for the hospital, and vision of its future. Later the decision-makers started to restructure and redefine what actually had taken place during the deliberations so that the events seemed to fit the myth of rational decision making. The later, nonrational (ritual) phase of the process served two important purposes for the hospital personnel. It allowed them to emerge from what often had been highly competitive, heated discussions with a revised image of themselves as tough but cooperative members of a functioning team. In addition, their symbolic strategies allowed them to gain a sense of psychological closure on the process—to feel that the decision had been made, the battle was over, and their attention could now turn toward using the new equipment effectively. In effect these groups had used the communication strategies that bind cultures together—myths, rituals, and ceremonies—to reunify themselves into a cohesive minisociety.

In hospitals where the decision-makers used rational communication strategies throughout the process, the groups seldom reunified. Dissension continued, debates proliferated, and in some cases key staff members resigned and expensive new equipment was left sitting in the basement. Meyer's research suggests that rational communication strategies are neither always superior to nor always inferior to less rational processes. Making rational decisions and making decisions that people will support are separate but interrelated elements of decision-making processes. Thus, as Figure 9-4 suggests, organizational decision situations can be described by two interrelated continua. One continuum reflects the extent to which rational decision making is possible and appropriate. The second involves the extent to which gaining commitment to and support for a decision is important. Different combinations of concern for rationality and concern for commitment call for different combinations of communication pro-

FIGURE 9-4
Continua of Organization Decision Contexts

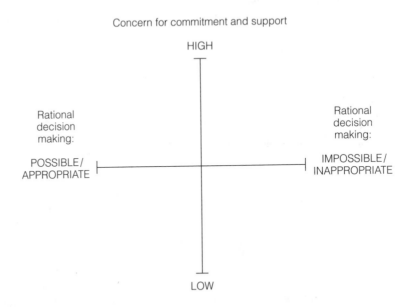

cesses. What is important is that the mixture of these two factors be appropriate to a particular context, not that decision-makers try to conform to social myths about how people ought to act or how organizational decisions ought to be made.

CASE STUDY
Koalas and Roos Flying through Chaos

We're overrun with information, but we're dying for lack of knowledge
—ALLAN MOORE, STRATEGIC PLANNING DIRECTOR FOR QANTAS

There probably is no industry that faces as chaotic an environment as airlines. The industry has faced a series of major, rapid, abrupt changes since the United States deregulated its airlines in 1979. By 1992 only three of the world's airlines (British Airways, Singapore Air, and Cathay Pacific) were profitable. Eastern Airlines, the largest carrier in the free world only ten years earlier, no longer existed. Worldwide deregulation of the industry was only one factor. Airport congestion, declining values of pre-owned airplanes, overcapacity created by the birth of a plethora of new airlines that were interested only in short-term profits, constant price wars (usually stimulated by the start-ups who could undercut established airlines because they did not have to invest in the future), and a patchwork of government policies that gave preference to some airlines—often the worst-managed ones—combined to create a situation that no airline decision-maker had ever before encountered.

To make matters worse, customers were also changing. Business travelers had begun using new communication technologies to reduce overseas travel; they had started to combine multiple destinations into one long trip instead of making several small ones, and they had started to demand low fares and enforce those demands by shopping around. On top of that, competitors were behaving irrationally. For example, the management personnel at Qantas once were able to predict what the management of Continental Airlines and Canadian Air would do. But now those airlines were going in and out of bankruptcy, announcing aircraft purchases and then changing their minds, and generally acting irrationally, and thus unpredictably. Qantas's motto had become "make sense, and quickly." *

Qantas faced its own sources of chaos. Because Australia is located at the end of international routes rather than in the middle, Qantas was affected more by the global chaos than other airlines. Qantas also had recently merged with Australia Airlines and was coping with trying to integrate two very different organizational cultures. The Australia Airlines people were a mystery to the Qantas people. Qantas feared that the newcomers would take over its territory, leaving it landing rights only at Hong Kong and Los Angeles. Qantas people thought the bushman's hats worn by AA's flight attendants were stupid and believed they were keeping them just to be different. In short, they felt, "We're different from them. We don't have the same history." Qantas management tried to deal with the culture clash by redistributing the workers so that all teams had members from both airlines. It seemed to be working, but the adjustment was slow, and the returns on the merger were so small that the airline had to seek outside funding.

A bigger problem was a breakdown in the circulation of knowledge through the organization. Things had become so chaotic that employees had started to protect themselves by focusing inward, on their own individual tasks and work groups. The communication networks that once extended throughout the organization had become fragmented; the organization's knowledge had become compartmentalized. Communication had become more formal, with all of the problems that accompany formalization (recall Chapter 3). Information, especially information that could be quantified, began to dominate decision making, because such information *seemed* to be stable. A new computer information system was installed to facilitate information flow; but it was so expensive that only a small percentage of the workforce had access to it. As a result it became more of a status symbol than a decision-making tool. One employee confided, "When you don't know where you're going any more, you want to hear someone's voice, you don't want to read about it. And when nothing is going right, you want to be face to face, not looking at a screen." †

But knowledge was something that Qantas desperately needed. It faced one of the most important decisions it had ever made: deciding whether to merge with

(continued)

(Case Study, continued)

Singapore Airlines or with British Airways. BA was easier to understand. Its strategy was to globalize, and to do so as quickly as possible. Its first step was to form an alliance with US Airways. Its second would be a merger with Qantas. SA's strategy was more ambiguous, even though it had made moves to globalize through alliances with Swissair and Delta Airlines. The key question for Qantas was, How will the airline we *don't* merge with respond? Time was short: Qantas's knowledge team had to make a recommendation to upper management soon. But how could they sort through the piles of data they had and make sense out of it—how could they transform information into knowledge? After consulting with two outside advisers, the knowledge team decided to use a decision-tree model: "We decided, I can't remember exactly when, to adopt the technique of decision trees. We were finally convinced that this was the direction to take," said Roger Robertson, strategic planning manager. The decision was made in favor of British Airways; but Robertson admitted that "it is not easy to think strategically at difficult moments. Something occurs in the environment, and one has a tendency to use it as an excuse."[‡]

Applying What You've Learned

1. To what extent was Qantas's decision to merge with BA rational? Why?
2. What aspects of nonrational decision making were present in the situation Qantas faced? How did they influence the decision process?

Questions to Think About and Discuss

1. How could Qantas's management have responded differently to the decision situations it faced?
2. What does your response imply about the possibility of rational organizational decision making?

This case is based on Philippe Baumard, *Tacit Knowledge in Organizations* (London: Sage, 1999).

[*]Baumard, p. 122.

[†]Baumard, p. 132.

[‡]Baumard, p. 132.

Rationalizing Organizational Nonrationality

The notion that good decisions need not be strictly rational decisions may seem counter to common sense. But, as we suggest throughout this book, the commonsense notions of a society are strategic, symbolic creations. And the notion that decision-makers must be as rational as possible is a core assumption in Western societies. In a provocative article aptly entitled "The Technology of

Foolishness," James March explained that Western societies embrace three primary articles of faith:

1. *The Preexistence of Purpose:* People begin with goals, make choices based on these goals, and can offer adequate explanations of their actions only in terms of their goals.
2. *The Necessity of Consistency:* People choose to act in ways that are consistent with their beliefs and with their roles in their social groups (families, organizations, communities, and so on).
3. *The Primacy of Rationality:* People make decisions by carefully projecting the probable effects of different courses of action, *not by intuition* (in which they act without fully understanding why they do what they do) or by tradition or faith (in which they do things because they always have been done that way).[28]

A major part of our socialization involves learning these three commandments. People learn that children act impulsively, irrationally, and playfully. Adults act calmly and rationally, making decisions by carefully considering a number of complicated factors, and are spontaneous only when they have calmly and rationally decided to be spontaneous. Because people are products of their societies, their individual identities and self-esteem are linked to the belief that they are rational people. As a result, when people do behave in ways that are not strictly rational, they need to pretend that they have not. People usually cooperate in maintaining the image that they all are rational adults, even if they sometimes doubt that they, their peers, and their organizations really are. People persist in pretending that they are rational actors, because doing so allows them to gain comfort from the knowledge that they live in a stable, predictable, rational world.

But by connecting to an underlying societal assumption, rationalizing human nonrationality has the effect of perpetuating social and organizational power relationships. Chapter 8 introduced social theorist Jürgen Habermas's distinction between practical and technical reasoning. All societies can be defined by the kind of balance they maintain between technical and practical reason. In traditional societies (some people use the pejorative term *primitive*), practical reason dominates technical reason. The experience of living is valued in itself; the meaning of an act lies more in the act itself than in what it might allow people to obtain. In industrial societies, technical reason dominates practical reason. For example, when Charley Conrad teaches time-management skills, he begins by asking people to play a simple "priority clarification" game: "Pretend that you just learned that you will live only one more year. Your situation will not change markedly—you will not become richer or poorer, smarter or dumber, and so on. What would you begin to do that you now do not do and what would you quit doing that you now are doing?" When he asks students this question, at least 80 percent say, "I'd quit school and start to travel or spend time with my family." Now it is possible that they could be in college primarily for practical reasons, for what school gives them in and of itself—because college piques and fulfills their curiosity about life or because it feeds their natural craving for knowledge (remember, Habermas's definition of "practical" is *not* the usual definition). Conrad's students tell him, however, that they *really* are going to school for technical reasons—because getting a degree is a means for obtaining other goals like getting a real job (recall Chapter 1), increasing their social status, or buying a BMW. School is merely a means of obtaining something (knowledge or a diploma) that is merely a means of obtaining something else. When these technical goals become irrelevant because of impending death, the students have no reason to stay in school. In Habermas's terms, technical reason dominates practical reason in their lives, just as it does in the lives of everyone in "modern" societies.

But like other societal assumptions, the particular balance of technical and practical reason that exists in a society privileges some people and some groups of people over others. In traditional societies those people who control symbolism—priests or shamans—are granted more power than other members of the culture. In technical societies people who control "rational" decision making are granted a privileged position. In the organizations of modern societies, the bias in favor of rational decision making favors managers. Upper-level male managers are in especially privileged positions. Men usually are assumed to be more rational than women. People in upper-level positions (usually men in U.S. organizations) have superior access to information. Their background and training give them greater facility with the language of rational decision making. So they *seem* to have a superior ability to decide what should be done, when, where, and by whom. As long as modern societies privilege technical reason (rationality, efficiency, effectiveness, and so on) and as long as decision-making rituals allow managers to *appear* to be rational actors, their superior power positions will be protected. Low-power people will tend to perceive that they have less power because they are "naturally" and "normally" less rational (recall the discussion of hegemony in Chapter 1). Rationalizing nonrationality helps preserve the deep structure of power in modern organizations and modern societies.

Summary: Communication and Decision Making

Contemporary models of decision making teach important lessons about the functions of communication in organizations. These models indicate that both the *processes* of communicating and the *products* of communication (decisions, plans, deals, and so on) allow members of organizations to *manage* ambiguous and confusing situations. If one embraces the assumptions of the rational-actor model uncritically, the ambiguity-management function of communication will seem inefficient and perhaps a little bit perverse. But blending rational and nonrational elements of decision making together in the same decision-making episodes may be neither strange nor ineffective. Doing so allows employees to *act,* and acting is often more important than reaching *optimal* decisions.

The danger facing organizational decision-makers is not that they will make decisions that are not strictly rational. Incorporating the ethical, political, personal, and interpersonal considerations that are excluded from the rational-actor model often—perhaps usually—leads to more productive outcomes than blindly following the dictates of rationality. The danger is that decision-makers may become trapped in their patterns of communicating and making decisions. Patterns of acting provide people with a great degree of stability. But, as Karl Weick has noted, the stability and predictability that come from tried and true ways of acting may themselves keep people from adapting to new needs and demands. Adaptation to past needs may prevent adaptability to future ones.

To avoid both of these problems—inappropriately imposing rational-actor models of decision making and becoming trapped in patterns of acting—employees must constantly monitor their communication and the communication patterns of their organizations, searching for strategies that can improve their ability to adapt. They must ask themselves, "Does strategy X work? Should I do it?" rather than asserting, "I know X works; it always has. We should use it." They must be able to obtain and accurately process information that casts doubts on their perceptions, beliefs, and interpretations. And they must be able to suspend their views of the "realities" of their organizations to understand how they can best respond to the situations they face.

Communication and the Management of Organizational Conflict

This section examines another practical reality of organizational life, that disagreement and conflict are inevitable aspects of working relationships, and the need to manage conflicts is always with us. For many years researchers and managers focused on the negative aspects of organizational conflict. Conflicts were assumed to reveal a weakness in the organization, a flaw in its design, operation, or communication. Conflicts needed to be resolved. Their sources had to be discovered and eliminated, and peace and stability had to be returned to the organization.[29]

Contemporary views regard organizational conflicts as inevitable and potentially valuable, both for individuals and for organizations. Conflicts give employees opportunities to publicize, test, and refine their ideas and to demonstrate their own competence and value to the organization. Conflicts also can help organizations adapt to changes, foster innovation, and integrate their diverse constituent groups into a functioning whole.[30] Conflicts are neither inherently good nor intrinsically bad, although they do vary in the degree to which they are *productive*. Conflicts that are relatively productive for the organization as a whole may be destructive for some of the participants. Similarly, episodes that are disruptive and damaging to the organization may be productive for many of the participants.

When people think about *organizational conflict,* they may conjure up images of executives shouting at one another in a boardroom, giant oligopolies bidding for a majority share of a competitor's stock, or, for the more fanciful of us, secret meetings on foggy nights when technological secrets are exchanged for chalets on the Riviera. Although overt and sometimes hostile confrontations are part of organizational conflict, they are only one part. We will define **conflict** more broadly, as communication between people who depend on one another and who perceive that the others stand between them and the realization of their goals, aims, or values.[31] This definition encompasses each of the examples listed earlier, as well as everyday discussions of organizational policies and projects, negotiations between employees or groups of employees (for instance, labor-management negotiations), and cooperative attempts to find mutually acceptable solutions to problems. In short, *conflicts* are communicative *interactions* among people who are *interdependent* and who perceive that their interests are *incompatible, inconsistent,* or *in tension.*

Theorist Louis Pondy developed an influential model of the *bases* and *phases* of organizational conflict, and our discussion is loosely based on his model. Pondy observed that conflicts move through phases from being latent in the organization to being perceived by members to being overtly enacted and finally leading to an aftermath. Our discussion is organized along these terms.[32]

Latent Conflict

In **latent conflict,** there is the potential for conflict but the parties have not yet framed the situation as a conflict. Grounds for conflict stem from at least three different sources. The most important is a real conflict of interests between parties. The divergence of interests between management and its subordinates is a good example. Management is motivated to keep the organization going in the most efficient possible manner, often no matter what, reducing costs and maintaining high quality. The interests of employees, however, more often center on personal concerns, such as compensation levels, amount of work required, working conditions, and quality of work life.

Any time different interest groups are created in an organization, latent conflicts arise. The particular set of groups that arises differs across organizations and over time in the same organizations. Possible oppositional groups include employees from two previously separate organizations in a newly merged organization; employees of different genders, ethnicities, or backgrounds; recently hired and experienced employees; and white-collar, blue-collar, and pink-collar employees. Depending on the organizational culture, the particular history of the organization, and trends in the surrounding society, any of these or dozens of other oppositions could create latent conflict in an organization.

There is a widespread myth in our society that most conflicts are due to communication problems. Although communication plays a vital role in conflicts, and although a second source of latent conflict is misunderstandings or poor communication, it is a mistake to assume that most conflicts are due to a lack of communication. In fact, organizations are shot through with conflicts of interest that may develop into open conflict. Acknowledging this is often the first step toward managing conflicts effectively.[33]

A third source of latent conflicts is the legacy of previous conflicts. Parties usually have both a history of interacting with one another in the past and the expectation that they will encounter one another in the future. Pondy noted that many latent conflicts are actually products of the aftermath of prior conflicts. A resolution in favor of one party may create resentment on the part of others that blooms into conflict at a later time. A mishandled conflict may sow seeds of discord at a later time. Unresolved grievances may suddenly reappear in the guise of issues completely unrelated to the original complaint.

Conflicts are most likely to develop among those employees who depend most on one another. Being interdependent means that there are many topics over which conflicts can arise—tangible objects, such as rewards and resources, or intangible factors, such as status and power. When people rarely interact with one another, they have few reasons or opportunities to fight. In organizational settings, the vast majority of conflicts arise in what theorists call **mixed-motive situations.** This means that the parties have opposed incentives both to cooperate and to compete. Even if employees have little incentive to cooperate during the discussion of a single issue, the fact that they will have to depend on one another in the future means that they always have incentives to reach a cooperative outcome to conflicts.

Several factors influence or shape the emergence of latent conflicts. One factor is the culture and climate of the organization. Some strategies of organizing simply tend to generate more conflicts than others. Organizations dominated by traditional strategies are often rife with conflicts, because they exaggerate distinctions among employees and interest groups; they also rely on a slow and balky communication system that creates misunderstandings and on a structure that creates tensions among the different positions in the hierarchy. In contrast, using a relational strategy that is legitimately empowering is less likely to promote conflicts. No organizational strategy eliminates conflict situations altogether, however. Conflicts always emerge.

Relationships among parties also influence the development of latent conflict. Trust developed during past interactions decreases the number of latent conflicts, because parties assume that they will be able to work through issues effectively. The opposite is true of distrustful relationships, which tend to breed conflict. The climate of an organization may encourage the parties either to cooperate or to compete with one another. Each of these factors is a latent aspect of the situation that surrounds a particular conflict.[34]

Ironically, attempts to improve communication can sometimes crystallize conflicts by defining opposing interests or bringing them to the surface. While still in graduate school, Charley Conrad was asked to mediate between a university administration (not his university) and the African American Students' Association. The more he talked with both sides, the clearer it became that they had almost no objective reason to cooperate and many reasons to compete with each other. They still were talking largely because they did not know how they really felt about each other. The situation was exceptionally volatile, because "getting them to talk to one another"—the task he had been called in to perform—almost certainly would have made it clear to everyone that a latent conflict actually did exist. If continued, "improving communication" easily could have transformed a latent conflict into a perceived one.

Another function of communication in organizations runs counter to open expression; communication often functions to hide and downplay latent conflicts, particularly conflicts of interest. Almost all organizations experience the conflicts of interest discussed earlier in this section. Dealing with them usually requires a large amount of time and resources, resulting in a decrease in resources devoted to organizational effectiveness and efficiency. As a result, management has incentives to paper over or obscure conflicts of interest. It may do this through messages that deny conflict and differences: company newsletters, for example, may carry the theme "We're all in this together." Other messages may highlight different interests that draw attention away from oppositions between groups within the organization. One tactic is to define an outside threat that serves to unite people within the organization and focuses their attention on differences in interests between the organization and outside groups. For example, a school administration might inform teachers that the legislature is going to cut appropriations to public schools.

Perceived Conflict

Perceived conflict occurs when one or more parties believe that someone stands between them and achieving their goals. This perception can be created in a number of ways. Sometimes an outsider explicitly tells an employee that his or her interests are incompatible with someone else's. More often, the perception stems from a "precipitating event." One employee criticizes another or makes a demand that the second person perceives is not legitimate. Or an employee makes what she or he considers a legitimate request and is rebuffed. Or a long period of annoyance builds up until the employee realizes that a conflict exists. *Perceived* conflict can exist when *latent* conflict does not, as when siblings fight over a serving of rapidly melting ice cream so large that they cannot possibly eat all of it. There is no objective reason for conflict in this situation, although the children *believe* that their interests are incompatible. Also, *latent* conflict can exist without *perceived* conflict, as when siblings are given an actually (but not apparently) inconsumable mound of ice cream.

In organizations, perceived conflict exists without latent conflict if employees believe that someone else is their enemy even when their interests really do coincide. Conflicts between *"line"* and *"staff"* personnel are quite common in all kinds of organizations. Often they exist because both groups ignore or de-emphasize their need to cooperate and instead focus their attention on their incentives to compete. Latent conflict also exists without perceived conflict if people overlook minor day-to-day frictions or if they concentrate so completely on routine or easily resolved disagreements that they suppress major problems.

Perhaps more than any other factor, employees' perceptions influence what happens during conflicts and what effects conflicts have on organizations. Table 9-3 summarizes ways in which employees may perceive a conflict. If they define

TABLE 9–3
Defining Conflict

Definitions That Make Conflicts Easier to Manage Productively	Definitions That Make Conflicts Difficult to Manage Productively
1. "Mixed motive" (or non-zero-sum) definitions: Each party perceives that it can obtain desired outcomes without the others losing the same amount of reward.	1. Zero-sum: Parties perceive that whatever one gains the other loses. The outcome will grant them either complete success or complete failure.
2. Empathic definition of the issue: Parties perceive the issue from both their own and the other parties' perspectives.	2. Egocentric definition of the issue: Parties perceive the issue only in their own frame of reference.
3. Broad contextualization of the issue: Parties search for underlying concerns that place the overt issue in a broad, organizational context.	3. Narrow focus on a single issue and its immediate effects.
4. "Commercial" issue: The issue is defined as problem-centered.	4. "Ideological" issue: The conflict is defined as a moral struggle between forces of good and evil.
5. Large number of possible solutions are available.	5. Small number of alternative solutions are available.

the situation as all or nothing, or see only a small range of alternatives as acceptable solutions, or believe that they can win only if the other parties lose, or believe that the difference of opinion has a strong moral or ethical dimension, they tend to try to impose their wills on others. They also perceive others as hostile and untrustworthy and adopt a narrow and inflexible course of action during overt conflicts.[35]

An important influence on the perceived conflicts are the frames of reference that employees bring with them into conflict situations. Through past experiences, both in their organizations and in their outside lives, people develop certain ways of making sense out of situations and issues.[36] **Conflict frames** include assumptions about what a conflict or issue is about, predictions about the costs and rewards associated with different outcomes, definitions of one's position on a particular issue or group of issues, and preferences regarding how the conflict should be managed. When people "frame" a conflict as an opportunity to achieve some kind of gain, they tend to use more open communicative strategies; when they "frame" it as an event that may lead to losses, their communicative strategies tend to be less flexible, and the likelihood of reaching an impasse is increased.

Frames also involve a complex set of expectations—about how the parties in a conflict will and should act, what kinds of persuasive strategies can legitimately be used to influence the outcome of the conflict, and how the conflict episode will unfold. For example, employees' perceptions of how well they handled past conflicts seem to influence the way they handle future conflicts. People who expect to handle a conflict well tend to employ more open and cooperative orientations and communication strategies; people who expect that they will not handle conflicts well tend to avoid conflicts or adopt competitive orientations and strategies.

Conflict Interaction

The parties' response to a perceived conflict constitutes conflict interaction. Conflicts are made up of communication, of *interactive* cycles of messages, responses, and counterresponses. Once these cycles commence, their development and outcomes are not within the control of any single participant. A conflict tends to have its own *momentum;* it is a cocreation by the parties and their interpretations, arguments, definitions, and strategies. Parties make choices about how they respond (communicate) based in part on their interpretations of the communicative strategies used by the other parties. They look to the other parties' communication for clues about how they are likely to respond to available communicative strategies. In a real sense, neither party controls interaction during conflict. The interaction often seems to take on a life of its own.

For example, after much delay and the gathering of a great deal of evidence, Elias decided to confront one of his subordinates about his use of illegal drugs. Elias's orientation was collaborative; he wanted to help the man get professional help for what seemed to be a serious addiction and was willing to go to great lengths to see that he could keep his job during and after the treatment. Elias called the worker in and explained his concerns. The worker denied using drugs, which made Elias a little angry; but Elias's emotions were tempered by his knowledge that drug and alcohol addicts almost always deny their dependence. He presented all the evidence that he had collected, assuming that doing so would help facilitate an open and honest discussion of the problem. Suddenly the worker blew up, shouting about Elias's dual standard. Everyone knew, he said, that Elias had taken a three-month leave of absence in 1982 to enter a treatment program for alcoholism after the company had tolerated his tardiness, absenteeism, and excuses for three years.

Elias, he said, had a "lot of gall" confronting him. As suddenly, Elias lost his temper. He had been promised that the referral would be kept secret and thought that it had been. He felt betrayed and projected his quite justifiable anger on the employee. He started screaming too and ended the episode by firing the worker and throwing him out of the office. His intention to be cooperative and collaborative had dissolved during a communicative interaction that he could never have predicted.

In conflicts that have productive outcomes, communication is both flexible and strategic. Parties begin with a wide range of acceptable outcomes and believe that everyone will be able to get something out of the episode (a "win-win" orientation). Initially, all parties generally do (and should) make lengthy statements that clearly state their positions on the key issues and the reasons for those positions (in the jargon of conflict research they *differentiate* their positions from those of the other parties). The parties engage in short cycles of different kinds of communication. Periods of coercion, cooperation, joking, relaxation, threats, and promises are mixed together as the parties move toward a solution that will be mutually acceptable. Of course, the movement is rarely smooth or easy. Tension between the parties' incentives to cooperate and to compete lasts throughout the interaction. As a result, the balance shifts back and forth, and the parties' communication also shifts from cooperative strategies to competitive strategies and back again. As long as it seems that progress is being made, a positive interchange will continue. When the interaction turns in a positive direction, parties respond with supportive statements or tension-reducing strategies, such as jokes, which in turn move the interaction in productive directions.

If, however, one party seems to be excessively stubborn or noncompliant, the other party is likely to shift to more competitive communication strategies, especially if he or she has more power in the organization. If the other party reciprocates, they may both suddenly become trapped in escalating cycles of competitive communication, transforming a productive interaction into a destructive one.[37] It is this fear of uncontrolled escalation that encourages people to try to avoid conflicts. Ironically, avoiding conflicts often tends to make uncontrolled escalation likely, because it allows people to develop a deeply held anger that may explode once a conflict does occur. The same thing may happen if two parties have accommodative orientations and real differences. They tend to repeatedly ignore their problems and over time build up a large reservoir of unexpressed hostility.

In contrast, in *destructive* conflicts, the parties usually begin with a win-lose orientation and view only a small number of outcomes as acceptable. Their communication is rigid and *reflexive* (mirroring the other parties' communication) rather than flexible and strategic.[38] Long periods of competitive strategies dominate the interaction, with few or no periods of joking, relaxation, or cooperation. For example, a labor union that used *Robert's Rules of Order* called a meeting to decide whether to stop work in support of a grievance against the plant's management. Although most of the members favored the proposal, a minority used parliamentary tactics long past the point where the outcome was in any doubt. The longer they argued against the proposal, the more polarized the group became and the more committed the majority became to winning the battle. The dispute left such a bitter legacy that the minority group eventually left the organization. Although the parties' orientations to the conflict set the stage for a destructive escalation, it was their way of communicating that led to a negative outcome.

Avoidant Strategies   Table 9-4 summarizes the communicative strategies that have most often been observed in organizational conflicts.[39] One group of strategies allows parties to *avoid* a divisive issue. Delaying or procrastinating can be overt ("I don't have time to talk about it now") or subtle. Employees can manipulate procedural rules to delay or avoid sustained confrontations. For instance, they can refer an issue to a committee or manipulate agendas so that it is either excluded from the discussion or discussed too late in a session to be

TABLE 9-4
Communication Strategies in Conflicts

Confrontive Strategies	Avoidant Strategies

1. Coercion: Overt Displays of Power
  Formal rank
  Coalitions
  Expertise
	1. Delay/Procrastination
	  Manipulating procedures
	  "Putting off" communication
	  Focusing on rules of interaction

2. Coercion: Threats or Promises	2. Regression

3. Personalization
  Moral accusations
  Ad hominem
  Revelation of secrets
	3. Commitments to revenge

4. Toughness
  Pure form
  Reformed sinner
	4. Refusing to admit existence of conflict

5. Compromise	5. Accommodation
6. Problem solving	
7. Superordinate goal	

taken seriously. Or they can focus the discussion so completely on establishing proper rules of interaction that the issue itself is never addressed. For example, when peace talks started during the Vietnam War, the two sides argued for months about the shape of the bargaining table, the proper display of flags, and rules for speaking times and turns. Although these topics were important for symbolic reasons (round tables symbolize that the participants are of equal status; rectangular tables do not), discussion of them delayed the consideration of key differences.

Sometimes parties regress to childlike tactics or quietly make commitments to "let this one go by but get revenge later on." Commitments to get revenge, silently obsessing about felt conflicts, running away, unproductively worrying, begging, and pouting all are far too common among adults and children alike. Often one or more parties avoid conflicts by refusing to admit that there is an issue between them. They may make statements like "I really think we basically are in agreement on this," or they may transcend to a level at which agreement does exist: "I know we both have the welfare of the students at heart."[40] A final avoidant strategy is accommodation, in which one party avoids the conflict simply by giving in to the other.

Southern High School is a rural school led by a principal who makes virtually every decision and watches teachers and students like a hawk. Like many small, service-oriented organizations, the school had a family atmosphere. However, an issue arose over a failing grade given to an all-state fullback in a required history course. The principal, who was also the football coach, asked the teacher to let the student do some remedial work. When she refused, he quietly changed the student's grade in the main office. Eventually the teacher discovered the change (on Friday night, when she saw the fullback start an important game) and confronted the principal in private. The principal minimized the event, arguing that the fullback would drop out of school if he could not play, and that his dropping out would weaken the teachers' negotiating position in upcoming contract talks. He apologized but argued that for the good of the student and for the good of the family, he had little choice.

Unconvinced, the teacher brought the issue up at the next meeting of the history department. Many of them agreed with the teacher, feeling that all of them had been insulted when the principal went over the teacher's head. They also were concerned about the contract talks, however, and encouraged her to forget the matter. But the anger didn't go away. Eventually the history teachers started to take sides over the issue and fight among themselves over what really were trivial issues. Others became quietly dissatisfied and started to disengage from their work. Morale dropped, as did the quality of teaching. But they did win the state football championship.

The moral of this story is really quite simple. There are cases in which avoidant strategies are productive. Avoidance may be the best response if issues really are trivial, if organizational power relationships make successful resistance impossible, if the parties lack the communication skills necessary to prevent destructive escalation, if the circumstances surrounding the issue are likely to change in ways that will eliminate the bases of the conflict, or if there is insufficient time to work through the issue adequately. But avoidant strategies usually only delay confrontations; they do not manage or resolve differences. When people use avoidant strategies, those who raised the issue are frustrated. They have taken risks without having an opportunity to realize any gains. Consequently, avoidant strategies may only generate hostilities that will come out in conflicts over other issues, making it more difficult to manage those conflicts productively.

Confrontive Strategies   Another approach is to *confront* the conflict directly. Although confrontation sounds competitive, it refers to directly addressing the issues at hand. It can be done in a competitive manner or in an integrative, problem-solving manner. Both competitive and integrative confrontation can work hand in hand: in some cases, for example, to motivate other parties to cooperate in an integrative solution, one must show them that one is willing to compete and will extract considerable costs unless they cooperate.

First, consider the more competitive approaches to confrontation. *Personalization* and *coercion* probably are best known, more because they are so often used than because they are the strategically wisest or most productive. Attacking the *person* of one's opponent(s), especially when the attack impugns morals, reveals secrets, or makes accusations of assorted -isms (racism, sexism, fascism, communism, and so on), denies the opponent any defense except counterattacking or acquiescing. *Coercion* comes in two forms, *overt displays of power* and *threats or promises.*[41] These function in essentially the same way; they depend on the same conditions for their success and are, in effect, two sides of the same coin. Three conditions must be present for coercion, threats, or promises to succeed. First, the *sources* must be perceived to have sufficient organizational power to be able to carry out the threat or promise. The threat or promise must also be communicated in a way that makes the *desired responses clear and specific* and the *consequences of compliance or noncompliance "vivid."* Both "I'm gonna cover you with honey and tie you to a hill of biting red ants in a glaring Arizona sun" and "I'm gonna cover you with whipped cream and . . ." are vivid threats or promises. Finally, the consequence must be *perceived as being fair, equitable, and appropriate to the magnitude of the action that is requested.* Consequences that are either trivial or horrendous compared to the request will not be taken seriously.

Threats are risky because they always insult the other party (although if they are worded as promises, the insult is reduced). They do help the other party understand the threatener's priorities and thus may increase the potential to avoid misunderstandings. The problem with threats and promises is that people's perceptions about what is credible, equitable, fair, and appropriate differ widely. In addition, the *act* of threatening or promising may influence those perceptions in unpredictable ways. Threats and promises tend to provoke counterthreats and promises, creating a sometimes comical response ("My mommy will beat up your daddy"). They often lead to destructive cycles of escalation.

A final competitive strategy is *taking a tough stance.* In its pure form, where all parties initially refuse to concede their positions, it can lead to productive results. Because no party appears to be willing to acquiesce or be intimidated, all parties are forced to take one another seriously and search for a mutually acceptable resolution of their differences. The key is knowing when to make an initial concession. If it is made too early, the other parties will see it as a sign of weakness and become more intransigent. If made too late, the conflict may have already escalated to a destructive level. If two parties are careful not to fall into a cycle of escalation—for example, if each one pauses and thinks strategically for a while before matching the other party's offer—matching can allow both parties to appear simultaneously to be both tough and reasonable.[42]

A more integrative, but related, strategy has been called *playing the reformed sinner.* In the reformed-sinner strategy, one party takes a tough stance until the negotiation reaches an impasse and then makes a significant concession. This signals that the party could compete but is willing to cooperate. Generally the issue on which the concession is made is important but not vital to the party. In societies with strong norms of reciprocity, the act of conceding creates strong psychological pressures for the other parties to concede something in response. In 1982, during the worst housing market in recent memory (mortgage interest rates were around 21 percent), Charley Conrad's wife's career led the Conrads to decide to move. Fortunately, BJ (Charley's wife) had purchased a nice, middle-priced, brick ranch house that had appreciated a bit, thanks primarily to her renovation work. She also had negotiated a 6.5 percent loan that was assumable by any buyer. As long as they asked a somewhat reasonable price, they had a strong negotiating position. Their first potential buyer was a newly hired assistant professor in the psychology department of a major private southeastern university; the person's primary research area was conflict management. This situation created a wonderful opportunity to watch conflict strategies in action.

The assistant professor and his wife said they were delighted with the house but somewhat concerned with the deterioration of an exterior brick staircase into the basement. But they would go home and talk about it and call the next day. Because this concern was over what could be perceived as a major problem but actually was not, it provided an excellent opportunity for the new professor to use the reformed-sinner strategy—taking a tough stance and then conceding on the staircase to force a reciprocal concession on a more important issue, like price. The next day Conrad had two contractors come by and give him written estimates for repairing the stairs ($200 and $800, which should tell you something about why you should always get multiple bids on construction and home repair projects). That night the assistant professor called and explained that they were excited about the house but very concerned about the stairs and what their condition might suggest about the structural integrity of the foundation. They had talked about the problem with his father-in-law, who "knew a lot about construction," and learned that it could cost $4,000 or $5,000 to repair the stairs. So they would be happy to buy the house for $3,000 below the asking price. After the Conrads told the buyer about their written estimates, the buyers quickly agreed that they would love to move in next week (after paying the asking price, of course).

We provide this example for two reasons. One is to explain the reformed-sinner strategy. In studies of conflict and negotiation, it has proved to be a useful strategy for motivating others to shift from competitive to cooperative (integrative) approaches. Another reason is to illustrate that being able to identify the communication strategies that are being used by other parties is often as important as being able to use those strategies oneself. There is substantial evidence that conflicts become destructive when there is a major power imbalance between the parties. Understanding communication strategies in conflicts provides a potent source of power, which can lead to unfair domination of powerless people. Empowerment—the creation of the power balances that generate productive outcomes in conflicts—begins with training all parties in the use of strategic communication.

There are also more cooperative confrontive strategies. One of these is compromise. When parties compromise, they work together to find a resolution that partly satisfies both parties. One common formula for compromise is splitting the difference fifty-fifty. Each party gives up some of what he or she wants in exchange for getting some of what he or she wants. Compromise requires some degree of willingness to sacrifice individual goals, but it also involves some assertiveness in that parties will not settle for a compromise that gives them nothing. It involves more open communication than toughness or the more competitive strategies, but it does not require that parties exchange information fully, because compromises can be reached just by trading offers, and some degree of assertiveness. Compromise is a useful way to resolve conflicts when differences in parties' interests are substantial but there is a balance of power such that neither party can force the other to comply. However, because neither party fully satisfies her or his interests, problems may still remain, and over the long haul parties may become dissatisfied with the resolution.

The most open confrontive strategy is *problem solving,* in which the parties utilize one of the decision-making models defined earlier in this chapter to work jointly through the conflict issues and identify options that meet both parties' needs. Problem solving requires open communication in which parties work to understand one another and conduct an honest search for mutually acceptable solutions. This often requires parties to put aside their initial interpretations of the conflict and to reframe the conflict in a new, different way.

Two counselors in a halfway house, Jeff and Lois, repeatedly engaged in tense confrontations in which each challenged the other's professional competency and blamed the other for problems with residents. When their supervisor sat down to discuss this with Jeff and Lois, it came out that Jeff felt stressed from overwork and wanted a more flexible schedule so he could be with his newborn daughter more. He believed that Lois was being inflexible in drawing up their work schedule. Lois believed that Jeff was trying to take advantage of her and wanted her to take on some of his patients for no extra compensation. These differences were framed in professional terms through questions about handling of patients, which were regarded as legitimate in this organization, rather than in terms of meeting personal needs, which were not regarded as legitimate issues in the halfway house. Once the supervisor had helped Jeff and Lois cut through the "acceptable" framing of the issue and better understand the grounds of their differences, the two developed a solution: Jeff would take a pay cut and work five hours a week less, and Lois would take on some of his patients and work five more paid hours, which she was glad to do.

Problem solving is a very constructive mode of conflict resolution. Successful attempts at problem solving build trust among parties and pave the way for future collaboration. Problem solving also, however, requires a great deal of time and energy, both of which may be in short supply. Furthermore, it is not very effective when parties' interests are mutually inconsistent.

A common strategy for problem solving is to identify a *superordinate goal:* parties find a common goal significant to both that gives them some common ground. A classic experiment by Muzafer Sherif was one of the first studies of this technique.[43] Sherif and his colleagues first created two opposing groups in a summer camp, the Bulldogs and the Red Devils. These groups engaged in a number of competitions, and members developed a strong sense of the value of their own group, while devaluing the competing group. Sherif and colleagues then devised several emergencies that required both groups to work together to overcome problems at the camp. For example, they had to cooperate to get a truck unstuck from the mud. This common activity in service of a valued shared goal significantly reduced competition between the groups, as well as undermining the strong boundaries between them. The superordinate-goal approach works only if the goal is truly desired by both parties and if accomplishing it is beyond the capacities of any single party or group. Moreover, it is not a foolproof integrator: if the parties fail to achieve the superordinate goal, they may go back to blaming one another for the failure, polarizing even more.

In some cultures, confrontive strategies are not as highly valued as they are in the United States. In some non-Western cultures saving face, preserving the honor and self-esteem associated with one's position in the social order, is a primary concern in conflict management. Stella Ting-Toomey has described the complicated face-saving system that characterizes Japanese approaches to conflict management. One principle of this system is the concept of *Nemawashi,* the subtle process of achieving consensus and support for a proposal. Extensive informal communication eventually involves every relevant member of the organization but never includes a "group confrontation" in which everyone meets in a formal negotiating session. Another principle is the Ringi System, a way of preventing open conflicts by circulating a document widely and getting everyone's seal of approval. This system diffuses responsibility and saves face for those people who initially may oppose the proposal, and it saves face for everyone, should the proposal fail. A third principle is the go-between system, in which people with different opinions seek out a third party to mediate. This complex, time-consuming, indirect system of conflict management is appropriate for Japanese organizations because the demands and constraints of Japanese culture make it more important to prevent conflicts than to manage them in the open.[44]

In summary, conflicts do not consist of one party, using one strategy. They are made of interactions, of patterns of communication, response, and counterresponse. In *productive conflicts* these patterns comprise numerous brief episodes during which the parties adopt a wide range of strategies. Coercion, threats, promises, redefinition, relational comments, digressions, joking, and relaxing are intermixed in a variety of proportions. No single strategy takes over; no sustained cycle of threat and counterthreat, coercion and regression distorts parties' perceptions or clouds their analysis of the situation. In *destructive conflicts* a narrow range of communicative strategies is used. Escalating cycles of threat, coercion, expansion of issues, and personalization lock parties into competitive, zero-sum patterns of interaction. Sometimes—perhaps often—destructive cycles are accidentally initiated by more powerful employees. They misperceive less powerful people as jealous, resentful, or hostile, and they overreact, adopting confrontive, competitive strategies when other approaches would have been more appropriate. Or they inadvertently place weaker people in positions where they feel they must either fight or be humiliated. But conflict cycles are never under any one member's control. It is the participants' ability to manage and control tendencies for escalation that determines whether a conflict will be productive or destructive.

CASE STUDY
The Bargaining Case

Bargaining is a special kind of conflict management. It looks like compromise, but it involves negotiating shared rules and cooperation within these rules to gain a competitive advantage. It focuses on the exchange of formal offers; but making offers is only one kind of communicative interaction in bargaining sessions. As Chapter 1 explains, a major function of communication is the creation of "realities" that guide and constrain further communication. But "realities" are constantly changing throughout processes of communicative interaction. These processes—and the way in which "history" is defined and redefined through communication—are illustrated nicely in the following case of bargaining between teachers and the school board in a small rural, midwestern district. This account is based on the research of Linda Putnam and her associates.*

The state teachers association provided the 133 teachers with a professional bargainer, Doug. The school board hired its own pro. Usually teacher bargaining (and most formal labor-management negotiation) is limited to an exchange of money (salaries and fringe benefits) versus teachers' control over their working conditions. The teachers' "reality-creation" process involved three stories (see Chapter 5). One story was about "the bad old days" of bargaining. For years the two sides had experienced hostile bargaining: long and heated arguments over rules of negotiation, threats, fist-pounding, name-calling, and refusals to settle had dominated yearly discussions. One year the two sides' initial offers were thinly veiled insults: the board offered a one-dollar raise; the teachers demanded a 25 percent increase. Four years ago the hostility erupted into a strike.

The townspeople supported the teachers—telephoning the board members at home and insulting and haranguing them as they walked down the streets. But the story the teachers told one another was about the immaturity that they had shown during the strike. They prided themselves in their newfound maturity, which essentially meant that they would now cooperate with the board and do everything possible to avoid another strike. Their reasoning was simple and self-fulfilling: We must avoid antagonistic bargaining because it could result in a strike, which is unacceptable because it would show that we are immature bargainers. Because we have matured, we will not strike. Of course, accepting this story eliminated the only threat the teachers had; but it created a comfortable reality that would guide and constrain their communication.

The second story was about Doug. He had started working with the teachers during the strike, and although no one remembered exactly what he did to achieve it, he negotiated an acceptable settlement. Telling this story reinforced the teachers' trust for Doug and led them to accept his goals, strategies, and decisions throughout the negotiation. Doug told the third story. He had faced Jim, the board's pro, many times in the past and found him to be "a bear" on power issues—he just would not give in on these issues. The teachers adapted the story and applied it to their board. One said, "It'll be a cold day in hell before that board will give us any policy issues (control)." The fact that Doug failed to tell them that their district was far behind the other districts in the state in terms of teacher control of working conditions added to the power of the story. So the teachers decided to introduce power issues but drop them early during the bargaining. Unfortunately, the "reality" they had created was inaccurate. Jim had advised the board to be ready to give up some policy issues to minimize financial costs in the new contract. In fact, the board was surprised when Doug dropped these items; but of course it had no reason to say so.

The teachers told and retold these three stories throughout the bargaining session. They asked for, and thus received, less than they could have gotten. But they communicated in a way that maintained the reality that they had created—they behaved maturely, reached an acceptable settlement (70–75 percent of the teachers supported the final contract), and avoided a strike. Of course, if you consider only the offers they made and accepted, they took a very soft bargaining position. But they compensated for that kind of softness through a ritual that proved they were tough negotiators. Negotiations regularly continued night after night, extending into the early morning hours. The bargaining team even enjoyed going to breakfast together after a long night of negotiations, arriving at school just in time to go to class. This ritual, repeated every year, proved to the negotiators and the other teachers that their representatives were tough bargainers. (Sometimes late-night negotiations are more than ritual. Charley Conrad once was on a teacher bargaining committee that stayed late to exhaust the opposition. We enlarged the teachers' committee so that no one member had to attend more than one late-night meeting, knowing that the school board did not have this flexibility. After five weeks of negotiating, when rumor had it that four board members were on the verge of divorce, we obtained what we wanted: the transfer of a much-hated principal and the largest salary increase in the district's history. But that was a different situation, a very different "reality.")

Applying What You've Learned

1. How did the parties' definitions of "reality" influence communication? The relative power of the bargainers?
2. In this situation, could an individual teacher or member have argued successfully for taking a tougher negotiating position?

Questions to Think About and Discuss

1. What functions did the "staying-all-night" ritual play in addition to demonstrating toughness?

(continued)

(Case Study, continued)

2. What long-term effects is this negotiation likely to have on the teachers' perceptions of reality? Doug's image and role? the board's negotiating strategies? the outcomes of subsequent negotiations?

---

*See similar analyses in the following papers and publications: Linda Putnam and Shirley Van Hoeven, "Teacher Bargaining as a Cultural Rite of Conflict Reduction," paper presented at the Central States Speech Association Convention, Cincinnati, Ohio, 1986; Linda Putnam and Shirley Van Hoeven, "The Role of Narrative in Teachers' Bargaining," paper presented at the Temple University "Discourse Conference on Conflict Intervention," Philadelphia, 1987; Linda Putnam, Shirley Van Hoeven, and Connie Bullis, "The Role of Rituals and Fantasy Themes in Teachers' Bargaining," *Western Journal of Speech Communication* 55 (1991): 85–103; and Linda Putnam, *Negotiation of Intergroup Conflict in Organizations,* Hallie Mande Neff Wilcox Published Lecture (Waco, TX: Baylor University, 1987).

The Aftermath of Conflicts

The final phase is the **aftermath** of the conflict. Two criteria are appropriate for evaluating the short-term effects of conflicts: the quality of the final decision and the effect of the conflict on working relationships. If a sensible solution emerges that meets the needs of every party or is supported by a legitimate consensus, the short-term effects will be positive. However, such integrative solutions are difficult to reach, and consensus is often elusive. In fact, in many cases a conflict will move from issue to issue with no real resolution. When new issues arise, the same patterns of communicative interaction recur.[45]

The more common modes of managing conflicts—compromise, majority vote, and acquiescence by one or more parties—leave residual frustrations that prompt future conflicts and complicate their management. Similarly, the dynamics of conflict episodes may leave behind changed perceptions of each party, unmanaged emotions, and commitments to get revenge, all of which influence working relationships. If they are repeated often, escalating conflicts may lead employees to view their relationships with one another as competitive rather than cooperative. Because their tasks are interdependent, competitive relationships may undermine the participants' performance and the organization's success.[46]

This potential for long-term negative effects on working relationships has led many organizations to use formal procedures and make structural changes to minimize the impact of unproductive conflicts. Some have tried to reduce unit or employee interdependence, both to minimize the number of issues over which differences might occur and to decrease the adverse effects of long-term relational problems. But interdependence cannot be reduced beyond a certain point, and when it is reduced, the parties' incentives to cooperate with one another are also reduced. Other organizations appoint formal conflict managers or establish formal procedures for handling even minor disagreements. Third-party interventions *can* prevent escalation, as long as the third party is skilled in conflict management and has sufficient formal power.[47] Formal rules and procedures can structure conflicts in ways that reduce ambiguity and prevent the use of the communication strategies that prompt escalation. Although there are limits to the effectiveness of structural changes, their use accents the need to evaluate the productiveness of each episode within the long-term perspective of the organization's operation.

Conflicts can be valuable and productive for organizations and employees alike. For organizations, conflict can stimulate creative problem solving; it can generate or publicize superior ideas and adjust perceived power relationships to better fit the skills and abilities of employees. For individual employees, conflict can provide opportunities to test, expand, and demonstrate their skills; better understand their organizations; and develop their self-esteem and confidence. If conflicts are kept within civil bounds and if satisfactory solutions to problems can be found, the total impact of each conflict can be positive.

Two implications emerge from the preceding discussion. First, organizational conflicts must be evaluated in terms of many considerations. Open conflicts are invariably disruptive and leave behind negative legacies. But their impact on the long-term effectiveness of the organization may, on balance, be favorable. Attempting to suppress or repress conflicts often damages organizations more than allowing them to surface and be managed. Second, controlling processes of escalation is the key to productive conflict management. The aftermath of organizational conflicts depends on maintaining patterns of communication that allow people to simultaneously demonstrate their competencies and solve problems. Escalation robs the participants of these opportunities and establishes the bases of nonproductive legacies. The strategic use of communication is the key to productive conflict management.

Organizational Dispute Resolution Systems

Conflict is so common in organizations that they typically develop characteristic procedures or structures for handling it. William L. Ury, Jeanne M. Brett, and Stephen B. Goldberg argue that the structure and culture of organizations influence the development of their **dispute resolution systems,** their preferred ways of managing conflicts.[48] Some organizations have formally established dispute resolution systems, such as a grievance procedure or a mediation program. Other organizations rely on informal dispute management systems; they may let it fall to managers to handle conflicts. Some dispute resolution systems, such as the courts or community mediation services, are provided by the government or the larger community.

Three types of dispute management systems can be distinguished in U.S. organizations. *Interest-based* dispute resolution systems attempt to help parties find a resolution that satisfies their needs or interests. One example of a formal interest-based system is the dispute mediation services that are increasingly being implemented in large organizations. For example, the University of Michigan has an Office of Dispute Mediation where parties can file formal cases that go through a multistep conflict management procedure. Interest-based systems tend to favor the problem-solving and compromising styles.

Rights-based dispute resolution systems attempt to determine which party's position is more valid based on independent standards that parties accept as legitimate and fair. The legal code is one such standard. Another type of standard is a socially accepted norm, such as seniority or equity. The most familiar rights-based dispute resolution system is the courts of law, in which a judge or jury determines the correct outcome based on arguments and evidence from the parties. Participating in this system requires the assistance of an attorney, because its procedures are so technical and complex. However, a manager who stops an argument over a new computer between two employees by giving it to the more senior employee is also engaged in rights-based dispute resolution. Rights-based dispute resolution systems tend to promote competitive and compromise conflict strategies. Parties make their best cases to the adjudicator—whether judge, parent, or manager—and rely on him or her to make the call. And if parties are fearful that the decision will not go their way, they may reach a side agreement before the rights-based adjudication is final.

In *power-based* dispute resolution systems, each party attempts to coerce the other into doing what the party wants. Examples of power-based dispute resolution are strikes by workers and lockouts by employers, a manager ordering an employee to do a task the employee finds unpleasant, and one employee browbeating another into doing what he wants. Power-based dispute resolution tends to occur in the absence of interest- and rights-based systems. It is the "default" mode of dispute resolution in most organizations. In power-based systems, competing, avoiding, and accommodating styles are most common.

The three dispute resolution systems are not necessarily independent of one another. Rights-based systems often evolve to correct for the problems and abuses of power-based systems. For example, the labor mediation system evolved because of the damage caused by strikes and labor-management conflict. Interest-based dispute resolution systems are often established as alternatives or supplements to rights-based systems. Today mediation is commonly offered as an alternative to trial in divorce courts, on the grounds that it offers both parties a chance to satisfy their interests, whereas a judge's or jury's decision may favor the interests of one side over the other.

Ury, Brett, and Goldberg's research suggested that in most organizations the majority of conflicts are handled through power-based approaches, a goodly portion through rights-based approaches, and the least number through interest-based approaches. In organizations that do not have formal interest-based systems or organizational cultures that encourage interest-based approaches, power-based and rights-based conflict management will prevail. Even in organizations with formal dispute resolution systems, power-based approaches are common. Parties may fear being labeled as trouble makers if they formally complain or as incompetent for not being able to manage their own affairs. Those with power may avoid formal systems because they believe they can get their way in any case and that the formal system may not decide in their favor.

Ury, Brett, and Goldberg recommend that organizations try to change so that they manage most of their conflicts using interest-based approaches. This may require not only establishing a formal dispute resolution system based on problem solving, but also changing the organization's culture and employee attitudes. Organizational dispute resolution practices generally develop gradually over the years and are grounded in deep-seated habits of thought and action.

For example, Bryant High School in Oakland, California, implemented a mediation program to help students manage conflicts more constructively. Tension and violence among students and between students and teachers were growing increasingly common at Bryant, and its administration decided to implement the mediation program to defuse a potentially dangerous situation. A major barrier to the success of the mediation program was lack of communication, negotiation, and problem-solving skills among students. One student put it this way: "All I ever wanted to do was fight. If someone said something to me I didn't like, I didn't think about talking, I just thought about fighting."[49] To bring about a change, the school undertook a major training effort, providing workshops and classes in problem-solving and nonviolence techniques to more than three thousand students and staff. The workshops were designed to develop attitudes and skills that promoted nonviolent dispute resolution. After several years of training and demonstration projects, the mediation program was successfully implemented. It is used to manage a significant number of conflicts, and violence has been reduced at Bryant.

A Feminist View of Communication and Conflict

Linda Putnam and Deborah M. Kolb recently articulated a **feminist approach** to conflict and negotiation that represents a significant departure from the approach to conflict taken so far in this chapter.[50] Traditional perspectives on negotiation and conflict management rest on a limited set of basic assumptions about the nature of conflict, negotiation, and conflict management. This set of assumptions and related understandings reflects the predominant perspective in the United States and Western Europe. It underlies almost all the hundreds of studies and books that have been published on conflict in the past forty-five years. Those assumptions are as follows:

1. The goal of parties in conflict is mutual gain that helps them achieve their interests.
2. Conflicts are best managed through setting up conditions whereby parties can make tradeoffs that enable them to realize their goals. The ultimate outcomes of conflicts should be assessed in terms of winning and losing, with the preferred outcome being win-win results (that is, all parties gain).
3. Relationships between parties in conflicts are seen in terms of one party related to another with different interests. Parties view each other

instrumentally, in terms of how they are either a barrier against or means for achieving their goals. Trust, which refers to the degree to which parties uphold their agreed-upon bargains, is a critical dimension of relationships.

4. Conflict management and negotiation occur in the form of proposals and counterproposals, with each side suggesting courses of action that benefit its own interests. The conflict is regarded as a problem that must be solved by the parties who are in conflict or by third parties brought in to help them reach an acceptable resolution.

5. Communication in conflicts functions largely to exchange information about parties' positions and interests that can be used to develop a final solution. Communication should play a largely informational role in effective conflict management and should not inflame the situation by injecting counterproductive emotions.

Like all accepted assumptions, this frame automatically excludes other legitimate perspectives. Based on feminist perspectives, Putnam and Kolb argue that the goal of conflict management and negotiation can be more than achieving a mutually beneficial outcome in the short term. It also can transform a situation so that parties understand themselves and their world better and develop stronger relationships for the long term. This alternative view criticizes the traditional perspective on conflict for its short-sighted and overly narrow focus on satisfying immediate interests. Instead, the alternative view would advocate that the entire point of engaging in conflict and negotiation is not simply to fulfill immediate needs, but to work toward a better life. Focus on immediate needs may in fact detract from bettering oneself.

For example, in the bargaining case, introduced previously, the negotiators took a traditional approach to their conflict, assuming that it had to be settled in terms of a contract addressing the issues that the parties thought important. Doug and Jim worked out a contract that resulted in a mutually acceptable solution. However, as the case shows, the stories the teachers told themselves led them finally to obtain less than they might have. Consider what might have happened if the parties had taken the alternative view offered here: They would not have focused on immediate, concrete issues, but rather on the nature of the relationship between teachers and the board. Both parties would have entered the negotiation interested in improving their relationship and in understanding the best ways to educate children. This would have eventually led the discussion to the degree of control teachers should have over working conditions. Teachers would likely have argued that they needed more control over their work to have the flexibility needed to meet student needs. The board would have had to face the hard fact that though keeping control was comfortable for them, the degree of control they had was probably too great. The end result might have been that the board granted the teachers more control. The teachers' respect for the board would have increased because it was giving up something that gave it a clear advantage. This admittedly hypothetical discussion could not have occurred if the parties had restricted themselves to talking about issues only, because control over work would have been reduced to an issue—recall that this is exactly how Doug had treated it—and therefore as something to trade away or win rather than discuss.

The longer-term, more general goals of the alternative perspective imply that the ultimate end of negotiation is not a settlement of immediate issues, but instead transformation of the situation and the people in it. Conflict and negotiation aim to transform the situation by creating new understandings and new ways for members to work together. They aim to transform the parties by giving them insights into themselves, insights into how they are contributing to the conflict and how they might change to improve the situation, and also deeper insights that help them live their lives better. The emphasis shifts from winning and losing to how to develop actions that parties can undertake together to move to a new level of collaboration. It also assumes that there may be no fundamentally opposed interests, in the sense that novel, transforming actions may allow seemingly different interests to be reconciled. In our hypothetical extension of the bargaining case, this is exactly what would happen. Through open discussion, parties come to understand each other better and see the situation differently. The result in this case would be that the board of its own accord would give up some of its power, thus fundamentally transforming how education occurred in the district. Such a resolution of the conflict would also fundamentally transform and build the relationship between teachers and board.

In the bargaining case the board and the teachers—through their intermediary bargainers Doug and Jim—viewed each other in instrumental terms. Each saw the other as someone who could be convinced or enticed to give in on one or more issues of interest or, if the worst happened, as a barrier to achieving their ends. Trust had been achieved between Doug and Jim; but it was not a trust based on appreciation of each other and on the importance of the relationship between board and teachers; instead, their trust was based on living up to prior commitments on issues and on a contract hammered out in the negotiations. On the alternative view of conflict, the board and the teachers would try to understand each other's motivations and needs, not with an aim of finding out what sort of offer to make, but with true concern for the others as people each group had a long-term relationship with. Their communication would not aim at finding points of agreement, but at understanding the other side and at figuring out how to improve the current situation and relationship. This could then be the basis for future cooperation that went well beyond the immediate contract negotiations.

Conflict management and negotiation are viewed as problem-solving processes in the traditional perspective: each side has to define the requirements for a good solution, and these then constitute a problem that the sides have to solve by finding a course of action that meets the requirements. The alternative perspective would not give problem solving primacy, but rather dialogue between the parties whereby they communicate with each other with the goal of achieving understanding and transformation. This communication might take the form of a deep I-and-thou discussion in which parties bare their souls; but it could also be more restrained as parties regard their counterpart as other and try to appreciate this other from their own point of view. Once effective communication has been established, the best course of joint action might simply suggest itself in the flow of discussion. Problem solving would be reserved for jointly defined issues that did not have readily apparent solutions.[51]

In the bargaining case the teachers and the board might have promoted communication by demoting (in a sense) their professional bargainers to be members of a team of people who met in an open communication forum to simply discuss their points of view. The goal of this forum would be to understand, not to solve things or define problems, or to reach any other instrumental goal. Simple understanding would be the goal, and it would be expected that this understanding would lead to sympathetic interactions that would generate joint actions endorsed by all parties.

The alternative, feminist view of conflict is fundamentally different from the confrontive, problem-oriented "let's-make-a-deal" traditional approach. In fact, it is so different that it may seem utopian in a world full of hard bargainers. However, traditional strategies often fail. Instead of leading to mutually acceptable outcomes, they often produce conflict situations that are increasingly difficult to resolve. The intransigence and polarization that results often has disastrous consequences for organizations and for their employees. Perhaps a different perspective is needed, one that would not make it more difficult to manage conflicts by restricting the flexibility of negotiators. Unfortunately, the traditional perspective is so deeply embedded in the political, societal, and legal context surrounding organizations that it is difficult to implement or even imagine any alternative. But in an era of globalization, when alternative forms of organizing are rapidly emerging, alternative forms of conflict management may be viable. For example, the alternative perspective seems particularly well suited for the network strategies of organizing described in Chapter 6. In these organizations, open communication and the establishment of long-term relationships is of fundamental importance. In view of the complexity of their structures and how often they must change them, network organizations are best coordinated in exactly the sort of communicative exchanges that the alternative model envisions. This enables them to continuously improve and address the actual, often ill-defined problems the network encounters, rather than simply react to well-defined issues handed down from previous groups and leaders.

Summary: Communication and Conflict

Conflicts are inevitable parts of organizational life. Whenever people depend on one another and interact with one another, grounds for cooperation and competition exist. Although there is substantial evidence that it is counterproductive to try to avoid or suppress conflicts, especially in the long term, our fear of conflict escalation and the accepted assumptions of some organizational cultures make it difficult to deal with conflicts openly and productively. Fortunately, a wide variety of communicative strategies are available to employees before and during overt conflicts. Understanding those strategies and using them *strategically* determines whether a particular conflict will be productive or destructive.

Conclusion

Organizational decision making and conflict management involve the pursuit of impossible dreams. The long-standing ideal of decision making—perfect rationality—is extremely difficult to attain. Individual, group, and organizational limitations set up powerful barriers to rational decision making. The ideal goal of conflict management—a resolution that meets the needs of all parties—is equally difficult. Individual tendencies, unfortunate framings, preexisting power relations, and lack of imagination work against problem solving. In both cases, our organizations rarely live up to expectations.

What then, should we do? Some would argue that we should be realistic and set our sights on other goals—to make decisions that are good enough and make adjustments later on or to resolve conflicts in ways that enable us to go on with our work and lives. Others would argue that, despite the fact that the goals of rationality and complete resolution of conflicts are rarely realized, they still represent worthy targets that we should shoot for.

What do you think?

Notes

[1] Dennis Mumby and Linda Putnam, "The Politics of Emotion," *Academy of Management Review* 17 (1992): 465–487. For a summary of research on nonrational aspects of organizational decision making, see Kathleen Sutcliffe, "Organizational Environments and Organizational Information Processing," in *The New Handbook of Organizational Communication,* Fredric Jablin and Linda Putnam, eds. (Thousand Oaks, CA: Sage, 2000); and Philippe Baumard, *Tacit Knowledge in Organizations* (London: Sage, 1999).

[2] James March and Herbert Simon, "The Concept of Rationality," in *Human Behavior and International Politics,* David Singer, ed. (Chicago: Rand-McNally, 1965), p. 343.

[3] Karl Weick, *The Social Psychology of Organizing,* 2nd ed. (Reading, MA: Addison-Wesley, 1979); and *Sense-Making in Organizations* (Thousand Oaks, CA: Sage, 1995); James March and Johann Olson, *Ambiguity and Choice in Organizations* (Bergen, Norway: Universitetsforlaget, 1970); and G. Westerlund and S. Sjostrand, *Organizational Myths* (New York: Harper and Row, 1979). These four works are important sources for the ideas presented in the remainder of this chapter.

[4] This survey is based largely on Randy Hirokawa and Marshall Scott Poole, eds., *Communication and Group Decision Making,* 2nd ed. (Thousand Oaks, CA: Sage, 1996). For more extensive summaries of research, see Randy Y. Hirokawa and Abran J. Salazar, "Task-Group Communication and Decision-Making Performance" in *Handbook of Group Communication Theory and Research,* Larry Frey, Dennis Gouran, and Marshall Scott Poole, eds. (Newbury Park, CA: Sage, 1999).

[5] Marshall Scott Poole and Carolyn Baldwin, "Developmental Processes in Group Decision-Making," in Hirokawa and Poole, 2nd ed. Also see Marshall Scott Poole, "Decision Development in Small Groups," parts I, II, and III, in *Communication Monographs* 48 (1981): 1–24; 50 (1983): 206–232; and 50 (1983): 321–341; and Henry Mintzberg, Duru Raisinghani, and Andre Theoret, "The Structure of 'Unstructured' Decision Processes," *Administrative Science Quarterly* 21 (1976): 246–275.

[6] Dennis Gouran and Randy Hirokawa, "Functional Theory and Communication in Decision-Making and Problem-Solving Groups: An Expanded Perspective," in Hirokawa and Poole, 2nd ed.

[7] Hirokawa and Poole, 2nd ed., p. 105. Also see Ernest Bormann, "Symbolic Convergence Theory and Communication in Group Decision-Making," in Hirokawa and Poole, 2nd ed.

[8] David Seibold and Renee Meyers, "Communication and Influence in Group Decision-Making," in Hirokawa and Poole, 2nd ed. Also see Tim Cline and Rebecca Cline, "Risky and Cautious Decision Shifts in Small Groups," *Southern Speech Communication Journal* 44 (1979): 252-263; S. M. Alderton and Larry Frey, "Effects of Reactions to Arguments on Group Outcomes," *Central States Speech Journal* 34 (1983): 88-95; and Frank Boster and Michael Mayer, "Differential Argument Quality Mediates the Impact of Social Comparison Process of the Choice Shift," paper presented at the International Communication Association Convention, San Francisco, May 1984; Irving Janis, *Victims of Groupthink* (Boston: Houghton Mifflin, 1972); "Sources of Error in Strategic Decision-Making," in *Organizational Strategy and Change,* Johannes Pennings and associates, eds. (San Francisco: Jossey-Bass, 1985); and Irving Janis and L. Mann, *Decision Making* (New York: Free Press, 1977).

[9] Julia Wood, Gerald Phillips, and Douglas Pederson, *Group Discussion,* 2nd ed. (New York: Harper and Row, 1989), p. 103.

[10] Nancy Harper and L. Askling, "Group Communication and Quality of Task Solution in a Media Production Organization," *Communication Monographs* 47 (1980): 77-100; Thomas Schidel, "Divergent and Convergent Thinking in Group Decision-Making," in *Communication and Group Decision-Making,* Randy Y. Hirokawa and Marshall Scott Poole, eds., 1st ed. (Thousand Oaks, CA: Sage, 1986); Randy Y. Hirokawa and Dirk Scheerhorn, "Communication in Faulty Group Decision Making," in Hirokawa and Poole, 1st ed.; Harold Guetzkow and J. Gyr, "An Analysis of Conflict in Decision-Making Groups," *Human Relations* 7 (1954): 367-381.

[11] Gouran and Hirokawa, p. 61.

[12] Many such procedures are available, including brainstorming, Nominal Group Technique, and Multi-Attribute Decision Making. See Susan Jarboe, "Procedures for Enhancing Group Decision Making," in Hirokawa and Poole, 2nd ed., for a good introduction and references to various group decision-making procedures.

[13] Karl Weick and Larry Browning, "Argument and Narration in Organizational Communication," *Journal of Management* 12 (1986): 243-259. For a comparison of individual and organizational decision making, see C. R. Schwenk and M. A. Lyles, "Top Management, Strategy, and Organizational Knowledge Structures," *Journal of Management Studies* 29 (1992): 155-174.

[14] Linda L. Putnam and Deborah M. Kolb, "Rethinking Negotiation," in *Rethinking Organizational and Managerial Communication from Feminist Perspectives* (Thousand Oaks, CA: Sage, 2000).

[15] Markus Vodosek and Kathleen Sutcliffe, "Overemphasis on Analysis," in *Pressing Problems in Modern Organizations (That Keep Us Up at Night),* Robert Quinn, R. M. O'Neill, and L. St. Clair, eds. (New York: American Management Association, 2000).

[16] The chess example is from A. Newell and Herbert Simon, *Human Problem Solving* (Englewood Cliffs, NJ: Prentice Hall, 1972). Memory and managerial decision making are examined by Kathleen Sutcliffe in "Commentary on Strategic Sensemaking," in *Advances in Strategic Management,* J. Walsh and A. Huff, eds. (Greenwich, CT: JAI Press, 1997). Also see Henry Mintzberg, *The Rise and Fall of Strategic Planning* (New York: Free Press, 1994); and Vodosek and Sutcliffe.

[17] Weick, *Sense-Making,* p. 60.

[18] Charles O'Reilly, "Variations in Decision-Makers' Use of Information Sources," *Academy of Management Journal* 25 (1982): 756-771. Analyses of how acting changes situations are available in Marshall Scott Poole and Andrew Van de Ven, "Using Paradox to Build Management and Organization Theories." *Academy of Management Review* 14 (1995): 562-578; and Andrew Van de Ven and M. S. Poole, "Explaining Development and Change in Organizations," *Academy of Management Review* 20 (1995): 510-540.

[19] Alan Teger, *Too Much Invested to Quit* (New York: Pergamon, 1980); M. Cohen, J. March, and J. Olson, "A Garbage-Can Model of Organizational Choice," *Administrative Science Quarterly* 17 (1972): 2.

[20] Weick, *Social Psychology.*

[21] Cohen, March, and Olson; O'Reilly; and Richard Butler, David Hickson, David Wilson, and R. Axelsson, "Organizational Power, Politicking, and Paralysis," *Organizational and Administrative Sciences* 8 (1977): 44-59. For a revision of the original garbage-can model, see Michael Masuch and Perry LaPotin, "Beyond Garbage Cans," *Administrative Science Quarterly* 34 (1989): 38-68.

[22] Richard Butler, Graham Astley, David Hickson, Geoffrey Mallory, and David Wilson, "Strategic Decision Making in Organizations," *International Studies of Management and Organization* 23 (1980): 234-249. The example is based on George Farris, "Groups and the Informal Organization," in *Groups at Work,* Roy Payne and Cary Cooper, eds. (New York: Wiley, 1981).

[23] Weick, *Social Psychology,* p. 10. The first four of the functions noted in subsequent sentences of the text are discussed by Weick; the fifth is drawn from C. Lindblom, "The Science of Muddling Through," *Public Administration Review* 19 (1959): 412-421.

[24] Tom Peters and Nancy Austin, *A Passion for Excellence* (New York: Random House, 1985).

[25] Lindblom. Henry Mintzberg and Alexandra McHugh, "Strategy Formation in an Adhocracy," *Administrative Science Quarterly* 30 (1985): 160-197, provide an excellent example of a successful "muddling through" organization.

[26] Weick, *Social Psychology;* and *Sense-Making.*

[27] Of course, our brief summary oversimplifies Meyer's research. See Alan Meyer, "Mingling Decision-Making Metaphors," *Academy of Management Review* 9 (1984): 231-246. Karl Weick takes an even more explicit position, concluding that a search for "accurate" conclusions sacrifices commitment and motivation. *Sense-Making,* p. 60.

[28] James March, "The Technology of Foolishness," in *Ambiguity and Choice in Organizations,* James March and Johann Olson, eds. (Bergen, Norway: Universitetsforlaget, 1970). Also see Michael Cohen and James March, *Leadership and Ambiguity,* 2nd ed. (Boston: Harvard Business School Press, 1974). Harrison Trice and Janice Beyer take an even more direct position, arguing that rationality is *the* core assumption of organizations in Western societies, including the United States. See *The Cultures of Work Organizations* (Englewood Cliffs, NJ: Prentice Hall, 1993), especially chapter 2.

[29] This section is based primarily on four sources: Louis Pondy, "Organizational Conflict: Concepts and Models," *Administrative Science Quarterly* 12 (1967): 296-320; Morton Deutsch, *The Resolution of Conflict* (New Haven, CT: Yale University Press, 1973); Linda Putnam, "Conflict and Dispute Management," in *The New Handbook of Organizational Communication,* Fredric Jablin and Linda Putnam, eds. (Thousand Oaks, CA: Sage, 1997); and Joseph Folger, Marshall Scott Poole, and Randall Stutman, *Working through Conflict,* 5th ed. (New York: Longman, 2004).

[30] Stella Ting-Toomey, "Toward a Theory of Conflict and Culture," in *Communication and Culture,* William Gudykunst, ed. (Beverly Hills, CA: Sage, 1985).

[31] Putnam, "Conflict and Dispute Management"; Charles Franz and K. Gregory Jin, "The Structure of Group Conflict in a Collaborative Work Group during Information Systems Development," *Journal of Applied Communication Research* 23 (1995): 108-127.

[32] Pondy, "Organizational Conflict." For an excellent summary of phase models and their strengths and weaknesses, see Linda Putnam, "Reframing Integrative and Distributive Bargaining," in *Research on Negotiation in Organizations,* Blair Shepard, M. Bazerman, and R. Lewicki, eds., vol. 2 (Greenwich, CT: JAI Press, 1990); Michael Holmes, "Phase Structure in Negotiation," in *Communication and Negotiation,* L. Putnam and M. Roloff, eds. (Newbury Park, CA: Sage, 1993). A number of phase models are summarized in Folger, Poole, and Stutman.

[33] See Folger, Poole, and Stutman, chapter 1.

[34] Psychological models of conflict call this process "displacement" (see Folger, Poole, and Stutman). It is examined at length later in this chapter, in "The Bargaining Case" and in the section entitled "The Aftermath of Conflicts." Also see Steven R. Wilson, "Face and Facework in Negotiation," in *Communication and Negotiation,* L. Putnam and M. Roloff, eds. (Newbury Park, CA: Sage, 1993). An excellent book on mediation that points to its transformative potential is R. Baruch Bush and Joseph P. Folger, *The Promise of Mediation: Responding to Conflict through Empowerment and Recognition* (San Francisco: Jossey-Bass, 1994).

[35] M. Neale and M. Bazerman, *Cognition and Rationality in Negotiations* (New York: Free Press, 1991).

[36] T. Simons, "Speech Patterns and the Concept of Utility in Cognitive Maps," *Academy of Management Journal* 36 (1993): 139-156. An excellent summary of frame-oriented conflict research is available in Linda Putnam and Majia Holmer, "Framing and Reframing," in *Communication and Negotiation,* L. Putnam and M. Roloff, eds. (Newbury Park, CA: Sage, 1993). For summaries of the impact that frames have on conflict behavior, see R. Fisher and W. Ury, *Getting to Yes* (Boston: Houghton Mifflin, 1981); Linda Putnam, S. Wilson, and D. Turner, "The Evolution of Policy Arguments in Teachers' Bargaining," *Argumentation* 4 (1990): 129-152; Daniel Canary and Brian Spitzberg, "A Model of the Perceived Competence of Conflict Strategies," *Human Communication Research* 15 (1990): 630-649; and Putnam, "Reframing."

[37] W. L. Felsteiner, R. L. Abel, and A. Sarat, "The Emergence and Transformation of Disputes," *Law and Society Review* 33 (1980-1981): 631-654; Putnam, "Reframing."

[38] Timothy Leary, *Interpersonal Diagnosis of Personality* (New York: Ronald, 1957); Kenneth Thomas and Richard Walton, *Conflict-Handling Behavior in Interdepartmental Relations* (Los Angeles: UCLA Graduate School of Business Administration, 1971).

[39] This summary is based on a number of sources. The most important are Alan Sillars, "Stranger and Spouse as Target Persons for Compliance-Gaining Strategies," *Human Communication Research* 6 (1980): 265-279; Bertram Raven and Arie Kruglanski, "Power and Conflict," in *The Structure of Conflict,* Paul Swingle, ed. (New York: Academic Press, 1970); and Folger, Poole, and Stutman.

[40] David F. Bush, "Passive-Aggressive Behavior in the Business Setting," in *Passive-Aggressiveness,* Richard Parsons and Robert Wicks, eds. (New York: Brunner-Mazel, 1983). Also see Deborah Kolb, ed., *Hidden Conflict in Organizations* (Newbury Park, CA: Sage, 1991). The list of regressive strategies is taken from Michael Roloff, "Roloff's Modes of Conflict Resolution and Their Items," in *Explorations in Interpersonal Communication,* Gerald Miller, ed. (Beverly Hills, CA: Sage, 1976).

[41] Julia Wood and Barnett Pearce, "Sexists, Racists, and Other Classes of Classifiers," *Quarterly Journal of Speech* 66 (1980): 239–250. Also see Wilson, "Face and Facework"; J. Tedeschi, "Threats and Promises," in *The Structure of Conflict,* Paul Swingle, ed. (New York: Academic Press, 1970); and W. Schenck-Hamlin and G. Georgacarakos, "Response to Murdock, Bradac, and Bowers," *Western Journal of Speech Communication* 50 (1986): 200–207.

[42] Wilson, "Face and Facework"; R. Axelrod, *The Evolution of Cooperation* (New York: Basic Books, 1984). Also see Folger, Poole, and Stutman.

[43] Muzafer Sherif, O. J. Harvey, B. J. White, W. R. Hood, and Carolyn W. Sherif, *Intergroup Conflict and Cooperation: The Robber's Cave Experiment* (Norman, OK: University Book Exchange, 1961). Also see Folger, Poole, and Stutman, p. 262.

[44] Ting-Toomey; Wilson, "Face and Facework"; also see T. Lim and J. W. Bowers, "Face-Work: Solidarity, Approbation, and Face," *Human Communication Research* 17 (1990): 415–450; and M. Roloff and J. M. Jordan, "Achieving Negotiation Goals." In *Communication and Negotiation,* L. Putnam and M. Roloff, eds. (Newbury Park, CA: Sage, 1993).

[45] Folger, Poole, and Stutman.

[46] William Donohue and R. Kolt, *Managing Interpersonal Conflict* (Newbury Park, CA: Sage, 1992).

[47] Putnam, "Conflict and Dispute Management."

[48] William L. Ury, Jeanne M. Brett, and Stephen B. Goldberg, *Getting Disputes Resolved: Designing Systems to Cut the Costs of Conflict* (San Francisco: Jossey-Bass, 1988).

[49] Ury, Brett, and Goldberg, p. 34.

[50] Putnam and Kolb.

[51] See Bush and Folger.

Chapter 10

Communication
and Diverse Workplaces

*As a result of changes in economic policy and technologies, economies that were once
separated . . . now are linked in an increasingly dense network of economic interactions.
This veritable economic revolution over the last 15 years has come upon us so suddenly
that its fundamental ramifications for economic growth, the distribution of income and
wealth, and patterns of trade and finance in the world economy are only dimly understood.*
—Jeffrey Sachs

*By the end of the 1980s, over two thirds of the American [U.S.] workforce was employed
in organizations with international connections. . . . Indeed, it is now virtually impossible
to conceive of a completely domestic, unicultural organization or organizational
communication practices that do not have inter-cultural dimensions. The Hudson report,
Workforce 2000, highlights the increasing racial, gender, ethnic, cultural, lifestyle,
and age mix of American organizations; the open borders of the European Union
have diversified their workforces; the political upheavals across Europe, Asia, and
Africa have increased immigration, and communication technologies have minimized
the saliency of geographical boundaries and national borders.*
—Cynthia Stohl

Central Themes

- The dominant perspective on organizations focuses on homogeneity and separation. Managers are separated from workers; organizations are separated from their environments; and employees are separated from their families and members of other organizations.
- Two processes—diversification and globalization—have challenged the dominant perspective by collapsing time and space. Organizations are increasingly heterogeneous, and "different" peoples are working in closer and closer proximity with one another.

343

- Organizational responses to increased diversification can be arrayed along a continuum from *denying* that it has occurred, to reducing its impact by attempting to *homogenize* the "others," to accepting their presence but *marginalizing* them, to confronting it as a positive development.
- In the long term, strategies of balanced innovation may effect significant change. They are sufficiently subtle to generate little resistance; although they make small changes, they can have major unintended consequences. Eventually, these small wins may actually change the dominant perspective and the power structure of organizations.
- Societal expectations and organizational processes combine to limit the organizational power and upward mobility of "other" employees.
- Confronting the dominant perspective begins in legitimate efforts to value "others'" ways of acting and leading and by treating flexibility as more important than consistency.
- A number of factors have combined to make it increasingly difficult to balance home and work. Both organizations and individuals can take steps to enhance that balance.

Key Terms

essentializing	flexplace
role encapsulation	glass walls
quid pro quo sexual harassment	mentors
hostile-environment sexual harassment	familism
glass ceilings	machismo
flextime	*simpatía*

In Chapter 2 we introduced the concept of *hegemony,* the idea that the hierarchical relationships that exist within a society come to be treated as *natural* (that is, inevitable) and *normal* (that is, expected and morally correct). Within each society, a set of related basic assumptions develop about organizations and organizational life. At least since the Industrial Revolution, and especially since traditional strategies of organizing were first articulated, organizations have been defined as sites where managers control workers in an effort to maximize performance through rational decision making and the efficient use of resources. In such organizations, thinking is separated from doing, and the people responsible for one activity are assumed to be very different from the people charged with the other. Each group is relatively homogeneous in gender, education, class, and race. This homogeneity enhances communication within each group and makes it unlikely that a member of one group will ever occupy a position within the other. When combined with underlying assumptions, homogeneity simplifies and stabilizes organizations, making organizational life more comfortable and predictable.

However, this dominant perspective has not gone unchallenged. One does not have to observe organizations closely to realize that the doers possess a great deal of task-related expertise and that the thinkers often act in nonrational ways. Personal interests and political considerations often lead them to sacrifice efficiency and organizational performance. Organizational power and managerial control are constantly resisted in many different ways. Instead of being the smoothly oiled machines depicted in the dominant perspective, organizations are sites where contradictions, fissures, and tensions are constantly being played out. During the past two decades, this has been challenged further by two processes—*diversification* and *globalization.* As people from different backgrounds and experiences enter organizations, and especially as they move into powerful positions in those organizations, and as Western organizations enter into societies with different assumptions, tensions are very difficult to ignore. The most important effect is that the heterogeneity that results can lead people to recognize that dominant organizational strategies are neither natural nor normal. They reflect a group of *choices* that societies and their members have made and continually reinforce through their everyday activities. People come to view the choices they have made as normal and natural and tend to forget that other forms of organizing are possible, such as relational, cultural, and networking strategies. Moreover, organizations' success with alternative forms of organizing indicates that the assumptions themselves may be inaccurate. With change comes resistance, and strategic responses to that resistance.

Resisting "Others"

During the 1960s, women started to move into professional and managerial roles throughout northern Europe. During the 1970s and 1980s this trend reached the United States, the United Kingdom, and former Commonwealth countries (Canada, Australia, and New Zealand). Almost simultaneously, white women were joined by members of racial and ethnic minority groups. Today virtually every economy in the world is experiencing workforce diversification to some degree. Organizational responses can be arrayed along a continuum from denying that it has occurred, to trying to reduce its impact by attempting to homogenize the "others," to accepting their presence but attempting to marginalize them, to confronting diversification as a positive development. Different organizations and different societies respond in their own unique ways to the presence of different "others," just as employees have unique experiences with diversification and develop distinctive strategies for dealing with resistance to the process. When discussing diversification, it is important to not **essentialize** the widely varying experiences and responses of individual members of different organizations, genders, classes, races, or individuals. Broad generalizations invariably obscure important differences in the experiences of the members of different societal groups. Employees' perceptions and actions are influenced by their culture, gender, race, and economic class; but they also are influenced by family values, personality characteristics, life history, and a host of other individual attributes. Conversely, it is also important to recognize that there are similarities in the strategic options that are available to employees in different organizations and different societies. Consequently, their strategic choices also may be quite similar.[1]

Denying "Others" a Legitimate Place in the Organization

The simplest response to diversification, and the one that seems to be most common when an organization or economy is just beginning the process, is to deny the legitimacy of "others'" presence. In some cases, denial is not intentional. People interact with one another based on the whole person, which includes race and gender as well as organizational position, task assignments, and professional expertise. Because managers and professional personnel in U.S. organizations still are disproportionately white and middle-class, they often have not had much experience communicating with people who are different from themselves and feel uncomfortable doing so. Or they may fear that if they do offer advice or help, the newcomer will view their efforts as patronizing, sexist, or racist. So they withdraw from him or her, and it takes longer for newcomers who are not white males to form effective interpersonal relationships, if they ever do. In highly paternalistic societies such as Latin America or traditionally Confucian cultures, young women often find that their suggestions are ignored by their superiors and that they are ostracized by their peers.[2]

Current employees also may expect non-white-male employees to occupy low-power positions in their organizations and as a result are less accommodating about providing inside information to newcomers who are in positions outside of those stereotypical roles. In spite of narrowing educational gaps in the United States between genders and races, women still tend to be located in nurturing careers, which are incredibly important to the society but typically carry limited power—nursing, sales, and teaching among college-educated employees and clerical or service occupations for women without college degrees. Similarly, nonwhite college-educated men tend to be in staff positions, whereas those without degrees are disproportionately situated in lower-level production positions.[3] In ambiguous situations, people rely on stereotypes to guide their interactions—stereotypes that may be very inaccurate and misleading.[4] The newcomer experiences **role encapsulation,** a process through which individual employees are perceived through racial or sexual stereotypes. For example, some women simply are not warm, supportive, nurturing people and do not want to be, in spite of what dominant stereotypes suggest (and some men are warm, supportive, nurturing people and do want to be). Nurturance, like any other behavior, is learned, not innate. But the stereotype is so powerful that supervisors and peers often try to negotiate women into support-oriented organizational roles (both formal and informal) or train them to behave in more stereotypical ways, frequently without realizing that they are doing so. In the same way, some male engineers negotiate roles that allow them to focus on their families and avoid burnout, even in organizations where burnout and devaluing family life is both normal and a sign of masculinity.[5] Indeed, 75 percent of male employees say that they would exchange promotion opportunities and raises for more time to spend with their families. They are unable to do so, because of the negative impact on their careers, status, and job security.[6] As the maternity/ paternity leave discussion later in this chapter explains in more detail, it may be even more difficult for men to escape encapsulated masculine roles than it is for women to escape traditional feminine roles.

Denial also may be conscious and intentional. In these cases it is accomplished through exclusion, overt discrimination, or harassment (or sometimes all three). The goal is to keep "others" out of the organization, persuade them to leave it prematurely, or force them to submit completely to the demands of dominant employees. In the West, discrimination usually is thought of in terms of overt bias in hiring and promotion decisions. First in northern Europe, then in Canada and the United States, and later in Australia, New Zealand, and southern Europe, laws have been passed that make this kind of discrimination illegal. However, as the 1996 Texaco Oil lawsuit (described in Chapter 12) indicated, organizations often devise complicated strategies to circumvent or ignore these laws. Major corporations worldwide are regularly convicted of discriminating on the basis of race, sex, age, religion, or disability, or choose to settle cases out of court. Perhaps the most visible recent case in the United States involved Coca Cola, which in November 2000 accepted a record $192.5 million out-of-court settlement of a case in which 2,000 current and former employees alleged that they were "systematically bypassed for raises and promotions" because of their race (the previous U.S. record was $176 million in the Texaco litigation). The plaintiffs complained of a closed promotion system in which job openings were filled by less qualified and less experienced white employees without ever being announced in public. Plaintiffs also complained of Coca Cola's strategy of refusing promotions for minority employees on the grounds of budget constraints while finding ways to circumvent those constraints to promote whites. Plaintiff Elvenyia Barton-Gibson noted, "It's so unfortunate that in the year 2000, we are still fighting this kind of case. These should be dead issues."[7]

However, discrimination often goes far beyond formal hiring and promotion decisions, and in many countries employees have little legal recourse when they are discriminated against. For example, during the 1980s and 1990s many governments in Asia (for example, Hong Kong, Taiwan, South Korea, and Singapore) and Latin America acted to weaken labor movements and legal protections afforded workers, sometimes in the guise of anticommunism. Their goal was to create the "industrial peace" necessary to attract investment by Western organizations. In turn, Western corporations who were moving their production operations to Latin America and Asia sought out a labor force of young single women, who they believed would be easy to control. For example, a manager of a maquiladora said that he preferred young and inexperienced female workers because they are "easier to shape to our requirements" and have a higher capacity for "eating bitterness."[8] Supervisors and labor contractors, almost all of whom are men, refer to women workers as "daughters" and treat them as "children" who should always "obey their parents (supervisors)." In societies where daughters are viewed as poor long-term investments, families and organizations often collude to have workers work long hours at low pay because a substantial proportion of their income is returned to the family. These payments help compensate for the expenses of raising a female child, considered to be of lower value than a male child in traditional Chinese culture. A Taiwanese worker reported that the system left her feeling trapped, like a "frog beneath a coconut shell."

Control systems also spawn resistance. Aihwa Ong's studies of women working in factories established by multinational corporations in agricultural areas of Asia found that workers often view their jobs and income as a means of gaining independence, a measure of self-esteem, and a way to improve their technical skills and obtain better jobs. Outside of work, they reject traditional mores regarding dress; they form friendships with co-workers from communities with very different societal standards; and young women demand the right to select their own husbands and begin to act like Western consumers. For example, in Malaysia sales of cosmetics quadrupled in only two years, in spite of a traditional link between cosmetics and prostitution. (Asia is now by far the fastest-growing market for Avon products). Of course, with increased independence have come an increase in economic and personal insecurity and increased efforts by local societies to more tightly control women's behavior. In Asia and Latin America, the creation of a large single-female labor force has led to increased public pressure for women to behave "properly." Malay women, as well as women workers in West Java and Thailand, are perceived as invading male (public) places, and their social activities are closely monitored and controlled. Transnational companies in Islamic countries hold religious classes in the workplace in an effort to enhance "moral discipline," including working hard and obeying orders without question. In both Latin American and Asian countries, multinational corporations control workers by appealing to feminine sex roles through beauty pageants and cooking classes.[9]

In industrialized economies, denial is more frequently expressed in various forms of harassment than in overt discrimination. Racial harassment and **quid pro quo sexual harassment** (whereby a person is promised rewards in exchange for sexual activity or threatened with punishment or job loss if they reject sexual proposals) have been illegal for some time. In 1994 Australia, following Europe, Canada, and the United States, also made **hostile-environment harassment** illegal. Two landmark cases from Australia help explain this concept. In 1989 a woman who was employed by Effective Cleaning Services to clean the Brisbane K-Mart store was told by K-Mart manager Brian Drysdale that she was a "naughty little girl who needed her bare bum smacked." He forced her to kneel beside him, ostensibly to clean under some cooking equipment, placed a hand on her head, lifted her t-shirt, and pulled down her pants and panties. On other occasions he lifted her off the ground, chased her around the room, made comments about her legs and bottom and repeatedly referred to her as a "naughty girl." When she complained to upper management, they believed Drysdale's denials of the events. The worker, who had been sexually abused as a child and as an adult, took her case to the Human Rights and Equal Opportunity Commission and won her case. Because Drysdale never demanded sexual activity, the case was not covered under laws regarding quid pro quo harassment. But his behavior clearly created a hostile work environment based on her sex.

In virtually all Western countries, hostile-environment laws were eventually expanded to encompass co-workers' actions that are known to management.[10] Again, Australia provides a typical case. Heather Horne and Gail McIntosh received compensation after being subjected to two years of verbal abuse, graffiti, and the display in their workplace of soft- and hard-core pornography, some of which the Western Australian Equal Opportunity Tribunal found to be grossly offensive and degrading. The workers' union sided with the organization, but the Tribunal did not. Damian Grace and Stephen Cohen explain the basis of the decision and why harassment often should be interpreted as a denial strategy:

> The display of pornography was anything but innocent. The two workers were bullied because they were different. This difference happened to be one of sex. It might as easily have been one of religion. . . . [T]he harassment is a particularly nasty display of sexism; the women were attacked as *women*. There was a clear assumption that women did not qualify for equal esteem with men . . . that they were powerless, and that they could be degraded through ridicule of their sex.[11]

As in similar cases in other industrialized countries, episodes such as these helped establish the illegality of hostile-environment sexual harassment. Unfortunately, as the following case study indicates, harassment is still prevalent in organizations in the industrialized world, and the legal system is still developing ways to deal with it. In the United States, same-sex harassment was not ruled illegal until 1999, and educational institutions were not held liable for harassment of students until 2000. Laws regarding religious and age-based harassment are only now emerging in the United States and Canada as workforces become more diverse. Many societies—in Scandinavia, Southern Europe, Africa, and Asia—attempt to create conditions in which the distinctive contributions made by both males and females can be combined and rewarded. But in the United States, the United Kingdom, and Commonwealth countries, treating members of different groups in similar ways is valued, and those values are enforced through antidiscrimination laws. Consequently, legal gaps and inequities create greater disadvantages than they might in more communitarian societies.

In addition, there is some evidence that harassment—in both nonviolent and violent forms—is on the rise in Europe and in the United States. Overt hostility in the workplace—racist, sexist, and homophobic slurs expressed in conversations, hate mail, graffiti, and faxes; sabotage of work projects and computer files; and physical assaults—may be increasing, suggesting that attitudinal barriers to diversity may be on the upswing.[12]

CASE STUDY
The Harassment Case

The 1990s provided substantial, repeated evidence of how pervasive sexual harassment and racial harassment are in U.S. organizations. Professor Anita Hill's testimony during the U.S. Senate confirmation hearings for Supreme Court Justice

(continued)

(Case Study, continued)

Clarence Thomas brought the problem into the living room of everyone who owns a television set. The U.S. Navy's Tailhook scandal, in which a number of female officers were shoved down a crowded Las Vegas hotel hallway and molested by a large group of Navy aviators; and the forced resignation of Senator Robert Packwood for repeatedly harassing female staff members over more than a decade provided compelling evidence of the extent of the problem for those people who had doubted the veracity of Professor Hill's testimony. By the middle of the decade media reports of allegations of sexual harassment, out-of-court settlements, or convictions became commonplace. In August 1995, Del Labs of Farmingdale, New York, agreed to pay $1.2 million to settle a lawsuit in which CEO Dan Wasong was charged by fifteen employees with touching their breasts and buttocks, asking for oral sex, and using abusive sexual language. In April 1996, the U.S. Equal Employment Opportunity Commission filed a lawsuit against Mitsubishi Motors Corporation for allowing sexual harassment to continue at its Normal, Illinois, assembly plants. In November 1996, charges of rape, coerced sex, and sexual harassment of women trainees at the U.S. Army's Aberdeen (Maryland) Proving Ground led to the publication of past or ongoing sexual harassment cases at Fort Leonard Wood (Missouri) and Fort Hood (Texas). A toll-free hotline set up by the army after the Aberdeen case became public received more than four thousand calls reporting cases of harassment during its first ten days of existence. In January 1997, the Publix Grocery store chain announced an out-of-court settlement of a sexual discrimination and harassment case that dwarfs the Del Labs settlement and, in turn, was dwarfed by the Mitsubishi settlement even though the plaintiffs eventually were awarded only a fraction of their $150 million claim. During 2003 and 2004 the U.S. Air Force Academy was embroiled in a highly publicized investigation of rape and sexual harassment that goes back decades.

However, our purpose in this case study is not to examine the frequency of racial or sexual harassment. The available evidence suggests that virtually all women and persons of color work in a hostile environment much of their lives, although it is clear that harassment is more likely in organizations that have developed a "conspiracy of silence" about harassment.* Surveys have indicated that at least one-third of female students and employees experience overt sexual harassment; the figure increases to 70–90 percent if researchers explain the legal definition of sexual harassment to their respondents. Whereas *quid pro quo* harassment is widely understood and unambiguously illegal, *hostile-environment* harassment is more difficult to define and prevent. During the late 1990s, U.S. courts consistently ruled that repeated physical affronts—touching, groping, or pinching—are illegal. Symbolic actions—written or oral comments including sexual jokes or lewd comments, or displays like nude pinups or obscene or pornographic displays in electronic media—are especially difficult to interpret. These activities are illegal only if they are sufficiently extreme and pervasive that a reasonable person would conclude that they create a *hostile and intimidating work environment,* if they were unwanted, and if the plaintiff's supervisor knew about them or reasonably could be expected to have known about them. Consequently, what constitutes a hostile environment varies across different courts and different cases. Some courts still use a reasonable-person standard: Would a reasonable person interpret the behaviors in question as constituting a hostile work or educational environment? Other courts have substituted a "reasonable-woman" standard, because there is clear research evidence indicating that women generally perceive a wider range of symbols and behaviors to be unwanted, hostile, or intimidating than men do. The Mitsubishi Motors case provided an excellent example of the range of activities that may be illegal. The suit alleged that male workers called their female peers "sluts, whores and bitches"; they placed drawing of genitals and breasts and various sexual acts labeled with female employees' names on car fenders and cardboard signs along the assembly lines; explicit sexual graffiti such as "kill the slut Mary" were scrawled on rest-area and bathroom walls, and one supervisor declared, "I don't want any bitches on my line. Women don't belong in the plant"; anonymous callers made threats like "You better watch your back, bitch" or "Die bitch, you'll be sorry." Women were subjected to groping, forced sex play, and male flashing; one complainant found her car defaced; another was forced off the road as she drove home from work; and in another case a worker put an air gun between a woman worker's legs and pulled the trigger. However, only one of these actions—the supervisor's comment—is *in itself* illegal. Peer harassment is illegal only if supervisors are directly involved or know about, or could be expected to know about, the harassment. The allegations at Mitsubishi also claimed that plant management was repeatedly told of the actions and failed to take corrective measures.

Because of the threat of retaliation and intimidation if the victim complains, and because of the low likelihood of winning harassment cases (it is *very* difficult to produce sufficient evidence to meet the legal requirements), only about 10 percent of targets of harassment actually report the incidents. Fewer still file formal complaints. But our goal is not to examine the legal barriers that exist when women or persons of color attempt to find redress for their grievances, although those barriers are significant and important. The sources listed at the end of this case study provide excellent analyses of both of these issues. Instead, our goal is to briefly summarize the ways in which organizations hide harassment and suppress complaints of harassment. Not all cases of organizational efforts to suppress complaints are as blatant as Rear Admiral John Snyder's response to helicopter pilot Paula Coughlin's complaints about behavior at the Tailhook convention: "That's what you get when you go to a hotel party with a bunch of drunk aviators." Once Coughlin told her story to the press, the Navy conducted an investigation that was so sloppy that a year later the Navy was not even certain which of its pilots were among the seventy or so involved in the incident. In the end, the Navy investigation recommended punishment for only two aviators, one Australian and one U.S. Marine. Eventually, and again in response to public reports about the sloppiness of the investigation and resulting pressure from the House Armed Services Committee, a number of officers (including Admiral Snyder) were dismissed, and the Pentagon took over the

(continued)

(Case Study, continued)

investigation.[†] Because few readers of this case are autoworkers or ever will be naval officers, these examples of harassment may not seem terribly relevant. But there is substantial evidence that college and university students are frequent targets of racial and sexual abuse and that their experiences and their university's responses are very much like those faced by career women. In fact, the most visible case of harassment in the United States during the first years of the twenty-first century has involved the U.S. Air Force Academy. In early 2003 investigators uncovered a pattern of sexual harassment, rape, abuse, cover-ups, and systematic punishment of women who spoke out against abuse. Eventually investigations by the Air Force, the Department of Defense, and U.S. Congress led to the forced resignation of the academy's top four officers and a complete revamping of its system for dealing with sexual harassment and abuse. In general, the victims who have come forward—including the thirty-nine rape victims—have expressed doubt that the changes made to date will do much to change the climate or practices at the academy.[‡]

In all kinds of organizations, harassment is most likely when (1) the organization accepts and reinforces the view that "normal" employees are white and male; (2) the number of "other" employees is small, and people who are not Anglo men have few sources of support; (3) the organization is loosely coupled, making it difficult to obtain timely corrective action; and (4) the power relationships between supervisors and their subordinates are highly unequal. Of course, each of these factors is present in most colleges and universities. In 1992 the *Journal of Applied Communication* published a special issue on sexual harassment that included twenty extended verbatim narratives written by people in the discipline of communication who have been sexually harassed.[§] These stories are quite typical of instances of harassment in the academic (and organizational) world. Some of the cases provided summaries of the responses of the survivors' peers and of university administrations that are not unlike the response of the Navy or Mitsubishi's management; three are illustrative.

One new graduate student experienced unwanted sexual advances by three different professors. Soon after the third event, she confided in a senior Ph.D. student. Unknown to her, he called a meeting of the other doctoral students to discuss sexual harassment in the department. Although he protected the names of the professors, he revealed her identity. The doctoral students took no action, because many of them were working closely with a professor who had a reputation for harassment, and they did not want to make him uncomfortable. (He was not one of the three.) Because she could not even count on support from her peers, she decided not to pursue the matter any further.[**]

In a second case, the chair of a department told about a case that is still in progress. A woman student complained about actions by a professor that were both improper and illegal, although she did not file criminal charges. When the department chair first heard about the charge, she did not believe it. After all, the professor projected the image of an innocent choirboy and had recently published an essay in the school newspaper that provided a "feminist" analysis of sexual harassment. His outspoken support of women's issues had earned him strong support among women faculty. After a lengthy hearing, during which the professor received a leave of absence with pay (in most universities, these are highly sought-after awards, not punishments), he signed a statement admitting guilt and was allowed to return to normal duties provided he had no further contact with the student, would do nothing else to create an intimidating environment for women students, and would not socialize with students for a year. Although he has already violated the latter two terms, the administration has taken no action. His department chair has been "gagged" by the university's administration. If she were to warn any potential employers about his history, she could lose her job, although she now knows he has been guilty of similar behavior at other universities. He was even dismissed from graduate school for sexual harassment; but that case too was kept confidential. Soon he will be looking for a new professorship. She concludes: "He will do a wonderful interview. You (other professors) will like him. Chances are you will hire him."

In a third case, a new assistant professor accepted a job in a department with a department chair who was reputed to be politically liberal. After two years on the job, she felt secure enough to complain about her chair's repeated sexist comments and jokes: "Once, when I was advising a senior major, he stopped by my opened door, looked at me, and then turned and asked the student, 'Are there any cute girls in your (sorority) house?' She blushed and turned to me. 'You shouldn't say that!' I retorted. 'Oh, I'm sorry. Are there any cute tarts? Are there any cute wenches?' He quipped. I yelled his name emphatically, 'You know that's inappropriate.' 'I guess you think it's harassment (it is) and you're writing it down.' He responded as he smiled and walked away." The professor complained about the event in a private meeting with the affirmative action officer and asked specifically that her identity not be revealed. Less than an hour later, the officer revealed her identity to the department chair. Eventually her department recommended that she not be reappointed to her position, although her performance had been excellent, and she was refused access to written evaluations of her work. The university administration alerted the professor to irregularities in her case, but it did not want to overrule the department. As a compromise she was granted a probationary contract. Later, one of her female colleagues filed a sexual harassment complaint against the department chair. The female provost (a position equivalent to vice president in private-sector organizations) advised the professor not to support the colleague who had filed the complaint. With no support, her colleague resigned. The following year the professor was denied tenure. But in this case, the university administration overruled the department's decision and not only granted her tenure, but appointed her chair of her department.

In general, research on harassment in academic organizations indicates that successful complaints against professors for sexual harassment occur but are quite rare. By the time action is taken, students have often completed their coursework with the harasser or have graduated. Universities often conduct harassment inves-

(continued)

(Case Study, continued)

tigations in private; they do not notify victims of the date and times of hearings or allow them to testify, and they fail to inform the students of any actions taken against the harasser. The rationale for maintaining secrecy typically is that the matter is a personnel action and that the accused harasser deserves the protection of academic due process. If the university is a public institution, the professor also may be afforded some protection by free speech considerations. But given the unequal power relationship that exists between harassers and targets, this conspiracy of silence primarily protects the university and the harasser from public embarrassment. More important, it lulls people into a complacent view that harassment is not a problem, creates skepticism and mistrust of the system among students (which militates against victims filing complaints), and leads victims to believe that they are alone in having been harassed, thus encouraging them (and others) to blame themselves. A Latina university employee explained that nonfaculty and nonstudent women have similar experiences:

> Everyone likes to pretend it doesn't happen. When you go from one position to the next in this university it's so small that bosses know each other and say, "Hey, this woman—watch out for her." So, you get blackmailed that way.[††]

The cult of secrecy ensures that the university will never face any organized pressure to eliminate harassment of students.

For these reasons, in the landmark *Meritor v. Vincent* case, the U.S. Supreme Court ruled that targets of harassment can take legal action against their employers (or universities, in later rulings) without following internal procedures, although not doing so makes it more difficult to demonstrate that supervisors knew or should have known about the harassment. The reason for the court's decision is simple: it realized that those procedures rarely work.

Applying What You've Learned

1. What is quid pro quo harassment? Hostile-environment harassment?
2. Why is harassment considered to be an issue of power or coercion?

Questions to Think About and Discuss

1. At a number of points in this book we have suggested that bureaucratic organizations typically suppress dissent, avoid conflicts, and restrict the flow of negative information. To what extent is the silence surrounding sexual or racial harassment simply another example of communication breakdowns in organizations? To what extent is it a function of racist or sexist attitudes? How might the two be interrelated?
2. Recently the U.S. Supreme Court ruled that sexual harassment of students violates Title IX of the Civil Rights Act and that women can now collect

monetary damages from universities if they are harassed. What impact is this ruling likely to have on universities and their handling of sexual harassment cases?

---

*Charles Conrad and Bryan Taylor, "The Contexts of Sexual Harassment: Power, Silences and Academe," in *Conceptualizing Sexual Harassment as Discursive Practice,* Shereen Bingham, ed. (Westport, CT: Praeger, 1994); Joann Keyton, Pat Ferguson, and Steven Rhodes, "Cultural Indicators of Sexual Harassment," Southern Communication Journal 67 (2001): 33-50.

†Michelle Violanti, "Hooked on Expectations: An Analysis of Influence and Relationships in the Tailhook Reports," *Journal of Applied Communication Research* 24 (1996): 67-82.

‡"Paper Finds Air Force Academy Negligence," *New York Times on the Web,* June 15, 2003, http://www.nytimes.com/.

§William Eadie and Julia Wood, eds., *Journal of Applied Communication Research* 20 (1992): 349-436.

**Eadie and Wood, p. 367.

††Eadie and Wood.

General Sources

Bingham, S., ed. *Conceptualizing Sexual Harassment as Discursive Practice.* Westport, CT: Praeger, 1994.

Clair, Robin. "The Use of Framing Devices to Sequester Organizational Narratives." *Communication Monographs* 60 (1993): 113-136.

Eadie, William, and Julia Wood, eds. *Journal of Applied Communication Research* 20 (1992): v418.

Keyton, Joann, Pat Ferguson, and Steven Rhodes. "Cultural Indicators of Sexual Harassment." *Southern Communication Journal* 67 (2001): 33-50.

Kreps, G., ed. *Sexual Harassment: Communication Implications.* Cresskill, NJ: Hampton Press, 1993.

Terpstra, David, and Douglas Baker. "Outcomes of Sexual Harassment Charges." *Academy of Management Journal* 31 (1988): 185-194.

Specific Cases

"Paper Finds Air Force Academy Negligence." *New York Times on the Web,* June 15, 2003, http://www.nytimes.com/. Virtually any major newspaper has a readily accessible archive of articles about the Air Force Academy scandal on its Web site. Transcripts of congressional hearings are available through the U.S. Government Web site or can be easily located through the Lexis-Nexis search engine, available in virtually all university libraries.

Violanti, Michelle. "Hooked on Expectations: An Analysis of Influence and Relationships in the Tailhook Reports." *Journal of Applied Communication Research* 24 (1996): 67-82.

Colleges and Universities

Clair, Robin. "The Bureaucratization, Commodification, and Privatization of Sexual Harassment through Institutional Discourse." *Management Communication Quarterly* 7 (1993): 128-157.

Conrad, Charles, and Bryan Taylor. "The Contexts of Sexual Harassment: Power, Silences and Academe." In *Conceptualizing Sexual Harassment as Discursive Practice,* edited by Shereen Bingham. Westport, CT: Praeger, 1994.

Dziech, B. W. *Sexual Harassment in Higher Education.* New York: Garland, 1998.

Dziech, B. W., and L. Weiner. *The Lecherous Professor.* 2nd ed. Urbana: University of Illinois Press, 1990.

Lash, Steve. "Court Holds Educators Liable for Harassment." *Houston Chronicle,* September 7, 1999, A1.

Mongeau, Paul, and Jennifer Blalock. "Student Evaluations of Instructor Immediacy and Sexually Harassing Behaviors: An Experimental Investigation." *Journal of Applied Communication Research* 22 (1994): 256-272.

Paludi, M. A., and R. B. Barickman. *Academic and Workplace Sexual Harassment.* Albany: State University of New York Press, 1991.

Segura, Denise. "Chicanas in White-Collar Jobs." In *Situated Lives,* edited by Louise Lamphere, Helena Razoné, and Patricia Zavella. New York: Routledge, 1997.

Differences in Perceptions of What Constitutes Harassment

Keyton, Joann, and Steven Rhodes. "Organizational Sexual Harassment." *Journal of Applied Communication Research* 27 (1999): 158-173.

Solomon, Denise Haunani, and Mary Lynn Miller Williams. "Perceptions of Social-Sexual Communication at Work." *Journal of Applied Communication Research* 25 (1997): 196-216.

———. "Perceptions of Social-Sexual Communication at Work as Harassing." *Management Communication Quarterly* 11 (1997): 147-184.

Homogenizing "Others"

A second possible form of resistance to diversification is to accept it while trying minimize its impact. If "other" employees can be persuaded (or forced) to
mimic the beliefs, values, and actions of organizational power-holders, their entry into an organization will lead to little or no change. "Old-timers" in organizations have numerous reasons for wanting newcomers to change to "fit in" to
existing organizational roles and practices instead of changing, themselves, to
accommodate the newcomers. These incentives are especially strong when the
newcomer is "different."

The Discourse of Accommodation   Regardless of the country that is involved, one of the most common responses to "different" employees is to encourage them to minimize their differentness, to accommodate themselves to
the norms of their organizations, to learn and use the communicative strategies
of Anglo men. But people who are different (and in U.S. organizations this term
encompasses people from lower socioeconomic classes, as well as African
Americans, Latinos, Asian Americans, people with disabilities, and women) all
find it immensely difficult to fit in. They clearly *are* different from the educated
middle-to-upper-class white males who dominate their organizations. In many
cases, their lack of familiarity with the communication style of bureaucratic discourse makes fitting in all the more difficult.[13]

One means of accommodating is always to *appear to be rational.* Because
societal myths depict women, African American men, and Latinos as emotional
(nonrational), using highly rational (that is, unemotional) forms of communication is especially important. A key part of the language of rationality is justifying
decisions or proposals in data-based terms (recall Chapter 9) or in terms of the
dominant values of the organizational culture. A second way of fitting in is to
create an image of loyalty to the organization. In an era of rapid job turnover (recall the case study on generational differences in Chapter 1), perceived loyalty is
an even more powerful image. The most common method of creating perceptions of loyalty is to repeatedly signal that the organization is one's highest priority. Although the symbols of loyalty differ in various organizations, there seems
to be one common component: subordinating all other activities and relationships to one's career and one's work relationships. Consistently taking work
home, seeking and accepting promotions or transfers even when they would be
disadvantageous to one's family, and limiting social ties to business contacts all
seem to be widely accepted indexes of loyalty. Of course, there is little evidence
that these activities are either a reliable sign of loyalty or necessary to the successful operation of organizations. But they are part of the symbolic reality that
guides perceptions. In traditionally structured middle- and upper-class families
(Ward and June Cleaver of *Leave It to Beaver* or Reverend and Mrs. Camden of
7th Heaven), creating these impressions is possible. The professional's wife is
available to serve as hostess, secretary, child-care specialist, and therapist. But
for unmarried professionals or married women professionals, there often is no

one available to play this "wifely" role. As a result, it is very difficult, if not impossible, for women to act like men who are part of traditional single-earner families—they simply do not have the resources necessary to continually demonstrate that their careers are their only, or at least their most important, priorities.

Presumably, the husbands of women professionals could help women demonstrate loyalty to their organizations by taking on a greater proportion of the family's workload. However, studies of time allocation have found that they often spend no more time doing home-related work than husbands whose wives do not work outside of the home. In many families, women are able to negotiate more equitable distributions of household work. For example, in separate studies Denise Segura and Beatríz Pesquera examined how Latinas negotiated workload arrangements at home. Because Latin cultures strongly support traditional sex-role arrangements, they expected that Latinas would find these negotiations to be especially difficult. They did find that it was a struggle for Latinas to negotiate more equitable arrangements, just as it is a struggle for non-Latin women. The title of Pesquera's study is taken from a comment made by one of the women she interviewed: "In the Beginning He Wouldn't Even Lift a Spoon," or, as they say in Spanish, *no levanta ni una cuchara.* But both researchers found that over time, couples often do negotiate more equitable task sharing and that the dominant factors in their being able to do so are income and task requirements as much as culture.

White-collar Latinas bring a great deal of work home and have frequent evening meetings. Blue-collar Latinas often work evening or night shifts, or work more than one job. In both cases, the visible evidence of work spillover into family life makes it easier for them to negotiate more equitable arrangements with their husbands. Similarly, the closer a wife's income is to her husband's, the more bargaining power she has. But they still have to negotiate. Pesquera observed that "women also utilize a variety of strategies in their daily struggle: they retrain, coach, and praise husbands for a job well done. At times they resort to slowdowns or work stoppages, so that eventually men are forced to contribute more to household labor." Husbands respond by stalling, doing slipshod work, or discrediting their wives by comparing them to women who do even more household work.[14] Many women find it easier to give up the struggle and do the work themselves. In fact, the total number of nonleisure hours worked by women employed full time is almost double the total for traditional housewives.[15] As a result, the Center for Creative Leadership found that 25 percent of the women they interviewed said that balancing work and family concerns was one of the greatest challenges they faced, while only 10 percent of the men shared this concern.

Of course, discourse that advises women and minority employees to strive to fit in often fails to recognize how complicated it is to do so. Employees are told to actively seek promotions that involve relocation and assignments that require travel, to stay with the same firm for long periods of time, and to make decisions about their nonorganizational life that put their careers and organizations first—choosing not to marry, to delay marriage, or to wait to begin a family until after they are well established in their careers.[16] If they do marry or form long-term partnerships, they are advised to negotiate a lifestyle with their partners that allows them to pursue their careers and simultaneously participate in a fulfilling family life.

Given the very real difficulties involved in following this advice, it is somewhat surprising that so many women in U.S. firms have been able to do so. Executive women change jobs for career, not family, reasons and are as likely as male executives to relocate to further their careers—if not more likely; and they take the same number of vacation days. Ironically, in spite of this evidence, upper managers still *perceive* that women put family before career and *believe* they will turn down assignments involving travel or relocation, and so on. Therefore, when women *do* experience career interruptions, the interruptions have a disproportionately negative effect on their careers. Women lose seniority, opportunities for training, and salary: "The first year back your wages are 33 percent lower than women who didn't leave. Over time, that difference diminishes (to 20 percent over 3–5 years and 10 percent after 11–20 years) but it never disappears." [17]

A final strategy that women and minority employees are told will help them fit in is to develop an exceptional performance record. Virtually all studies of the upward mobility of successful women, African Americans, and Latinos in U.S. firms have found that their performance had to be better and more consistent than the performance of Anglo men. A Latina white-collar worker told Denise Segura:

> I've seen it! In interviews with a white candidate, they see it written on the paper and they say, "Isn't this great!" But, when you bring a Latina in, it's almost like they're drilled: "Tell us"; "Give us examples"; "How long did you do it?" . . . You always have to prove yourself. . . . You almost have to fight harder to demonstrate that you can do a job just as well. [18]

This pattern is explained in part by overt discrimination. But it also is related to the weak link between performance and rewards that exists in most organizations. Excellent performance is rewarded only if it also is *visible* to the organization's power holders and only if they *perceive* that it provides evidence of exceptional competence. But how does one make her or his performance visible? The simplest way is to tell others about it. Even simple strategies are complicated by societal assumptions. In many societies, openly talking about one's successes is unacceptable. An employee must rely on communication through informal networks. "Different" employees often are excluded from those networks, however. In Western societies, men typically learn to be more comfortable talking about their exploits than most women do. In fact, they tend to exaggerate their successes ("I caught a fish/made a sale/won a case that was *this* big") and to express them in comparative and competitive terms. Women brag less frequently; they tend to understate their accomplishments and attribute their successes to other members of their team. As a result, males' bragging creates impressions of competence, confidence, pride, and success (all positively valued in managerial settings), whereas females' bragging makes people like them more and praise them for being sensitive, not for being successful. [19]

For women and members of minority groups, visibility is paradoxical in other ways. In organizations or units that have small numbers of women, African Americans, or Latinos (Rosabeth Moss Kanter has suggested that 15 percent is a crucial level), the ones who are there often live in "glass houses." As one woman executive explained, "There is an element of derailment built into the system for women—the pressure created by having to be a role model and a 'first' along with personal competency. Men don't have to deal with this added pressure." Another admitted, "I feel that if I fail, it will be a long time before they hire another woman for the job. . . . Carrying that burden can lead women to play it safe, to be ultraconservative, to opt out if a situation looks chancy." Everyone makes mistakes. If power holders focus on an employee's mistakes instead of successes, or if they attribute an occasional error to a person's race or sex, visibility becomes a barrier, not an advantage.[20]

Differential Perceptions and Attributions   The visibility paradox is further complicated by perceptual and attributional processes. Societal myths about race, gender, and ethnicity create perceptual sets through which people *interpret* events and actions. Researchers have long recognized that in general, subordinates receive significantly higher ratings from persons of their own race and sex, even when objective performance standards are used. This results in part from the continuation of overtly racist attitudes and behaviors, as the Texaco, Coca Cola, and other cases so clearly indicate. But differential evaluation also seems to occur even when overt racial biases are not evident.[21] Societal assumptions also influence attributions. Even when excellent performance by women, African American men, or Latinos is made visible, it may be attributed to factors outside of the employee's control—luck, special advantages, the help of other employees, the effectiveness of the organization as a whole, or high motivation and effort (which cannot be sustained over the long term)—rather than to skill and expertise. Even when performance is attributed to the same factors, it may have different effects. If a white male's success is attributed to hard work, it usually helps his career because evaluators assume that he is also competent. But when a woman's or a minority employee's success is attributed to hard work, evaluators tend to assume that it disguises limits to her or his competence, so it may do little to help him or her advance in the organization.[22] In addition, supervisors also seem to feel and express less confidence in their evaluations of women and minority subordinates than of their white male subordinates. When evaluators express a lack of confidence in their judgments about an employee's performance, it creates less positive perceptions than the performance merits. In organizations, as in the rest of life, perceptual "realities" are more important than actual performance.

Finally, Anglo male supervisors tend to base their evaluations of African American and Latino/Latina subordinates more on the extent to which they *conform* to the organization's norms of behavior than on their performance (the reverse is true for Anglo subordinates). As a result, "fitting in" is transformed from a means to an end. In general, Anglo male supervisors and employers feel more comfortable with people whom they perceive as similar to themselves, and they tend to promote similar people. Because Latinas and African American women are the most dissimilar, they are the least likely to be promoted. To complicate matters further, Anglo male supervisors are often unaware of their perceptions or the role that those perceptions play in their actions toward and evaluations of women and African Americans and Latinos.[23] "Different" employees experience a complex web of double binds as they try to fit into organizations in which being a white male is perceived to be "normal" and "natural."

Dealing with Homogenization   There is substantial evidence that white women in northern European, U.S., and Commonwealth organizations are beginning to break through the **glass ceiling** successfully. Although this concept is most often associated with women, it also applies to members of ethnic and religious minority groups and to people with disabilities. And it is a worldwide phenomenon. Progress for Latino, African American, and Asian American men has been slower but still is substantial. At least in the United States, the progress seems to have continued through the recession of 1999–2003 (job and income losses in previous U.S. recessions have been greatest for non-white-male employees).[24] Members of all groups seem to have found ways to balance the conformity demands of organizations while maintaining their own distinctive styles of leading and managing, although the leadership and management strategies used by people at the very top of organizations seems to vary little by race, gender, or ethnicity.[25] They may accept the overall constraints imposed by their organizations but find ways to create cohesive, high-performing work groups within those constraints. For example, they may maintain a highly structured, unemotional mode of communicating with people outside of their units but encourage openness and honest communication with their subordinates while providing them with support for creative risk taking.[26] Educated Muslim immigrants in U.S. firms seem to adopt the attitudes and behaviors of their organizations while at work but retain their original culture outside of work (especially if they are highly committed to their faith).

African American and Asian American women, as well as Latinas, have experienced less progress, in part because they are doubly (or triply, if socioeconomic class is included) "different" from the white male norm. Consequently, even politically conservative commentators admit that the progress has been slow and mixed. The glass ceiling once was assumed to be located at the level of middle management. Above that point in an organization's hierarchy, the number of openings falls rapidly, and performance evaluation becomes much more subjective. However, recent research has found that the ceiling is even lower than middle management for Anglo women, and lower still for African Americans and Latinos/Latinas. This does not mean that the ceiling cannot be penetrated—there are a number of noted successes—but it does suggest that the combination of differences in opportunity and societal attitudes makes it difficult to break through it. And "the barriers to the upper rungs of the corporate ladder for minority women appear to be nearly impenetrable"; the percentage of Latinas and African American and Asian women in the corporate offices of Fortune 500 firms (1.3 percent) has not changed in recent years.[27]

In the long term, the various strategies of balanced innovation have the potential for effecting significant change. They are sufficiently subtle to generate little resistance, while making small changes that over the long term will have major unintended consequences. Eventually, these small wins may actually change the power structure of bureaucratic organizations. For example, if the supervisor of one division of an organization successfully implements structural changes, such as **flextime** (allowing employees to work schedules that fit their needs) or **flexplace** (allowing people to work at home whenever possible), those policies may serve as a model for other divisions and eventually for the organization as a whole. When significant numbers of "different" employees enter organizations, the organizations themselves will truly be different, and they eventually and inevitably will have to make fundamental changes. When the upper levels of organizational hierarchies begin to include some people who are not Anglo men, new perspectives, values, and ideas will become part of the discourse of upper management. When substantial numbers of Anglo men have worked successfully with women and persons of color as peers below the glass ceiling, they will bring more positive attitudes with them when *they* move into upper management.[28]

Marginalizing "Others"

A third possible organizational response to increased diversification is to accept "different" others' presence in the organization but to isolate them in "spaces" that have relatively low levels of power. In some societies these spaces often are literal—in Mongolia, South America, India, the Philippines, and North Africa, women workers tend to be segregated in homes or "out-of-the-way" places in their organizations—and serve to isolate the employees from potential sources of power and influence. In U.S. organizations, "different" employees are more likely to be placed in relatively powerless departments.[29] Obtaining power is crucial to upward mobility. It also is necessary to achieve other personal and career goals, such as effectively serving one's customers and clients, successfully obtaining and completing challenging and meaningful projects, and so on. As Chapter 8 explains, power is closely related to one's place in the formal structure of one's organization.

Manipulating Opportunity Structures   Latinos, African Americans, and Anglo women often work in industries that provide little opportunity for advancement and in divisions of organizations that have low levels of power. As indicated earlier in this chapter, this location results in part from broad socialization processes that encourage non-white-male employees to enter fields with limited organizational power—"nurturing" or "people-oriented" fields for women, and "applied" or "practical" (as opposed to theoretical or managerial) careers for African American men and Latinos. Even when African American men, Latinos, and women do not "choose" staff-related careers, organizations tend to shunt them in those directions. For example, only 7.3 percent of *line* divisions (those that contribute directly to the profitability of the firm) in Fortune 500 firms (the largest 500 firms in the United States) have women managers, although this represents a significant increase over the 5.3 percent in 1997. Because virtually all organizations require upper managers to have line experience, being limited to staff positions reduces one's organizational power and may prevent promotion. Virtually all the 1,622 women among the 12,945 corporate officers (12.5 percent, up from 8.7 percent in 1995) in Fortune 500 firms have had substantial line experience. Staff positions seem to be surrounded by **glass walls,** and these walls may be the greatest barrier to upward mobility for women and minority managers.[30]

Of course, creating racially segregated and gender-segregated sectors of an organization also reduces organizational effectiveness. People who have the same backgrounds and experiences are more prone to problems of trained incapacity, groupthink, and communication breakdowns. Organizations with one unit or subculture composed of all upper-class Anglo males and other units or subcultures made up of people with widely differing attributes and experiences tend to have low levels of cross-sector cooperation and high levels of cross-unit communication breakdowns.[31] But upper managers' preferences for co-workers with whom they are comfortable seem to be more important in promotion decisions than concerns about efficient communication or "objective" decision making.

Dealing with Marginalization   To compensate for glass walls and glass ceilings, women and members of racial or ethnic minority groups adopt various strategies. Two of them involve obtaining information about the organization, its culture, and its practices through mentors and by cultivating informal communication networks. There is widespread agreement that newcomers who successfully navigate the entry experience do so largely because they are able to establish close, personal mentoring relationships with one or more senior employees early in their careers.[32] From these **mentors** newcomers obtain all the different kinds of information discussed in this chapter. However, like all interpersonal relationships, mentor-mentee relationships are difficult to form and maintain, especially when the mentees are of a different gender, race, or ethnic background than their mentors. Informal mentoring systems tend to exclude African Americans and Latinos/Latinas and, to a somewhat lesser degree, white women. A study by Catalyst, a New York–based research organization, found that half of African American women had been unable to establish a mentoring relationship, compared with one-third of white women who failed to do so.[33]

Both mentor and mentee may feel awkward, especially at first. Once the relationship is established, it may be difficult to avoid creating an actual or perceived dependency relationship. In U.S. firms, so few women or members of minority groups occupy positions near the top of organizations that the vast majority of mentors will be European-American men. In general, these supervisors seem to be willing to mentor or assist male subordinates if they are sufficiently competent. However, they seem to be willing to mentor European-American women, Latinos, and African American men only if the potential mentees are near the bottom of the organizational hierarchy. Once they are promoted and become possible threats to the supervisors, the supervisors withdraw their help, even if they espouse egalitarian attitudes.

Traditional sex-role stereotypes also complicate mentoring relationships; it is difficult for the parties to know how to act toward each other or how to interpret each other's actions. The relationship may be strained and communication may be less open and spontaneous than in same-sex relationships. Cross-sex (or cross-race or -ethnicity) mentoring relationships also seem to be weaker, less stable, and more limited to discussions of task issues than are same-sex (and same-race or -ethnicity) relationships. European-American male mentees also seem to obtain access to other relationships through their mentors, whereas this is much less true for women, African American men, and Latinos. As a result, establishing and maintaining positive mentoring relationships is more difficult for women, African American men, and Latinos than it is for Anglo men, and the mentoring relationships that they do establish seem to be less beneficial to their career advancement. The complicated nature of mentoring is one reason why women and minority men often do not become fully integrated into their organizations but instead eventually move on.[34]

Another mechanism for helping newcomers make sense of their organization is to encourage them to become linked to informal communication networks. For the reasons described in the previous paragraphs, "different" employees often find it difficult to become integrated into the informal networks that exist within their firms. An alternative is to resort to external networks. Most major cities and many smaller ones now have active networks for women, African American, and Latino managers and professionals. External networks have proved to be valuable to all three groups. Contacts made in networks provide a wide variety of information about how organizations work as well as offering social and emotional support. Employees who have experienced overt discrimination or racial or sexual harassment are supported by people who have had similar experiences and have learned how to deal with those problems. Networks share information about which firms have good (and which have poor) records of advancing women and minority employees. They provide advice about handling everyday work-related problems and exchange information about when and where vacancies are anticipated. At times, networks can become elitist, shifting their focus from aiding all their members to assisting a selected few. But when they work effectively, they can provide members with all the information that European-American men traditionally have gained through informal good-old-boy networks. In short, external networks help compensate for the fact that Latinos, Latinas, European-American women, and African Americans are often excluded from the internal networks of their organizations.[35]

"Different" employees also can deal with marginalization by adopting particular career strategies. They can actively prepare for, seek out, and accept assignments in traditionally Anglo male occupations, industries, and specializations. Although doing so often means that they will suffer temporary financial losses or personal dislocation and will have to deal with more extensive sexism/ racism and sexual/racial harassment than they would experience in service/ staff positions, their long-term career prospects will increase.[36] Interestingly, many women seem to have recognized that these barriers continue to exist and have responded by starting organizations of their own. During the 1980s a much larger number of women—one of three MBAs in one study—have left large organizations to start their own businesses. Their decisions were motivated in part by anticipation of the freedom, excitement, and feelings of achievement that accompany succeeding in running one's own business in a highly competitive environment. But they also stemmed from frustration with gender-related barriers in their old firms that kept them from being rewarded adequately and equitably for their contributions, and from moving into positions of greater challenge and creativity.

The growth of these firms has been remarkable. In 1980 there were 2 million women-owned businesses with $25 billion in sales or receipts; in 1999 there were 9.1 million with 27.5 million employees and $3.6 trillion in sales or receipts. Thirty-eight percent of U.S. businesses are now owned by women. In California the number of women-owned companies has increased 164 percent since 1992. In 1996, 405,200 African American women owned businesses with 261,400 employees and sales of $24.7 billion, a 137 percent increase over 1986. In Australia about one-half of small businesses are owned by women, and their growth rate is double that of small businesses owned by men. Women entrepreneurs are just as successful as male entrepreneurs; they provide better benefits packages for their employees (especially in the United States and Mexico) and play an increasing role in traditionally male sectors of the economy such as construction, transportation, agriculture, and manufacturing.[37] Consequently, as a result of their inability or unwillingness to meet the personal and career needs of professional women, large, complex organizations have lost a great deal of talent and expertise and in the process have created a large number of effective competitors. Unfortunately, limited access to investment capital makes it difficult for women or persons of color to become entrepreneurs; but they are slowly overcoming those barriers. Banks are reticent to make loans to women entrepreneurs, and only 2 percent of loans made by venture capitalists (the individuals or organizations who fund start-ups) go to women (far less than 1 percent go to minority entrepreneurs). As a result, most women draw on personal assets or loans from friends and family to start their businesses in the United States, Europe, and the Commonwealth countries.[38]

Confronting the Dominant Perspective

Organizations have a variety of strategies available to resist workforce diversification. Each of these strategies sacrifices the potential benefits of diversity but allows the organization to avoid making changes. "Other" employees use an equally varied group of strategies to overcome organizational resistance. An alternative approach is for organizations to recognize the potential benefits of diversity and devise strategies for confronting the dominant perspective.

Valuing "Others'" Ways

Researchers have noted that the people who make up the workforce of today's organizations in the industrialized world have a different set of core values than those that are included in the dominant perspective. Virtually absent are an unquestioning loyalty to the organization and an obsession with the pursuit of money. Instead, today's workers value recognition, feelings of accomplishment, being treated with respect and dignity, psychological involvement and pride in meaningful work (recall Chapter 4), and quality of life, including opportunities for self-development, health, and wellness. These values are inconsistent with traditional, bureaucratic strategies of organizing and instead are consistent with the more flexible relationship-, culture-, and network-oriented strategies described in Unit II. They underlie a pattern of acting and a set of leadership strategies that are especially appropriate to the turbulent and globally competitive environments faced by modern organizations.

In a now-classic study, Sally Helgessen compared the day-by-day work activities of (primarily Anglo) male managers to those of (primarily Anglo) female managers. She found that males tend to work at an unrelenting pace, with no scheduled breaks during the day. Their days are characterized by interruptions, discontinuity, and fragmentation. They spend little time in long-term planning or reflecting on their goals or the effectiveness of the strategies they use. They prefer face-to-face communication to written messages but have difficulty sharing information with co-workers and subordinates. Anglo women, Helgessen observed, also tend to prefer face-to-face interactions. They work at a steady pace and schedule small breaks during the day; they take a broader and longer-term perspective instead of focusing solely on day-to-day activities; they actively share information with others and gain satisfaction from *both* the process of working *and* its results. They define power as the ability to *act with* others to accomplish goals that could not be achieved by individuals acting alone, rather than as *power over* others (recall Chapter 8). Leadership involves empowering others, being at the *center* of a group rather than in front of it. Leaders' claims to expertise and authority must be justified continually and be explained to other employees in terms they can readily understand. A decade later communication researchers Diane Kay Sloan and Kathleen Krone's study of thirty women managers in multiple sectors of the U.S. economy found similar results—feminine leadership styles that focused on openness and support and a much more widespread masculine style that focused on closedness and intimidation.[39]

Research with Latinos and Latinas also suggests a preference for a particular form of leadership. Latin cultures are grounded in the concepts of familism, machismo, and *simpatía*. **Familism** involves strong values attached to family and community and a commitment to hard work and achievement as a way of honoring one's family. It also values aiding others who are in need. It is for this reason that having a job that pays low wages is even more stressful for Latinos than for other males. **Machismo,** a concept that is widely misunderstood by non-Latinos/Latinas, embraces a strong sense of loyalty and duty to other members of the community and a sense of honor and duty, not to an impersonal organization, but to other people. *Simpatía* is a complex concept that involves engaging in positive, agreeing behaviors whenever possible, showing respect for one's superiors by conforming to their wishes, and avoiding conflict and confrontation *in public settings.* But it does not mean conformity and blind obedience, because it also requires superiors to show respect to their subordinates, especially in public. These values lead to a high level of concern for interpersonal relationships and the feelings of other people, a participatory, open-door leadership style, and a preference for face-to-face communication. They also generate a desire for fair treatment and high levels of freedom and autonomy. Latino/Latina supervisors tend to feel a responsibility for developing their subordinates' skills and abilities. Latin culture also encourages a high level of flexibility in leadership strategies, including a willingness to ignore the formal chain of command when it is inefficient. African Americans and Asian Americans also seem to lead by developing cooperative work teams, openly sharing information, encouraging participation in decision making, and helping to develop all employees' expertise.[40]

In sum, Anglo men tend to use what Chapter 4 calls transactional leadership. Women, Latinos, and African American and Asian American men prefer what Chapter 5 calls transformational leadership, an approach that is particularly well suited to the turbulent environment of a competitive, global economy. Of course, individual employees have had their own distinctive developmental experiences and may have developed leadership styles that deviate from both their general cultural backgrounds and the norms of their organizations. However, if organizations pressure "others" to adopt transactional leadership styles, as they seem to do much more frequently in U.S. firms than in European organizations, they sacrifice the strengths that can come with diversity.[41]

Challenging the Underlying Attitudes of the Dominant Perspective

Instead of resisting diversification, organizations can confront the dominant perspective directly by valuing attitudes that are appropriate to a diverse workforce in a global environment. The key assumptions of the dominant perspective are that thinking and doing should be separated; that the thinking function should be treated as superior and should be conducted by a group of people who are similar to one another in every possible respect; and that actions should be guided by stable policies and procedures that are arrived at through rational decision making. Hiring decisions should be based largely on how well potential employees fit into the existing organization, and once they start work, they should be encouraged to adapt to an existing organizational role. Of course, attempting to assimilate employees into existing organizational practices and valuing diversity are contradictory ideas.[42]

The most important attitudinal change in confronting the dominant perspective is to celebrate *flexibility*. It has two components: *recognizing* that achieving goals of equity and effectiveness does not mean treating everyone in the same way but does mean treating them all fairly; and *believing* that organizations should be adapted to fit the needs and develop the talents of every individual employee, instead of demanding that every employee adapt to the organization. An organization needs to make very different adjustments to utilize fully the talents of a single mother of two preschoolers, a computer programmer who is confined to a wheelchair, a deaf investment counselor, a group of Latina production workers, or a middle-aged Anglo male who has *plateaued* (reached the highest level in the organization that he will ever reach). For example, the Aluminum Company of America (ALCOA) hired Kevin Kennedy, an operations engineer who had a degenerative eye condition that restricted his peripheral vision and would eventually lead to blindness. Instead of declaring that Kevin inevitably would be incapable of doing his job, ALCOA's management asked how the organization could enable Kevin to continue to contribute. They assigned an assistant to help him when his job involved operating large industrial machinery or visiting plants with which he was unfamiliar. When his vision deteriorated further, the organization responded by redefining his duties so that they focused on computer modeling; they provided special lighting for his workspace and a large magnifying glass to help him read and purchased a large-screen computer and software for converting written texts to Braille. In this way the company was able to retain a highly competent employee at a cost far below the cost of hiring and training a replacement.[43] In the process, they discovered what researchers have known for some time—meeting the needs of disabled workers is far less expensive than managers tend to believe that it will be.

The Hallmark Corporation no longer encourages members of its artistic staff to specialize. Instead it rotates new employees through different assignments to give them a wide range of actual job experiences. If potential candidates for a promotion lack a specific set of skills, the organization may assign them to a different department for six months or so to give them a chance to develop the skills necessary to move up. In some cases, the employees may discover that they are better suited for the division to which they are temporarily assigned, and the organization does everything possible to facilitate a move to that division. Traditionally, promotion has meant abandoning one's technical specialty and becoming a manager. But many people who have exceptional technical skills do not have the interests or abilities necessary to become successful managers. So they are forced to either remain in the same unchallenging positions or move into a role with which they are uncomfortable. Diversity management proposes that organizations create alternative career paths, so that people can stay within their specialties but receive promotions and increasingly complex technical assignments, or they can cycle in and out of management positions.

Another attitudinal change involves focusing on *outcomes* instead of constraints. Different employees produce the best outcomes if they are enabled to do their jobs in their own ways. Jim James, a research engineer, had promised his wife that he would retire in two months. He knew he would not be able to finish the project that he was working on in that amount of time. His supervisor decided that his expertise on the project was too valuable to lose, so he arranged to have James spend twenty hours a week as a consultant to the firm and to be assigned a co-op student from the local university as a research assistant. He was able to arrange his own working schedule, keep his commitment to his wife, and offer his firm expertise on specified projects that only he could provide.

Developing Supportive Policies

The single most important step that an organization can take to challenge the dominant perspective is to change its reward system. Rewarding employees for conforming to organizational norms merely serves to perpetuate dominant attitudes and behaviors. Rewarding them for performance not only generates change, but it adds credibility to change efforts. Performance-based systems involve collecting data on the number and proportion of people who are promoted, breaking that data down by gender, race, and ethnicity, and *publicizing* the data throughout the firm. This is because upper managers tend to *overestimate* the success of diversity programs, leading to complacency, and Anglo males who are competing with newcomers tend to *underestimate* their own opportunities, leading to unnecessary resistance and backlash. Like all organizational change efforts, diversity will succeed only if it is strongly, honestly, and openly supported by individuals in upper management. *They* must establish policies and procedures that target women, African American men, and Latinos for recruitment, professional development, and advancement. *They* must support the development of internal advocacy groups and task forces to provide emotional support for diverse groups of employees, and *they* must keep the organization's diversification goals at the forefront of everyday activities. Policies and programs alone are meaningless. After all, Texaco and Coca Cola had a number of diversity management and fair-employment practices, policies, and procedures on the books and had even won awards for them. The same was true of San Diego Gas and Electric Company when, in 1994, the courts ordered it to pay $3 million to a former worker who had been repeatedly called "nigger," "coon," or "boy" and subjected to threats and racial and sexual graffiti about him. And the same was true of Wal-Mart when it recently lost a $50 million sexual harassment suit (reduced to $5 million on appeal) in spite of the company's "strong" commitments, policies, and procedures. In all of these cases, there was no evidence that the commitments and policies had ever been translated into action— no one had been disciplined for any of the activities included in the cases.[44]

CASE STUDY
Is That Term "Childless" or "Childfree"?

Numerous polls and surveys conducted in the United States during the past decade
have found that one of employees' greatest concerns is balancing work and family.
This tension results in part from the downsizing of U.S. organizations during the
1980s and 1990s. Especially for white-collar employees, downsizing has meant that
a smaller number of workers must do the same amount of work that was previously
done by a larger workforce. The tension also results from U.S. public policy—according to United Nations data, the United States is one of only six industrialized
nations that do not guarantee paid maternity leave (the others are New Zealand,
Papua New Guinea, Australia, Lesotho, and Swaziland).* The 1993 Family and Medical Leave Act does not cover businesses with fewer than fifty employees (such
businesses employ almost half of the U.S. workforce) and does not require maternity or paternity leave (or sick leave, or care for a sick relative) to be paid—only
that leave must be granted. Consequently, it tends to be used by upper-middle-class
and upper-class workers, because lower-income workers simply cannot afford to
forgo a paycheck for an extended period of time. California did enact a paid-leave
requirement in September 2003, but the prognosis for it to stay on the books over
the long term is not good. The upshot is that relatively few U.S. organizations offer
paid leave or other family-friendly policies like flexwork (which can involve either
flexible work times or flexible places of work—telecommuting, for example) or
dependent care. Those that do tend to be in industries in which the workforce is
largely composed of women—in particular, women who have relatively strong bargaining positions with management, either because they have hard-to-find skills or
because they are in tight labor markets, which give workers a stronger bargaining
position on all issues.

However, even when companies have favorable policies, it may be difficult for
employees to use them. Managers may not tell their subordinates about the policies or may pressure them into not using them. People who use these policies tend
to be perceived as less ambitious, committed, and professional than those who
forgo them, even though these employees typically are more efficient and productive than their colleagues. Even before people accept a job, they should try to find
out whether family-friendly rhetoric represents policies that are actually followed.
After accepting the job, they should try to determine the extent to which the organization rewards managers for being flexible. They should also make their own
values clear to their co-workers. Although these strategies are often thought of as
relevant to women, they may be even more important for men. *Chicago Tribune*
columnist Carol Kleiman summarizes the available evidence rather bluntly: "The
workplace gives a lot of lip service to family-friendly policies, but when it comes
to crunch time and a male employee isn't there, he's considered disloyal. In fact, if

(continued)

370	Chapter 10	*Communication and Diverse Workplaces*

(Case Study, continued)

he puts his family first, he's considered a wimp."† When Maryland State Trooper Kevin Knussman won a four-year legal battle for paternity leave in 1999, only a few co-workers congratulated him; many made snide comments. As a result of these pressures, only one-half million of the two million people who have taken parental leave under the 1993 U.S. Family and Medical Leave Act have been men. In spite of these barriers, the average amount of time that U.S. fathers spend with their children has increased from 1.8 hours a day in 1977 to 2.3 hours in 1996 (compared to 9–17 minutes a day in Japan and less than one hour in Britain and Germany). But the change is mixed—there is an increasing number of U.S. men who have nothing to do with their children and an increasing number who are becoming very actively involved. The ones who are spending more time do it because they want to be more involved in their children's lives than their fathers were involved in theirs, because their wives are working full time, and because they can do so. Sometimes being involved in one's family requires creative resistance. One new father parks his car at the far corner of the parking lot so that he can disappear (to go home) at five o'clock; another leaves his desk lamp and computer on when he takes his child to the physician; many fathers cobble together vacation and sick leave time so that they can spend time with their children without admitting it. One noted, "I know other men who are doing the same thing" and compared these fathers to Alcoholics Anonymous: "We know who we are and why we're doing this, but we don't give our names."‡

Choosing to have family as a top priority is a difficult decision because it often requires that people violate powerful social norms. For example, although Japanese workers are officially allotted eighteen paid vacation days each year; on average they take only nine. They have learned to see vacation time as a burden on their co-workers, not as an entitlement they have earned. When holidays are institutionalized—meaning that everyone takes them off—Japanese workers actually take them. Even in northern Europe, where lengthy paid vacations have been mandated by law for decades, people hesitate to take them for fear that they will be viewed as disloyal. But in the United States, a trend toward maintaining a greater balance between work and family seems to be taking hold. The post–baby boom generational groups consistently list work-family balance as a high priority, suggesting that there will be increasing pressure for organizations to change. It also is clear, however, that many organizations will strongly resist those changes, so choosing an organization with values similar to your own will continue to be important.

Because long-term career advancement (and lifetime income) is reduced by taking leaves, particularly for men, these policies tend to be underused, especially by single workers, men, and career-oriented women.§ In fact, in organizations that offer paid paternity leave (about 13 percent do) and take steps to ensure that employees are not penalized for taking it, a surprising number of fathers actually take the leave. For example, accounting firm KPMG of Montvale, New Jersey, expected that about 5 percent of its fathers would take paternity leave. But when the firm implemented its program, 30 percent of the fathers did so. J. P. Morgan Chase and Company had a similar experience.**

Underlying assumptions about the "proper" economic roles that women and men should play, and about government noninterference in the free market, influence family-related public policies and managerial choices about organizational policies and practices. But those assumptions go even deeper, into the ways people communicate with one another at work. Erika Kirby and Kathleen Krone recently studied an organization that had adopted rather liberal family-friendly policies, at least by U.S. standards. They found a very complicated pattern of communication surrounding the use of those policies. Regulatory Alliance (a pseudonym for the organization they studied) is a government agency charged with making sure that banks follow legal requirements. Employees have to travel a great deal, and their tasks are sufficiently technical that it is impossible to hire and train replacement personnel to cover for an employee when she or he is out on leave, unless everyone knows that the leave will be for an extended period of time. As a result, when people take leave, other employees have to pick up the workload.

Kirby and Krone found that two themes dominated conversations about leave policies. The dominant theme involved perceptions of preferential treatment for employees who had children and resentment on the part of employees who did not. The resentment focused on women who took maternity leave, primarily because very few men took paternity leave. But when women did take maternity leave, people perceived that new mothers "have got it a little bit easier" than new fathers: new fathers "may have had two hours of sleep the night before and yet soon after the birth they're expected to go into work the next day and perform like nothing ever happened." But the feelings of unequal treatment went beyond leave itself. Employees perceived that single workers were assigned a disproportionate amount of travel, especially long trips: "If we've got a big complicated bank coming up, I can pretty well guarantee it's not going to be a new mother in charge of it."[††] Similarly, people working part-time (all of them were mothers) were not as dedicated as those who worked full time. And again, there were gender differences in the perceptions:

> If a man went part-time, the "question would be, 'Well, why is he only working part-time?' as opposed to if it's a mother there's kind of a reason." A male examiner agreed that "realistically, I think it's much more difficult for probably the male to go part-time. . . . I think it just kind of goes against the norm." This perception that part-time was just a program for women could be problematic. A female [Regulatory Alliance] member illustrated that "if the only really good [reason] is women having children, that fosters that resentment. . . . 'She wants to go part-time and I am going to have to pick up more work' and then you get that backlash."[‡‡]

Interestingly, the part-timers worked very hard in order to counter this perception, but it was pervasive enough that it reduced the likelihood that employees would

(continued)

(Case Study, continued)

request part-time status. There really was an "us versus them" attitude about the issues.

The second theme that Kirby and Krone discovered involved a distinction between using the policies and abusing them. People who were perceived as abusing the policies were targeted for a great deal of peer pressure. As often is the case (see Chapter 5), it was the work team, more than supervisors, that exerted control over employees. Workers told one another stories about people who had abused the system and about the reactions they received. According to one story, a female manager who had recently had a baby went to her supervisor "horrified that people were going to think that she was getting preferential treatment in staying in town longer, when in fact it was a mere coincidence. She didn't want anybody to think that she was asking for special accommodations."[§§] This climate of opinion made it difficult for managers to approach employees about the policies that were in place and for workers to know when and to what extent they should use the policies. They often resorted to "testing the waters" to see how co-workers would respond to the idea of their using the policies.

Using What You Have Learned

1. What underlying assumptions are "played out" at Regulatory Alliance? Be sure you go deeper than the obvious issues. For example, some organizations have the same leave policies for adopting a baby and for giving birth to one. Some do not. Others treat elder-care leave the same way they treat maternity/paternity leave. Others do not. What are the differing assumptions underlying each of these policy options?
2. How are those assumptions related to one another? For example, if a policy reduces organizational efficiency but enhances worker job satisfaction, which should take priority? Why?

Questions to Think About and Discuss

One of the clearest demographic trends of the past twenty years has been the falling reproductive rate of people around the world, but especially in northern Europe (which has had negative population growth rates for some time) and among whites in the United States and Canada (both of which will have negative population growth rates within a very few years if current trends continue). Of U.S. women aged forty to forty-four, 19 percent are childless, twice as high a percentage as twenty years earlier. Some of this shift results from increasing infertility rates, and some of it results from a reduction in the percentage of adult women who are married. But nearly 7 million U.S. women define themselves as voluntarily childless (or "childfree," to use a popular term), up from 2.4 million in 1982. The rates are substantially higher among educated, professional workers. In part because of a general feeling of being discriminated against, and in part because it is more difficult for childless/childfree employees to locate one another, support groups for "childfree" workers have mushroomed (for example, the organization named No Kidding, which now has seventy-one chapters in the United States).***

1. Who should take responsibility (individual employees, organizations, government, and so on) for encouraging or enabling workers to have and care for children? Why? What groups of people will be treated unfairly if your answer becomes social policy? What groups will be given preferential treatment? Can you justify those differences? How?

2. Design an organizational benefits package that is likely to maximize the potential tensions and conflicts among the various employee groups at Regulatory Alliance. Be sure to include the indirect effects of policies (for example, if the company's health care policy is designed to minimize costs of "family" coverage, it is likely to reduce the scope of coverage for workers themselves; if it covers pregnancy care as a medical condition instead of an elective condition, health care costs borne by the company and employees who participate in the program will be higher, and so forth). Then design a benefits package that is likely to minimize those tensions.

---

*Shannon Buggs, "Maternity Leave Can Cost a Great Deal More Later," *Houston Chronicle*, December 2, 2002, E1.

†"Men Still Suspect If Priority Is Family," *Houston Chronicle*, April 9, 2000, D2; also see Suzanne Braun Levine, *Father Courage* (New York: Harcourt, 2000).

‡Trooper Knussman's story is told in "Dad Wins Legal Fight for Time Off," *Houston Chronicle*, February 5, 1999, A19.

§L. Bailyn, J. K. Fletcher, and D. Kolb, "Unexpected Connections: Considering Employees' Personal Lives Can Revitalize Your Business," *Sloan Management Review* 38 (1997): 11–19.

**L. M. Sixel, "Paid Paternity Leave More Popular Than Expected," *Houston Chronicle*, May 16, 2003, C1.

††Erika Kirby and Kathleen Krone, "'The Policy Exists but You Can't Really Use It': Communication and the Structuration of Work-Family Policies," *Journal of Applied Communication Research* 30 (2002): 61.

‡‡Kirby and Krone, p. 62.

§§Kirby and Krone, p. 65.

***For an extended analysis of this data, and a list of additional support services, see Ellen Metter, *Cheerfully Childless* (New York: Browser Press, 2001).

Taking a Holistic Perspective

The final element of the dominant perspective is the notion that organizations are "containers," places that are separated by time and space from the places where employees live their nonwork lives. Of course, this notion has never been accurate for professional and managerial employees. Taking work home, being on call, and spending sleepless nights pondering work-related problems have all been normal parts of white-collar employees' lives in the industrialized world. However, the advent of many new technologies—laptop computers, the Internet, cell phones, paging systems, and so on—mean that many people never actually leave work. It is ironic that technologies that have promised people more control over their time—from the telephone to the personal computer—usually have not provided the promised control. Instead they often have increased organizations' ability to limit or invade employees' private time. Organizational downsizing throughout the world has created a situation in which a smaller number of workers are available to complete the same amount of work. Increased organizational demands to work overtime since the early 1990s have created a situation in which balancing work and family is one of the greatest problems faced by modern employees. Overall, the average U.S. workweek increased only two hours between 1982 and 1996, but that figure is misleading. The vast majority of new workers added during that time were women, who average less than forty hours per week. Underemployment among blue-collar workers also artificially reduces the average. As a result, as the new century started, the U.S. workforce was divided into two disparate groups: those who are unable to work full time because the jobs are not there, and those whose workload has skyrocketed. For the latter group the experience of Elizabeth Oaks, a lawyer who works in the oil and gas industry, is typical: "We come home, we barely get something to eat, and we're exhausted. . . . I can't imagine what people do who have children."[45]

For example, in the United States, one-third of adults average less than seven hours of sleep a night, although most people need eight or nine hours. Bureau of Labor statistics show that the average number of paid vacation days per year in U.S. firms is 6.8, rising to 10 for professional employees. These figures are comparable to those of the Philippines, Hong Kong, and Mexico but substantially below those for Saudi (15 days), German (18 days), Italian (28–42 days), or British (35 days) workers. The rapid movement of women into the professional labor force since the early 1980s has significantly increased the number of people who experience work-home spillover. The percentage of women who chose to not have children almost doubled between 1976 and 1995, and the figure is even higher among women with college degrees. More than half of new mothers return to the workforce within a year of giving birth. Two-thirds of women with some college do so, as do three-quarters of women with graduate or professional degrees. In general, mothers with higher incomes are more likely to return (two-thirds of those making $75,000 or more do so, compared to half of those earning less than $20,000). These differences result in part from personal goals; educated, upper-income mothers have usually postponed having children until they have completed their education, become established in their careers, and moved up through their organizational hierarchies. The high level of career commitment that results gives them extra incentives to return to work. But it also has to do with their greater ability to afford high-quality child care and their enhanced bargaining power with their employers.

"Family-friendly" policies are rarely made available to all members of an organization. Instead they are offered to employees who are difficult to replace or who have other sources of organizational power.[46] Lower-level, lower-income workers, those who need benefits the most, often are not eligible for them. It is for this reason that *Working Mother* magazine, whose annual list of the "100 Best Companies for Mothers to Work For" is the most comprehensive survey of "family-friendly" policies, entitled its 2000 study "Nice Perks, If You Can Get 'Em." In short, employees have multidimensional lives, each part of which demands their time, energy, and commitment. Unfortunately, some organizations refuse to take a holistic perspective, one that recognizes these multiple responsibilities. Fortunately, some do.

One of the easiest ways to get a sense of the kinds of programs and policies that can be valuable to a diverse workforce is to peruse *Working Mother*'s "100 Best" list. Firms are evaluated in part on the fairness of their salary schedules and their record of promoting women. But they also gain points for having programs such as child-care assistance (including backup day care for children who are ill or out of school for a holiday, vacation, or snow day), flextime, flexplace, and flexible benefit plans. But *Working Mother* also warns readers about surveys that look *only* at a company's policies, because they are often either not implemented or implemented in a way that penalizes employees who use them. As Jennifer Chatman, a professor in the School of Business at the University of California—Berkeley notes, "The policies provide a good image and attract employees, but they're not practiced because people get informally penalized for doing anything that takes away from a one-hundred-percent effort." As the childless/childfree case study indicates, even if upper managements support the policies—and a growing percentage do, because it is very clear that these policies really do increase productivity and reduce costs related to absenteeism and turnover—middle- or lower-level managers and peers may not. For example, Dupont has struggled for years to persuade its managers to support family-friendly policies. In 2000 the company spent $200,000 to train managers in locations away from the home office to assess their employees' needs and develop appropriate policies, but it continues to face resistance.[47]

In spite of these challenges, there are many examples of programs and policies that seem to have been implemented successfully. Ben and Jerry's Homemade Holdings Inc. pays health club fees and reimburses parents for adoption fees (up to the cost of a hospital delivery of a baby); Beth Israel Hospital in Boston provides breast pumping stations for returning mothers who are nursing their babies; Arthur Andersen and Company provides on-site day care for employees during the peak tax-preparation season; Barnett Bank in Florida provides round-trip transportation for employees' children to summer day camp at the local YMCA; Lincoln National Insurance has trained 300 family day care providers to be employed by their workers; and Colgate-Palmolive pays the full cost of in-home emergency care for ill children for its employees. At the Bureau of National Affairs Inc., employees with ten years of service are eligible for six-month sabbaticals at half pay, and Consolidated Edison of New York has a new training program to attract women to higher-paying jobs traditionally held by men (such as utility repair work).[48] The list could be extended almost endlessly.

Even small and medium-sized businesses can help. They often lack the funds to establish expensive benefits, such as on-site day care or scholarships for employees' children. But they can provide flexibility. Cross Country Staffing, a Boca Raton, Florida, firm with only 284 employees (84 percent of whom are women) made the *Working Mother* list for the first time in 2000. The company instituted job-sharing in 1991 and a variety of flextime systems during the 1990s. Because more than half of U.S. employees work in small companies (those with fewer than 500 employees), and two-thirds of the new jobs created in the next five years will be in small firms, these steps are especially important. And they demonstrate that any organization can consult with employees about what *their* needs are and design flexible programs that *individualize* policies, procedures, and benefits, while staying within the constraints imposed by budgets and concerns for fairness.

Conclusion

On the one hand, in the United States and many other countries, substantial progress has been made in changing organizations to meet the challenges of a diverse workforce. Today there are far more women, African Americans, and Latinos in entry-level professional and managerial positions than there were twenty years ago. Between 1970 and 1985 the proportion of female managers in the U.S. economy as a whole increased from 15 percent to 36 percent, and the number of female managers grew 400 percent. In 2000, 49 percent of management and professional jobs were held by women, and that figure is projected to grow to 54 percent by 2030. Two-thirds of all managers hired between 1965 and 1985 were women. In 1992, 55 percent of the people earning bachelor's degrees were women, as were 35 percent of new M.D.'s and 42 percent of new attorneys, suggesting that there are sufficient numbers of women receiving advanced training to continue these trends. A majority of students in U.S. medical and law schools are women. The percentage of women in upper management grew from 3.5 in 1970 to 6.8 in 1980 to 14 percent in 1996 but leveled off during the recession of the late 1990s and early 2000s.

However, people who are not Anglo males are still concentrated at the lower levels of organizations and in sectors with lower salaries and fewer mobility opportunities. In 1991, 25 percent of officers and managers in small firms were Anglo women, 5 percent were African Americans, 3 percent were Latinos or Latinas, and 2 percent were Asian Americans. In the 100 largest of firms in the Fortune 500 firms, fewer officers and managers are women (about 18 percent), and only 7 percent are African Americans, Latinos, or Asian Americans. In the Fortune 500 as a whole, upper management still is almost exclusively the province of Anglo males—90 percent of these firms do not have a woman among the five most compensated officers.[49]

Salaries for all women in the labor force have been around 69 percent of men's salaries for decades. In 1992 the figure reached a high of 72 percent, subsequently fell back to 69 percent, and in 2003 reached its highest level ever, 80 percent. The gap is smaller for women aged 25–34 (82 percent) and smaller still for women aged 27–33 who have never had children (98 percent). Surveys in 2003 by the National (U.S.) Association for Female Executives and the General Accounting Office found that "no matter how much you try to explain it away there is somewhere between a 12 percent to 20 percent wage gap that can only be attributed to discrimination."[50] Among professional occupations, the gap varies, and it changes with different economic conditions. In contrast, African American men still earn approximately 50 percent of Anglo men's salaries; African American women earn approximately 30 percent of Anglo men's incomes and approximately 60 percent of the income of Anglo women. Overall, Latinos earn two-thirds of the salaries of Anglo men. Of course, many of these gaps are still significant, even if the data are corrected for education, experience, or seniority within the firm.

Attitudes about a diverse workforce also have improved but still serve as barriers to change. And as the U.S. workforce becomes more diverse, other groups of employees have started to confront the dominant perspective. For example, age discrimination has become an increasing problem during the 1990s and is likely to grow in importance as the baby boomers age. Like other forms of differential treatment, ageism is both pervasive and subtle. It is grounded in the cultural assumption that older people are inherently less capable than younger workers. For example, when managers described thirty-year-old and sixty-year-old workers, they used the terms "more productive, capable of working under pressure, flexible, able to learn, and decisive" for the younger workers and "reliable, honest, committed to quality, have good attendance records, and use good judgment" for the older ones in spite of consistent research evidence indicating that intellectual skills do not decline substantially with age. They also tend to assume that younger workers will stay with the company for twenty-five to thirty years, in spite of substantial evidence that long-term connections to a single organization no longer can be assumed for *any* group of employees (recall the Generation X case study in Chapter 1).[51] Negative attitudes about gay and lesbian employees persist even though a number of organizations have taken steps to reduce differential treatment. In 1996 IBM announced that it would extend health benefits to partners of its homosexual employees. More than 500 major U.S. companies now have policies forbidding discrimination and ensuring equivalent benefits for gay employees, up from 250 in 1995 and including Apple Computer, Ben and Jerry's, Dayton Hudson, Eastman Kodak, Fox Broadcasting, Glaxo Wellcome, Hewlett-Packard, Seagram and Sons, Levi Strauss, Microsoft, NYNEX, Time Warner, Walt Disney, Wells Fargo, and Xerox.

So, at least in the United States, Europe, and the Commonwealth countries, there is evidence that some organizations have started to confront the dominant perspective while others engage in resistance. The barriers that traditionally have separated different groups of employees have started to dissolve. But it is not yet clear whether the vestiges of those barriers will continue to exist, new barriers will be created, or the dominant perspective will disappear.

Notes

[1] Radha S. Hegde, "A View from Elsewhere," *Communication Theory* 8 (1998): 271–297; John Oetzel and Keri Bolton-Oetzel, "Exploring the Relationship between Self-Construal and Dimensions of Group Effectiveness," *Management Communication Quarterly* 10 (1997): 289–315; A. R. Jan Mohamed and J. Lloyd, eds. *The Nature and Context of Minority Discourse* (Oxford, UK: Oxford University Press, 1990). J. Sullivan and S. Taylor's study of Korean and Japanese employees illustrates the combined influence of cultural and individual characteristics: "A Cross-Cultural Test of Compliance-Gaining Theory," *Management Communication Quarterly* 5 (1991): 220–239. The quotations at the beginning of this chapter were taken from the following sources: Jeffrey Sachs, "International Economics: Unlocking the Mysteries of Globalization," *Foreign Policy,* 110 (Spring, 1998): 168–206; Cynthia Stohl, "Globalizing Organizational Communication," in *The New Handbook of Organizational Communication,* Fredric Jablin & Linda Putnam, eds. (Thousand Oaks, CA: Sage, 2000), p. 324.

[2] Julia Kwong, "Ideological Crisis among China's Youths: Values and Official Ideology," *British Journal of Sociology* 45 (1994): 247–264.

[3] Genaro Armas, "Educational Gaps between Genders, Races Diminish," *Houston Chronicle,* March 21, 2003, A27; American Association of University Women, "'Pink Collar' Jobs Still Lure Most Women, Study Finds," *Houston Chronicle,* May 5, 2003, A5; Luis Valdivia, "A Burgeoning Hispanic Middle Class? Doubtful," *Houston Chronicle,* September 5, 2003, A25.

[4] Brenda Allen, "A Black Feminist Standpoint Analysis," in *Rethinking Management and Organization Communication from Feminist Perspectives,* Patrice Buzzanell, ed. (Thousand Oaks, CA: Sage, 2000); E. L. Bell, "The Bicultural Life Experience of Career-Oriented Black Women," *Journal of Organizational Behavior* 11 (1990): 459–477; P. H. Collins, "Comment on Hekman's 'Truth and Method,'" *Signs* 22 (1997): 375–381; D. C. Hine, "The Future of Black Women in the Academy," in *Black Women in the Academy: Promises and Perils,* L. Benjamin, ed. (Gainesville: University Press of Florida, 1997); P. S. Parker and D. Ogilvie, "Gender, Culture, and Leadership," *Leadership Quarterly* 7 (1996): 189–214.

[5] D. E. Eyer, *Mother-Infant Bonding: A Scientific Fiction* (New Haven, CT: Yale University Press, 1992); Gideon Kunda, *Engineering Culture* (Philadelphia: Temple University Press, 1992); Dennis Mumby, "Organizing Men," *Communication Theory* 8 (1998): 164–183.

[6] Julia Wood, *Gendered Lives* (Belmont, CA: Wadsworth, 1994); Judy DeHaven, "Aggressive Women Get Help," *Houston Chronicle,* September 22, 2002, D5.

[7] David Ivanovich, "$192.5 Million Settles Coca-Cola Race Suit," *Houston Chronicle,* November 17, 2000, A1, 20. As is typical in out-of-court settlements, Coca Cola's management denied that discrimination was systematic or consistent with the values of the organization. Also see Sheri Prasso, "Study: Stereotypes Hinder Female Executives," *Houston Chronicle,* February 29, 1996, B1.

[8] This hiring preference came as a surprise to local governments who had hoped that the new factories would provide jobs for a potentially much more troublesome group—young males who recently had migrated from rural areas to the cities in search of employment.

[9] The preceding examples were taken from the work of Aihwa Ong. See *Spirits of Resistance and Capitalist Discipline* (Albany: State University of New York Press, 1987); "The Gender and Labor Politics of Postmodernity," *Annual Review of Anthropology* 20 (1991); and "Spirits of Resistance," in *Situated Lives,* Louise Lamphere, Helena Razoné, and Patricia Zavella, eds. (New York: Routledge, 1997). Also see Stohl, "Globalizing."

[10] And, in some countries, co-worker actions that could reasonably have been expected to be known by management.

[11] Damian Grace and Stephen Cohen, *Business Ethics* (Melbourne, Australia: Oxford, 1995), pp. 42, 148 (emphasis in the original).

[12] Susan Faludi, *Backlash: The Undeclared War against American Women* (New York: Crown, 1991); Charlene Solomon, "Keeping Hate Out of the Workplace," *Personnel Journal* 71 (July 1992): 30–36; M. W. Zak, "It's Like a Prison in There," *Journal of Business and Technical Communication* 8 (1994): 282–298; Kathleen Kelley Reardon, *They Don't Get It, Do They?* (Boston: Little, Brown, 1995); Michele Galen and Ann Therese Palmer, "White, Male and Worried," *Business Week,* January 31, 1994, pp. 50–55; A. Edwards and C. Polite, *Children of the Dream: The Psychology of Black Success* (New York: Doubleday, 1992); and Anne Fisher, "When Will Women Get to the Top," *Fortune,* September 21, 1992, 44–56.

[13] A. Rizzo and C. Mendez, *The Integration of Women in Management* (New York: Quorum Books, 1990); Barbara Reskin and Irene Padavic, *Women and Men at Work* (Thousand Oaks, CA: Pine Forge Press, 1994).

[14] Beatríz Pesquera, "In the Beginning He Wouldn't Even Lift a Spoon"; and Denise Segura, "Chicanas in White-Collar Jobs," both in *Situated Lives,* Louise Lamphere, Helena Razoné, and Patricia Zavella, eds. (New York: Routlege, 1997), p. 307.

[15] See Arlie Hochschild and Anne Machung, *The Second Shift* (New York: Avon Books, 1997); A. Hochschild, *The Time Bind* (New York: Metropolitan Books, 1997); Janie Carter, *He Works, She Works* (New York: AMACOM, 1995); and Jean Potuchek, *Who Supports the Family?* (Palo Alto, CA: Stanford University Press, 1997).

[16] See Ann Morrison, Randall White, and Ellen Van Velsor, *Breaking the Glass Ceiling* (Greensboro, NC: Center for Creative Leadership, 1992).

[17] Korn/Ferry International, "The Decade of the Executive Woman," *Houston Chronicle,* February 19, 1996, B1.

[18] Segura, "Chicanas in White-Collar Jobs," p. 301.

[19] Lynn Miller, Linda Cooke, Jennifer Tsang, and Faith Morgan, "Should I Brag?" *Human Communication Research* 18 (1992): 364-399.

[20] Morrison, White, and Van Velsor, p. 137. For extended analyses of the visibility paradox, see Tom Daniels, Barry Spiker, and Michael Papa, *Perspectives on Organizational Communication,* 4th ed., (Madison, WI: Brown and Benchmark, 1997); Katherine Miller, *Organizational Communication* (Belmont, CA: Wadsworth, 1994); Philomena Essed, *Everyday Racism,* Cynthia Jaffe, trans. (Claremont, CA: Hunter House, 1990); and *Understanding Everyday Racism* (Newbury Park, CA: Sage, 1991). Kanter's analysis is presented in Rosabeth Moss Kanter, *Men and Women of the Corporation* (New York: Harper and Row, 1977) and *A Tale of "O": On Being Different in and Organization* (New York: Harper and Row, 1980).

[21] This is likely to be true for Latinos/Latinas as well as for others, but there is little directly relevant research. See John Dovidio, Samuel Gaertner, Phyllis Anastasio, and Rasyid Sanitioso, "Cognitive and Motivational Bases of Bias," in *Hispanics in the Workplace,* P. Knouse, P. Rosenfeld, and A. Culbertson, eds. (Newbury Park, CA: Sage, 1992); and Essed, *Everyday Racism.*

[22] M. F. Karsten, *Management and Gender* (Westport, CT: Quorum Books, 1994); Marjorie Nadler and Larry Nadler, "Feminization of Public Relations," in *Communication and Sex-Role Socialization,* Cynthia Berryman-Fink, D. Ballard-Reich, and L. H. Newman, eds. (New York: Garland, 1993). Supervisors' confidence in their evaluations is examined in Stella Nkomo, "The Emperor Has No Clothes: Rewriting Race in Organizations," *Academy of Management Review* 17 (1992): 487-512. Problems related to perceptions and explanations of success are the bases of advice often given women who enter careers in sales or merchandising. The assumption is that these occupations provide employees with quantifiable and easily communicated evidence of their success. To the extent that objective data are available, differential attribution of success is a less serious problem.

[23] Martin, *Hearings,* p. 29. For summaries of perceptions of women and persons of color, see Denise Segura, "Walking on Eggshells: Chicanas in the Labor Force"; and Dovidio et al., both in *Hispanics in the Workplace,* S. Knouse, P. Rosenfeld, and A. Culbertson, eds. (Newbury Park, CA: Sage, 1992).

[24] Grace and Cohen, p. 143. For data on U.S. workers breaking through the glass ceiling, see Marianne Bertraud, "Female Executives Make What Men Do," *Houston Chronicle,* October 21, 2000, C2; L. M. Sixel, "Women Climb Corporate Ladder—but Slowly," *Houston Chronicle,* November 19, 2002, B1; Catalyst, "Women of Color Making Strides," *Houston Chronicle,* July 17, 2002; Mary Williams Walsh, "Women Given Entrée into the Boardroom," *Houston Chronicle,* August 13, 2002, B6; Kelly Crow, "Staying Focused on Diversity Goals," *New York Times on the Web,* October 28, 2003, http://www.nytimes.com/. For an extended analysis of the effects of the recession, including some sectors of the economy in which gains of the 1990s have been reversed, see Robert Mishel and Heather Boushey, *The State of Working America, 2002-2003* (Washington, DC: Economic Policy Institute, 2004).

[25] Peter Kuitenbrouwer, "Female Executives Not So Different: Study," *Calgary Financial Post,* August 11, 2003, FP8.

[26] F. Dickens and J. Dickens, *The Black Manager* (New York: AMACOM, 1991), argue that eventually all African American employees will need to confront their supervisors over issues of racism, and these authors provide extended advice about when, how, and over what specific issues to do so. Many of the other sources cited in this chapter offer similar advice. Interestingly, self-help books oriented toward white women rarely provide advice about how subordinates should confront their supervisors over issues of sexism, except perhaps in cases of overt sexual harassment, perhaps because they are written from a more completely accommodationist perspective. For an analysis of how African American women implement the balancing act, see Bell.

[27] Paul Page, "African Americans in Executive Branch Agencies," *Review of Public Personnel Administration* 14 (1994): 28. Also see Khalid Mohammed Alkhazraji, W. Gardner, J. Martin, and J. Paolillo, "The Acculturation of Immigrants to U.S. Organizations," *Management Communication Quarterly* 11 (1997): 217-265; "Num-

ber of Female Executives Continues to Rise, Survey Says," *Houston Chronicle,* November 14, 2000, C3; Cindy Reuther and Gail Fairhurst, "Chaos Theory and the Glass Ceiling," in *Rethinking Organizational and Managerial Communication from Feminist Perspectives,* Patrice Buzzanell, ed. (Thousand Oaks, CA: Sage, 2000); Patrice Buzzanell, "Reframing the Glass Ceiling as a Socially Constructed Process," *Communication Monographs* 62 (1995): 327-354; Peter T. Kilborn, "For Many in Work Force, Glass Ceiling Still Exists," *New York Times,* March 16, 1995; Pan Suk Kim and Gregory Lewis, "Asian Americans in the Public Service," *Public Administration Review* 54 (1994): 285-290; U.S. Department of Labor, *The American Workforce: 1992-2005,* USDL Bulletin N. 2452 (Washington, DC: Government Printing Office, 1994); Gary Powell and D. A. Butterfield, "Investigating the 'Glass Ceiling' Phenomenon," *Academy of Management Journal* 37 (1994): 68-86.

[28] See Linda Putnam, "Feminist Theories, Dispute Processes, and Organizational Communication"; and Betsy Bach, "Making a Difference by Doing Differently: A Response to Putnam," papers presented at the Arizona State University "Conference on Organizational Communication: Perspectives for the 1990s," Tempe, AZ, April 1990; and Connie Bullis, "At Least It's a Start," in *Communication Yearbook 16,* Stanley Deetz, ed. (Newbury Park, CA: Sage, 1993).

[29] D. Spain, *Gendered Spaces* (Chapel Hill, NC: University of North Carolina Press, 1992).

[30] "Just 10% of Senior Managers for Fortune 500 Are Women," *Houston Chronicle,* January 7, 2000, C3; Eileen Alt Powell, "Women are Hitting the 'Glass Wall,'" *Houston Chronicle,* November 12, 1999, C1; "Number of Female Executives Continues to Rise," C3. Also see G. Moore, "Structural Determinants of Men's and Women's Personal Networks," *American Sociological Review* 55 (1990): 726-735; Sonia Ospina, *Illusions of Opportunity* (Ithaca, NY: Cornell University Press, 1996); Reskin and Padavic; and L. Smith-Lovin and M. J. McPherson, "You Are Who You Know," in *Theory on Gender/Feminism on Theory,* Paula England, ed. (New York: Aldine, 1993).

[31] Jorge Chapa, "Creating and Improving Linkages between the Tops and Bottoms," paper presented at the "Organizational Innovation Conference," Humphrey Institute of Public Affairs, University of Minnesota, Minneapolis, September 1992; Ospina; B. Schneider, S. Gunnarson, and J. Wheeler, "The Role of Opportunity in the Conceptualization and Measurement of Job Satisfaction," in *Job Satisfaction,* C. J. Crannay, P. Smith, and E. Stone, eds. (New York: Lexington Books, 1992); *Houston Chronicle,* October 18, 1996, C3; Korn/Ferry; Julie Lopez Amparano, "Study Says Women Face Glass Walls as Well as Glass Ceilings," *Wall Street Journal,* March 3, 1992.

[32] See Kathy Kram, *Mentoring* (Chicago: Scott, Foresman, 1986); and R. Michael Bokeno and Vernon Gantt, "Dialogic Mentoring," *Management Communication Quarterly* 14 (2000): 237-270. For work on African Americans, see David Thomas and Clayton Alderfer, "The Influence of Race on Career Dynamics," in *Handbook of Career Theory* (New York: McGraw-Hill, 1989); and Dickens and Dickens; and on Latinos, see Stephen Knouse, "The Mentoring Process for Hispanics," in *Hispanics in the Workplace,* S. Knouse, P. Rosenfeld, and A. Culberson, eds. (Newbury Park, CA: Sage, 1992).

[33] "Little Upward Help for Minority Females: Executive Women Say Mentors Needed," *Houston Chronicle,* July 14, 1999, C3; M. Maynard, "Diversity Programs Work, Where They Exist," *USA Today,* September 15, 1994, p. 5; R. Scherer, "First National Survey of Minority Views Shows Deep Racial Polarization," *Christian Science Monitor,* March 16, 1994, p. 4.

[34] Bullis and Rohrbacuk Stout; John Dovidio et al.

[35] "Little Upward Help"; Herminia Ibarra, "Personal Networks of Women and Minorities in Management," *Academy of Management Review* 18 (1993): 56-87; and "Race, Opportunity, and Diversity of Social Circles in Managerial Settings," *Academy of Management Journal* 38 (1995): 673-703; Judi Marshall, *Women Managers Moving On* (London: Routledge, 1995); B. Milwid, *Working with Men* (East Rutherford, NJ: Berkley, 1992); Edwards and Polite.

[36] Morrison, White, and van Velsor; Laura Mansnerus, "Why Women Are Leaving the Law," *Working Woman,* April 1993. The problems seem to be especially pronounced in high-tech jobs. "Study Finds Women Denied Top High-Tech Jobs," *Houston Chronicle,* November 13, 2002, B3.

[37] The best single source of information on women-owned businesses in the United States is the Web site of the National Foundation of Women Business Owners, http://www.nfwbo.org. Australian data is presented in Grace and Cohen. Also see Anita Blair, *Houston Chronicle,* July 8, 1996, A15; Charles Boisseau, "Ranks of Female Businesses Soar," *Houston Chronicle,* January 30, 1996, C1; Arne Kalleberg and Kevin Leicht, "Gender and Organizational Performance," *Academy of Management Journal* 34 (1991): 157; "Women Owned Firms See Huge Growth," *Houston Chronicle,* May 11, 1999, C5.

[38] "Financing," *Houston Chronicle,* May 23, 1999, D5; Grace and Cohen.

[39] Sally Helgessen, *The Female Advantage: Women's Ways of Leadership* (New York: Doubleday, 1990); Diane Kay Sloan and Kathleen Krone, "Women Managers and Gendered Values," *Women's Studies in Communication* 23 (2000): 111-130. Also see Judith Rosener, "Ways Women Lead," *Harvard Business Review* (November-

December 1990): 119–125; and Marlene Fine and Patrice Buzzanell, "Walking the High Wire," in *Rethinking Organizational and Managerial Communication from Feminist Perspectives,* Patrice Buzzanell, ed. (Thousand Oaks, CA: Sage, 2000).

[40] For a summary of Latino/Latina leadership styles, see Bernardo Ferdman and Angelica Cortes, "Culture and Identity among Hispanic Managers in an Anglo Business," in *Hispanics in the Workplace,* S. Knouse, P. Rosenfeld, and A. Culbertson, eds. (Newbury Park, CA: Sage, 1992), especially p. 265. Also see G. Marin and B. V. Marin, *Research with Hispanic Populations* (Newbury Park, CA: Sage, 1991); Richard Cervantes, "Occupational and Economic Stressors among Immigrant and United States–Born Hispanics," in *Hispanics in the Workplace,* S. Knouse, P. Rosenfeld, and A. Culbertson, eds. (Newbury Park, CA: Sage, 1992); and Dickens and Dickens.

[41] B. W. Wilkins and P. A. Anderson, "Gender Differences and Similarities in Management Communication," *Management Communication Quarterly* 5 (1991): 186–211. Also see Ann Harriman, *Women—Men—Management* (Westport, CT: Greenwood Press, 1996); Gary Powell, *Women and Men in Management* (Newbury Park, CA: Sage, 1993); Frederica Olivares, "Ways Men and Women Lead," *Harvard Business Review* 69 (January–February 1991): 2–11.

[42] D. P. Blanchette, "Technology Transfer in a Culturally Diverse Workforce (Part I)," *Industrial Management,* July–August 1994, 31–32.; and H. Sussman, "Is Diversity Training Worth Maintaining?" *Business and Society Review* 89 (1994): 48–49.

[43] David Jamieson and Julie O'Mara, *Managing Workforce 2000* (San Francisco: Jossey-Bass, 1991), p. 89.

[44] Ann Morrison, *The New Leaders* (San Francisco: Jossey-Bass, 1992).

[45] Daniel Creson, cited in Jeannie Kever, "Life in the Tired Lane," *Texas Magazine,* August 13, 2000, p. 8; also see "Overworked America?" September 6, 1999, *The Online (PBS) Newshour,* http://www.pbs.org/.

[46] See Faye Fiore, "New Mothers Now Return to Work Sooner, Study Says," *Houston Chronicle,* November 27, 1997, A2; and "More New Mothers Returning to Work," *Houston Chronicle,* October 24, 2000, A6.

[47] The survey's results are presented in each October issue.

[48] Many of these policies have been mandated by law for decades outside of the United States. In Ecuador, for example, firms must provide women with three months of paid maternity leave and schedule them for only six hours of work at a time during the next three months so that they can nurse their babies. Most European and Canadian firms have on-site day care and provide special breaks for nursing mothers.

[49] Jennifer Holt, "Women's Status Improving, but Slowly," *Houston Chronicle,* November 16, 2000, C2; L. M. Sixel, "Pay Gap Narrower, but Far from Closed," *Houston Chronicle,* February 26, 1999, C12. "Female Executives Make What Men Do," *Houston Chronicle,* October 21, 2000, C2; Jilian Mincer, "Women Managers Will Hold Most Jobs," *Houston Chronicle,* June 17, 2003, B1.

[50] Betty Spence, president of the National Association for Female Executives, cited in "Women's Pay Gap Widens in Some Fields," *Houston Chronicle,* December 10, 2003, B4.

[51] L. M. Sixel, "Race and Rewards at Texaco," *Houston Chronicle,* July 19, 1996, B1. Also see L. J. Bradford and C. Raines, *Twentysomething* (New York: Master Media, 1992).

Chapter 11

Communication, Globalization, and Organizations

The times, they are a changin'.
—BOB DYLAN

All of this [globalization] creates a problem for democracies. Democracy and capitalists have very different core values. Democracy is founded on equality—one vote per citizen regardless of his intelligence or work ethic. Capitalism, however, is motivated by inequality: differences in economic returns create the incentive structure which encourages hard work and wise investment. . . . The economically fit are expected to drive the economically unfit out of existence; there are no equalizing feedback mechanisms in capitalism.
—LESTER THUROW

[Today] is the first time in history that virtually every individual at every level of society can sense the impact of international changes. . . . [D]uring the next decade [the global labor pool] will absorb nearly 2 billion workers from emerging markets, a pool that currently includes close to 1 billion unemployed and underemployed workers. . . . These people will be earning a fraction of what their counterparts in developed countries earn and will be only marginally less productive. You are either someone who is threatened by this change or someone who will profit from it, but it is almost impossible to conceive of a significant group that will be untouched by it.
—DAVID ROTHKOPF

How we learn to strike the right balance between globalization's inherently empowering and humanizing aspects and its inherently disempowering and dehumanizing aspects will determine whether is it reversible or irreversible, a passing phase or a fundamental revolution in the evolution of human society.
—THOMAS FRIEDMAN

Central Themes

- There is little question that since the early 1990s the world economy has become increasingly globalized, creating new challenges and new opportunities for organizations, workers, and governments.
- A key to dealing with globalization is understanding cultural differences—and understanding that differences are not deficiencies.
- Free trade is based on the "theory of comparative advantage," a concept that has become increasing politicized during the past decade.
- As the theory of comparative advantage predicts, globalization has led to massive increases in economic inequality, both within and between nations.
- Globalization forces organizations to become *responsive,* not just reactive.

Key Terms

culture	Confucian dynamism
power distance	low-context cultures
uncertainty avoidance	high-context cultures
masculinity-femininity	theory of comparative advantage
individualism-collectivism	responsive organizations

One of the dominant themes of this book is that there is an important and complex relationship between organizations and the societies from which they draw their members. Up to this point we have focused on one side of that relationship—the ways in which societal assumptions, structures, and processes influence organizations and organizational communication. For millennia, those processes encouraged homogeneity, separation, and often antagonism—workers versus managers; men versus women; racial and ethnic majorities versus minorities; Europeans versus Americans versus Africans versus Asians; and upper class versus middle class versus lower class. Homogeneity and separation were sustained through human-made social barriers and through the seemingly natural realities of time and space.

However, at least since the time of the Industrial Revolution and the democratization of Europe and North America, there also have been pressures toward heterogeneity. During the past twenty years, those pressures have become progressively more potent. Workforces have become more diverse, and the barriers that exist within organizations to separate different groups of "others" have started to break down. As a result, new assumptions, structures, and processes are beginning to emerge. As Chapter 10 explains, this increased proximity *within* organizations demands the development of new systems and communicative strategies.

At least since the beginning of the 1980s, organizations and their members have been challenged to deal with a second kind of proximity, an unprecedented collapsing of the barriers of time and space. Of course, this is not the first time that economic activity has taken on a global dimension. Extensive trade networks extending from the Persian Gulf to North Africa flourished thousands of years before the Christian era; even larger systems existed among Asia, Africa, and Europe at the time of Alexander the Great (around 300 BC), and these were expanded during the Roman Empire. Extensive systems developed in Meso-america soon after. The mercantile system of the fifteenth through the nineteenth centuries established a worldwide economic system dominated by Europe.[1] Even some specific issues give a sense of déjà vu. Since the 1990s U.S. econo-mists, politicians, and CEOs have seemed obsessed with the burgeoning Chi-nese market—U.S. and European luxury auto makers are expanding their oper-ations in and near Shanghai as fast as they can—just as their equals in the 1890s and the early twentieth century were obsessed with the opportunity to make "shoes for the Chinese."[2] The current situation does seem to be historically unique, however, at least in terms of the magnitude of changes. Technological developments have fundamentally altered the way that information and expert-ise is disseminated around the globe. As important, the level of education of people throughout the world has substantially increased. For example, in the thirteen largest poor countries, male illiteracy rates fell from 19 percent to 12 percent between 1980 and 1997; for women they fell by more than one-third, from 36 percent to 22 percent. In China and Indonesia, illiteracy declined by more than 75 percent. Increases in school enrollment suggest that the trends will continue. Thus, even in the Third World, populations are increasingly capable of using new technologies and the information and expertise that they provide.[3]

As a result, today it is almost impossible to predict where a given organiza-tion (or its many divisions) will be located. People who log on to AOL's help desk to straighten out a bill or correct a technical glitch will be talking to a Filipino techie working at what used to be Clark Air Force Base in the shadow of Mount Pinatubo. People who dial the Mexico tourism hotline may talk with someone who is located in Bend, Oregon, and employed by Destination Ventures. The odds are less than fifty-fifty that she or he is from Mexico. McDonald's Restaurants of Canada and the Moscow (Russia) City Council have established joint ventures. Managerial decisions made in small savings and loans in Ohio are tightly linked to British oil stocks. Swissair moved its entire accounting division to India to take advantage of lower labor costs for secretaries, accountants, and programmers; British Air's office that corrects reservation errors and keeps track of frequent flyer miles is located in Mumbai, India. IBM may have the most complex global network: programmers at Tsinghua University in Beijing write Java-based soft-ware; they send it to an IBM facility in Seattle via the Internet, where the pro-gramming is revised and forwarded to the Institute of Computer Science in Be-larus and the Software House Group in Latvia, from where it is sent back to Beijing; there the process starts over and continues in a never-ending cycle. IBM calls the system "Java around the Clock" and prides itself at having created a "forty-eight hour day" via the Internet.[4]

Although globalization has been driven by technology and increased edu-cation, it has been guided and directed by institutions of international trade and finance. Within a decade, the barriers to global production and economic activity that existed during the cold war have largely disappeared, to be replaced by international economic bodies (largely controlled by the United States and Europe) like the World Trade Organization (WTO) and the International Monetary Fund (IMF). Both critics and defenders of globalization have noted that these changes have significantly shifted power away from individual citizens and governments and toward large multinational organizations.[5] The effects of the changes have been decidedly mixed—some people, countries, and societies have benefited in many ways; others have suffered. In fact, Mexico's President Vicente Fox, under increasing opposition within his own country because of his proglobalization ideology and policy proposals, recently warned that the global economy is at a crucial turning point, facing a road leading to continued increases in a worldwide gap between the rich and poor with related social unrest, and another leading to equitable and sustainable economic growth throughout the world.[6]

Whatever the specific results of globalization may turn out to be, it is clear that organizations now have a significantly increased ability to influence the societies from which they draw their members. It is too early to make any firm predictions about the outcomes of globalization. Instead, our goal in this chapter is to outline the changes that have taken place and to explore the ongoing debate about their consequences. We begin by examining the challenges faced by organizations because of the multicultural nature of the global economy. Then we look at its economic and organizational dimensions.

Culture, Difference, and Organizational Communication

Organizational communication scholar Cynthia Stohl recently chided her colleagues for being so parochial in their research and writing, working almost completely from a Western, usually a U.S., perspective. Even on those rare occasions when scholars take an international or intercultural focus, she argues, they are oriented toward helping people from white, Western, industrialized societies better manage people or organizations from "other" societies. The goal is to get everyone, regardless of background, values, or interests, to sing together in a harmonious chorus, and to sing predetermined notes, rather than "letting all voices, on and (arguably) off key, into the choir."[7] "Managing" diversity becomes yet another exercise in organizational control. This orientation is not surprising, because U.S. citizens and U.S. organizations have long been noted for their cultural parochialism, and U.S. organizations for their preoccupation with control. For example, in 1979 the first major U.S. government report that advised academic organizations to increase training in foreign (non-English) language and international cultures was published. A decade later only 23,000 U.S. college students were studying Japanese, while 20 million Japanese were studying English. Today the figures are not significantly different, although the number of Anglos learning Spanish has increased in the five states with the largest

Latino populations (New York, California, Texas, Florida, and Arizona). Change has been almost as slow in noneducational organizations. U.S. firms spend a small percentage of their training budgets on international or intercultural education (10-15 percent). Even though American employees are critical of their international colleagues' errors when speaking English and believe that these breakdowns hurt productivity, they often make no attempt to learn even the simplest foreign phrases.[8] In contrast, international firms take language learning much more seriously. In fact, the two major Japanese banks spend 50 percent of their training funds on international training.

However, increasing cross-cultural understanding is a worldwide challenge. A survey of 1,300 Japanese managers and their Southeast Asian subordinates found that the managers thought their local colleagues were illogical, indecisive, and inflexible, and the local managers perceived that their Japanese supervisors were secretive, intolerant, and inflexible. As the "Going South" case study (Chapter 4) shows, major cultural differences exist within countries.[9] Important linguistic and cultural differences have existed between northern and southern China for centuries, and between rural and urban China for decades. Rice University in Houston, Texas, conducts popular training programs that are designed to explain Texas and Texan culture to "expatriates" who have been transferred to the "Republic" from the rest of the United States. And, as the "Can You Trust Anyone under Thirty?" case studies (in Chapter 1 and later in this chapter) indicate, cultures are constantly changing, both because of globalization and because of other factors. An alternative view is expressed in the concept of celebrating diversity, of recognizing that multiple backgrounds and perspectives can enrich organizations and organizational life, far beyond the financial advantages that may come from diversification. The first step in celebrating diversity involves understanding the concept of culture and cross-cultural differences.

Defining Culture

In Chapter 5 we introduced the concept of **culture** as a learned system of beliefs, values, and meanings that guide, usually nonconsciously, the ways in which people make sense of their surroundings and choose how to act in those surroundings. Management scholar Edgar Schein conceptualizes culture at three levels: the most basic level is composed of core beliefs and values that members of the culture take for granted. The second level is a group of norms governing how people are to behave. It also is nonconscious, unless someone (usually a newcomer or someone who is outside of the "mainstream" of the culture) behaves in unexpected (and abnormal and unnatural) ways. The final level is composed of artifacts—tangible items like building designs or dress and symbolic forms like rituals and ceremonies. As Chapter 5 explains, artifacts express and reproduce the underlying levels of culture, but they are not the culture itself.

Cultures are learned by their members, so presumably they can be learned by outsiders, however complex the process might be. Whereas this is obviously true of the artifacts of a culture—it is easy to teach outsiders how to present their business cards to Japanese associates, or under what circumstances one should entertain Korean colleagues in one's home instead of taking them to a restaurant—it is much more difficult to explain the deeper levels of culture, especially when there simply is no word in one language that captures the meaning of a core concept in another culture. In fact, it is very difficult to accurately access deeper levels of culture from artifacts alone. For example, wearing the traditional Muslim *hijab* (veil and head cover), or not wearing it, has become an issue in schools and businesses in many countries. But women make their decisions about the *hijab* for a variety of reasons. Some refuse to wear it because it symbolizes patriarchal subjection of women; others, including converts to Islam, from the United States to Japan, wear it for the same reason—it allows women to minimize the likelihood that they will be viewed (literally) as sex objects. In other situations it symbolizes class differences. Social and organizational theorist Anthony Giddens concludes: "The *hijab* has no unitary meaning. It reflects the diversity of women's experience and aspirations around the world." [10] As a result, trying to draw conclusions about the values and beliefs underlying this very important artifact is virtually impossible. Indeed, because so much of a person's culture is taken for granted, it is even difficult to teach people to be sensitive to their own cultural biases. For example, few white people in U.S. organizations think of themselves as members of a "white" culture, although nonwhite members of those same organizations have very clear views of the values, communication styles, and behavior that they associate with "whiteness." [11] In some ways it is easier to learn to accurately interpret "other" employees' actions—a white male supervisor can quickly learn that he may misinterpret an Asian American's (or a Latino or Latina's) respect for modesty and deference to authority as evidence of lack of leadership skills or managerial competence. [12]

The most influential model of cultural differences is Geert Hofstede's study of IBM employees in fifty-three different nations during the 1970s and 1980s. His model differentiates cultures based on their **power distance** (the amount of power that supervisors can acceptably exercise over their subordinates—high in China, low in Israel or Austria), their **uncertainty avoidance** (the degree to which people are uncomfortable with ambiguity and risk and therefore prefer to work with long-term acquaintances or friends rather than with strangers—high in Japan, low in the United States), their **masculinity-femininity** (the extent to which the culture values the stereotypically masculine traits of assertiveness and competitiveness or the stereotypically feminine attributes of cooperativeness and interdependence—high in Latin America and Japan, low in Scandinavia), and their **individualism-collectivism.** Asian, Latin, Middle-Eastern, and African cultures tend to be collectivist, which means that people in those societies learn to place a high value on solidarity, cooperation, and concern for others. Their communication tends to be guided and constrained by concerns about hurting the other person's feelings, minimizing impositions placed on the other person, and avoiding negative evaluations of the other person. A person's identity is closely tied to his or her membership in important referent groups. In contrast, western European and North American societies tend to be individualistic; people learn to value competition and independence from other people or groups. They like communication that is clear, efficient, and effective, and they adapt their own communication to correspond to those guidelines. It is not surprising that organizations in collectivist societies (and organizations located in individualist societies but dominated by people from collectivist societies) tend to operate according to collectivist principles and that organizations in individualistic societies operate in accord with the core values of those societies.[13] Subsequent research indicates that the individualism-collectivism distinction may be the most important, especially in communication between members of Western and Eastern cultures.

During the 1980s, Hofstede added to his system a fifth concept, **Confucian dynamism,** which differentiates cultures in which people learn to take a short-term time orientation (low Confucian, as in the United States) from cultures where a long-term one is preferred (as in China). Hofstede's model has been critiqued on a number of grounds, from the research methods that were used, to its tendency to equate nationality and culture, thereby ignoring subcultural differences. For example, people from industrialized parts of a country tend to be more individualistic than rural residents, although they may very well be part of collectivist societies. Hofstede's model also fails to recognize that cultures change over time and that the leaders of the key institutions in a society may overtly, even blatantly, try to mold popular values and assumptions. For example, during the Maoist era in China, the government attempted to replace Confucian ideas with Marxist/Leninist doctrine. Both are collectivist, although the most important referent "group" in Confucianism is one's family, whereas the most important referent group for Maoists is the party or the state. Under the leadership of Deng Xiaoping, the government rejected Maoist collectivism and encouraged Confucian values and individualism. Both were seen as necessary to opening the Chinese economy to the West. Similarly, Saudi Arabia's leaders have been trying, with limited success, to persuade its young men to engage in work that is now largely performed by immigrants. Perhaps the most important criticism comes from research indicating that individualism and collectivism are separate dimensions, so that cultures can be both highly individualistic and highly collectivist, and so on.[14]

An additional, also popular, concept was developed by Edward Hall. In **low-context** cultures people focus their attention on the explicit content of a message when they try to make sense out of it; in **high-context** cultures, much of the meaning is extracted from the context in which the message is uttered, and the message itself is much more ambiguous. As a result, the messages constructed by people from low-context cultures seem to be blunt and excessively detailed to people from high-context cultures; messages from high-context cultures seem to be excessively vague, confusing, or noncommittal to people from low-context cultures. Cultures also differ in the time orientation that is taught to their members. Some value precision and exactness (for example, Germany) and view violations of "normal" schedules as a serious affront; others value flexibility (for example, Latin societies, although the influx of multinational employees is rapidly changing this norm in urban areas). In some cultures, obeying "promptness" rules depends on one's rank, age, or status; in others everyone is expected to use the same clock. When New York's Corning Corporation began collaborating with the Mexican firm Vitro, Mexican employees sometimes felt that Corning moved too fast to integrate the two operations. (They also found the Americans to be too blunt and direct.) The Americans felt that Vitro was moving too slowly (and that their dogged pursuit of politeness kept them from acknowledging problems that needed to be dealt with).[15]

In some cultures, relationships are defined solely by organizational rank and expertise; in others they are influenced by nonorganizational considerations, such as age, kinship, sex, and wealth. In some societies, intimate relationships are expected to be monogamous; in others polygyny (multiple wives) and polyandry (multiple husbands) are normal. In some, providing alcohol and prostitutes is a normal part of business entertaining (for example, Thailand and some parts of Nevada); in others it is a capital offense. That is to say, people in different cultures are pleased, worried, annoyed, and embarrassed by different things; seemingly identical conventions and rituals mean very different things from one society to another, and showing respect and deference vary in importance. Different societies socialize their members to accept different attitudes about work, tasks, the division of labor, and various practices, punishments, and rewards.

Increasing Cultural Understanding

Well-designed intercultural training programs focus on communication itself. For example, the Canadian International Development Agency's predeparture program for its expatriates provides training in seven core communication skills:

- Communicating respect (in the language/behavior of the host society)
- Being nonjudgmental (of others' attitudes, beliefs, and behaviors)
- Recognizing the influence of one's own perceptions and knowledge
- Being empathic (trying to understand the other's point of view and life situation)
- Being flexible (being able to accomplish a task in a manner and time frame that is appropriate to the host culture and the others' needs)
- Demonstrating reciprocal concern (actually listening and promoting shared communication)
- Tolerating ambiguity, especially about cultural differences

The goal of this program is to persuade managers not to define *differences* as *deficiencies*. All organizational change efforts are difficult to implement; diversification training is more difficult than most. After years of designing and conducting such programs, A. P. Carnavale and S. C. Stone warn that

> In most organizations, valuing and managing diversity requires nothing less than cultural transformation. This is a prodigious task, for it requires people—especially those in the dominant culture—to let go of the assumptions about the universal rightness of their own values and customary ways of doing things in order to become receptive to other cultures.[16]

And even well-designed and well-conducted training can have unintended negative consequences. If organizations focus solely on *differences* among employees, the values, beliefs, and experiences that they have *in common* may be obscured. The result is to perpetuate stereotypes and polarize the workforce. For example, Ellen Castro became a successful consultant after she left her job as a manager of 500 employees in a $90 million retail profit center in response to her boss's use of ethnic slurs. She explains how her experience led to her current approach to consulting:

> [At first] I did it the man's way, the Anglo man's way. I've [since] learned that if you don't let people be who they are, they won't be authentic or creative. I know what it's like to be in an environment where you can't be yourself. It took a toll on my spirit. I don't think employers can afford to do that today. . . . [So you have to value differences. But] what you [often] do with these programs is emphasize how we're different, that people can get their feelings hurt. But what about how we're alike? All employees want respect. We all want to be involved in decision making. By emphasizing "diversity" we've created a chasm. Instead, let's look at people for who they are, what's their best skill? What can she bring to the table as a female? Diversity is not going to work until you have a culture where everyone is given respect and dignity.[17]

Of course, none of what we have said suggests that everyone from a particular society has the same core beliefs and values; gender, age, economic background, educational level, and individual experiences all influence the ways in which people interpret and incorporate the messages that they receive into their own views of the world and ways of communicating. But the complete package of beliefs and values that people bring with them into their organizations exerts a powerful influence on their communication and is difficult to change. As a result, members of organizations must find ways to manage what often are complex webs of differences in beliefs, values, and modes of communicating.

CASE STUDY
Can You Trust Anyone under Thirty? Part II

The People's Republic of China has always been an economic giant. For most of human history it was the world's largest economy and most advanced civilization. China started to decline after 1450, but even as late as the early 1800s it accounted for one-third of the world's Gross Domestic Product (GDP). During the late twentieth century, it revived—its GDP grew at an astounding 10 percent per year from 1978 until 2002, and almost all projections suggest that it will continue to do so in the near term. It now is the third largest consumer economy in the world. Although Western organizations have flocked to China, their managers constantly complain about how difficult it is to deal with Chinese culture and the Chinese economic system—after all, China invented bureaucracy more than four thousand years before Max Weber started writing about it as the most appropriate organizational form for the Protestant nations of Europe. But Chinese society has repeatedly undergone profound social change throughout the past century. If one's attitudes, values, interpretive frames, and ways of acting are a function of one's experiences at key times in one's life (as we suggest in the Generations case study in Chapter 1), then generational differences, and the potential for cross-generational conflict, should be even greater in China than they are in the United States. If members of non-Chinese organizations hope to deal successfully with China, they must understand these changes and the differences they have spawned.

Of course, China has been a Confucian society for more than two thousand years. Although Western interpretations of Confucianism focus on its long-term time orientation, it has other important dimensions as well. Its fundamental principles include the belief that society is made stable by unequal and complementary relationships (ruler-subject, father-son, older brother–younger brother, husband-wife, and senior friend–junior friend); that the family is the prototype of all social organizations; and that all people are responsible for "virtuous behavior" (which includes being benevolent, charitable, and humane *toward other members of one's referent group*—family and friends, but *not* outsiders—and treating other members of that referent group as one would like to be treated) and pursuing virtue (acquiring skills and education, working hard, living a frugal life, being patient, and persevering in the face of adversity).

Confucian principles lead to a distinctive concept of authority, *li,* and a distinctive mode of organizing, labeled *guanxi. Li* dictates that during social interactions people must follow proper social obligations, especially toward people higher in the social hierarchy—a "harmony through hierarchy." *Guanxi* focuses on traditional Confucian role relationships and considers mutual, reciprocal exchanges as the basis for business interactions. Unlike the Western approach of regulating business through legal contracts—which is inherently offensive from a Confucian perspective—*guanxi* is grounded in developing trust through time-consuming, long-term relationships; it views "pulling strings" as entirely legitimate in order to help people with whom one has those relationships. Although *guanxi* is more flexible than Western legalism, it also is more cumbersome, because it creates a complex and changing maze of obligations. During the Republican era (1911-1948), Confucianism was encouraged by the government, although there was also a strong Western presence in commercial areas such as Shanghai.

During the Maoist era (1949-1965) and the Great Cultural Revolution (1966-1976), the government attempted to discredit everything Western and to substitute doctrines of communist collectivism, which focused on loyalty to the state and the society as a whole, for Confucian loyalty to the family. Maoism advocated an austere lifestyle defined by self-sacrifice and simple living. Under Deng Xiaoping and his successors (1977-present), Maoist thought has been discredited, and policy has focused on reviving Confucian ideas, while introducing Western individualism under the notion that "being rich is glorious." The Maoist concept of equal distribution of wealth has been denounced for retarding economic progress, comfort and material rewards have been celebrated, and efficiency has been stressed. However,

(continued)

(Case Study, continued)

nationalism and pride in country have also been stressed. Evidently, the government hopes for a society in which individualism, entrepreneurship, and materialism go hand-in-hand with Confucian values of altruism, helpfulness, generosity, and eagerness to work for the collective society.

After 1970 China also implemented in urban areas its "one child" policy, which has had some unintended consequences for the culture. As a result, today's Chinese culture is a complex mixture of Confucianism, collectivism, and individualism. Differential experiences across generations combine with other influences—gender, geographic location during one's formative years, company size, industry—in ways that make cross-generational tensions very likely. An Older Generation (currently aged fifty or older) was primarily influenced by Maoism and communist/ collectivist cultural assumptions; a Current Generation (now in their forties) was encouraged to return to the tenets of Confucianism; and a New Generation has been taught to value China's emerging form of capitalism while holding on to more traditional values. Some research has found differences between the Older and the Current generations, but the primary contrast seems to be between them, with their notions of collectivism, and the individualistic New Generation, particularly young men who were raised in industrialized parts of the country.

Surveys of the New Generation in Fujian and Anhui provinces found that only 15 percent aspired to "serve the people" in 1981, and the percentage dropped to zero by the end of the decade. A different study found that about the same percentage (37 percent) of young people listed "good job, good careers, and comfortable lives" as their highest priorities as listed "to make our motherland rich and powerful" (36 percent). By the end of the 1990s only 21 percent put national interests at the top of their priority list, while almost two-thirds focused their attention on personal gain. However, the New Generation has not completely abandoned China's Confucian values. Many of China's 292 million young people (roughly equal to the entire population of the United States today) were willing to sacrifice some material gain if it meant that they could stay near their families or hold jobs that they found to be intrinsically satisfying. But by the end of the 1990s, collectivism was becoming less important—almost half of New Generation members admitted that they would take time and energy to help someone else only if it did not interfere with their own, individual success. The New Generation also seems to worship everything foreign, especially if it comes from the United States; some even envy Japan, in spite of the history of enmity between the two peoples. Although they still support China's political system, they are cynical about their leaders, in part because corruption has been a serious problem as China has moved toward capitalism, and politically well-connected families have been the primary beneficiaries of that corruption.

Members of the older generations and even people in their late twenties, see the New Generation as hedonistic. They tend to believe that, instead of achieving their leaders' goals of creating a New Generation with "one foot in the new economy" and "one foot in Confucianism," China has created a "spoiled one child," "Chinese me," or "Chuppie" (Chinese yuppie) generation that focuses on conspicuous consumption and self-indulgence. However, other observers note that outside of cities and towns, the change has not been so marked. Outside of the cities, China has had a two-child policy. This is because incomes are much lower in rural areas (perhaps as much as 20 percent lower), and one child is not likely to be able to support his or her parents. Consequently, the rural system retains a more traditional family arrangement. As a result, both the two older generations and the rural New Generation may provide a continuing challenge to the new individualism. Even in the cities, Chinese students try to stay near family if it is at all possible to do so, and connections with cousins, nieces, and nephews in extended families maintain traditional relationships even for only children. Chinese schools retain traditional hierarchical relationships, so there are many Confucian and collectivist influences still in place to counter the pressures of individualism.

Applying What You've Learned

1. What expectations do each of these generational groups have about life and about organizations?
2. What messages and experiences have contributed to those expectations?
3. Over what issues are the three groups likely to have conflicts? Why?

Questions to Think About and Discuss

1. Which Chinese generational group has had experiences and values that are most like yours? (Remember, it's the experiences you've had more than your age that influences generational membership). How do your expectations and experiences correspond to the various generational groups in China? Over what issues are you likely to have conflicts with members of the three groups? Why?
2. Which of the (U.S.) generational groups described in the "Under Thirty" case in Chapter 1 are most like the New Generation in China? Which ones are most unlike the New Generation?
3. There is an alternative explanation for the generational differences noted in both the U.S. (Chapter 1) and the Chinese "generations" case studies. When people age, their values change because of a complex set of psychological, sociological, and economic factors. This is why as far back as ancient Egypt, Assyria, India, and China, there is evidence of older generations despairing the lost values of their children and grandchildren. For example, there is a two-thousand-year old Chinese expression, "The newer generation is always not as good as the older one," that is used even by college sophomores in response to foolish actions by freshmen or freshwomen. We have pre-

(continued)

(Case Study, continued)

sented both case studies as if the economic and sociological/political factors were dominant. Could the changes we have outlined be primarily a function of psychological changes that accompany aging, and less related to experiences? Why or why not? What implications does your answer have for organizational interpersonal relationships across generations?

We would like to thank three graduate students for their input into this case study. Two were enrolled in our classes at Texas A&M University—Xiaowei Tan and Yuchun Yuan, both from Shanghai. The third, Kaibin Xu, was at the University of Alabama when he helped us write this case study, but has moved to the University of Colorado. He was raised in Hubei Province (central China) and Sichuan Province (southwest China).

Sources

Chen, Ling. "Connecting to the World Economy." *Management Communication Quarterly* 14 (2000): 152–160.

Child, John. *Management in China during the Age of Reform.* Cambridge, UK: Cambridge University Press.

Ching, C. C. "The One-Child Family in China." *Studies in Family Planning* 13 (1982): 208–212.

Hassard, John, Jackie Sheehan, and Jonathan Morris. "Enterprise Reform in Post-Deng China." *International Studies of Management and Organization* 29 (1999): 107–136.

Hong, Jianzhong, and Yrjo Engstrom. "Changing Principles of Communication between Chinese Managers and Workers." *Management Communication Quarterly* 17 (2004): 553–587.

Kristof, Nicholas. "Will China Blindside the West?" *New York Times on the Web,* December 3, 2002, http://www.nytimes.com/.

Kwong, Julia. "Ideological Crisis among China's Youths: Values and Official Ideology." *British Journal of Sociology* 45 (1994): 247–264.

Ralston, David, Carolyn Egri, Sally Stewart, Robert Terpstra, and Yu Kaicheng. "Doing Business in the 21st Century with the New Generation of Chinese Managers." *Journal of International Business Studies* 30 (1999): 415–428.

Varg, Paul. "The Myth of the China Market, 1890–1914." *American Historical Review* 73 (1968): 742–758.

Economics, Globalization, and Organizational Communication

The theoretical justification of globalization is free-market (laissez-faire) capitalism, introduced in Chapter 2. Although the theory of free-market capitalism was developed to explain a nation's internal economic system, it is easily applied to international economics.

Globalization and the Discourse of Free Trade

The key link is a concept called the **theory of comparative advantage.** This theory starts with the observation that different areas of the globe have different *natural* economic advantages. Some areas have abundant natural resources; some have an especially productive labor force; some are strategically located on trade routes, and so on. If the economy of an area relies on its natural advantages, it will be more efficient than if it tries to develop industries in which it does not have an advantage. With increased efficiency come increased profits, incomes, and wealth. If every area focuses on its advantages and refuses to develop industries in which it does not have a comparative advantage, the entire global economy benefits. Conversely, if governments interfere with these natural processes by adopting tariffs, quotas, or currency values that artificially support industries in which their country does not have an advantage, or if they create artificial barriers to the free flow of trade, finance, and labor, they reduce the wages and wealth of their own people and make the whole world's economy less efficient than it otherwise would be.[18]

Even the strongest advocates of free trade recognize that it may be socially disruptive and create serious economic inequities for short periods of time. Industries in which an area does not have a competitive advantage will be unable to compete. Companies in nonadvantaged industries will go bankrupt, and workers will either have to shift to advantaged industries or move to areas where their old companies have a comparative advantage. These areas are likely to have lower standards of living and incomes than workers enjoyed when their companies were being artificially supported. Within each country, inequities in income and wealth are likely to grow as groups with ready access to the basis of each country's "advantage" benefit, and other groups are disadvantaged. Capital will flow to advantaged industries or to countries that are effectively exploiting their advantages. But, the theory argues, eventually each area will be dominated by organizations that produce the products or provide the services in which it has a comparative advantage, and all of the employees of those organizations will benefit.

If the wealth that is created by exploiting these newfound advantages is invested wisely, each economy will begin to grow. The system will self-correct, and wage rates will rise, eventually creating an equilibrium. For example, there is evidence that many counties are investing more in their educational systems to more effectively compete in a global market. In the industrialized countries, this means increasing the percentage and number of residents who go to college and encouraging college students to focus on technologically oriented careers. Doing so gives them and their countries a comparative advantage in the high-tech sectors of the world economy. In developing countries, it means increasing literacy rates and the number and percent of their residents who are in school. In both cases, the primary beneficiaries of these trends are women, for they have historically received weaker educations, especially in technical fields. In some cases the international organizations charged with implementing free trade act in ways that defeat this cycle. For example, the World Bank and the International Monetary Fund impose strict austerity plans on most of the countries to which they provide assistance. The resulting budget cuts make it difficult for them to make necessary adjustments. For example, the benefits of globalization in Latin America have been very unequally distributed, in large part because the governments of Latin American countries have not had the funds necessary to improve public education in ways that give the bulk of their citizens the skills needed for them to compete in the global economy.[19] In parts of both the developed and developing world, these strategies already seem to be increasing incomes and wealth. However, the correction occurs only if the newly acquired capital stays in the home country. Because investors can now easily shift their funds to any country in the world at the touch of a button, much of the wealth created by exploiting a country's comparative advantage leaves the country. From South Asia to Europe, the fruits of economic advantage in the global economy largely have wound up in the U.S. stock and bond markets, in which only about half of U.S. families participate.[20] Without increased capital, development is stunted and the corrective functions of the free market are short-circuited.

Of course, even the strongest advocates of free trade admit that in some cases there may be good noneconomic reasons for violating the tenets of the theory. For example, a government may wish to support its own computer or steel industry as a matter of national defense, or it may want to protect a fledgling industry from foreign competition until it is sufficiently well-established to compete successfully, or it may wish to restrict migration across its borders for political reasons. But, the theory argues, any artificial barrier reduces the efficiency of the national (and world) economy and reduces wealth, wages, profits, and employment in the long run. Artificial barriers to free trade should be continued only as long as the noneconomic advantages clearly outweigh the economic disadvantages. Too many barriers to the free movement of trade, capital, and labor—whether imposed by government, labor organizations, or cultural norms—upset the global free market and reduce the total amount of wealth that is created. It is for this reason that some proponents of free trade, such as British philosopher-educator John Stuart Mill, advocated having governments pay compensation to workers and industries that lose out to global competition. Doing so reduces social costs and potential social unrest but does not interfere with market processes. The modern version of this tactic is seen when governments invest funds for retraining of employees who have lost their jobs due to globalization.[21]

The debate over "exceptions" and compensation makes a very important point about free trade and globalization—although it is discussed in economic terms, its implementation is a highly political process and can only be understood fully from that perspective. For example, in early 2002 the Bush administration announced that it would impose import duties of up to 30 percent on a number of types of steel. It was quite clear that the measure was structured to help steel industries in Pennsylvania and Ohio, likely battleground states in the 2004 presidential election (in fact, the measure actually hurt U.S. steel manufacturers in other states, especially after other countries retaliated). Free-trade purists, like Secretary of the Treasury Paul O'Neill, complained loudly that the action harmed U.S. economic interests because it interfered with free trade. Protected from foreign competition, the affected companies almost immediately increased the prices they charged U.S. manufacturers for the steel they bought. European countries immediately filed complaints with the World Trade Organization, which eventually ruled that the U.S. action was illegal, and threatened to retaliate. In late 2003, the administration reversed its position, and European countries immediately announced that it would file complaints against U.S. tax breaks that they believe unfairly restrict European imports. Taking a cue from the administration, the actions target areas that will be important in the 2004 election: Florida, Pennsylvania, and Ohio.

A more important issue, at least to developing countries, is U.S. agriculture policy. In 1997 the U.S. government adopted the Freedom to Farm Act, which reversed many subsidies and protections for farmers and ranchers. The primary rationale for the change was the theories underlying free trade and comparative advantage. The shift had a devastating effect on many sectors of U.S. agriculture and led to a bipartisan effort to repeal the act.[22] The result was the $180 billion Farm Security Act, passed in the fall of 2002. It revived and even expanded many of the protective provisions and was wildly popular in heavily agricultural states, even though approximately 80 percent of the benefits will go to giant agribusinesses and wealthy farmers (Ted Turner and Arthur Schwab often are singled out as examples) rather than struggling rural families. The bill immediately encountered threats of litigation and retaliation by our trading partners, criticism by free-trade purists, and ridicule at home. Humorist Dave Barry focused on the mohair subsidy. Initiated during World War II to provide warm coats for soldiers, in 1997 the subsidy, which primarily helps ranchers in the Texas hill country, was eliminated as being antiquated (modern military coats are made with synthetic fibers). However, it was reinstated in 2002. Barry responded, "If you're like most American taxpayers, you often wake up in the middle of the night in a cold sweat asking yourself, 'Am I doing enough to support mohair producers?'" The new bill even subsidizes U.S. firms to buy subsidized U.S. agricultural products.

The U.S. position on immigration has oscillated in much the same way. At times immigrants are actively sought out—for example, computer experts from Asia during the "dot com" boom of the 1990s or laborers from Mexico since 2000—and at times they are banned. The shifts result almost wholly from political pressures.[23] Indeed, immigration currently is a highly contentious political issue throughout the world, as is outsourcing of high-tech jobs—financial analysis, medical transcription, interpretations of X rays and CT scans all are increasingly being done for Western firms in Asia. Current projections are that one in ten technology jobs in the United States will move overseas by the end of 2004 and at least 3.3 million white-collar jobs, paying $136 billion in wages, will shift from the United States to developing countries by 2015. Backlash in the developed world has become enough of a problem that it was a major issue at a recent summit of thirty Asian countries held in Hyderabad, India. Anti-outsourcing Web sites like OutsourceCongress.org and professional organizations like the Information Technology Professionals Association of America are becoming an important political trend.[24]

Similarly, Japanese banks, whose careful lending policies were instrumental to that country's miraculous recovery after World War II, have become progressively more political as the country stays mired in recession. Instead of supporting companies willing to take reasonable risks in order to grow, credit is increasingly going to politically well-connected companies on the verge of bankruptcy. Worldwide, although the rhetoric may be strongly in favor of free trade, public policy is more along the lines of "support free trade, except in the case of" important political considerations. In each of these cases, economic policy is made for political reasons but justified on economic grounds. The lesson for managers is clear—there are two ways to deal with the dislocations of globalization: become more competitive, or become more politically active (see Chapter 12 for more detail). But even that lesson is complicated because some companies benefit and some companies suffer from any trade-related policy.[25]

Organizations, Discourse, and the Effects of Globalization

In many ways, globalization has worked precisely as the theory of comparative advantage predicts. Areas with comparative advantages are experiencing unparalleled economic growth. The economy of Taiwan and parts of India—Bangalore and Hyderabad—are booming, The Malaysian economy continues to expand, as do China's and the economies of much of Southeast Asia.[26] International firms have moved to the United States, for the same reasons that U.S. firms move jobs offshore. For example, both Mercedes-Benz and BMW decided to build vehicles in the southern United States in order to be closer to that market, but also because of lower wages and weaker worker and environmental protection laws than those in Germany. Chinese appliance manufacturer Haier Group moved to South Carolina in order to reduce transportation costs and in order to gain status among China's growing economic elite. An increasing number of immigrants to the United States, especially from Asia, now are returning home because their economic prospects are better there, just as almost half of the immigrants to the United States during the nineteenth century returned home when they found that U.S. life was not as good as they had expected. Similarly, Polish immigrants who moved to Germany looking for work now are returning home, even though wages in Poland are one-third of those in Germany. Amid a general decline in the economy of the U.S. Great Plains, some towns have responded creatively and successfully to attract new jobs. The rural poverty rate in Vietnam has been slashed from 70 percent to 30 percent. One of its great success stories was the catfish industry, which benefits from Vietnam's warm climate, abundant water, and cheap labor. It quickly captured 20 percent of the U.S. frozen catfish market and drove prices down, at least until U.S. catfish farmers persuaded Congress to place tariffs of 37 to 64 percent on Vietnamese fish imports. The Philippines, Poland, and much of southern Europe also have been caught in the middle of shifts toward free trade, and then away from it, by more industrialized countries.[27]

However, areas and industries that do not enjoy a "natural" advantage have been devastated. Mining towns in New Mexico and Arizona cannot compete with offshore operations, often owned and managed by U.S. firms. Cotton farmers from Arizona to Georgia no longer were able to compete with African and Latin American producers. The giant Lifesavers Candy plant in Holland, Michigan, closed because its managers could save at least $90 million over the next fifteen years by moving to Canada, where sugar is cheaper as a result of the North American Free Trade Agreement (NAFTA). The Domino sugar plant in Sugarland, Texas, recently announced that it would be moving its operations out of the United States. The heavy industries in Monterrey, Mexico, can no longer compete with foreign imports, including steel, and are slowly disappearing. News reports of additional U.S. blue-collar and lately white-collar jobs being moved overseas appear weekly. At least the "destruction" aspect of "creative destruction" is clearly in evidence, although its impact sometimes is exaggerated— about 30 percent of recent U.S. manufacturing job losses can be attributed to foreign competition (the rest resulted from new technologies and the recession).[28]

Over time, companies that shifted production to low-wage countries have been able to shift production again to even lower-wage countries. This movement erases many of the gains of developing countries and short-circuits the corrective effects of free trade. South Korea is an example of a society that was able to become strong enough to sustain its growth when foreign countries shifted to lower-wage countries; Mexico appears to have not had sufficient time to do so. Much of the Mexican economic gain that was stimulated by NAFTA has disappeared as companies have moved their Mexican operations to Asia and Central America. Poverty rates declined in parts of Latin America throughout the 1990s (while increasing in Venezuela and Paraguay), but the trend was reversed after 1997. In five years almost 20 million additional poor people were added to the region. But it is clear that in the process of shifting jobs from country to country, the managers of multinational corporations have been able to increase the incomes of their nonproduction workers and their investors.[29]

In short, globalization has had major effects on the power relationships that exist among nations and between groups within nations. As we indicate throughout this book, with the exercise of power or with changes in power relationships comes resistance. Some countries are attempting to cushion or offset the adverse effects of globalization. The European Economic Union and the European Trade Union Confederation are implementing strategies designed to increase productivity (and thus support wages) and attract investment capital while adjusting their social support programs. At the same time, they have passed new environmental, worker-protection, and tax laws that target U.S. firms operating on the Continent. China refuses to devalue its currency relative to the U.S. dollar, making its products more attractive to U.S. consumers and the Chinese workforce more attractive to U.S. companies. Developing countries, primarily in Latin America, are discussing ways to pool their resources to insulate themselves against currency fluctuations and the capital markets, much as Europe has done with the Euro. Developed nations in Asia are taking similar steps. Many anti-free-trade politicians have been elected—in Spain, Ecuador, Brazil, Venezuela—even in countries like Chile, which is in the process of negotiating new trade agreements. Recent trade negotiations, which invariably are met with protests in the streets of the host countries, have ended when developing countries decided to go home. Even some of the strongest economies in some areas have balked at new trading arrangements, and protests occur almost daily throughout the world, even in closed societies like China. But at this point no region has devised strategies that promise to protect its economies from the pressures of globalization successfully over the long term, and no region has fully embraced the concept of "creative destruction" that underlies the theory of comparative advantage.[30]

Organizational Practices and Strategies of Organizing   Globalization
has also had a major impact on organizations themselves. Throughout this book,
we have noted that some strategies of organizing are better suited for turbulent,
highly competitive environments than others. Relational, cultural, and networking strategies all increase the speed of information flow and the quality of organizational decisions. Each strategy creates a communication system that allows
an organization to rapidly respond to environmental pressures. But in a global
economy, being able to *react* quickly and decisively may not be enough. Globalization demands that an organization *anticipate* change and move *proactively.*
In these **responsive organizations** (in contrast to reactive ones) structures
and procedures develop that allow the organization's members to understand its
competitive advantages and disadvantages and use that knowledge to create opportunities and anticipate environmental changes.[31] One of the realities of globalization is that minor differences in an organization's ability to exploit its environment have major effects on its performance. The most effective firm in a
given sector of the economy can completely dominate the market; being second
best may not mean having a smaller share of the market it may mean having no
share at all.[32] Global organizations have two options—to become *the* dominant
force in their field, or to become a highly selective niche player. Organizational
size has a number of advantages—it allows an organization to dominate governments, suppliers, and workers. This is why corporate mergers, both within
the core countries and between them, occur today on almost a daily basis.

But historically, size also has meant bureaucratization, and as we have seen
in earlier chapters, bureaucratization has meant inflexibility. The optimal strategy for global organizations, therefore, is to be both large and nimble, a combination that requires new and different strategies of organizing. It means that
some activities need to be centralized and others need to be decentralized.
There are various ways to accomplish this. As we point out in Chapter 3, an organization that wishes to maintain a traditional strategy can use information and
communication technologies to monitor employees in decentralized units.
However, this strategy is ultimately limited in its flexibility. Eventually organizations facing circumstances like these will be pressured to move to networked
structures that incorporate centralized and decentralized components. Dell
Computer Corporation, now the world's largest PC manufacturer, has centralized the billing, inventory management, and distribution networks for its European operations in a single site in Ireland. But it has decentralized decision making to its individual sales and service centers in European countries. A large
European food corporation requires all its European branches to interact with
the Italian branch for their own ice cream marketing because the Italian market
is so complex. But the Italian director of manufacturing must interact with her
or his French colleague who is responsible for European manufacturing. Every
national manager has several bosses worldwide and also is a worldwide supervisor for some specific practices.

Monsanto still is searching for the optimal mix of centralization and decentralization, specialization and "global vision." Its CEO, Robert Shapiro, realizes
that any strategy that denies information to its employees, or encourages the

firm to hire people because they take orders well, will not survive. He also realizes that the final strategy will reduce his control over the organization and even reduce his awareness of "what's going on." Monsanto has not yet settled on a final strategy, but it is clear that it cannot be a traditional bureaucracy. The best strategy will involve a form of "radical decentralization," one that focuses on enhancing internal and external communication. Globalization does not mean that every organization will develop radically new strategies of organizing. For example, the family-business model that long has dominated Taiwan and Hong Kong seems to be especially well-suited to globalization—the members of such businesses are highly motivated and more committed, more flexible, and less bureaucratic than the state-owned businesses with which they compete. In China, where government agents still operate as supervisors, the challenge is to find ways to combine the socialist model and the family firm in a way that balances "the modern and the traditional while remaining competitive in the global economy."[33] Alternative forms of organization may also be useful. The heterarchy should be effective in environments that are changing extremely rapidly. The cooperative and feminist forms are useful because they shelter their employees from some of the negative effects of hostile and changing environments. However, whatever strategy a given organization develops, it must deal effectively with the pressures of globalization.

In sum, the economic theories underlying laissez-faire capitalism and free trade predict many of the observed effects of globalization. Although these theories predict that the resulting economic dislocations will eventually be corrected, there is reason to doubt those predictions. Neither theory adequately anticipates the effects of a free market on capital, and both assume that multinational organizations will be less monopolistic than they are becoming. Both factors may undermine the corrective mechanisms noted in economic theory. If these mechanisms do fail, economic inequality is likely to increase further; social tensions are likely to continue to grow, and the democratizing pressures of globalization will be undermined. Organizations and their members could find themselves in a world that is both chaotic and increasingly hostile and divided.

CASE STUDY
Small Company, Global Approach

Organizations internationalize in different ways. Some traditionally national firms discover international opportunities and move incrementally by expanding to neighboring markets in nearby countries, then throughout their region, and then to the rest of the world. During their expansion they learn more and more about how to operate internationally and thereby minimize the risks involved in making mistakes. Others, for example Logitech, take a global perspective from the outset—they are "born global."* Gayle Warwick Fine Linen was born global.

(continued)

(Case Study, continued)

In 1990 U.S. citizen Gayle Warwick found herself in London, where her husband had relocated as part of a new job. An art history major with some coursework in law school and some experience in corporate public relations, she had no experience running a business. That is not to say that she had no experience—she had managed a family on two continents and was from an entrepreneurial family. Her grandfathers ran their own plumbing and contracting companies on Long Island (New York), and she had worked as a teenager in her father's lumber business. She knew that "going global" is all the rage among U.S. small businesses these days—during the previous ten years the number of companies with fewer than 100 workers who export their products had doubled to 213,000 (generating almost $130 billion in sales). But she really hadn't thought about creating a global business.

Then at a social engagement with the Vietnamese wife of one of her husband's business associates, she saw a hand-embroidered tablecloth and received an invitation to visit the couple's home country. The two made the trip in 1995, and Ms. Warwick had some samples made and shipped them home to sell at charity Christmas fairs. After her friend moved away the following year, she decided to go to Vietnam and explore the possibility of setting up a linen business. She conducted more research and spent $16,000 of her savings to travel to Italy, Ireland, and Switzerland to talk with linen and organic-cotton spinners, weavers, and finishers; to France and Germany to attend textile trade fairs; and to Vietnam to find embroiderers, and she decided to become an entrepreneur. The most important thing she learned during her research was that to make an idea work, you have to be very tenacious.

Her new expertise and contacts started to pay off. Executives of a French quality-control company whom she met while in Ho Chi Minh City put her in touch with exporters in Hanoi, who helped her find the skilled craftspeople in rural Vietnam who would work on her designs. She hired a French company to handle shipping, an accounting firm to handle taxes, a consulting firm to market her table linens, and an artist to help design them. Together they spent hours studying textiles in London museums.

She incorporated the business in 1998 and began selling from a converted dining room in her London home. Gayle Warwick Fine Linen are designed to be sold to an international economic elite—people in multiple countries who are becoming increasingly connected with one another. A set of organic-cotton sheets and pillow shams sells for $625; napkins and place mats start at $75 each. Thanks to favorable reviews in the *Times* of London and the *Financial Times,* she began to receive orders from internationally known interior designers. She also started selling to upscale stores on the U.S. East Coast. As a result, she has overcome one of the biggest problems facing any small company—the lack of name recognition. Sales have increased from $40,000 in 1998 to an estimated $300,000 for 2004, allowing her to make a profit for the first time. She is planning a new range of products, from children's pajamas and women's silk loungewear made in Vietnam to cashmere bed throws made in Italy.

Advocates of globalization cite Ms. Warwick's record as an example of the virtues of world trade. Donna Sharp, executive director of the World Trade Institute of New York's Pace University, said, "With a little know-how, creativity and confidence, even the smallest business can find opportunities around the globe. Almost everyone can take advantage of trade-lead Web sites, or go to global conferences or trade shows. The small businesses of today are the multinationals of tomorrow."[†]

Applying What You Have Learned

1. What characteristics of the global economy allowed Gayle Warwick to successfully build her company?
2. What barriers did she have to overcome in order to succeed? What strategies did she employ in order to do so?

Questions to Think About and Discuss

1. Advocates of globalization point to successes like Gayle Warwick's as evidence of its positive value. What factors will influence the success of her business over the long term?
2. Now that you know the Gayle Warwick Fine Linen story, devise a strategy for competing with that organization. What can you do to overcome her "head start" in the industry? What will Gayle Warwick Fine Linen need to do in order to compete successfully with you?

This case study is based on Jane L. Levere, "A Small Company, a Global Approach," *New York Times on the Web*, January 1, 2004, http://www.nytimes.com/.

[*]Michael Rennie, "Born Global," *McKinsey Quarterly* 4 (1993): 45–52; Tage Koed Madsen, Erik Rasmussen, and Per Servais, "Differences and Similarities between Born Globals and Other Types of Exporters," *Advances in International Marketing* 10 (2000): 247–265.

[†]Levere, p. 4.

Globalization, Ethics, and Organizational Democracy   Although we discuss ethics at length in Chapter 12, it is important to note here that it has become increasing important because of globalization. Historically, U.S. organizations have been decidedly undemocratic institutions. And throughout U.S. history formal organizations have exerted strong influences on political decision making, increasingly out of sight of the public eye. When combined with widespread acceptance of the assumptions underlying laissez-faire capitalism, these realities have created a social situation in which powerful organizations can operate freely, without being held responsible to the larger society. For example, Stanley Deetz concludes that in the contemporary United States, "commercial corporations function as public institutions but without public accountability." Given U.S. residents' commitments to openness and democracy, this is somewhat surprising. The tension between democracy and autonomous, nondemocratic organizations is the basis of a distinctive view of corporations' responsibilities to the larger society.[34] Conversely, it is in the most democratic societies in the world that opposition to globalization has been strongest and most effective.

One clear result of globalization is that worker power worldwide has declined substantially. This results in part from structural factors—labor organizations are highly bureaucratic and thus are unable to respond rapidly to changes in overall power relationships. In addition, they have traditionally relied on political action. As governments have become progressively less powerful relative to multinational organizations, workers' ability to influence corporate practices through political action has declined. The policy decisions that are most important to workers now are made by international organizations, not national governments. Corporations have shifted their operations to areas in which labor's influence is weak, for example, the developing world and the southern United States. International trade economist Dani Rodrik concludes:

> Employers are less willing to provide the benefits of job security and stability, partly because of increased competition but also because their enhanced global mobility makes them less dependent on the good-will of their local work force. Governments are less able to sustain social safety nets, because an important part of their tax base has become footloose because of increased mobility of capital. . . . Globalization creates an inequality in bargaining power that 60 years of labor legislation in the U.S. has tried to prevent.[35]

As a result, a two-tiered labor force has emerged throughout the developed and developing world. One tier is composed of highly educated workers in stable, high-paying jobs that provide substantial benefits and job security. Their skills and their ability to move from company to company provide them with relatively strong bargaining positions, as long as the economy is strong. The other tier is composed of workers who typically (but not always) have less education or education that is not relevant to high-tier jobs, and who are in various kinds of contingent positions that may (but often do not) provide high salaries but no benefits or job security. Of course, even in the United States, there have been notable instances of labor resistance to the creation of a two-tiered system—successful strikes against United Parcel Service and General Motors over the use of part-time workers and outsourcing and Microsoft's multimillion settlement in December 2000 with "permatemp" workers who had long-term jobs with the company but were denied fringe benefits, such as health insurance and stock options. But the global trend toward a two-tiered workforce seems to be quite clear. Although different stakeholders are increasingly affected by the actions of multinational corporations, they are increasingly powerless to affect those actions.

Notes

[1] John Parry, ed. *The Establishment of the European Hegemony, 1415–1715* (New York: HarperCollins, 1967); Kevin O'Rourke and Jeffrey Williamson, *Globalization and History* (Cambridge, MA: MIT Press, 1999); Louis Uchitelle, "Some Economic Interplay Comes Nearly Full Circle," *New York Times on the Web,* April 30, 1998, http://www.nytimes.com/; Roland Robertson, *Globalization* (London: Sage, 1992).

[2] Paul Varg, "The Myth of the China Market, 1890–1914," *American Historical Review* 73 (1968): 742–758.

[3] Alan Heston and Neil Weiner, "Dimensions of Globalization," *Annals of the American Academy of Political and Social Science* 570 (2000): 8–18. However, substantially less progress has been made in sub-Saharan Africa.

[4] These examples are taken from Cynthia Stohl, "Globalizing Organizational Communication," in *The New Handbook of Organizational Communication,* Fredric Jablin and Linda Putnam, eds. (Thousand Oaks, CA: Sage, 2000); Harry Shattuck, "Mexico Offers Better Assistance," *Houston Chronicle,* November 12, 2000, G1; and Thomas Friedman, "You've Got Mail—from the Philippines," *Houston Chronicle,* September 30, 2000, A36; and *The Lexus and the Olive Tree* (New York: Farrar, Straus and Giroux, 1999).

[5] Dani Rodrik, "Has Globalization Gone Too Far?" *Challenge* 41 (1998): 81–94. Also see Gary Burless, R. Lawrence, and R. Shapiro, *Globaphobia* (Washington, DC: Brookings Institution Press, 1998); Friedman, *Lexus;* and George Soros, *The Crisis of Global Capitalism* (New York: Public Affairs, 1998); and *The Open Society* (New York: Public Affairs, 2000).

[6] Vicente Fox, "At a Turning Point in Closing the Rich-Poor Gap," *Houston Chronicle,* March 21, 2002, A37.

[7] Stohl, "Globalizing"; Susan Hafen, "Cultural Diversity Training," p. 127; and Debashish Munshi, "Through the Subject's Eye," both in *Organization—Communication: Emerging Perspectives,* George Cheney and George Barnett, eds., vol. 7 (Cresskill, NJ: Hampton Press, 2003).

[8] Stohl, "Globalizing." Also see C. Hilton, "International Business Communication," *Journal of Business Communication* 29 (1992): 253–265; Charles Bantz, "Cultural Diversity and Group Cross-Cultural Team Research," *Journal of Applied Communication Research* 20 (1993): 1–19. Both Richard Shuter, "Communication in Multinational Organizations," in *Communication and Multinational Organizations,* R. Wiseman and R. Shuter, eds. (Thousand Oaks, CA: Sage, 1994); and Fred Casmir, "Third Culture Building," in *Communication Yearbook 16,* Stanley Deetz, ed. (Newbury Park, CA: Sage, 1993), have argued that intercultural effectiveness depends on building blended or multicultural workplaces in which ethnic, racial, and cultural differences are celebrated.

[9] Philip Harris and Robert Moran, *Managing Cultural Differences,* 5th ed. (Houston: Gulf, 2000). For an excellent case study of cross-cultural conflict between Japanese managers and Anglo-U.S. engineers and human resource officers, see Stephen Banks and Patricia Riley, "Structuration Theory as an Ontology for Communication Research," in *Communication Yearbook 16,* Stanley Deetz, ed. (Newbury Park, CA: Sage, 1993).

[10] " 'Hijab' Debate Isn't Just a French Affair," *Houston Chronicle,* January 11, 2004, C4.

[11] Diane Grimes, "Putting Our Own House in Order: Whiteness, Change, and Organization Studies," *Journal of Organizational Change Management* 14 (2001): 132–149; Jolanta Drzewiecka and Kahleen Wong (Lau), "The Dynamic Construction of White Ethnicity in the Context of Transnational Cultural Formations," in *Whiteness: The Communication of Social Identity,* Thomas Nakayama and Judith Martin, eds. (Thousand Oaks, CA: Sage, 1999).

[12] An interesting exception is Martin Gannon, *Understanding Global Cultures,* 2nd ed. (Thousand Oaks, CA: Sage, 2001), which does a wonderful job of showing how a key ritual of a culture reveals a great deal about deeper levels of culture—American football, the Mexican fiesta, the German symphony. J. Dovidio, S. Gaertrer, P. Anastasio, and R. Sanitioso, "Cognitive and Motivational Bases of Bias," in *Hispanics in the Workplace,* P. Knouse, P. Rosenfeld, and A. Culbertson, eds. (Newbury Park, CA: Sage, 1992). D. Jamieson and J. O'Mara, *Managing Workforce 2000* (San Francisco: Jossey-Bass, 1991), list Hewlett-Packard and Hallmark as organizations with especially effective training programs. Unfortunately, there is little evidence that education itself will overcome racism or sexism. K. Kraiger and J. Ford, "A Meta-Analysis of Ratee Race Effects in Performance Ratings," *Journal of Applied Psychology* 70 (1985): 56–65.

[13] For summaries see Khalid Alkhazraji, William Gardner, Jeanette Martin, and Joseph Paolillo, "The Acculturation of Immigrants to U.S. Organizations," *Management Communication Quarterly* 11 (1997): 217–265; Taylor Cox, S. Lobel, and P. McLeod, "Effects of Ethnic Cultural Differences on Cooperative and Competitive Behavior on a Group Task," *Academy of Management Journal* 34 (1991): 827–847; and M. Kim, J. E. Hunter, A. Miyahara, A. Horvath, M. Bresnahan, and H. Yoon, "Individual- vs. Culture-Level Dimensions of Individualism and Collectivism," *Communication Monographs* 63 (1996): 29–49; and N. Adler, *International Dimensions of Organizational Behavior,* 2nd ed. (Boston: Kent, 1991).

[14] Henry Triandis, R. Bontempor, M. Villareal, M. Asai, and N. Lucca, "Individualism and Collectivism: Cross-Cultural Perspectives on Self-Ingroup Relationships," *Journal of Personality and Social Psychology* 21 (1988): 323–338; David Ralston, D. Holt, Robert Terpstra, and Yu Kaicheng, "The Impact of National Culture and Economic Ideology on Managerial Work Values," *Journal of International Business Studies* 28 (1997): 177–208; and Michael Marti, *China and the Legacy of Deng Xiaoping: From Communist Revolution to Capitalist Evolution* (Washington, DC, Brassey's, 2002).

[15] A. DePalma, "It Takes More Than a Visa to Do Business in Mexico," *New York Times,* June 26, 1994, A16–17.

[16] A. P. Carnavale and S. C. Stone, "Diversity: Beyond the Golden Rule," *Training and Development,* October 1994, p. 24.

[17] Hector Cantu, "Racial Slur Helped Form New Career," *Houston Chronicle,* March 21, 1999, D3. Also see Stephen Paskoff, "Ending the Workplace Diversity Wars," *Training: The Human Side of Business* (August 1996): 3. Also see Al Gonzalez, J. Willis, and C. Young, "Cultural Diversity and Organizations," in *Organizational Communication,* Peggy Yuhas Byers, ed. (Boston: Allyn and Bacon, 1997); A. Rizzo and C. Mendez, *The Integration of Women in Management* (New York: Quorum Books, 1990); Barbara Reskin and Irene Padavic, *Women and Men at Work* (Thousand Oaks, CA: Pine Forge Press, 1994).

[18] The theory of comparative advantage was first proposed in 1817 by David Ricardo in *Principles of Political Economy and Taxation* (Buffalo, NY: Prometheus Books, 1996). It is summarized at length in any good economics textbook and is examined at length by Douglas Irwin in *Against the Tide* (Princeton, NJ: Princeton University Press, 1996).

[19] John Otis, "Ailing Schools Can't Set Free Peru's Youth," *Houston Chronicle,* December 22, 2003, A1.

[20] Richard Freeman and Lawrence Katz, "Rising Wage Inequality," in *Working under Different Rules* (New York: Russell Sage Foundation, 1994); Jim Hoagland, "Can't Leave Backyard Politics Out of Globalization," *Houston Chronicle,* October 22, 2000, C3; and Soros, *Crisis.*

[21] D. Irwin.

[22] Dave Barry, "Rest Easy Knowing the Mohair Business Is Thriving," *Bryan/College Station (TX) Eagle,* June 23, 2002, D3; Nicholas Kristof, "America's Failed Frontier," *New York Times on the Web,* September 3, 2002, http://www.nytimes.com/; "Welfare Reform for Farmers," *New York Times on the Web,* November 10, 2003; Elizabeth Becker, "U.S. Subsidizes Companies to Buy Subsidized Cotton," *New York Times on the Web,* November 4, 2003; "The Hypocrisy of Farm Subsidies," *New York Times on the Web,* December 1, 2002.

[23] U.S. Senator John Cornyn, "Pragmatic Reasons for the Guest-Worker Proposal," *Houston Chronicle,* January 8, 2004, A29; Ruben Navattette Jr., "Grandson of Immigrant Now to the Right of Rove," *Houston Chronicle,* January 8, 2004, A29; William F. Buckley, "Face It, We Surrendered on Immigration," *Houston Chronicle,* January 10, 2004, A36.

[24] "Critics of Outsourcing Hope to Start Movement," *Houston Chronicle,* January 20, 2004, B4.

[25] Joseph Kahn and Richard Stevenson, "Treasury Official Is Said to Fault Steel Tariff Move," *New York Times on the Web,* March 16, 2002, http://www.nytimes.com/; Dan Nephin, "Domestic Steel Prices Head Higher," *Houston Chronicle,* March 31, 2002, D5; Elizabeth Becker and David Sanger, "President in Political Vise over Steel Tariff Decision," *New York Times on the Web,* December 2, 2003; Alan Cowell, "Europeans Plan to Press for Tariffs against U.S.," *New York Times on the Web,* December 6, 2003. For an assessment of Japanese banking policies, see Akio Mikuni and R. Taggert Murphy, "Would Reform Ruin Japan?" *New York Times on the Web,* October 29, 2002; David Rosenbaum, "They Support Free Trade, Except in the Case of . . . ," *New York Times on the Web,* November 16, 2003; Edmund L. Andrews, "A Civil War within a Trade Dispute," *New York Times on the Web,* September 20, 2002.

[26] Keith Bradsher, "A High-Tech Fix for One Corner of India," *New York Times on the Web,* December 27, 2002, http://www.nytimes.com/; Amy Waldman, "Despite Widespread Poverty, a Consumer Class Emerges in India," *New York Times on the Web,* October 20, 2003.

[27] Thomas Friedman, "Globalization Movement Alive and Well, "*Houston Chronicle,* September 22, 2002, C3; Pete Engardio, "Corporate America's Silent Partner: India," *Business Week Online,* December 15, 2003, http://www.businessweek.com/; "Tech Leaders Urge Congress Not to Act to Keep Jobs in U.S.," *Houston Chronicle,* January 8, 2004; Kevin O'Brien, "Unusual Pattern on Polish Border," *Houston Chronicle,* January 11, 2004, D6; Yilu Zhao, "When Jobs Move Overseas (to South Carolina)," *New York Times on the Web,* October 26, 2003, http://www.nytimes.com/; Timothy Egan, "Amid Dying Towns of Rural Plains, One Makes a Stand," *New York Times on the Web,* December 1, 2003; Jennifer Beauprez, "A Better Life, but Not in the U.S.," *Houston Chronicle,* August 17, 2003, D2; Ian Fisher, "As Poland Endures Hard Times, Capitalism Comes under Attack," *New York Times on the Web,* June 12, 2003; "The Rigged Trade Game," *New York Times on the Web,* July 20, 2003; "The Great Catfish War," *New York Times on the Web,* July 22, 2003.

[28] Edmund Andrews, "Imports Don't Deserve All That Blame," *New York Times on the Web,* December 7, 2003, http://www.nytimes.com/; Louis Uchitelle, "A Missing Statistic: U.S. Jobs That Went Overseas," *New York Times on the Web,* October 5, 2003. Summaries of the effects on the candy industry are available in Jenalia Moreno, "Mexico Takes a Bite Out of the Market," *Houston Chronicle,* November 25, 2003, B1; and Dean Reynolds, "Sticky Situation," ABC News, March 25, 2002, http://www.abcnews.go.com/. Excellent summaries of the economic effects of NAFTA are available in Joseph Stiglitz, "The Broken Promise of NAFTA," *New York Times on the Web,* January 6, 2004; a November 11, 2002, broadcast of Bill Moyer's *NOW* television show (a transcript is available on the PBS Web site), and a multipart investigation published in the *Houston Chronicle* in November and December 2002, available on the newspaper's Web site.

[29] See Soros, *Crisis;* Jenalia Moreno, "China Replaces Mexico as Land of Cheap Labor," *Houston Chronicle,* October 25, 2002, C1; Eduardo Mocada, "Made in China: Educational Lesson for Mexico," *Houston Chronicle,* No-

vember 18, 2002, A23; Frank Rampersad, "Coping with Globalization," *Annals of the American Association of Political and Social Science* 570 (2000): 115-125; and Jeffrey Sachs, "Making It Work," *Economist,* September 12, 1998, available at http://www.economist.com/; Jane Bussey, "Reduction in Poverty Stalls in Latin America," *Houston Chronicle,* December 1, 2002, D6.

[30] Amy Chua, "Power to the Privileged," *New York Times on the Web,* January 7, 2003, http://www.nytimes .com/; Samuel Loewenberg, "Europe Gets Tougher on U.S. Companies," *New York Times on the Web,* April 20, 2003; Dudley Althus, "Voters Rejecting Free-Trade Model," *Houston Chronicle,* November 24, 2002; David Leonhardt, "Globalization Hits a Political Speed Bump," *New York Times on the Web,* June 1, 2003; Elizabeth Becker and Larry Rohter, "U.S. and Chile Reach Free Trade Accord," *New York Times on the Web,* December 12, 2002; Elisabeth Rosenthal, "Workers' Plight Brings New Militancy in China," *New York Times on the Web,* March 10, 2003; Louis Uchitelle, "When the Chinese Consumer Is King," *New York Times on the Web,* December 14, 2003.

[31] Lynda St. Clair, Robert Quinn, and Regina O'Neill, "The Perils of Responsiveness in Modern Organizations," in *Pressing Problems in Organizations (That Keep Us Up at Night),* Robert Quinn, R. O'Neill, and L. St. Clair, eds. (New York: American Management Association, 2000), p. 245.

[32] Robert Frank and Philip Cook, *The Winner Take All Society* (Reading, MA: Addison-Wesley, 1998).

[33] Charles Sheehan, "Steelworkers Roll with the Changes," *Houston Chronicle,* November 12, 2003, D8; Ling Chen, "Connecting to the World Economy," *Management Communication Quarterly* 14 (2000): 152-160. The other examples in this paragraph are from Ruggero Cesaria, "Organizational Communication Issues in Italian Multinational Corporations," *Management Communication Quarterly* 14 (2000): 161-172; and Friedman, *Lexus.*

[34] Stanley Deetz, "Transforming Communication, Transforming Business," *International Journal of Value-Based Management* (1995): 2. Also see Stanley Deetz. *Transforming Communication, Transforming Business* (Cresskill, NJ: Hampton Press, 1995).

[35] Dani Rodrik, "Sense and Nonsense in the Globalization Debate," *Foreign Policy* 107 (Summer 1997): 17, 19; for a brief but excellent analysis, see Richard Harvey Brown, "Global Capitalism, National Sovereignty, and the Decline of Democratic Space," *Rhetoric and Public Affairs* 5 (2002): 347-357.

Chapter 12

Communication, Ethics, and Organizational Rhetoric

*What I found was really disappointing. Before undertaking this research I believed
that people's personal values made a big difference in how they behave [ethically]
in the workplace. But now I'm convinced they don't.*
—Arthur Brief

Our conversations about corporations need to change for us to truly create the good society.
—R. Edward Freeman and Jeanne Liedtka

Central Themes

- Unethical and illegal organizational behavior has become a recurring theme in U.S. economic history. Organizational ethics should be viewed through a societal frame of reference because organizational actors draw upon cultural assumptions to legitimate their behaviors, and engage in rhetorical acts designed to mold favorable cultural assumptions.
- At least from the time of Adam Smith, societies with capitalist economies have struggled with the need to constrain greed while not undermining the economic advantages of free-market systems. This tension is reflected in the primary models of organization-society relationships: social responsibility, social responsiveness, and multiple stakeholders.
- Organizational rhetoricians have many strategies available that can be used to protect their organizations from external pressures.
- The early years of the twenty-first century witnessed a series of corporate scandals, the best known of which involved the Enron corporation. The history of that scandal provides an informative case study in many of the concepts discussed in this chapter and in this book.

Key Terms

charity principle   stewardship principle

Since the turn of the twenty-first century, some of the "hottest" topics in U.S. society have been fraud, corruption, and ethical malfeasance in major corporations. Stimulated by the two largest bankruptcies in U.S. history—Enron and WorldCom—academics, journalists, and even the politicians who helped create the conditions that allowed these corporate scandals to happen have been shocked by the machinations of corporate executives who seem to be devoid of any personal code of ethics. But this era of corruption clearly is not a new phenomenon. The "robber baron" era of the late 1800s, which led to Theodore Roosevelt's "trust busting" legislation; revelations of profiteering by U.S. munitions companies during World War I, which culminated in jail sentences for some of the worst offenders; the corruption of politics by organizational money during the 1920s, which led to the reforms of the "Progressive Era"; and the investment scandals of the 1980s—all these indicate that unethical behavior by corporations and their leaders is a continuing aspect of U.S. society. Between 1975 and 1990, two-thirds of the Fortune 500 firms were *convicted* of serious crimes ranging from price fixing to illegal dumping of hazardous wastes. In late 1996 Archer Daniels Midland ("supermarket to the world," according to its commercials) was fined a record $100 million by the U.S. Justice Department for illegally fixing prices of citric acid and lysine (an additive in animal feeds), but this figure was eclipsed by fines levied in response to the "corporate meltdown" of the early 2000s. Many other organizations reached out-of-court settlements or were convicted of misdemeanors. In some sectors of the economy, pressures to engage in illegal or unethical actions are so intense and the actions are so frequent that they have come to be seen as the normal way of doing business (for example, financial fraud in defense contracting, sexism in the military, and racism and homophobia in the petroleum/petrochemical industry).[1]

Initially, it may seem strange that we have decided to discuss organizational ethics and organizational rhetoric in the same chapter. In some ways it is a strange decision for us as well, because in previous editions of this book—and in Chapter 8 of this edition—we talked about ethics as an aspect of organizational power and politics. But for readers who are familiar with rhetorical theory, the link will not seem strange at all. At least since the time of Plato, ethics, politics, rhetoric, and economic institutions have been linked to one another. Plato's student Aristotle told his students that they must consider politics and rhetoric as two sides of the same coin, and the treatise on ethics that he wrote for his own son is filled with links to politics and rhetoric. Contemporary rhetorical theorists have continued the association.[2]

Organizational ethics and organizational rhetoric are intertwined in two ways. First, as we have done throughout this book, we will argue that organizations can be understood only with reference to the social, political, and economic climate within which they operate. When managers choose a particular strategy of organizing, they do so within the guidelines and constraints imposed by their societies. They legitimate their choices by drawing on the underlying assumptions of their society. However, leaders of organizations do not merely adapt to the environmental pressures they face (as we explain in Chapter 7); they also act to mold those pressures. One way they do this is by establishing a favorable image of themselves and their organizations in the minds of their audiences. At the same time, they can use rhetoric to reinforce the societal assumptions that privilege managerial and organizational interests over those of other individuals and groups.

A second means of controlling environmental pressures, one that has become increasingly complex because of globalization, is to persuade politicians to pass favorable laws. Competing in the global marketplace is an incredibly difficult undertaking. Persuading governments to protect one's company from global competition, or to require citizens to pay some of the costs of competition, often makes things easier. For example, at the height of the Enron-inspired scandals in the United States, John Bogle, the founder of the Vanguard group of mutual funds, explained that it is much more rational for corporate executives to spend their money influencing politicians than it is for them to use it to build new plants or purchase new equipment. A new plant will return at most 10 to 20 percent of the money invested in it each year during its lifetime, Bogle argued. Political donations, in contrast, return 300–500 percent, and do so with much less risk. Of course most communication between organizations and political officials occurs in private, through lobbying, for example. But even political decisions that are arrived at in private eventually have to be legitimated in public, no matter how hard the parties try to keep them secret. This is especially true in democratic societies. Consequently, the two primary functions of organizational rhetoric are (1) to strategically mold popular opinions, attitudes, and values in ways that create support for organizational practices or undermine opposition to them (or both), and (2) to strategically influence public policies. Both are inherently ethical activities, and both serve as the basis for ethical judgments about organizational policies and practices.[3]

Ethics and Organizational Rhetoric

Over time, capitalists and scholars alike have struggled to deal with the moral and ethical dilemmas created by laissez-faire capitalism. For example, free-market purists (financier George Soros calls them "free market fundamentalists" because of their steadfast commitment to their faith in spite of abundant disconfirming evidence) almost always trace their views back to Adam Smith's concept of the "invisible hand." In *The Wealth of Nations* Smith (who never used the term *laissez-faire*) argues that people are indeed motivated by the desire to maximize their individual economic gains. However, a free, open, and informed competition among potential buyers and sellers will lead to optimal deals among them and eventually to a society that balances economic needs in the most efficient way possible. The challenge for market societies is to appropriately constrain those individual motivations. Greed may be good as a motivator, but if left unchecked, it can destroy societies and economies. It does so in two ways. First, it encourages people to undermine and short-circuit the key element of the market economy, competition, by creating monopolies. Greed also serves to undermine rational decision making by customers, investors, and government officials because it encourages managers to hide or distort information about the quality of products being sold, the production processes being used, or the financial health of companies. Finally, celebrating greed undermines societies by encouraging people to celebrate and sympathize with the rich and powerful while denigrating the poor, the lowly, or the wise.

Second, unrestrained greed leads to the "tragedy of the commons." The phrase harks back to the Middle Ages, when communities held an area in common where every citizen could graze his or her livestock. The "tragedy" is that free-market incentives led everyone to use the commons as much as possible in order to save her or his own pastureland. Eventually the commons became overgrazed and useless to everyone. This process is the basis of much contemporary concern about the environmental effects of market economies—that unbridled use of natural resources will eventually exhaust them, especially because organizations rarely pay (or pay full value) for the resources themselves. Economists call costs like public education, transportation systems, military security, and cleaning up environmental damage "externalities" because they are not normally included in the costs of a transaction between a buyer and a seller. They thus are "external" to the value of the exchange. Of course, both parties in an economic exchange have absolute incentives to treat as many of their costs of doing business as possible as "externalities." Doing so means that they are not responsible for bearing those costs and can pass those costs on to others, thereby maximizing their economic gains. In short, "what's good for General Motors" (and any other organization) is to get taxpayers, suppliers, and competitors to pay for as much of its "external" costs as possible and to minimize the amount that it has to pay through taxes and other fees.

Smith realized that free-market economies faced inevitable ethical challenges, and he discussed them in a companion book to *The Wealth of Nations,* entitled *The Theory of Moral Sentiments.* In its multiple editions, Smith struggled with how a society can constrain greed without undermining the economic advantages of the free market. In early editions he argued that informal constraints are adequate. People develop a sense of right and wrong and a commitment to the welfare of other people as they mature in their communities. The potential shame that would come from excessive greed or unfair economic behavior would constrain the actions of even the greediest people. Smith assumed that market economies depended on the values of prudence and self-control and that those values could be taught. Some people learn these lessons completely and become saints (Smith noted that this is "a select, though, I am afraid, a small party"). The "average" person also is constrained by his or her own conscience but needs the additional constraint of public opinion and pressure. Some people, unfortunately, have neither conscience nor a capacity to feel disgraced. Free of these restraints, those people engage in vicious economic behavior that is destructive to their society and, in the long run, to themselves because one cannot have a full and meaningful life without a connection to one's community (the lesson that Ebenezer Scrooge learned one cold winter night). Regrettably, Smith concluded, those people would have to be constrained by the power of the state. The potential for excess is greatest for people working in the capital markets—banking, international finance, and trade. Consequently, Smith believed, government would have to be most active in that sector of the economy, a view that is especially ironic given the central role that the capital markets have played in recent unethical corporate behavior.

However, during Smith's lifetime England became more and more industrialized and more and more urban. He realized that with these trends came increased geographic mobility, decreased opportunities for surveillance by members of a person's community, and decreased likelihood that "average" people would internalize the values of prudence and self-control. Unlike Smith's economic theory, which stayed virtually the same throughout various editions of *The Wealth of Nations,* Smith's social theory changed as he struggled with his changing society and the declining ability of informal social processes to regulate human greed. Although today's free-market fundamentalists tend to ignore *The Theory of Moral Sentiments* almost completely, it establishes the fundamental ethical issue facing societies with free-market economies: How can a free society simultaneously obtain the economic advantages of the "invisible hand" while avoiding the excesses of human greed?[4]

Societal Assumptions and Organizational Rhetoric

The proper relationship between organizations and society has been a highly contested concept since the creation of the corporation in the 1800s. By the end of that century widespread anger about the excesses of large corporations had led to the creation of a new industry—public relations—and a new ideology about the proper relationship between organizations and society. One of the most visible organizational rhetoricians during the "gilded age" was Andrew Carnegie, the founder of U.S. Steel. Carnegie argued that two principles needed to be accepted if laissez-faire capitalism was to succeed over the long term. One was the **charity principle,** which required more fortunate members of the society to assist its less fortunate members, either directly through philanthropy or indirectly through corporate support of social service organizations. Carnegie roundly criticized other "captains of industry" (the term "robber barons" was an equally popular epithet at the time) for ignoring broader social concerns in their narrow pursuit of wealth and power. Somewhat ironically, Carnegie seemed to be less concerned about the wealthy industrialists' treatment of their employees, but his commitment to the society as a whole was clear. Carnegie was also committed to the **stewardship principle,** which suggested that businesses and wealthy people had an obligation to try to increase the wealth of the society as a whole by wisely investing the resources they controlled. For the following fifty years, Carnegie's assumptions were accepted and codified into a concept of "corporate social responsibility," a belief that organizations had a responsibility to assist in the solution of social problems in addition to making money, especially if they had helped to create those problems. But by the 1960s this model of *corporate social responsibility* was being challenged.[5]

A group of conservative theorists, led by economist Milton Friedman of the University of Chicago, argued that the only responsibility corporations have is to pursue their own economic self-interest. Managers have no particular expertise in defining social problems and no incentives for trying to solve them, and capitalism provides no means of holding managers accountable for the effects of their purportedly "socially responsible" activities. To the extent that they *do* invest the organization's capital in such activities, they make it vulnerable to competitors who invest all their resources in enhancing their firms' economic position. Thus, in the long run, they threaten the jobs of their employees and violate the trust of their investors. In short, Friedman argued, Carnegie's two principles are contradictory: in an economy defined by competitive, laissez-faire capitalism, corporate *charity* reduces the economic viability of a firm, thus violating the *stewardship* principle. In a democratic society, only government is responsible for dealing with social problems, because only government can be held accountable for doing or not doing so. Organizations should be concerned with *generating* wealth, and government should not interfere in that process. Governments should concern themselves with *distributing* wealth and not leave that task to corporations.[6] Furthermore, when government works to solve social problems, it must do so without interfering with the operation of economic markets (recall the discussion of the futility, jeopardy, and perversity theses in Chapter 2).

Debates over the social responsibility doctrine continued until the late 1970s, eventually leading to a new doctrine of "social responsiveness." From the social responsiveness perspective, managers are responsible for monitoring an organization's environment and strategically responding to environmental pressures. Most of these pressures are economic, as Unit I explains. But others are more social than economic. For example, the growing environmental movement of the 1970s and 1980s placed new pressures on managers, pressures that, ironically, were enforced by governmental action. The advantage of the social responsiveness perspective is that it does give managers some guidelines for making socially relevant choices: obey the law, fulfill regulations, and placate powerful external interest groups.

But the social responsiveness doctrine is problematic in two ways. First, it establishes an adversarial relationship between managers and both government agencies and external interest groups. Instead of fostering a cooperative effort to deal with social and economic problems, it encourages competitive and hostile orientations. Second, it encourages managers to find ways to proactively manage external pressures. In many cases it is easier to circumvent or overpower external pressures than to be responsive to them. Contributing to the political campaigns of candidates who promise to weaken environmental standards is often much less expensive than meeting those standards. Exploiting weaknesses in governmental monitoring or the legal system may be more cost-effective than acting in legal and ethical ways. Recall the $100 million fine against Archer Daniels Midland that was described at the beginning of this chapter. Because price fixing short-circuits the competitive mechanisms of the free market, this is precisely the kind of governmental action that is sanctioned by laissez-faire economic theory. However, the government's ability to punish ADM paled in comparison to the estimated $200–$600 million in extra profits that the company made by engaging in the illegal activities.

These problems with the corporate social responsibility doctrine eventually led to the development of "multiple-stakeholder" models of organizational ethics. Advocates of multiple-stakeholder perspectives argue that many groups have a legitimate stake in the decisions made by managers and the actions taken by the organizations they control. Management is responsible for finding ways to meet the needs and consider the interests of all legitimate stakeholders in the company. Workers, suppliers, consumers, host communities, stockholders, and the general community often have taken more risks and made greater long-term investments in their organizations than upper management has. Through their taxes, *they* have paid to educate the workers hired by the organization, built the infrastructure needed for the organization to function (roads, airports, electric systems, and so on), and invested *their* labor and capital in the organization. And *they* are harmed most when the organization downsizes, despoils the environment, engages in discriminatory actions, and so on.

In rare cases, societies consider these issues openly and honestly. For example, now that the system of apartheid has been dismantled, South Africa is attempting to develop a "code of ethics" for organizations operating within its borders. The 2002 *King Report* lists ten core values for South African society and organizations:

*   Collectivism over individualism.
*   Consensus instead of dissensus.
*   Humility and helping others instead of criticizing them.
*   Nondiscrimination.
*   *Ubuntu,* which expresses a social contract that extends beyond one's immediate family to encompass society as a whole; the literal meaning is "I am because you are, you are because we are."
*   Trust and belief in the essential fairness of all human beings.
*   High standards of morality.
*   A close kinship system.
*   Consultation as the basis of labor-management relations.
*   Belief in the existence of an omnipresent, omnipotent, superior creator being.

Of course, codifying these values into a code of ethics and a legal system for organizations is an exceptionally complex task, one that still is under way.[7] The *King Report* and efforts to implement it are based on the assumption that all groups have the same interests—sustaining a profitable and socially responsible organization. But few societies are attempting to deal with these issues as explicitly as South Africa is. In all societies, the interests of multiple stakeholders conflict with one another, and organizations—as well as societies—must find ways to manage those conflicts. It is that reality that underlies the key rhetorical problem faced by organizations.

Reactive Image Management: Managing Organizational Crises   Organizational image management is most complicated during crises.[8] Of course, in the case of organizational scandal, one can offer a legitimate apology—admit error, accept responsibility, suggest remedies or reparations, and promise not to repeat the sin. Doing so may assuage one's guilt and minimize the effects on the organization's image, but it also invites sanctions. Victims are likely to initiate lawsuits, using the apology as evidence of guilt, and insurance companies are likely to invoke clauses that allow them to avoid paying claims in cases of knowing malfeasance. Consequently, in organizational discourse, legitimate apologies are relatively rare. It is more likely that an employee will simply *deny* having made the error or being responsible for it. Denial is most successful when the crisis resulted from an accident rather than a scandal, especially if combined with expressions of sympathy for victims and offers of restitution. Consequently, organizational rhetoricians usually try to define an event as an accident—an unintentional and unavoidable event—rather than an intentional unethical or illegal act. The most common means of doing so is to point to the bureaucratic structure of organizations. As we explained in Chapter 3, there are a number of different sources of communication breakdowns in bureaucracies. Because everyone "knows" that, individuals in upper management can argue that they were not aware that unethical or illegal activities were going on in the organization. In fact, management can "plan ahead" to use this strategy by actively discouraging employees from talking about ethical issues, especially when possibly illegal activities are involved. There is a substantial amount of evidence that in most organizations upper management is more likely to fire employees for *talking about* ethical/legal issues than for committing unethical/illegal actions on behalf of the organization. Then, if employees *do* act in unethical or illegal ways, management can plead ignorance of the activities and escape responsibility. Operatives in the administration of President Reagan gave the name "plausible deniability" to this strategy. Although more and more companies are stating publicly their commitment to ethics in management, few of their employees find it comfortable to raise such concerns either in public or in the privacy of their offices. B. E. Toffler concluded that "there seems to be a sense among managers that talking about ethics is 'just not done here.' And, unfortunately, they are usually right."[9]

If the tactic of denial is unavailable, organizations may offer a *quasi-theory,* one that is used to explain away errors. In our culture commonly used quasi-theories include "Boys will be boys" and "We had a falling out." Or one may offer an *excuse,* in which one acknowledges making an error but denies any harmful intent or claims that she or he had no choice in the matter ("The devil made me do it"). One may *justify* one's actions by blaming them on some socially accepted rule of conduct, on organizational policies, or on a higher authority. One can offer *counterclaims,* in which one asserts that his or her actions have been misunderstood (or distorted by a biased media in the case of public scandals) and that he or she really had the other person's interests at heart ("I really wasn't trying to sell you more life insurance; I was just telling you what I do for a living," or "This policy is such a wonderful deal that I really had to share it with you"). When it was revealed that Toshiba of the United States sold advanced submarine technology to the Soviet Union during the late stages of the cold war, the organization responded that it never had any intent to undermine U.S. security but instead was trying to help the United States by providing good jobs for American workers. Another strategy is *bolstering,* in which the accused person (or company) accepts the charges but attempts to overcome them by linking herself or himself to relationships, concepts, or objects that the audience values.[10]

Earlier in this book (Chapters 6, 8, and 10) we mentioned a highly publicized case of racial discrimination at the Texaco Oil Company. What started as an exposé of incredibly offensive corporate practices became a case study in effective crisis management. Initially, Texaco *denied* that any discrimination had taken place. Federal law requires plaintiffs to produce hard evidence both that their treatment was discriminatory and that the discrimination was because of their race. There are many ways for a company to hide evidence of discrimination—obscuring discriminatory decisions in larger downsizing moves, changing job descriptions to make a qualified minority applicant seem unqualified, or (as Texaco did) simply keeping one set of records for private use and another for government agencies, courts, and the public. As a result, it is almost impossible to obtain direct evidence of discrimination, so denial is a very effective strategy. Without direct evidence, the 1994 suit had languished, although in early 1996 the Equal Employment Opportunity Commission issued a preliminary decision in favor of the plaintiffs. This decision triggered what was to become a fateful meeting among Texaco executives.

It was a frank and wide-ranging discussion of issues related to Texaco's affirmative action programs. Worried about the suit, David Keough (senior assistant treasurer) discussed ways to *carefully* destroy company documents so that evidence of discrimination was eliminated but evidence supporting Texaco's case was retained. The secret appraisal documents and minutes of meetings during which they were discussed were the biggest concern. Robert Ulrich, the company treasurer, concluded, "You know, there is no point in even keeping the restricted version anymore. All it could do is get us in trouble." After reviewing Texaco's promotion history, Ulrich noted that "all the black jelly beans seem to be glued to the bottom of the bag." Eventually the executives discussed their feelings about the suit and the employees who had filed it. Ulrich complained that those "niggers" were causing difficulties for them.

None of this would ever have become known except for two events. Richard Lundwall, the coordinator of personnel in Texaco's finance department, had been assigned to keep minutes on the meeting and had tape-recorded it to have an accurate record. In August 1996 Texaco fired Lundwall in a downsizing move, and he turned his tapes over to the plaintiffs' attorneys, who released them to the *New York Times.* They broke the story on November 4.

Denial was no longer a viable response; and there simply were no quasi-theories, excuses, or justifications readily available. Texaco immediately shifted strategies to a barrage of *bolstering.* Texaco attorney Andrea Christiansen was "shocked and dismayed" by the tapes; CEO Peter Bijur announced, "The rank insensitivity demonstrated in the taped remarks . . . offends me deeply. . . . This alleged behavior does not represent the way the company feels about any of our employees. This alleged behavior violates our code of conduct, our core values, and the law. . . . Wherever the truth leads, we'll go." He also announced that Texaco would hire an outside attorney to assist the authorities with the investigation and would spend $35 million on outside evaluations and enhancement of Texaco's affirmative action and diversity management programs, and that the company had hired an outside expert to evaluate the tape. On November 14 Texaco announced a new scholarship program for minority students but said that "the program has nothing to do with recent negative publicity concerning published reports of racial slurs used by company executives." Faced with a boycott of its products by civil rights groups, Texaco settled the two-year-old suit within two months and accepted external oversight of hiring and promotion programs as part of the settlement. Virtually everything that a company and its spokespersons can say or do to bolster its image as a nondiscriminatory employer was said and done between November 1996 and January 1997.

In addition, the company briefly offered a *counterclaim.* The independent specialist hired and paid by Texaco to analyze the tape reported that the word that had initially been translated as "nigger" really was "St. Nicholas." But this strategy was short-lived, because, as CEO Bijur admitted when the finding was announced, "these preliminary findings merely set the record straight as to the exact words spoken in the conversations; but they do not change the categorically unacceptable context and tone of these conversations." [11] Although it is too early to assess the extent to which Texaco has altered its discriminatory culture and practices, the organization's responses did succeed in diverting attention and rebuilding the organization's image. Its new challenge is to sustain that positive image over the long term. Research by Melissa and David Baucus shows that over the long term, organizations that fail to sustain an effective image-management campaign suffer significant economic losses. [12] Those that succeed in doing so can avoid those losses.

CASE STUDY
Competence or Connections?

Even before Inauguration Day, the Bush administration's ties to the oil industry had become a volatile political issue. As the administration developed its energy policy in secret, and Vice President Dick Cheney delayed divesting himself of stock in energy giant Halliburton, which he had once run, that tie became a rallying point for critics. No company has been more successful in attracting government contracts,

(continued)

(Case Study, continued)

or in minimizing the amount of money paid in U.S. taxes. When the Department of Defense announced in the spring of 2003 that it had awarded Halliburton a billion-dollar contract to transport fuel from Kuwait to Iraq without allowing other companies to compete for the contract, the firestorm escalated. The attention given the story intensified in late 2003 when accountants at the Pentagon's Defense Contract Audit Agency suggested that Halliburton may have overcharged the U.S. taxpayers $61 million for the shipping contract. In one way, the accusations were not all that new. Halliburton had been accused of overcharging the U.S. government throughout the 1990s and in 2002 agreed to pay a $2 million settlement to dismiss charges that it had defrauded the U.S. government. Critics immediately attacked Halliburton for profiteering while troops are dying. President Bush announced that if the allegations were true, he felt that Halliburton should reimburse the federal government for the overcharges.

On January 15, 2004, Halliburton notified the Pentagon that some of its employees may have obtained illegal kickbacks from Kuwaiti firms involved in the contract. The notification was not made public. The next day, the Pentagon awarded Halliburton an additional $1.2 billion contract, this time after competitive bidding. On January 23, Halliburton ran a half-page newspaper ad. Originally we planned to reproduce the ad verbatim in order to ensure accuracy of our report. However, in March 2004, we were denied permission to do so, forcing us to paraphrase its content. The ad takes up about one-third of a newspaper page and is composed of nine paragraphs. The first asserts that Halliburton is one of only a few companies in the world that is capable of assisting in the rebuilding of Iraq. No details regarding those competencies are provided. It then notes, in boldfaced type, that the company was rewarded its second contract, to help rebuild Iraq's oilfields, after competitive bidding. Paragraph 2 says that some critics attributed the contracts to special interests, labels such claims as political advertising, and denies the charges. The longest paragraph comes third. It is presented as a "fact check" and states that the company has worked for administrations of both major parties (again in boldfaced type) since World War II, currently has contracts in Bosnia and Kosovo that were granted by the Clinton administration, and has a workforce of 100,000 people in 100 countries who have special skills that make them uniquely qualified for these projects. The concluding sentence repeats the claim that the company is not a special interest and suggests that it has two special goals in Iraq. Paragraphs 4 and 5 describe the goals at length: to complete the restoration of Iraq's infrastructure and oil fields as quickly as possible, in order to return normalcy to the country's people, and to continue working to make soldiers comfortable and secure. Paragraph 5 describes the diversity of the company's work: it simultaneously prepares thousands of omelets to feed the troops and implements plans to build Iraq's oil system. The remaining paragraphs are brief, expressing management's pride in Halliburton's employees and their skills. The ad concludes with a restatement of its title.

Applying What You've Learned

1. What claims does Halliburton make in the ad? What evidence does it provide to support those claims?

2. What does the ad *not* say (remember, in Chapter 7 we explained the concept of "deconstruction," which suggests that what communicators choose to ignore often is as important as what they choose to talk about)? For example, does it deny overcharging, or that political connections could have influenced both the closed and competitive bidding processes, and so on.

3. What rhetorical strategies are used in the ad? What cultural values come into play? What values are de-emphasized or ignored?

4. How are key terms defined? For example, the ad repeatedly claims that Halliburton has "special" skills? What makes them "special?" Is it likely that no other firms have them?

Late on the evening of January 22, the night before the ad ran, the *Los Angeles Times* broke the story of the illegal kickbacks. On January 24, after the ad was published, Halliburton announced that it had fired the two employees involved in the kickback scheme. Later in the day Randy Hurl, CEO of KBR (the Halliburton subsidiary involved in the initial contract) also announced, "We will bear the cost of the potential overcharge—not the government."* Ross Adkins, spokesman for the Corps of Engineers, which has consistently defended Halliburton during the crisis, claimed that "it is not the company that did anything wrong" and concluded that the company should not be blamed for the actions of former employees. Democratic politicians again called for an independent investigation of the Iraq contracting process; the Bush administration (White House spokesman Scott McClellan) attributed the calls to political processes: "I think there's, obviously, a lot of election-year politicking going on," a sentiment echoed by Halliburton spokeswoman Wendy Hall: "We've been saying all along we think political influence is best kept out of the contracting process. We understand it is an election year and the war will be an important part of the election. But worrying about election coverage doesn't repair oil fields or feed soldiers." Hall's statement was prophetic. A week later (February 1) the *Wall Street Journal* reported that Halliburton had overcharged the Department of Defense $27.4 million for meals served to U.S. troops at five bases in Iraq and Kuwait during 2003. The following day the Pentagon announced that Halliburton would repay the U.S. government for the overcharges and that the Pentagon was initiating a review of the fifty-three additional dining facilities operated by Halliburton subsidiaries in the Persian Gulf. On February 6, Halliburton started running television ads in selected markets that featured CEO Dave Lesar speaking the text of the newspaper ad while pictures of smiling soldiers being served meals and camels crossing the desert in front of burning oil wells were shown. Lesar does not mention the recent accusations made against Halliburton or

(continued)

(Case Study, continued)

its ties to Vice President Cheney. The closest he comes to doing so is the line, "Will things go wrong? Sure they will. But when we do, we'll fix them."

Questions to Think About and Discuss

1. Answer each of the questions listed above for the statements made after the new revelations were made public.
2. Under what circumstances are political connections an advantage for an organization? Under what circumstances are they a liability? (Keep your answers to these questions. Then answer the questions again after you read about the Enron saga later in this chapter).

Subsequent ads of the same size and in the same format were published at roughly one-month intervals. The most recent one as this book went to press appeared on March 31, 2004. Entitled "The Halliburton Success Story Improving Lives in Iraq," it begins by noting that Halliburton's employees experience a success whenever a soldier thanks them for clean clothes or a hot meal. It then lists the total numbers of these stories: tens of thousands of living spaces with showers and toilets, four meals a day served to thousands of soldiers, millions of pounds of mail delivered and bundles of laundry cleaned. The second section lists contributions to the Iraqi people: restoring the country's oil industry to more than its prewar capacity, and doing so ahead of schedule; eliminating hazards to the environment caused by the industry; and solving the problem of sabotage-related wasted resources. It closes with an expression of management's pride in its employees and its ability to serve U.S. troops and the Iraqi people.

Questions to Think About and Discuss

1. Answer the questions we asked about the first ad in response to this one.

---

*The original ad appeared in the *Houston Chronicle*, January 23, 2004, C3. The follow-up story, and all of the quotations that appear in the second part of this case study come from David Ivanovich, "Halliburton Gives Refund to Pentagon," *Houston Chronicle*, January 24, 2004, C1, 7; and Joel Brinkley and Eric Schmitt, "Halliburton Will Repay U.S. Excess Charges for Troops' Meals," *New York Times on the Web*, February 3, 2004, http://www.nytimes.com/. A concise summary of Halliburton's relationship with the U.S. government is available in Bob Herbert, "The Halliburton Shuffle," *New York Times on the Web*, January 30, 2004. The television ads are described in David Ivanovich, "Halliburton Defends Its Iraq Work," *Houston Chronicle*, February 6, 2004, 2C. The second ad that is described at length appeared in the *Houston Chronicle* on March 31, 2004, B3.

Proactive Image Management   All people and all organizations have images. The question is not whether or not an image exists; the question is whether the image is developed carefully over time through strategic communication, or whether it is developed haphazardly in response to organizational crises. Proactive image management advocates the former. We have already discussed most of the key concepts underlying this perspective—organizations must legitimate themselves and their activities by drawing links to the core values of the societies in which they operate. For example, mainstream U.S. society seems to be composed of people who are "ethical segregationists," applying very different standards to the operations of organizations, politicians, and "regular" people.[13]

In general, organizations are evaluated in almost completely economic terms—if they produce jobs and tax revenues for a community, they are allowed to engage in a much wider range of questionable activities than politicians or individuals and still be seen as legitimate. U.S. citizens have come to believe an "organizational imperative," that everything good in life comes through private-sector organizations. So, as "institutional theory" (recall Chapter 7) would predict, organizations can create the image that they are expert, economically successful, innovative, and up-to-date. By doing so they can gain a great deal of support. Unfortunately, it does not seem to matter that many innovative strategies are short-term managerial fads that soon disappear, or that the "reality" of the organization's operations is inconsistent with the image that has been constructed. For example, Margarete Arndt and Barbara Bigelow studied a group of hospitals that were updating their organizational structure. The organizations did not face a crisis; in fact they had a very solid long-term reputation for efficiency and quality care. The hospitals' managers successfully claimed that the changes would improve organizational flexibility and efficiency, even though they actually reduced it. Management also claimed that they had been forced to make the changes by "oppressive" regulators, even though there was no evidence that regulatory pressure actually took place. Furthermore, Arndt and Bigelow found that hospital management was inconsistent in its focus on innovation. When they believed that innovation would be perceived favorably by important stakeholders, they talked about being innovative. When they believed that there was little rhetorical value in being innovative, they did not. The strategy was successful because it was based on the hospital's positive reputation and its stakeholders' belief in the virtues of progress, the competence of professional managers, and the evils of government "intervention" (recall Chapter 2).[14]

Organizational rhetoricians also are aided by the incoherent nature of societal values. For example, health care policymakers in the United States traditionally have faced an unavoidable "trilemma" (a dilemma with three poles instead of the normal two). U.S. citizens value quick and easy access to health care. But they also value high quality and low prices. Unfortunately, for economic and structural reasons, these values cannot all be achieved simultaneously because they work against one another. To complicate matters further, U.S. citizens also strongly oppose government involvement in the health care marketplace and have a deep respect—almost a worshipful attitude—for health care providers, especially medical specialists. They also are willing to pay great sums for acute care, although they prefer that costs be borne by someone else, but largely ignore preventive medicine.

When politicians attempt to address one of these values, organizations that are threatened by the proposal are able to draw on the other values to defeat reform. Controlling costs can easily be depicted as reducing access to or the quality of care; increasing quality is expensive and is likely to reduce access by pricing health care beyond the means of some people and some organizations, and so on. When the Clinton administration attempted to address all of these issues in the same proposal, insurance companies, which were most threatened by the plan, created a series of television ads featuring an intelligent and concerned owner of a small business and her slightly clueless husband. All of these so-called Harry and Louise ads expressed opposition to government interference in the "best medical system in the world." Each ad focused on a part of the proposal that was designed to deal with one part of the trilemma and argued that implementing it would harm the other parts.[15]

When organizations face multiple stakeholders, proactive image management is more complicated. As a result, the rhetoric addressed to one stakeholder group often is very different from the rhetoric developed for other stakeholders. Audiences with particular technical expertise are swayed most by institutional arguments, members of the media are most influenced by the firm's long-term track record, and the general population is most influenced by appeals to broader social values. Dealing with multiple stakeholders is especially complicated for companies that operate internationally, because the core values of one society may be very different from the core values held by stakeholders in the other societies in which the organization operates. Modern communication technology, which allows messages that are carefully crafted for one stakeholder group to be instantly disseminated among other stakeholders, who may have completely contradictory values, complicates the process further.[16]

Consequently, managers (or the corporate communication specialists to which image-management activities often are delegated) often must choose which stakeholder groups to accommodate, knowing full well that an image that satisfies one group may alienate others. Stakeholders differ from one another in terms of their access to sources of power (recall Chapter 8), their legitimacy in the eyes of other stakeholders, and the extent to which their concerns are urgent.[17] Proactive image management would focus on the core values of groups that are powerful and legitimate and make contingency plans for events in which the demands of other groups might suddenly become urgent. For example, the optimal paradigm case of successful proactive image management is the Malden Mills corporation and its CEO Aaron Feuerstein. For literally decades, Malden Mills has been the best possible corporate citizen. It contributes to its community in every possible way, and its CEO is known worldwide for his personal and professional ethics. In an industry that is known for closing plants and shifting jobs out of the United States, Malden Mills has innovated in order to continue operating in Massachusetts. When it faced bankruptcy in the mid-1980s, Feuerstein was forced to lay off many of his workers, but he rehired them as soon as possible. When a fire devastated the plant in the mid-1990s, he tapped his personal fortune to pay a full salary to his out-of-work workers. Because of the high level of trust developed over time, his customers (companies like Lands End and L.L. Bean) honored their contracts while the factory was being rebuilt. During the crisis Feuerstein drew upon his existing stakeholder relationships and acted in ways that strengthened them. When the plant reopened, the ceremony was covered by almost every national news organization. In short, Malden Mills had the best possible relationship with virtually every stakeholder group, except one. When the recession of 1999–2003 hit, Malden Mills again faced bankruptcy. Feuerstein, whose personal reserves had not been rebuilt since the fire, could not support the company and was forced into bankruptcy. The court gave him extra time to seek funds to pay off his creditors, but he was unable to do so. Malden Mills still exists, but it no longer is managed by its heroic CEO. When bankruptcy hit, the most important stakeholders were its creditors, and no amount of goodwill with other stakeholders overcame their power.[18]

Proactive image management has a final function, to reproduce and support the societal values underlying organizational rhetoric. In the United States no industry has been more successful in doing this than the petroleum industry. For decades the industry largely had been reactive to a string of crises, from Standard Oil's abuses at the turn of the twentieth century to the Teapot Dome scandal of the 1920s to the energy crisis and charges of price gouging during the 1970s. But by the end of the 1970s the industry realized that consumer and environmental groups had become strong enough to present a continuing challenge. Even the industry's very successful depiction of nuclear power as a safe, nonpolluting, technologically sophisticated solution to the nation's long-term energy needs was threatened by the 1979 accident at Three Mile Island. So the industry took a lesson from its nuclear power campaign and embarked on a long-term strategy to develop an image as the irreplaceable "engine" that drives the American economy.[19] By depicting themselves as primarily concerned with balancing economic and environmental needs, these firms drew on cultural values regarding managerial and scientific expertise. By casting themselves as calm and rational in the face of extremism, they increased their credibility. By focusing attention on the economic necessity of energy, they elevated those concerns in the popular mind, and they continue to do so.

CASE STUDY
Made in America?

As an example of organizational rhetoric, the "Made in America" label is a home run. But, it also is a highly contested term. For example, in April 2002 a court in American Samoa ordered a Daewoosa garment factory on Saipan to pay $3.5 million to 270 workers from China and Vietnam. American territories in the Pacific are attractive sites for textile companies because they can wear the label and be shipped to the U.S. mainland without paying tariffs or being subject to import quotas. The 15,000 workers on Saipan are mostly Chinese women, who have paid recruiters as much as $8,000 to get jobs in the factories. That is money usually obtained by mortgaging family farms. Given the investment they and their families

(continued)

(Case Study, continued)

have made, they put up with almost any abuse—which court records indicate includes being cheated out of their wages, beaten, and deprived of food—in order to keep their $3.05-per-hour jobs. Thanks to the efforts of antisweatshop groups and the U.S. Department of Labor, working conditions have improved. However, the workers are unlikely to see any money from the court decision—the factory on Saipan, like a similar factory in California, has declared bankruptcy in order to avoid paying the judgment. Moves to bring U.S. territories under U.S. minimum wage and labor laws have been blocked by House Republican whip Tom DeLay, who argues that Saipan is being unfairly singled out because sweatshops also operate on the mainland—in California, New York, and Texas. Customers at the Gap, Dayton Hudson, and The Limited will be able to continue purchasing products made by Daewoosa, comfortable in the knowledge that they were "Made in the USA."*

Just after Christmas 2003, Charley Conrad took his children to a local athletic store to buy new tennis shoes. For the past few years he has preferred shoes made by New Balance even though they are a little pricey, because they are comfortable, seem to last a long time—even on the feet of his very active kids—and are made in the United States. (He still remembers a difficult time during his childhood when his aunt and uncle lost their jobs because the shoe factory they worked at closed and moved its operations out of the country). This year one pair of the shoes he bought had a six-sided message, folded to about the size of a credit card.

The front page had the phrase "a commitment to U.S. manufacturing" printed prominently above a large NB logo. The next four pages contained the following message (the words that are italicized here were printed in red but not italicized in the original).

> Many of our shoes are produced in one of six United States factories. While most of the footwear industry has moved its production overseas to take advantage of low labor costs and generally cheaper production costs, *we continue to have many of our shoes made in the United States* and have expanded production substantially. Since 1995, we have increased our manufacturing jobs by 65%. *We at New Balance are proud to provide jobs to the U.S. workforce,* and proud of our well educated, high quality associates who can compete with anyone in the world. Through their hard work, we are able to make many of our models of shoes in the United States despite the competition from lower cost imports.
>
> Unfortunately, we are not able to obtain all materials and components that are needed for these shoes in the United States. In some cases, they are simply not available. In other situations, economic and quality considerations dictate foreign sourcing. However, *New Balance remains committed to providing jobs for American workers* and to supporting domestic manufacturers and suppliers where possible.
>
> The Federal Trade Commission has attempted to determine what it means to say a product is "made in" the United States. While this seems like a simple question, the answer is not always obvious given the global nature of the economy. We believe most consumers think "Made in USA" means that real manufacturing jobs

were provided to U.S. workers in order to make that product. *The shoes produced in our U.S. factories are made by U.S. workers using both U.S. and imported materials.* Where the level of domestic value is at least 70%, we have labeled the shoe "Made in USA." Where it falls below that level, we have qualified it as containing both domestic and imported materials. This determination is based in part on a survey of consumers conducted by the FTC. The Federal Trade Commission's analysis of the Made in USA issue can be found on the internet at FTC's web site www.ftc.gov, or for a copy write to New Balance Athletic Shoe, Inc., Brighton Landing, 20 Guest Street, Boston, MA 02135-2088, Attention: Communications.

The final page (which appears as the back of the card when it is folded up) carries the well-known logo for recycling, the words "Printed in the USA on recycled paper," and this message: "*New Balance* has proven that high quality, width sized athletic footwear can be made by Americans for discriminating customers. We are proud of this fact. For more information about New Balance products, visit our web site at *www.newbalance.com* or call *1-800-622-1218.*"

Applying What You Have Learned

1. Which of the rhetorical strategies described in this chapter are used in the New Balance pamphlet?
2. What does the company seem to assume about the beliefs, values, and thought processes of its audience?

Questions to Think About and Discuss

1. Does the rhetoric succeed? Would customers who base their purchasing decisions at least in part on the "Made in USA" label prefer New Balance shoes after reading the pamphlet? What image would customers who do not base decisions on items being "Made in the USA" have of the organization and its products after reading the pamphlet?
2. Can "mixed" messages (in this case, "We're committed to manufacturing in the U.S., but sometimes can't") succeed? Why or why not?

---

*"Sweatshops under the American Flag," *New York Times on the Web*, May 10, 2002, http://www.nytimes.com/.

Public Policy and Organizational Rhetoric

Organizations influence public policies in two ways, by pressuring policy-makers to enact favorable legislation and by blocking unfavorable laws. Molding legislation assists organizations directly by allowing them to engage in profitable activities that disadvantage other groups or by insulating themselves from competition. It also helps them indirectly by allowing them to shift responsibility for unethical actions to the legal system. If organizations can persuade legislators to pass favorable laws, they subsequently are able to argue that their actions were legal. Although actions can be both legal and unethical (for example, slavery or apartheid), or illegal and ethical (nonviolent protest), if an action can be shown to be legally permissible, it is much easier to defend.

Political scientists long have recognized that elite groups, including executives in organizations, have clear advantages in influencing public policy. Much of that influence is exercised in private, through constant, quiet lobbying of regulators and policymakers. Representatives of organizations advocate, sometimes for years, waiting for opportunities to argue that their pet proposal is appropriate to a particular problem. If they fail, they merely wait for the next opportunity. For example, during the 1960s, when it was politically viable to advocate expanding social service programs, advocates of HMOs touted them as a means of increasing access to care by the poor. Later, when the Nixon administration focused on cost containment, HMO advocates argued that health care inflation was driven by the fee-for-service payment system and could be controlled by increased reliance on managed care. Still later, when the public health community sought to focus on preventive care, HMOs were touted as a solution to that problem as well. After the defeat of the Clinton administration's health care program in the early 1990s, and a continued escalation of health care costs, HMOs once again were praised as an effective means of cost containment. Today they are advocated as a more efficient alternative to Medicare and Medicaid, in spite of abundant evidence that for-profit HMOs have much higher administrative costs than the public programs do.[20] The fact that most people *believe* that private sector HMOs are more efficient than the public programs is testimony to the effectiveness of the health insurance industry's rhetoric.

However, events sometimes overwhelm these processes, and an issue that interests organizations does reach the public agenda. Again, organizations have advantages. Probusiness groups are more tightly organized than groups representing other interests. As a result, when their interests are threatened, they are better able to quickly mobilize their resources to remove threatening proposals from the policymaking agenda. Mobilization depends on advocates' rhetorical skills, on their ability to define a particular proposal as beneficial to a sufficiently large group of people to gain policymakers' attention and respect, and on their ability to energize their coalition. In fact, developing public policy *in public* is threatening to power elites. Open policy conflicts can lead to the formation of coalitions among low-power actors that may upset political power balances.[21]

For example, at the height of the Enron scandal, the public learned about a common practice in U.S. firms in which organizations purchased life insurance policies for their employees or retirees and listed the organization, or selected upper-level executives, as beneficiaries. As a rule, employees are not informed that these policies exist, although they usually are a matter of public record because the premiums paid by the corporation are deductible from federal and state income taxes. Incensed by the existence of these so-called dead-peasant policies, labor and consumer groups unified sufficiently to persuade members of Congress to draft legislation that would require management to get employees' permission before taking out such policies. Other proposals would have required management to divide the proceeds with the workers' families. Lobbyists from the insurance industry and corporate advocacy groups quickly made it clear that the proposal had no chance of even being discussed, much less passed. First, the proposals were modified to drop the dual-payment requirement, and eventually to require management only to notify employees. Even this watered-down proposal was defeated without ever being debated in public.[22]

Another advantage for organizational rhetoricians is time. If they can delay action until the attention and emotional fervor accompanying calls for reform subside, they can maintain the status quo. This is especially true of issues like corporate unethical behavior, because it is newsworthy for only a brief period of time. In addition, such matters are usually too complex to be explained in thirty-second news clips. Media, and thus popular, attention quickly shifts to other issues. For example, within months of learning that major mutual funds managers had allowed questionable or illegal activities that cost small investors billions of dollars in lost investment returns, most of those investors were no longer concerned about the scandal. The stock market had sustained a rally, their investment plans were showing gains, and their outrage had dissipated.[23]

On the other hand, if popular attention is sustained for a long enough period of time, organizational rhetoricians may have to engage in public rhetoric. In those rather rare cases, they have a number of socially acceptable arguments available. They can define socioeconomic "problems" as "private sector" concerns, not matters for government policy. This argument gains credibility from the cultural assumptions that free-market capitalism is inherently superior to any other economic system and that government "interference" in the free-market system is inherently futile and perverse (recall Chapter 2). This strategy long has been successful in blunting pressure for increased government regulation after periods of business corruption and malpractice. In most cases, corporate rhetoric is creative, sophisticated, and effective. For example, during the late 1990s the U.S. Congress debated the McCain-Feingold bill, which would have regulated the tobacco industry. The bill's sponsors used recently released evidence to argue that the industry had for a long time hidden the addictive nature of its product and had even purposely maximized the addictive power of cigarettes. However, when the McCain-Feingold bill was debated, the industry was able to use the same argument to their advantage. Because the funding mechanisms in the bill relied on increased tobacco taxes, industry rhetoricians were able to define the proposal as a tax bill in disguise, one that unfairly penalized precisely those poor and middle-class victims that the bill's proponents had demonstrated were incapable of shaking their addiction.

Even if public rhetoric fails, organizational rhetoricians can quietly advocate for the passage of "hollow laws" that seem to solve problems but do not make substantive changes. Because bills almost always pass the U.S. Senate and House of Representatives in different forms, they are referred to "conference committees," which iron out differences between the bills in private, where organizational rhetoricians (lobbyists) have a great advantage.

Finally, in the unlikely event that substantive laws are enacted, organizational rhetoricians can shift their attention to the implementation process, which largely takes place in private. For example, the Bayh-Dole Act is a provision of U.S. patent law that requires pharmaceutical firms that receive federal research grants to make the drugs that are developed with those funds available at a reasonable price. (About 80 percent of the drugs developed in the United States were supported by federal grants.) However, the law has never been enforced because the industry has successfully described it as an anticompetitive price-control measure. Similarly, within hours after the signing of the 2002 Corporate Accountability Act, the Bush administration announced that it would interpret the act's whistle-blower protection provisions as narrowly as possible, thereby robbing regulators of much of the information they need to prosecute corporate corruption. Organizations often quietly negotiate arrangements with regulators that minimize the impact of policies, a process that political scientists have labeled "regulatory capture."[24] For example, in at least seven countries on three continents, the beef industry has long succeeded in fighting regulations designed to prevent the spread of "mad cow" disease. In the UK, where the disease was discovered, the first government memo on the disease from the Ministry of Agriculture demanded that all news of the disease be kept confidential because of its potential adverse impact on beef exports, and declared that "British beef is wholly safe." Once the scandal broke, France, Spain, Italy, Germany, and Japan banned imports of British beef and denied that there was any risk among their own cattle. Each agriculture ministry was able to make these claims because they refused to conduct widespread testing of their own herds. Subsequent investigations by the French Senate and the Japanese legislature concluded that the agriculture ministries "constantly sought to prevent or delay the introduction of precautionary measures" (France) because they "might have had an adverse effect on the competitiveness of the agri-foodstuffs industry" (Japan).

In the United States the regulatory situation is a bit more complicated because the Department of Agriculture has the dual and often contradictory mandate to promote the sale of beef and other agricultural products at home and abroad, on one hand, and to ensure the safety of those products, on the other. In addition, many of the highest-ranking executives in the department previously worked for the industry. Consequently, it is not surprising that the U.S. regulatory agencies used the same strategies that had been used in other countries to minimize their interference with the industry—overt denial of any risks, refusing to collect data that might be embarrassing, and delaying enforcement of bans on practices that consumer groups long have argued are risky—allowing "downer" cattle (those that cannot walk) to be included in the food chain and not requiring the removal of high-risk materials like spinal cords from processed meats. In addition, the industry was able to persuade regulators to not require them to develop a potentially costly system for quickly tracing infected cattle to the ranches where they were born. Once other countries banned the import of U.S. beef in 2003, many of these precautions were implemented.

Even after those bans were initiated, the industry was able to blunt calls for increased regulation. In January 2004 the U.S. Senate and the Bush administration, under pressure from the beef industry, decided to delay until 2006 the implementation of a 2002 law that would have required producers to place a country-of-origin label on all beef. The industry's arguments were drawn directly from laissez-faire theory—a mandatory labeling program was an expensive, cumbersome bureaucratic incursion into the free market; a voluntary program would be cheaper and less burdensome. Consumer groups responded that for years the industry had had the ability to establish a voluntary program but had refused to do so. In addition, the Department of Agriculture lacks the power to mandate more stringent measures, for example, the recall of diseased beef, and there is no indication that testing by an independent laboratory is in the offing. At this point the issue really is not the likelihood that any individual will contract the disease—those odds are almost infinitesimally small. But, as the Japanese minister of agriculture noted when his country refused to lift its ban on imported U.S. and Canadian beef in late January 2004, both the beef industry and the regulatory agencies have developed an image of putting profits above safety, and it is that image that drives continued bans on beef imports.[25]

Summary   Throughout Unit I we discussed the challenges created for organizations by pressures in the environments surrounding them, a discussion that culminated in our summary of contingency design theory in Chapter 7. In this chapter we have argued that organizations are able to proactively manage environmental pressures, by influencing popular attitudes and molding public policies. We also have asserted that it is impossible to fully understand organizational ethics unless one takes a systemic perspective (recall Chapter 1), in order to grasp the complex matrix of forces and processes that influence employees' ethical choices. We conclude this chapter with an extended case study that applies these concepts further—perhaps the most visible example of corporate illegality in recent U.S. history.

Enron as a Paradigm Case of Organizational Ethics and Rhetoric

The Enron saga serves as both a conclusion to our discussion of organizational rhetoric and ethics and a conclusion to this book. Unlike most of the instances of managerial corruption uncovered during the initial years of the twenty-first century, which were simple cases of executives using company resources to support extravagant lifestyles, the Enron story is exceptionally complex. In fact, as U.S. Justice Department spokespersons pointed out when they announced executive Andrew Fastow's guilty plea in January 2004, it was *supposed* to be complex. Enron executives invested an incredible amount of time and energy, and spent literally millions of dollars on accountants and lawyers, in order to make their activities so complex they were not likely to be discovered, much less understood or successfully prosecuted against. The story itself has generated a library full of book-length analyses, but we can provide only a brief sketch here. However, even an abbreviated summary illustrates many of the core concepts that we have developed throughout this book.[26]

Setting the Stage

Understanding Enron must start where we started, with an analysis of the discourse of laissez-faire capitalism (recall Chapter 2 and the first part of this chapter). By the end of the 1970s, federal government policy started to be more and more controlled by people who believed in free-market fundamentalism. One effect of this shift was a wave of deregulation that started with the airlines in 1978 under President Jimmy Carter. During the Reagan and Bush administrations of the 1980s, more and more sectors of the U.S. economy were removed from federal regulation, and even in those sectors that were not deregulated, government oversight and control was scaled back. In addition, proponents of deregulation argued, globalization, technological development, and "high-speed management" had combined to create a fundamentally "new" economy, one that could not function effectively if saddled with the demands imposed by government regulators on the organizations of the "old economy." Government regulation, they argued, makes little sense when capital flows across political boundaries at the speed of light; production facilities can readily be moved from country to country as multinational firms search for the most profitable environmental laws, regulatory environments, and labor arrangements; and corporations are organized in forms that were not even envisioned when the regulatory schemes were created. Indeed, it is *futile* for governments to try to resist the power of the international markets, and their efforts to do so will *inevitably* reduce the competitiveness of their firms, thereby disadvantaging their own citizens.

By the time the economic boom of the 1990s had started, there was a patchwork quilt of policies and practices in place that allowed organizations to exploit deregulation in some sectors, avoid some sectors that still were regulated, and pressure regulators, legislators, and local, state, and federal executives to create favorable rules and regulations in others. Indeed, the genius of Enron's management, which eventually became its undoing, was to devise ways to manipulate this regulatory maze, pushing for deregulation in areas in which it had a competitive advantage and for increased regulation where it was at a disadvantage.[27]

Closing the Courts   At the same time, corporations used litigation and political influence to weaken other forms of external control over their actions. The process began with a series of court decisions, the most important of which were the *Lampf* (1991) decision, which denied private investors the right to bring lawsuits against individuals who aid and abet a fraud, even if they did so knowingly; *Reves v. Ernst & Young* (1993), which narrowly limited the RICO statute (a law that was enacted to help federal agencies deal with organized crime but eventually was expanded to apply to a wide range of "white collar" offenses) to exclude external advisers (primarily accounting firms that audit company books and law firms that provide legal advice to management from liability in fraud cases); *Raab v. General Physics* (1993), which created highly specific evidence requirements to demonstrate fraud; and *Central Bank of Denver, N.A. v. First Interstate Bank of Denver, N.A.* (1994), which ruled that private plaintiffs could not initiate an aiding and abetting suit under the Securities and Exchange Act section 10(b).[28] Each of these restrictions was written into law in the 1995 Private Securities and Litigation Reform Act. The bill was passed over President Clinton's veto after an intense campaign led by Democratic National Chairman and Senator Christopher Dodd (Conn.), who received almost a quarter of a million dollars in donations from the accounting industry during the 1995–1996 election cycle, even though he was not up for reelection. The primary justifications offered for these changes were that litigation had gotten out of hand and was destroying necessary capital formation; companies were routinely sued for stock declines even if no fraud or malfeasance was involved; frivolous lawsuits were rampant and expensive, in spite of recent reforms; and companies were forced to settle groundless suits in order to avoid the costs of litigation. Although there was little empirical evidence to support any of these claims, they are consistent with the fundamentalist view that no outside forces should be allowed to interfere with managerial prerogatives. In the fundamentalist climate of the 1990s they were easily rationalized.[29]

Disciplining the Regulators   Consequently, by the late 1990s, federal agencies and private-sector associations (for example, the Federal Accounting Standards Board [FASB]) were the only potential sources of control over managerial behavior. Because private-sector agencies have no enforcement power, they must rely on the Securities and Exchange Commission to initiate legal action, and the SEC must rely on the U.S. Department of Justice to carry those actions out. However, SEC enforcement funding was significantly reduced throughout the 1990s through legislation sponsored by members of both parties who received significant campaign contributions from business lobbies and the accounting industry. After 1995, complaints filed with the SEC increased by 60 percent, perhaps because of increased illegality, but primarily because securities tort reform had left aggrieved investors with no other recourse. The combination of reduced funding and increased complaints created a massive workload problem for the agency, so that by the end of the decade it was forced to abandon its policy of examining the reports of Fortune 500 companies every year, and instead do so only every three years.

In addition, Congress repeatedly rejected SEC proposals to more tightly regulate the investment and accounting industries. In 1995 FASB and the SEC proposed that stock options be expensed (reported as debts on corporate balance sheets), and in 2000–2001 the SEC proposed to ban consulting by accounting firms with companies that they audit. Critics had long argued that the potential income from consulting contracts, granted by upper management with little or no oversight, would discourage accounting firms from revealing questionable accounting practices in their audits. For example, in 2001 the Arthur Andersen corporation received $25 million from Enron for auditing its books, but also received $27 million in non-audit-related consulting fees. Enron CEO Ken Lay wrote to then SEC chairman Arthur Levitt in opposition to the proposed limits, basing his position on standard claims of efficiency: "Enron has found that . . . its 'integrated audit' arrangement to be more efficient and cost-effective than the more traditional roles of separate internal and external auditing function." In both cases, members of Congress, most of whom had received major campaign funding from the accounting and investment industries, forced the agency to back down, usually by threatening to further cut its funding. The public rationale for each of these changes was the argument that markets are efficiently self-regulating and that government interference in managerial prerogatives *inevitably* reduces organizational efficiency, increases costs, and stifles creativity.[30]

Creating an Obsession with Stock Values   The second change also involves basic free-market assumptions. The key concept is called the "efficient market hypothesis." It asserts that at any given point in time, stock prices are not only an accurate measure of the future value of a company; they are the best available measure. Although research on the actual correlation between stock price and corporate valuation is mixed, there is no question that the efficient market hypothesis was accepted uncritically by economists and public policymakers throughout the 1990s.[31] In the production-oriented "old economy," there are measures of a company's value that are independent of its stock prices—inventories, plant, equipment, and so on. In a service or "knowledge" economy, however (recall Chapter 6), organizations have few tangible assets. So the value of the company is based almost completely on its image, and the key to a favorable image is the value of its stock. Of course, one way to create a favorable corporate image is to build a valuable company. But images also can be constructed rhetorically. During the 1990s the value of U.S. stocks skyrocketed. Current estimates are that at least 80 percent of the increased value was an illusion. Presumably, various people are supposed to help investors and employees differentiate "real" and fictional company value. But in the atmosphere of the 1990s, all of those supposedly objective and "independent" groups—accountants and auditors, investment advisers and their research teams—were in positions in which their own rewards depended heavily on their *not* discovering or revealing information that would lead their clients to sell the stocks or choose not to purchase the stocks of a particular firm.[32]

The Rise of the Secular Savior   The final basic assumption involved corporate executives. In the United States, managers and executives already had a privileged position. Beginning with scientific management (recall Chapter 3), managers have commanded high levels of power and compensation based on their presumed superior expertise. The beliefs that "what's good for corporations is good for the U.S." and "what's good for managers is good for everyone else" have long been taken for granted. As a result, U.S. firms have a far larger number of managers relative to nonmanagers, and a much bigger gap between

managerial compensation and worker compensation, than firms in other industrialized nations. Moreover, during the 1980s and 1990s, CEOs were elevated to
the status of cultural icons. It may have started with Lee Iacocca's intervention
to save the nearly bankrupt Chrysler Corporation. The press portrayed him as a
frankly speaking white knight, an American cultural icon who briefly was talked
about as a possible U.S. presidential or vice-presidential candidate.[33] In any case,
the enhancement of CEOs' status was aided by distortions of many of the theories that we have described throughout this book. According to those theories,
managers monitor environmental pressures or changes and make changes necessary to compete successfully in those ever-changing contexts. They do so almost miraculously, in the face of imperfect information, political constraints, organizational inertia, "heavy opposition and seemingly bleak odds." It is for that
reason, according to the secular savior mythology, that "top executives matter."
The "charismatic" or "transformational" models of leadership popular during
the 1990s depicted the CEO as at least a hero, if not divine:

> These illusions are furthered by organizational folklore. . . . [O]rganizations ac-
> tively foster beliefs in the control exercised by managers. . . . Efforts associated
> with successful outcomes tend to be more popular stories. These stories focus
> on the successful outcome as if it were an inevitable outcome of individual and
> organizational actions, ignoring many likely (but not experienced) paths to-
> ward failure.[34]

At the same time, two changes were made in the way CEOs' compensation was
determined. First, a new industry of "compensation consultants" was created,
whose income was based on a percentage of the income granted their clients by
various boards of directors. Until the 1980s, boards compared executive salaries
to the incomes of other employees within their companies. Although the gap
between executive salaries was much greater in the United States than in other
countries (a ratio of around 150:1 compared to ratios one-tenth as large in the
other major economies), internal comparisons did serve as a constraint on executive salaries. But during the 1980s, compensation consultants persuaded
boards to start comparing their executives' salaries with those of other executives. Eventually a bidding war began, much like the bidding war that exists
among media stars and professional athletes, but with no salary caps or revenue-
sharing rules, and with no concrete measures of success or failure (no box-office
receipts or win-loss records). Because compensation consultants are paid on a
percentage basis, and because boards of directors tend to be composed of executives from other firms, whose incomes would rise as the incomes of other
executives rose, the sky quickly became the limit.

The second change provides an excellent example of the unintended consequences of organizational actions. During the late 1980s revelations of corporate corruption, popular outrage over skyrocketing CEO compensation, and a
recognition that there was little correlation between executive compensation
and organizational success combined to generate pressure for reform. The "solution" was to tie executive compensation to stock values, on the assumption

that doing so would make executives more accountable.[35] As a result, by 1999 more than 60 percent of CEOs' compensation came from stock and stock options. In 1992 CEOs owned about 2 percent of all outstanding stock; today they own more than 12 percent.

However, basing executive compensation on stock values via options has two unintended consequences—it encourages managers to ignore or de-emphasize the interests of stakeholders other than investors (employees, the communities within which a corporation operates, and so on), and it gives them incentives to sacrifice long-term organizational stability and growth for short-term stock appreciation.[36] The negative effects are greatest in firms that offer massive options to executives, particularly if they also reissue options in order to protect managerial compensation when stock values fall. The new system encouraged executives to take inordinate risks and, in extreme cases, engage in unethical and illegal practices. As a result, even some of the most ardent proponents of the stock options theory, like Harvard economist Michael Jensen, now admit that "what we learned from the 1990's is that when a company's stock is overvalued it sets in motion a set of organizational pressures that can destroy rather than create shareholder value." Honest managers were so swept up by the need to produce rising profits just to keep their jobs, and their small fortunes, that they stepped over the line. Dishonest managers had an almost unlimited opportunity to manipulate the system in their favor. Virtually everyone involved—executives, accountants, investment advisers—had massive financial incentives to create an illusion of value while effective regulation became less and less possible.[37] None of these changes, by themselves, would have encouraged or allowed the wave of unethical and illegal executive activities that engulfed the United States at the beginning of the twenty-first century. However, as Chapter 1 explained, systems are defined by the complex interactions among their components, not by the components themselves. By 2000, the United States had created a "fraud-inducing-system," much like the "accident-inducing system" that Charles Perrow observed in the maritime industry (recall the electrical blackout case in Chapter 2).

The Enron Saga

Enron was born in the 1984 merger of two traditional, rather boring energy companies, Houston Natural Gas and Internorth. In order to complete the merger and gain control of the company, Kenneth Lay, a Horatio Alger story from rural Missouri, had to defeat a competing bid by Irwin Jacobs. To do so he used funds in his company's employee pension funds to purchase the necessary stock. Although perfectly legal, the maneuver was a harbinger of less legal things to come. Lay knew that the deregulation mania of the 1980s had created an opportunity for Enron to move into a much more exciting, and potentially much more lucrative, arena of energy trading. For this purpose he hired Jeffrey Skilling, who knew that the first thing Enron needed was capital and that in order to get capital he needed to improve the company's apparent strength. But the energy industry was saddled with some very restrictive accounting rules, ones that tied corporate value very tightly to the worth of the company's tangible assets. In order to make Enron's balance sheets look more positive, Enron needed to persuade regulators to change existing accounting rules.

The two most obvious examples involved the use of "mark-to-market" accounting, and "derivatives." Prior to Jeffrey Skilling's arrival at Enron, the company used standard "cost" (also called "accrual") accounting, in which a company is allowed to record the value of a transaction only when it actually takes possession of the assets that are exchanged. Cash accounting does not work well when a company deals in highly complex contracts or contracts that extend over a long period of time. For those companies—for instance, Wall Street stock or commodities traders—a more flexible system (called "mark-to-market") is needed because it is the future value of stocks or commodities that is important, not their current value. As long as the assets being traded are "fungible" (easily bought or sold on the open market), and as long as the firms make realistic predictions of their future value, mark-to-market accounting may work well. But if for tax or image purposes a company needs to be able to show a large gain (or a large loss) in a particular year, it is very tempting for management to creatively adjust its price estimates for the different years of the contract. Enron's management realized that accounting is a rhetorical act. Manipulating accounting results is an especially powerful form of rhetoric because they *seem* to be objective, scientific, and reliable.[38] Executives can get by with distorting the company's record as long as their internal accountants, external auditors, the investment community, and regulatory agencies accept their estimates. For this reason the SEC long had limited the use of mark-to-market accounting to firms in highly regulated (state and federal) markets.

Skilling knew that shifting to mark-to-market accounting would allow Enron and its many divisions to better manage their ledger books to create the image that they desired. In 1991 Enron quietly adopted mark-to-market accounting. In 1993, after extensive lobbying by Enron and its auditor, Arthur Andersen, the SEC officially allowed the shift. The rationale offered by Enron and Andersen was a simple application of the ideology of the "new economy."[39] Because no energy trading company had ever used the system, no outsiders really knew how to evaluate the contracts made with it. Some of Enron's insiders knew, though. On a single transaction, a $1.3 billion contract with the New York Power Authority, Skilling received a $65 million bonus because mark-to-market accounting allowed him to book most of the gain on a twenty-three-year-long deal in one quarter. Under an accrual system, his bonus would have been less than 1/23 of that amount. As important, the shift meant that Enron would never again use an accounting system based on the actual value of its assets.

The second change involves "derivatives," financial contracts between two or more parties that are structured in ways that allow managers to keep them off of their companies' official books. Before 1992 derivatives were limited to quasi-public agencies like the New York Mercantile Exchange and the Chicago Board of Trade, which were closely regulated by state agencies and the Commodity Futures Trading Commission (CFTC). In 1992 Enron asked the CFTC's chair,

Wendy Gramm, to grant it an exemption that would allow it to operate its own unregulated energy trading market using its own standards and without CFTC oversight. During her last days as CFTC chair, Gramm granted the exemption, and included a clause that eliminated CFTC oversight of energy traders even when contracts were designed to defraud or mislead buyers.[40] The exception was written into law in the Commodity Futures Modernization Act of 2000, sponsored by Senator Phil Gramm, Wendy's husband. It was passed by the Senate on a unanimous vote after virtually no debate and signed into law by President Clinton on December 13, 2002. The rationale for both actions was the argument that regulatory structures needed to be adapted to the new global economy. After her resignation from the CFTC, Ms. Gramm joined Enron's board of directors at a salary of $300,000 per year.

Changes were made within Enron as well. At Harvard Business School and McKinsey & Co. Consulting, Skilling had been trained to use a reward system originally developed by General Electric. Each year the various divisions of the company are labeled as "stars," "dogs," or "cash cows," based on their reported earnings for the year. Their budgets for the next year are adjusted accordingly, and if the "dogs" do not show improvement, they are eliminated. The system forces each division to be accountable to upper management, but it also encourages short-term thinking and fraud. It had those effects at Enron. Skilling created a similar reward system, expanded by Andrew Fastow, for individuals. Labeled "rank and yank," it established short-term paper profits as the only economic basis for evaluating employees, and it also demanded complete conformity:

> Enron has been described by many employees as having an absolutely cutthroat culture that pitted one employee against another. . . . where most employees were afraid to express their opinions or to question unethical and potentially illegal business practices. Because the rank-and-yank system was both arbitrary and subjective, it was easily used by managers to reward blind loyalty and quash brewing dissent.[41]

Of course, there was dissent, but dissenters soon were fired or transferred to remote locations, or they resigned (recall the discussion of dissent and whistleblowing in Chapter 8). Once "old-style" managers like Rich Kinder and J. Clifford Baxter, who valued positive manager-employee relationships and opposed questionable accounting practices, left the firm, there were no internal limits to fraud. In 1998 Enron discovered the Internet and Internet trading, a sector of the economy where there also were no external limits.

Most of the actions taken by Enron's management after 1998 created an illusion of success. In spite of failing projects on four continents, Enron was the darling of the investment community. The company touted its returns in press releases, and analysts praised Enron on business and finance television shows. It became a symbol of the new economy. Even after Enron's losses started to mount, and its stock price started to plummet, investment analysts remained loyal. In April 2001 Enron announced that it had lost $35 million on its broadband unit alone during the previous quarter. In spite of those losses, Merrill Lynch analyst Donato Eassey, repeated his buy recommendation in a report entitled "Raising the Bar—Again" and predicted that Enron's stock would almost double in value to an all-time high of $100 a share within a year. Almost every investment analyst followed his lead.

There were a few doubters, but Enron management dealt with them as forcefully as it dealt with internal dissenters. Enron's artificially elevated stock prices became the primary form of collateral used in its deals. For a year or so after the dot.com stock bubble burst in 1999 and 2000, Enron's management was able to maintain the illusion. But in late 2000 its stock price started to decline, and the house of cards started to collapse. In August 2001 Skilling resigned, taking his multi-million-dollar stock options with him. Kenneth Lay immediately deluged Enron's employees with e-mails telling them that he thought the company's stock was still an "incredible value," although he had been systematically selling his for some time. In January 2002 Sherron Watkins sent a memo to Kenneth Lay expressing her fear that Skilling's departure would lead to a full-scale investigation of the company's accounting practices. Although the memo was anonymous, the identity of its author spread rapidly through the grapevine at Enron. Fastow attempted to have Watkins fired for her prophetic dissent, but he failed. By mid-October Enron's stock had lost 80 percent of its value, but ten of the seventeen investment analysts who were experts on the firm still rated it as a "strong buy." In fact, only Carol Coale of Prudential Securities advised her investors to sell the stock. On October 22 the SEC announced that it was starting to investigate some of the deals made by Andrew Fastow; two days later he was fired. Lay desperately sought a bailout, but neither his old friends in the Bush administration nor the investment community would help. As a final resort he sought a merger with cross-town rival Dynegy Energy. They reached a tentative deal, but after more closely inspecting Enron's books, Dynegy canceled the deal. On December 2 Enron filed for bankruptcy protection under Chapter 11 of the federal bankruptcy code. It immediately fired 4,000 workers; other firings soon followed. Heavily invested in Enron stock, almost all lost their life savings and their retirement plans. Outside investors also sustained heavy losses. Enron's management staff had brilliantly manipulated gaps in the U.S. regulatory system to build a house of cards. Their political connections allowed them to quietly weaken the regulatory system that had been seriously undermined during the 1990s. Their public rhetoric also was compelling. It drew on the faith in "progress" and in managerial saviors that long has characterized mainstream U.S. culture, while articulating the tenets of free-market fundamentalism and the promises of the "new economy." Ironically, Enron's political connections eventually became its undoing, because once those connections became public knowledge, its allies could not justify bailing Enron out.

Stemming the Tide

Other bankruptcies soon followed, including the largest in U.S. history at WorldCom. With polls indicating that upwards of 80 percent of Americans supported reform, upcoming elections at the state and congressional levels, and a plethora of proposed "solutions" to issues of corporate malfeasance,[42] 2002 would seem to have had all of the ingredients needed for a major change in U.S. economic policies. However, to date public policy reform has been quite modest. Even during the frenetic congressional activity of mid-July 2002 (about which Senator Phil Gramm complained, "In this climate anything can pass"), significant change was stymied. Senators John McCain and Carl Levin proposed that corporations be required to expense stock options. On the day after Alan Greenspan described unexpensed options as "avenues to express greed," [43] (Democratic) Senate leaders, responding to intense pressure from the Business Roundtable and from Silicon Valley firms operating as the Stock Options Coalition, manipulated Senate rules in order to keep the proposal from even being discussed. Similarly, Senator Byron Dorgan proposed an amendment that would have required executives to return any performance bonuses they had received within the six months prior to their firms declaring bankruptcy. It too was rejected by the Senate (within minutes) without being discussed. Even the strongest supporters of fundamental change now admit that no further legislation on corporate governance seems likely. Even casual observers are left to ask, "What happened to the best opportunity for fundamental reform since the New Deal?"

During the six months immediately after Enron's declaration of bankruptcy, policymakers engaged in two kinds of discourse—a highly public competition in comparative outrage, and a progressive narrowing of the definition of "victims" of corporate malfeasance. The Enron scandal created a serious rhetorical problem for policymakers. Enron executives had been major contributors to the Bush presidential campaign and had donated funds to a large majority of the members of Congress. Although it was not clear what decision-makers should do, it was abundantly clear that they had to do something. Virtually every congressional committee and every state and local officeholder appeared on television to express his or her vehement opposition to everything that had happened at Enron. Many commentators noted that these congressional hearings were not hearings at all. Congresspersons asked few questions, and all but one of the people they called in to testify refused to do so, claiming their right to protection against self-incrimination under the Fifth Amendment of the U.S. Constitution. The hearings quickly deteriorated into a political ritual, in which a defendant claimed his Fifth Amendment rights and long harangues by congresspersons ensued. This outrage rhetoric did have two effects—it identified the congresspersons with their constituents through their apparently shared anger, and it deflected attention from the sizable campaign contributions that they had received from Enron and other suspect firms.

Some business leaders argued that no new laws were necessary. In a statement that could easily have been written by Adam Smith in his early, optimistic years, *New York Times* CEO Russell Lewis told professors at the Academy of Management convention that

> the leaders of corporate America can, in my humble opinion, heal themselves. They can do it . . . by being crystal clear about their companies' purpose and core values. And lastly, successful CEOs will need to work their butts off to make certain they communicate all of this to every employee. . . . My personal

philosophy is not one that says that mankind is inherently drawn toward evil, and therefore we need a societal framework, a legal framework, and religious prescriptions [perhaps proscriptions] that scare the hell out of people so they never do anything wrong. For some people, all that and more is necessary. . . . I think people are essentially good and want to do the right thing. But they have to be helped, and they have to be guided, and they have to be taught, and they have to be reminded, and they have to be cajoled. . . . That the strength of those institutions, or more to the point, the flagging strength of some of those institutions, if those were beefed up, along with the, appealing to our angels, as Lincoln put it, I think both those things would make for a better business climate and for a better America.

The position of the business community was summarized by Tom Donohue, president of the U.S. Chamber of Commerce:

The issue facing Congress and the administration is simple: Will government actions and rhetoric make things more certain or more uncertain? Will business reforms be given a chance to work, or will there be more beating up and piling on? Will government policies make business leaders so risk-averse that we lose our creativity, innovation, and competitiveness?

Grady Rosier, CEO of McLane Company of Waco, Texas, and chairman of the National Association of Wholesale Distributors, echoed Donohue's comments, warning policymakers to "resist throwing the baby out with the bath water" through excessive regulation, and calling for "good apple" CEOs to "step up and run their businesses and watch the total game, just not what's going on one play at a time."[44] In short, increased government regulation will inevitably have perverse economic consequences.

Some legal reforms were enacted, but attention soon shifted away from Congress to the criminal justice system. Because U.S. society is so highly individualistic, social problems usually are viewed as the results of individual failings. From welfare reform to motorcycle helmet laws to health policy, individuals rather than systems are held responsible for social ills. During the debate over corporate governance at Enron, systemic problems were individualized through the metaphor of "a few bad apples." Everyone involved vowed to see that wrongdoers would serve hard time. Prosecutors arranged to arrest criminals in front of television cameras, timed to coincide with morning television news shows. Seeing executives being led away in handcuffs is a powerful form of political-legal theater, but it also serves to assuage popular anger and undermine pressure for reform. Perhaps most important, it ignores the simple fact that all but a small fraction of the actions leading to the "corporate meltdown" were perfectly legal, as Jeffrey Skilling has consistently argued in their defense. For politicians, the crisis soon passed. Poll data indicates that the issue of corporate corruption had no impact on the 2002 elections, even in Houston, Texas, where the largest number of people lost their jobs and savings. As more information became available, the scandal widened, eventually encompassing major investment banks, stockbrokers, and the mutual fund industry.

Organizational Life after Enron

By the fall of 2002, Enron had disappeared from the television screens; except for an occasional indictment, plea bargain, or conviction, the story of organizational ethics has been decidedly "good news and bad news." The 2002 Corporate Accountability Act plugged some loopholes in U.S. accounting law and increased the enforcement budget of the SEC, although not to pre-1990 levels. Congress increased the SEC's power further in the spring of 2003. In spite of utter chaos at the outset, the agency now seems to have leadership that is committed to reform, although its recent history leaves many observers skeptical. Still, the federal government continues to take actions designed to reign in both federal and state regulatory agencies. Measures of occupational prestige consistently indicate that the level of respect afforded corporate executives, accountants, and stockbrokers has joined that of attorneys, insurance executives, and automobile salesman near the bottom of the lists. Boards of directors are more independent of corporate executives than they were before Enron's bankruptcy, but for every example of a board reining in excessive executive compensation, there seems to be an example of "business as usual" as CEOs and willing boards find new ways to privilege their interests.[45] Ex-Enron employees and a number of advocacy groups continue to advocate legislation to protect workers' rights as workers.

Business schools have rediscovered ethics, although insiders question the impact of requiring students to take additional modules on ethics. The Harvard Business School, alma mater of Jeffrey Skilling and Andrew Fastow, has gotten the ethics religion. Robert A. G. Monks, Harvard Law School alumnus and corporate governance reformer, concludes,

> God bless them for trying. . . . But you have to look at an ethics program within the context of the Harvard Business School culture, which is a very pro-management culture. The single most ethically challenging question in business for the last 10 years is the issue of CEO pay. What is Harvard going to teach its students about CEO pay?"[46]

In its revised curriculum Harvard Business School does plan to have its students study how executive compensation and other incentives influence a corporation's ethics, just as it did when Skilling and Fastow were on campus.

Similar scandals have been uncovered in other countries, most notably the Parmalat agriculture product corporation in Italy, which may be an even larger corruption-related bankruptcy than WorldCom. In those cases the same systemic factors that contributed to the U.S. "corporate meltdown" seem to have been operating—a government committed to deregulation, "outside accountants" who seem to have looked the other way, excessive executive pay and consumption, complex operations on multiple continents, and so on. Individuals are indeed going to jail. But the system that generated the crisis seems to have changed little.[47]

Conclusion

The 1990s were dominated by a realization that the organizations in today's global economy are both very different than they were a generation ago and even less like they will be a generation from now. Like all times of social and cultural change, the 1990s and early 2000s have witnessed a great deal of anxiety and controversy about the directions that societies, economies, and organizations will take. It is clear that people now work in closer proximity to one another than ever before. Increased proximity comes in the form of a diverse workforce and in the form of a global economy. Some of the strategies of organizing that were discussed in Unit I may soon become obsolete; others may experience a resurgence. Alternative forms of organizing have emerged and will continue to do so. They will dominate some sectors of the global economy for a time and then be eclipsed by others. Each of the challenges described in Unit III will become more relevant and more pronounced. Technological change will continue; organizational power and politics will become more complex; decision making will be more difficult; and conflict management will be more important; diversity and corporate ethics will be increasingly important issues.

It also is clear that social and organizational power relationships continue to privilege the interests of some groups while failing to meet even the basic needs of others. Indeed, with globalization and worldwide deregulation, these gaps seem to be growing rapidly. None of this is especially surprising, because it results from the fundamental tensions described in Chapters 1 and 2. The problem—and the challenge—is that societies and their organizations can deal with these fundamental tensions in one of two ways. They can focus on *individuality*, domination, and control and become more competitive and divided, with one group of members turning against others and magnifying long-held antagonisms based on organizational rank, nationality, class, race, ethnicity, and gender. Or they can focus on creating a meaningful *global community* that represents the interests of multiple stakeholders and meets the needs of all of their members. But "societies" and "organizations" do not make choices—people do. Human beings are, after all, choice-making beings. It is *our* choices that will determine the road our society and our organizations take. The strategies that *all of us* choose will determine the kind of organizations that *we* live in for the rest of our lives and the kind of society that *we* will create for ourselves and for our children. Make good choices.

Notes

[1] Amatai Etzioni, cited in C. Gorman, "Listen Here, Mr. Big!" *Time,* July 3, 1989, 40–45. Also see Lawrence Hosmer, "The Institutionalization of Unethical Behavior," *Journal of Business Ethics* 6 (1987): 439–447. The ADM case is summarized by Joseph Menn in "ADM Fine Criticized as Too Low," *Houston Chronicle,* December 1, 1996, C13.

[2] Ernest Barker, ed. and trans., *The Politics of Aristotle* (London: Oxford University Press, 1976). For an updated analysis of the role that rhetoric plays in politics, see Deborah Stone, *Policy Paradox* (New York: Norton, 1997).

³John Bogle, "Interview with Bill Moyers," *NOW,* July 19, 2002. A transcript of this interview is available on the Web site http://www.pbs.org/. Former Senator William Proxmire estimated the payoff from political donations at a much higher level, 1,000 percent. See his introduction to Philip Stern, *Still the Best Congress Money Can Buy* (Chicago: Regnery, 1992); also see Greg Palast, *The Best Democracy Money Can Buy* (New York: Plume Books, 2001). An excellent summary of the role that lobbying plays in public policy formation is Frank Baumgartner and Beth Leech, *Basic Interests* (Princeton, NJ: Princeton University Press, 1998).

⁴This very, very brief summary of Smith's very complex ideas is based on our reading of Smith's work and on four secondary sources: Joseph Cropsey, *Polity and Economy* (South Bend, IN: St. Augustine's Press, 2001); David Gore, "Adam Smith's Rhetorical Sympathy" (master's thesis, Texas A&M University, 2001); Jerry Muller, *Adam Smith in His Time and Ours* (Princeton, NJ: Princeton University Press, 1993); John Peters, "Publicity and Pain: Self-Abstraction in Adam Smith's *Theory of Moral Sentiments,*" *Public Culture* 7 (1995): 657-684. For an analysis of the tragedy of the commons, see Garrett Hardin, "The Tragedy of the Commons," *Science,* December 13, 1968, pp. 1243-1248.

⁵Roland Marchand, *Creating the Corporate Soul: The Rise of Public Relations and Corporate Imagery in American Big Business* (Berkeley: University of California Press, 1998).

⁶Milton Friedman, *Capitalism and Freedom* (Chicago: University of Chicago Press, 1962); and "The Social Responsibility of Business Is to Increase Profits," *New York Times Magazine,* September 13, 1970, pp. 122-126. Also see Milton Friedman and Rose Friedman, *Free to Choose* (San Diego, CA: Harcourt Brace, 1980): and Thomas Friedman, *The Lexus and Olive Tree* (New York: Farrar, Straus and Giroux, 1999), p. 86.

⁷See Stella Nkomo, "Teaching Business Ethically in the 'New' South Africa," *Management Communication Quarterly* 17 (2003): 128-135.

⁸A. Marcus, and R. Goodman, "Victims and Shareholders," *Academy of Management Journal* 42 (1998): 479-485. The key source for the following section is William Cupach and Sandra Metts, *Facework* (Newbury Park, CA: Sage, 1994). For detailed analyses of what we will label "counterclaims," see Joe Folger, Marshall Scott Poole, and Randall Stutman, *Working through Conflict,* 4th ed. (New York: Addison-Wesley, 2000); and for "conversational repairs," see Michael McLaughlin, *Conversation* (Beverly Hills, CA: Sage, 1984). For an application to the communication of public figures, see B. L. Ware and W. A. Linkugel, "They Spoke in Defense of Themselves," *Quarterly Journal of Speech* 59 (1973): 273-283.

⁹B. E. Toffler, *Tough Choices* (New York: Wiley, 1986). When managers *do* talk about ethics, it usually is to avoid taking responsibility for ethical choices. Matt Seeger, "Responsibility in Organizational Communication," in *Proceedings of the 1992 National Communication Ethics Conference,* J. Jaska, ed. (Annandale, VA: Speech Communication Association, 1992). Gary Weaver, Linda Klebe Trevino, and Philip Cochran analyze this "decoupling" process as a managerial strategy for avoiding responsibility in "Integrated and Decoupled Corporate Social Performance," *Academy of Management Journal* 42 (1999): 539-552. Excellent examples of these processes are available in Adrienne Christiansen and Jeremy Hanson, "Comedy as Cure for Tragedy," *Quarterly Journal of Speech* 82 (1996): 157-170; Kimberly Elsbach and Robert Sutton, "Acquiring Organizational Legitimacy through Illegitimate Actions," *Administrative Science Quarterly* 35 (1992): 699-738; and James Patterson II and Myria Watkins Allen, "Accounting for Your Actions," *Journal of Applied Communication Research* 25 (1997): 293-316. For analyses of general processes that make people feel that ethics "is someone else's job," see William G. Scott and D. K. Hart, *Organizational America* (Boston: Houghton Mifflin, 1979); and *Organizational Values in America* (New Brunswick, NJ: Transaction, 1989).

¹⁰Jeffrey Hobbs, "Treachery by Any Other Name," *Management Communication Quarterly* 8 (1995): 323-346. For additional case studies in the strategies that organizational rhetoricians use to maintain the images of their firms, see Elizabeth Lance Toth and Robert Heath, eds., *Rhetorical and Critical Approaches to Public Relations* (New York: Praeger, 1992).

¹¹This example is based on Kurt Eichenwald, *New York Times on the Web,* November 4, 1966, http://www.nytimes.com/; and "Texaco Reeling from Racial Scandal," *Houston Chronicle,* November 5, 1996, C1; Sharon Walsh, "Plaintiffs Say Texaco Tough in Bias Cases," *Houston Chronicle,* November 14, 1996, C1; L. M. Sixel, "Workplace Racism Cases Hard to Win," *Houston Chronicle,* November 13, 1996, C1; and Salatheia Bryant, "Texaco Initiates Scholarship Program to Help Minorities," *Houston Chronicle,* November 12, 1996, A17. For an extended analysis, see Susan Brinson and William Benoit, "The Tarnished Star, "*Management Communication Quarterly* 12 (1999): 483-510.

¹²Melissa Baucus and David Baucus, "Paying the Piper," *Academy of Management Journal* 40 (1997): 129-151.

¹³Robert Sims, "The Challenge of Ethical Behavior in Organizations," *Journal of Business Ethics* 11 (1992) 501-513; Robert Jackall, "Moral Mazes: Bureaucracy and Managerial Work," *Harvard Business Review* 61 (September-October 1983): 99-123.

[14] Scott and Hart, *Organizational America;* Barry Staw and Lisa Epstein, "What Bandwagons Bring: Effect of Popular Management Techniques on Corporate Performance, Reputation, and CEO Pay," *Administrative Science Quarterly* 45 (2000): 523–556; David Deephouse, "Does Isomorphism Legitimate?" *Academy of Management Journal* 39 (1996): 1024–1039; Margarete Arndt and Barbara Bigelow, "Presenting Structural Innovation in an Institutional Environment," *Administrative Science Quarterly* 45 (2000): 494–522. For an analysis of the discourse surrounding managerial fads, see Timothy Clark and David Greatbach, "Management Fashion as Image-Spectacle," *Management Communication Quarterly* 17 (2004): 396–424.

[15] Charles Conrad and Holly McIntush "Communication, Structure, and Health Care Policymaking," in *Handbook of Health Communication,* A. Dorsey, K. Miller, R. Parrott, and T. Thompson, eds. (Hillsdale, NJ: Lawrence Erlbaum, 2003).

[16] Deephouse. For excellent case studies of organizations dealing with multiple audiences, see Myria Watkins Allen and Rachel Caillouet, "Legitimation Endeavors," *Communication Monographs* 61 (1994): 44–62; and William Benoit, "The Cola Wars: Coke versus Pepsi," *Accounts, Excuses, and Apologies* (Albany, NY: State University of New York Press, 1995); Tatiana Kostova and Srilata Zaheer, "Organizational Legitimacy under Conditions of Complexity: The Case of the Multinational Enterprise," *Academy of Management Review* 24 (1999): 64–81. Two multiple-stakeholder models have been developed, one by Stan Deetz, *Transforming Communication, Transforming Business* (Cresskill, NJ: Hampton Press, 1995); and another by Richard Freeman, *Strategic Management: A Stakeholder Approach* (Boston: Pitman, 1984). For an extension of Freeman's model, see Jeff Frooman, "Stakeholder Influence Strategies," *Academy of Management Review* 24 (1999): 191–205.

[17] B. Agle, R. Mitchell, and J. Sonnenfeld, "Who Matters to CEOs?" *Academy of Management Journal* 42 (1999): 507–525.

[18] John Milne, "Mill Owner Says He'll Pay Workers," *Boston Globe,* December 15, 1995, B50; Robert Ulmer, "Effective Crisis Management through Established Stakeholder Relationships," *Management Communication Quarterly* 14 (2000): 590–615; Matthew Seeger and Robert Ulmer, "A Post-Crisis Discourse of Renewal," *Journal of Applied Communication Research* 30 (2002): 126–142.

[19] George Diosonopolous and Steven Goldzwig, "The Atomic Power Industry and the NEW Woman," in *Rhetorical and Critical Approaches to Public Relations,* Elizabeth Toth and Robert Heath, eds. (Hillsdale, NJ: Lawrence Erlbaum, 1992); Robert Farrell and G. Thomas Goodnight, "Accidental Rhetoric," *Communication Monographs* 48 (1981): 271–300; Robert Crable and Steve Vibbert, "Mobil's Epideictic Advocacy," *Communication Monographs* 50 (1983): 380–396; W. Marc Potter, "The Environment of the Oil Company," in Toth and Heath; and Nancy Stutts and Randall Barker, "The Use of Narrative Paradigm Theory in Assessing Audience Value Conflict in Image Advertising," *Management Communication Quarterly* 13 (1999): 209–244; George Diosonopolous and Robert Crable, "Definitional Hegemony as a Public Relations Strategy," *Central States Speech Journal* 39 (1988): 134–145.

[20] Theodore Marmor, *The Politics of Medicare,* 2nd ed. (New York: Aldyne de Gruyter, 2000).

[21] This section is based on Conrad and McIntush. Also see Frank Baumgartner and Bryan Jones, *Agendas and Instability in American Politics* (Chicago: University of Chicago Press, 1983); and Stone.

[22] L. M. Sixel, "Wal-Mart Settles Insurance Lawsuit," *Houston Chronicle,* January 9, 2004, C1.

[23] "As Funds Gain, Scandal Concerns Fade," *Houston Chronicle,* January 26, 2004, D3.

[24] Billy Hall and Bryan Jones, "Agenda Denial and Issue Containment in the Regulation of Financial Securities"; and John F. Mahon and Richard A. McGowan, "Making Professional Accounting Accountable," both in *Cultural Strategies of Agenda Denial,* Richard W. Cobb and Marc H. Ross, eds. (Lawrence: University Press of Kansas, 1997).

[25] Eric Schlosser, "The Cow Jumped over the U.S.D.A.," *New York Times on the Web,* January 2, 2004, http://www.nytimes.com/. Also see Schlosser's *Fast Food Nation* (Boston: Houghton-Mifflin, 2001). For an extended case study of regulatory capture, see R. Richard Ritti and Jonathan Silver, "Early Processes of Institutionalization," *Administrative Science Quarterly* 31 (1986): 25–42. The country-of-origin policy shifts are described in "Country-of-Origin Labels Can Wait, Congress Says," *Houston Chronicle,* January 23, 2004, G10.

[26] More extensive analyses are available in Peter Fusaro and Ross Miller, *What Went Wrong at Enron* (New York: Wiley, 2002); Robert Bryce, *Pipe Dreams* (New York: Public Affairs Press, 2002); and Loren Fox, *Enron: The Rise and Fall* (New York: Wiley, 2003). Many of the ideas in this section are developed in more detail in Charles Conrad, "Setting the Stage," *Management Communication Quarterly* 17 (2003): 5–19; and Charles Conrad, "Stemming the Tide," *Organization* 10 (2003): 549–560.

[27] See Bryce; and Fusaro and Miller. For a more general analysis, see George Soros, *The Crisis of Global Capitalism* (New York: Public Affairs Press, 1998); and Nobel-prize-winning economist George Stiglitz, *Globalization and Its Discontents* (New York: Norton, 2002).

[28] "Bigger than Enron," *Frontline,* WGBH, Boston, June 28, 2001, transcript available at http://www.pbs.org/; Arthur Levitt, *Take on the Street* (New York: Pantheon, 2002).

[29] W. S. Lerach, Testimony before the Subcommittee on Telecommunications and Finance, House Committee on Commerce, Legislation on Securities Fraud Litigation (H.R. 10) (January 19, 1995), 103rd Cong., 2nd sess.; J. Seligman, "The Merits Do Matter," *Harvard Law Review* 108 (1994): 438–457. It is important not to view these processes as limited only to the 1990s. Bryan Hall and Bryan Jones have shown that the business lobby has long been effective in blunting calls for increased regulation after periods of business malpractice. In addition, by arguing that the private sector–free market has a built-in self-corrective mechanism, the SEC has repeatedly been able to avoid taking a more active regulatory role. Hall and Jones. Similarly, J. F. Mahon and Richard McGowan have demonstrated that the accounting industry has long been able to avoid increased government regulation or oversight by claiming that accounting practice is too complex and individualized for government to be able to effectively intervene in the industry. Mahon and McGowan.

[30] "Bigger than Enron"; Levitt. The Center for Responsive Politics found that the accounting industry gave more than $50 million to candidates for federal offices during the 1990s, with 56 percent going to Republicans and 43 percent going to Democrats. However, this data is a bit misleading: at the beginning of the decade these contributions were almost identical across party lines; by 1999 Republican candidates were receiving about twice as much accounting industry money as Democratic candidates.

[31] A negative analysis based on a long-term data base is provided by R. J. Shiller, *Irrational Exuberance* (Princeton, NJ: Princeton University Press, 2000). A favorable analysis, based on data from 2002, is provided by Indiana University finance department professor Utpal Bhattacharya and graduate students Peter Groznik and Bruce Haslem. A summary of this study is available in Michael Hulbert, "The Bad News on Certification Was Old News to the Market, *New York Times on the Web*, March 2, 2003, http://www.nytimes.com/; the complete paper is available at http://papers.ssrn.com/so13/papers.cfm?abstract-id=332621.

[32] A. Larry Elliott and Richard J. Schroth, *How Companies Lie: Why Enron Is Just the Tip of the Iceberg* (New York: Crown Business, 2002); Rakesh Kuhrana, *Searching for a Corporate Savior* (Princeton, NJ: Princeton University Press, 2002).

[33] Stanley Deetz, *Democracy in the Age of Corporate Colonization* (Albany: State University of New York Press, 1992); David Gordon, *Fat and Mean* (Ithaca, NY: Cornell University Press, 1996); Matt Seeger, "C.E.O. Performances: Lee Iacocca and the Case of Chrysler," *Southern Speech Communication Journal* 52 (1986): 52–68.

[34] David Levinthal and James March, "The Myopia of Learning," *Strategic Management Journal* 14 (1993): 97. Also see John Child, "Managerial and Organizational Factors Associated with Company Performance," *Journal of Management Studies* 11 (1974): 13–27; James Thompson, *Organizations in Action* (New York: McGraw-Hill, 1967); Dianne Hambrick, "Top Management Groups," in *Research in Organizational Behavior*, B. Staw and L. Cummings, eds., vol. 15 (Greenwich, CT: JAI Press, 1994); Dianne Hambrick and P. Mason, "Upper Echelons," *Academy of Management Review* 9 1984): 193–206; Barry Staw and John Ross, "Commitment in an Experimenting Society," *Journal of Applied Psychology* 65 (1980): 249–260; Barry Staw and John Ross, "Behavior in Escalation Situations," in *Research in Organizational Behavior*, B. Staw and L. Cummings, eds. (Greenwich, CT: JAI Press, 1987).

[35] David Leonhardt, "Options Do Not Raise Performance, Study Finds," *New York Times on the Web*, August 11 2002, http://www.nytimes.com/. The interests of other stakeholders had been defined out of the equation by free-market fundamentalism.

[36] Daniel Altman, "How to Tie Pay to Goals, Instead of the Stock Price," *New York Times on the Web*, September 8, 2002, http://www.nytimes.com/; Bogle; Warren E. Buffett, "Who Really Cooks the Books?" *New York Times on the Web*, July 24, 2003. Based on an analysis of thirty years of research (1960–1990), R. Dalton, K. Daily, C. Certo, and R. Roengpitya found that executives' stock holdings are not significantly related to corporate performance. "The Relationship between Stock Options and Organizational Performance," paper presented at the Academy of Management Convention, Denver, CO, August 2002. Comparable conclusions emerged from a similar analysis of data from 1992 to 2001: Joseph R. Blasi and Douglas L. Kruse, *In the Company of Owners* (New York: Basic Books, 2002).

[37] Walter M. Cadette, "How Stock Options Lead to Scandal," *New York Times on the Web*, July 12, 2002, http://www.nytimes.com/; Jeff Madrick, "A Theory on Corporate Greed," *New York Times on the Web*, February 20, 2003.

[38] Robin Roslender, *Sociological Perspectives on Modern Accountancy* (London: Routledge, 1992); also see Michael Power and Richard Laughlin, "Critical Theory and Accounting," in *Critical Management Studies*, Mats Alvesson and Hugh Willmott, eds. (London: Sage, 1992).

[39] Bryce.

[40] Bryce.

[41] Fusaro and Miller, pp. 51–52. For an assessment of the GE system, see Charles Conrad, "The Ethical Nexus," in *The Ethical Nexus*, Charles Conrad, ed. (Norwood, NJ: Ablex: 1993). The best summary of Enron's lobbying activities is Bryce.

[42]*New York Times* Editorial Board, *New York Times on the Web,* February 2, 2002, http://www.nytimes.com/.

[43]Leslie Wayne, "Tighter Rules for Options Fall Victim to Lobbying," *New York Times on the Web,* July 20, 2002, http://www.nytimes.com/. Also see *New York Times* Editorial Board, "Congressional Cowardice," *New York Times on the Web,* July 18, 2002; Senator Carl Levin was quoted in Louis Uchitelle, "Broken System? Tweak It," *New York Times on the Web,* July, 28, 2002.

[44]See Russell Lewis, "A CEO's Lot Is Not a Happy One," Academy of Management Annual Convention, Denver, Colorado, August 11, 2002, p. 6. A transcript of the Lewis speech is available from http://www.nytco.com/pdf-reports/Academy_Russ_20020811.pdf; the subsequent question-and-answer session was transcribed from videotaped C-SPAN coverage of the event. The Donohue and Rosier comments are available in transcripts of the "Panel on Economic Recovery and Job Creation," President's Economic Forum, moderated by Treasury Secretary Paul O'Neill, Baylor University, Waco, Texas, August 13, 2002. Transcript available online from Federal News Service via *Lexis-Nexis Academic.*

[45]Paul Krugman, "Business As Usual," *New York Times on the Web,* October 22, 2002, http://www.nytimes.com/; Gretchen Morgenson, "Buybacks Aren't Always a Good Thing," *New York Times on the Web,* January 18, 2004.

[46]Cited in Robert Weisman, "Harvard Digs Deeper on Ethics," *Houston Chronicle,* January 4, 2004, D3.

[47]Richard Oppel Jr., "Senate Votes to Strengthen S.E.C.'s Hand," *New York Times on the Web,* April 10, 2003, http://www.nytimes.com/; Landon Thomas, "Memo Shows MFS Funds Let Favored Clients Trade When Others Couldn't," *New York Times on the Web,* December 9, 2003; and "Calpers Sues the Big Board," *New York Times on the Web,* December 17, 2003; *Wall Street Journal,* "SEC Turned Timid As Corruption Became More Complex," *Houston Chronicle,* December 26, 2003, D4; Stephen Labaton, "Defying Election-Year Tradition, S.E.C. Draws Up a Busy Agenda," *New York Times on the Web,* January 2, 2004; Patrick McGeehan, "Quick, What's the Boss Making?" *New York Times on the Web,* September 21, 2003; "Get Independents to Chair Boards of Funds, SEC Says," *Houston Chronicle,* January 15, 2004, B4; Kurt Eichenwald, "In String of Corporate Troubles, Critics Focus on Boards' Failings," *New York Times on the Web,* September 21, 2003; Patrick McGeehan, "Top Executives' Lucrative Deals Tie the Hands That Pay Them," *New York Times on the Web,* June 28, 2003; [Reuters], "Spitzer Threatens to Sue U.S. Regulator over Loan Exemption," *New York Times on the Web,* December 11, 2003; David Kaplan, "Fighting for Workers' Rights," *Houston Chronicle,* January 15, 2004. For an assessment of business school ethics programs, see the "Forum" on "Teaching Business Ethically" in the August 2003 special issue of *Management Communication Quarterly,* 17:126–164. Harvard's program is examined in Weisman.

Bibliography

*Indicates items particularly appropriate for graduate students.

Abrahamson, E. "Management Fashion." *Academy of Management Review* 21 (1996): 254–285.

Abrahamsson, B. *Bureaucracy or Participation.* Beverly Hills, CA: Sage, 1977.

Acker, J. "Feminist Goals and Organizing Processes." In *Feminist Organizations,* edited by M. M. Ferree and Y. Martin. Philadelphia: Temple University Press, 1995.

———. "The Gender Regime in Swedish Banks." *Scandinavian Journal of Management* 10 (1994): 116–142.

Adams, R., and R. Parrot. "Pediatric Nurses' Communication of Role Expectations of Parents to Hospitalized Children." *Journal of Applied Communication Research* 22 (1994): 36–47.

Adler, G. S., and P. Tompkins. "Electronic Performance Monitoring." *Management Communication Quarterly* 10 (1997): 259–288.

Adler, N. *International Dimensions of Organizational Behavior.* 2nd ed. Boston: Kent, 1991.

Agle, B., R. Mitchell, and S. Sonnenfeld. "Who Matters to CEOs?" *Academy of Management Journal* 42 (1999): 507–525.

Aiello, J. R. "Computer-Based Work Monitoring." *Journal of Applied Social Psychology* 23 (1993): 499–507.

Aiello, J. R., and C. M. Svec. "Computer Monitoring of Work Performance." *Journal of Applied Psychology* 23 (1993): 537–548.

*Aktouf, O. "Defamiliarizing Management Practice." In *Understanding Management,* edited by S. Linstead, R. G. Small, and P. Jeffcutt. London: Sage, 1996.

*Albrecht, T. "An Overtime Analysis of Communication Patterns and Work Perceptions." In *Communication Yearbook 8,* edited by R. Bostrom. Beverly Hills, CA: Sage, 1984.

Albrecht, T., and M. Adelman. *Communicating Social Support.* Newbury Park, CA: Sage, 1988.

Albrecht, T., and B. Bach. *Organizational Communication: A Relational Perspective.* Ft. Worth, TX: Harcourt, 1996.

*Albrecht, T., and B. Hall. "Facilitating Talk about New Ideas." *Communication Monographs* 58 (1991): 273–288.

———. "Relational and Content Differences between Elites and Outsiders in Innovation Networks." *Human Communication Research* 17 (1991): 535–561.

Albrecht, T., and J. Halsey. "Mutual Support in Mixed Status Relationships." *Journal of Social and Personal Relationships* 9 (1992): 237–252.

Alderton, S. M., and L. Frey. "Effects of Reactions to Arguments on Group Outcomes." *Central States Speech Journal* 34 (1983): 88–95.

Aldrich, H. E. *Organizations and Environments.* Englewood Cliffs, NJ: Prentice Hall, 1979.

Alexander, E., L. Penley, and I. E. Hernigan. "The Effect of Individual Difference on Managerial Media Choice." *Management Communication Quarterly* 5 (1991): 155–173.

*Alkhazraji, K., W. Gardner, J. Martin, and J. Paolillo. "The Acculturation of Immigrants to U.S. Organizations." *Management Communication Quarterly* 11 (1997): 217–265.

Allen, B. "A Black Feminist Standpoint Analysis." In *Rethinking Organizational and Managerial Communication from Feminist Perspectives,* edited by P. Buzzanell. Thousand Oaks, CA: Sage, 2000.

*———. "Feminist Standpoint Theory." *Communication Studies* 47 (1996): 257–271.

Allen, M. W. "The Relationship between Communication, Affect, Job Alternatives, and Voluntary Turnover Intentions." *Southern Communication Journal* 61 (1996): 198–209.

Allen, M. W., and R. Caillouet. "Legitimation Endeavors." *Communication Monographs* 61 (1994): 44–62.

Althus, D. "Voters Rejecting Free-Trade Model." *Houston Chronicle,* November 24, 2002.

Altman, D. "How to Tie Pay to Goals, Instead of the Stock Price." *New York Times on the Web,* September 8, 2002, http://www.nytimes.com/.

*Alvesson, M. "Organizations, Culture, and Ideology." *International Studies of Management and Organization* 17 (1987): 4-18.

*———. *Organization Theory and Technocratic Consciousness.* New York: Walter de Gruyter, 1987.

Alvesson, M., and H. Wilmott, eds. *Critical Management Studies.* Newbury Park, CA: Sage, 1992.

American Association of University Women. "'Pink Collar' Jobs Still Lure Most Women, Study Finds." *Houston Chronicle,* May 5, 2003, A5.

Amparano, J. L. "Study Says Women Face Glass Walls as Well as Glass Ceilings." *Wall Street Journal,* March 3, 1992.

*Ancona, D. G., and D. F. Caldwell. "Beyond Task and Maintenance: Defining External Functions in Groups." *Group and Organization Studies* 13 (1988): 468-494.

Ancona, D. G., T. Kochan, J. Van Maanen, M. Scully, and D. Westney. "The New Organization: Taking Action in an Era of Organizational Transformation." In *Managing for the Future: Organizational Behavior and Processes.* Cincinnati: South-Western College Publishing, 1999.

Andrews, E. L. "Imports Don't Deserve All That Blame." *New York Times on the Web,* December 7, 2003, http://www.nytimes.com/.

———. "A Civil War within a Trade Dispute." *New York Times on the Web,* September 20, 2002, http://www.nytimes.com/.

Andrews, P. H., and R. Herschel. *Organizational Communication.* Geneva, IL: Houghton Mifflin, 1996.

Ansari, S., and K. Euske. "Rational, Rationalizing, and Reifying Uses of Accounting Data in Organizations." *Accounting, Organizations, and Society* 12 (1987): 549-570.

Applegate, L. M., R. Austin, and F. W. McFarlan. *Corporate Information Strategy and Management,* 6th ed. Boston: McGraw-Hill, 2003.

Arendt, H. *The Human Condition.* Chicago: University of Chicago Press, 1958.

Armas, G. "Educational Gaps between Genders, Races Diminish." *Houston Chronicle,* March 21, 2003, A27.

Arndt, M., and B. Bigelow. "Presenting Structural Innovation in an Institutional Environment." *Administrative Science Quarterly* 45 (2000): 494-522.

Arnold, L. "Sharing of Terror Intelligence Still 'Haphazard,' Study Finds." *Houston Chronicle,* December 3, 2003, A8.

Arquilla, J., D. Ronfeldt, and M. Zanini. "Networks, Netwar, and Information Age Terrorism." In *Countering the New Terrorism,* edited by A. Lesser, B. Hoffman, J. Arquilla, D. Ronfeldt, and M. Zanini. Santa Monica, CA: Rand, 1999.

"As Funds Gain, Scandal Concerns Fade." *Houston Chronicle,* January 26, 2004, D3.

Ashcraft, K. L. "Organized Dissonance: Feminist Bureaucracy as Hybrid Form." *Academy of Management Journal* 44 (2001): 1301-1322.

Ashcraft, K., and A. Kedrowicz. "Self-Direction or Social Support?" *Communication Monographs* 69 (2002): 88-110.

Aune, J. *Selling the Free Market.* New York: Guilford Press, 2001.

Axelrod, R. *The Evolution of Cooperation.* New York: Basic Books, 1984.

*Axley, S. "Managerial and Organizational Communication in Terms of the Conduit Metaphor." *Academy of Management Review* 9 (1984): 428-437.

Bach, B. "The Effect of Multiplex Relationships upon Innovation Adoption." *Communication Monographs* 56 (1991): 133-148.

———. "Making a Difference by Doing Differently: A Response to Putnam." Paper presented at the Arizona State University "Conference on Organizational Communication," Tempe, AZ, February 1990.

*Banks, S., and P. Riley. "Structuration Theory as an Ontology for Communication Research." In *Communication Yearbook 16,* edited by S. Deetz. Newbury Park, CA: Sage, 1993.

Bantz, C. "Cultural Diversity and Group Cross-Cultural Team Research." *Journal of Applied Communication Research* 20 (1993): 1-19.

Barber, B. "Jihad vs. McWorld." *Annals of the American Academy of Political and Social Science* 570 (2000): 23-33.

Barber, B. R. *Jihad vs. McWorld.* New York: Random House, 1995.

Barber, D. *Power in Committees.* Chicago: Rand McNally, 1966.

*Barge, J. K. *Leadership.* New York: St. Martin's, 1994.

Barge, J. K., and G. W. Musambria. "Turning Points in Chair-Faculty Relationships." *Journal of Applied Communication Research* 20 (1992): 54-77.

Barker, E., ed. and trans. *The Politics of Aristotle.* London: Oxford University Press, 1976.

*Barker, J. R. "Tightening the Iron Cage: Concertive Control in Self-Managing Teams." *Administrative Science Quarterly* 38 (1993): 408-437.

Barker, J. R., and G. Cheney. "The Concept and Practices of Discipline in Contemporary Organizational Life." *Communication Monographs* 61 (1994): 20-43.

Barker, J. R., and P. Tompkins. "Identification in the Self-Managing Organization: Characteristics of Target and Tenure." *Human Communication Research* 21 (1994): 223–240.

*Barker, J. R., C. W. Melville, and M. E. Pacanowsky. "Self-Directed Teams at Xel: Changes in Communication Practices during a Program of Cultural Transformation." *Journal of Applied Communication Research* 21 (1993): 297–313.

Barley, S., and D. B. Knight. "Towards a Cultural Theory of Stress Complaints." *Research in Organizational Behavior* 14 (1992): 1–48.

*Barley, S., and G. Kunda. "Design and Devotion: Surges of Rational and Normative Ideologies of Control in Managerial Discourse." *Administrative Science Quarterly* 37 (1992): 363–399.

*Barley, S., G. W. Meyer, and D. Gash. "Cultures of Culture." *Administrative Science Quarterly* 33 (1988): 24–60.

Barlow, J. "Ethics Can Boost the Bottom Line." *Houston Chronicle,* October 31, 1996.

Barnard, C. *The Functions of the Executive.* 30th anniversary ed. Cambridge, MA: Harvard University Press, 1968.

Barry, D. "Rest Easy Knowing the Mohair Business Is Thriving." *Bryan/College Station (TX) Eagle,* June 23, 2002, D3.

Barstow, D. "California Leads in Making Employer Pay for Job Deaths." *New York Times on the Web,* December 23, 2003, http://www.nytimes.com/.

Barstow, D., and L. Bergman. "Criminal Inquiry under Way at Large Pipe Manufacturer." *New York Times on the Web,* May 15, 2003, http://www.nytimes.com/.

———. "Deaths on the Job; Slaps on the Wrist." *New York Times on the Web,* January 10, 2003, http:// www.nytimes.com/.

Bartunek, J. M., and M. Moch. "Multiple Constituencies and the Duality of Working Life." In *Reframing Organizational Culture,* edited by P. Frost, L. Moore, M. R. Louis, C. Lundberg, and J. Martin. Newbury Park, CA: Sage, 1991.

Bass, B. *Bass and Stogdill's Handbook of Leadership.* 3rd ed. New York: Free Press, 1990.

———. *Leadership and Performance beyond Expectations.* New York: Free Press, 1985.

Bastien, D. "Change in Organizational Culture." *Management Communication Quarterly* 5 (1992): 403–442.

Baucus, M., and D. Baucus. "Paying the Piper." *Academy of Management Journal* 40 (1997): 129–151.

Baumard, P. *Tacit Knowledge in Organizations.* London: Sage, 1999.

Baumgartner, F., and B. Jones. *Agendas and Instability in American Politics.* Chicago: University of Chicago Press, 1983.

Baumgartner, F., and B. Leech. *Basic Interests.* Princeton, NJ: Princeton University Press, 1998.

Baxter, L. "'Talking Things Through' and 'Putting It in Writing.'" *Journal of Applied Communication Research* 21 (1994): 313–328.

Beauprez, J. "A Better Life, but Not in the U.S." *Houston Chronicle,* August 17, 2003, D2.

Becker, E. "U.S. Subsidizes Companies to Buy Subsidized Cotton." *New York Times on the Web,* November 4, 2003, http://www.nytimes.com/.

Becker, E., and L. Rohter. "U.S. and Chile Reach Free Trade Accord." *New York Times on the Web,* December 12, 2002, http://www.nytimes.com/.

Becker, E., and D. Sanger. "President in Political Vise over Steel Tariff Decision." *New York Times on the Web,* December 2, 2003, http://www.nytimes.com/.

Behr, P. "Blackout Report Cites Ohio Utilities: Michigan Panel Points to Failure to Isolate System." *Washington Post,* November 6, 2003, E5.

Bell, E. L. "The Bicultural Life Experience of Career-Oriented Black Women." *Journal of Organizational Behavior* 11 (1990): 459–477.

Bellah, R., R. Madsen, W. Sullivan, and S. Tipton. *Habits of the Heart.* 2nd ed. Berkeley: University of California Press, 1995.

Bennis, W., J. Parikh, and R. Lessem. *Beyond Leadership: Balancing Economics, Ethics, and Ecology.* Cambridge, MA: Basil Blackwell, 1994.

Benoit, W. "The Cola Wars: Coke versus Pepsi." In *Accounts, Excuses, and Apologies.* Albany, NY: State University of New York Press, 1995.

Benson, S. "The Clerking Sisterhood." In *Gendering Organizational Analysis,* edited by A. J. Mills and P. Tancred. Newbury Park, CA: Sage, 1992.

Bergen, P. "Al Qaeda's New Tactics." *New York Times,* November 15, 2002.

———. "Defining Al-Qaida: Is It a Group? Is It a Movement?" *Houston Chronicle,* January 4, 2004

*Berger, C. "Power, Dominance, and Social Interaction." In *Handbook of Interpersonal Communication,* edited by M. Knapp and G. Miller. 2nd ed. Thousand Oaks, CA: Sage, 1994.

Bertraud, M. "Female Executives Make What Men Do." *Houston Chronicle,* October 21, 2000.

Bettman, J., and B. Weitz. "Attributions in the Board Room." *Administrative Science Quarterly* 28 (1983): 165–183.

"Bigger than Enron." *Frontline.* WGBH, Boston, June 28, 2001, transcript available at http://www.pbs.org.

*Bingham, S., ed. *Conceptualizing Sexual Harassment as Discursive Practice.* Westport, CT: Praeger, 1994.

Bitzer, L. "Functional Communication." In *Rhetoric in Transition,* edited by E. White. University Park: Pennsylvania State University Press, 1980.

———. "The Rhetorical Situation." *Philosophy and Rhetoric* 1 (1968): 1–14.

Blalock, D. "Workplace Ethics Take a Vacation." *Houston Chronicle,* March 31, 1996, D3.

Blanchette, D. P. "Technology Transfer in a Culturally Diverse Workforce (Part I)." *Industrial Management,* July–August (1994): 31–32.

Blasi, J. R., and D. L. Kruse. *In the Company of Owners.* New York: Basic Books, 2002.

Blau, J. *Illusions of Prosperity.* New York: Oxford University Press, 1999.

Bogle, J. "Interview with Bill Moyers." *NOW,* July 19, 2002, transcript available on the Web site http:// www.pbs.org/.

Boisseau, C. "Ranks of Female Businesses Soar." *Houston Chronicle,* January 30, 1996.

Boje, D. "The Storytelling Organization." *Administrative Science Quarterly* 36 (1991): 106–126.

Bokeno, R. M., and V. Gantt. "Dialogic Mentoring." *Management Communication Quarterly* 14 (2000): 237–270.

Bormann, E. *Small Group Communication: Theory and Practice.* 3rd ed. New York: HarperCollins, 1990.

*———. "Symbolic Convergence Theory and Communication in Group Decision-Making." In *Communication and Group Decision Making,* edited by R. Hirokawa and M. S. Poole. 2nd ed. Thousand Oaks, CA: Sage, 1996.

Boster, F., and M. Mayer. "Differential Argument Quality Mediates the Impact of Social Comparison Process of the Choice Shift." Paper presented at the International Communication Association Convention, San Francisco, May 1984.

Botan, C. "Communication, Work, and Electronic Surveillance." *Communication Monographs* 63 (1996): 294–313.

———. "Examining Electronic Surveillance in the Workplace." Paper presented at the International Communication Convention, Acapulco, Mexico, May 2000.

Bradford, L. J., and C. Raines. *Twentysomething.* New York: Master Media, 1992.

Bradsher, K. "A High-Tech Fix for One Corner of India." *New York Times on the Web,* December 27, 2002, http://www.nytimes.com/.

Brandel, M. "Distant Messages." *Computerworld,* December 9, 2002.

Braverman, H. *Labor and Monopoly Capital.* New York: Monthly Review Press, 1974.

Bridge, K., and L. Baxter. "Blended Relationships: Friends as Work Associates." *Western Journal of Communication* 56 (1992): 200–225.

Brinkley, J., and E. Schmitt. "Halliburton Will Repay U.S. Excess Charges for Troops' Meals." *New York Times on the Web,* February 3, 2004, http://www.nytimes.com/.

Brinson, S., and W. Benoit. "The Tarnished Star." *Management Communication Quarterly* 12 (1999): 483–510.

Brockner, J., T. R. Tyler, and R. Cooper-Schneider. "The Influence of Prior Commitment to an Institution of Reactions to Perceived Unfairness." *Administrative Science Quarterly* 37 (1992): 254–271.

Brown, R. H. "Global Capitalism, National Sovereignty, and the Decline of Democratic Space." *Rhetoric and Public Affairs* 5 (2002): 347–357.

*Browning, L. "Lists and Stories in Organizational Communication." *Communication Theory* 2 (1992): 281–302.

Browning, L., J. Beyer, and J. Shetler. "Building Cooperation in a Competitive Industry: SEMATECH and the Semiconductor Industry." *Academy of Management Journal* 38 (1995): 113–151.

Bryant, S. "Texaco Initiates Scholarship Program to Help Minorities." *Houston Chronicle,* November 12, 1996.

Bryce, R. *Pipe Dreams.* New York: Public Affairs Press, 2002.

Buckley, W. F. "Face It, We Surrendered on Immigration." *Houston Chronicle,* January 10, 2004, A36.

Buffett, W. E. "Who Really Cooks the Books?" *New York Times on the Web,* July 24, 2003, http:// www.nytimes.com/.

Buggs, S. "Maternity Leave Can Cost a Great Deal More Later." *Houston Chronicle,* December 2, 2002, E1.

*Bullis, C., and B. W. Bach. "Socialization Turning Points." *Western Journal of Speech Communication* 53 (1989): 273–293.

Bullis, C., and P. Tompkins. "The Forest Ranger Revisited." *Communication Monographs* 56 (1989): 287–306.

*Burawoy, M. *Manufacturing Consent.* Chicago: University of Chicago Press, 1979.

Burgoon, J., D. Buller, and W. G. Woodall. *Nonverbal Communication: The Unspoken Dialogue.* New York: Harper and Row, 1995.

Burke, R., and C. Cooper, eds. *The Organization in Crisis: Downsizing, Restructuring, and Privatization.* Oxford: Blackwell, 2000.

Burless, G., R. Lawrence, and R. Shapiro. *Globaphobia.* Washington, DC: Brookings Institution Press, 1998.

*Burns, T., and G. M. Stalker. *The Management of Innovation.* London: Tavistock, 1961.

Bush, D. F. "Passive-Aggressive Behavior in the Business Setting." In *Passive-Aggressiveness,* edited by R. Parsons and R. Wicks. New York: Brunner-Mazel, 1983.

*Bush, R. B., and J. P. Folger. *The Promise of Mediation: Responding to Conflict through Empowerment and Recognition.* San Francisco: Jossey-Bass, 1994.

Bussey, J. "Reduction in Poverty Stalls in Latin America." *Houston Chronicle,* December 1, 2002, D6.

*Butler, R., G. Astley, D. Hickson, G. Mallory, and D. Wilson. "Strategic Decision Making in Organizations." *International Studies of Management and Organization* 23 (1980): 234-249.

*Butler, R., D. Hickson, D. Wilson, and R. Axelsson. "Organizational Power, Politicking, and Paralysis." *Organizational and Administrative Sciences* 8 (1977): 44-59.

Buzzanell, P. "Gaining a Voice: Feminist Organizational Communication Theorizing." *Management Communication Quarterly* 7 (1994): 339-383.

———. "Reframing the Glass Ceiling as a Socially Constructed Process." *Communication Monographs* 62 (1995): 327-354.

———, ed. *Rethinking Organizational and Managerial Communication from Feminist Perspectives.* Thousand Oaks, CA: Sage, 2000.

Cadette, W. M. "How Stock Options Lead to Scandal." *New York Times on the Web,* July 12, 2002, http:// www.nytimes.com/.

"Calpers Sues the Big Board," *New York Times on the Web,* December 17, 2003, http:// www.nytimes.com/.

Cameron, K., and M. Thompson. "The Problems and Promises of Total Quality Management." In *Pressing Problems in Modern Organizations (That Keep Us Up at Night),* edited by R. Quinn, R. O'Neill, and L. St. Clair. New York: American Management Association, 2000.

Canary, D., and B. Spitzberg. "A Model of the Perceived Competence of Conflict Strategies." *Human Communication Research* 15 (1990): 630-649.

Cantu, H. "Racial Slur Helped Form New Career." *Houston Chronicle,* March 21, 1999.

Cappelli, P. *The New Deal at Work: Managing the Market-Driven Workforce.* Boston: Harvard Business School Press, 1999.

Carnavale, A. P., and S. C. Stone. "Diversity: Beyond the Golden Rule." *Training and Development* 48 (October 1994): 21-26.

Carnegie, S. "The Hidden Emotions of Tourism: Communication and Power in the Caribbean." Master's thesis, Texas A&M University, 1996.

Casey, M., V. Miller, and J. Johnson. "Survivors' Information-Seeking Following a Reduction in Force." *Communication Research* 24 (1997): 755-781.

Casmir, F. "Third Culture Building." In *Communication Yearbook 16,* edited by S. Deetz. Newbury Park, CA: Sage, 1993.

Catalyst, "Women of Color Making Strides," *Houston Chronicle,* July 17, 2002, B2.

Cawelti, J. *Apostles of the Self-Made Man.* Cambridge, MA: Harvard University Press, 1974.

Cervantes, R. "Occupational and Economic Stressors among Immigrant and United States–Born Hispanics." In *Hispanics in the Workplace,* edited by S. Knouse, P. Rosenfeld, and A. Culbertson. Newbury Park, CA: Sage, 1992.

Cesaria, R. "Organizational Communication Issues in Italian Multinational Corporations." *Management Communication Quarterly* 14 (2000): 161-172.

Chae, B., and M. S. Poole. "A Tale of Two Systems: Technology Acceptance of Mandated Technologies." Department of Management, Kansas State University, 2003. Unpublished manuscript.

Chapa, J. "Creating and Improving Linkages between the Tops and Bottoms." Paper presented at the "Organizational Innovation Conference," Humphrey Institute of Public Affairs, University of Minnesota, Minneapolis, September 1992.

Chen, L. "Connecting to the World Economy." *Management Communication Quarterly* 14 (2000): 152-160.

Cheney, G. "Democracy in the Workplace." *Journal of Applied Communication Research* 23 (1995): 167-200.

———. *Values at Work.* Ithaca, NY: Cornell University Press, 1999.

Cheney, G., L. Christensen, T. Zorn Jr., and S. Ganesh. *Organizational Communication in an Age of Globalization.* Prospect Heights, IL: Waveland Press, 2004.

Cheney, G., and G. Frenette. "Persuasion and Organization." In *The Ethical Nexus,* edited by C. Conrad. Norwood, NJ: Ablex, 1993.

Chesboro, J. W. "Communication Technologies as Cognitive Systems." In *Toward the 21st Century: The Future of Speech Communication,* edited by J. Wood and R. B. Gregg. Cresskill, NJ: Hampton, 2000.

Child, J. *Management in China during the*

Age of Reform. Cambridge, UK: Cambridge University Press.

———. "Managerial and Organizational Factors Associated with Company Performance." *Journal of Management Studies* 11 (1974): 13–27.

Chiles, A. M., and T. Zorn. "Empowerment in Organizations: Employees' Perceptions of the Influences on Empowerment." *Journal of Applied Communication Research* 23 (1995): 1–25.

Ching, C.C. "The One-Child Family in China," *Studies in Family Planning* 13 (1982): 208–212.

Christiansen, A., and J. Hanson. "Comedy as Cure for Tragedy." *Quarterly Journal of Speech* 82 (1996): 157–170.

Chua, A. "Power to the Privileged." *New York Times on the Web,* January 7, 2003, http://www.nytimes.com/.

Clair, R. P. "The Bureaucratization, Commodification, and Privatization of Sexual Harassment through Institutional Discourse." *Management Communication Quarterly* 7 (1993): 128–157.

———. "The Political Nature of the Colloquialism, 'A Real Job.'" *Communication Monographs* 63 (1996): 249–267.

*———. "The Use of Framing Devices to Sequester Organizational Narratives." *Communication Monographs* 60 (1993): 113–136.

———. "Ways of Seeing." *Communication Monographs* 66 (1999): 374–381.

Clair, R. P., and K. Thompson. "Pay Discrimination as a Discursive and Material Practice." *Journal of Applied Communication Research* 24 (1996): 1–20.

Clark, T., and D. Greatbach. "Management Fashion as Image-Spectacle." *Management Communication Quarterly* 17 (2004): 396–424.

*Clegg, S. *Frameworks of Power.* Newbury Park, CA: Sage, 1989.

*———. *Modern Organizations.* Newbury Park, CA: Sage, 1990.

*———. *Power, Rule, and Domination.* London: Routledge and Kegan Paul, 1975.

*———. "Power, Theorizing, and Nihilism." *Theory and Society* 3 (1976): 65–87.

*Cohen, M., and J. March. *Leadership and Ambiguity.* 2nd ed. Boston: Harvard Business School Press, 1974.

*Cohen, M., J. March, and J. Olson. "A Garbage-Can Model of Organizational Choice." *Administrative Science Quarterly* 17 (1972): 1–25.

Cohen, S. *Failed Crusade.* New York: Norton, 2000.

Collins, P. H. "Comment on Hekman's 'Truth and Method.'" *Signs* 22 (1997): 375–381.

Collinson, D. *Managing the Shop Floor.* New York: DeGruyter, 1992.

Comer, D. "Organizational Newcomers' Acquisition of Information from Peers." *Management Communication Quarterly* 5 (1991): 64–89.

Connelly, J. "Youthful Attitudes, Sobering Realities." *New York Times on the Web,* October 28, 2003, p. 3, http://www.nytimes.com/.

Conrad, C. "The Ethical Nexus." In *The Ethical Nexus,* edited by C. Conrad. Norwood, NJ: Ablex, 1993.

———. "Review of *A Passion for Excellence.*" *Administrative Science Quarterly* 30 (1985): 426–429.

———. "Setting the Stage," *Management Communication Quarterly* 17 (2003): 5–19.

———. "Stemming the Tide," *Organization* 10 (2003): 549–560.

———. "Was Pogo Right? Communication, Power, and Resistance." In *Communication Research in the 21st Century,* edited by J. Wood and R. Gregg. Cresskill, NJ: Hampton Press, 1995.

Conrad, C., and H. McIntush. "Communication, Structure, and Health Care Policymaking." In *Handbook of Health Communication,* edited by A. Dorsey, K. Miller, R. Parrott, and T. Thompson. Hillsdale, NJ: Lawrence Erlbaum, 2003.

Conrad, C., and B. Taylor. "The Contexts of Sexual Harassment: Power, Silences, and Academe." In *Conceptualizing Sexual Harassment as Discursive Practice,* edited by S. Bingham. Westport, CT: Praeger, 1994.

Coolidge, S. D. "Boomers, Gen-Xers Clash." ABC News, September 1, 1999, http://www.abcnews.go.com/sections/business.

Coopersmith, J. "Facsimile's False Starts." *IEEE Spectrum,* February 1993, pp. 46–49.

Cooren, F., and J. Taylor. "Organization as an Effect of Mediation: Redefining the Link between Organization and Communication." *Communication Theory* 7 (1997): 219–260.

Cornyn, J. "Pragmatic Reasons for the Guest-Worker Proposal." *Houston Chronicle,* January 8, 2004, A29.

"Corporate Women." *Business Week,* June 8, 1992.

"Country-of-Origin Labels Can Wait, Congress Says," *Houston Chronicle,* January 23, 2004, G10.

Courtright, J., G. Fairhurst, and L. E. Rogers. "Interaction Patterns in Organic and Mechanistic Systems." *Academy of Management Journal* 32 (1989): 773–802.

Cowell, A. "Europeans Plan to Press for Tariffs against U.S." *New York Times on the Web.* December 6, 2003, http://www.nytimes .com/.

Cox, T., S. Lobel, and P. McLeod. "Effects of Ethnic Cultural Differences on Cooperative and Competitive Behavior on a Group Task." *Academy of Management Journal* 34 (1991): 827–847.

Crable, R., and S. Vibbert. "Mobil's Epideictic Advocacy." *Communication Monographs* 50 (1983): 380–396.

"Critics of Outsourcing Hope to Start Movement," *Houston Chronicle,* January 20, 2004, B4.

Cropsey, J. *Polity and Economy.* South Bend, IN: St. Augustine's Press, 2001.

Crow, K. "Staying Focused on Diversity Goals." *New York Times on the Web,* October 28, 2003, http:// www.nytimes.com/.

Crozier, M. *The Bureaucratic Phenomenon.* Chicago: University of Chicago Press, 1964.

Cupach, W., and S. Metts. *Facework.* Newbury Park, CA: Sage, 1994.

*Czarniawska-Joerges, B. *Exploring Complex Organizations.* Newbury Park, CA: Sage, 1992.

"Dad Wins Legal Fight for Time Off." *Houston Chronicle,* February 5, 1999,A19.

Daft, R. *Organization Theory and Design.* 3rd ed. St. Paul, MN: West, 1989.

Dalton, R., K. Daily, C. Certo, and R. Roengpitya. "The Relationship between Stock Options and Organizational Performance." Paper presented at the Academy of Management Convention, Denver, CO, August 2002.

Dana, L. P. "Small Business as a Supplement in the People's Republic of China (PRC)." *Journal of Small Business Management* 37 (1999): 76–81.

*Dandeker, C. *Surveillance, Power, and Modernity.* New York: St. Martin's Press, 1984.

Davis, K. "Management Communication and the Grapevine." *Harvard Business Review* 31 (September–October 1953): 43–49.

Deal, T., and A. Kennedy. *Corporate Cultures.* Reading, MA: Addison-Wesley, 1982.

DeBrosse, J. "The Y's Have It." *Houston Chronicle,* February 17, 1998.

*de Certeau, M. *The Practice of Everyday Life.* Berkeley: University of California Press, 1984.

Deephouse, D. "Does Isomorphism Legitimate?" *Academy of Management Journal* 39 (1996): 1024–1039.

*Deetz, S. "Critical Theories of Organizational Communication." In *The New Handbook of Organizational Communication,* ed-ited by F. Jablin and L. Putnam. Thousand Oaks, CA: Sage, 2000.

*———. *Democracy in the Age of Corporate Colonization.* Albany: State University of New York Press, 1992.

———. "Representation of Interests and the New Communication Technologies: Issues in Democracy and Policy." In *Communica-tion and the Culture of Technology,* edited by M. Medhurst, A. Gonzales, and T. R. Pe-terson. Pullman: Washington State Univer-sity Press, 1990.

———. *Transforming Communication, Trans-forming Business.* Cresskill, NJ: Hampton Press, 1995.

———. "Transforming Communication, Trans-forming Business." *International Journal of Value-Based Management* (1995): 1–18.

DeHaven, J. "Aggressive Women Get Help." *Houston Chronicle,* September 22, 2002, D5.

DePalma, A. "It Takes More than a Visa to Do Business in Mexico." *New York Times,* June 26, 1994.

Derrida, J. *Speech and Phenomenon.* Evans-ton, IL: Northwestern University Press, 1976.

*DeSanctis, G., and B. Gallupe. "A Foundation for the Study of Group Decision Support Systems." *Management Science* 33 (1987): 589–609.

Deutsch, M. *The Resolution of Conflict.* New Haven, CT: Yale University Press, 1973.

Deutsch, M., and R. Krauss. "Studies in Inter-personal Bargaining." *Journal of Conflict Resolution* 61 (1962): 52–76.

Dickens, F., and J. Dickens. *The Black Man-ager.* New York: AMACOM, 1991.

Diosonopolous, G., and R. Crable. "Defini-tional Hegemony as a Public Relations Strat-egy." *Central States Speech Journal* 39 (1988): 134–145.

Diosonopolous, G., and S. Goldzwig. "The Atomic Power Industry and the NEW Woman." In *Rhetorical and Critical Ap-proaches to Public Relations,* edited by E. Toth and R. Heath. Hillsdale, NJ: Lawrence Erlbaum, 1992.

Dovidio, J., S. Gaertrer, P. Anastasio, and R. Sa-nitioso. "Cognitive and Motivational Bases of Bias." In *Hispanics in the Workplace,* ed-ited by P. Knouse, P. Rosenfeld, and A. Cul-bertson. Newbury Park, CA: Sage, 1992.

Downs, A. *Corporate Executions.* New York: AMACOM, 1995.

Downs, C., and C. Conrad. "A Critical Incident Study of Effective Subordinancy." *Journal of Business Communication* 19 (1982): 27–38.

Drohan, M., and A. Freeman. "English Rules."

Annals of the American Academy of Political and Social Science 570 (2000): 428-434.

Drzewiecka, J., and K. Wong (Lau). "The Dynamic Construction of White Ethnicity in the Context of Trans-national Cultural Formations." In *Whiteness: The Communication of Social Identity,* edited by T. Nakayama and J. Martin. Thousand Oaks, CA: Sage, 1999.

Duncan, R. B. "Characteristics of Perceived Environments and Perceived Environmental Uncertainty." *Administrative Science Quarterly* 17 (1972): 313-327.

Dziech, B. W. *Sexual Harassment in Higher Education.* New York: Garland, 1998.

Dziech, B. W., and L. Weiner. *The Lecherous Professor.* 2nd ed. Urbana: University of Illinois Press, 1990.

Eadie, W., and J. Wood, eds. *Journal of Applied Communication Research* 20 (1992): 349-436.

Edley, P. "Discursive Essentializing in a Woman-Owned Business." *Management Communication Quarterly* 14 (2000): 271-306.

Edwards, A., and C. Polite. *Children of the Dream: The Psychology of Black Success.* New York: Doubleday, 1992.

Edwards, R. "Sensitivity to Feedback and the Development of Self." *Communication Quarterly* 38 (1990): 101-111.

*Edwards, R. *Contested Terrain.* New York: Basic Books, 1978.

Egan, T. "Amid Dying Towns of Rural Plains, One Makes a Stand." *New York Times on the Web,* December 1, 2003, http://www.nytimes.com/.

Eichenwald, K. "In String of Corporate Troubles, Critics Focus on Boards' Failings." *New York Times on the Web,* September 21, 2003, http://www.nytimes.com/.

———. "Texaco Executives, on Tape, Discussed Impeding a Bias Suit." *New York Times on the Web,* November 4, 1996, http://www.nytimes.com/.

———. "Texaco Reeling from Racial Scandal." *Houston Chronicle,* November 5, 1996, C1.

Eisenberg, E. "Ambiguity as Strategy in Organizational Communication." *Communication Monographs* 51 (1984): 227-242.

Eisenberg, E., and H. L. Goodall Jr. *Organizational Communication: Balancing Creativity and Constraint.* Boston: Bedford/St. Martin's Press, 2001.

Eisenberg, E., P. Monge, and K. Miller. "Involvement in Communication Networks as a Predictor of Organizational Commitment." *Human Communication Research* 10 (1983): 179-201.

Eisenberg, E., and S. Phillips. "Miscommunication in Organizations." In *"Miscommunication" and Problematic Talk,* edited by N. Coupland, H. Giles, and J. Wieman. Newbury Park, CA: Sage, 1991.

Eisenberg, E., and P. Riley. "Organizational Culture." In *The New Handbook of Organizational Communication,* edited by F. Jablin and L. Putnam. Thousand Oaks, CA: Sage, 2000.

Elliott, J. "High Court Rulings Favor Business, Group Says." *Houston Chronicle,* October 31, 2003, A30.

Ellis, B. "The Effects of Uncertainty and Source Credibility on Attitude about Organizational Change." *Management Communication Quarterly* 6 (1992): 34-57.

Elsbach, K., and R. Sutton. "Acquiring Organizational Legitimacy through Illegitimate Actions." *Administrative Science Quarterly* 35 (1992): 699-738.

Emerson, R. M. "Power-Dependence Relations." *American Sociological Review* 27 (1962): 31-41.

Emmett, R. "Vnet or Gripenet." *Datamation* 27 (1981): 48-58.

Engardio, P. "Corporate America's Silent Partner: India." *Business Week Online,* December 15, 2003, http:// www.businessweek.com/.

Essed, P. *Everyday Racism.* Translated by C. Jaffe. Claremont, CA: Hunter House, 1990.

———. *Understanding Everyday Racism.* Newbury Park, CA: Sage, 1991.

"Executive Pay Remains Tops." ABC News, August 30, 1999, abcnews.go.com/sections/business.

"Executive's Concern Led to Investigation of Funds." *Houston Chronicle,* December 10, 2003, B3.

Eyer, D. E. *Mother-Infant Bonding: A Scientific Fiction.* New Haven, CT: Yale University Press, 1992.

Ezzamel, M., and H. Willmott. "Accounting for Teamwork: A Critical Study of Group-Based Systems of Organizational Control." *Administrative Science Quarterly* 43 (1998): 358-396.

*Fairhurst, G. "Dialectical Tensions in Leadership Research." In *The New Handbook of Organizational Communication,* edited by F. Jablin and L. Putnam. Thousand Oaks, CA: Sage, 2000.

Fairhurst, G., and R. Sarr. *The Art of Framing: Managing the Language of Leadership.* San Francisco: Jossey-Bass, 1996.

Falbe, C., and G. Yukl. "Consequences of Managers Using Single Influence Tactics and Combinations of Tactics." *Academy of Management Journal* 32 (1992): 638-652.

Faludi, S. *Backlash: The Undeclared War*

against American Women. New York: Crown, 1991.

Farrell, A. Y. "Like a Tarantula on a Banana Boat." In *Feminist Organizations,* edited by M. M. Ferree and P. Y. Martin. Philadelphia: Temple University Press, 1995.

Farrell, T. R., and G. T. Goodnight. "Accidental Rhetoric." *Communication Monographs* 48 (1981): 271–300.

Farris, G. "Groups and the Informal Organization." In *Groups at Work,* edited by R. Payne and C. Cooper. New York: Wiley, 1981.

*Felsteiner, W. L., R. L. Abel, and A. Sarat. "The Emergence and Transformation of Disputes." *Law and Society Review* 33 (1980–1981): 631–654.

"Female Executives Make What Men Do." *Houston Chronicle,* October 21, 2000.

"FERC Says Grid Fix Can't Wait for New [Energy] Bill." *Houston Chronicle,* January 8, 2004, B2.

Ferdman, B., and A. Cortes. "Culture and Identity among Hispanic Managers in an Anglo Business." In *Hispanics in the Workplace,* edited by S. Knouse, P. Rosenfeld, and A. Culbertson. Newbury Park, CA: Sage, 1992.

Ferguson, K. *The Feminist Case against Bureaucracy.* Philadelphia: Temple University Press, 1984.

Ferleger, L., and J. Mandle. Special Issue on Globalization. *Annals of the American Academy of Political and Social Science* 557 (July 2000).

Ferree, M. M., and P. Y. Martin, eds. *Feminist Organizations.* Philadelphia: Temple University Press, 1995.

"Financing." *Houston Chronicle,* May 23, 1999.

Fine, M., and P. Buzzanell. "Walking the High Wire." In *Rethinking Organizational and Managerial Communication from Feminist Perspectives,* edited by P. Buzzanell. Thousand Oaks, CA: Sage, 2000.

Fineman, S. "Emotion and Organizing." In *Handbook of Organization Studies,* edited by S. Clegg, C. Hardy, and W. Nord. Thousand Oaks, CA: Sage, 1999.

———. "Organizations as Emotional Arenas." In *Emotion in Organizations,* edited by S. Fineman. London: Sage, 1993.

Finholt, T., and L. Sproull. "Electronic Groups at Work." *Organization Science* 1 (1990): 41–64.

Fiore, F. "New Mothers Now Return to Work Sooner, Study Says." *Houston Chronicle,* November 27, 1997.

Fisher, A. "When Will Women Get to the Top?" *Fortune,* September 21, 1992, 44–56.

Fisher, C. "On the Dubious Wisdom of Expecting Job Satisfaction to Correlate with Performance." *Academy of Management Review* 5 (1980): 607–612.

Fisher, I. "As Poland Endures Hard Times, Capitalism Comes under Attack." *New York Times on the Web,* June 12, 2003, http://www.nytimes.com/.

Fisher, M. "What's the Proper Etiquette for a Scarlet E-Mail?" *Houston Chronicle,* June 1, 1999.

Fisher, R., and W. Ury. *Getting to Yes.* Boston: Houghton Mifflin, 1981.

Fisher, W. "Narration as a Human Communication Paradigm." *Communication Monographs* 51 (1984): 1–22.

Fishman, J. "The New Linguistic Order." *Foreign Policy* 113 (Winter 1998–1999): 116–142.

Flam, H. "Fear, Loyalty, and Greedy Organizations." In *Emotion in Organizations,* edited by S. Fineman. London: Sage, 1993.

*Fleishman, E., and associates, eds. *Studies in Personnel and Industrial Psychology.* 1st ed., 1961. Rev. ed., Homewood, IL: Dorsey, 1967.

*Fligstein, N. *The Architecture of Markets.* Princeton, NJ: Princeton University Press, 2001.

*———. *The Transformation of Corporate Control,* Cambridge, MA: Harvard University Press, 1990.

Folger, J., M. S. Poole, and R. Stutman. *Working through Conflict.* 5th ed. New York: Longman, 2004.

"Ford, Union to Open 30 Child-Care and Family-Service Centers for Workers." *Houston Chronicle,* November 22, 2000.

Foreman, C. "The Reality of Workplace Democracy: A Case Study of One Company's Employee Involvement Process." Paper presented at the International Communication Association Convention, Chicago, May 1996.

*Forester, J. *Planning in the Face of Power.* Berkeley: University of California Press, 1989.

Foss, S., and C. Griffin. "Beyond Persuasion." *Quarterly Journal of Speech* 62 (1995): 2–18.

*Foucault, M. *Discipline and Punish: The Birth of the Prison.* Translated by A. Sheridan. 1977. New York: Vintage, 1990.

*———. *The History of Sexuality.* Translated by R. Hurley. Vol. 1. 1978. New York: Vintage, 1990.

*———. *Power/Knowledge.* Translated by C. Gordon. New York: Pantheon, 1980.

Fox, L. *Enron: The Rise and Fall.* New York: Wiley, 2003.

Fox, V. "At a Turning Point in Closing the Rich-Poor Gap." *Houston Chronicle,* March 21, 2002, A37.

Frank, R., and P. Cook. *The Winner Take All Society.* Reading, MA: Addison-Wesley, 1998.

Franken, S. "Corporations' Quest to Create a Happy Workplace." *Houston Chronicle,* October 15, 2000, D3.

*Franz, C., and K. G. Jin. "The Structure of Group Conflict in a Collaborative Work Group during Information Systems Development." *Journal of Applied Communication Research* 23 (1995): 108-127.

Freeman, J. "The Tyranny of Structurelessness." In *Women in Politics,* edited by J. S. Jaquette. New York: Wiley, 1974.

Freeman, R. *Strategic Management: A Stakeholder Approach.* Boston: Pitman, 1984.

Freeman, R., and L. Katz. "Rising Wage Inequality." In *Working under Different Rules.* New York: Russell Sage Foundation, 1994.

Freeman, R. E., and J. Liedtka. "Corporate Social Responsibility: A Critical Approach." *Business Horizons,* July–August 1991, pp. 89–96.

Friedman, M. *Capitalism and Freedom.* Chicago: University of Chicago Press, 1962.

———. "The Social Responsibility of Business Is to Increase Profits." *New York Times Magazine,* September 13, 1970, pp. 122-126.

Friedman, M., and R. Friedman. *Free to Choose.* San Diego, CA: Harcourt Brace, 1980.

Friedman, T. "Globalization Movement Alive and Well." *Houston Chronicle,* September 22, 2002, C3.

———. *The Lexus and the Olive Tree.* New York: Farrar, Straus and Giroux, 1999.

———. "You've Got Mail—From the Philippines." *Houston Chronicle,* September 30, 2000.

Frooman, J. "Stakeholder Influence Strategies." *Academy of Management Review* 24 (1999): 191-205.

*Frost, P. "Power, Politics, and Influence." In *Handbook of Organizational Communication,* edited by F. Jablin, L. Putnam, K. Roberts, and L. Porter. Newbury Park, CA: Sage, 1987.

Frost, P., L. Moore, M. R. Louis, C. Lundberg, and J. Martin, eds. *Reframing Organizational Culture.* Newbury Park, CA: Sage, 1991.

Fukuyama, F. "The End of History?" *National Interest* 481 (1989): 117-142.

Fulk, J. "Social Construction of Communication Technology." *Academy of Management Journal* 36 (1993): 921-950.

*Fulk, J., and L. Collins-Jarvis. "Wired Meetings: Technological Mediation of Organizational Gatherings." In *The New Handbook of Organizational Communication,* edited by F. Jablin and L. Putnam. Thousand Oaks, CA: Sage, 2000.

*Fulk, J., and G. DeSanctis. "Articulation of Communication Technology and Organizational Form." In *Shaping Organization Form: Communication, Connection, and Community,* edited by G. DeSanctis and J. Fulk. Newbury Park, CA: Sage, 1999.

Fulk, J., and S. Mani. "Distortion of Communication in Hierarchical Relationships." In *Communication Yearbook 9,* edited by M. McLaughlin. Newbury Park, CA: Sage, 1986.

Fulk, J., C. Steinfield, J. Schmitz, and J. G. Power. "A Social Information Processing Model of Media Use in Organizations." *Communication Research* 14 (1987): 529-552.

Fusaro, P., and R. Miller. *What Went Wrong at Enron.* New York: Wiley, 2002.

Galbraith, J. "Organizational Design." In *Handbook of Organizational Behavior,* edited by J. Lorsch. Englewood Cliffs, NJ: Prentice Hall, 1987.

Galen, M., and A. T. Palmer. "White, Male, and Worried." *Business Week,* January 31, 1994, pp. 50–55.

Gallupe, B., L. Bastianutti, and W. H. Cooper. "Unblocking Brainstorms." *Journal of Applied Psychology* 76 (1991): 137-142.

Gannon, M. *Understanding Global Cultures.* 2nd ed. Thousand Oaks, CA: Sage, 2001.

Gardner, W., and D. Cleavenger. "The Impression Management Strategies Associated with Transformational Leadership at the World-Class Level." *Management Communication Quarterly* 12 (1998): 3–41.

Garko, M. "Persuading Subordinates Who Communicate in Attractive and Unattractive Styles." *Management Communication Quarterly* 5 (1992): 289-315.

Garson, B. *The Electronic Sweatshop: How Computers Are Transforming the Office of the Future into the Factory of the Past.* New York: Penguin, 1988.

George, C. *The History of Management Thought.* Englewood Cliffs, NJ: Prentice Hall, 1972.

"Get Independents to Chair Boards of Funds, SEC Says." *Houston Chronicle,* January 15, 2004, B4.

Gibson, M., and M. Papa. "The Mud, the Blood, and the Beer Guys." *Journal of Applied Communication Research* 28 (2000): 72-91.

Gibson, M., and N. Schullery. "Shifting Meanings in a Blue-Collar Worker Philanthropy Program." *Management Communication Quarterly* 14 (2000): 189-236.

*Giddens, A. *Beyond Left and Right.* Cambridge, UK: Polity Press, 1994.

*———. *The Consequences of Modernity.* Cambridge, UK: Polity Press, 1990.

*———. *Modernity and Self Identity.* Palo Alto, CA: Stanford University Press, 1991.

*Gioia, D., and H. Sims. "Cognition-Behavior Connections: Attribution and Verbal Behavior in Leader-Subordinate Interactions." *Organizational Behavior and Human Performance* 37 (1986): 197–229.

Global Healthcare Exchange, http://www.ghx .com.

Goffman, E. "On Face Work." *Psychiatry* 18 (1955): 213–231.

———. *The Presentation of Self in Everyday Life.* New York: Doubleday, 1959.

*Golding, D. "Management Rituals." In *Understanding Management,* edited by S. Linstead, R. G. Small, and P. Jeffcutt. London: Sage, 1996.

Gonzalez, A., J. Willis, and C. Young. "Cultural Diversity and Organizations." In *Organizational Communication,* edited by P. Y. Byers. Boston: Allyn and Bacon, 1997.

Gordon, D. *Fat and Mean.* Ithaca, NY: Cornell University Press, 1996.

Gore, D. "Adam Smith's Rhetorical Sympathy." Master's thesis, Texas A&M University, 2001.

Gould, J. *Deadly Deceit: Low Level Radiation, High Level Coverup.* New York: Four Walls Eight Windows, 1990.

Gould, J., and E. Sternglass. *The Enemy Within: The High Cost of Living near Nuclear Power.* New York: Four Walls Eight Windows, 1996.

Gouran, D., and R. Hirokawa. "Functional Theory and Communication in Decision-Making and Problem-Solving Groups: An Expanded Perspective." In *Communication and Group Decision Making,* edited by R. Hirokawa and M. S. Poole. 2nd ed. Thousand Oaks, CA: Sage, 1996.

*Gowler, D., and K. Legge. "The Meaning of Management and the Management of Meaning." In *Understanding Management,* edited by S. Linstead, R. G. Small, and P. Jeffcutt. London: Sage, 1996.

Grace, D., and S. Cohen. *Business Ethics.* Melbourne, Australia: Oxford, 1995.

Granovetter, M. *Getting a Job.* Cambridge, MA: Harvard University Press, 1974.

"The Great Catfish War." *New York Times on the Web,* July 22, 2003, http://www .nytimes.com/.

*Gregory, K. "Native-View Paradigms." *Administrative Science Quarterly* 28 (1983): 360–372.

Grimes, D. "Putting Our Own House in Order: Whiteness, Change, and Organization Studies." *Journal of Organizational Change Management* 14 (2001): 132–149.

*Guetzkow, H., and J. Gyr. "An Analysis of Conflict in Decision-Making Groups." *Human Relations* 7 (1954): 367–381.

Guzley, R. "Organizational Climate and Communication Climate." *Management Communication Quarterly* 5 (1992): 379–402.

*Habermas, J. *Communication and the Evolution of Society.* London: Heinemann Educational Books, 1979.

*———. *Knowledge and Human Interests.* London: Heinemann Educational Books, 1972.

Hackman, J. R. *Groups That Work (And Those That Don't).* San Francisco: Jossey-Bass, 1990.

Hackman, M. Z., and C. E. Johnson. *Leadership: A Communication Perspective.* Prospect Heights, IL: Waveland Press, 1991.

Hafen, S. "Cultural Diversity Training." In *Organization—Communication: Emerging Perspectives,* vol. 7, edited by G. Cheney and G. Barnett. Cresskill, NJ: Hampton Press, 2003.

Hall, B., and B. Jones. "Agenda Denial and Issue Containment in the Regulation of Financial Securities." In *Cultural Strategies of Agenda Denial: Avoidance, Attack, and Redefinition,* edited by R. W. Cobb and M. H. Ross. Lawrence: University Press of Kansas, 1997.

Hambrick, D. "Top Management Groups." In *Research in Organizational Behavior,* edited by B. Staw and L. Cummings. Vol. 15. Greenwich, CT: JAI Press, 1994.

Hambrick, D., and P. Mason. "Upper Echelons." *Academy of Management Review* 9 (1984): 193–206.

Hananel, S. "Whistle-Blowers Lack Protection." *Houston Chronicle,* September 2, 2002, A19.

Handy, C. "Trust in Virtual Organizations." *Harvard Business Review* 73 (1995): 40–51.

Hannerz, U. *Cultural Complexity.* New York: Columbia University Press, 1992.

Hardin, "The Tragedy of the Commons." *Science,* December 13, 1968, pp. 1243–1248.

Harper, N., and L. Askling. "Group Communication and Quality of Task Solution in a Media Production Organization." *Communication Monographs* 47 (1980): 77–100.

Harriman, A. *Women—Men—Management.* Westport, CT: Greenwood Press, 1996.

Harris, P., and R. Moran. *Managing Cultural Differences.* 3rd ed. Houston: Gulf, 1991.

Harrison, T. "Communication and Interdependence in Democratic Organizations." *Communication Yearbook 17,* edited by S. Deetz. Newbury Park, CA: Sage, 1995.

———. "Communication and Participative Decision-Making." *Personnel Psychology* 38 (1985): 93–116.

Hassard, J., J. Sheehan, and J. Morris. "Enterprise Reform in Post-Deng China," *International Studies of Management and Organization* 29 (1999): 107-136.

Hatch, M. *Organization Theory.* Oxford: Oxford University Press, 1997.

*Hegde, R. S. "A View from Elsewhere." *Communication Theory* 8 (1998): 271-297.

*Held, D. *Introduction to Critical Theory.* London: Hutchinson, 1980.

Helgessen, S. *The Female Advantage: Women's Ways of Leadership.* New York: Doubleday, 1990.

Hellman, P. "Her Push for Prevention Keeps Kids out of ER." *Parade,* April 19, 1995, 8-10.

Helm, M. "Former Director Defends FBI." *Houston Chronicle,* October 9, 2002, A7.

Herbert, B. "The Halliburton Shuffle." *New York Times on the Web,* January 30, 2004, http:// www.nytimes.com/.

Heston, A., and N. Weiner. "Dimensions of Globalization." *Annals of the American Academy of Political and Social Science* 570 (2000): 8-18.

"'Hijab' Debate Isn't Just a French Affair." *Houston Chronicle,* January 11, 2004, C4.

Hill, E. *The Intelligence Community's Knowledge of the September 11 Hijackers Prior to September 11, 2001.* Washington: Government Printing Office, September 2002.

Hilton, C. "International Business Communication." *Journal of Business Communication* 29 (1992): 253-265.

Hine, D. C. "The Future of Black Women in the Academy." In *Black Women in the Academy: Promises and Perils,* edited by L. Benjamin. Gainesville: University Press of Florida, 1997.

Hirokawa, R., and A. Miyahara. "A Comparison of Influence Strategies Used by Managers in American and Japanese Organizations." *Communication Quarterly* 34 (1986): 250-265.

Hirokawa, R., and M. S. Poole, eds. *Communication and Group Decision Making.* 2nd ed. Thousand Oaks, CA: Sage, 1996.

*Hirokawa, R., and A. Salazar. "Task-Group Communication and Decision-Making Performance." In *Handbook of Group Communication Theory and Research,* edited by L. Frey, D. Gouran, and M. S. Poole. Newbury Park, CA: Sage, 1999.

Hirschman, A. *Exit, Voice, and Loyalty.* Cambridge, MA: Harvard University Press, 1970.

———. *The Rhetoric of Reaction.* Cambridge, MA: Belknap Press, 1991.

Hitt, M., B. W. Keats, G. H. Harback, and R. D. Nixon. "Rightsizing: Building and Maintaining Strategic Leadership and Long-Term Competitiveness. *Organizational Dynamics* 23 (1994): 18-32.

Hoagland, J. "Can't Leave Backyard Politics out of Globalization." *Houston Chronicle,* October 22, 2000.

Hobbs, J. "Treachery by Any Other Name." *Management Communication Quarterly* 8 (1995): 323-346.

Hochschild, A. *The Managed Heart.* Berkeley: University of California Press, 1983.

———. *The Time Bind.* New York: Metropolitan Books, 1997.

Hochschild, A., and A. Machung. *The Second Shift.* New York: Avon Books, 1997.

Hollihan, T., and P. Riley. "The Rhetorical Power of a Compelling Story." *Communication Quarterly* 35 (1987): 11-20.

Holmes, M. "Phase Structure in Negotiation." In *Communication and Negotiation,* edited by L. Putnam and M. Roloff. Newbury Park, CA: Sage, 1993.

Holt, J. "Women's Status Improving, but Slowly." *Houston Chronicle,* November 16, 2000.

Homans, G. *The Human Group.* New York: Harcourt Brace, 1950.

Hong, J., and Y. Engstrom. "Changing Principles of Communication between Chinese Managers and Workers." *Management Communication Quarterly* 17 (2004): 553-587.

Hosmer, L. "The Institutionalization of Unethical Behavior." *Journal of Business Ethics* 6 (1987): 439-447.

Howe, N., and W. Strauss. *Millennials Go to College.* Washington, DC: American Association of Collegiate Registrars and Admissions Officers, 2003.

———. *Millennials Rising: The Next Great Generation.* New York: Vintage, 2000.

*Howes, D., ed. *Cross-Cultural Consumption.* London: Routledge, 1996.

Hulbert, M. "The Bad News on Certification Was Old News to the Market." *New York Times on the Web,* March 2, 2003, http:// www.nytimes.com/.

Huntington, S. "The Clash of Civilizations?" *Annals of the American Academy of Political and Social Science* 570 (2000): 3-22.

*Huspek, M. "The Language of Powerlessness." Ph.D. diss., University of Washington, 1987.

"The Hypocrisy of Farm Subsidies." *New York Times on the Web,* December 1, 2002, http://www.nytimes.com/.

Ibarra, H. "Personal Networks of Women and Minorities in Management." *Academy of Management Review* 18 (1993): 56-87.

———. "Race, Opportunity, and Diversity of Social Circles in Managerial Settings." *Academy of Management Journal* 38 (1995): 673-703.

Infante, D., and W. Gordon. "How Employees See the Boss." *Western Journal of Speech Communication* 55 (1991): 294–304.

Irwin, D. *Against the Tide.* Princeton, NJ: Princeton University Press, 1996.

Irwin, H. *Communicating with Asia.* Sydney, Australia: University of New South Wales Press, 1997.

Ivanovich, D. "$192.5 Million Settles Coca-Cola Race Suit." *Houston Chronicle,* November 17, 2000.

———. "Halliburton Ads Defend Iraqi Work." *Houston Chronicle,* February 4, 2004, 2C.

———. "Halliburton Gives Refund to Pentagon." *Houston Chronicle,* January 24, 2004, C1, C7.

*Jablin, F. "Communication Competence and Effectiveness." In *The New Handbook of Organizational Communication,* edited by F. Jablin and L. Putnam. Thousand Oaks, CA: Sage, 2000.

*———. "An Exploratory Study of Subordinates' Perceptions of Supervisory Politics." *Communication Quarterly* 29 (1981): 269–275.

*———. "Formal Organizational Structure." In *Handbook of Organizational Communication,* edited by F. Jablin, L. Putnam, K. Roberts, and L. Porter. Newbury Park, CA: Sage, 1987.

*———. "Organizational Entry, Assimilation, and Exit." In *The New Handbook of Organizational Communication,* edited by F. Jablin and L. Putnam. Newbury Park, CA: Sage, 2000.

———. "Superior-Subordinate Communication." In *Communication Yearbook 2,* edited by B. Ruben. New Brunswick, NJ: Transaction Books, 1979.

*———. "Task/Work Relationships." In *Handbook of Interpersonal Communication,* edited by M. Knapp and G. Miller. Beverly Hills, CA: Sage, 1985.

*Jablin, F., and M. Kramer. "Communication-Related Sense-Making and Adjustment during Job Transfers." *Management Communication Quarterly* 12 (1998): 155–182.

Jackall, R. "Moral Mazes: Bureaucracy and Managerial Work." *Harvard Business Review* 61 (September–October 1983): 99–123.

Jackson, M. "Business Bends to Include Generation X Workforce." *Bryan/College Station (TX) Eagle,* January 31, 1999.

Jamieson, D., and J. O'Mara. *Managing Workforce 2000.* San Francisco: Jossey-Bass, 1991.

Janis, I. "Sources of Error in Strategic Decision-Making." In *Organizational Strategy and Change,* edited by J. Pennings and associates. San Francisco: Jossey-Bass, 1985.

———. *Victims of Groupthink.* Boston: Houghton Mifflin, 1972.

Janis, I., and L. Mann. *Decision Making.* New York: Free Press, 1977.

Jarboe, S. "Procedures for Enhancing Group Decision Making." In *Communication and Group Decision Making,* edited by R. Hirokawa and M. S. Poole. 2nd ed. Thousand Oaks, CA: Sage, 1996.

*Jehensen, R. "Effectiveness, Expertise, and Excellence as Ideological Fictions." *Human Studies* 7 (1984): 3–21.

Johansen, R. *Teleconferencing and Beyond.* New York: McGraw-Hill, 1984.

Johnson, B. *Communication: The Process of Organizing.* Boston: Allyn and Bacon, 1977.

Johnson, K. "Many Companies Turn Workers into High-Tech Nomads." *Minneapolis Star-Tribune,* April 3, 1994.

"Just 10% of Senior Managers for Fortune 500 Are Women." *Houston Chronicle,* January 7, 2000.

Kahn, J., and R. Stevenson. "Treasury Official Is Said to Fault Steel Tariff Move." *New York Times on the Web,* March 16, 2002, http://www.nytimes.com/.

Kalleberg, A., and K. Leicht. "Gender and Organizational Performance." *Academy of Management Journal* 34 (1991): 155–163.

Kaplan, D. "Fighting for Workers' Rights." *Houston Chronicle,* January 15, 2004.

Kaplan, R. D. "The Coming Anarchy." *Annals of the American Academy of Political and Social Science* 570 (2000): 34–60.

Karsten, M. F. *Management and Gender.* Westport, CT: Quorum Books, 1994.

Kassing, J. "From the Look of Things." *Management Communication Quarterly* 14 (2001): 442–470.

Kassing, J., and T. Armstrong. "Someone's Going to Hear about This." *Management Communication Quarterly* 16 (2002): 39–65.

Katzenbach, J. R., and D. K. Smith. *The Wisdom of Teams.* New York: HarperCollins, 1993.

Kennedy, G. *Classical Rhetoric in Its Christian and Secular Traditions from Ancient to Modern Times.* Chapel Hill: University of North Carolina Press, 1980.

Kerr, J., and J. Slocum. "Managing Corporate Culture through Reward Systems." *Academy Management Executive* 1 (1987): 99–108.

Kerr, S. "On the Folly of Rewarding A While Hoping for B." *Academy of Management Journal* 19 (1975): 769–783.

Kersten, A. "Culture, Control, and the Labor Process." In *Communication Yearbook 16,* edited by S. Deetz. Newbury Park, CA: Sage, 1993.

Kets deVries, M., and K. Balazs. "The Downside of Downsizing." *Human Relations* 50 (1997): 11–50.

Kever, J. "Life in the Tired Lane." *Texas Magazine,* August 13, 2000, p. 8.

Keyton, J., and S. Rhodes. "Organizational Sexual Harassment." *Journal of Applied Communication Research* 27 (1999): 158–173.

Kidwell, R. E., Jr., and N. Bennett. "Employee Reactions to Electronic Control Systems." *Group and Organization Management* 19 (1994): 203–219.

*Kiesler, S., J. Siegel, and T. W. McGuire. "Social Psychological Aspects of Computer-Mediated Communication." *American Psychologist* 39 (1984): 1123–1134.

Kilborn, P. T. "For Many in Work Force, Glass Ceiling Still Exists." *New York Times,* March 16, 1995.

*Kim, K., H.-J. Park, and N. Suzuki. "Reward Allocations in the United States, Japan, and Korea." *Academy of Management Journal* 33 (1990): 188–198.

Kim, M., J. Hunter, A. Miyahara, A. Horvath, M. Bresnahan, and H. Yoon. "Individual- vs. Culture-Level Dimensions of Individualism and Collectivism." *Communication Monographs* 63 (1996): 29–49.

Kim, P. S., and G. Lewis. "Asian Americans in the Public Service." *Public Administration Review* 54 (1994): 285–290.

*Kim, Y. Y., and K. Miller. "The Effects of Attributions and Feedback Goals on the Generation of Supervisor Feedback Message Strategies." *Management Communication Quarterly* 4 (1990): 6–29.

Knouse, S. "The Mentoring Process for Hispanics." In *Hispanics in the Workplace,* edited by S. Knouse, P. Rosenfeld, and A. Culbertson. Newbury Park, CA: Sage, 1992.

"Knowledge Center: Security." *Computerworld,* July 14, 2003, pp. 30–40.

*Knuf, J. "'Ritual' in Organizational Culture Theory." In *Communication Yearbook 16,* edited by S. Deetz. Newbury Park, CA: Sage, 1993.

Kolb, D., and J. Bartunek, ed. *Hidden Conflict in Organizations.* Newbury Park, CA: Sage, 1991.

Korn/Ferry International. "The Decade of the Executive Woman." *Houston Chronicle,* February 19, 1996, B1.

Kostova, T., and S. Zaheer. "Organizational Legitimacy under Conditions of Complexity: The Case of the Multinational Enterprise." *Academy of Management Review* 24 (1999): 64–81.

*Kraiger, K., and J. Ford. "A Meta-Analysis of Ratee Race Effects in Performance Ratings." *Journal of Applied Psychology* 70 (1985): 56–65.

Kram, K. *Mentoring.* Chicago: Scott, Foresman, 1986.

*Kramer, M. "Communication after Job Transfers: Social Exchange Processes in Learning New Roles." *Human Communication Research* 20 (1993): 147–174.

*———. "A Longitudinal Study of Superior-Subordinate Communication during Job Transfers." *Human Communication Research* 22 (1995): 39–64.

*Kramer, M., R. R. Callister, and D. B. Turban. "Information-Receiving and Information-Giving during Job Transitions." *Western Journal of Communication* 39 (1995): 151–170.

Kramer, M., and V. Miller. "A Response to Criticisms of Organizational Socialization Research." *Communication Monographs* 66 (1999): 360–369.

Kreps, G., ed. *Sexual Harassment: Communication Implications.* Cresskill, NJ: Hampton Press, 1993.

Kristof, N. "America's Failed Frontier." *New York Times on the Web,* September 3, 2002, http:// www.nytimes.com/.

———. "Will China Blindside the West?" *New York Times on the Web,* December 3, 2002, http:// www.nytimes.com/.

Krugman, P. "Business As Usual." *New York Times on the Web,* October 22, 2002, http:// www.nytimes.com/.

———. "The Death of Horatio Alger." *Nation,* December 18, 2003, http://www.thenation.com/.

Kruml, S., and D. Geddes. "Exploring the Dimensions of Emotional Labor." *Management Communication Quarterly* 14 (2000): 8–49.

Kuhrana, R. *Searching for a Corporate Savior.* Princeton, NJ: Princeton University Press, 2002.

Kuitenbrouwer, P. "Female Executives Not So Different: Study." *Calgary Financial Post,* August 11, 2003, FP8.

*Kunda, G. *Engineering Culture.* Philadelphia: Temple University Press, 1992.

Kuttner, R. *Everything for Sale.* Chicago: University of Chicago Press, 1999.

Kwong, J. "Ideological Crisis among China's Youths: Values and Official Ideology." *British Journal of Sociology* 45 (1994): 247–264.

Labaton, S. "Defying Election-Year Tradition, S.E.C. Draws Up a Busy Agenda." *New York Times on the Web,* January 2, 2004, http:// www.nytimes.com/.

Lamude, K., T. Daniels, and K. White. "Managing the Boss." *Management Communication Quarterly* 1 (1987): 232–259.

Larkey, L., and C. Morrill. "Organizational Commitment as Symbolic Process." *West-

ern Journal of Communication 59 (1995): 193–213.

Larson, C. E., and F. M. J. LaFasto. *TeamWork: What Must Go Right/What Can Go Wrong.* Newbury Park, CA: Sage, 1989.

Lash, S. "Court Holds Educators Liable for Harassment." *Houston Chronicle,* September 7, 1999, C25.

Leary, T. *Interpersonal Diagnosis of Personality.* New York: Ronald, 1957.

Legg, N. A. "Other People's Kids: Decision-Making about Sexual Education." Master's thesis, Texas A&M University, 1992.

Leonhardt, D. "Globalization Hits a Political Speed Bump." *New York Times on the Web,* June 1, 2003, http:// www.nytimes.com/.

———. "Options Do Not Raise Performance, Study Finds." *New York Times on the Web,* August 11, 2002, http://www.nytimes.com/.

Lerach, W. S. Testimony before the Subcommittee on Telecommunications and Finance, House Committee on Commerce, Legislation on Securities Fraud Litigation (H.R. 10), January 19, 1995, 103rd Cong., 2nd sess.

Levere, J. L. "A Small Company, a Global Approach," *New York Times on the Web,* January 1, 2004, http:// www.nytimes.com/.

Levine, S. B. *Father Courage.* New York: Harcourt, 2000.

Levinthal, D., and J. March. "The Myopia of Learning." *Strategic Management Journal* 14 (1993): 95–112.

Levitt, A. *Take on the Street.* New York: Pantheon, 2002.

Liebeskind, J. P., A. L. Oliver, L. Zucker, and M. Brewer. "Social Networks, Learning, and Flexibility: Sourcing Scientific Knowledge in New Biotechnology Firms." *Organization Science* 7 (1996): 428–443.

Likert, R. *New Patterns of Management.* New York: McGraw-Hill, 1961.

*Lim, T., and J. W. Bowers. "Face-Work: Solidarity, Approbation, and Face." *Human Communication Research* 17 (1990): 415–450.

Lindblom, C. "The Science of Muddling Through." *Public Administration Review* 19 (1959): 412–421.

"Little Upward Help for Minority Females: Executive Women Say Mentors Needed." *Houston Chronicle,* July 14, 1999, B6

Locke, E. "The Ideas of Frederick Taylor." *Academy of Management Review* 7 (1982): 14–24.

———. "The Nature and Causes of Job Satisfaction." In *Handbook of Industrial and Organizational Psychology,* edited by M. Dunnette. Chicago: Rand-McNally, 1976.

Loewenberg, S. "Europe Gets Tougher on U.S. Companies." *New York Times on the Web,* April 20, 2003, http://www.nytimes.com/.

"The Lordstown Auto Workers." In *Life in Organizations,* edited by R. M. Kanter and B. Stein. New York: Basic Books, 1979.

Lott, C. "Redwood Records: Principles and Profit in Women's Music." In *Women Communicating,* edited by B. Bate and A. Taylor. Norwood, NJ: Ablex, 1988.

Louis, M. R. "Acculturation in the Workplace." In *Organizational Climate and Culture,* edited by B. Schneider. San Francisco: Jossey-Bass, 1990.

———. "Surprise and Sense-Making in Organizations." *Administrative Science Quarterly* 25 (1980): 226–251.

*Lucas, H. C. *The T-Form Organization: Using Technology to Design Organizations for the 21st Century.* San Francisco: Jossey-Bass, 1996.

Lukes, S. *Power: A Radical View.* London: Macmillan, 1974.

Madrick, J. "A Theory on Corporate Greed." *New York Times on the Web,* February 20, 2003, http:// www.nytimes.com/.

Madsen, T. K., E. Rasmussen, and P. Servais. "Differences and Similarities between Born Globals and Other Types of Exporters." *Advances in International Marketing* 10 (2000): 247–265.

Mahon, J. F., and R. A. McGowan. "Making Professional Accounting Accountable." In *Cultural Strategies of Agenda Denial: Avoidance, Attack, and Redefinition,* edited by R. W. Cobb and M. H. Ross. Lawrence: University Press of Kansas, 1997.

Mansnerus, L. "Why Women Are Leaving the Law." *Working Woman,* April 1993, pp. 21–24.

Manusov, V., and J. M. Billingsley. "Nonverbal Communication in Organizations." In *Organizational Communication: Theory and Behavior,* edited by P. Y. Byers. Boston: Allyn and Bacon, 1997.

March, J. "The Technology of Foolishness." In *Ambiguity and Choice in Organizations,* edited by J. March and J. Olson. Bergen, Norway: Universitetsforlaget, 1970.

*March, J., and G. Sevon. "Gossip, Information, and Decision Making." In *Advances in Information Processing in Organizations,* edited by L. Sproull and P. Larkey, vol. 1. Greenwich, CT: JAI Press, 1982.

*March, J., and H. Simon. "The Concept of Rationality." In *Human Behavior and International Politics,* edited by D. Singer. Chicago: Rand-McNally, 1965.

Marchand, R. *Creating the Corporate Soul: The Rise of Public Relations and Corporate Imagery in American Big Business.* Berkeley: University of California Press, 1998.

Marcus, A., and T. Goodman. "Victims and

Shareholders." *Academy of Management Journal* 42 (1998): 479–485.

Marin, G., and B. V. Marin. *Research with Hispanic Populations.* Newbury Park, CA: Sage, 1996.

Marmor, T. *The Politics of Medicare.* 2nd ed. New York: Aldyne de Gruyter, 2000.

Marrow, A., D. Bowers, and S. Seashore. *Management by Participation.* New York: Harper and Row, 1967.

Marshall, J. "Viewing Organizational Communication from a Feminist Perspective: A Critique and Some Offerings." In *Communication Yearbook 16,* edited by S. Deetz. Newbury Park, CA: Sage, 1993.

——. *Women Managers Moving On.* London: Routledge, 1995.

Marti, M. *China and the Legacy of Deng Xiaoping: From Communist Revolution to Capitalist Evolution.* Washington DC: Brassey's, 2002.

Martin, J. *Cultures in Organizations: Three Perspectives.* New York: Oxford University Press, 1992.

Martin, J., K. Knopoff, and C. Beckman. "An Alternative to Bureaucratic Impersonality and Emotional Labor: Bounded Emotionality at the Body Shop." *Administrative Science Quarterly* 43 (1998): 429–469.

Martin, J., and M. Powers. "Truth or Corporate Propaganda: The Value of a Good War Story." In *Organizational Symbolism,* edited by L. Pondy, P. Frost, G. Morgan, and T. D. Dandridge. Greenwich, CT: JAI Press, 1993.

Martin, L. *Pipelines of Progress.* Washington, DC: U.S. Department of Labor, August 1992.

Masuch, M., and P. LaPotin. "Beyond Garbage Cans." *Administrative Science Quarterly* 34 (1989): 38–68.

Mattson, M., R. P. Clair, P. A. C. Sanger, and A. D. Kunkel. "A Feminist Reframing of Stress." In *Rethinking Organizational and Managerial Communication from Feminist Perspectives,* edited by P. Buzzanell. Thousand Oaks, CA: Sage, 2000.

Maynard, M. "Diversity Programs Work, Where They Exist." *USA Today,* September 15, 1994.

Mayo, E. *Social Problems of an Industrial Civilization.* Boston: Graduate School of Business Administration, Harvard University, 1945.

McAllister, D. J. "Affect- and Cognition-Based Trust as Foundations for Interpersonal Cooperation in Organizations." *Academy of Management Journal* 38 (1995): 24–59.

McFarlin, D., and P. Sweeney. "Distributive and Procedural Justice as Predictors of Satisfaction with Personal and Organizational Outcomes." *Academy of Management Journal* 35 (1992): 626–637.

McGeehan, P. "Quick, What's the Boss Making?" *New York Times on the Web,* September 21, 2003, http:// www.nytimes.com/.

——. "Top Executives' Lucrative Deals Tie the Hands That Pay Them." *New York Times on the Web,* June 28, 2003, http://www.nytimes.com/.

McKinlay, A., and P. Taylor. "Power, Surveillance, and Resistance: Inside the Factory of the Future." In *The New Workplace and Trade Unionism,* edited by P. Ackers, C. Smith, and P. Smith. London: Routledge, 1996.

McLaughlin, M. *Conversation.* Beverly Hills, CA: Sage, 1984.

McMillan, J. "Legal Protection of Whistleblowers." In *Corruption and Reform,* edited by S. Prosser, R. Wear, and J. Nethercote. St. Lucia, Queensland: University of Queensland Press, 1990.

*McPhee, R. "Vertical Communication Chains: Toward an Integrated View." *Management Communication Quarterly* 1 (1988): 455–493.

McPhee, R., and S. Corman. "An Activity-Based Theory of Communication Networks in Organizations, Applied to a Local Church." *Communication Monographs* 62 (1995): 132–151.

*McPhee, R., and M. S. Poole. "Organizational Structure, Configurations, and Communication." In *The New Handbook of Organizational Communication,* edited by F. Jablin and L. Putnam. Thousand Oaks, CA: Sage, 2000.

Meindl, J. "Managing to Be Fair." *Administrative Science Quarterly* 34 (1989): 252–276.

Melymuka, K. "Going for Broke." *Computerworld,* March 26, 2003.

——. "Smarter by the Hour." *Computerworld,* June 23, 2003, pp. 43–44.

"Men Still Suspect If Priority Is Family." *Houston Chronicle,* April 9, 2000.

Menn, J. "ADM Fine Criticized as Too Low." *Houston Chronicle,* December 1, 1996.

Metter, E. *Cheerfully Childless.* New York: Browser Press, 2001.

*Meyer, A. "Mingling Decision-Making Metaphors." *Academy of Management Review* 9 (1984): 231–246.

Meyer, M. "Here's a 'Virtual' Model for America's Industrial Giants." *Newsweek,* August 13, 1993.

Meyerson, D. "Interpretations of Stress in Institutions." *Administrative Science Quarterly* 39 (1994): 628–653.

Miceli, M., and J. Near. *Blowing the Whistle: The Organizational and Legal Implications for Companies and Employees.* New York: Lexington Books, 1992.

Mikuni, A., and R. T. Murphy. "Would Reform

Ruin Japan?" *New York Times on the Web,* October 29, 2002, http://www.nytimes.com/.

Miller, K. *Organizational Communication.* Belmont, CA: Wadsworth, 1994.

Miller, L., L. Cooke, J. Tsang, and F. Morgan. "Should I Brag?" *Human Communication Research* 18 (1992): 364–399.

*Miller, V., and F. Jablin. "Information Seeking during Organizational Entry." *Academy of Management Review* 16 (1991): 92–120.

Mills, K. "Northwest on a Flier-Satisfaction Mission." *Houston Chronicle,* May 14, 2000.

Milne, J. "Mill Owner Says He'll Pay Workers." *Boston Globe,* December 15, 1995, B50.

Milwid, B. *Working with Men.* East Rutherford, NJ: Berkley, 1992.

Mincer, J. "Women Managers Will Hold Most Jobs." *Houston Chronicle,* June 17, 2003, B1.

*Mintzberg, H. *Power in and around Organizations.* Englewood Cliffs, NJ: Prentice Hall, 1983.

*——. *The Rise and Fall of Strategic Planning.* New York: Free Press, 1994.

*Mintzberg, H., and A. McHugh. "Strategy Formation in an Adhocracy." *Administrative Science Quarterly* 30 (1985): 160–197.

*Mintzberg, H., D. Raisinghani, and A. Theoret. "The Structure of 'Unstructured' Decision Processes." *Administrative Science Quarterly* 21 (1976): 246–275.

Mishel, L., J. Bernstein, and H. Bousley. *The State of Working America, 2002/2003.* Ithaca, NY: Cornell University Press, 2003.

Mocada, E. "Made in China: Educational Lesson for Mexico." *Houston Chronicle,* November 18, 2002, A23.

Mohamed, A. R. J., and J. Lloyd, eds. *The Nature and Context of Minority Discourse.* Oxford, UK: Oxford University Press, 1990.

*Mohrman, S. A., S. G. Cohen, and A. M. Mohrman. *Designing Team-Based Organizations: New Forms for Knowledge Work.* San Francisco: Jossey-Bass, 1995.

*Monge, P., and N. Contractor. "Emergent Communication Networks." In *The New Handbook of Organizational Communication,* edited by F. Jablin and L. Putnam. Thousand Oaks, CA: Sage, 2000.

——. *Theories of Communication Networks.* New York: Oxford, 2003.

Mongeau, P., and J. Blalock. "Student Evaluations of Instructor Immediacy and Sexually Harassing Behaviors: An Experimental Investigation." *Journal of Applied Communication Research* 22 (1994): 256–272.

Moore, G. "Structural Determinants of Men's and Women's Personal Networks." *American Sociological Review* 55 (1990): 726–735.

Morand, D. A. "The Role of Behavioral Formality and Informality in the Enactment of Bureaucratic versus Organic Organizations." *Academy of Management Review* 20 (1995): 831–872.

Moreno, J. "China Replaces Mexico as Land of Cheap Labor." *Houston Chronicle,* October 25, 2002, C1.

——. "Mexico Takes a Bite Out of the Market." *Houston Chronicle,* November 25, 2003, B1.

——. "Old-Fashioned Savings, Loans." *Houston Chronicle,* September 17, 2002, B1.

Morgenson, G. "Buybacks Aren't Always a Good Thing." *New York Times on the Web,* January 18, 2004, http://www.nytimes.com/.

Morrill, C. "The Private Ordering of Professional Relationships." In *Hidden Conflict in Organizations,* edited by D. Kolb and J. Bartunek. Newbury Park, CA: Sage, 1992.

*Morris, G. H., S. C. Gaveras, W. L. Baker, and M. L. Coursey. "Aligning Actions at Work." *Management Communication Quarterly* 3 (1990): 303–333.

Morris, J. "Whistle-Blower Claims Settled." *Houston Chronicle,* November 20, 1996.

Morrison, A., R. White, and E. Van Velsor. *Breaking the Glass Ceiling.* Greensboro, NC: Center for Creative Leadership, 1992.

Mulder, M. "Power Equalization through Participation?" *Academy of Management Journal* 16 (1971): 31–38.

Mulder, M., and H. Wilke. "Participation and Power Equalization." *Organizational Behavior and Human Performance* 5 (1970): 430–448.

Muller, J. *Adam Smith in His Time and Ours.* Princeton, NJ: Princeton University Press, 1993.

*Mumby, D. *Communication and Power in Organizations.* Norwood, NJ: Ablex, 1988.

*——. "Communication, Organization, and the Public Sphere." In *Rethinking Organizational and Managerial Communication from Feminist Perspectives,* edited by P. M. Buzzanell. Thousand Oaks, CA: Sage, 2000.

*——. "Organizing Men." *Communication Theory* 8 (1998): 164–183.

*——. "Power, Politics, and Organizational Communication." In *New Handbook of Organizational Communication,* edited by F. Jablin and L. Putnam. Thousand Oaks, CA: Sage, 2000.

——, ed. *Narrative and Social Control: Critical Perspectives.* Newbury Park, CA: Sage, 1993.

*Mumby, D., and L. Putnam. "The Politics of Emotion." *Academy of Management Review* 17 (1992): 465–486.

*Mumby, D., and C. Stohl. "Power and Discourse in Organization Studies." *Discourse and Society* 2 (1991): 313–332.

Munshi, D. "Through the Subject's Eye." In *Organization—Communication: Emerging Perspectives,* vol. 7, edited by G. Cheney and G. Barnett. Cresskill, NJ: Hampton Press, 2003.

Murphy, A. "Hidden Transcripts of Flight Attendant Resistance." *Management Communication Quarterly* 11 (1998): 499–535.

Nadler, M., and L. Nadler. "Feminization of Public Relations." In *Communication and Sex-Role Socialization,* edited by C. Berryman-Fink, D. Ballard-Reich, and L. H. Newman. New York: Garland, 1993.

Nathan, B., A. Mohrman, and J. Milliman. "Interpersonal Relations as a Context of the Effects of Appraisal Interviews." *Academy of Management Journal* 34 (1991): 352–369.

National Foundation of Women Business Owners, http://www.nfwbo.org, January 6, 2001.

Navattette, R., Jr. "Grandson of Immigrant Now to the Right of Rove." *Houston Chronicle,* January 8, 2004, A29.

Neale, B., and M. Bazerman. *Cognition and Rationality in Negotiations.* New York: Free Press, 1991.

———. "Negotiating Rationally." *Academy of Management Executive* 6 (1992): 42–65.

Nephin, D. "Domestic Steel Prices Head Higher." *Houston Chronicle,* March 31, 2002, D5.

Neumark, D., ed. *On the Job: Is Long-Term Employment a Thing of the Past?* New York: Russell Sage Foundation, 2000.

Newell, A., and H. Simon. *Human Problem Solving.* Englewood Cliffs, NJ: Prentice Hall, 1972.

New York Times Editorial Board. "Congressional Cowardice." *New York Times on the Web,* July, 18, 2002, http://www.nytimes.com/.

*Nkomo, S. "The Emperor Has No Clothes: Rewriting Race in Organizations." *Academy of Management Review* 17 (1992): 487–512.

———. "Teaching Business Ethically in the 'New' South Africa." *Management Communication Quarterly* 17 (2003): 128–135.

Nohria, N., and J. D. Berkley. "Allen-Bradley's ICCG Case Study." In *The Post-Bureaucratic Organization: New Perspectives on Organizational Change,* edited by C. Heckscher and A. Donnellon. Newbury Park, CA: Sage, 1994.

"Number of Female Executives Continues to Rise, Survey Says." *Houston Chronicle,* November 14, 2000.

*Nunamaker, J. F., A. Dennis, J. George, J. Valacich, and D. Vogel. "Electronic Meeting Systems to Support Group Work." *Communications of the ACM* 34 (1991): 40–61.

O'Briant, D. "Move Over, Gen-Xers." *Houston Chronicle,* August 13, 2003, D1.

O'Brien, K. "Unusual Pattern on Polish Border." *Houston Chronicle,* January 11, 2004, D6.

O'Conner, E. "Discourse at Our Disposal." *Management Communication Quarterly* 10 (1997): 395–432.

Oetzel, J., and K. Bolton-Oetzel. "Exploring the Relationship between Self-Construal and Dimensions of Group Effectiveness." *Management Communication Quarterly* 10 (1997): 289–315.

Olgren, C., and L. Parker. *Teleconferencing Technology and Applications.* Dedham, MA: Artech House, 1983.

Olivares, F. "Ways Men and Women Lead." *Harvard Business Review* 69 (January–February 1991): 2–11.

Ong, A. "The Gender and Labor Politics of Postmodernity." *Annual Review of Anthropology* 20 (1991): 196–214.

———. "Spirits of Resistance." In *Situated Lives,* edited by L. Lamphere, H. Razoné, and P. Zavella. New York: Routledge, 1997.

———. *Spirits of Resistance and Capitalist Discipline.* Albany: State University of New York Press, 1987.

Onions, C. T., ed. *The Oxford Dictionary of English Etymology.* Oxford, UK: Oxford University Press, 1966.

Oppel, R., Jr. "Senate Votes to Strengthen S.E.C.'s Hand." *New York Times on the Web,* April 10, 2003, http://www.nytimes.com/.

Orbe, M. "An Outsider within Perspective to Organizational Communication." *Management Communication Quarterly* 2 (1998): 230–279.

O'Reilly, C. "Variations in Decision-Makers' Use of Information Sources." *Academy of Management Journal* 25 (1982): 756–771.

Organ, D. "Linking Pins between Organizations and Environments." *Business Horizons* 14 (1971): 73–80.

O'Rourke, K., and J. Williamson. *Globalization and History.* Cambridge, MA: MIT Press, 1999.

Ospina, S. *Illusions of Opportunity.* Ithaca, NY: ILR/Cornell University Press, 1996.

Otis, J. "Ailing Schools Can't Set Free Peru's Youth." *Houston Chronicle,* December 22, 2003, A1.

Ouchi, W. "The Relationship between Organizational Structure and Control." *Administrative Science Quarterly* 22 (1977): 95–113.

———. *Theory Z.* Reading, MA: Addison-Wesley, 1981.

Ouchi, W., and A. Jaeger. "Type Z Organization." *Academy of Management Review* 3 (1978): 305–314.

Ouchi, W., and A. Wilkins. "Efficient Cultures." *Administrative Science Quarterly* 28 (1983): 468–481.

"Overworked America?" *The Online (PBS) Newshour,* http://www.pbs.org/, September 6, 1999.

Pacanowsky, M. "Communication in the Empowering Organization." In *Communication Yearbook 11,* edited by J. Anderson. Beverly Hills, CA: Sage, 1987.

———. "Creating and Narrating Organizational Realities." In *Rethinking Communication: Paradigm Exemplars,* edited by B. Dervin, L. Grossberg, B. O'Keefe, and E. Wartella., vol. 2. Beverly Hills, CA: Sage, 1989.

Page, P. "African Americans in Executive Branch Agencies." *Review of Public Personnel Administration* 14 (1994): 24–51.

Palast, G. *The Best Democracy Money Can Buy.* New York: Plume Books, 2001.

Paludi, M. A., and R. B. Barickman. *Academic and Workplace Sexual Harassment.* Albany: State University of New York Press, 1991.

Papa, M., M. Auwal, and A. Singhai. "Dialectic of Control and Emancipation in Organizing for Social Change." *Communication Theory* 5 (1995): 189–223.

*Papa, M., and W. Papa. "Competence in Organizational Conflicts." In *Competence in Interpersonal Conflict,* edited by W. R. Cupach and D. J. Canary. New York: McGraw-Hill, 1996.

"Paper Finds Air Force Academy Negligence." *New York Times on the Web,* June 15, 2003, http://www.nytimes.com/.

Pardo, M. "Doing It for the Kids." In *Feminist Organizations,* edited by M. M. Ferree and Y. Martin. Philadelphia: Temple University Press, 1995.

Parker, P. S., and D. Ogilvie. "Gender, Culture, and Leadership." *Leadership Quarterly* 7 (1996): 189–214.

Parry, J., ed. *The Establishment of the European Hegemony, 1415–1715.* New York: HarperCollins, 1967.

Paskoff, S. "Ending the Workplace Diversity Wars." *Training: The Human Side of Business,* August 1996, pp. 2–8.

Patterson, J., II, and M. W. Allen. "Accounting for Your Actions." *Journal of Applied Communication Research* 25 (1997): 293–316.

*Pavitt, C., G. G. Whitchurch, H. McClurg, and N. Petersen. "Melding the Objective and Subjective Sides of Leadership: Communication and Social Judgments in Decision-Making Groups." *Communication Monographs* 62 (1995): 243–264.

Pena, D. "Tortuosidad." In *Women on the U.S.-Mexico Border,* edited by V. L. Ruiz and S. Tiano. Boston: Allen and Unwin, 1987.

Perrow, C. *Complex Organizations.* 3rd ed. New York: Random House, 1986.

*———. "A Framework for the Comparative Analysis of Organizations." *American Sociological Review* 32 (1967): 194–208.

———. *Normal Accidents.* New York: Basic Books, 1984.

———. *Organizing America.* Princeton, NJ: Princeton University Press, 2002.

Pesquera, B. "In the Beginning He Wouldn't Even Lift a Spoon." In *Situated Lives,* edited by L. Lamphere, H. Razoné, and P. Zavella. New York: Routledge, 1997.

Peters, J. "Publicity and Pain: Self-Abstraction in Adam Smith's *Theory of Moral Sentiments.*" *Public Culture* 7 (1995): 657–684.

Peters, T., and N. Austin. *A Passion for Excellence.* New York: Random House, 1985.

Peters, T., and R. Waterman. *In Search of Excellence.* New York: Harper and Row, 1982.

Pettigrew, A. "Information Control as a Power Resource." *Sociology* 6 (1972): 187–204.

*Pfeffer, J. *Managing with Power.* Boston: Harvard Business School, 1992.

*———. *Power in Organizations.* Marshfield, MA: Pitman, 1981.

*Pfeffer, J., and A. Davis-Blake. "The Effect of the Proportion of Women on Salaries." *Administrative Science Quarterly* 32 (1987): 1–24.

*Pfeffer, J., and N. Langton. "Wage Inequality and the Organization of Work." *Administrative Science Quarterly* 33 (1988): 588–606.

Phillips, K. *The Politics of Rich and Poor.* New York: Broadway Books, 1990.

———. *Wealth and Democracy.* New York: Broadway Books, 2002.

Planalp, S. *Communicating Emotion.* Cambridge, UK: Cambridge University Press, 1999.

———. "Communicating Emotion." *Communication Theory* 9 (1999): 216–228.

Pollock, T., R. Whitbred, and N. Contractor. "Social Information Processing and Job Characteristics." *Human Communication Research* 26 (2000): 292–330.

Pondy, L. "Organizational Conflict: Concepts and Models." *Administrative Science Quarterly* 12 (1967): 296–320.

———. "The Role of Metaphors and Myths in the Organization and the Facilitation of Change." In *Organizational Symbolism,* edited by L. Pondy, P. Frost, G. Morgan, and T. D. Dandridge. Greenwich, CT: JAI Press, 1993.

*Poole, M. S. "Decision Development in Small

Groups I." *Communication Monographs* 48 (1981): 1–24.

———. "Decision Development in Small Groups II." *Communication Monographs* 50 (1983): 206–232.

———. "Decision Development in Small Groups III." *Communication Monographs* 50 (1983): 321–341.

———. "Organizational Challenges for the New Forms." In *Shaping Organization Form: Communication, Connection, and Community,* edited by G. DeSanctis and J. Fulk. Newbury Park, CA: Sage, 1999.

Poole, M. S., and C. Baldwin. "Developmental Processes in Group Decision-Making." In *Communication and Group Decision Making,* edited by R. Hirokawa and M. S. Poole. 2nd ed. Thousand Oaks, CA: Sage, 1996.

Poole, M. S., and J. Roth. "Decision Development in Small Groups IV." *Human Communication Research* 15 (1989): 323–356.

Poole, M. S., and A. Van de Ven. "Using Paradox to Build Management and Organization Theories." *Academy of Management Review* 14 (1995): 562–578.

Posner, B. Z., and W. H. Schmidt. "Values and the American Manager." *California Management Review* 26 (1984): 202–216.

Potter, W. M. "The Environment of the Oil Company." In *Rhetorical and Critical Approaches to Public Relations,* edited by E. L. Toth and R. Heath. New York: Praeger, 1992.

Potuchek, J. *Who Supports the Family?* Palo Alto, CA: Stanford University Press, 1997.

Powell, E. A. "Women Are Hitting the 'Glass Wall.'" *Houston Chronicle,* November 12, 1999.

Powell, G. *Women and Men in Management.* Newbury Park, CA: Sage, 1993.

Powell, G., and D. A. Butterfield. "Investigating the 'Glass Ceiling' Phenomenon." *Academy of Management Journal* 37 (1994): 68–86.

Powell, W., and P. DiMaggio, eds. *The New Institutionalism in Organizational Theory.* Chicago: University of Chicago Press, 1990.

Powell, W. W., K. Koput, and L. Smith-Doerr. "Interorganizational Collaboration and the Locus of Innovation: Networks of Learning in Biotechnology." *Administrative Science Quarterly* 41 (1996): 116–145.

Power, M., and R. Laughlin. "Critical Theory and Accounting." In *Critical Management Studies,* edited by M. Alvesson and H. Willmott. London: Sage, 1992.

Powers, D. *The Office Romance.* New York: American Management Association, 1999.

Prasso, S. "Study: Stereotypes Hinder Female Executives." *Houston Chronicle,* February 29, 1996.

Pratt, M. "The Good, the Bad, and the Ambivalent." *Administrative Science Quarterly* 45 (2000): 456–493.

Putnam, L. "Conflict and Dispute Management." In *The New Handbook of Organizational Communication,* edited by F. Jablin and L. Putnam. Thousand Oaks, CA: Sage, 1997.

———. "Conflict in Group Decision Making." In *Communication and Group Decision Making,* edited by R. Hirokawa and M. S. Poole. Newbury Park, CA: Sage, 1986.

———. "Feminist Theories, Dispute Processes, and Organizational Communication." Paper presented at the Arizona State University "Conference on Organizational Communication: Perspectives for the 1990s," Tempe, AZ, April 1990.

———. *Negotiation of Intergroup Conflict in Organizations.* Hallie Mande Neff Wilcox Published Lecture. Waco, TX: Baylor University, 1987.

———. "Preference for Procedural Order in Task-Oriented Small Groups." *Communication Monographs* 46 (1979): 193–218.

———. "Reframing Integrative and Distributive Bargaining." In *Research on Negotiation in Organizations,* edited by B. Shepard, M. Bazerman, and R. Lewicki, vol. 2. Greenwich, CT: JAI Press, 1990.

Putnam, L., and M. Holmer. "Framing and Reframing." In *Communication and Negotiation,* edited by L. Putnam and M. Roloff. Newbury Park, CA: Sage, 1993.

Putnam, L., and T. Jones. "Reciprocity in Negotiations." *Communication Monographs* 49 (1982): 171–191.

Putnam, L., and D. M. Kolb. "Rethinking Negotiation: Feminist Views of Communication and Exchange." In *Rethinking Organizational and Managerial Communication from Feminist Perspectives,* edited by P. Buzzanell. Thousand Oaks, CA: Sage, 2000.

Putnam, L., N. Phillips, and P. Chapman. "Metaphors of Communication and Organization," in *Handbook of Organization Studies,* edited by S. Clegg, C. Hardy, and W. Nord. London: Sage, 1996.

Putnam, L., and S. Van Hoeven. "The Role of Narrative in Teachers' Bargaining." Paper presented at the Temple University "Discourse Conference on Conflict Intervention," Philadelphia, 1987.

———. "Teacher Bargaining as a Cultural Rite of Conflict Reduction." Paper presented at the Central States Speech Association Convention, Cincinnati, Ohio, October 1986.

*Putnam, L., and C. Wilson, C. "Communicative Strategies in Organizational Conflicts." In *Communication Yearbook 6,* edited by M. Burgoon. Newbury Park, CA: Sage, 1982.

Putnam, L., S. Wilson, and D. Turner. "The Evolution of Policy Arguments in Teachers' Bargaining." *Argumentation* 4 (1990): 129-152.

Putnam, R. *Bowling Alone.* New York: Simon and Schuster, 2000.

Rafaeli, A., and R. Sutton. "The Expression of Emotion in Organizational Life, II." *Research in Organizational Behavior* 11 (1989): 1-42.

*Rahim, M. "Referent Role and Styles of Handling Interpersonal Conflict." *Journal of Social Psychology* 126 (1986): 79-86.

Ralston, D., C. Egri, S. Stewart, R. Terpstra, and Y. Kaicheng. "Doing Business in the 21st Century with the New Generation of Chinese Managers," *Journal of International Business Studies* 30 (1999): 415-428.

Ralston, D., D. Holt, R. Terpstra, and Y. Kaicheng. "The Impact of National Culture and Economic Ideology on Managerial Work Values." *Journal of International Business Studies* 28 (1997): 177-208.

Ralston, S., and W. Kirkwood. "Overcoming Managerial Bias in Employment Interviewing." *Journal of Applied Communication Research* 23 (1995): 75-92.

Rampersad, F. "Coping with Globalization." *Annals of the American Association of Political and Social Science* 570 (2000): 115-125.

Raven, B., and A. Kruglanski. "Power and Conflict." In *The Structure of Conflict,* edited by P. Swingle. New York: Academic Press, 1970.

Reardon, K. K. *They Don't Get It, Do They?* Boston: Little, Brown, 1995.

Redding, W. C. "Rocking Boats, Blowing Whistles, and Teaching Speech Communication." *Communication Education* 34 (1985): 245-258.

Remland, M. "Leadership Impressions and Nonverbal Communication." *Communication Quarterly* 19 (1987): 108-128.

Rennie, M. "Born Global." *McKinsey Quarterly* 4 (1993): 45-52.

Reskin, R., and I. Padavic. *Women and Men at Work.* Thousand Oaks, CA: Pine Forge Press, 1994.

[Reuters]. "Spitzer Threatens to Sue U.S. Regulator over Loan Exemption." *New York Times on the Web,* December 11, 2003, http://www.nytimes.com/.

*Reuther, C., and G. Fairhurst. "Chaos Theory and the Glass Ceiling." In *Rethinking Organizational and Managerial Communication from Feminist Perspectives,* edited by P. Buzzanell. Thousand Oaks, CA: Sage, 2000.

Reynolds, C. W., and R. V. Norman, eds. *Community in America: The Challenge of Habits of the Heart.* Berkeley: University of California Press, 1988.

Reynolds, D. "Sticky Situation." ABC News, March 25, 2002, http://www.abcnews.go.com/.

*Ricardo, D. *Principles of Political Economy and Taxation.* Buffalo, NY: Prometheus Books, 1996.

Rice, R. "Evaluating New Media Systems." In *Evaluating the New Information Technologies,* edited by J. Johnstone. San Francisco: Jossey-Bass, 1984.

——. *New Communication Technologies.* Beverly Hills, CA: Sage, 1984.

*Rice, R., and C. Aydin. "Attitudes toward New Organizational Technology." *Administrative Science Quarterly* 36 (1991): 219-244.

*Rice, R., and U. Gattiker. "Communication Technologies and Structures." In *The New Handbook of Organizational Communication,* edited by F. Jablin and L. Putnam. Thousand Oaks, CA: Sage, 2000.

*Rice, R., and G. Love. "Electronic Emotion." *Communication Research* 14 (1987): 85-108.

Richmond, V. P., and J. C. McCroskey. "The Impact of Supervisor and Subordinate Immediacy on Relational and Organizational Outcomes." *Communication Monographs* 67 (2000): 85-95.

Richmond, V. P., and K. D. Roach. "Willingness to Communicate and Employee Success in U.S. Organizations." *Journal of Applied Communication Research* 20 (1992): 95-115.

Riebling, M. *Wedge: From Pearl Harbor to 9/11.* New York: Touchstone Books, 2002.

"The Rigged Trade Game." *New York Times on the Web,* July 20, 2003, http://www.nytimes.com/.

Ritti, R. R., and J. Silver. "Early Processes of Institutionalization." *Administrative Science Quarterly* 31 (1986): 25-42.

Ritzer, G. *The McDonaldization of Society.* Newbury Park, CA: Pine Forge Press, 1993.

Ritzer, G., and A. Liska. "McDisneyization and Post-Tourism." In *Touring Cultures,* edited by C. Rojek and J. Urry. London: Routledge, 1997.

Rizzo, A., and C. Mendez. *The Integration of Women in Management.* New York: Quorum Books, 1990.

Robb, D. "Unified Messaging Boosts Productivity." *Computerworld,* November 4, 2002, pp. 32-33.

*Roberts, N. "Organizational Power Styles." *Journal of Applied Behavioral Science* 22 (1986): 443–455.

Robertson, R. *Globalization.* London: Sage, 1992.

Rodrik, D. "Has Globalization Gone Too Far?" *Challenge* 41 (1998): 81–94.

———. "Sense and Nonsense in the Globalization Debate." *Foreign Policy* 107 (Summer 1997): 15–24.

Rohter, L. "Workers in Argentina Take Charge of Abandoned Factories." *New York Times on the Web,* July 6, 2003, http://www.nytimes.com/.

*Roloff, M. "Roloff's Modes of Conflict Resolution and Their Items." In *Explorations in Interpersonal Communication,* edited by G. Miller. Beverly Hills, CA: Sage, 1976.

*Roloff, M., and J. M. Jordan. "Achieving Negotiation Goals." In *Communication and Negotiation,* edited by L. Putnam and M. Roloff. Newbury Park, CA: Sage, 1993.

Rosen, M. "Breakfast at Spiro's." In *Reframing Organizational Culture,* edited by P. Frost, L. Moore, M. R. Louis, C. Lundberg, and J. Martin. Newbury Park, CA: Sage, 1991.

———. "You Asked for It: Christmas at the Bosses' Expense." *Journal of Management Studies* 25 (1988): 463–480.

Rosenbaum, L. "They Support Free Trade, Except in the Case of. . . ." *New York Times on the Web,* November 16, 2003, http://www.nytimes.com/.

Rosener, J. "Ways Women Lead." *Harvard Business Review* 68 (November–December 1990): 119–125.

Rosenthal, E. "Workers' Plight Brings New Militancy in China." *New York Times on the Web,* March 10, 2003, http://www.nytimes.com/.

Roslender, R. *Sociological Perspectives on Modern Accountancy.* London: Routledge, 1992.

Roth, B. "Information Gap between FBI, CIA Closed, Bush Says." *Houston Chronicle,* June 5, 2002.

Rothkopf, D. "In Praise of Cultural Imperialism?" *Foreign Policy* 107 (Summer 1997): 107–199.

Rothschild-Whitt, J., and J. A. Whitt. *The Cooperative Workplace.* Cambridge, UK: Cambridge University Press, 1986.

Russo, T. C. "Organizational and Professional Identification." *Management Communication Quarterly* 12 (1998): 72–111.

Sachs, J. "International Economics: Unlocking the Mysteries of Globalization." *Foreign Policy* 110 (Spring 1998): 168–206.

———. "Making It Work." *Economist,* September 12, 1998, available at http://www.economist.com/.

*Said, E. *Orientalism.* New York: Penguin, 1978.

*Sambamurthy, V., and M. S. Poole. "The Effects of Variations in Capabilities of GDSS Designs on Management of Cognitive Conflict in Groups." *Information Systems Research* 3 (1993): 224–251.

Sampson, E. E. "Justice, Ideology, and Social Legitimation." In *Justice in Social Relations,* edited by H. W. Bierhoff, R. L. Cohen, and J. Greenberg. New York: Plenum, 1986.

Sayles, L. "Work Group Behavior and the Larger Organization." In *Research in Industrial Human Relations,* edited by W. F. Whyte. New York: Harper, 1957.

*Schenck-Hamlin, W., and G. Georgacarakos. "Response to Murdock, Bradac, and Bowers." *Western Journal of Speech Communication* 50 (1986): 200–207.

Shenon, P. "Chief of Sept. 11 Panel Assesses Blame but Holds Off on Higher-Ups." *New York Times on the Web,* December 19, 2003, http://www.nytimes.com/.

Scherer, R. "First National Survey of Minority Views Shows Deep Racial Polarization." *Christian Science Monitor,* March 16, 1994.

Schlosser, E. "The Cow Jumped over the U.S.D.A." *New York Times on the Web,* January 2, 2004, http:// www.nytimes.com/.

———. *Fast Food Nation.* Boston: Houghton Mifflin, 2001.

Schneider, B., S. Gunnarson, and J. Wheeler. "The Role of Opportunity in the Conceptualization and Measurement of Job Satisfaction." In *Job Satisfaction,* edited by C. J. Crannay, P. Smith, and E. Stone. New York: Lexington Books, 1992.

*Schweiger, D., and A. Denisi. "Communication with Employees Following a Merger." *Academy of Management Journal* 34 (1991): 110–135.

*Schwenk, C. R., and M. A. Lyles. "Top Management, Strategy, and Organizational Knowledge Structures." *Journal of Management Studies* 29 (1992): 155–174.

Scott, C. "Communication Technology and Group Communication." In *Handbook of Group Communication Theory and Research,* edited by L. Frey, D. Gouran, and M. S. Poole. Newbury Park, CA: Sage, 1999.

———. "Identification with Multiple Targets in a Geographically Dispersed Organization." *Management Communication Quarterly* 10 (1997): 491–522.

*Scott, C., S. Connaughton, H. Diaz-Saenz, K. McGuire, R. Ramirez, B. Richardson, S. Shaw, and D. Morgan. "The Impacts of Communication and Multiple Identifications on Intent to Leave." *Management Communication Quarterly* 12 (1999): 400–435.

*Scott, C., S. Corman, and G. Cheney. "Development of a Structurational Model of Identification in the Organization." *Communication Theory* 8 (1998): 298–336.

Scott, J. *Domination and the Arts of Resistance.* New Haven, CT: Yale University Press, 1990.

Scott, W. G., and D. K. Hart. *Organizational America.* Boston: Houghton Mifflin, 1979.

———. *Organizational Values in America.* New Brunswick, NJ: Transaction, 1989.

Seeger, M. "C.E.O. Performances: Lee Iacocca and the Case of Chrysler." *Southern Speech Communication Journal* 52 (1986): 52–68.

———. "Responsibility in Organizational Communication." In *Proceedings of the 1992 National Communication Ethics Conference,* edited by J. Jaska. Annandale, VA: Speech Communication Association, November 1992.

Seeger, M., and R. Ulmer. "A Post-Crisis Discourse of Renewal." *Journal of Applied Communication Research* 30 (2002): 126–142.

Segura, D. "Chicanas in White-Collar Jobs." In *Situated Lives,* edited by L. Lamphere, H. Razoné, and P. Zavella. New York: Routledge, 1997.

———. "Walking on Eggshells: Chicanas in the Labor Force." In *Hispanics in the Workplace,* edited by S. Knouse, P. Rosenfeld, and A. Culbertson. Newbury Park, CA: Sage, 1992.

*Seibold, D., and R. Meyers. "Communication and Influence in Group Decision-Making." In *Communication and Group Decision Making,* edited by R. Hirokawa and M. S. Poole. 2nd ed. Thousand Oaks, CA: Sage, 1996.

*Seibold, D., and C. Shea. "Participation and Decision-Making." In *The New Handbook of Organizational Communication,* edited by F. Jablin and L. Putnam. Thousand Oaks, CA: Sage, 2000.

Seligman, J. "The Merits Do Matter." Harvard Law Review 108 (1994): 438–457.

Senge, P. *The Fifth Discipline: The Art and Practice of the Learning Organization.* New York: Double-day, 1990.

Sennett, R., and J. Cobb. *The Hidden Injuries of Class.* New York: Vintage, 1972.

Series on the Immigration and Naturalization Service. *Houston Chronicle,* December 15, 2000.

Sewell, G. "The Discipline of Teams: The Control of Team-Based Industrial Work through Electronic and Peer Surveillance." *Administrative Science Quarterly* 43 (1998): 397–428.

Sgro, J., P. Worchel, E. Pence, and J. Orban. "Perceived Leader Behavior as a Function of

Trust." *Academy of Management Journal* 23 (1980): 161–165.

Shattuck, H. "Mexico Offers Better Assistance." *Houston Chronicle,* November 12, 2000.

Sheehan, C. "Steelworkers Roll with the Changes." *Houston Chronicle,* November 12, 2003, D8.

Sherif, M., O. J. Harvey, B. White, W. Hood, and C. W. Sherif. *Intergroup Conflict and Cooperation: The Robber's Cave Experiment.* Norman, OK: University Book Exchange, 1961.

Shiller, R. J. *Irrational Exuberance.* Princeton, NJ: Princeton University Press, 2000.

Shuler, S., and B. D. Sypher. "Seeking Emotional Labor." *Management Communication Quarterly* 14 (2000): 50–89.

Shuter, R. "Communication in Multinational Organizations." In *Communication and Multinational Organizations,* edited by R. Wiseman and R. Shuter. Thousand Oaks, CA: Sage, 1994.

*Sias, P. "Constructing Perceptions of Differential Treatment." *Communication Monographs* 63 (1996): 171–187.

*Sias, P., and F. Jablin. "Differential Superior-Subordinate Relations, Perceptions of Fairness, and Coworker Communication." *Human Communication Research* 22 (1995): 5–38.

*Sillars, A. "Stranger and Spouse as Target Persons for Compliance-Gaining Strategies." *Human Communication Research* 6 (1980): 265–279.

Simons, T. "Speech Patterns and the Concept of Utility in Cognitive Maps." *Academy of Management Journal* 36 (1993): 139–156.

Sims, R. "The Challenge of Ethical Behavior in Organizations." *Journal of Business Ethics* 11 (1992): 501–513.

*Sitkin, S. B., K. M. Sutcliffe, and J. R. Barrios-Choplin. "A Dual-Capacity Model of Communication Medium Choice in Organizations." *Human Communication Research* 18 (1992): 563–598.

Sixel, L. M. "Race and Rewards at Texaco." *Houston Chronicle,* July 19, 1996.

———. "Forced Arbitration Closing Court Doors to Employees." *Houston Chronicle,* December 27, 2002.

———. "Paid Paternity Leave More Popular than Expected." *Houston Chronicle,* May 16, 2003, C1.

———. "Pay Gap Narrower, but Far from Closed." *Houston Chronicle,* February 26, 1999.

———. "Sign Here If You're Injured—Or You Won't Get Treatment." *Houston Chronicle,* November 2, 2003.

———. "Wal-Mart Settles Insurance Lawsuit," *Houston Chronicle,* January 9, 2004, C1.

——. "Women Climb Corporate Ladder—but Slowly." *Houston Chronicle,* November 19, 2002, 1B.

——. "Workplace Racism Cases Hard to Win." *Houston Chronicle,* November 13, 1996.

Sless, D. "Forms of Control." *Australian Journal of Communication* 14 (1988): 57–69.

Sloan, D., and K. Krone. "Women Managers and Gendered Values." *Women's Studies in Communication* 23 (2000): 111–130.

Smith, D. "Stories, Values, and Patient Care Decisions." In *The Ethical Nexus,* edited by C. Conrad. Norwood, NJ: Ablex, 1993.

*Smith, K. "The Movement of Conflict in Organizations." *Administrative Science Quarterly* 34 (1989): 1–20.

Smith, K., and V. Simmons. "The Rumpelstiltskin Organization." *Administrative Science Quarterly* 28 (1983): 377–392.

Smith, R. "How to Be a Good Subordinate." *New York Times,* November 25, 1970.

*Smith-Lovin, L., and M. J. McPherson. "You Are Who You Know." In *Theory on Gender/Feminism on Theory,* edited by P. England. New York: Aldine, 1993.

*Snyder, R., and J. Morris. "Organizational Communication and Performance." *Journal of Applied Psychology* 69 (1984): 461–465.

Solomon, C. "Keeping Hate out of the Workplace." *Personnel Journal* 71 (July 1992): 30–36.

Solomon, D. H., and M. L. M. Williams. "Perceptions of Social-Sexual Communication at Work." *Journal of Applied Communication Research* 25 (1997): 196–216.

——. "Perceptions of Social-Sexual Communication at Work as Harassing." *Management Communication Quarterly* 11 (1997): 147–184.

Soros, G. *The Crisis of Global Capitalism.* New York: Public Affairs, 1998.

——. *The Open Society.* New York: Public Affairs, 2000.

Spain, D. *Gendered Spaces.* Chapel Hill: University of North Carolina Press, 1992.

Spence, L. *The Politics of Social Knowledge.* University Park: Pennsylvania State University Press, 1978.

*Sproull, L., and S. Kiesler. *Connections: New Ways of Working in the Networked World.* Cambridge, MA: MIT Press, 1992.

*——. "Reducing Social Context Cues." *Management Science* 32 (1986): 1492–1512.

Stark, D. "Ambiguous Assets for Uncertain Environments: Heterarchy in Post Socialist Firms." In *The Twenty-First Century Firm: Changing Economic Organization in International Perspective,* edited by P. Dimaggio. Princeton, NJ: Princeton University Press, 2001.

——. "Heterarchy: Distributing Authority and Organizing Diversity." In *The Biology of Business: Decoding the Natural Laws of Enterprise,* edited by J. H. Clippinger III. San Francisco: Jossey-Bass, 1999.

Staw, B., and L. Epstein. "What Bandwagons Bring: Effect of Popular Management Techniques on Corporate Performance, Reputation, and CEO Pay." *Administrative Science Quarterly* 45 (2000): 523–556.

*Staw, B., P. McKechnie, and S. Puffer. "The Justification of Organizational Performance." *Administrative Science Quarterly* 28 (1983): 582–600.

Staw, B., and J. Ross. "Behavior in Escalation Situations." In *Research in Organizational Behavior,* edited by B. Staw and L. Cummings. Greenwich, CT: JAI Press, 1987.

——. "Commitment in an Experimenting Society." *Journal of Applied Psychology* 65 (1980): 249–260.

St. Clair, L., R. Quinn, and R. O'Neill. "The Perils of Responsiveness in Modern Organizations." In *Pressing Problems in Organizations (That Keep Us UP at Night,* edited by R. Quinn, R. O'Neill, and L. St. Clair. New York: American Management Association, 2000.

Stern, P. *Still the Best Congress Money Can Buy.* Chicago: Regnery, 1992.

Stiglitz, J. "The Broken Promise of NAFTA." *New York Times on the Web,* January 6, 2004, http:// www.nytimes.com/.

Stohl, C. "Bridging the Parallel Organization: A Study of Quality Circle Effectiveness." In *Communication Yearbook 10,* edited by J. Burgoon. Beverly Hills, CA: Sage, 1985.

——. "European Managers' Interpretations of Participation." *Human Communication Research* 20 (1993): 108–131.

——. "Globalizing Organizational Communication." In *The New Handbook of Organizational Communication,* edited by F. Jablin and L. Putnam. Thousand Oaks, CA: Sage, 2000.

——. *Organizational Communication.* Thousand Oaks, CA: Sage, 1995.

*——. "The Role of Memorable Messages in the Process of Organization Socialization." *Communication Quarterly* 34 (1983): 231–249.

Stohl, C., and G. Cheney. "Participatory Processes/Paradoxical Practices." *Management Communication Quarterly* 14 (2001): 349–407.

Stohl, C., and M. Stohl. "Networks, Terrorism, and Terrorist Networks." Paper presented at the National Communication Association Organizational Communication Preconference, Washington, DC, November 20, 2002.

Stolberg, S. G., and J. Gerth. "Drug Makers Fight Generic Rivals and Raise Questions of Monopoly." *Houston Chronicle,* July 23, 2000.

Stone, D. *Policy Paradox.* New York: Norton, 1997.

Straziuso, J. "New Doctors Find Hours Still Long, but Abuses Fewer." *Houston Chronicle,* January 13, 2004, B10.

"Study Finds Women Denied Top High-Tech Jobs." *Houston Chronicle,* November 13, 2002, B3.

Stutts, N., and R. Barker. "The Use of Narrative Paradigm Theory in Assessing Audience Value Conflict in Image Advertising." *Management Communication Quarterly* 13 (1999): 209-244.

*Sullivan, J., and S. Taylor. "A Cross-Cultural Test of Compliance-Gaining Theory." *Management Communication Quarterly* 5 (1991): 220-239.

Sussman, H. "Is Diversity Training Worth Maintaining?" *Business and Society Review* 89 (1994): 48-49.

Sutcliffe, K. "Commentary on Strategic Sensemaking." In *Advances in Strategic Management,* edited by J. Walsh and A. Huff. Greenwich, CT: JAI Press, 1997.

*———. "Organizational Environments and Organizational Information Processing." In *The New Handbook of Organizational Communication,* edited by F. Jablin and L. Putnam. Thousand Oaks, CA: Sage, 2000.

"Sweatshops under the American Flag." *New York Times on the Web,* May 10, 2002, http://www.nytimes.com/.

Tannenbaum, A. "Control in Organizations." *Administrative Science Quarterly* 7 (1962): 17-42.

Taylor, F. "The Principles of Scientific Management." In *Classics of Organizational Theory,* edited by J. Shafritz and P. Whitbeck. Oak Park, IL: Moore, 1978.

Taylor, J., and E. van Every. *The Emergent Organization: Communication as Its Site and Surface.* Mahwah, NJ: Lawrence Erlbaum, 2000.

"Tech Leaders Urge Congress Not to Act to Keep Jobs in U.S." *Houston Chronicle,* January 8, 2004.

*Tedeschi, J. "Threats and Promises." In *The Structure of Conflict,* edited by P. Swingle. New York: Academic Press, 1970.

Tegar, A. *Too Much Invested to Quit.* New York: Pergamon, 1980.

*Terpstra, D., and D. Baker. "Outcomes of Sexual Harassment Charges." *Academy of Management Journal* 31 (1988): 185-194.

"Texaco Reeling from Racial Scandal." *Houston Chronicle,* November 5, 1996.

"Texaco Whistle-Blower: Much Trouble, Little Reward." *USA Today,* December 20, 1999.

*Therborn, G. *The Ideology of Power and the Power of Ideology.* London: Verso, 1980.

Thomas, D., and C. Alderfer. "The Influence of Race on Career Dynamics." In *Handbook of Career Theory,* edited by M. Arthur, D. Hall, and B. Lawrence. New York: McGraw-Hill, 1989.

Thomas, K., and R. Walton. *Conflict-Handling Behavior in Interdepartmental Relations.* Los Angeles: UCLA Graduate School of Business Administration, 1971.

Thomas, L. "Memo Shows MFS Funds Let Favored Clients Trade When Others Couldn't." *New York Times on the Web,* December 9, 2003, http://www.nytimes.com/.

*Thompson, J. *Organizations in Action.* New York: McGraw-Hill, 1967.

Thurow, L. "New Rules: The American Economy in the Next Century." *Harvard International Review* 19 (Winter 1997-1998): 7-42.

Ting-Toomey, S. "Toward a Theory of Conflict and Culture." In *Communication and Culture,* edited by W. Gudykunst. Beverly Hills, CA: Sage, 1985.

Toffler, B. E. *Tough Choices.* New York: Wiley, 1986.

Tomlinson, J. *Globalization and Culture.* Chicago: University of Chicago Press, 1999.

Tompkins, P. *Organizational Communication Imperatives: Lessons from the Space Program.* Los Angeles: Roxbury House, 1993.

Tompkins, P. K., and G. Cheney. "Communication and Unobtrusive Control in Organizations." In *Organizational Communication: Traditional Themes and New Directions,* edited by R. D. McPhee and P. Tompkins. Beverly Hills, CA: Sage, 1985.

"Top, Junior Officers Vie, Study Says." *Houston Chronicle,* November 19, 2000, A11.

Toth, E. L., and R. Heath, eds. *Rhetorical and Critical Approaches to Public Relations.* New York: Praeger, 1992.

Tourish, D., N. Paulsen, and P. Bordia. "The Downsides of Downsizing." *Management Communication Quarterly* 17 (2004): 485-516.

*Tracy, K., and E. Eisenberg. "Giving Criticism." *Research on Language and Social Interaction* 24 (1990-1991): 37-70.

Tracy, S. "Becoming a Character for Commerce." *Management Communication Quarterly* 14 (2000): 90-128.

Tracy, S., and K. Tracy. "Emotion Labor at 911." *Journal of Applied Communication Research* 26 (1998): 390-411.

*Tretheway, A. "A Feminist Critique of Disciplined Bodies." In *Rethinking Organizational and Managerial Communication from Feminist Perspectives,* edited by P. Buzzanell. Thousand Oaks, CA: Sage, 2000.

*Trevinio, L., R. Lengel, and R. Daft. "Media Symbolism, Media Richness, and Media Choices in Organizations." *Communication Research* 14 (1987): 553–574.

Triandis, H., R. Bontempo, M. Villareal, M. Asai, and N. Lucca. "Individualism and Collectivism: Cross-Cultural Perspectives on Self-Ingroup Relationships." *Journal of Personality and Social Psychology* 21 (1988): 323–338.

Trice, H., and J. Beyer. *The Cultures of Work Organizations.* Englewood Cliffs, NJ: Prentice Hall, 1993.

———. "Studying Organizational Cultures through Rites and Ceremonials." *Academy of Management Review* 9 (1984): 653–669.

Uchitelle, L. "Broken System? Tweak It." *New York Times on the Web,* July 28, 2002, http://www.nytimes.com/.

———. "A Missing Statistic: U.S. Jobs That Went Overseas." *New York Times on the Web,* October 5, 2003, http://www.nytimes.com/.

———. "Some Economic Interplay Comes Nearly Full Circle." *New York Times on the Web,* April 30, 1998, http://www.nytimes.com/.

———. "When the Chinese Consumer Is King," *New York Times on the Web,* December 14, 2003, http:// www.nytimes.com/.

Ulmer, R. "Effective Crisis Management through Established Stakeholder Relationships." *Management Communication Quarterly* 14 (2000): 590–615.

Ury, W., J. M. Brett, and S. Goldberg. *Getting Disputes Resolved: Designing Systems to Cut the Costs of Conflict.* San Francisco: Jossey-Bass, 1988.

*"U.S.-Canada Power System Outage Task Force, Washington, D.C." November 19, 2003. Available at http://www.energy.gov.

U.S. Senate Select Committee on Intelligence and U.S. House Select Committee on Intelligence. *Joint Inquiry into Intelligence Community Activities before and after the Terrorist Attacks on September 11, 2001.* S. Rpt. 107-351, JH. Rpt. 107-792, 107th Cong., 2nd sess. The full report is available at www .gpo.access.gov.

Valdivia, L. "A Burgeoning Hispanic Middle Class? Doubtful." *Houston Chronicle,* September 5, 2003, A25.

Vanderford, M., D. Smith, and W. Harris. "Value Identification in Narrative Discourse." *Journal of Applied Communication Research* 20 (1992): 123–161.

van Maanen, J., and E. Schein. "Toward a Theory of Socialization." In *Research in Organizational Behavior,* edited by B. Staw, vol. 1. Greenwich, CT: JAI Press, 1979.

Varg, P. "The Myth of the China Market, 1890–1914." *American Historical Review* 73 (1968): 742–758.

Vaughn, D. *Controlling Unlawful Organizational Behavior.* Chicago: University of Chicago Press, 1992.

Verton, D. "Employers OK with E-Surfing." *Computerworld,* December 18, 2000.

———. "Senator Attacks Data Sharing." *Computerworld,* December 11, 2000.

Violanti, M. "Hooked on Expectations: An Analysis of Influence and Relationships in the Tailhook Reports." *Journal of Applied Communication Research* 24 (1996): 67–82.

Vodosek, M., and K. M. Sutcliffe. "Overemphasis on Analysis." In *Pressing Problems in Modern Organizations (That Keep Us Up at Night),* edited by R. Quinn, R. M. O'Neill, and L. St. Clair. New York: American Management Association, 2000.

Vroom, V. H., and P. W. Yetton. *Leadership and Decision Making.* Pittsburgh: University of Pittsburgh Press, 1973.

Wald, M. "Few Indications That Efforts to Cut Blackout Risks Are under Way." *New York Times on the Web,* December 13, 2002, p. 2, http://www.nytimes.com/.

Waldman, A. "Despite Widespread Poverty, a Consumer Class Emerges in India." *New York Times on the Web,* October 20, 2003, http://www.nytimes.com/.

*Waldron, V. "Achieving Communication Goals in Supervisor-Subordinate Relationships." *Communication Monographs* 58 (1991): 289–306.

*Waldron, V., and K. Krone. "The Experience and Expression of Emotion in the Workplace." *Management Communication Quarterly* 4 (1991): 287–309.

Walker, C., and E. Moses. "The Age of Self-Navigation." *American Demographics* 18 (September 1996): 36–42.

Wall Street Journal. "SEC Turned Timid As Corruption Became More Complex." *Houston Chronicle,* December 26, 2003, D4.

Walsh, M. W. "Women Given Entrée into the Boardroom." *Houston Chronicle,* August 13, 2002, 6B.

Walsh, S. "Plaintiffs Say Texaco Tough in Bias Cases." *Houston Chronicle,* November 14, 1996.

Walther, J. B. "Interpersonal Effects in Computer-Mediated Interaction." *Communication Research* 19 (1992): 52–90.

Ware, B. L., and W. A. Linkugel. "They Spoke in Defense of Themselves." *Quarterly Journal of Speech* 59 (1973): 273–283.

*Watzlawick, P., J. Beavin, and D. Jackson. *Pragmatics of Human Communication.* New York: Norton, 1967.

Wayne, L. "Tighter Rules for Options Fall Victim to Lobbying." *New York Times on the Web,* July 20, 2002, http://www.nytimes .com/.

Weaver, G., L. K. Trevino, and P. Cochran. "Integrated and Decoupled Corporate Social Performance." *Academy of Management Journal* 42 (1999): 539–552.

*Weber, Max. *The Protestant Ethic and the Spirit of Capitalism.* New York: Scribner's, 1958.

Weick, K. *Making Sense of the Organization.* London: Blackwell, 2000.

———. "Organizational Culture and High Reliability." *California Management Review* 29 (1987): 112–127.

*———. *Sense-Making in Organizations.* Thousand Oaks, CA: Sage, 1995.

*———. *The Social Psychology of Organizing.* 2nd ed. Reading, MA: Addison-Wesley, 1979.

*Weick, K., and L. Browning. "Argument and Narration in Organizational Communication." *Journal of Management* 12 (1986): 243–259.

Weidlich, T. "Who Says Unions Must Dislike the Chief?" *New York Times on the Web,* December 15, 2002, http://www.nytimes .com/.

Weisman, R. "Harvard Digs Deeper on Ethics." *Houston Chronicle,* January 4, 2004, D3.

"Welfare Reform for Farmers." *New York Times on the Web,* November 10, 2003, http://www.nytimes.com/.

*Westerlund, G., and S. Sjostrand. *Organizational Myths.* New York: Harper and Row, 1979.

*Westley, F. "Middle Managers and Strategy." *Strategic Management Journal* 11 (1990): 339.

Wilkins, A. *Managing Corporate Character.* San Francisco: Jossey-Bass, 1989.

Wilkins, B. W., and P. A. Anderson. "Gender Differences and Similarities in Management Communication." *Management Communication Quarterly* 5 (1991): 186–211.

Willinghanz, S., J. L. Hart, and G. Leichty. "Telling the Story of Organizational Change." In *Responding to Crisis,* edited by D. Millar and R. Heath. New York: Lawrence Erlbaum, 2003.

Wilson, S. "Face and Facework in Negotiation." In *Communication and Negotiation,* edited by L. Putnam and M. Roloff. Newbury Park, CA: Sage, 1993.

*Wilson, S. R., J. O. Greene, and J. P. Dillard. "Introduction to the Special Issue on Message Production." *Communication Theory* 10 (2000): 135–138.

*Winter, S. J., and S. L. Taylor. "The Role of Information Technology in the Transformation of Work: A Comparison of Post-Industrial, Industrial, and Proto-Industrial Organizations." In *Shaping Organization Form: Communication, Connection, and Community,* edited by G. DeSanctis and J. Fulk. Newbury Park, CA: Sage, 1999.

"Women Owned Firms See Huge Growth." *Houston Chronicle,* May 11, 1999.

"Women's Pay Gap Widens in Some Fields." *Houston Chronicle,* December 10, 2003, B4.

Wood, J. "Engendered Relationships." In *Processes in Close Relationships,* edited by S. Duck, vol. 3. Beverly Hills, CA: Sage, 1993.

*———. *Gendered Lives.* Belmont, CA: Wadsworth, 1994.

Wood, J., and B. Pearce. "Sexists, Racists, and Other Classes of Classifiers." *Quarterly Journal of Speech* 66 (1980): 239–250.

Wood, J., G. Phillips, and D. Pederson. *Group Discussion,* 2nd ed. New York: Harper and Row, 1989.

Woolls, D. "Al-Quaida Suspects Had Normal Lives." *Houston Chronicle,* January 20, 2004, A9.

Wyatt, N. "Shared Leadership in a Weavers' Guild." In *Women Communicating,* edited by B. Bate and A. Taylor. Norwood, NJ: Ablex, 1988.

*Yates, J., and W. J. Orlikowski. "Genres of Organizational Communication." *Academy of Management Review* 17 (1992): 299–326.

Youker, R. "Organization Alternatives for Project Managers." *Project Management Journal* 8 (March 1977): 18–24.

*Young, E. "On the Naming of the Rose." *Organization Studies* 10 (1989): 187–206.

Zak, M. W. "It's like a Prison in There." *Journal of Business and Technical Communication* 8 (1994): 282–298.

Zalzenik, A. "Power and Politics in Organizational Life." *Harvard Business Review* 48 (May–June 1970): 47–60.

*Zand, D. E. "Trust and Managerial Problem-Solving." *Administrative Science Quarterly* 17 (1972): 229–239.

Zhao, Y. "When Jobs Move Overseas (to South Carolina)." *New York Times on the Web,* October 26, 2003, http://www.nytimes.com/.

Zipkin, A. "Bosses Become Nice to Try to Keep Employees from Leaving." *Houston Chronicle,* June 4, 2000.

Index

D

Daft, Richard, 238
"Dead-peasant" policies, 428–429
Dean, James, 282–283
Decentralization, 75, 109–110; participation and, 110–112
Decentralized structures, 147
Decision making: centralization of, 69; distribution of, 75; group, 136–138; intuition and, 300–302; multiple aims and events in, *308;* nonrational, 300–310; participatory, 110–112; PDM and, 112; at Qantas, 313–314; rationalization in, 303; rational model of career, *291,* 291–292; understanding in, 302–303. *See also* Ambiguity; Organizational decision making
Deconstruction, 240
Deep acting, 172
Deep structure of power, 257
Deetz, Stanley, 403
Degradation ceremonies, 167
DeLay, Tom, on sweatshop products, 424
Del Labs, harassment at, 350
Dell Computer Company, 47; Code of Conduct at, 83; outsourcing by, 60
Deming, J. Edwards, 114
Democracy: globalization and, 382; organizational, 403–404
Deng Xiaoping, 388, 391
Denial, 150; of legitimacy of "others," 345–349
Density, 121
Deregulation: corporations and, 440; Enron and, 434; free-market capitalism and, 430
Derivatives, Enron and, 435–436
Desanctis, Gerardine, 188
Design. *See* Contingency design theory; Organizational design
De-skilling, 126–127
Destructive conflicts, 329
Developing countries: resource pools for, 399; U.S. agriculture policy and, 397
Dewey, John, 295
Differences, vs. deficiencies, 389–390
Disabled workers, meeting needs of, 367
Disciplinary power, 256
Discourse, of accommodation, 356–359
Discrimination, 347; against gays, 377. *See also* Texaco Oil
Display rules, 172
Dispute resolution systems, 333–339
Dissent, 277–278; in nuclear power industry, 281–283; whistle-blowers and, 280
Distorted communication, 149
Distribution of wealth, in China, 391
Distributive justice, 84
Diversity, 343–377; advantages of, 41–44; challenging dominant perspective on, 366–377; communication and, 81–82; essentializing experiences and, 345–346; in feminist organizations, 245; holistic perspective on, 373–376; organizational control and, 385–386; organization strategies of resistance to, 364–368; resisting "others"

and, 345–364; rewards for, 368; of workforce, 375
Dodd, Christopher, 431
Domination, by power, 256
Donohue, Tom, 439
Downsizing: emotional reactions to, 172; meaning of, 284; work/family needs and, 369
Drucker, Peter, 47
Drugs, industry and, 428
Dual-authority systems, 193, *194*
Dynamic networks, 200

E

Eassey, Donato, 436–437
Economic boom (1990s), deregulation and, 430
Economic development, in areas with comparative advantages, 398
Economic sectors, organizations in, 17
Economic system, nature of, 39
Economy: of China, 390–392; comparative advantage and, 394–395; generation born 1982–2002 and, 12; globalization of, 384–385; network organizations in, 219; social myths about, 39–40
EDI. *See* Electronic data interchange (EDI) systems
Education: children and, 374; globalization and, 384–385
Efficiency: criteria of, 284–285; Taylor and, 70–71
Efficient market hypothesis, stock values and, 432
Egocentric influence, 298–299
Eisenberg, Eric, 240
Electricity, blackout and, 34–37
Electronic data interchange (EDI) systems, 55–56, 197
Electronic media: relational strategies and, 138–143; telework and, 102–103
Electronic surveillance, 90
Electronic Sweatshop, The (Garson), 98–101
Elites: global economic, 45; language of, 93; public policy and, 426
E-mail, 59, 138–139; user's relationships and, 139
Emotions: display rules for, 172; message meaning and, 268; regulation of, 171–173; surface and deep acting of, 172; of tourism, 173–177
Employee-based knowledge, 57
Employees: choices of, 345–346; communication style of, 147; enforcing company policies and, 96–97; ICTs and, 94–96; job satisfaction of, 144; Mexican concept of, 113–115; monitoring of, 94; motivation of, 83–85; PDM resistance by, 111–112; power relationship with employers, 272–275; private information about, 97; strategic communication by, 18–20; as teleworkers, 103; temporary careers in network organizations, 217; trained incapacity of, 75–76; treatment of, 68
Employment at will doctrine, 90
Empowerment, 133–134, 247; critical thinking about, 150–151; self-managed teams and, 130–132
Enactment-selection-retention, 309

Enforcement, of company policies, 96–104
English, Vera, 282
Enhancement ceremonies, 167
Enrichment, job, 127
Enron, 409; executive life insurance and, 428; hearings about, 438; organizational ethics, rhetoric, and, 434–440; organizations after, 440
Enterprise resource planning (ERP) systems, 58, 197
Entrepreneurs: women as, 364; Xers as, 11
Environment: communication across organizational boundaries and, 232; design and communication structures and, 229–231; ethics and, 410. *See also* Organizational environments
Environmental complexity, 190, 229, 231
Environmental movement, corporate social responsibility and, 413
Environmental stability, 190, 230
Equal Employment Opportunity Commission: Mitsubishi and, 350; Texaco and, 416
Equilibrium, economic, 39
Equity: Mexican concept of, 114; of rewards, 84–85
ERP. *See* Enterprise resource planning (ERP) systems
Essentializing, 345
Ethical communication, 246–247
Ethics, 409–410; context of, 410; Enron and, 434–440; globalization and, 403–404; at Halliburton, 418–420; image management and, 415–417; multiple-stakeholder models of, 414; organizational rhetoric and, 410–429; proactive image management and, 420–423; whistle-blowers and, 278
Ethnicity: mentoring and, 363. *See also* Discrimination; Minorities; *specific groups*
European Economic Union (EEU), productivity and, 399
European Trade Union Confederation, productivity and, 399
"Exceptions," free trade and, 396
Executives: accountability of, 433–434; compensation of, 433; life insurance for, 428; power of, 432–434
Expectations, strategic ambiguity and, 265
Expertise, 57; in messages, 266; as power source, 258–259
Expressive messages, 264
Externalities, 411
Externalization, 158
External networks, for marginalized groups, 363
Extranet, 50; of American Hospital Supply, 56, 58–59

F

Face management, 84
Fairhurst, Gail, 181
Familism, 365–366
Family: policies friendly to, 374–376; work needs and, 369–372
Family-business model, in Taiwan and Hong Kong, 401